P9-DGZ-984

Hey Mom,
Can I Ride My Bike Across America?

Five Kids Meet Their Country

John Seigel Boettner

Seigel Boettner Fulton
Brea, California

Thanks to John Bartholomew and Son Limited for their beautiful *World Travel Series United States of America Map* and the permission to reproduce a portion of it on the cover. Also thanks to J.S. Holliday for bringing William Swain to life in his wonderful book, *The World Rushed In*. Copyright ©1981 by Simon & Schuster, Inc. Excerpts from William's journal and Mr. Holliday's text reprinted by permission of Simon and Schuster, Inc.

Copyright © 1990 by John Seigel Boettner
Edited by Bob Leroy, Mike Orman, Dad, and Dunn Middle School '89
Photographs by John and Lynn Seigel Boettner
Illustrations by John Seigel Boettner
Cover Photography by Aidan Bradley

Published by Seigel Boettner Fulton
570 W. Central, Bldg. 4A
Brea, CA 92621
All rights reserved. No part of this book may be used or reproduced in any manner whatsoever without written permission from the publisher except in the case of brief quotations embodied in articles and reviews.
Publishers Cataloging-in-Publication Data

Boettner, John Seigel, 1953 —
Hey mom, can I ride my bike across America?
1. United States — Description & Travel 1981 — 2. Bicycle Touring — United States.
3. Pioneers — California — Biography. 4. Boettner, John Seigel, 1953 — I. Title.
Library of Congress Catalog Card Number: 90-80522
ISBN 0-9625707-7-X Hardcover
ISBN 0-9625707-6-1 Softcover

Printed in the United States of America

10 9 8 7 6 5 4 3 2 1

BOOK DESIGN BY FRITZ+BOETTNER DESIGN

For Jimmy, Heather, Joy, Carl, Ethan and Lynn . . .
Hey you guys, I love you.

Contents

"*The pioneers decorated their wagons with slogans and mottos painted in axle grease. We used pieces of ripped-up sheet and magic markers and pinned our mottos to the back of our loaded bikes. My motto was:*
'The more I see the country,
The less I call this work.'"

Joy Fulton, age 12
August 14, 1986

1

"Shoot, Dorothy, we aren't even in Kansas yet."

Jimmy
Jacksonport State Park, Arkansas

When I was 12, I was afraid of the dark. My pudgy 150 pounds were no match for all the noises that lurked in the blackness. Every night, I used to hike down our hallway to crawl in between Mom and Dad, and I was a sleepless, wide-eyed disaster on nights spent at friends' houses or summer camp. I often wondered if I would ever be able to live on my own. Who would protect me from those noises in the night when I was physically too big to fit in between my parents?

How memories of a younger me managed to squeeze their way into my consciousness the night of our Arkansas tornado, I'll never know. But somehow, with all the emergency messages pouring through my brain, there I was — if only for a second — the frightened little John on his way down the hallway again.

KABOOM!!! A bolt of lightning brought me back to the present as it struck just across the river.

"Hey John, I didn't even get past one thousand on that one," yelled a frightened Heather. "That means the lightning is pretty close!" Heather was trying to calculate the distance of the strike by counting the time between the light and the thunder, while at the same time trying to hold down her tent from the howling wind. Next to her was her friend and tentmate, Joy, who was also spread-eagle on the floor, trying to keep them and their tent from blowing to Oz.

"Hey John, what should we do?" cried Joy.

"Ethan, Carl, you guys hold down the tent." It was Jimmy yelling at his partners in the boys' tent. While I was watching home movies and listening to the girls, he was taking action.

"I'm gonna go see if anything's left on the clothesline. I have a feeling our choners are off to see the wizard! You guys wait here and hold down the tent."

"Jimmy, you're crazy!" yelled Carl. "Don't go out there!"

CRACK!!! Jimmy's response was drowned out by another explosion.

"Shoot, Dorothy, we aren't even in Kansas yet."

"Jimmy, is that you out there?" I yelled.

"Yeah dude, it's me. I was trying to take our laundry off the clothesline. You better think of something pretty quick because I don't think this is just a thunderstorm."

4

"John, what should we do?" said Heather and Joy.

"Yeah John, what should we do?" echoed Carl and Ethan.

I didn't say anything as I quickly unzipped our tent and poked my head outside. With lightning flashing constantly around us, I had no trouble surveying the damage or seeing the black, boiling sky heading our way. It looked like a huge tidal wave, and its roar shook the ground. The boys' tent had lost all of its stakes and was heaving with each blast of wind. All of its "expedition-proven" poles had buckled, and it was being jerked around like some empty hot air balloon. When its roof was thrown to the ground, I could see the shapes of Ethan and Carl outlined in nylon against the floor. Next door, the girls' smaller tent was in much the same condition, and they were hugging the floor with all their strength, trying not to be blown away by the twister.

Joy and Carl were twelve, Heather and Ethan were thirteen and Jimmy was, as he said, "thirteen—but almost an adult." They didn't have Mom or Dad down the hall. In fact, to get a hold of their parents would be a long distance call spanning a few time zones. I, that one-time-so-very-scared little boy, and my wife Lynn were the closest folks they had, and as *our* tent stakes exploded out of the ground and *our* nylon home buckled beneath the sky, Lynn finally woke up and moaned, "John, what should we do?"

"Yeah John, what should we do? . . . ."

It was the summer of 1986 and I was 33-years-old. I had outgrown my parents' bed sometime before I started shaving and begun to get more sleep on those overnights. I had even lived by myself for six years. I was still a light sleeper, but slept well enough to dream amidst the nightnoises of my own bedroom. My wife Lynn, five young friends, and I were living one of those dreams that summer. We were riding our bicycles across America.

By that stormy night in Arkansas, we had already been on the road for six weeks and had traveled 1600 miles. Every one of those days and every one of those miles had shown me how different living a dream was from just dreaming it.

In my dreams I didn't have to do any leading. I just woke up having been on some incredible adventure or having traveled to some amazing land. In my dreams I just magically got there. There was always some shadow to lead me — just like in Dickens' "*Christmas Carol*" — and when times got really tough, I just woke up.

Crossing America, I was that shadow, that spirit of what was next around the bend — and I was supposed to have all the answers. In six weeks I had been asked a thousand times in words and longing looks: "John, how much further is it?" . . . "What's the next mountain like?" . . . "Do you think we'll need our rain gear today?" I, unlike Dickens' ghosts, hadn't been to the next town yet or been over that next mountain before. I had grown up my whole life in Southern California where my only clothing consideration was what color shorts to wear and where lightning was something that never struck twice (in one year.) I wasn't a very knowledgeable guide, but I was the only one we had.

The question that Lynn and the kids most often asked was, "John, what should we do now?" And in the midst of that tornado in Arkansas, Lynn's fingernails in my arms and her wide open brown eyes spoke for herself and all the kids.

It had started out such a beautiful evening. We rode into camp at Jacksonport State Park where the Black and White Rivers come together in western Arkansas. Our campsite sat on a beautiful green bluff above the water. The only trees around us were the ones on the island that separated the two rivers. Other than the bathrooms, which for some unknown reason sat up on fifteen-foot stilts, our tents were the tallest things in camp.

"Hey John, it sure is quiet out here tonight," said Heather as I hung the clothesline and she wrung out the shorts that had carried her 70 miles that day.

"Yeah, it's kinda weird it's so still," said Joy. "It's almost like the world stopped spinning."

The sky was clear except for the south's summer haze of humidity. The only weather it seemed we'd be dealing with that night was the constant stickiness that never would let our clothes — or us — get completely dry. I told the kids to put their rainflies on their tents "just in case", and they answered in their usually cheerful, end-of-the-day fashion, "Oh John, there's not a cloud in the sky and it's so hot and sticky. Do we have to?" A "yup" from me took care of that question.

Darkness offered little relief from the sticky heat, and as dinner ended and camp was secured, even the hint of a breeze that had been whispering across the river stopped. As Joy and Heather crawled into their tent and Jimmy, Ethan and Carl crawled into theirs, Lynn and I took one last look over our camp. The bikes were locked and covered, all the food was packed securely in its Ziploc bags and placed on the table in blue stuff sacks, and the girls' laundry was organized and hung neatly on the line. The guys, who had taught us all in our first week the difference between "washed" laundry and "clean" laundry had theirs hanging haphazardly, some inside out, some rolled half out/half in, on the line. Learned or otherwise, there were some obvious differences between the ways the guys and girls did certain things, and even without any wind, I expected at least one of the boys to be picking up his damp socks or undies off the grass in the morning.

With flashlights hung inside, the kids' tents glowed and revealed small silhouettes in the darkness. Their two domes looked like spaceships touched down on the southern plain. I could see Joy's and Heather's familiar shadows in their nighttime journal-writing positions — lying on their stomachs and resting on their elbows, they religiously recorded the day's events and emotions before they were lost to the night. I walked over to their tent, tapped on their rain fly and said good night.

"'Night, John. It sure is hot with this rain fly on," they answered.

Walking over to the guys' tent, I could see no silhouettes, only the occasional flash of one of their flashlights, used to emphasize some point in one of their private jokes or to see how much they could get each other's mouths to glow — Ethan could fit three flashlights in his. Although the boys kept journals too, I'd learned by then to expect about as much organization in their journal writing as I could from their laundry.

I rattled their tent poles at a quiet moment and whispered, "See you in the morning guys." I hoped I didn't ruin their light experiment.

"Not too early, John," answered Ethan.

"Yeah, why don't you be a pal and let us sleep in 'til 5 AM tomorrow," suggested a sarcastic Carl.

"'Night, Johnny Boy," laughed Jimmy.

The boys were quickly back to their business. I just hoped they remembered some of today so that they could record it in their journals at our breakfast meeting.

When I got to our tent, Lynn already had everything set up. I tried to cheat the heat a little by not zipping up our rainfly. As I laid my head down next to Lynn's, I noticed that our Arkansas night had become even more still. The already oppressive air had thickened and the nocturnal concert of the local bug band stopped. Even the song of the two rivers hushed.

Lynn's body moved closer to me and stuck in the sweaty suction of my greasy, sunburned arms. After many nights in our nylon sauna, we were used to embraces and good nights that smelled and felt different than ones at home. At night we usually talked of our days, saving our journal time for the morning. We'd often stare up at the blue ceiling of our tent and talk about how well the kids were doing and how proud we were of the way they had ridden a particularly difficult stretch of road. Other nights, we wouldn't talk at all. If I had seemed to push us one town too far, fifteen miles too long or promised a bathroom stop that never seemed to materialize, Lynn would silently turn from me and let me know she was less than pleased with my leadership. That day's ride had been a hot, but wonderful, backcountry road day of riding through Arkansas. It had been complete with free breakfast bought by a local farmer, a lunch sampling of our first catfish and hush puppies at Betty's BBQ, and Lynn's find of some old cigar boxes at the Birdeye, Arkansas Country Store & Post Office. She was excited that they had pictures of Lincoln and the White House on them and thought they'd be perfect for her first grade classroom. The man at the store sold her all he had for a buck each and said he would wrap them for mailing and make sure they would arrive home before the first day of Lynn's school.

"My kids will really like them—" Lynn was interrupted by a flash of light and the sudden rustling of our loose rainfly.

"What was that?" I said, sitting up suddenly.

"It's only a little breeze," she said pulling me back down. "Do you really think the boxes will get to Santa Barbara by the first day of school? Don't you think I should have asked him if he had any more?" The rainfly began to flap more like a flag in the wind and the flashes outside seemed to be happening more frequently.

"I'm going to go outside and check things out," I interrupted.

"Oh John, don't get up now. The breeze feels good. Do you think I could have gotten more boxes?"

Lynn slid off my chest and onto her pad as I rose to see what was causing the flashes of light.

The bugs and river were still eerily silent, and a warm wind whipped gently through camp. The guys' underwear was still on the line, and on the horizon, above the island, I saw what was causing the flashing. There still weren't any clouds in the sky, only a black haze flashing gray from the distant strobes of lightning.

"Everything's okay, Lynn. It looks like there may be a thunderstorm way northwest of here. It's so far away I can't even see any clouds." Before getting back in the tent, I noticed that the girls' light was out, their journal session over. A few feet away, the guys' tent seemed quiet too. Maybe they did need that extra sleep.

If there was ever a contest for who could fall asleep the fastest, I think I could make a lot of money entering Lynn, because she can fall asleep in mid-syllable. That night was no different; in the seconds between my description of the weather and my return to her side, she was already asleep dreaming of crayon-filled cigar boxes.

I was barely down and sweating again when the rainfly changed from its gentle flapping to a violent slapping at the entrance to our tent. I sat up, unfastened our door and zipped the fly closed. Meanwhile, it seemed that the flashes of that far off thunderstorm were getting closer and brighter. I even thought I was beginning to hear the thunder — "Nah John, it's only your imagination; like that old boogie man outside your bedroom. Go to sleep," I told myself. "Yeah, go to sleep."

Everything that happened next happened so quickly. Suddenly, our whole tent started to lurch violently from side to side. Those distant flashes of light were now bright enough to light up the inside of the tent. With each flash I could see the sides of our home jerking wildly like sails ripped loose from their rigging.

"Ignore the weather, John," I told myself. "Everyone else is asleep, these are three-season tents, and it's only a summer thunderstorm. Enjoy being out in nature and being protected by the best in modern outdoor technology."

Just as I had convinced myself of our safety and protection, the ceiling of our tent, which normally stands about four feet high, flattened and pressed against my face. Then the other side of the tent, Lynn's side, did the same. The sky, that just seconds before had been so still and quiet, was now flogging our home.

Lynn drowsily mumbled something to the effect of 'What's happening?' and I told her to go back to sleep, it was just a thunderstorm. As she rolled over I decided to unzip the door and the rainfly and see what was happening outside.

Our tent was lurching so violently I had to aim my head out the door. The scene that awaited me was even worse than all the ones my nighttime imagination had conjured up. The still and hazy sky over the island and the two rivers was now a boiling mass of black and white clouds spitting wind, lightning and rain. It looked like the biggest wave I had ever seen, and it was coming down the river and towards us faster than any wave I had ever tried to out-swim or out-run.

Looking over at the kids' tents I saw that they were blown completely flat by the now constant swirl of wind, and it was at this point that I saw Jimmy trying to rescue everyone's laundry. Socks, underwear and aerodynamic biking clothes were either now in his embrace or heading with the wind toward the Mississippi. Joy and Heather were trying to keep their tent from joining the flying laundry; Ethan and Carl were following Jimmy's orders to stay put; and I finally found what it took to wake Lynn in the middle of the night.

I didn't have any warm bed down the hall to crawl into. Heather's lightning count was becoming shorter and shorter, and the largest waves of the storm were now building just across the river. With each second I waited to decide what to do, another part of someone's tent would explode out of the ground or rip through its casing. The wind was only getting meaner, and since Heather and Joy combined weighed less than I did, I had to do something fast. As Jimmy ran and dove into his tent and the kids all laid flat trying to hold down their homes, I heard everyone silently waiting for my directions.

I remembered that, in addition to the stilts around the bottom of the bathrooms, there was also a line of junipers. I decided that we would abandon camp and drag our tents under the bathrooms; maybe those bushes would provide a windbreak. I yelled as loud as I could, hoping everyone could hear me above the roar. The clouds and the electricity were now almost upon us. Leaves, branches and other debris swirled our way as the first big wave of the storm was about to break over our side of the river. I could see a wall of a million raindrops blowing sideways as it was lit up by the constant explosions of lightning. Heather had stopped counting.

"JIMMY! You and Ethan and Carl leave all your stuff inside the tent and try to drag it across the field underneath the bathrooms. Do you understand?"

Jimmy answered by yelling my orders to Ethan and Carl, and before I got over to the girls, the guys were already on their way out of their house and beginning their attempt to move it.

"Joy and Heather, are you two all right?"

"Yeah John, but what should we do?"

"Leave everything inside and come outside and help me drag your tent underneath the bathrooms. I think we might get some protection there."

"Okay, we'll be right out."

I ran back over to Lynn. "Lynn, spread yourself out along the floor of the tent. The stakes have all blown out of the ground and won't hold anymore. We're all going to move underneath the bathrooms. The boys are moving their tent now and I'm going to help Joy and Heather move theirs. I'll be right back to help you." I could see that our once flexible aluminum tent poles were now permanently bent. Our tent would fill up with a gust of air like a parachute and then be sucked back to the ground, outlining Lynn's sprawled figure on the floor. I could even see the outline of our panniers as they were smothered by the blue nylon.

"I love you and I'll be back real soon. Just spread out and act HEAVY!"

I never imagined the sky could be so violent. Dodging bolts and doing our best not to become airborne, we all made it underneath the bathrooms, but the electricity, wind and deafening crack of the lightning put my adrenaline gland on overload. Standing underneath the bathroom, with five wide-eyed kids and my wife staring up at me and more waves about to break, I had no time to be as scared as some voices inside me were suggesting.

I thought that once under the bathrooms and behind the junipers, we might be safe, but we were still in the impact zone. I had never been able to outrun my California ocean's anger and I doubted I would be able to outrun the Arkansas sky. The lightning and wind hadn't calmed at all, and I looked down, during one of the bursts of bright light, to notice a small lake was forming underneath us.

The kids and Lynn went inside their crumpled tents trying to keep them from blowing away when the gusts of wind funnelled through our windbreak. I was standing outside surveying our situation when I remembered something about electricity's attraction for tall metal objects and water. Each metal stilt that supported the bathroom now stood in about three inches of water, and the tents containing my wife and kids were floating in that same water. It looked like it was time for *Abandon Camp Plan: Phase Two* — whatever that was.

"Okay everyone, we're going to have to leave our tents and things down here. We need to get up into the bathrooms."

"But what about all of our gear in the tents?" Heather's voice came from somewhere beneath her tent that now looked more like a two-person stuff sack.

"Just grab your handlebar bags and valuables and leave everything else. I'm going to try and wrap your tents around these posts so that the wind will keep them here. Hopefully your gear inside will help weigh them down. You guys just get upstairs as fast as you can."

The kids and Lynn ran up the bathroom stairs and I tried my best to secure our homes and much of our gear. As I danced in the gusts and the lightning and the thunder that rattled my insides, another one of my internal advisors asked: "John, are you sure you want to cast much of what you'll need to complete your journey to this Arkansas wind? Shouldn't you just hold your breath and go under a few more waves? Beaching everyone here might give you more of a chance against the breaking sky, but these tall bathrooms might also be the first thing to be carried off in a tornado. After all, what do *you* know about tornadoes?"

There may have been other "right" decisions, but it wasn't until the next morning that I learned about the"Severe Thunderstorm/Tornado Watch" that had been posted for our spot on the map. Once finished with us, the storm had uprooted trees and killed two people in town.

After wrapping the gear-filled tents around the stilts, I ran up the stairs to the bathrooms that were rocking in the storm. The kids and Lynn were sitting in a circle on the tile floor of the Ladies Room, and Heather and Jimmy scooted over to give me a place in the puddle next to them. Each crack of lightning made the building shudder, and as the storm rattled our only place of refuge, we all huddled closer and closer together.

"Hey John, remember that time you were reading us Peter Jenkins' book, *A Walk Across America*, and Barbara and him were camped out in that lightning storm?" asked Joy between cracks of thunder.

"Yeah, when the lightning struck right next to their tent and they tried to take off all their metal jewelry and squeezed each other so tight?" added Heather.

"I think we're just like them," continued Joy as she hugged Heather and Lynn closer to her.

"Yeah, or that time you read us about Barbara and Larry Savage riding their bikes around the world in that book, *Miles From Nowhere* . . . all those times Barbara thought she was going to die?" said Carl. "I don't know what would be worse: her being chased by that ape in India or us trying to run away from this storm."

"Or them using branches to fight off those Egyptians who threw rocks at them," added Ethan.

"Yeah, but you can't scare a tornado away with sticks," laughed Jimmy. "I think we *are* like those people, and, John, you should write a book about our adventures . . . if we make it."

We did make it.

I nodded along with the kids that night as they told stories of the people who had inspired them to take their journey. With each crack seeming like it would split the building into pieces, we huddled closer and closer together for what seemed like an eternity. In between explosions, the kids continued to reminisce. Finally, as the storm reluctantly roared off in the distance like a slow semi-truck, the kids found themselves places to sleep around the small room: Joy and Heather ended up wrapped tightly around each other next to the toilet covered by Joy's blanket; Carl and Ethan were wedged tightly into the corner over by the trash can; and Jimmy curled up and snored on top of the counter, head in one sink and bottom in the other. Lynn and I spent the rest of the night watching over the kids and waiting for the storm to pass completely. We held each other tight and looked down in amazement at the five kids who had joined us for our bike ride across America.

Morning dawned as usual, and like Peter and Barbara Jenkins,' and Larry and Barbara Savage's, our journey could continue, better for the telling. We bravely and confidently gathered up what was left or our scattered and tattered gear —

Ethan borrowed back a pair of his socks being worn by a cow in the field nearby
— and then we circled, hand in hand, where our tents had begun the night.
    "Hey John, we only got forty miles to ride today?" said Carl.
    "Yup."
    "No problem, man; that will be easy."
    Just like when I was 12, somehow everything felt safer in the light of day.

FROM SEA TO SHINING SEA

2

"No Joy, it's not even up for discussion. I'm not letting you ride your bike across America. Four months is just too long, and I don't want to hear any more about it."

Joy's mom
Fall/Winter, 1985-86

Hey Mom . . .

"Hey John! I can ride my bike and scratch my face at the same time," shouted Ethan, grinning from ear to ear.

It was early October of 1985 and, two weeks earlier, Ethan had received his first multi-speed bicycle. Ethan was 12-years-old and his mom, Sue, had asked me to be very watchful of him on his first ride: "Ever since he was little, Ethan has had trouble with his equilibrium and balance, so please be careful. I'm worried about him on his bicycle."

"Just another worried mom," I said to myself. Having taught kids Ethan's age for several years and having met many mothers nervous at their babies' initial adventures out of the driveway, I comforted Sue with my usual, "Oh sure, we'll be careful. We'll take it easy and take roads with very little traffic, don't worry." As soon as Sue left school, I dismissed her fears and descriptions of Ethan's abilities, and prepared the Dunn Middle School Bike Club for their first Monday afternoon ride of 1985-86.

Bike Club veterans from the year before confidently mounted their steeds and volunteered to lead the pack. Having ridden at the back many times, I didn't think there was anything unusual about Ethan wanting to be the last one to take off on his first school ride. I soon found out how wrong I was — and how right his mom was.

"Okay Ethan, it's your turn. Just follow the group, I'm right behind you."

His brand-new, shiny, blue 18-speed bicycle, with all its levers and cables and curving handlebars, seemed to confuse Ethan. He had trouble finding his way into his pedals which had toe straps, so I said, "Don't worry about those, Ethan. Just ride on the bottom of your pedals without straps; we'll learn to use those later."

Next, he needed help deciding where to put his hands on the handlebars. As much as he had studied how each of his classmates had done it, he found that for him this was something that was much harder than it looked. I got off my bicycle and showed him how to place his hands so that they would always be close enough to squeeze the brake levers, and he silently nodded his head, trying to remember everything. I shifted his bike into a nice cruising gear and told him

16

that he didn't need to worry about shifting for a long time. "Just relax and get used to your new bike, and then we'll learn how to shift."

With all systems go, little Ethan Turpin — all 80 pounds and 12 years of him — was off down the school driveway on his first *real* bike ride. He wiggled and he wobbled, as he and his bike zig-zagged at the slowest possible speed. Sue was right about his balance. Watching the intense look of concentration on Ethan's face as he completed each pedal stroke, I could tell that every inch of that maiden voyage was a giant accomplishment for him. He made it about 100 yards — if you add up all the zigs and the zags — before he wobbled off the side of the blacktop and crashed with a cloud of dust into the ditch under the big oak tree. He was surprised at what the soft dirt would do to his skinny tires. In Ethan's cloud of dust, I remembered my own first solo flight down the sidewalk. My ditch had been the neighbors' geranium patch, and as Ethan lay tangled in his frame tubes, I yelled, "Alright Ethan!" Goosebumps danced up my spine, and tears welled up in my eyes as I watched him pull his helmet off his nose and search in the dirt for the thick glasses that had flown off his face. Finding them, he got up, dusted himself off, waved over at me and smiled. Soon he was back on top of his bike, zigging and zagging to try and catch up with his friends.

I don't remember how many more times Ethan crashed that day. I do remember that everyone cheered him into our traditional midway cookie and water stop. When the ride was over and his mom picked him up, she asked me how he had done.

"Great!" was my honest and enthusiastic answer.

Little did Ethan, Sue or I know that soon Ethan would be daringly lifting one of his hands off his handle bars to scratch that itch, to shift those gears and to grab one of his water bottles for a drink — while he was pedaling! And Sue and I had no idea that her little guy would soon be asking to ride himself, his bicycle and 40 added pounds of food and gear 5,000 miles across America.

Soggy Granola

People are always asking me when I first started planning for our journey across the United States: "What ever made you decide to go across America? . . . on a bicycle? . . . with KIDS?!" My long answers usually get edited out of TV interviews and cut up by those who squeeze words into printed columns.

As a kid growing up in Santa Barbara, California, I couldn't wait to get my first bicycle, and as long as I can remember I loved America. My dad used to take my five brothers and sisters and me to all the parades downtown and whenever the color guards carrying the flag were in sight, we would all follow Dad's lead in standing up. If we were too young to stand — and with six kids there always seemed to be at least one of us who was — my dad would put us up on his shoulders. In school, I always got wet eyes and funny bumps all over when I heard the *Battle*

Hymn of the Republic. I called it the *"Glory, Glory Song,"* and I knew right where it was in our classroom songbook. Whenever we went to Disneyland, I always went to Great Moments with Mr. Lincoln first, and by the time I was 12, in 1965, I was sure I was going to go to college at the Naval Academy. I watched John Wayne movies and was proud to be an American.

The late sixties changed a lot of things for me. I traded in my butch wax and navy cap for long hair and a draft card that said Conscientious Objector. Instead of going to parades with Mom and Dad, I was arguing for my right to go to rock and roll concerts. I was always staying at the dinner table late and loud to "discuss" with my folks what it really meant to stand up for our flag. Still, I loved my country. With draft card in my wallet, I dragged my girlfriend to visit my old friend Mr. Lincoln on High School Grad Night at Disneyland. His auditorium wasn't too crowded , but the *Glory, Glory Song* still gave me chills as it played in the background.

Something else that never changed as I grew up was my love for two wheels. There was always some bicycle nearby. I got my first ten-speed — a gold Schwinn Continental — for my tenth birthday, and I wore out many tires riding with my baseball glove hooked on its handlebars or my newspapers stuffed in the bags on my shoulders. Even when I graduated to a 63 VW, I still kept my bicycle close by. Every time I hopped on my bike, I got to relive a piece of the freedom I felt that first time I rode down the sidewalk and crashed into those geraniums.

College found me riding my bicycle to classes. As I studied my country — I was an American Studies major — our participation in the Vietnam War ended. It was just in time for me to be able finish school and get my teaching credential. Teaching seemed to be just the right thing for me. Having grown up in a household with so many brothers and sisters, I knew what it was like to have to raise my hand to ask for the milk; I was a pro at waiting in line for the bathroom; and I figured after all the family outings to those parades, I'd have no problem with field trips. Kids would roll to school with lunchbox in one hand, handlebars in the other, and maybe I could find one of those old songbooks in some dusty closet. Despite the 60's, I knew a song I'd like to share with a new generation of kids.

My wide, college eyes weren't prepared for how different the classrooms of 1975 would be from my own, and I didn't realize that the changes in me went so much deeper than my hairstyle. School had been so easy and predictable for me when I was a kid. Teachers held conferences with Ozzie *and* Harriet, everyone knew or at least remembered JFK; and it seemed, to my young eyes, that everyone loved America. You learned reading, writing and arithmetic from books, and you learned about the world and anatomy from a National Geographic Magazine hidden in your desk. In my classroom, I wanted my third graders to read and write and add, but I also wanted them to get those National Geographic magazines out on the top of their desks and ask questions about them. I didn't want my kids to grow up and have to go to war, but I did want them to stand up when our flag went by. And although battle hymns were definitely not the vogue, I wanted to hear them singing an emotional rendition of the *Glory, Glory Song*. Some of my colleagues were even questioning Abraham Lincoln's reputation, and while so many of them were going off to see faraway, foreign lands, I, the old American Studies romantic, was trying to convince my kids and my communities to stay proud of America. Despite its flaws, it hurt me to see so many of my friends with an American inferiority complex.

In the summer following my fifth year of teaching, I decided it was time to do something I had always dreamed of. I packed up my bicycle and flew to New England to see the land of covered bridges, Pilgrims and Paul Revere. For six weeks I pedaled, and, somewhere, on some back road in Maine, I dreamt of bringing some students back to the same place. I wanted them to see their America from the unique vantage point of their bicycles.

That dream moved from dream to opportunity to reality much faster than I ever expected. The very day I got back to California I met Lynn Seigel, who two years later would become my wife. Months later, when I proposed marriage to her at our favorite Italian restaurant, I also proposed two bicycle trips as honeymoon options. When she said yes, I don't think she knew how many post honeymoon bicycle trips she was getting herself into.

By the time we were married, I had changed teaching jobs and was working at a middle school just north of Santa Barbara, California. My teaching partner, Jim Brady, saw our middle school as a doorway for kids to see the world, and he started a summer program called Educational Safaris. I had brought my bicycle with me to my new school and together we started brainstorming all the possibilities two wheels might give our kids. In my first year at Dunn, we began our Monday Biking Club. That summer I took five of my pedaling friends and students on my first group bicycling tour. Dine, Peter, Mike, Kate, Christy and I spent five days bicycling the coast of Big Sur, and although my inexperience in leading a group tour resulted in self-destructing rear racks, wobbly rear wheels and nearly losing Kate and fearless leader (me) to a riptide, we all came back with hopes of where we might go on our bicycles the following summer.

That next summer came quickly, and Jim and I planned two biking Educational Safaris. Jim and his wife, Robin, would be taking a group of middle schoolers to southern England to ride old Roman roads; and when Lynn and I returned from our honeymoon bicycle tour in the Canadian Rockies, we would be taking eight kids back to my favorite roads in New England. Kate, Christy and Mike were three of those eight kids, as was David Blanchard who eight years before had been in my first third grade class — I was his first "boy teacher." We all sat on a beach on Cape Cod and wrote our own Mayflower Compact, and as we pedaled into Plymouth and Boston and Lexington, I saw my books and my America come alive for those eight kids. The goose bumps flowed freely as I watched them meeting their fellow Americans past and present, and all the questions they asked about their history and their customs were better than I had in any textbook on my shelf at school.

In the summers to follow, Lynn and I returned to New England and Canada with more kids and, in our most daring adventure, we took six kids and their bicycles with us to see Japan.

Four years spanned the time from the first Dunn Middle School Biking Club meeting to that Educational Safaris Japan Bicycle Tour. Lynn and I were becoming pretty well versed in group bicycle touring, having spent each of our wedding anniversaries in separate dormitories of distant youth hostels. I always kept a year ahead of each of our journeys, and one fall morning in 1984, I stopped in the middle of my granola and looked across the table at Lynn. I guess I must have had much the same look on my face that I had that night a few years before at that Italian restaurant — or maybe it wasn't a look. Maybe my stopping in mid-meal was the warning signal, because Lynn knew once I started eating, I only came up for air on very special occasions.

"Okay, John, what is it?"

"What do ya mean, what is it?"

"Well, I can tell from the strange way you're acting that something is on your mind. Do you want *another* new bicycle?"

"No, you know I already have two."

"Well, I remember when I thought one was enough! Really John, what's going on? We've both got to get going to school. You're not pregnant are you?" (As much as Lynn loved the chromosomes she was dealt, she still said she would gladly let me get fat and carry our children for their first nine months. So far in our two years of marriage neither of us had that opportunity.)

Soggy granola and cold toast are two of my least favorite ways to begin my day, so I finally grinned up at her and said, "I think I know where we should go on our next Educational Safari." It wasn't my most convincing voice, but it was about par for whenever I proposed another adventure.

I think Lynn knew that my "thinking" of a journey almost guaranteed that very soon, she, about a half-dozen kids, and I would be straddling our bicycles in the very place that had not-too-long-before interrupted our granola or pasta.

"But John, we haven't even been to Canada and Japan yet and you're already thinking about the summer after this one?! A lot can happen over the next year and a half."

I *was* pregnant, and I knew the dream inside me this time would need a lot of gestation time.

"Lynn," — she knew it was serious whenever I preceded anything with "Lynn" — "what would you think about taking a group of kids across America on bicycles?"

"I was wondering when you'd ask. Sure, why not? How long do you think it will take? How far is it?"

She acted like we'd already talked about it.

"I'm not sure how long it would take us. I know that Bikecentennial takes adult groups in 3 months, but I'm not sure if we would take their same route, or if we could do it in the same amount of time. Those are all things I need to take these next 18 months figuring out. But what's important is that you'll go?"

"Sure, I always thought we talked about 'doing the whole thing' someday, and I knew with your plan for us to have our first child before your 35th birthday, I figured we would be having this conversation either very soon or very much later."

At that, I dove back into my cereal and gobbled down my toast. It was a little soggy and cold, but it tasted fine to me that morning.

"Let's talk some more at dinner tonight, but right now we'd better finish our breakfast or we'll both be late for school."

Months of granola and many discussions later, Lynn and I found ourselves home from a summer where we had taken kids from the freezing, snow-covered solitude of the Canadian Rockies to the hot and humid crowdedness of Japan. On my desk sat maps of the entire United States, and soon our phone would ring with the first parents asking about our next adventure.

It was about that time that I stood at the end of the school driveway and witnessed Ethan Turpin's first bike ride. Although not in my wildest dreams did I expect Ethan to be one of the kids who would eventually join Lynn and me on our transcontinental trek, I did scan that first day's group of young bicyclists trying to figure out who among them, first, might be interested and second, might be up to such an undertaking. Ethan's cloud of dust didn't let me daydream for long and was a reminder for me — the one who always plans so far in advance — to take first things first.

In November, I planned making a presentation to the middle school kids and parents about our upcoming journey. I needed to have things like route, times, and costs tentatively planned. I needed to be prepared to answer the hundreds of "what ifs???" that parents can ask so well. And I needed to present this journey in a way that I had never presented one of our Educational Safaris before. New England had been 500 miles and 3 weeks, Canada 400 miles in 2 weeks and Japan — as far away from home as it might have been — was only 300 miles in 4 weeks. *From Sea to Shining Sea* (as our across America journey was called), according to my preliminary estimates, would take us 4500 miles and 4 months. I felt I needed to create a picture of our journey that was equal parts romance and reality: romance to interest kids in the crossing and reality to weed out the ones who could never make it. It was bound to be the most incredible and most unbearable thing that Lynn and I had ever done, and I was sure it would be that way for the kids as well. I wouldn't accept anyone who just wanted to see if they liked it. We weren't going to ride for a couple of weeks, then sit down and discuss how much we liked things and then take a vote to see if we wanted to continue west. Everyone needed to have a commitment to riding the entire journey, and as wonderful and exciting and unforgettable as I was sure it would be, I also knew that at times we might feel as though our commitment had committed us to some insane asylum on wheels.

Before making that presentation, I only had one kid who'd already signed on. Jimmy West, born and raised in Memphis, Tennessee, had moved to Santa Barbara at the beginning of his sixth grade year and decided to come to Dunn Middle School. He loved California where "you can wear anything you want to school. It's soooo rad!" A year before, on his first day of middle school biking atop his brand new 18-speed, he, like Ethan, had found a nice brown dusty ditch off the blacktop with his name on it. He spent the whole year learning about his bicycle and wearing different costumes to school. I drove him up to school everyday, and each morning at 7, Jimmy would peek around our door in some new disguise.

Lynn does pretty well with my revelations in the morning, but she did have trouble with Jimmy's trick-or-treating. One morning he'd be King Tut, the next a Ninja, and the next a break dancer, complete with blaring music. It took a lot of convincing, but Jimmy ended up being one of our Japan bicycling family. Lynn was more than a little hesitant to have Jimmy knocking at our tent every morning for a month that summer, but one evening, after an especially delicious dinner and a few glasses of wine, Lynn consented to Jimmy's joining us.

It turned out that Jimmy and Lynn entered a life-long friendship that month in Japan, and she was really excited at the prospect of spending four more months with him crossing America. Spending his earliest years growing up along the Mississippi, I think a little Huckleberry Finn had rubbed off on our young Jimmy. His cocky, adventurous spirit was something that took a while for people to get used to, but once they took the time to get to know him, they usually ended up loving him almost as much as Lynn and I did. We had no reservations about Jimmy being part of our *From Sea to Shining Sea* family.

79 Pictures

"I sure hope we get some interested kids and parents tonight," I said to Lynn as I set up the projectors. It was the night of our recruiting slide show. Everyone at school now knew of Lynn's and my plan to cross America, and so far the only firm commitment was from our Ninja friend, Jimmy. I'd spent many late night and early morning hours putting together a show that I hoped would get us some more families. We were hoping for six to eight kids.

As the schoolhouse slowly filled up, I got more and more nervous in anticipation of which families and kids would show up. My only predictable prospects were Joy and Heather, who had gone to Canada with us. I knew that Heather and her folks were very interested in her going. Lynn and I enjoyed her company so much we had already made a plan in our minds that would allow Heather to go even if it took her and her family 50 years at $5 a month to pay her way.

Heather was about four and a half feet tall, with blonde hair, blue eyes and freckles. She had a sparkle in her smile and a spunk in her spirit that made you want to run up and give her a great big hug. I remember one of my first doses of Heather in Canada. We were climbing to the teahouse above Lake Louise. It was only our third day in Canada, and Heather, armed with her brand-new camera, was already known as the group photographer. If it was colorful, Heather would take a picture of it, and she was always making us stop. "Oh . . . Oh . . . you guys wait a minute! Let me get a picture of you in front of those beautiful wildflowers." . . . "Did you see those neat clouds? Wow! Will you wait here while I get a picture?" In three days, she took more pictures than any busload of Japanese tourists, and by now, everyone hiked hesitantly in preparation for Heather's call for a pose. Anyway, as we were walking up to the teahouse that sat right on the edge of a small lake and just above a waterfall, Heather nonchalantly asked, "Hey John, how many pictures will I get with one roll of film? I've never used this camera before."

"Well, Heather, you should get 36, but sometimes, if you're lucky, you can get 38 or 39. Why, how many have you taken so far?"

"I must have a special roll, because this is still my first one. Ya know where the numbers are on the top, that show how many pictures you've taken? Well, they disappeared a couple days ago in the Calgary Airport. According to my best count I think I've got 79 pictures on this roll so far. This is a pretty neat camera!"

I walked over to Heather and put my arm around her as we hiked on up the trail. I almost didn't have the heart to tell her. "Uh, Heather . . . I'm sorry, but are you sure you've got film in there?"

"Oh sure, I've got 6 rolls."

"No, I mean are you sure you have film in your camera? Did you put a roll in yourself?"

"No, but *I'm* pretty sure my mom or dad did back in the LA Airport. Why?"

"Well, because *I'm* pretty sure there's no film in your camera. I don't know of any roll of film that can take 79 pictures." I didn't know whether to laugh or cry. Matt and Joy, two of Heather's sometimes unwilling subjects, were hiking with us. Listening to our conversation, they had a little trouble holding back their laughter.

Heather's only answer was a smiling, "Whoopsie, maybe there *isn't* any film in there. Let's look and find out."

Her camera was empty and the discovery drew a big giggle from her tent-mate, Joy. Matt — still in the primitive stages of diplomacy — grabbed his head and said, "Heather, I can't believe you did that. You're sooo stupid."

While Matt was laughing his way all over the trail, I was thinking of all the pictures Heather had taken but would now never make it into her Canadian Rockies scrapbook. I didn't have much time to dwell in my sadness, because Heather quickly interrupted my indulgence with, "Oopsie . . . Well, I guess we better put some film in it then. John, would you show me how to put film in my camera?"

Film loaded and giggles and laughter beginning to die down, it wasn't long before I heard Heather again: "Hey, Joy and Matt, slow down and come back here. The trees and the waterfall are so beautiful, I've just got to get a picture of you guys in front of it."

From that moment on, I knew I had to have Heather along on our trip across America. I knew there would be plenty of times when I would need her to teach me how to say "Oopsie" in the face of disaster. I knew the whole group — whoever they were — would need her spunky spirit to continue down the road.

Happy Valentine's Day

"How far will you ride?" . . . "How long will it take you?" . . . "Well, if it's going to take you four months, what about school?" . . . "How much will it cost?" . . . "What if somebody gets hurt out in the middle of nowhere?" . . . "What if someone gets sick?" . . . "Will you have a vehicle following you as a sag wagon?" . . . "Don't you think kids only 11 or 12 are too young?" . . . "You mean you're not going to go to Yellowstone?! You've *got* to see Yellowstone."

The slide show was over and it was question and answer time. I felt like it was the 1840's and I was on the back of a wagon in Ohio or New York trying to get my wagon train together. I hoped my answers, in their honesty and enthusiasm, didn't make me sound like some snake oil salesman wanting to swipe some unsuspecting youngsters from their loving parents.

Heather did sign on after that slide show. I promised I would make sure she had film in her camera.

I didn't do so well with Joy — or should I say, I didn't do so well with her mom. In contrast to my long journey, Jim Brady was offering a three week bicycle tour in England. During our presentation that night, I saw Sulie, Joy's mom, lean over and tell her that she was going on Jim's England trip and that there would be no "discussions" of "America." Rumor had it that Joy always won "discussions". . . .

Ever since Canada, Joy had been thinking of crossing America on her bicycle. She and Heather had become tent sisters in their two weeks in the Rockies, and while Heather was taking pictures with her camera all day long, Joy was taking pictures with her mind. Heather would stop to take a picture and Joy would stop to take notes on an especially yellow Columbine or an exceptionally tall mountain. They were always stopping alongside the road for some exploration and conversation:

"Heather, I think we should be on the lookout for bears. This looks like bear country to me. I bet you could get a really neat picture of one. John says they walk right along the side of the road."

Joy was blonde too, but where Heather was short and full of freckles, she was tall and tan. Joy's was a gentle and soft sparkle, and the two of them complemented each other perfectly. On our crisp and clear Canadian nights, you could hear the two of them in their tent comparing notes on all they'd seen that day.

Then they would fall asleep atop their journals, or keep everyone else awake with one of their sleeping bag fights — we didn't carry pillows, so they improvised.

Even though their enjoyment of our evenings made them the hardest ones to wake up in the morning, I hoped I would be waking the both of them up out in the middle of Nebraska somewhere. But, as much as Joy's mom trusted Lynn and me, and as wonderful as she thought our journey would be, the reality of four months away from her baby turned me into that snake oil salesman. Realizing her Joy was rapidly approaching womanhood, Sulie wanted to be the one who got to tuck her daughter in and wake her up while she was still young enough to let someone do it. Sulie knew that once Joy turned the corner from being a kid, she wouldn't have the chance again.

My granola and toast didn't taste very good the morning after our meeting. My wonderful slide show and question and answer session had netted Lynn and me just one more rider. It was time for us to start asking ourselves some questions. Would we go with just two kids? . . . If Jimmy and Heather would go, who would sleep with whom? . . . Was I willing to let Heather sleep with Lynn for four months, and, as much as I loved Jimmy, did I want to sleep with him as my tentmate from June thru October? . . . If Jimmy and Heather decided not to go and be the only kids, would Lynn and I set off on our journey just the two of us?

"John, we've still got time before we have to make our final decision. I'm sure there's more kids and parents who might be interested."

"Yeah, but we need to have the group together by February so we can do all the preparation we need to do."

"Well, it's only November. You've still got a couple months."

Sometime that morning I got out my calendar and penned in the first Saturday in March as the day when Lynn and I would gather all the kids and their families for our first *From Sea to Shining Sea* orientation meeting. That night, before I crawled under the covers with Lynn, I sat on the edge of our bed and changed my alarm ahead to 4 AM — I knew I was going to need all the hours I could possibly get to do all I had to do for my wife, my classroom and my dream.

In my classroom, every day began with my reading ten or fifteen minutes of Peter Jenkins' *Walk Across America*. The rest of our class time was spent studying and simulating the opening of the American West. We had Rendezvous with fur traders and Indians in the Rockies; we acted out the journals of pioneers coming west in the mid-nineteenth century; and we homesteaded on horseback, wagon and foot with our ancestors who first plowed the plains. I had written to every one of the states along our planned route, and the fruits of those letters were beginning to find their way to Santa Barbara. Each week, when I got home from school, I would discover a new manilla envelope in my mailbox containing maps and information on biking through one of the states on our cross country trek. Some of the envelopes contained the usual form letters, maps and tourist brochures, but many of them contained enthusiastic personal letters. It seemed some folks out there were excited about the prospect of a group of kids pedaling through their state. One man from Nebraska even wrote us a couple of times, filling his envelopes with books and brochures. He apologized for always filling my mailbox and ended one of his letters with, "I'm just so excited that you'll be coming through our state!" It seemed that not too many people were interested in pedaling across Nebraska. I knew how he felt, because Jimmy and Heather were the only kids I had signed up to ride.

I hoped what we were doing in my classroom, along with our Monday Bike Club rides — stocked with an extra supply of cookies and cheer — would naturally recruit some more kids to join my dream. As we read about Peter and his dog Cooper crossing the Blue Ridge Mountains or rolled on our wagons along the Platte River, I hoped a few of my students would feel the itch to see for themselves what America was like. The more we studied and the more maps and enthusiastic letters I received from people I'd never met, in places I'd never been, the more I longed for the group that could share in my planning and enthusiasm.

It was Valentine's night, two weeks before my March calendar date, and Lynn and I were having a candlelight dinner of our own at home, when the phone rang: "Shoot, who would be calling on Valentine's night?" I growled. "Some people . . . ."

"Why don't you just let the answering machine answer it?" said Lynn.

"No. I'd better answer it." I got up and walked over to the phone.

"Hello, John?" I recognized Joy's voice.

"Hi, this is John. Happy Valentine's Day, Joy. What's up?"

"Well, I was wondering if you had any room left on your America trip?"

Room left?!!! I don't think Joy realized if we didn't get more kids soon, I didn't know if there would be a trip. "Yeah, Joy, we have room left. Why? Do you have a friend or know someone who wants to go?"

"Yeah, me!"

I almost swallowed the phone.

"But I thought your mom wanted you to go on Jim's trip to England."

"Well, yeah, she did. Tomorrow's the deadline to sign up for Jim's trip and we just had a discussion. I told them how much I really wanted to cross America on my bicycle and be like Peter Jenkins and see what it was really like to be a pioneer and everything . . . and they finally said I could go. So, is it okay with you and Lynn if I sign up for your trip?"

"OKAY?! Joy, at first I was upset that someone would be calling Lynn and me in the middle of our Valentine dinner, but this is the best possible Valentine's present we could get!!! Of course we'd love to have you come with us. Ever since Canada, Lynn and I hoped that you could come with us. I just gave up hope after I found out how your mom felt about it."

"Yeah, I noticed you changing the subject whenever I was around. Well, she still doesn't want to let go of me for four months, but she knows how much your trip means to me, so she said okay. She still doesn't feel too good about my being away."

I heard her mom and dad in the background, and finally Bob, her dad, got on the phone. "Well, John, Sulie always said if she got into a discussion with Joy that Joy would win. Biking across America has been off limits on our discussion agenda, but tonight, Joy brought it up anyway.

"Sulie was right. Joy won."

Hitchhiking Spiders

The week before Joy's phone call, *From Sea to Shining Sea* had acquired its third and youngest member, eleven-year-old Carl Fagerlin. It was his first year at the Middle School and to say I was surprised by his interest in pedaling a bicycle 4500 miles would be an understatement. He had joined the bicycle club less than enthusiastically earlier in the year, and every Monday, I'd have to play cheerleader to convince Carl that he should join us for our 15 mile cruise. Part of his reluctance had to do with his bicycle. It was an orange, sometimes ten-speed, that looked as if it had been built from galvanized pipe by a plumber. What was once chrome was now rust, it weighed twice as much as anyone else's bike, and Carl's machine had at least one resident spider.

On the Bike Club's first overnight outing, Carl was usually at least 30 minutes behind everybody, sweating in his crotch-crunching Levi's. He completed that weekend trip only through the constant encouragement and companionship of Lynn. Carl's desire to join the America trip surprised me and drew some moans and groans from Heather and Jimmy. They couldn't quite envision Carl going 40 miles, much less 4,000. Lynn, or anyone else who had ever ridden with Carl, couldn't either.

One morning in early February, Carl, his mom, dad and little brother met with me at school at dawn. We sat around my giant relief map of America and talked about *From Sea to Shining Sea*. Going into that meeting I had some of the same fears that Jimmy and Heather had. I knew Carl shared our vision, but I wasn't sure he had what it took physically and emotionally. Still, I needed kids, not at any cost, but at almost any cost. Lynn and I had decided that it probably wouldn't be a good idea for just the four of us — Heather, Jimmy, her and me — to cross the country. I'd either have to get more kids, or we would have to reconsider our dream.

I went into that meeting with the Fagerlins armed with descriptions of many of the harsh realities I was sure we would encounter in four months of bicycling. I also was adamant in saying that anyone who signed on wasn't signing on for any trial period, but was making a commitment to himself and the group. Continuing down the road was not up for a vote, and I explained how I was sure there would be times where, given that choice, we would all vote not to continue. I think Carl got my message that morning, and still he and his parents were more than willing to sign on. A new bicycle was on the agenda, as were shorts instead of blue jeans, and Carl's dad, mom and little brother were going to each get bicycles to help Carl with the training schedule I had planned for everyone. I still wasn't completely sure about Carl, but with the support and encouragement from his family, I was ready to take a chance. My next step was to sit down with my friends Jimmy and Heather and convince them that I wasn't crazy.

77 Miles?!

The first Saturday in March, the day of our first meeting, finally dawned. My sleepless nights of planning and recruitment schemes were over. My trip booklets were finished and printed, complete with calendars, maps, conditioning programs and checklists. In a cold, blowing rain, Lynn, Jimmy and I drove up to school ready to meet the families soon to become part of ours.

Carl and his family showed up first. He'd already purchased his new touring bicycle, racks, and panniers (saddle bags) and wanted to check them out with me before the meeting. I'd never seen him so excited. Heather, along with her mom, dad and two sisters, was next. Then came Joy and her mom and dad. Although Lynn had prepared bagels and hot drinks for everyone, the nervous group that gathered in my classroom that morning didn't taste much of her offerings.

"Okay everyone, why don't we circle our desks like covered wagons and get started." My months of planning and conferring with friends were now capsulated into my thirty-page booklet. On its cover was our trip logo: a blue outline of the continental United States filled with caricatures of American folks. There were politicians in Washington, oystermen in the Chesapeake, banjo pickers in Appalachia, and surfers in California. Bold and black, going from east to west across the middle, was a covered wagon, followed by a tall, curly-haired man atop a heavily-loaded bicycle. Behind him, was a group of small kids atop heavily-loaded bicycles of their own. Those loaded bicycles were as significant as anything else in our logo, because many people thought I was nuts to make the kids carry their own gear. In my trip planning, many other cyclists, teachers and some parents had suggested that a sag wagon be added to our journey — that surely just pedaling the 4500-plus miles was enough for the kids.

"Don't you think it would be easier and safer to have a vehicle following you? Thirty pounds of added weight will surely make things more difficult."

"Yeah, and with a sag wagon if someone gets hurt or the weather gets real bad, you'd always have the vehicle to fall back on."

Whenever I heard those comments, I wondered how the pioneers would have ever made it west today. The only things I wanted us to be able to fall back on were ourselves and the people living in the land around us. We needed our vulnerability to get the most out of our journey. Our only sag wagon would be provided by some unknown, friendly local folks who I was sure were waiting to meet us all across America. Yes, the weather would be bad — probably worse than any of us Californians imagined — but I was also putting money on my hunch that the Americans out there were going to prove more friendly and helpful than we could ever dream. I didn't want any sag wagon preventing those Americans from getting their full chance.

Just as all of us sat down to begin going over our booklets, in walked a surprise . . . Ethan Turpin and his dad. Ethan was no longer crashing his bike into ditches regularly, he knew how to do things like shift or itch or get a drink while riding, and he'd even successfully completed our weekend bike club ride of 70 miles.

"Hey Ethan, what are you doing here?" asked Jimmy. "Did you leave something in your locker?"

" . . . " (Ethan always paused before any words came out of his mouth) " . . . well . . . I was thinking about crossing America with you guys . . . . "

Ethan didn't crack a smile as he announced his intentions to a disbelieving group, and all the heads in the room turned to look at Ethan and then back at me. Ethan was already a bicycling legend at our school and I was sure even the other kids' parents had heard of Ethan's big adventures. Everyone knew how far Ethan had come since his first day atop his blue bicycle, just five months earlier. All the kids really liked Ethan's mellow personality, but no one had any idea that he was actually considering going across America.

I handed Ethan and his dad a booklet and a colored marker. They joined our circle and we all spent the next two hours tracing our way across America. As we rolled our pens across the maps, I spoke of heat and humidity in the Southeast and of towns and places like the Blue Ridge Parkway, the Great Smokey Mountains, the Ozarks, the Platte River and Jackson Hole. With all my descriptions of elevation and weather and mileage, I was surprised that no one walked out before we reached the Pacific — everyone seemed to feel what took us under two hours to trace with markers couldn't be that tough.

It must not have sounded that tough to Ethan and his dad either, because after that meeting our campaign to win over his mom began. Joy's mom, Sulie, was easy to convince compared to Sue. She still saw Ethan closer to training wheels than transcontinental journeys — "My gosh, John, he's only twelve-years-old! He still crawls in bed with Bill and me . . . . And besides, even if you could ever convince me, where would we get the money to pay for his trip?"

In spite of his mom's objections, Ethan joined our three month training program. It involved riding after school and on weekends getting in shape and getting used to a loaded, touring bicycle. Our conditioning motto was: "We're only as fast as our slowest rider," and although we weren't intending to race across America, we wanted to have a pace comfortable and agreeable to all.

While Ethan was getting himself into better condition, I spent at least one evening a week, for about a month, trying to get his mom into shape to give him permission. First, I had to convince her that I thought he could make it; then I had to talk to Ethan's doctor to get him to okay his going. Ethan was born with a large lump of blood vessels, nested like an egg, in the small of his back. Why they were there, no one knew, and Sue wanted to be especially sure that no bike ride, during the growth spurt that was sure to accompany Ethan's 13th summer, would endanger his health. After Dr. Lou said go for it, Sue began leaning towards letting Ethan go.

It was time to work on getting sponsors, so I printed up some sponsor sheets. It was now up to Ethan to start writing letters and going door to door to raise some of his own money for the trip. Some people pledged money for each mile, some bought every mile in a particular state, some donated equipment, some just gave money, and one friend even gave him a transcontinental supply of vitamins! Grandparents, aunts, uncles and neighbors who had all seen little Ethan wiggle and wobble caught his contagious determination to cross America on his bike. Before he left, poor Ethan had a list of sponsors that would haunt him. In return for their donations, he promised he would write them from somewhere out on the road. Ethan had about as much fun writing as he had that first day on his bicycle, and he would be forever behind in his part of the pledge bargain. Now, years later, I think he has a couple people he still owes letters.

While plane reservations were being confirmed, little bicycling shorts being specially sewn, tents and equipment being ordered and checklist after checklist stacking up on my desk at home, Lynn, Jimmy, Heather, Joy, Carl, Ethan and I were getting ourselves and our bicycles in shape to ride. We needed to be able to ride an average of fifty miles per day, day after day after day for four months, on bicycles that would have thirty to forty extra pounds of gear on them. One of our first major tests occurred halfway through our conditioning program. We were going to pedal a half-century. A half-century is where a large group of bicyclists gather for a Saturday ride of fifty miles. Along the way, there are food stops and water stops. Riding with a large group of people always seems to make the miles go by easier and faster, so I chose one for us.

We arrived at the beginning of the ride proudly decked out in our new *From Sea to Shining Sea* t-shirts. Our bikes had shiny new racks all in place, but our first fifty-miler would be without gear. Most of the people at the starting line were over 18 and all decked out in their weekend riding togs. When my group of kids walked up with their bikes, the disbelieving questions began immediately:

"Are you riding today?" . . . "My gosh how old are you?" . . . "Do you really think you can do it?" . . . "Do your parents know you're doing this?"

No one suspected that, in less than two months, these same little people would be riding half centuries almost every day for four months — I don't know if I realized it myself.

One guy jokingly leaned down to Heather and said sarcastically, "What's that say on your shirt about *'From Sea to Shining Sea'?*"

"Well, me and my friends and my teacher and his wife are riding our bicycles across America this summer and the name of our trip is From Sea to Shining Sea. We're just doing this ride to get in shape."

"Yeah, we're just doing this to get in shape," chimed Carl and Ethan with grins on their faces.

Their smiles and nonchalant tones surprised the man in the lycra. He was so shocked he rode away mumbling something to himself. I saw him ride over to a group of his friends and point back to my motley band who had disappeared in the direction of the registration booth. I wondered if his friends believed him.

Our second "half-century," a month later, turned out to be more of a test than I had bargained for. I knew it was going to be hotter than our first one, and I knew it contained a lot more traffic and a lot more hills. Still, with another four weeks' conditioning under our shorts, I figured it would be just enough of a challenge to bring us to our next plateau of fitness and confidence. After checking in at the registration counter though, I wasn't so sure. First, they had changed the name of our ride from a "Half Century" to a "Metric Century," which meant instead of fifty miles the course would be sixty-two. Then, when I looked at the map and read the distances that accompanied the directions, I noticed that the end was posted not at Mile 62, but at the 77-mile-mark. I only hoped that the kids wouldn't look at the map, that they would just follow me and listen to my directions. I was going to try and lie the distance down to 50 or 60 miles. I forgot that Carl had his cycle computer installed and ready to measure our mileage — and my credibility.

"What took you so long? I've been here for at least 15 minutes!" Jimmy stood at the first rest stop, sucking on his water bottle and boasting of his first twenty miles.

"Yeah, and Heather and me have been here for a while too," said Joy. "They've got lots of bananas but they're already out of water! Boy John, you are slow."

Lynn, Ethan and Carl were also waiting at that rest stop, and I could see my first strategy was working so far. I'd ride very slowly at the back and always try to be the last in our group to reach the stops. When the kids would see me way off the back, they would figure they were getting stronger.

"John, you're a wimp!" Carl loved getting the final jab.

"You guys are just getting too quick for me. I hope I can keep up with you across America." I looked across at Lynn and we smiled quietly to each other. The kids were too busy complimenting themselves to see us exchange winks.

As the day wore on and the heat, wind and traffic increased, my method of staying way behind the kids became more and more difficult. Carl was the first to wither. The lunch stop was at the 35-mile-mark. Just past the sandwich station, the road climbed up into the sun. The blacktop seemed to vibrate in the heat and any water that we had put in our water bottles quickly got hot enough to brew tea. I was hoping that the lunch provided would help us make it through the last half of our ride, but the water was warm and the sandwiches were so dry from being out in the sun that they almost gagged the kids as they tried to force them down. The lunch stop did little to lift the groups' rapidly sagging spirits.

"John, I can't keep my eyes open."

"C'mon Carl, it's one in the afternoon. It's not your bedtime yet."

"No John, I'm not kidding. It's hard for me to keep my eyes open while I'm riding."

Carl was slowly weaving up the hill, his head drooped down over his handlebar bag.

"Just drink some water and put your mind on something else. You're just feeling the deadies after lunch."

Carl moaned pathetically and weakly reached down to pull his bottle from the cage on his bike.

"Pour some on your face and down through your helmet. Don't worry about running out. When you run out, I'll give you one of *my* water bottles. It is really hot today and I know that lunch wasn't very good. We've gone over forty miles already and you've done great."

"How much farther do we have to go?" The keep-them-talking technique was working. Carl was now riding a line that was much straighter than when we first left lunch, and I thought I noticed a little more strength in his pedal stroke and a little more lift in his head.

"Oh, I'm not sure, Carl. I think this map is about as bad as that lunch. How's your new bike riding? . . ."

In about five miles, we were back up with the pack of Ethan, Lynn and the girls.

"Hey John, you didn't tell us we would be riding through a desert today," said a red-cheeked Joy.

"Yeah John, it's so hot out here that even the lizards are resting in the shade," added Heather. "They won't even cross the road, because they know they would fry their little feet!"

We rode on through some hot, dusty badland east of Los Angeles. Ethan was hunched over his handlebars laboring with each turn of his pedals, Joy and Heather were going much slower than their usual pace, and Lynn, our master of on-the-road conversation, was out of encouraging words. I decided it was time for a little afternoon thundershower, so I played rainmaker with one of my water bottles.

"Hey, Ethan," I whispered. "Let's go squirt Joy and Heather with water."

Ethan suddenly perked up and followed me in pursuit of the dragging females.

I rode up behind them. With a water bottle in the hand hidden behind my back, I said in my sweetest voice, "Hi, girls! You two are sooo cute!" Squirting them awake with most of my bottle, I rode off with a parting, "Especially when you're wet!"

Just as they were yelling, "We're going to get you back, John!" Ethan sped by with attack number two.

Our water bottle shower made the next ten miles somewhat more bearable, and all of us, except for Jimmy, rode through the desert and sagebrush talking about imaginary ice cream parlors and Dairy Queens. We took orders for our favorite flavors and imagined what it would be like to soak in bathtubs of frosted Slurpees. Ethan decided he would coat his entire body with freezing cold rocky road ice cream. Jimmy had to hallucinate on his own, because he was somewhere way out in front.

As I listened to someone's fantasy of a massive lemon slush, I wondered if this was the way Wyoming was going to be. Would these kids have enough imagination and determination to get themselves across the hundreds of miles of high desert that surely awaited us sometime in August and September? And as the heat and miles began to take their toll on me that afternoon, I wondered if water bottle thunderstorms and frosty fantasies would be enough to get me across.

Carl, now up front, interrupted my thoughts with a yell from up around the bend. "Hey you guys. I see something red, white and blue lying over in the weeds. I think it's Jimmy."

Carl stood on the shoulder of the road pointing to the other side. Not known for soft tone or subtlety, Carl yelled: "Hey you guys, I think Jimmy's passed out in the bushes! HE LOOKS LIKE HE'S DEAD."

I hoped that Jimmy had just decided to wait for us and take a nap. With Carl's shrieking announcement, I was sure even the snoozing lizards had been awakened from their siestas, and as the rest of the group joined Carl on the side of the road, I coasted over to Jimmy who still hadn't moved.

His bike was leaned against a tree, so I knew he hadn't crashed. Before I had a chance to gently nudge him, the whole group was standing around our silent leader. Heather, as you can guess, had her camera (with film) out and was snapping pictures. Joy was giggling at how cute Jimmy looked when he was asleep, and Ethan and Carl had water bottles primed and ready for their own style of greeting for their downed comrade. Lynn, our nurse, had her bandana dampened and ready to mop his brow, and as we all stood over him, Jimmy slowly moaned. He opened his eyes and then stretched his arm over his face.

"Boy, you guys are slow. I was feeling hot, so I stopped here to wait for you all. I must have been here so long that I fell asleep."

Before I could stop them, Ethan and Carl responded to Jimmy's evaluation of their biking speed with a stream of warm water. Jimmy was definitely up then, and he tried to jump up and retaliate. Before letting him get all the way up, I commanded a cease fire and Heather snapped another picture. Lynn told Jimmy to sit back down, and started stroking his pale forehead with her wet bandana.

"Are you sure you're all right, Jimmy?" Joy kneeled down and checked her friend.

"Yeah, I think I'm okay. I just got really hot and the water didn't help to cool me off. The shade of this tree felt really good."

After Lynn finished treating Jimmy, everyone walked back across the road. There seemed to be more life in their legs and faces than I had seen since the first rest stop. Carl looked at his computer and said, "Hey, we've already gone fifty miles! We should be done with this ride."

All eyes suddenly turned to me. It was time for me to break the news about the "Half Century."

"Well, you guys, I'm sorry to say that this isn't a fifty-mile ride. When I got the map this morning, I noticed it said 'Metric Century,' and then when I looked at the mileage, I saw it said '77 miles.' I didn't tell you earlier because I didn't want to discourage you. You guys are really doing great!"

"77 miles! Are you kidding?" Carl was the first to react.

Joy softly followed. "We almost did that many miles in one day in Canada, so I think I can make it. They shouldn't have called this a 'half century' though . "

"Yeah, I agree with Joy, I think we can make it." Heather added.

Jimmy, who's nap hadn't robbed him of any confidence, boasted, "Let's go for it, dudes. I bet we'll have to do some 77-milers across the USA, so why not do our first one now?"

Ethan's eyes got really big at the thought of 77 miles. He didn't say anything. He just adjusted the chinstrap on his helmet, sucked up a little water from his bottle, and shrugged his shoulders. Without saying another word, we were off down the road.

It was getting late in the afternoon and we still had 15 miles to go. At the beginning of the ride, there were always other riders riding near us or passing us, but at 4 o'clock there weren't too many other riders passing us anymore. All seven of us were riding in a group now and the sag wagon, assigned to sweep the course for tired stragglers, suddenly pulled up behind us. The driver slowed down and his companion in the passenger seat stuck his head out the window:

"Hey, do you kids need a ride?"

Before I had a chance to answer, everyone of the kids had their own replies. As usual, Carl was first. "Hey, are you kidding? I came here to ride my *bike!*"

"No way, man. I'm not finishing in no sag wagon!" yelled an angry Jimmy.

"No thanks, I'm okay." said Joy.

"Yeah, we're okay," smiled Heather.

Ignoring the van, Ethan didn't even look up.

The sag wagon crew didn't ask us again if we wanted their help. I'm sure if they had, that guy in the passenger seat would have been showered with water from five well-aimed bottles.

Heather, Joy and I were the last to finish that half-century. After seeing the sag wagon, Jimmy, Ethan and Carl decided to play *Race Across America* (RAAM.) Jimmy was Lon Haldeman, Ethan was Michael Secrest, and Carl was Jonathan Boyer. All the kids had recently watched the *RAAM* on TV, so the three boys decided to act as if they were the guys who rode across America in less than ten days. Somehow they found some reserves of energy, and the three of them sprinted the best they could over those last ten miles. Lynn, who usually stayed near the back, was out there sprinting too. She was riding her brand-new custom bike and she wanted to ride fast with the guys. I rode in the back with my friends, Joy and Heather.

The girls and I decided we needed some extra finishing energy, so we stopped for our own private popsicle, cookie and cold drink stop soon after everyone else left us. The three of us were the last ones to finish the ride — besides our popsicle stop, Joy and Heather insisted on a couple stops of their own. First, there was a patch of "especially beautiful wildflowers, don't you think, Joy?" just five miles from the finish, and two miles later, there was "a patch of green grass just made for lying on and looking up at the whispy clouds, wouldn't you agree, Heather?" I really enjoyed riding with the girls and seeing the world at their pace, but I paid the price of my pace with the ribbing I received from three young male friends of mine at the finish:

"Man John, you sure were slow today."

"Yeah John, you're getting old. You finished dead last out of hundreds of people!"

"Thanks for your support, guys . . . ."

As we walked our bicycles to the car, I overheard the girls talking to Lynn: "Yeah, and we couldn't believe it. John leaned over to us and said, 'Hey girls, let's stop at that store for some refreshments.' We never thought John would stop for popsicles. He always just says 'keep going.' We sat there eating fig bars and juice and we couldn't believe it."

After our 77 mile "Half Century" through mountains, desert and cruddy sandwiches, the guys, the girls and Lynn wanted to celebrate. We decided on a feast at the local Taco Bell, and Ethan called his mom between burritos:

"Hi, Mom, I'm going to be home a little late . . . The ride was a little longer than we expected. I rode 77 miles!" The look on Ethan's and all the other kids' faces told me they were feeling ready to cross the continent. As I gobbled down my third burrito, I was feeling that way too.

3

I ordered a chocolate sprinkle and a rainbow sprinkle with five rainbow sprinkle donut holes. When we arrived at LA Airport, there was lots of hugs and kissing going on and I could see the sadness in my parents' eyes. But, I just couldn't get it through my mind what I was doing . . . .

Joy's Journal
June 18, 1986

Four Pairs of Undies

"I think my mom is paranoid," sighed Ethan, shaking his head and continuing the scrubbing of his freewheel. It was Monday, June 16th, and I had set aside the final two days before our departure to have private packing sessions with each of the kids and their parents.

Ethan was shaking his head because his mom had a role of fluorescent orange reflectors and she was sticking little squares and triangles all over his bike. She covered the handlebars, toe clips, seat, and all the tubes — she even started to put some on the tires! Finished with his bike, she began to attack his panniers and clothes. Day-glo triangles on the front, back and sides of each bag and rectangles on his helmet. Ethan ignored his mom the best he could until she began covering his shoes with the stickers. Knowing how close his mom already was to tears, he rolled his eyes and wisely waited until she left the room before pronouncing his mom's condition.

In the other room of the schoolhouse lay Ethan's necessities for four months on the road. I had given each of the kids a checklist specifying and limiting what they could bring, and many of my last forty-eight hours were spent checking off each allowed pair of underwear, each sock, towel, toothbrush and tube of toothpaste. Somewhere amidst all their clothing, camping gear and bike tools there had to be room for all the food that we would have to carry, and my preliminary estimates showed that at times we would be so far from civilization, we would have to carry five days supply of provisions.

As we checked off each item, we organized them into Ziploc plastic bags. Not only would the bags keep things dry, but they would also separate clean clothes from honey jar meltdowns and misplaced dirty socks.

I must have been crazy thinking two hours would be enough time to pack each kid. I had seen my dad try to get my family packed and in our station wagon enough times to know better.

"I've got one sock, and I'm sure I had the other one with it when we left the house this morning," mumbled Ethan as he rummaged through his pile on the floor.

"These heavy duty Ziplocs sure aren't very heavy duty," he continued, as

38

his mom drove home to find the sock and he ripped another bag attempting to stuff his three shirts inside. It was his fourth bag, and I was not only running out of time, but I was also running out of bags.

By the time we found all of Ethan's socks and found a place for his ten pounds of vitamins — remember, the vitamin pledge? Whatever happened to one-a-days anyway? — he had been with me for over three hours. His face was so full of grease, it looked as if he had cleaned his chain and freewheel with it, but at least everything was cleaned, packed and ready.

"See you at the airport," I waved from the same porch where just months before, I had talked with Sue about her son's first ride. Before going back inside, I whispered, "Good job, Mom," and watched the Turpin family drive home together the last time for a long time. Sue had done a good job not crying in those three hours.

"Okay, Heather, how many pairs of underwear are you packing? I love you a lot and I love how organized you are, but I know you always bring too many pairs of underwear."

"But, John . . . . "

"No 'But, Johns!' We need room for peanut butter and jelly where those extra pairs of underwear would be. We can't eat your Calvin Kleins."

"Oh, John . . . Okay Mom, here's a pair you'll have to take home. Boy John, you're mean."

Little did Heather know that Lynn and I had already had our underwear *and* sock *and* shirt *and* shoe confrontation months before, when I'd originally composed the checklist. On every trip we'd ever taken, our girl members overestimated their need for clothes. Originally, I had wanted to allow even less in terms of clothes, but after some stern ultimatums from my spouse, I padded the list.

"No discussion, Heather. How many pairs of shoes?"

"Well . . . I can't really decide which pair of shoes to take along with my biking shoes. Should I take these white tennis shoes . . . or should I take these white leather sandals? Or maybe . . . I could take them both?"

"Sorry, Heather, your smile's not going to do you any good with clothes." I couldn't believe she had had the packing checklist for four months and hadn't yet decided which pair of shoes to bring. Still, I was such a sucker for her smile, I let her take both pairs of shoes. She promised to send one pair home from Washington, D.C., after we had gone out "nice" in the Capitol.

After having made that compromise, I figured we would proceed quickly and easily through our lists and we did — except for pants and shirts.

"Should I bring this plain cotton t-shirt or that colorful blouse with the buttons?" Although I was used to going through the same wardrobe dilemma every morning with Lynn, with all I had to do in the next 48 hours, I didn't have much patience for Heather. "And, John, what do you think of these shorts? Do you like the black ones or the tan ones better?"

How could women be so oblivious? I was beginning to wonder if Heather was already learning the female technique I knew so well. They get you so frustrated that you say something like: "I don't care! Just take whatever you want."

Heather's smile told me she wouldn't be surprised if I let her take both shirts and both shorts. I moaned, looked the other way and continued packing her bike into its padded bag. I would discover the secrets of Heather's wardrobe somewhere down the road, but if I discovered anything extra getting in the way of food, some rhododendron bush in North Carolina would be wearing some of Heather's extra attire!

By late Monday afternoon, I had Carl, Heather and Ethan packed up and ready to meet us at the airport Wednesday morning. My buddy, Jimmy, was waiting for me back at my house in Santa Barbara to pack up his stuff. I figured that he'd be the easiest to pack because he had been with me throughout the year on our drives to school and knew that I meant business with my checklist. Also, because his dad lives in Memphis and he lives with his mom, I had done a lot of his shopping and preparation with him. Jimmy was the closest I had to a son.

The only item I knew wasn't completely specific was under the toiletries section. It read *Personal Items*, and I had created it mostly for the benefit of Lynn, Heather and Joy. I had nightmarish visions of what such freedom might bring, because even though Lynn didn't wear make-up, I still couldn't figure out all the stuff she kept in her special little bag. In packing up Joy and Heather, I didn't dare look into their "*Items*," but their bags weren't nearly as big or bad as I had expected. Then, along came Jimmy.

" 3 pair shorts?"

"2 biking, 1 sports. Check."

"1 pair casual pants."

"Check."

"4 pairs underwear."

"I only need two. Check."

Jimmy and I were proceeding through the packing list like John Glenn and Mission Control. As we packed and Jimmy's pile of gear disappeared into Ziplocs and panniers, I was proud of how I had prepared him. All the time we were packing, though, I noticed this big, white plastic bag that I couldn't figure out. When we got to "*Personal Items*," I found out.

"Hey Jimmy, what's in the white bag?"

"Oh nothing, man, just my toiletries."

"Mind if I take a look?"

"Not at all. Go 'head."

Designer shampoo, designer rinse, designer conditioner, designer setting lotion, designer mousse, designer body lotion, cologne, after shave, two kinds of deodorant and some things . . . I never even heard of! The contents of that white bag were unbelievable. I thought to myself: Jimmy didn't sound the least bit worried when I asked to take a look. . . Does he really smell that bad, or am I just being old fashioned?

Sounding more like his old man than his dad, I yelled, "Jimmy, are you crazy? You've got more junk in this bag than a girl!"

"John, you said 'Personal Items' were up to us."

"But—

"Hey dude, remember what you taught us about *ex post facto* laws?"

"Yeah, you're right. I did say toiletries were up to you. As long as you have room to carry your share of food. Just remember you have to pedal all of this stuff."

"I know, I know . . . Hey John, if you're nice, I'll even show you how to use some of this stuff. Remember, man, this is the eighties."

"The eighties . . . Check."

Tuesday night found Lynn and me side by side in our own bed for the last time for many months. All the kids' stuff was neatly packed, checked off and sitting in our garage. Tomorrow, Lynn and I would take care of all the odds and ends that needed to be done for our trip and for our being away from home. Even with all the preparation and planning that had consumed me for the past year and a half, I knew that tomorrow's final chores would probably continue all through the night, so I snuggled up extra close to Lynn.

"John . . . thanks for taking me."

"What do you mean? You're my partner."

"Yeah, but you've done most of the planning. You've spent all the time getting the kids and the maps and the tickets and everything else. So thanks for taking me." With that, Lynn rolled over and kissed me. Drawing back and placing her fingers on my chin, she looked up at me and said, "John, we're about to have five kids, and, for the next 5,000 miles we won't have many pillows or much privacy. Promise you'll meet me back here in October?"

"Promise."

Bye Mom

I was right about me not making it to bed the next night, because Thursday, June 18 didn't dawn, it was just a blurry, caffeine-inspired continuation of Wednesday, the 17th. I was up loading 120 rolls of film and organizing my desk for my brother, Jay, who would be running *From Sea to Shining Sea Headquarters*, making sure our bill collectors — who somehow didn't see any reason to put us on hold for four months — stayed satisfied. He would also keep parents and friends posted of our weekly progress and be our lifeline — sending us supplies and cash at pre-planned rendezvous points.

Lynn did get one more night under her home covers. She rarely let anything interfere with her right to sleep, and *From Sea to Shining Sea* eve was no exception.

I loaded my last film cassette and downed a gulp of coffee that had been sitting on my desk for an hour. Its awful taste kept me awake as much as its caffeine, and as I called out, "Mrs. Olsen, where are you?", the alarm on my watch went off. It was 3:30 AM, time to wake up sleeping beauty. My other brother, Dan, would soon be in the driveway ready to load our two pick-up trucks with the bikes. We were meeting all the kids and their families at Los Angeles International Airport at 6:30.

Sleepy-eyed Ethan was one of the first to meet us at the airport. "How're ya doin', Eeth?" I asked.

"Okay, I guess, but my mom sure is acting weird this morning. It's like she's mad at me or something."

I looked over at Sue and when I saw the look on her face, I was taken back to the morning I left my mom in the driveway as I moved away to college. I had expected my mom to be sad, but that morning she looked at me like I had killed the dog, yelled at my sisters and warped all her Robert Goulet records. I'm sure Ethan's mom didn't have any Robert Goulet records, but the look on her face was definitely familiar. Time had taught me that my mom really wasn't mad so, taking a deep breath, I whispered to Ethan that it would be okay, and walked over to his family to say good morning. Bill Turpin's pride in his son was getting the best of his sadness, and he gave me a smiling "Good morning, John, how are you?" But when Sue shot me her quick "Good morning, John," I knew her pride was on hold.

Ethan was his sister's best friend, and she didn't seem to be too happy with me for taking her friend and brother away for "the whole summer!!!" Acting like I was invisible, she gave me the same non-look my sisters used to give me — the one reserved for moments of the highest displeasure. I had lots to do checking on seven passengers and seven bicycles, and checking in with five families, so with my best "Good morning, Amber," I was on with business:

"Now let's see . . . I'm holding onto Ethan's spending money . . . and he's supposed to keep a record in his journal of how he spends it. Got it. And . . . if he needs more money, we'll call home and, Sue, you'll send it . . . Oh sure, Lynn and I will loan him some money if he needs it before he can get hold of you.... "

"Heather, have I got it right that you have all your own spending money?. . . Is $100 enough for four months? Yes, Becky (Heather's mom), I think so. All of her entertainment and food are covered in the group budget . . . .

"So, Fagerlins, you want me to take care of Carl's money like I do Ethan's, and I'll keep a record of it . . . A separate budget for his spending money and his film money??? Sure, I think I can handle it.

"Hi, Fultons! Sulie, I hope you're kidding about still wanting Joy to go to England . . . Oh, you're not? — Well, Bob, how was the fishing last week? . . . .

"Jimmy, has your mom got her phone number in Uruguay yet? . . . You think so?! Audrey (Jimmy's mom), let me have that phone number!"

Lynn handed out our final roster, mail drops and information sheet to each of the parents. While the parents were momentarily distracted, the kids got a chance to hit the bathroom and snack bar, and the two of us got a few moments to make sure we had what we needed.

"Lynn, you've got the food budget travelers checks?"

"Right here with the budget book in my handlebar bag along with our personal money for my quilt collection." Lynn knew it was a perfect time to slip that one in.

"And I've got the plane tickets in my front pocket and the entertainment budget travelers checks here in my bag. Here's Ethan's money and Carl's spending money and Carl's film money. Have you taken any pictures yet? I told you to take pictures, didn't I?"

"Yes, John."

"Flight #558, first call. Would all passengers for Braniff Flight 558 to Washington, D.C. please report to your gate for departure with your boarding passes ready."

"John! John! What boarding passes? I don't have any boarding pass!"

"It's okay, Carl, *I* have your passes. I'll give them to you as soon as its time to board."

Somewhere in between that first call and the last call, almost all of the last minute questions got answered. At some secret cue, each family circled its members for the last time and huddled up, oblivious to anyone else. Tears fell hard from mothers' eyes and dads' pride was dampened a bit too, as they said good-bye to their kids. As each of the kids walked over to me to get their boarding pass, I couldn't help but wonder who were the braver ones . . . the kids who were going to ride their bikes across our country, or the parents who were letting them.

"Good morning, ladies and gentleman. This is your captain speaking. Braniff Airlines Flight 558 would like to extend a very special welcome to James West, Heather Deutsch, Joy Fulton, Carl Fagerlin, Ethan Turpin and John and Lynn Seigel Boettner, the *From Sea to Shining Sea* bicycle group. These five kids and their teachers are flying with us to Washington, D.C. They will begin their journey in Washington and ride their bicycles some 4,500 miles back to California. Their trip will take them four months, and we wish them the best of luck."

I guess the parents had made some contact with the cabin, because this announcement caught the kids and me completely by surprise. Carl, Jimmy and Ethan interrupted their first of many cokes to listen, and Joy stopped writing all over Heather's arm with her ball-point pen long enough to hear everyone's name. The man in the seat next to them leaned over to Joy and asked if she was one of the famous bicyclists.

"Uh, Uh." Joy was so articulate sometimes.

"Well, I think that's just great. Ridin' y'all's bicycles all the way across the U.S.A. Would y'all give me your autographs for my young boy back in Dallas? I really think what y'all are doin' is just wonderful. My son would be real excited to have y'all's autographs."

While Joy and Heather started the autographs, Jimmy leaned over at me and said, "Hey John, did you see that guy up in first class when the announcement came over the loudspeaker?"

"You mean, the guy with the three-piece suit and the *Wall Street Journal?*"

"Yeah, that's the one. Well, did you see what he did when he heard we were going to ride across the USA?"

"No, I didn't. What did he do?"

"Too bad, 'cuz, man, it was great. He folded up his paper, looked out at the window, then back at us and then back out the window again. He just kept staring out the window. I think he'd like to trade his desk for one of our bikes . . . Man, John, you should have seen him . . . ."

Every so often I looked over at the kids, and if they weren't answering some admirer's questions or sipping a coke or writing on each other, they were usually silently gazing out the window, like the guy in first class.

"Hey Ethan, look down there! Can you believe we're really gonna ride all the way across that?"

A wide-eyed Ethan leaned over Jimmy's shoulder, scratched his fresh haircut and looked out the window. His jaw dropped open, his eyes got even bigger, but no words came out of his mouth. Ethan's silent gaze was a look we would soon all get used to, but on Day 1, Jimmy wasn't prepared for it.

"Yo, Ethan!" Jimmy wanted his answer. "I said, can you believe we're going to ride across all that?"

Still not getting an answer from Ethan, Jimmy sat back and said to himself, "Ethan, you're in space . . . . "

Each one of the kids took some time to look down from the jet and stare at the America that had looked so much smaller on our classroom map.

"Hey, John! Do you know what state we're flying over? Jimmy says it's Tennessee, but he's from Tennessee and I think he's just saying that. Heather says it's Virginia, Carl says it's North Carolina, and Ethan, he's still staring out the window. Whatever it is, it sure is green."

"Well, Joy, I'm not sure what state it is. I've never been to any of the states we're going to be riding through, except Oregon and California, so I can't help you. How are you feeling?"

"Other than getting tired of everyone asking us if we're the kids biking across America and why we're doing it and stuff, I'm doing okay. It sure looks big down there, though, and I think I'm getting a little nervous."

"Know what, Joy? So am I."

4

We went to the Lincoln Memorial and I counted the steps . . . fifty-eight. I thought that it would be neat to sit in Abe's lap . . . .

Joy's Journal
June 19, 1986

Uncle Steve

We flew from the Pacific to the Atlantic in less than six hours — time flies when you fly. Leaving a trail of Coca-Cola cans, plastic cups and M&M wrappers behind them, the kids left the plane with an admiring flight crew all lined up at the exit to give them special good-byes and good-lucks. Lynn and I brought up the rear, making sure no traveler's checks, wallets or journals were left amid the rubble.

I'm always nervous when one of our groups arrives at an airport, worrying if our bicycles have made the air journey as well as we have. Visions of missing panniers and mangled bicycle frames always occupy my imagination as I walk towards the baggage area. The kids didn't seem to share my concern as they ran and slid on the waxed linoleum and searched for any escalators going their way. They managed to find every set of moving stairs between us and our baggage check, and went up and down each one as many times as they could before Lynn and I disappeared from sight.

One, two, three, four, five, six, seven blue bike bags. I saw our precious cargo standing straight and seemingly unharmed off to the side of the luggage conveyor. The kids were hoping to see their bikes come tumbling down the ramp along with all the Samsonite, but I was glad to see they had received some special handling.

Transportation into Washington for us and our bikes was arranged by Carl's dad who had business associates there, and standing right next to our bike bags were three very official looking men in suits and ties. Mr. Edson, the man Carl's dad had put in charge of Operation *From Sea to Shining Sea*, introduced himself and his companions, then informed us that a company van and semi-truck were awaiting us just outside the glass doors of the baggage area. When Carl's dad said that they would have a truck ready to take our bikes into the city, I envisioned a pickup, so when I stepped outside and saw the awaiting semi, I couldn't believe it. It could have carried fifty bicycles, and I envisioned our seven bags crashing all around the back of its enormous trailer.

"Hey John, can we ride in the back?" Carl wanted to crash around with them.

"Yeah! You and Lynn go in the van and we'll go in the back of the truck," grinned Ethan.

"Sorry, guys."

"Oh, John."

"Nope, let's all stick together."

We were going to spend four days in DC, staying with Joy's Uncle Steve and Aunt Shirley who lived and worked downtown. Mr. Edson would escort our bikes to the DDI warehouse, while Brian Hodges would drive us to Uncle Steve's house.

"There it is, you guys, over there on the right, the Washington Monument. As soon as we get around this corner, you'll be able to see the White House and the Capitol. It's not on the way to 'Uncle Steve's' but I'll drive us around the mall if you want." Brian was enjoying being our tour guide.

"Yeah, sure, we're not in a hurry." I was so excited being in Washington, D.C. for the first time, I led the unanimous vote.

"Go for it, Mr. Hodges." Jimmy did have good manners. I was glad he substituted our driver's name for his usual "dude."

My first drive in front of the Capitol brought all the pictures from old textbooks and encyclopedias and evening news to life. Off to one side was the White House, and there on the other side of the grass, over by the Air and Space Museum, was The Smithsonian. Hundreds of people were playing softball on the giant grassy area that made up "the Mall," and off at one end, casting its long shadow, was the Washington Monument. I had to stick my head out the window to get a full view. I was so excited I wanted Brian to drive around it at least one more time.

"John, let's go to my uncle's house now."

"Yeah John, I've got to go to the bathroom."

Lynn leaned up to me and touched me on the shoulder. "It's okay, John, we'll be here for a few more days and you'll get to see everything. We really should get to Steve and Shirley's. You know, you're kinda cute when you get excited. You're more of a little kid than the kids are."

Steve and Shirley lived in the Eastern Market section of Washington. Trees formed shady archways over bumpy streets lined with ivy-covered brick houses in the process of yuppie urban renewal. Brian dropped us off on the corner and we walked to Steve and Shirley's.

"Hey John, how come there are so many junk cars parked next to new BMWs around here?" asked Carl.

"Yeah, and one house will be all fixed up and nice, and the two on each side of it will look like a bomb blew them up . . ." said Jimmy.

"I don't know you guys . . . . " I wondered too as we walked past German sports cars advertising their alarm systems next to their college alma maters. Right next to them were broken-down and dented Dodges and Cadillacs. Black women stood at the bus stop with recycled shopping bags, and shiny, black bodies soared skyward in their hightops over the netless hoops of the nearby school playground.

I remembered watching a *60 Minutes* story once on the plight of Washington's predominantly black population, and as we walked through the Eastern Market, I couldn't help but wonder if the brick faces lining those streets were surviving the urban renewal better than the black ones walking them.

"Ooooh, how neat!" I was sitting out in the patio enjoying a beer, some chips and the garden, when I heard Heather excitedly talking to herself. Lynn was inside talking with Shirley, and Joy and the boys were visiting with Uncle Steve. Heather was following a blinking yellow dot of light around the back of the garden in a world of her own.

"Please slow down, you little bug or whatever you are. I'm from California and I've never seen one of you before. I promise I won't hurt you. Oooh, nice bug, that's better. Yeah, just stay there for a minute. Do you think you could possibly leave your light on a little longer so I can get a better look? You're a cute little bug. How do you do that anyway?" I didn't say anything but I hoped Heather didn't mind me eavesdropping on her private nature study.

Pretty soon the rest of the group came outside to help cut up onions and tomatoes. They also knew that if they didn't get their paws in the chips and dip soon, that I would single-handedly take care of both bowls. After grabbing a chip and spilling a little onion dip down his chin, Carl asked, "What's Heather doing?"

"Oh, she's watching fireflies. Let her be, Carl."

Pretty soon Uncle Steve, Aunt Shirley, Lynn and I were left to the onions and the tomatoes and buns, as the kids chased dots of light around the garden. Carl wasn't content to observe, and like most guys his age he had to catch each one he saw. He was even able to capture them one handed, with burger in one hand and firefly in the other. Heather and Joy disapproved of Carl's treatment of their cute flying friends, and quick to catch the political spirit of Washington, the two of them formed the SPCF, the Society for the Prevention of Cruelty to Fireflies. They puffed up their chests and arm-in-arm walked up to Carl and objected vociferously to his alleged mistreatment of one of our nation's "neatest" resources. In order to enjoy my dinner, and to preserve some fireflies for future generations, I stood up for Joy and Heather's cause by giving Carl a quota: "Okay Carl, one more."

"But, John . . . . "

"I'm doing it for your own good, Carl. If you don't stop catching fireflies and get over here to the table, I'm going to finish all the chips." My threat seemed to help things out. Carl immediately stopped his hunt and sat down at the table.

The kids watched the light show as they ate their dinner, and Lynn and I got a chance to visit with Steve and Shirley as we ate ours. Joy's mom called Steve her "hippie younger brother," and I already knew that he had worn sideburns and had played football alongside O.J. Simpson at USC. Now, Steve was the Chief of Staff for the Senate Committee on Aging, and I tried to find out how a child of the sixties ended up in Washington with short hair, three-piece-suit and a Republican senator for a boss. Lynn was enjoying her visit with Shirley, a tall, pretty woman who, too, had weathered some earlier radical times and was now a successful working woman. She held a very respected position with a government research agency, played evening softball, and had a wonderful house she was fixing up. Both Lynn and I were just settling in for a long visit, when we noticed the kids nodding off in their patio chairs. We'd almost forgotten all that the kids had been through that day. They had risen before dawn on the other side of America, and had to say good bye to their families and sign autographs on a big metal bird. Ethan's big brown eyes were having trouble staying open; Heather's freckled face lay eyes closed against Joy's shoulder, as they both somehow balanced their dozing figures on the picnic bench; Jimmy was conked out and snoring on his chair; and Carl's eyes were open, but he was so out of it he didn't even notice the fireflies buzzing around his head. We'd have to visit with Steve and Shirley later. It was time to put our kids to bed and for me to get my first sleep in a couple nights.

With five drowsy but sincere, "Good night, Aunt Shirley"s and "Good night, Uncle Steve"s, all the kids told their surprised new relatives they'd see them in the morning. Soon Heather and Joy were crawling into their sheetsacks on the hard linoleum floor in the bedroom, while the boys, Lynn and I crawled into ours on the floor in the next room. After everyone said goodnight to everyone else, before Jimmy started snoring and before Lynn fell into her nightly coma, I rolled up behind her and whispered in her ear, "Happy Anniversary, dear." It was our third anniversary, and for the first time, we were sleeping in the same room. Lynn, not expecting any romantic advances with Jimmy at our heads and Ethan and Carl within reach, squeezed my hand and was quickly off to never never land.

"John . . . What should we wear to Steve's committee meeting today?"

"Well Heather, I don't have too many choices. I'm going to wear my long nylon pants and my shirt with buttons. I told the guys to wear their long pants and a clean shirt. People will find out we're biking and realize we can't carry fancy clothes."

"Yeah, but we still should look nice."

"Heather, I *always* look nice, but sometimes Lynn doesn't always agree with my opinion. I think you'd better go over your choices with her or Joy. Enjoy having to make a decision while you can, because once we get on our bikes in Maryland in a couple of days, you won't have the extra clothes you brought with you for the airplane. We'll be sending them home. I was serious when I told you back at school that you'd have to lighten your load after Washington."

Before I finished my lecture, Heather was back in the bathroom with Joy and Lynn discussing the fashion statement for the day. The guys and I just sat shaking our heads.

"Those girls are crazy . . . Man, I would wear what I got on right now even if we had an appointment with President Reagan himself," said Carl.

"Even though you wore them on the plane all day yesterday and slept in them last night?" asked Jimmy.

"Yup!"

"Well, I don't know about that, but what I can't understand about girls is why they always have summit conferences in the bathroom . . . Girls never go to the bathroom by themselves; there's always at least two of them, and usually four or five . . . How can they read a magazine on the pot when they're always talking?"

I leaned over to Jimmy and said, "Maybe that's why God created man so that he could easily relieve himself just standing next to a bush. I mean, there are certain times when all the bathrooms are full of women, and without our advantage, this world could have some major problems."

"John, you're brilliant." Jimmy enjoyed my early morning revelations with his usual hint of sarcasm.

"I think you're gross!" was Carl's reaction. Ethan sat silently, contemplating what problems might indeed arise if our anatomy was different.

" . . . Whoa, dude . . . that would be serious . . . ." Ethan *was* serious, but Jimmy threw a pillow at him anyway.

It was less than a mile from Steve and Shirley's place to the Capitol and the Senate office building where Steve's committee met, so we decided to walk.

As soon as we left the neighborhood and came upon our first marble columns and buildings, Heather's camera started to click. She was soon followed by everyone else. We took pictures of unknown government buildings and climbed up to walk on the tops of the short walls that separated the lawns and gardens from the sidewalks. Streams of official looking men and women poured towards the Capitol. The men were almost all dressed in gray suits and black shoes, and the women wore long skirts with jackets and scarfs. I had worried earlier that we might get lost on our way to the government center, but I needn't have. Although nothing was marked, ours was a one-way sidewalk. No one was walking away from wherever these people were headed, and if anyone had dared walk the other way, they would probably have been involved in a three briefcase collision.

"Lynn, why do some of the women wear jogging shoes with their nice outfits? They look kinda silly."

Having experienced this same phenomenon on one of our trips to Boston, Lynn explained to Joy and Heather how the women would wear their comfortable shoes to walk to and from work and change into their pumps at the office.

"Oh, I understand now," said Heather. "Hey, wait everybody. There's the White House. Everyone stop so I can take a picture."

"Sorry, Heather, that's not the White House, that's the Capitol," said Jimmy.

"Well, isn't that the place where the President lives?" Heather was still confused.

"Don't you know anything, Heather?" It was Carl's turn. "The President lives in the White House." Ethan and Joy were remaining silent, but listening intently to this impromptu and informative lesson on Federal architecture.

"Well, what happens in the Capitol then?" Heather wanted to know.

Carl's answer didn't help much. "I'm not sure, but I know that the President lives in the White House, and the White House doesn't have a dome like that."

Jimmy soon put everyone's confusion to rest. Slowly and deliberately he offered his expert knowledge: "Carl's right. Ron and Nancy live in the White House, and I don't think you can see it from here. The Senate and the House of Representatives meet in the Capitol."

"Oh, you mean that's where we're going to see Uncle Steve's Senate committee meeting?"

Jimmy looked over at me. "No, Heather, that's not where we are going to see the committee meeting. We're going to the Dirksen Senate Office Building."

"Oh well, I'm sure I'll figure it out in a couple of days. I think I'll just take pictures for now. Hey everybody, will you all stop so I can take a picture of you guys with *the Capitol* in the background?" As Heather took our picture, I heard Ethan and Joy whispering about their not knowing the difference between the Capitol and the White House either.

By the time we stopped for Heather's—and everyone else's—pictures, we were a little late for our appointment at Uncle Steve's office. My getting us a little lost en route to the Dirksen Building didn't help matters much, but it wasn't taking long for all the surrounding gray office buildings to look the same to me. The first time we entered Dirksen we had to have our handlebar bags searched by security, and the kids enjoyed imagining they were secret agents being screened for electronic bugging devices. Making it past checkpoint one, we proceeded down the labyrinth of hallways filled with more gray flannel officials. We couldn't tell anyone's rank because everyone looked the same.

"I think red and yellow ties are in this summer," Heather noticed.

"You're right, and I think the people who wear topsiders must be not quite so important. They look younger," added Joy.

We must have been quite a sight as we scratched down the hall in our colorful nylon pants, Hawaiian shirts, and California tans. Somehow, what had been appropriate in LA International stuck out like a sore thumb in the Dirksen Building. Maybe Lynn was right this time.

The official looking sign on Steve's office door said:

SENATE COMMITTEE ON AGING — SENATOR HEINZ, CHAIRMAN.

We opened the door and squeezed ourselves into the waiting area. The little cubicle of carpet had all of two chairs in it and on the small end table there were a couple of magazines I had never even heard of.

"Yes, may I help you?" Steve's secretary sounded a bit uncomfortable as we shut the door behind us. She looked more used to visits from gray-haired octogenarians than from freckle-faced adolescents.

Carl and Ethan immediately grabbed the two chairs and began thumbing through the magazines. While I told the secretary that Steve was expecting us, poor Ethan couldn't contain himself. "Man . . . these magazines are boring! They don't even have any pictures." Lynn tried to whisper something about whispering as Ethan's magazine review broke the library-like silence, while Steve's secretary desperately tried to get hold of the only person who could identify the motley crew crowding around her desk.

Much to her relief, Uncle Steve soon appeared from behind one of the doors. She managed a nervous smile as Steve introduced us and what we were doing for the next four months. She was glad that we were headed west.

"What happened to you guys?" asked Steve.

The secretary changed her look from panic to pain, as each of the kids simultaneously gave him their explanation for our tardiness. Steve somehow understood, deciphering what everyone had to say.

"Well, kids, we'd better be getting to the Committee hearing. Grab your bags and cameras and follow me."

The kids rushed out the door following Steve, while Lynn and I said goodbye to his secretary.

"Nice meeting you," was Lynn's farewell.

I followed Lynn out the door and just before I closed it I said,"See ya later." From the look on that poor secretary's face, I was afraid I'd said something wrong.

Even though Uncle Steve didn't have any kids of his own, he sure was a natural around them. Lynn and I enjoyed trailing behind the kids who were crowded around him, as he led them down the hallways and up the stairs like the pied piper. Steve's six-foot figure towered above them, and their necks were craned at full extension every time he spoke. Steve had an answer for each one of their many questions and he always took time to stop and point out special people and places in his building. He explained that today's hearing was about mandatory retirement. Lynn and I smiled as we listened to him first teach the kids how to pronounce "man-da-tory re-tire-ment" and then explain what it was. By the time we reached the conference room, the kids were primed to listen to what was going on. No one needed to warn them to be quiet and pay attention; Steve had them ready. In fact, if Senator Heinz had called on one of them for their opinion, I'm sure they would have gladly testified. Before the hearing was called to order, we all sat down and tried to figure out who was a senator and who were just staff or witnesses.

"It's easy, man," said Jimmy. "First rule out the young guys and girls, I think they are pages. Then look for the gray suits, and see who has the most people standing around them. Then, if they have that high and mighty, aloof look — you know, like they are always looking over the heads of everyone else — then I say they are senators."

We each cast our votes for who was a senator and who was not. We'd know who was the best judge when everyone took their places.

Just before everything began, Uncle Steve motioned us over to one of the men in a gray suit and red tie. He had received our unanimous vote as being a real senator and when Uncle Steve introduced him to us as our own California Senator, Pete Wilson, we all smiled proudly at our insight. As Steve went around the circle saying our names, Heather whispered to Ethan, "I told you he was a senator." Senator Wilson managed a weak handshake and tried to sound impressed with our journey across America, but seemed preoccupied with some other, more important business. I thought that my five kids taking four months of their young lives to pedal across their country to meet fellow Americans and learn about where and how they live was pretty impressive, but I guess I didn't understand what was really important in Washington. Anyway, we got our handshake and photograph with our senator, and then went back to our front row seats.

Senators came and went during the hour of testimony we witnessed. The kids had to contain themselves from raising their hands to ask questions about what was going on. Finally Joy leaned over to me and whispered, "It sounds like everyone who's talking is against mandatory retirement, so what's the problem? If everyone agrees on not having a mandatory retirement age, then why take so much time with a discussion?"

I reached over, put my arm around her shoulder and said, "You're right, Joy. I wish you could stand up and tell the committee that." She smiled and returned to listening to the testimony.

Just about then, Senator John Glenn walked in and took his seat on the panel. He looked a little more weathered and wrinkled than the John Glenn I grew up with in Life magazine, but he was still unmistakably John Glenn. Heather got all excited and tried her best to control herself, but I think everyone around her noticed when she began pointing at the bald, athletic-looking man, who had just walked in. Finally, unable to contain herself any longer, she got up out of her seat and tiptoed over to me.

"John, John! Do you see the senator who just walked in?" She held her pointed finger up close against her chest, but she wanted me to be sure I knew who she was talking about. I nodded my head and Heather excitedly continued, "Well, he looks just like the guy in the movie! You know, he looks just like the guy in *The Right Stuff*. I can't believe it. He looks so much like the guy in the movie!"

Before I could say anything, Jimmy grabbed Heather by the shirt-tail and sat her down next to him. In the same authoritative voice he had used to explain the Capitol, Jimmy this time informed her: "Heather, that man up there is the guy the movie was *about*!" Jimmy shook his head in disbelief, and Heather went back to her seat to think about what Jimmy had said. About ten minutes later, a light went on in Heather's already bright eyes and she whispered to herself, but loud enough for us to hear, "Oh, I get it."

Jimmy just moaned.

After over an hour, the kids were convinced that mandatory retirement wasn't a good idea, and during a pause in the action, we decided to leave. Uncle Steve spoke to us in the corridor outside and mentioned that there would be some dissenting opinions coming up before the committee soon. Ethan said he'd like to stick around to hear what would be said, but he lost out in our own democratic decision process. We voted to go for a walk around the Capitol and meet Steve for lunch at 12:30 in the Dirksen Cafeteria.

"C'mon Ethan. I want to take some pictures outside." Heather's shutter finger was itching.

As soon as we got outside, Heather let loose with, "Can you guys believe how much John Glenn looked like the guy in *The Right Stuff*?!"

Jimmy's reaction wasn't very long in coming. "Heather, I can't believe you didn't know who he was! John Glenn, famous astronaut and senator? I can't believe it . . . ." We walked through the park separating the Senate office buildings from the Capitol, Heather, Jimmy and everyone else kidding each other the whole way.

As we walked around the Capitol towards the Mall, the kids spotted the huge lawn that unrolls like a green carpet towards the Washington Monument. They all got the escalator-look in their eyes, and Joy yelled, "Hey John, can we run?"

"Yeah, we've been in airplanes and vans and hearing rooms too long, let's run!" seconded Carl.

"Sure, go for it. Just keep us in sight." Lynn and I had made each of them put Steve and Shirley's address and phone number in their journals that morning, but we still didn't want to lose sight of them our first real day in Washington.

"John, will you hold my camera for me?" Joy's camera must have weighed five pounds.

"Sure, Joy."

"John, will you hold my handlebar bag?"

"No, Carl, I want everyone to carry their own. It's got all your important stuff in it, so you should get used to carrying it yourself. Sorry."

"Oookay."

As the kids ran down the steps and out onto the grass ahead of us, Lynn and I grabbed each other's free hand and squeezed. "They sure are neat kids, John. I'm really going to enjoy spending time with them. I don't think we could have a nicer family for four months."

"Yeah, Lynn, I think you're right. Even when Jimmy and Heather were kidding each other it was all in fun."

"And wasn't it neat when Ethan said he wanted to stick around for more testimony? He wasn't kidding. He really wanted to hear what the opposition was going to say."

"I think Steve had a lot to do with that. Did you see how the kids were glued to every word he said when he led them down the hall to the meeting? Staying with him and Shirley is sure a nice way to begin our trip."

"Yeah, the kids feel real at home with both of them. They would make neat parents."

"Hey Lynn! Hey John! We're over here!" Up here was more like it. All five of them were swarming over a statue of some old general atop a bronze horse. Joy was giving Heather a boost up his giant boot, Carl was climbing the horse's tail, and Ethan and Jimmy were trying to crawl out on his arm.

"You guys are crazy! Stay up there, while I take a picture," I yelled.

"John, are you sure it's okay for them to climb those statues?" asked Lynn.

"I don't see why not. Those statues look pretty solid to me. Let the kids have a good time." Lynn and I watched them climb three or four more of those colossal bronze statues from our seats along a nearby reflecting pool. My only worry, as they climbed the turquoise-streaked arms of history, was their handlebar bags filled with spending money, identification and journals. They had left them in a pile at the base of their first conquest. I still needed to teach them the importance of holding onto their bags in the city — they came from neighborhoods where you never locked your doors and left the keys in your unlocked car — but heck, you can't climb a statue with a bag around your neck, so I left that lesson for later.

Lynn interrupted her enjoyment of watching the kids climbing famous jungle gyms with periodic, "John, are you really sure it's okay for them to be climbing those things?" In her younger days, Lynn had visited more art museums than me, and before long I learned her concerns were right.

"Hey, you kids, get down off there! Don't you know those statues are to look at, not to climb on?! Get down off of there right now!" One of Washington's men in blue, sounding like my less-than-beloved junior high school art history teacher, had signalled the end of this recess, and the kids came back grumbling. It was people like that who, I thought, gave art a bad reputation, and I couldn't help but agree with the kids' disappointment.

"It's okay, you guys. It's almost time for us to meet Uncle Steve for lunch anyway."

"Yeah, but what are those statues for anyway? There's no way we could hurt those things. They're massively strong. If a hundred years of weather can't hurt them, how can we?" The rest of the group unanimously groaned their agreement with Ethan.

It didn't take long for the kids to move on to their next lesson in Washington. Again, Lynn and I followed them, watching as they pointed at something or suddenly stopped to circle up for a discussion. They were just about to make the left turn toward Steve's office at the edge of the Capitol, when they noticed a demonstration going on up on the steps. They paused a moment and, in formation, made a right turn up the steps toward the picket signs and protesters. I hoped Steve wouldn't mind our being a little late for lunch.

The demonstration we happened upon was a fairly tame one. It was a protest against rape and abortion by the Catholic Network Service. Nuns, priests and parishioners were quietly holding their placards, while one speaker at a time spoke at the microphone. The seven of us seemed like the only crowd, as everyone else who walked by paid little attention to sisters from Kansas calling for stronger penalties for rapists. Jimmy, Heather, Joy, Carl and Ethan hadn't developed their political callouses yet, and they were genuinely interested. While a young woman played her guitar and sang the Lord's Prayer, each of the kids walked around in front of the protesters and read each of their signs.

After reading as many as they could, Lynn and I watched the kids hold a committee meeting of their own. Joy was the first to speak:

"Well, senators, I think we should make a decision immediately on this problem of rape and abortion."

Heather agreed. "First of all, what do you think about rape? Mr. Senator West?" In just one morning, the kids had learned the proper protocol for addressing senators. They decided that at all subsequent meetings in the next four months, each of them would be addressed in the proper way.

"Well, I agree that the punishment for rape should be more severe."

"Well, what punishment do you think would be more appropriate?"

"I agree with the woman whose sign says, 'Castration for rapists.'"

Senator Fagerlin (Carl) didn't wait to be recognized. "Yeah! Castrate 'em!"

"Thank you, Mr. Senator Fagerlin, but next time could you kindly wait until I call on you."

"Mr. Senator Turpin(Ethan)?"

"Mr. Senator Turpin?!"

" . . . Well . . . uh . . . yeah, castration sounds cool to me."

Next Heather called on Joy. "Ms. Senator Fulton?"

"Castration. Yes, definitely castration."

It was time for Heather's vote, but she got that confused look on her face that I had already seen earlier. Joy interceded. "Yes Ms. Senator Deutsch, what do you think is the proper punishment?"

"Well, first of all what does 'castration' mean?" Heather was the only one of the group who hadn't grown up on a farm of some kind, and her face again showed her puzzlement with something that everyone else seemed to know about. The guys immediately burst into laughter, but for some reason neither Jimmy nor Carl offered their explanation.

Joy saw her chance. "Mr. Senator West? . . . Mr. Senator Fagerlin? . . . Mr. Senator Turpin? Would you like to explain to Ms. Senator Deutsch just what 'castration' means?" The guys' laughter suddenly turned to blushes, and their mouths went unnaturally silent.

The boys sudden shyness was matched by Joy's sudden confidence. "Well, if you can't, I can," and with that Joy explained just loud enough and with just enough detail to put our three male senators in pain.

Heather then raised her hand and proudly answered, "Castration seems right to me. Yes, I'll vote for castration."

I hated to end the historic session, but I knew Uncle Steve had a very busy schedule. "Excuse me . . . senators? I hate to interrupt your very important meeting, but do you think you could take a recess for lunch? We have a very important lunch engagement with a certain Uncle Steve, and we're already late. Could you continue your discussion after lunch?"

They looked at each other officially and Heather said, "Well yes, I think that might be arranged."

Abe's Lap

Somehow, the security check getting into Steve's Senate Office Building wasn't as exciting the second time around. As the guards emptied handlebar bags filled with film cannisters, gum wrappers, brushes and other adolescent contraband, Carl moaned, "Hurry up, you guys, I'm hungry!" The security guards, who seemed more used to briefcases filled with legal folders, shook their heads as they watched Ethan stuff everything back into his bag.

Steve was waiting for us and said he was going to take us downstairs to the Senate staff cafeteria. It was 12:30 and it looked like every well-dressed senate staff person was headed to the same place we were. None of the secretaries or office people on their way to lunch seemed to notice the kids–at least for a while.

Each of the kids' handlebar bags hung from their shoulders like large heavy purses, and my only concern about the kids carrying them so far had been that they didn't seem to realize that they needed to keep an eye on their bags when they laid them down somewhere in the city. The cafeteria was about to provide me with another concern. Before getting into the long line in the crowded cafeteria, Lynn gave each of the kids a five dollar bill from the food budget to buy their lunches. "Keep track of how much you spend, and we'll write it down in the budget book when we sit down. Don't go crazy on junk, but get what you'll eat. We'll see you at our table."

With their money in hand, the kids grabbed a place in line, and soon they were off with a brown plastic tray in their hands and their bags slung precariously over their shoulders. Ethan's bag kept slipping off his shoulder, requiring him to reach up with one of his hands to put it back. With an empty tray, it wasn't much of a problem, but loaded with food it might become the perfect launchpad for his lunch. I just hoped the drink he ended up choosing had a lid.

As I grabbed my salad, I noticed Heather, Joy and Carl over at the burger and fries counter patiently waiting for their cheeseburgers. I sighed with relief when I saw that their drinks were in cans. I was standing in the mass of people waiting for a cashier, when everyone towards the back of the merging mass of hungry staff people scattered and screamed. I looked over my shoulder, half-expecting to see someone being robbed or to see some secretary fainting from the day's heat. Instead, I saw Jimmy and Ethan standing alone in the middle of where the crowd had been. My kids were definitely no longer invisible. As young women checked their suits and dresses and men checked lapels and ties, there stood Ethan with his handlebar bag around his ankles. Jimmy and he had been to the "Build-your-own- Burrito-Bar" and their trays, which moments before had been stacked as high as humanly possible with tortillas, beans, tomatoes, onions, cheese and taco sauce, were now overturned at their feet. Chili was splashed all over them and the once-white cafeteria floor. I could tell by the look on Jimmy's face that he was embarrassed, but as I watched Ethan mourning his lost burrito, I realized he had a completely different reaction to things. The senate staffers, on the other hand, had a reaction of their own. They had napkins and ice water ready to remove any stains in world record time.

As if suddenly declared to be carrying some sort of plague, everyone in that crowded cafeteria made way for my five diseased little people. A wide path was cleared for the girls and Carl, allowing them to go right up to the cash register — in fact, they had their choice of any of the four registers. Being the first of our party to be on the lookout for a table, it seemed that wherever the three of them went, all tables in their area were suddenly vacant. Pretty good for a standing-room-only lunchtime. Jimmy and Ethan were given the red carpet treatment after they returned to the burrito bar to rebuild their lunches. Everyone near them made way and they too had a free path to the cashier on their return journey. Ethan couldn't believe how easy it was. "Man, you guys! Everyone gave Jimmy and me cuts when we got our second trays full!" Jimmy wanted to crawl inside his tortilla, and Steve, who was trying to act invisible himself, couldn't help laughing. Somehow, I didn't think lunch in that cafeteria had ever been so exciting.

"Fifty-six, fifty-seven, fifty-eight. Hey Heather, there are fifty-eight steps in the Lincoln Memorial." I watched Joy and Heather climb to their first meeting with the man on the pennies. It was my first live visit up these steps as well, but their eyes got so big and their stride became so excited as we approached the Memorial, I decided to let them lead the way.

"Hey Stick," (Heather called Joy, "Joy-stick", "Stick" for short) "come on over here. They've got some of his speeches carved in the walls. I want to take a picture."

Joy was standing at the great statue's feet looking up with her chin high and her jaw dropped wide open. Even though she was standing in a big crowd, she let out a big, "Wow . . . " causing more inhibited visitors to stare at her excitement. Interrupted by Heather's calling, she paused for one more moment, and then walked over to her tentmate. "Oh, how neat. Wait for me. You know what? I think it would be neat to sit in his lap."

"What do you mean?" asked Heather as she looked up at Mr. Lincoln.

"I mean, wouldn't it be neat to crawl up and sit in Abe's lap? . . . Not like we did with the statues, but to crawl up in his lap and talk to him for awhile. He looks so kind . . . . "

We spent three more wonderful days in Washington, and the kids were the best guides anyone could ever have. We rode as many escalators and subways as we could. We rented paddle boats to splash around in front of the Jefferson Memorial; the kids bought their Washington souvenirs — Joy and Heather bought art prints and books of art posters; the boys bought Slinkies, switchcombs and John Lennon granny glasses. And, although we didn't see any more burrito-bars, we did manage to spill at least one drink a day in one of Washington's many museum cafeterias.

The Capitol and the Mall gave us our views of Washington's political and historical culture, while our trips back home to Uncle Steve's and Aunt Shirley's taught us some of its people culture. Leaving the Senate behind Senator Kennedy one afternoon, we decided to go catch a movie near Uncle Steve's house. Unless you counted the ones on the screen, ours were the only white faces in the theater, and our skin felt like it glowed in the dark. As the lights went out we sat down to watch Rodney Dangerfield in *Back to School*. Sitting as inconspicuously as we could, we soon discovered that they watch movies differently in DC than back at home. Everybody seemed to know everybody else in the theater — except us — and loud, friendly conversations took place from the front row to the back and across the aisles. The audience was like a big family, and every time someone walked into the theater, they were greeted by the majority of the audience as if they were a long lost relative. When the movie finally started, we all expected the theater to get quiet, but were we wrong! All the conversations continued, regardless of what was happening on the screen. People would repeat Rodney Dangerfield's jokes to each other and yell back across the theater to friends, making sure that they had heard the last line. The guys in front of us somehow managed to repeat every joke of the movie, while doing their own re-enactment of all of Rodney Dangerfield's previous movies. At first the kids were confused by all the noise in the theater, but they soon got used to it. When it was all over and we walked out the alley to the street, Carl exclaimed, "Man, I've never been to a theater like that. You could hardly hear the movie."

" . . . Yeah, but I kinda enjoyed it even more . . . It was like a double feature. We got to see *Back to School* . . . and we got to see the people . . . watching *Back to School*. It was like two movies in one!" smiled Ethan.

There was a lot more to watch in Washington, D.C., but it was time to get on our bicycles. I felt like the kids had seen enough to make them want to come back again, and as much as I enjoyed seeing so many of the things I had read about, I was itching for us to ride. We had a few miles to pedal in order to make it home by October.

Welcome to **Maryland**

5

I ordered a soft-shell crab sandwich, and I didn't like it at all. When you open up the sandwich you just see two crabs sitting there, legs and all . . . I also took communion at the church. I've never done it before. It's really easy; you just dip the bread in the wine (or grape juice) . . . .

Heather's Journal
June 29, 1986

Looks Like Diarrhea

Early Monday morning, we were greeted by Carl's folks and the men from DDI who had met us upon our arrival at Dulles Airport. Carl's parents had driven to Washington to see us off on our bikes and to spend the rest of the summer at Mark's eastern office. Outside was a smaller truck carrying our still-bagged bicycles and the two cars that were going to take us to the Eastern Shore, where we would begin our bicycling. As we headed away from the curb in front of Uncle Steve's and Aunt Shirley's, we could see more gray-suited government workers strolling in the direction of the Capitol. Just across the block in the background, we could also hear the non-stop bouncing of basketballs as black hands dribbled towards their goal. We had grown familiar to those gray suits and those black hands, and it was tough to say good-bye to "DC."

We drove out across the Annapolis bridge to Tuckahoe State Park, Maryland. I had read that the Chesapeake Bay's Eastern Shore, with its collection of quiet country roads and sleepy fishing villages, was an ideal place to ride a bicycle. One writer even wrote: "It's so flat and near the water, that in some places you better make sure you ride only at low tide!" It sounded perfect.

In the summertime in California, if you don't have your computerized camping reservation months ahead of time, you can kiss off any chance of camping in any state or county park. So you can imagine how surprised I was when we arrived at Tuckahoe and were the only ones in the park. A thick green canopy of trees separated our campground from the surrounding cornfields, and the only signs of civilization we saw within miles of the park were a few dogs.

After unloading our bikes from the truck, we thanked Mr. Edson and his helpers for all their assistance in getting our bicycle trip started. We handed them an official *From Sea to Shining Sea* thank-you card, signed with personal thanks from each of the kids. Lynn gave them gas money and a little extra tip for a six-pack and a crab lunch on the way home. Earlier that morning, the kids had presented Aunt Shirley and Uncle Steve with another official thank-you card, accompanied by a bouquet of flowers that Joy and Heather had picked out.

While I helped the boys re-assemble their bikes, the Fagerlins, Heather, Joy and Lynn, drove to nearby Queen Anne to buy food for lunch, dinner, tomorrow's breakfast and other staples for down the road.

The Maryland summer sky that afternoon was a steamy gray. Stepping out of the car was like stepping into a sauna, and at one in the afternoon, even the shade of the trees offered no relief from the heat and stifling humidity. It didn't take long for my shirt to become saturated with a combination of my sweat and the hot Eastern Shore fog I was working in. By the time the KP crew returned from the store, I had finished re-attaching Ethan's racks and wheels, had pumped up his tires and made sure bike number one's systems were a go. In that same time, Jimmy and Carl had set up their tent for the first time outside of California.

"What's for lunch gang?" I yelled, as I struggled to take off the shirt that was stuck fast to my body. I hung it out to dry on a nearby branch — wishful thinking.

"Cold drinks, french bread, cheese and crab!" Carl's dad yelled back, holding a large clear plastic bag filled with at least 20 crabs. "Grab a beer and I'll give you a lesson on how to eat these things."

"Alright, beers!" smiled Jimmy.

"Not you, Jimmy! We got cokes for you guys," laughed Mark.

We all sat around the table stacked high in the middle with Chesapeake Bay crabs. They were a deep red-orange color and were covered with a combination of fuzzy beard and what looked like brown mud. I was hoping that America would show us that it was more than hot dogs and apple pie, and our first lesson on local cuisine was about to begin — unless you're counting our Build-Your-Own-Burritos.

As we prepared to declaw our lunch, Heather asked, "Do we eat that mud too?" Heather was game for almost anything, and if she learned that the folks on "the shore" spiced up their crab with mud, I'm sure she would have gone for it.

"Oh Heather, that's not mud, that's the special pepper they use to season the crab." Carl's dad, our crab expert, put Heather and the rest of us a little more at ease. "They just boil them up with the spices right in the water."

While Carl's dad was explaining the art of cooking crab, I looked over at Ethan. Ethan had defogged his wire-rimmed glasses and was having a staring contest with the crab that was pointing his way. He (Ethan, not the crab) was staring and turning his head, checking out his lunch's face, feelers and fingers. Slowly Ethan reached over to his crab as if to introduce himself, then picked it up and turned it upside down and sideways. Every so often, Dr. Ethan would poke at its underside or lift up a leg to check things out. He even pulled the crab up to his nose, face to feelers with his lunch, and if Carl's dad hadn't interrupted with, "Here's what you should do first . . .," Ethan probably would have lifted that old crustacean up to his mouth and took a big bite out of its shell. Insides, beard and all.

Mark Fagerlin's demonstration lasted until the first crab juice — or "crab yuck" as the kids called it — came squirting out the side of his crab and down his arm. From that point on, the kids decided to develop their own technique for mining the sweet pink crabmeat that lay hidden somewhere underneath the dirty, orange armor. How something seemingly so big could have so little meat inside was a mystery, and the crab yuck flowed freely down arms, faces and t-shirts that afternoon.

Carl got tired of the slim pickings that were to be found in the arms and small claws of our crabs, so he decided to go for what he thought had to be the crabmeat jackpot. He picked up the main body of his crab and cracked it on the side of the wooden picnic table. Then, as if he were cracking open an egg for frying, he tried to break the shell in half with his thumbs. It took a little more doing than an egg, and all the kids watched with baited breath as Carl peeled off the big chunks of crab shell. Well, suffice it to say that what lay beneath that armor of orange promptly caused my troops to drop their lunches and throw up flags of surrender.

"Ooh gross!"

"Yuck! What's that gooey brown and yellow stuff in there? It looks like diarrhea!"

Joy's description of Carl's discovery was a good one, but even Jimmy, in all his appreciation for the grosser things in life, had to respond, "Joy, that's gross!"

"Well, you tell me what it looks like then, Jimmy."

Jimmy was speechless for only the second time in four days. Carl's dad continued his lesson:

"Well, you guys, I hate to tell you this, but Carl's just discovered what some people consider to be the best part. They scoop out that stuff, which by the way isn't diarrhea, but the insides. They scoop it out and spread it on crackers."

Jimmy was the first to respond. "Well John, I'm going to have to flunk this examination. I think I'll pass on the . . . the diarrhea."

"Yes, well I think I'll have some bread and cheese, thank you," smiled Heather. "Maybe I'll try stomach and crackers some other time." Heather politely nudged her crab into the pile of untouched crabs, still stacked in the middle of the table.

Soon the rest of the kids had abandoned their local lunches and were dining on an old California favorite: cheese and french bread.

The table and they were a mess of crab shells, peppery mud, and crab juice. Mark and I were left with the spoils of the crab war of Tuckahoe State Park, and while Ethan alternated bread and cheese with an occasional inspection of some new portion of crab anatomy, I proceeded to suck, chew and poke my way through our mountain of local delicacies.

The kids finished their lunch long before I was ready to finish mine, and they were anxious to get their bikes ready to roll. In the time that it took me to find my way through one crab, Joy and Heather had their tent up, their pads rolled out and their nylon home decorated and arranged to their satisfaction. Those two were so quick and organized it was unbelievable. Joy walked over to the table and asked, "John, when can we do my bike? Heather and I want to do our laundry and go explore the park, so can we do mine pretty soon?"

"Sure Joy, just let me finish one more of these guys and then we'll go work on your bike."

"Okay. Thanks, John."

As I cracked open my last claw, I looked over at Heather who, at 4'6" tall, was trying to string a clothesline from two trees that were way out of her reach.

"Joy, would you do me a favor?"

"Sure, John."

"Would you tell Heather I'll help her with that clothesline? I know she has good intentions, but at the height she'll make that line, your underwear and socks will soon be dragging on the ground. They'll be getting dirty instead of drying."

I turned the rest of the crabs over to Mark, strung our clothesline across camp and returned to our makeshift bike shop. Carl's folks helped Lynn clean up the table and did the best they could trying to find things to help with. They were helpful, but as Carl became more and more preoccupied with his bike and his tent and his riding companions, I could see them getting the feeling that it was finally time to say good bye. Carl was ready to ride his bike home.

Carl was over with me, oiling his chain, when I whispered to him, "Hey Carl, I think it's time to go give your mom and dad a hug and a good bye." As I watched pale faced and skinny little Carl stubbornly leave his bike and walk over to his parents, I remembered again the first time I left home. I watched for a few moments and then returned to Joy.

"John, John, what's the matter? You really spaced out there for a minute. Can we finish my bike?" Joy handed me the wrench and held her front rack in place for me to attach.

Blood

By twilight, the kids had set up camp, Lynn had organized the kitchen, and I had finished all the bikes except "Bud", my own trusty steed. Bud and I had traveled many places together and even though I knew all his screws, scratches and adjustments well, I usually spent a little extra time with him. While I carefully attached Bud's fenders, racks and wheels, Lynn and the girls reminded the boys that they were to be cooking the night's spaghetti, salad and bread. "We went to the market, so you guys have to cook."

"Hey John, would you help us get the stove started?" As usual the kids didn't let me have much time to myself. "Yeah, and can I use your Swiss Army knife to open the tomato sauce?"

I looked over at the table and saw Jimmy hunched over the zucchini, carefully slicing it up in uniform size. Ethan, who had requested my help with the stove, was studying the package of spaghetti like he had earlier studied the crab, and Lynn was giving Carl one of her death stares.

"Carl . . . You already asked me if you could borrow my knife and I told you to use your own."

"Yeah, but it's somewhere in the bottom of my handlebar bag. Besides, I don't want to get it dirty."

This time Lynn added crossed arms to her death stare. Carl tried to avoid the evil eye and looked at me for some sympathy. "Sorry, Carl, but I think Lynn's right. You should use your own knife. Now's as good a time as any to get your handlebar bag organized so you can get at things you're going to be using often."

Carl got himself up from the table. "Man . . . ," he moaned. Before heading off to his bike, he managed to fire a death stare of his own my way.

"Hey Carl, I think that has got to be one of your best moans. I think I'll give it an 8.5."

"You're mean, John."

"You got it," I smiled. Carl went to get his knife and I pulled my rag one last time over Bud's blue frame. It was a ritual moment for me. I always rubbed him one last time after I assembled him on our trips. Whether it was a temple courtyard in Japan, a sidewalk in Boston or a parking lot in Canada, it always gave me a proud feeling to know that all the pre-trip planning was behind me and another adventure for Bud, some of my kids, Lynn and me was about to begin. *From Sea to Shining Sea* promised to be our biggest adventure to date, and I looked over my shoulder to see that no one was watching, punched my fist into the air and whispered, "Yeah Bud, here we go again."

"Hey John, I still need your help with the stove."

"Sorry, Eeth, I'll be right there."

As the sun headed west behind the haze toward California, we hoped that the approaching darkness would offer us some relief from the heavy sky. Instead, just as we squirmed to our seats at the dinner table in our damp shorts, the sky thickened even more. Hundreds of unidentified flying objects were joining us for dinner. It seemed that Tuckahoe State Park wasn't deserted after all. It had lots of residents; they were just nocturnal. And they had terrible table manners. Instead of joining us for dinner, it looked like they were going to *have* us for dinner.

As gross as the crabs looked, at least they were dead and motionless. Our uninvited dinner guests looked like crustacean cousins. They too had many legs, weird bodies and appendages built for removing chunks of flesh. They also had wings. One thing I could say for them, they certainly were as punctual as any guests I've ever shared dinner with. As soon as that hazy light in the sky went down, they were up. They didn't even wait for our dinner to be on the table because they immediately joined us in the kitchen.

First, it was Maryland mosquitoes who began to circle around our heads. The commanding officer of the Tuckahoe Air Command had assigned a squadron of blood suckers to each of us, and when the girls came back from another one of their bathroom conferences and started picking at the dinner preparations, he promptly assigned two more squadrons to our sector. Heather was the favorite target, as one giant skeeter set himself up on her nose as an air traffic controller. He didn't draw blood, he just waved in his buddies for landings on Heather's neck, legs and eyebrows. The first wave of bloodsuckers delighted in our sweaty bodies. Either they liked to wade in our perspiration, or it helped lubricate their entry into our flesh. Soon we were alternating our kitchen cutting and stirring with swatting and swearing. Everyone knew things were getting pretty bad when Lynn sounded the ultimate alarm: "I think it's time for . . . insect repellant."

"Oh no, not that stuff! That's worse than mosquitoes." Joy's opinion of our little bottles of goop summed up everyone's opinion of the stuff that was supposed to ward off the flying enemies. It was always the thickness of squeeze margarine, and regardless of its advertised "scent", it always reeked.

"That stuff is so awful!" she continued. "With the sweat all over me already and the way it stinks and spreads on . . . Every time I wear it, I think I know how the Indians felt when they used bear fat to keep the bugs away. It's gross!"

"I don't care what those labels say, I think all that stuff IS bear fat!" Jimmy summed up my feelings exactly. While Lynn went over to our tent to get her bottle of Cutters, I tried to teach the kids a battle technique that had given me satisfaction, if not victory, in many past battles with bugs of the world.

"Okay, you guys. Wait for one of them to land on your arm or leg." Heather's air traffic controller must have heard me, because for a while the mosquitoes only landed on our necks or tried to drill through our shirts. Finally, one landed on my forearm. "Just let him sink his drill in and start pumping blood. The guys who designed oil derricks must have been thinking of mosquitoes because they look just like them, don't you think?"

"Ouch!" Jimmy interrupted my demonstration with a swat of his hand. His blow splattered bits and pieces of mosquito mixed with blood on the back of his neck. "C'mon John, never mind the oil derrick jive. Get on with it!"

"Well anyway, let the ugly bugger suck a little blood, and then flex your muscle like this. It will send a big spurt of blood in its direction." Suddenly the mosquito, who just moments before had been enjoying some California cuisine, burst into bloody pieces right there on my arm. "Yeah . . . got him," I sighed with delight.

"Radical!" yelled Carl. "Come and get me, you stupid bugs!"

"Far out," gasped Ethan, joining Carl and waiting for his first victim.

"John, you're mean." Joy didn't seem to approve as she joined Lynn in her nonviolent application of our modern-day "bear fat." I just wrinkled my forehead and rolled my eyes her way, as I searched for another victim.

While waiting, I noticed Ethan gritting his teeth and looking like he was trying to pass a weeks worth of food. "Hey Ethan, what are you doing?!" He continued his concentrated grimace. "Hey, Ethan, you look like you're constipated. What are you doing?!"

Through his teeth, he managed, "There's this mosquito on my neck and I'm trying to flex my neck to kill him. For some reason it's not working."

Pretty soon the guys and I were all sweaty and flexed out from our hopeless battle. The Maryland mosquitoes were good. We all shared Lynn's Cutters and surrendered to the smell that would become our constant nighttime companion.

Our first camp dinner was ended prematurely when some more UFO's arrived. They weren't mosquitoes; they were too big. The giant, black bombers flew past our ears and decided to pass us up; they seemed to prefer spaghetti to our blood. The first one landed in Heather's plate, and soon everyone had big black buzzing bugs swimming slowly through their pasta. Wings and needle-like legs were trying to backstroke through the boys' great tomato and zucchini sauce.

"Hey John, do you think the Indians put bear fat on their spaghetti?" laughed Heather.

"The Indians didn't have spaghetti, Heather."

"I KNOW that, Jimmy; it was just a joke. And I know something else, we need something to get these bugs away from our spaghetti, because the Parmesan certainly isn't working . . . . "

Despite Heather's attempts to brighten our situation, we surrendered our dinner. We made a swift retreat from our table and set off for dishes, showers, laundry and the steamy, but mosquito-netted protection of our tents. We didn't know it but there were still some more Tuckahoe natives for us to meet before we zipped up our tents for the night. Waiting for us at the bathrooms were all kinds of weird flying creatures. Many of them were such accomplished campers, they had even learned where the bathroom was and how to use it. I'm certain the bug population was laughing hysterically as it heard us in the showers, on the toilet or at the sink as we encountered some new species of creepy crawler. Our surprise meetings were always accompanied by a loud shriek. The only species that seemed to be winning the battle were the many hidden spiders who had spun their webs wherever there was a corner — a corner of the room, of a stall, of a vent or of a dispenser. Their silky traps were everywhere, and many of their dead victims hung above us as we showered and got ready for bedtime. As Dr. Ethan brushed his teeth, he studied one particularly colorful adversary trapped near the mirror.

"Yeah," he mumbled, spilling toothpaste down his chin and onto his t-shirt. He paused his brushing session long enough to enjoy watching the bug squirm itself to death in the web above him.

As I watched my bespectacled friend from the throne in my doorless stall, Heather knocked on the boys' bathroom door. "Hey John, we need your help. I think Joy has a tick."

"Just a second, Heather. I'll be right there."

Lynn had a better stomach for things medical than I. She was always assigned the first aid kit and had acquired the nickname "Dr. Lynn." The few times I had tried to play doctor on one of our safaris, I had proved my incompetence almost immediately. On one memorable occasion in the Canadian Rockies, Lynn asked me to pick some gravel out of a bleeding knee. One of our kids had fallen and ripped a flap of skin open, and Lynn said all I had to do was lift that flap up with my fingers while I pulled out the tiny pebbles with my tweezers. RIGHT, LYNN! After trying to ignore the blood, I handed the tweezers over to Lynn, grabbed our bottle of Canadian whiskey — kept to numb our patients pain on such occasions — and took a big swig. While Susan held back her tears, I looked away and hoped not to faint. I had no idea why the girls were coming to me for help, and as I got up from the toilet I hoped my tick technique would be a bit better than my attempt at knee surgery.

"John, we called for Lynn first, but she must be back at camp, so . . . ," Heather explained as I came out the door.

"You remember Susan and Canada, huh."

"Yup. I sure hope you do better with Stick."

When we got to Joy, she looked at me calmly, with complete trust in her eyes. She lifted her shirt just above her belly button and said, "I think I have a tick. Can you get it off me?"

If all patients were like Joy, I think I'd look into medicine as a career. As it was, it was students like her that made me glad I got to be a teacher. She didn't know I was nervous and ignorant about how to get rid of the brown speck that was burrowing into her soft skin — or at least she didn't let on. She just stood there and waited for me to take care of her. Joy's trusting eyes were better than any Canadian pain killer, so I heated up the blade of my Swiss Army knife — just like I remembered the book had suggested — and placed the hot blade just above the tick. It took me a couple of matches and approaches with my blade to coerce that stubborn insect, but at last he started to wiggle and back out of one of my favorite people's skin. I quickly grabbed him with my tweezers and tossed him aside.

"Thanks, John. Man, you're really sweating." smiled Joy, and she and Heather returned to their shower. She probably figured the water pouring off my brow was just from the humidity. I knew it wasn't.

After my much needed shower, I walked up to the guys' and girls' tents. "Good night, you guys. Don't let the bed bugs bite."

"Good night, John," echoed the girls from their tent.

"Don't let the bed bugs bite . . . Very funny, John," snickered the boys. The three of them were rustling around in their tent trying to decide the best sleeping plan for their dome. I could hear them grumble as their sweaty bodies tried to get comfortable amidst their debris. It sounded as if switchcombs, Slinkies and stuffed animals had fallen out of their unzipped panniers and were vying for some of the already crowded floor.

The boys' jockeying for position died down as I laid down next to Lynn in our tent. Lynn had already crawled out of the cocoon of her sheetsack and was lying naked across the top of her sleeping pad. She blew on her forearms and mopped the sweat from her forehead with her damp bandana, trying to cool herself off. I leaned over and kissed her on the forehead.

"God, John, you smell horrible."

71

"How romantic . . . ," I answered, not telling her that she had seen more fragrant days herself. "Yeah, I know, but I sure look great!" Lynn pushed me over onto my damp pad.

"Who says so?"

"Aw c'mon, admit it. Aren't I the cutest, most handsome, most smelly doctor you've ever had the pleasure of spending such a gorgeous evening with?" As a result of my recent surgical success, I was feeling a bit cocky. "When was the last time you spent an evening under the stars with fine pasta, vintage red Crystal Light and in the company of such a fine surgeon?"

"What do you mean 'surgeon'?"

I went on to explain my tick operating procedure in great detail. Such great detail that Lynn was soon asleep. "So much for romance," I sighed.

I lay back on my pad and gazed up through the see-through netting in the roof. I dreamed of the line of kids on loaded bicycles that would soon be heading west. Maryland's welcome of heat, humidity and insects was invisible to me that moment. Not even the sounds of Joy and Heather being attacked by — and attacking — some large flying beetles in their tent next door could interfere with my dream that was about to begin. I woke up the next morning, still smiling up at the roof.

Only 4,500 Miles to Go

" . . . land that I love.
Stand beside her,
and guide her
through the night,
with a light from above . . . "

I heard Carl's voice singing his own rendition of *God Bless America* from the direction of where his bicycle was parked. He had risen even before my alarm clock and me and was already dressed and packing his panniers. I don't even know if he realized he was singing. I quietly sat up in our tent and watched him through the net windows, careful not to disturb his private concert. He'd roll up something in a plastic bag, stuff it down deep into his pannier and then continue singing. He was like a four-year-old, humming in a sandbox, and as I watched him, in his own little world, I prayed that God would bless us all as we set out across His land.

After listening to a couple more verses — a few of which Carl seemed to make up himself — I decided it was time to crawl out and wake up the rest of the troops. To give Carl warning of my presence, I stretched my arms and let out a morning sigh from inside my tent. At the sound of my stretching, he immediately ended his song, and as I stuck my ugly head out of our tent, he looked over at me.

"Good morning, John. Man, you look awful."

"Gee thanks, Carl. Good morning to you, too. How come you're up so early?"

"Well, it was hot inside our tent and Jimmy and Ethan were snoring, so I just decided to get up early and pack. I think I can fit all my stuff in my front panniers, so I have plenty of room in my rears to pack up all our food."

"Great, Carl. We'll pack up the food after we have breakfast. It seems a little cooler this morning."

"Yeah, but I think it might rain. When I walked over to the bathroom this morning, the sky looked awful dark and gray. I think I heard some rumbling off in the distance, too."

"Well, let's hope it doesn't rain on our first day riding."

The alarm on my watch interrupted us, and I looked to see it was 6:30 AM, time to wake everybody up. I was going to try 6:30 as our test wake-up time. I wanted us on the road early enough in the morning to get most of our riding done before the sun's awful heat forced all living things in this part of the country to find shady shelter. I hoped that a 6:30 wake-up would give us enough time to hit the bathrooms, have breakfast, pack up and get on down the road by 8:30.

Lynn and the other sleepy travellers moaned their morning greetings. They emerged from their tents, sweaty and crusty-eyed, and a line of four cute little zombies headed off toward the restrooms, toiletry kits and towels tucked under their arms. I cranked up the stove and began boiling the water for hot chocolate, coffee and oatmeal. Ethan, the last of the zombies, almost ran into a tree on his way to the boys' room. Some subconscious radar saved him just in time.

"Hey Ethan, need a helmet?" I laughed. He ignored my early morning humor.

"What can I do to help, John? Pack Rat, my bike, is all packed and ready to go."

"Sure, Carl, thanks. You can help me set the table for breakfast."

"I hope the locals don't like oatmeal as much as they like spaghetti," smiled Carl.

He proceeded to set the table with our breakfast supplies, and as each of the kids returned, looking much the better from their journeys to the bathroom, they helped us get breakfast ready. Heather opened the coffee and hot chocolate, Jimmy found out how to open the foil around our cream cheese, and Joy punctured the seals of our squeeze bottles of margarine and apple-raspberry jam. Lynn mixed up our jugs of Tang and instant milk, and soon our pot of boiling water was singing and adding to the already steamy morning.

I don't know who showed up first, Ethan or the storm, but as the kids waited for their oatmeal to cool off and as I toasted bread in our frying pan, peels of thunder started rumbling louder and louder towards us. The storm seemed to be coming from the direction of the bathroom, so Jimmy cracked a joke about Ethan doing his thing in the john. He didn't get a chance to finish because he was interrupted by a particularly loud CRACK right overhead. The trees above us started rocking and the sky darkened.

"I told you I thought it was going to rain—" FLASH! Carl's meteorological forecast was cut off by a burst of lightning that went off above the trees like a giant flashbulb.

"One thousand one, one thousand two, one thousand three, one thous—." A rumbling boom rolled through the heavy air as Heather tried to calculate how far away the lightning was.

I had hoped the short, relatively flat distances of the Eastern Shore would provide us with a week of basic training. I hoped that in our first easy miles the kids would be exposed to all the different conditions the sky of eastern America had to offer. But heat, humidity, bugs, rain, thunder and lightning, all in our first twenty four hours, was overdoing it.

"One thousand o—." CRACK!!! I had never heard thunder follow lightning so quickly. Every minute or so, that morning's nearby bolts split the sky open around us. The wind caused the trees to creak and tangle and the following explosions of sound and light rarely let Heather separate them by two counts. The kids were all enjoying letting their breakfast cool down to the sky's electrical show, until it started to dump water. The drops of rain started slowly and felt refreshing, but then gathered momentum like a downhill bicycle. Soon, my pile of toast was getting soggy, and kids were retreating to their tents. Jimmy and I thought we'd outlast the short downpour, but when the piece of toast I was working on started to float in the pool of water now in the frying pan, I turned off the stove, covered it and left Jimmy to his oatmeal and wheat sponge.

I wasn't in our tent but five minutes when I heard Joy and Heather outside talking with Jimmy. Their voices were muffled by the pouring rain, and occasionally their conversation was drowned out by the lightning's thunderous accompaniment. I peeled back our rainfly to see the three of them sitting around the breakfast table in their bright yellow rain jackets drinking steaming hot chocolate and leaning over their precious jellied toast like human umbrellas. Jimmy noticed me looking out of our tent.

"C'mon John, you wuss. We need more toast out here! Are you gonna let a little water scare ya? Besides, now no one can ever say this campsite has no electricity."

"Yeah John, just put on your rain jacket and join us. This is the first Maryland meal we've had without bugs." Heather was smiling, as she clutched her hot chocolate between her two little hands. This rain is also making things kinda cooler."

"Go 'head, join them fearless leader," smiled Lynn. "I'll wait here in our nice, dry tent. Just save me some breakfast."

"Thank you, dear." I kissed Lynn good morning and headed out to join my young friends in the rain.

"Only 4,500 miles to go you guys!!! You look great." The kids and Lynn were lined up shoulder to shoulder, atop their loaded bicycles. Their line filled the road that led out of Tuckahoe State Park. We all joined gloved hands and silently squeezed before setting off.

I was to ride the point as navigator and Dr. Lynn was to bring up the back. She was our doctor of motivation and psychology as well as of cuts and bruises, and we needed her as the caboose of our wagon train. For the first yards of our journey, I let Jimmy lead. I wanted to record this special departure with my camera. "Meet me where this road ends at that first intersection, okay Jimmy?"

"Gotcha, boss. See ya in California . . . . " Jimmy put both feet in his *From Sea to Shining Sea* pedals for the first time and was off down the puddled road.

After snapping his picture I walked over to Heather, gave her a hug, and whispered, "Go for it, Heather."

"4,500 miles, that should be fun!" Heather smiled and winked at me before she grabbed her handlebars and was off. One of my favorite sets of freckles was off towards California.

Next in order were Joy, Carl, Ethan and Lynn. It was a line that would become so familiar to us in the next three and a half months. When Ethan, the last of the kids, had safely navigated his first Eastern Shore body of water(the puddle five feet down the road), Lynn and I looked at each other silently.

"See you in Santa Barbara." Lynn cinched up her left toe strap, kissed me and was off after Ethan.

I watched everyone disappear around the corner, walked over to Bud, climbed up on his saddle and yelled, "Yahoo!" I hoped my shout woke up all the sleeping mosquitoes.

"Hey John, I think you're going the wrong way." Carl was questioning my navigational skills less than one mile into our trip, and being the hardheaded leader that I too often was, I ignored him and continued down the road. I looked behind me and saw that our single-file line had disintegrated. The kids were now riding side by side talking to each other and pointing out the new scenery. It looked like they were enjoying the solitude of the Maryland farmland.

I planned to backtrack out of the park the way we had driven in, but somehow the road didn't seem too familiar. My normally good sense of direction seemed off, and the backcountry roads had no signs. As I tried to get my bearings, I was interrupted by an attacking farm dog that suddenly appeared out of one of the rows of corn. I wasn't in the mood for any sudden change of course, so I yelled at him and continued down the road, studying the map atop my handlebar bag. I hoped the kids wouldn't have any trouble with him.

Weathered gray barns and farmhouses sat out amongst the fields every half mile or so. After about a half hour of riding, the houses began to get closer and closer together. Over the tops of the stalks of corn I thought I saw a gathering of power lines, and I hoped it was Queene Anne, the first town on my map. Jimmy and I got to the town first, but there wasn't any sign telling us what town it was, if it was one. It didn't look like much of a town. The only signs of business were a rusty old Coca-Cola thermometer hanging from a dilapidated wooden house on the corner and a group of men in overalls and ballcaps huddled under the hood of an old Ford parked in front of a barn next door.

I stopped at the intersection to try and figure out where we were, and as I studied my state map, each of the kids lined up behind me. Carl didn't wait long to ask, "Hey John, where are we? I thought you said our first stop was Queen Anne. This isn't Queen Anne. We were there yesterday."

Again I ignored Carl and coasted Bud over to the group of men, who, by then, had come out from under the hood to check us out. The group of local boys looked at me as if they had never seen tight lycra shorts, bicycling helmets and perforated gloves with no fingers. When I thought about where we were, I realized they probably hadn't.

"Excuse me, but could you tell me where we are?"

The three of them leaned back, looked us over once more and elbowed each other, as if they had just heard a joke. Then they all spoke at once in accents that were as thick as the muddy water irrigating their fields, "Well sir . . . you's in Ridgely, Mair'land. Yep, Ridgely, Mair'land. Where you folks headed?"

I looked down on my map quickly to find Ridgely and noticed that I had taken us the long—and wrong—way. "Well, I'm a teacher from California" — as I said California, I wondered if I should have kept our state of origin secret, but too late — "and my wife and I and five of our students are riding our bicycles across America. Today is our first day on the road and we're heading for Easton and St. Michael's. Could you tell me how we can get to Easton?"

From my quick glance at our map, Easton only seemed to be twenty-five or so miles away. Still, everyone of those guys scratched their heads, as if they had never been there. One of the men even seemed as if he had never heard of Easton.

"Bicyclin' 'cross America . . . well shoot, that shau is a might far ways to pedal," the man continued. "And with them kids 'n all. I never heard of nuthin' like that bafore."

"Ain't that just the truth," agreed one of his friends as he shook his head. The three of them lifted their caps and scratched their foreheads in disbelief.

The more wiry one of the bunch scratched his two day old beard. He pulled up his once white, now grease-stained t-shirt to wipe the sweat from his face. He looked over at me and said, "Now whur you been and whur you headed?"

"Well, we spent last night at Tuckahoe State Park and we're gonna ride our bicycles across America. Today we're trying to get to Easton and St. Michael's. I think I made a wrong turn coming out of the campground." At that point, he huddled up his friends and they began a discussion that, if judged by their tone of voice and their waving and pointing of arms, seemed to be the source of much disagreement. It was so loud that even the kids, who were across the road, had volume enough to try and translate.

While they argued and drew in the dirt, I studied my map. Finally after about five minutes of discussion, one of them — if I heard right, I think his name was Frank — stepped forward. "Well, you folks is now in Ridgely and by the ways we figgur it, you got a fair piece to travel on them there bicycles to get to Easton. We got a friend George, lives down in Matthewstown he does, and Herman and me thinks that is right close to Easton. We ain't never been to Easton 'cuz we never had any business to, but ifn you folks follow this here road that goes along the tracks, it'll take you to Queen Anne. When you get to the store there at the crossroads, you turn left and that road should take you folks to Matthewstown. What did ya say you thought it was from Queen Anne to Matthewstown, Herman?"

"Well, ole George, he's from Matthewstown and last time he was up here, I heerd him tell how it takes him near 20 minutes to make that drive. He says that's why he don't do it more often. You know George, he don't like wastin' time drivin' when he could be fishin'. 'Sides, he says his favorite hole's only an oyster's throw away from his back porch. Ain't got no reason to come here much, he don't."

"Ain't that the truth. I can't remember last time George came up this way." Ole Frank seemed to be getting ready to begin a discussion with his two buddies about George's last visit, so, before they began, I decided it was time to be off towards Queen Anne. Maybe there I could get some directions from George's Matthewstown to Easton.

"Thank you very much for your help. You guys have a good day." I put my foot into my left pedal and got ready push off to where the kids were waiting patiently. I don't know if Herman, Frank and the other Marylander, who's name I don't remember, ever returned to their work underneath that old Ford's hood, because no sooner had they waved good bye to us than they began another heated arm-waving and dust-kicking discussion of something of local importance.

Not long after their voices faded away to the north, we saw the familiar crossroads and market of Queen Anne. It was eleven o'clock in the morning and we had ridden about eight miles — four of which weren't a planned part of our day. I wanted to keep on going, but the girls needed to go to the bathroom.

The market had a hand painted sign that said: "Fresh Peelers and Steamed Crabs — By the Dozen." With its crooked and slanted letters, it looked as if it had been painted by the local first grade class. Right next to the sign stood a wood bench lined with rows of wooden baskets full of ripe, red tomatoes. We rolled our bicycles up against the back wall of the gravel parking lot. The hot sun behind the motionless gray sky was just beginning to evaporate the haze and our first patches of Maryland blue were beginning to show themselves on the Shore.

With its screen door and flower boxes, the small market looked more like someone's house than a market. At the back were two large tanks bubbling and gurgling. After the kids paused to gulp down some water from their bottles, they all walked over to check the tanks out. They were filled with tiny fish, and as the kids poked their fingers into the cool water, a green pick-up truck drove up. The driver backed into the stall next to the tanks.

A tall black man, in blue coveralls and red baseball cap, opened the truck's door and slowly pulled himself out. He looked to be in his fifties with some gray around his eyebrows, and was the blackest black man I had ever seen. The lines in his face were highlighted by the shine of his sweat, and his deep brown eyes twinkled when he saw the kids so interested in his fish tanks. They hadn't noticed him yet, and as I looked at him, he nodded and winked my way. I silently stepped back as he walked up next to them.

"My, my, what you little folks adoin'?" His voice was deep and his words came so slow they seemed to melt together. The kids, amazingly quick judges of character, all turned around and smiled up at the big man, as if he was an old and favorite relative.

"You knows what you be lookin' at?" he asked.

"Yeah, they are fish." Heather was the first to speak. "I don't know what kind they are, but they look a little small to eat. What do you use them for?"

"Well, honey, dem is minnows and we uses em for bait. You be right. Dey be much too small to be eatin'."

By this time Carl had noticed the bushel baskets in the back of his truck. They were full of something that seemed to be moving. "Hey you guys, come over here. Look what's in the back of his truck." The bed was stacked high with baskets teeming full of something that was moving. Blue-green claws and legs were poking and reaching out of the openings in the baskets. "Excuse me sir, but are those live crabs?!"

"Nothin' but, suh! You be lookin' at my catch of de finest crabs to be foun' in dis part of Mairland. Yes indeed. How would you like a little lesson in crabs and crabbin'? You folks don't seem to be from around dese parts, so how bouts I shows you a ting or two about dese jimmies and sooks?"

"Hey, my name's Jimmy," grinned Jimmy.

"Sorry suh, but in dis part of de country a jimmy also be a male blue crab. A female, she be called a sook." Pretty soon the kids were up in his truck and sitting on the sides of the bed. They were all eyes and ears listening to their black friend teach them all about crabs. "We got three ways to catch dese crabs. De ones here I catched wit' pots. Early dis mornin' I went and hauled up me pots from de bay. And now, before it gits real hot, I got to sort out de jimmies from de sooks. I got to sort out da peelers from de busters."

The kids were mesmerized by the big waterman. "What's a peeler? . . . And, what's a buster?" Heather even raised her hand as she asked her question.

"Well, honey, a peeler is a sook. Now who members what a sook be?"

"A sook is a female and a jimmy is a male, just like Jimmy." Heather laughed, as Jimmy, in one of his rare moments of confusion, tried to figure out his reaction.

"Right you be. A peeler is a sook that be gettin' ready to shed its hard shell, and a buster be a sook already sheddin'. And when a sook be done sheddin' it shell, it got to be one of de most delicious things to eat on God's good earth."

"Last night, we had a whole pile of crabs for dinner," said Ethan with surprising speed. "Except they weren't blue; they were bright orange. What kind of crabs were they?"

"Dey be blues just as well, only dey be steamed. When blue crabs be steamed dey turn a bright red color. Oooh, but de peelers . . . de soft-shells . . . dey be de best eatin'. Some city folk drive all de way out here just to eat 'em. You fry dem up real nice in meal and eat dem just as dey come out of de frying pan. Oh, dey taste just like candy. Some folk likes to put dem between two pieces of bread with a thick slice of tomato. I like 'em dat way too, but oooh my favorite be when dey just hop out of de pan."

Heather got this real funny look on her face and asked, "You mean you eat the whole crab? Do you just take big bites out of it?"

"Yes ma'am, some folks say it be like eatin' a spider; only tastes much better."

About that point, I wanted to know this man's name, but I felt any introduction now would be a rude interruption. Our professor of Maryland crabology was soon pulling his baskets down into the shade at the back of the store. "Suh", "ma'am", "honey", and "little folk" would have to do for names that afternoon.

"I bes' be cullin' today's catch before dat hot sun ruin' me catch soon. Bafore I does though, come on down from de truck and let me show yous de difference between sooks and jimmies."

Carl was already over one of the baskets lifting up a crab and turning it over. As he put his first one back, he noticed something unusual in the basket. "Hey, these two look like they're siamese twins!" He immediately lifted up two who were in passionate embrace.

"Carrrrl," Jimmy moaned, in his most disapproving voice. "Those aren't siamese crabs."

"Aaaah, you just foun' youself some doublers. Dey be a jimmy and a sook fixin' to make little jimmies and little sooks. I'll cull de jimmy into the cooking pot and check de sook to see if she be close to peelin'. If she be a buster, we clean her quick and get her ready for de pan. If she close to peelin', den we keep her in de tank and watch her til she do."

After getting a chance to pick up and examine some of his wiggling catch, the kids began to answer some of his questions about what they were doing and where they came from. He walked over with them to their bicycles and nodded his head in approval of their work and their cargo. Before going back to his work and before their bladders burst, he shook each of their hands and waved goodbye.

"You folks must sho' be journey proud today," he bellowed before we parted. The big black crabman's warm voice and smiling eyes lost nothing in the translation. The kids hadn't missed a thing he'd said.

Low Tide

It was already after 11, and we still had thirty miles to go. I hadn't planned on such an early snack break, but Lynn returned from her trip to the bathroom with a package of cookies and a half gallon of real milk. The kids didn't exactly have a love affair with the powdered kind we had at breakfast. She emerged from behind the screen door, singing something about calcium and carbohydrates and healthy growing bodies. Lynn would make a great mother, and a great Wonder Bread commercial. I looked down at my map and moaned.

"Okay, everybody, each person take three cookies and drink some milk. Do it quickly, because John wants us to get down the road," she said to her approving audience.

It wouldn't be the last time in the next few months that Lynn's nack for snacks would prove popular to the kids. To their credit, they all wolfed down their rapidly melting cookies and returned to their bikes, complete with white milk moustaches and ready to ride. All, I should say, except Ethan. He was the last to come out of the bathroom and the last to discover there was something to eat. Even with Lynn's urging, he couldn't help but examine each of his cookies before eating them.

"What's the matter, Eeth?" said Jimmy. "You afraid they left out one of the 'Os' in 'OREO'?"

We would soon discover that our final signal to be off down the road would become, "C'mon, Ethan!"

From the market, we crossed underneath the railroad tracks into the town of Queen Anne. As some local dogs accompanied us to the outskirts of town, I kept searching for the water that provided all the crabs our friend had talked about. I was expecting water creeping up to the sides of our roads on the Eastern Shore, but so far we had seen more green and amber waves of grain than any of the waves I had expected.

Corn rolled for as far as our eyes could see and soon we found ourselves rolling through Matthewstown — no sign of George, though, he must have been fishin'— and on into Easton. On my map, Easton had the rare distinction of receiving the accompanying phrase: "See Enlargement." It was one of the towns I had read about and was supposed to be the home of some very famous and beautiful colonial architecture.

We had travelled 25 miles by the time we reached Easton and it was close to one o'clock. Not being able to eat historic houses, the kids pointed out some notable architecture of their own. "Hey, there's a Hardees!" "Yeah, and there's a McDonald's!" "Let's go to Hardees. I've never been to one before." We weren't going to be eating meals at fast food places, but I could tell the troops needed something more than a Quaker meeting house to congratulate them for their first miles. I agreed to "drinks only" and hoped that at least we could ride past some of the old houses on our way to our lunch in town.

We picnicked on peanut butter and jelly sandwiches, bananas, trail mix, chocolate milk and lots of orange juice. The setting of our first Eastern Shore picnic lunch was a little different than I had first romanticized. I figured we'd buy our supplies and then bike to some nice bayside beach or shady public green. Instead we sat on a sticky sidewalk and leaned against shopping carts in front of the Easton Safeway. Views of native knees, ankles and hubcaps substituted for my anticipated visions of sailing ships and whitecaps.

The shade of that storefront, our all-we-could-eat luncheon, and the prospect — at least according to my map — of a real body of water at St. Michael's made the last dozen miles of our day a breeze. Just outside of Easton, we caught our first glimpse of water, the Miles River. As we crossed over an inlet at the bridge near Newcomb, I could feel the kids energy pushing me to go a little faster. Instead of being spread out for about a half a mile behind me, like they had done earlier in the morning, they were all in a line on my tail, pumping away like a machine. They weren't looking at me or staring at the pavement just in front of their wheels, but were, as Jimmy would say, "cruisin'." Smiling and gazing off at the shoreline, every so often, one of them would point something out and all their heads would turn to check out a shorebird or sailboat gliding along the water. The miles flew by, and soon we were in St. Michaels.

St. Michaels is famous as the home of the Chesapeake Bay Maritime Museum, and I decided it would be as good a place as any to begin my search for our place to stay. I'd heard that there was no place to camp in St. Michael's, but I figured a few questions might find us a welcoming church or school.

The museum sat right on the harbor, and with the shops and the docks to keep the kids busy, I set out to find us a place to sleep. I walked up to the girl who ran the information and ticket booth for the museum and explained who I was and what our group was doing. I tried to make "My name is John Seigel Boettner and I'm a teacher from California and . . . we are riding our bicycles across America." not sound like a recording, and as the girl's eyes lit up with excitement, I knew I had a lead.

"Are those your kids I just saw ride in? Wow! And those little kids are going to ride all the way across America? Gosh, I wish I could do that." She went on to explain how she went to college in Virginia and had always wanted to do something like we were doing. The farthest she had ever pedaled her bicycle was 25 miles, but she sure would like to take a tour someday. ". . . If I only had the time. With school and summer jobs and all, I just don't know when I'll ever find the time . . . Do you need another leader?"

"No, I'm sorry, but my wife is the other leader. You should do it sometime, though. One of the things we're doing on our trip is finding a place to stay when we get to a town — a church or a school or a campground or some place to set up our tents or sleep on the floor. My book says that there aren't any campgrounds in St. Michaels. Do you know of any place we could sleep?"

"Oh sure! Well . . . just a minute. Can you wait just a minute? I just need to make a phone call."

Before I knew it she was back with our night's lodgings and even morning showers all figured out. "I just talked to the director of the museum and she said you all could set up your tents over where they're building the new part of the museum. It's a green patch of grass just behind the parking lot, and we're constructing a replica of a colonial fishing village there. It's nice and green and sits right on the water. I called the local sheriff so he'll know you'll be there tonight. The only problem might be the construction workers. They're off now, but they get started by 7 in the morning. I hope that's okay. After you get up in the morning, just come and see me and I'll show you where the museum's showers are. Gee, I think it's so neat what you are doing . . . riding all the way across America and all . . . and being from California . . . I always wanted to go to California. Why did you decide to come out here to Maryland?"

I began to tell her that the reason we came to her state was to meet people like her and the boys in Ridgely and the crab professor in Queen Anne, but she didn't give me much of a chance. She interrupted with more bubbling enthusiasm for our group. She reminded me of an older Heather, and if it wasn't for a group of ladies trying to get her attention so they could buy their admission tickets to the museum, I probably would have had to make up some excuse to get back to my group. They had finished browsing the shops and were over on one of the docks studying something in the water.

"Thanks again. I really appreciate all your help. And go for that trip someday. See you in the morning." The two gray-haired ladies finally got their tickets.

"Boy, John, what happened to you?" asked Joy. "How come you've got such a big smile on your face?"

"What did you do find, some buried treasure or something?" laughed Carl.

"Guess what, you guys? Remember how I told you how we were going to rely on the local people's friendliness for where we would sleep at night?"

"Yeah."

"Well, I found us a place to set up our tents right next to the water, and . . . the woman who got us permission to camp there is even offering us a place to take a shower — with HOT water."

"HOT showers! Alright!!!" everyone shouted in agreement.

"Hey, how come you guys aren't in the water going for your first Chesapeake swim? Once we head west in Virginia, there won't be any ocean to swim in."

"Uh, John, I don't think we're going to be doing much swimming in the Chesapeake. At least I'm not." Carl had a disappointed look on his face.

"What dya mean you're not going for a swim? The water looks great."

"Look a little closer, John." Jimmy motioned me closer to the surface of the army-green water for a lecture. "See those little white things swimming around?"

"Yeah."

"Well, those are little jellyfish called sea nettles, and they sting just like jellyfish. So, I'm with Carl, I'm not going to go swimming either." Jimmy, who loved the ocean, had had his trunks primed and ready for his first swim, but now just stared at them hanging from his handlebars.

"Yeah, one of the fishermen told us that sea nettles are the worst when it's been a dry year and this year is setting a record so far for no rain. He says he's seen more nettles this year than he's seen in a long time." Heather, as usual, had the inside story.

" . . . Wow, these guys are pretty cool . . . They look just like ghosts dancing in the water." Ethan was on his stomach, head hanging off the dock studying the nettles.

Joy was next to him also observing their dance up close. "They are kinda pretty. I like the way they open and close and roll over so slowly . . . Oooh, did you guys see that one over there? He's big . . . bigger than my hand. I wonder how bad they sting? I sure would like to go for a swim."

After we all watched the dance for a while and had a who-can-spot-the-biggest-one contest, I decided we would continue our study of local cuisine by eating dinner at The Crab Claw Restaurant. Our envious friend at the museum ticket booth had recommended it. It sat over the bay right next to the museum.

"I know you guys probably want to get out the stoves and go to the market and cook something at camp, but I was wondering if maybe you might want to eat out tonight? I hear that the Crab Claw has the best Chesapeake Bay seafood in St. Michaels."

"Yeah dude. Go for it!" Somehow food prompted an immediate response from the usually contemplative Ethan.

"I don't want to decide for you guys, so why don't you take a vote."

Joy, who had become the president of our senate, automatically began to call the roll. "Mr. Senator West?"

"I'm in. Let's go for it."

"Mr. Senator Fagerlin?"

"Me too."

"Ms. Senator Deutsch?"

The result of the vote was a unanimous and uplifting yes. The only concern came from Ms. Senator Deutsch who asked Mrs. Senator Seigel Boettner if our food budget could handle an eat-out feast. Lynn, who was a master at bending the budget to meet dietary desires, smiled and said with just the right amount of hesitation, "Well, I think the budget can handle it if we only order what we'll eat and if we're careful keeping track the next few days. I also need today's Budget Book recorders."

Heather and Joy promptly volunteered to go over the day's records after dinner. We said good bye to the dancing sea nettles and were off to The Crab Claw.

It usually takes kids on our bike trips a few weeks to learn how important it is to fuel their bodies for all the energy they'll need on the road, but as the kids ordered their first meal after pedaling, I realized they'd have no problem filling their tanks. Lynn might be challenged with balancing her food budget, but not eating well wasn't going to be a problem with this group.

We ordered buckets and baskets of oysters, clams, fish and chips, french fries, clam chowder, shrimp, squid, crabcakes — you name it, if it was on the menu we ordered it. Everybody tried some of everybody else's and washed their catches of the day down with four pitchers of soda. The waiters who witnessed these small bodies downing all the food and the waitresses who took the second and third orders for more fries and more drinks stared at their pint-sized customers in disbelief. They were the first in what was soon to be a long line of American waitresses to marvel at the kids' appetites. Jimmy burped to signal the close of our meal and as we headed over to our camp on our bicycles, I noticed our waitress watching us leave. When she saw us get on our loaded bicycles, she sighed and continued with her work. The revelation of our bicycles helped her understand.

Once tents were up, it was time to do the day's laundry, so off to the bathrooms went the kids, clean clothes in one hand and bottle of liquid soap in the other. I tried to make our routine simple: 1) wash ourselves and what we had worn that day and 2) change into a fresh set of clothes before going to bed.

It was only our second night out, and I still had to remind the kids of all they had to do before they went to bed. After laundry was hung out hopefully to dry, we found seats on top of some pilings and rocks along the water. We spent a half hour writing about our day, with the bay playing our background music. The sun went down, casting its orange glow on our last pages, and I adjourned our meeting to give everyone a little free time before it was time for lights out. I sat and tried to write more in my journal, but was distracted by the kids.

Ethan was standing silently with Jimmy over at the point — "Hey John, will you watch our journals? We're going to go skip some rocks. The water is so still here, it's the perfect place . . . ." Carl, remnants of energy making it hard for him to sit still, was off by himself climbing his way along the water, turning pilings into balance beams, and Joy and Heather were sitting and watching the sun head home, its orange reflection on the mirrorlike water fading to a shiny black. As silhouettes turned into darkness, we were left only with the sounds of the bay — the bells on the swaying boats, the lapping of the tiny waves on the shore and the quacks of approaching ducks that stopped, suddenly silent, just before the splash of their landing. A gentle breeze cooled the sweat on our necks and fireflies danced, writing their fluorescent lines across the Chesapeake sky.

Without orders from me, the tired kids quietly headed for their tents. I hated to disturb the bay's lullaby, but I wanted to tuck everyone in. "Good night, Heather, good night, Joy. You guys sure did great today."

"Good night, Mr. Senator West, Mr. Senator Turpin and Mr. Senator Fagerlin. Sorry about that detour of mine this morning."

"Good night, Mommy and Daddy," chimed the boys in their most high-pitched voices. They always maintained some semblance of silliness before falling asleep, and Lynn, who was holding my hand, gave them a more acceptable reply, "Good night, babies." After a good laugh from the darkness of their blue cave, the boys elbowed each other good night and were soon snoring. Lynn and I stood outside our tent and gazed around at our camp. Groups of bikes were locked and covered with their orange plastic tarps, shorts and underwear were hanging from the handlebars, and the three tents were circled on the grass. Before crawling in ours, we hugged each other good night.

The girl at the booth was right about the workers getting started early, and I wasn't sure if it was them or the "Cockle doodle doing" of Lynn — our designated rooster — that had all five of them up at the crack of dawn the next morning. Soon we were eating Cheerios and bananas and drinking orange juice at a table we borrowed from the closed Crab Claw. After showers, we explored the lighthouses and shipyards of the Maritime Museum. The admission ticket to the museum was a little, round orange sticker, and Joy and Heather immediately stuck theirs on their helmets. Among other souvenirs of their journey, the girls were going to collect banana stickers and any other kind of sticker that would fit on their helmets.

"I hope we have enough room on these helmets," smiled Joy as she slapped hers on.

According to Carl's bicycle computer, our first day's ride was 36.16 miles. Including my scenic route to Queen Anne, just about right for a first day. I figured thirty to forty miles a day for the first week would be a good way to get ourselves acclimated to living on our bicycles. Our pace and mileage during that first week would give us time to get our camp set-up organized, our daily meetings into a routine, and also give us time to hold Who-Can-Find-The-Biggest-Sea-Nettle contests. Soon, though, our average would have to pick up to fifty miles a day — and more.

Heading south from St. Michaels, we soon discovered that the Eastern Shore was actually a collection of shores. In fact, we couldn't even tell if we ever saw the actual Chesapeake Bay. Always nearby—if not in sight, then in smell—was some body of water. Around every corner was the salty scent of the not-quite-sea water of the Miles River or the Avon or the Choptank. All the criss-crossings of the many unnamed creeks and marshes made us feel like we were riding on a maze. The water was the green color of pea soup, and creaky, planked bridges straddled the fingers of water like giant wooden xylophones. Large, steel drawbridges united more distant shorelines at towns named Cambridge and Vienna. Just outside of St. Michaels we discovered another way to cross water too deep to wade—the ferryboat.

The Tred Avon Ferry is America's oldest running cable-free ferry, and since 1683, it has united the Talbot County towns of Bellevue and Oxford. The little-traveled road leading to the ferry was a tunnel of green trees, and just past the sign announcing the ferry, the trees parted enough for us to get our first glimpse of the Avon River. The noontime sun had turned the surface of the river a shiny silver, and we could see an old black man fishing from its wide, sandy bank. Steam almost seemed to rise off the water and three kids, black and skinny, waded knee-deep near the fisherman.

Once out of our tunnel of green, we saw a long wooden pier. It was the entrance to the ferry. Across the water and heading towards the pier was what appeared to be a white wooden house, complete with one car garage floating on a barge. We coasted up to the pier, got off our bikes and pushed them along the splintery, uneven planks of the pier.

"Hey John, this smells like Santa Barbara," said Jimmy. ". . . like down at the beach."

The mixture of salt air and creosote on pilings took me back home too.

Ethan looked out at the kids, still wading off in the distance. ". . . Man, I wonder why those kids don't get stung by the jellyfish. Maybe there aren't any around here."

"Wrong, Ethan." Joy corrected Ethan as she leaned over the railing and studied the water. "There are hundreds of them here. Even more than we saw last night. And some of them are BIG! And Ethan, they are 'sea nettles' not 'jellyfish'."

"Well . . . all I know is that they look like jellyfish and they sting like jellyfish — at least that's what that fisherman said — and I know I won't be doin' any swimmin'. . . Man, I wonder why those kids aren't getting stung."

The floating house puttered up to the end of the pier and a lone car drove off the front. This was our ferry. Across the river was Oxford and I remembered reading that it had collection of colonial architecture possibly more beautiful than the one we had bypassed in Easton. I was hoping the ferry ride would put the kids in the mood to explore some old houses.

"Hey John, I'm hungry." Carl said, halfway across the river.

"Yeah, let's eat." Jimmy didn't often agree with his youngest tentmate, but his stomach often did. Soon my hopes for a walking tour of Oxford were dashed. At least this time we didn't eat in front of a Safeway. We parked our bikes near the ferry unloading ramp and ate our lunch of peanut butter and jelly, Crystal Light, and fig bars on a narrow stretch of shaded lawn that served as Oxford's waterfront park. After wolfing down their sandwiches, Joy, Carl, and Heather could resist the temptation of the water no longer. Throwing off their shoes and socks, they ran towards the river.

"You guys are crazy!" Jimmy munched his second sandwich and shook his head. His disapproval caused Carl to speed up his pace and be the first one in up to his knees. Heather and Joy walked in a bit more gingerly, searching constantly for the dancing ghosts.

"Hey Heather, let's try to get stung. These look like pretty small nettles around here."

"Okay, Stick," agreed Heather. "Let's just make sure we go for the small ones first."

Jimmy looked up from his sandwich. "Unbelievable."

"Yeah, I know. They're nuts trying to get stung. Man, I'd never go out there." Ethan seemed resigned to passing up his eastern swim. The girls and Carl baited the nettles for ten minutes with their sunburned legs, but returned unscathed and cocky.

"Maybe they just don't like California meat," Carl casually bragged, as he put on his smelly socks.

Just outside of Oxford, we approached another small town on my map named Trappe. Jimmy was riding ahead of me, and he announced to the group that we were approaching a town.

"Hey Jimmy, how do you know we're coming close to another town?" I asked. "You don't even have a map."

"Simple, John. You can tell we're coming to a town by that water tower over there. See it? Above the trees? Every town we've come to has had a water tower, and since there don't seem to be all that many roads out here, I figured the one we're on must lead to that town up ahead."

As Jimmy continued his explanation of local geography, Carl rode up fast and breathing hard. His face was red, and he had trouble trying to catch his breath and talk at the same time. "John! Joy fell! We were riding along . . . and all of a sudden . . . she crashed in the middle of the road."

"Is she okay?"

"She scraped herself up pretty good and she was crying; I'm not sure. Lynn just told me to ride up here and tell you and Jimmy to slow down and wait for us."

We weren't even fifty miles into our trip, and Joy was down. As we stood there and waited, I had visions of broken bones and broken bike parts. I knew that the possibilities of someone getting hurt in four months of cycling were real, but I didn't actually expect anything disastrous to happen — and not on our second day; not on a quiet Maryland country road with no cars.

Soon Lynn, Ethan and the girls rode up. Other than Joy's scraped leg, red eyes and ripped handlebar tape, she seemed to be okay. Lynn told me I was going too fast, so I promised to take a rest stop at the water tower ahead. It wasn't planned and I didn't really want to, but it looked like we would be having a second lunch. After Joy's fall, everyone's tanks seemed to be running low.

While Joy bit the peanut butter and jelly bullet, the rest of the kids watched. Doctor Lynn sponged Stick's wounds with her bandana soaked in ice water. Joy turned out to be the perfect patient again.

"Ethan, could you pass me a cookie?" was Joy's only special request during her visit to the "doctor's" office. Always satisfied by simple things, Joy was soon back atop her bicycle and quietly leading the rest of us down another unnamed road. Joy's stoic strength made it easier for each of the kids to pedal on.

Just shy of Henry's Crossroads, Maryland, on a dusty and gravel-strewn dirt road, we sat down to one of Lynn's most creative feasts. Spread out on her damp beach towel turned table cloth were gooey peanut butter fudge made from Rice Crispies mixed with hot chocolate powder, warm orange drink, and one even warmer light beer. Carl's computer had just beeped the signal for our 100-mile mark and regardless of the lack of facilities, I figured it was time for a celebration. We laid our bikes down in a nearby ditch and gathered in the middle of the deserted dirt road. Although the menu left a little to be desired — we never again repeated it — there was dancing and singing and cheering. After I anointed the road with the foamy beer, Jimmy grabbed his water bottle and poured it over Ethan's head. "Hey, you guys, we only have 4400 miles to go!!!" Every other water bottle in the area immediately aimed and fired at Jimmy.

Despite Joy's fall, the quiet roads through Maryland cornfields were the perfect beginning for us. The kids' hands began to relax on their handlebars and I could see them beginning to enjoy the land and the people more and more. One afternoon we passed fields made famous by Harriet Tubman, and marked by a

MARYLAND STATE HISTORIC SITE

marker. Miss Tubman, the founder of the Underground Railroad, had run away from the spot where we were riding.

"STOP, JOHN! STOP! yelled Joy. "I wrote a report about Harriet Tubman last year in school, remember? I can't believe we're riding past the same place I read about. Heather, get your camera, we need to take some pictures."

"Wow, I wonder which way she ran from here . . . ," said Joy as she looked around.

"Probably back the way we just came from, because we're heading south aren't we, John?" said Heather.

"Yeah, we're heading south," answered Carl. "I can tell because we have that stupid headwind. John says that the wind here comes from the south, and every time we turn a certain way, it's in our faces. If that woman you're talking about ran away from here in the summertime, at least she would have a tailwind."

Underneath the sign in the cornfield, Heather took pictures as Joy gave us her story of the woman who began the secret railroad to freedom.

In Vienna, Maryland, at the foot of the Nanticoke River Bridge, Heather and Joy met the white-haired Danish woman who ran Lebo's Market. Her pale face was a marked contrast to all the black faces we'd seen who had stayed in Maryland, and soon she was involved in an excited conversation with the two girls.

"You mean you are going to ride all the way to California?" she asked.

"Yes ma'am," answered the girls.

"Well, I never heard of such a thing. What do your mothers think?"

"My mom really wanted me to go." Heather was the first to answer.

"And my mom . . . well, it took a long time for her to let me go," blushed Joy. "She's still not too happy about my decision."

"Well, dear, you look like you already hurt yourself. Maybe your momma was right?"

"Oh no, I'm okay," insisted Joy. "I just fell and scraped myself a little bit. It doesn't even hurt anymore."

"Well, I still can't believe it. You be careful now. There are a lot of crazy drivers on the road. Please, you be careful."

"We will. Thank you." The girls came back to where we were having lunch and soon their Danish friend joined us. She had ice water for our water bottles, Danish whistle pops for the kids, and Danish bubble gum for Lynn and me. Before we left, she had Joy and Heather writing her address down in their journals. As we headed off towards the bridge, she yelled, "Now you all be sure and write me when you get to California, ya hear." I looked over my shoulder and saw her standing, one hand waving and the other held to her stomach, on the steps of her little store.

The old black man, with wrinkled face and dirty cap, honked at the band of ducks paddling ahead of his rusty old barge. His little boat looked even older than the one at Oxford; any paint that might have ever graced its hull and sides had long since been eaten away by the salt air.

"Hey John, we're going to ride across the water on THAT?" asked Carl. "Shoot, I hope they have life jackets."

"I doubt it, Carl," said Jimmy. "Look at that guy driving. I bet he's never even heard of life jackets. Besides, you could almost—well, I could almost—throw a rock from here to the other side, this river is so narrow."

"I think it's neat," said Joy. "Look at those ducks. I bet they ride back and forth in front of the ferry all day. And the man, he looks like he would be fun to talk to."

The ferryboat lurched to a stop on our side, and the banged-up gangway clanged down onto the road that disappeared down into the water. The ferryman didn't say anything, he just motioned us aboard. We squeezed our bikes in alongside a white pick-up, just barely having room on the two car ferry. The ferryman collected our fares, and the kids ran to the leading end of the boat. Joy was right about the ducks. The driver slammed the gangway shut, shifted into reverse, and the boat coughed its way into motion. We headed back across the channel led by our quacking escorts. The kids grabbed some fig bars out of their handlebar bags and spent the entire five minutes of our voyage feeding the ducks.

"Hey John, ducks need carbohydrates too," laughed Jimmy, seeing me shaking my head.

Just down the road, in Princess Anne, we continued our Transcontinental Pizza Survey(TPS) at the Princess Anne Pizza Hut. Just for old time's sake, we created another inland waterway when Ethan somehow managed to capsize a pitcher of Dr. Pepper all over our table. Napkins floated off the table onto our laps, and soon the Pizza Hut rescue crew were all around us, laughing and passing the napkins. Once the table and our laps were mopped up, the tall and slender ebony-faced employee, who seemed to be getting the biggest kick out of our group, was back with another pitcher of bubbly brown brew — "on the house."

"And you all don't be jivin' me when you says you be ridin' yo bikes all de way to Calfornya?"

He made it sound like we were riding to Mars.

"My oh my, I always be thinkin' 'bout goin' to Calfornya some day, but I don't know if I ever get to go. I sho' would like to, though. Are you all really from Calfornya? I still can't believe you kids be pedalin' that far."

He disappeared back into the kitchen, as we downed our two large pizzas and three pitchers of drink. This group left no leftovers, and as Joy was calling on Mr. Senator Turpin for his pizza rating on our only Maryland pie, Jerome, our disbelieving waiter, shyly returned to our table.

"Excuse me. I believes you all and everything, but would you write me when you all gets home to Calfornya? I never got any letters from dere and I sure would like it if you could send me one. I got an envelope here wit' my address and stamp and everything."

The kids could feel the fascination and envy in his request. Even Ethan didn't keep him waiting there too long with that envelope in his nervous hand.

"Sure man, we'll write you," and with Ethan's answer, Heather reached up and got Jerome's envelope. He smiled as if he had just received the biggest tip of his life. The kids continued to tell him about California, and I felt Lynn reach underneath the table. Finding my hand, she gave me a knowing squeeze.

Leaving Princess Anne the following afternoon, Jimmy and I rode across a short bridge, spanning a little blackwater pond. We were riding side by side when the sounds of our tires on the wood woke up some sunbathing turtles. Five little orange-bellied natives slid off the snag they were resting on and splashed into the water.

"Did you see that, Jimmy?" I asked as I pulled over.

"Yeah. I didn't think turtles could jump, but those little guys sure seemed like they got air to me! And man, did you see how orange their bellies were? They looked like ripe persimmons. Let's wait here and show the others." Jimmy scanned the water as we waited for the rest of the group.

On our last day of pedaling in Maryland, we were riding, strung far apart, on another deserted road. It wound through tree shrouded marshland, and moss hung from the thick stands of trees.

"Hey John, those trees have special roots."

"Why do you say that, Joy?"

"Well, look underneath them. There isn't much dirt. Mostly just gooey mud. I would think trees would fall over in it."

"How would you like to be a slave trying to run away through that stuff?" I asked.

"Yuck. They could never find you, but you probably couldn't get out either."

My map said our road would last for a little over five miles, so I told Jimmy he could lead. "Just wait for us at the first crossroads." Joy and I coasted to the back of the group by ourselves and we continued wondering out loud about how it would be to be a slave trying to escape through these swamps.

As we were trying to imagine crouching black runaways, we came around a corner to an old house and trailer propped up on the only dry piece of land we had seen in the last few miles. We didn't know it, but we were soon to be trying to manage an escape of our own.

In four days of Maryland cycling, we had been chased by a dozen or so of the local hounds. I don't know if they thought we were birds, raccoons or possums, but they sure seemed to enjoy chasing us smelly cyclists down the road. Luckily for us, all of them so far had all been all bark and no bite. Even with that track record, what emerged from underneath the house ahead didn't make us stop and ask questions.

As soon as the sound of our spinning wheels reached the house, a deep, snarling growl resonated from under the house. At the sound, my heart immediately pumped adrenaline to the far reaches of my body. My hair, fingernails, and toenails must have grown half an inch within seconds. I looked at Joy and she looked at me, our expressions frozen with fear. We instantly accelerated our bikes, and in one second, my brain scanned the yard for giant dog dishes and piles of human bones.

Before I got a chance to finish my examination, not one, but two giant black forms exploded out of the ground and were after Joy and me. When they emerged from the dust, we saw we were being chased by two full-grown Doberman pinschers. They were the kind of dogs I'd seen on TV — you know the kind that claw chain link fences, the kind trained to go for the necks of burglars. We weren't stealing anything, but from the bared teeth of those two canines, it didn't look like they were asking questions either.

In my loudest, meanest, most authoritative (and most scared) voice, I yelled: "GO HOME!"

I think I heard the lead Doberman laugh.

Joy definitely wasn't laughing, because both dogs seemed to like her perfume better than mine. They almost acted as if I wasn't there and confined their chase to her. In seconds, they were barking and snarling and showing Joy their dental work.

Joy responded with her usual, animal loving, "Nice dogs, nice dogs," and if I was a dog I would surely have been convinced of her sincerity. Joy really spoke kindly to those two hounds, but they didn't understand her California accent. They seemed more interested in lunch than new friends. Joy felt their hot breath on the back of her legs and looked over to me for some help. Neither my macho approach or her friendly one seemed to be working. I slowed my bike to a stop and told her to do the same.

"Get off your bike slowly and put it between you and the dogs. Then roll away very slowly. Hopefully, they'll get tired of hassling your wheels and go home."

It worked. Their low growls and occasional bark continued with decreasing emotion for the next hundred yards. Then, with a final loud authoritative snarl, they toothed their 'don't come backs', and headed back to their shade, strutting with victory. I thought we had seen the last of them, so I got on Bud and sped ahead to catch up with the rest of the group not too far away.

I hadn't been back on my bike but thirty seconds when I heard their barks again. They were getting louder and louder, as if they were after us, and I looked over my shoulder to see Joy, head down, riding as fast as she could towards me. A couple hundred yards behind her were our old buddies in hot pursuit. I slowed down and Joy flew past me screaming, "JOHN!" I had never heard her scream before and she looked terrified. I looked back at the dogs and got a little terrified myself. I stood on my pedals and rode up to Joy as fast as I could.

"Okay Joy, we're going to out run them this time, okay?"

Joy didn't say a word. She just put her head down and cranked as hard as she could.

We didn't look back; we just listened for the sound of their barks. At first they seemed to be gaining, then they stayed about the same distance away. Then, as Joy pumped even harder, their barks and growls faded behind us. Joy rode fast long after their echoes faded away. Finally, she pulled over, heaving and exhausted.

". . . John. . . I've never. . . pedaled so fast . . . on my bicycle . . . in my life . . . When I heard them . . . barking again . . . I screamed for you and . . . I looked up and you weren't there. I was so scared . . . I knew I didn't have the guts . . . to hit them with my pump. Without you there, I was also too scared to stop. I saw you ahead, so I just rode as fast as I could. I didn't know I could go that fast."

"I'm sorry I left you behind, Joy. Are you okay?" I put my hand on her sweaty shoulder. "I never thought they would come back after you. You must smell especially good, because it seems that you're the most popular one in our group for dogs to chase."

"Yeah, I know. Earlier today, when Heather and I were riding, this little dog ran up to us and didn't even bother with Head (Joy's nickname for Heather), he just chased after me."

Soon we were back on our bikes and reunited with the rest of the group. Lynn had stopped across the street at the little country market to buy some 10-cent popsicles. As I watched Joy alternate licks on her root beer popsicle with her high speed doberman chase story, I wondered if she realized she'd just experienced a little more of what it must have been like for Harriet Tubman when she ran from here as a young woman, and I couldn't help but wonder what kind of popsicle young Harriet would have liked.

Water Spiders

The large water tank on the horizon had a giant red crab painted on it. Crisfield, Maryland, "the crab capital of the world" and home of the Miss Crustacean Beauty Pageant, was to be our last stop in Maryland. We'd spent the night with the mosquitoes at Jane's Island State Park and had only two miles to ride to the end of the wharf at Crisfield, where we would catch the mail and supply boat to Tangier Island.

"Hey John, what time did you say our boat leaves?"

"It doesn't leave 'til 12:30, so why don't you guys explore the waterfront. First though, the captain of the mail boat says we can load our bikes aboard now, so come on over to the dock with me. Take off your handlebar bags, and anything else you might need, and help me get them aboard. After that, go ahead and look around."

"You mean we don't have to do a bike-watch?" asked Heather. (On bike-watches, each of us would be assigned a half hour to sit and watch the bikes, while everyone else went shopping or exploring. The kids knew it was necessary, but didn't enjoy it.)

"No, I think they'll be perfectly safe aboard the mail boat. Enjoy Crisfield and meet Lynn and me at The Kozy Korner Cafe for lunch at 11:30."

As much as I liked pizza and peanut butter and jelly, I was ready for some more local seafood, and if the smell of Crisfield was any indication, I knew I would soon find some lunch that had gone for a swim earlier in the day.

"Soft-Shell Crab, Soft-Shell Crab Sandwiches, World's Best Crab Cakes" read the signs in the restaurant and cafe windows near the wharf. I was dreaming of my first soft-shell crab, when another Jimmy interrupted me.

"Hey John, dig Ethan's hat." Jimmy and Ethan each held a large soft-scoop ice cream cone in their hands.

"C'mon you guys. Ice cream at ten o'clock? We just had breakfast." I shook my head at the guys who were battling to eat their cones before the hot sun melted the giant scoops down their arms. Ethan was wearing a new hat, but I focused more on the big splotch of melted vanilla ice cream moving down his t-shirt.

"Cool hat, Ethan, but did you notice the big spill on your only clean shirt?"

He didn't answer, he just tilted his hat a little more and looked down at the sticky stain that now looked like the continent of South America with a bad case of continental drift. Ethan stared at the spot for 30 seconds studying it, and only stopped his study when more of his cone dripped down his arm. He immediately licked his arm and rubbed it on his shirt. "Oh yeah, these cones are kinda hard to eat in this heat. You like my hat, huh? I've been looking for one like this for years. It looks like its from England, don't you think?"

"England . . . right Ethan." I shook my head as I answered Ethan. How in fifteen minutes he and Jimmy had found a hat shop and ice cream cones I didn't know and I wasn't going to ask. "See you guys in a while. Save some room for lunch."

"Right on, John," waved Jimmy. "See you later."

As I headed off in search of some camping supplies, I watched the guys lick and drip their way down the planked sidewalk. They traded off swiping Ethan's hat from each other's head, as they tripped towards some other treasure.

The seafood side of the menu at The Kozy Korner Cafe had me drooling as Lynn and I waited for the kids at our lunch rendezvous. The guys came in and sat in a booth with me, and the girls sat with Lynn.

"Hey John, can we get milkshakes?"

"Yeah, but you should really try their Cokes here. Remember when Peter Jenkins talked about drinking ice cold Coke from those thick, frosty, green bottles? Well, they have those kind of bottles here, and I think you'll find you've never tasted anything quite like them, especially on a hot day like today. Besides, I hear they really taste good with soft-shell crab sandwiches."

"Yuck! I'm going to have a hamburger." Joy wasn't too enthusiastic about my proposition.

"Yeah, with french fries," echoed Carl.

Heather was the only one to find the least bit of merit in my suggestion, and the best she could manage was, "John, I think I'm going to order fish and chips, but if it looks good, will you give me a taste of your sandwich?"

"Sure, Heather." I looked around at the rest of the group disapprovingly. "You guys are wimps! We bring you all the way to Crisfield—the crab capital of the known world—and you order hamburgers and french fries. Pathetic. Where's that old spirit of adventure?"

"Okay John, I'll have a Coke with my milk shake," grinned Jimmy. I was hoping a little guilt would change some orders, but Jimmy's change wasn't quite what I had in mind. Soon it was Cokes and shakes all around, but no more crustacean sandwiches. The soft-shell crab population of Crisfield slept a little more safely that evening.

When our orders finally came up and my sandwich made its much awaited appearance, the kids were even more convinced they had made the right decision. There on my plate, next to a slice of onion and tomato sat what looked like two slices of plain white bread stacked together. At closer inspection I noticed, as did Lynn and the five kids who were draped over my shoulders, a small green appendage peeking out from one of the sides of the bread. Seizing the opportunity to gross out my audience — and it wasn't easy to gross out twelve and thirteen-year-olds — I quickly lifted up the top slice of bread to reveal two small blue-green crabs pressed into a pool of mayonnaise.

"Ooh gross! They do look like spiders," exclaimed Carl.

"John, you're disgusting," groaned Jimmy. "You're not really going to eat that are you?"

"They're just babies," sighed Joy.

I had the kids just where I wanted them. I tossed in the onions and tomatoes, put the top slice of bread on top of my sandwich, and with just the right pause for dramatic effect, bit into the sleeping "babies."

I was hoping some juice would squirt out the sides of my sandwich, but my two babies weren't quite that juicy. Still, I succeeded in grossing out the entire group. After witnessing my premier bite, they immediately returned to their seats to wash down their distaste with milkshakes, just as if they were washing down a forced taste of lima beans. Needless to say, Heather didn't ask for a taste, and as the kids enjoyed their burgers, Cokes, fries and milkshakes in real glass soda glasses — "Just like *Happy Days*," said Heather — I enjoyed my first soft-shell crab sandwich all to myself.

Once finished with our last Eastern Shore lunch, we walked over to the boat. Heather managed to distance herself from the group and tiptoed back to me. She waved her arms, motioning me to bend down so she could whisper something in my ear.

"Hey John, did it taste any good?" I laughed and put my arm around her as I winked and nodded. I could tell, from the curious look on her always twinkling face, that soon Heather would be joining me for a "water-spider" sandwich of her own.

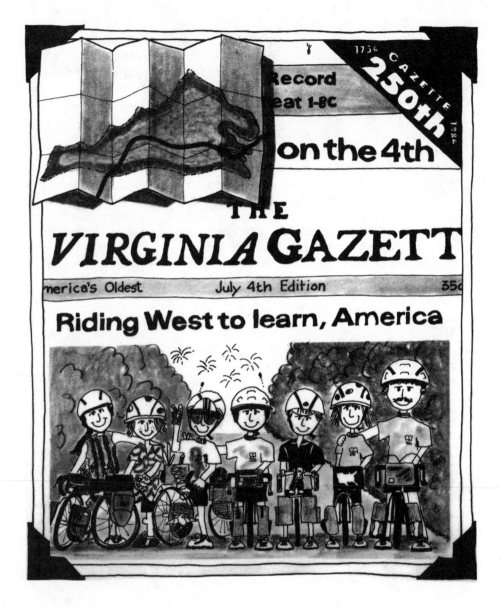

6

For breakfast, we went to The Steer. I had Biscuits and Gravy and Fried
Apples. They were definitely Southern Style. We went to Appomatox Court-
house and saw where the treaty was signed. It looked so realistic. I could see
Lee and Grant sitting in the room . . . .

Jimmy's Journal
July 6, 1986

Roight Heavy Soicles

A flock of Maryland sea gulls cawed their good-byes as the mail boat putt-putted its way out of the harbor.

"Hey John, most of those sea gulls have black faces," said Carl, as he pointed up at the birds riding the wind behind the boat. "Just like most of the people we saw in Maryland."

Another flock of sea gulls was the first to greet us as we neared our first piece of Virginia — Tangier Island. The Tangier gulls all had white faces, and we would soon find that so did all the people residents of Tangier.

"Those yo boikes?" The captain was on deck getting ready to dock at Mail-boat Harbor. "They sho' is quoight a soight."

"Yup, I guess they are," I said. "They're carrying all our possessions." I wondered if my brand of English sounded as strange to the captain as his did to me. As we approached the wharf and the captain gave his orders for docking, I listened harder, trying to figure out his version of our language. By the time we docked and were ready to unload our bikes, I still hadn't figured it out.

"These here soicles be roight heavy, they be." He lifted the small red one, with girls underwear hanging from the rear panniers, and handed it down to Heather.

"Thank you, skipper," saluted Heather, smiling up at his permanently tanned face.

"You be very welcome, ma'am." He tipped his cap back to her. She smiled up at the captain again and rolled her bike up the pier.

Ethan's was next. "And whur you be goin' with all you have hyar?" Ethan's bike had t-shirts, underwear, shorts and socks hanging wherever things could be hung. His stuffed pteradactyl hung out the side pocket of his front pannier, chains and charms dangled from his handlebar bag, a Slinky made its way out of the top compartment, and his Maryland flag and skull and crossbones flapped in the breeze from underneath bungee cords on his rear rack.

"Well ... uh ... we're riding our bicycles across America," stuttered Ethan as he reached up and received his blue bike from the skipper.

"Danged if I never heerd of such a thing bafore. We got lots of soicles on

Tangier, but I don't think any of 'em been 'cross the country. You have yourself a foine roide now, ya hyar."

"Thanks," smiled Ethan.

As the good captain helped me get the bikes to the kids, I kept working on a description for his accent. Our American language lessons were happening faster and more frequently than I ever imagined. Just when we were beginning to understand some DC street jive, along came the good ole boys and George from Matthewstown. Then came our professor of crabology. Now here we were at it again on Tangier Island. The native tongue on that small speck of land was the strangest brew of American English we would encounter in four months.

We all said good bye to the mail boat and rolled our bicycles onto the dirt path we hoped would lead us to Tangier's main street. The kids knew we were going to stay at a Bed and Breakfast and were very excited about the prospect — at least until they set eyes on the island.

"Hey John, why are we going to stay here? This whole island looks like it's falling apart." At first glance, I had to admit I agreed with Carl's impression.

There weren't any nostalgic museums in sight; no topsider-wearing historical society patrons with name tags strolling the waterfront on their way to work. All that greeted us that afternoon on Tangier were piers and shanties and boats, watermen and watermen's wives all scarred and grayed by the waters of the ocean.

The waters surrounding Tangier were not only weathering the boats and the buildings and the people, but were eating the entire island away. The British had camped on Tangier during the War of 1812 — in fact, Francis Scott Key spent the night before he wrote our national anthem on Tangier with his British captors — but those beach campsites were now underwater. No place on the island was more than five feet above bay level, and Tangier was indeed one of those places where you could only ride a bicycle when the tide was right. One storm was so bad that it flooded the entire island, literally forcing everyone to wait out the storm upstairs. Story has it that the island kids, while waiting for the bay to recede, made the best of their predicament by using second story windows for diving boards and the ocean as their front yard swimming pool.

"Hey John, where's this inn? I'm cooking in this heat!" Jimmy was looking pretty hot as he emptied his water bottle on his head. Heather didn't look too good either as she tied her hair up and prepared to fan herself with her journal.

"Well, you guys, it can't be far. Tangier is only two and a half miles long and less than one mile wide."

"What's the name of the inn again?" asked Joy, as she pushed her bicycle along the narrow path of asphalt.

"Hilda Crockett's Chesapeake House," I answered.

"Oh yeah . . . Can we ride our bikes? They're much harder to push."

The captain had said to turn left after leaving the dock and we would be on the main street. We had taken that left, but the blacktop we discovered was so narrow it seemed more like a path than a main street.

"Excuse me, ma'am, but is this Main Street, and is this the way to The Chesapeake House?" I asked a gray-haired woman heading our way. Before answering Joy, I figured I'd better be sure we were going the right way.

The woman looked a lot like most of the women we had seen since getting off the boat. She was wearing a flowered work dress and looked like she was someone's grandmother. She walked with a slight bend in her back and wore black plastic and wire glasses. She stopped and looked us over before she answered my question.

"Yes, son, this is Main Street ifn you loikes to call it such. And yes, you be headin' in the proper direction to foind Chesapeake House."

"Thank you, ma'am."

"Joy, I think it would be okay to ride if you're very careful. Ride single file and be careful of the gravel patches, you guys. Just look for a sign that says Hilda Crockett's. It should be a two-story, white wood house with shutters and a fence."

"See you there, boss," said Jimmy.

One by one the kids mounted their bikes and were off down the road. It was so narrow, I was afraid the kids, with all their gear and extra girth, might unintentionally knock someone over who was walking along the same road. The path was not only the main street, but was also the main sidewalk. Heather hesitated before being the last to leave. She looked up at me with a puzzled expression on her face. Having seen the same look before, I knew I was in for some more of Heather's wisdom.

"Uh . . . John . . . I know you told us to look for a white, two-story, wooden house with a fence in front, but . . . I've been noticing that most of the houses around here — if not all of them — are 'white, two-story, wooden houses.' The only difference seems to be that some have picket fences and some have chain-link ones . . . ."

I looked around and, as usual, she was right. Lynn was next to me laughing, and Heather had a big grin on her face. "You're right, Heather. Let's just hope it has a sign. You'll have to look for the white, two-story, wooden one with a fence *and* a sign."

"Okey dokey," chirped Heather. She fanned herself one more time, tightened her helmet and was off. Lynn and I decided to walk.

"This sure isn't Nantucket," said Lynn as we pushed our bikes after the kids. "But I kinda like it. It doesn't seem so fake and there's still some little shops. They look like they're part of people's homes. I think I'm going to have fun here."

Looking at the small gift shops, I didn't really see any way that she could overspend our own souvenir budget here. No credit card warning signs were hanging in the shop windows, but still—

"I hope not too much fun, dear . . ."

"Oh, John. I've spent hardly any money yet."

I wished she hadn't included that "yet", but I decided it was best not to say anything more.

Hilda Crockett's Chesapeake House did look an awful lot like all the other wood houses on Tangier, but luckily it did have a sign. After unloading our bikes and lugging all of our stuff upstairs, I gave the kids the afternoon off.

"Do whatever you want, you guys. Just meet back here for dinner at 5 o'clock."

We had three rooms: one for the guys, one for the girls, and one for Lynn and me. The thought of three hours of free time immediately brought grins of mischief to everyone's faces. The girls—including Lynn—couldn't wait to do some shopping, and the guys couldn't wait for some mischief they hadn't thought of yet. All I wanted to do was fall into my much-too-soft bed and drool my way through a much-needed afternoon nap.

Just as I was about to collapse onto the mattress, a loud KABOOM!!! rattled the whole house. I looked out my second story window and saw that the steamy gray Chesapeake sky had suddenly changed. Giant clouds were blowing over the harbor a few blocks away, and the trees outside were being whipped by the wind. Another eastern thunderstorm was heading our way. It was already raining silver sheets over the water, and the hair on my arms started dancing to the electricity accompanying the damp air. Another bolt of lightning cracked somewhere nearby, and just as suddenly, rain was pelting against the window, making it impossible to see outside. Our bicycles were leaning against the fence downstairs, and tied to their racks were our tents and panniers, filled with food and clothes we didn't think we'd need for our overnight stay. The sky had been so hot and still, we just loosely covered everything with our orange plastic tarps. As the storm slammed against the house, I imagined those tarps blowing across the island and out to sea with it. Soon, plastic bags of underwear, oatmeal, and bagels would be floating in flooded panniers. It looked like my nap was going to be put on hold. I ran over to the guys' room to tell them to go downstairs and get their gear.

"Knock, knock," I said as I tapped on the boys' door.

"Who's there?" Jimmy poked his head out from behind the door he only opened to a crack. "Oh, hi John . . . what's happening?"

There was something in Jimmy's tone that told me that the guys had found their mischief and weren't too excited about me joining in. The tiny wad of toilet paper stuck precariously to the tip of his nose didn't help his secrecy much either. "Gosh, I hate to interrupt your journal writing session guys, but we'd better move our stuff inside and out of this storm."

Jimmy waved his hand behind him and slowly opened the door. The guys had saved a few straws from our afternoon lunch. The straws, teamed up with a roll of toilet paper from the bathroom, provided them with all the weapons and ammunition needed to have an afternoon of one of young America's favorite national pastimes — a spit wad fight. As Jimmy continued his slow opening of the door, he slipped his straw into his back pocket. Once the door was completely open, I was greeted with a full view of the battlefield. The boys' room was strewn with hundreds of little white balls. On the far side of the room, Ethan was just surfacing from behind a mattressed bunker, and in the opposite corner, Carl was standing next to the roll of toilet paper. He had a pillow shield in one hand and a straw in the other.

"Yeah, you guys, I'm really sorry to interrupt your journal meeting, but let's go move our bikes and stuff. It's really raining out there." I watched them whisper their way downstairs and laughed as I went to look for the girls.

Lynn and Heather were inside the bathroom washing clothes and getting ready to hit the shops of Tangier, and Joy was downstairs. Soon, we were all outside getting drenched and jumping, as the lightning crashed over the tiny island. Just as we got our dripping stuff up underneath the porch, the rain stopped. The wind blew the clouds, and as quick as it had come, the storm was gone. The sky turned a deep blue, washed momentarily of its gray humidity by the storm. Joy and Heather stayed outside to look for a rainbow, Lynn headed back up to the bathroom, and the guys headed back to the war zone. I almost hated to do it, but just before I headed off to the land of Nod, I asked the guys to declare a cease-fire and mop up.

The dining room at Hilda Crockett's reminded me of the one I grew up with, except that instead of one large picnic style table there were several. Checkered vinyl tablecloths hung over the sides and were topped with bowls and platters piled high with a traditional Tangier Island meal. It was served family-style, and the kids bravely filled their plates with first helpings of everything: country ham, cole slaw, cream corn, crab cakes, oyster fritters and chocolate cake, accompanied by tall plastic tumblers of iced tea. It was all-you-could-eat, as advertised, and although the kids didn't go for seconds on fritters and crab cakes, they did try everything without Lynn or my having to encourage them to. The other guests sharing our table were almost as impressed with the kids' manners and appetites as they were with our bicycle adventure — and no one even spilled any iced tea!

"Hey John, it's Saturday night and it's summertime. Let's go cruisin'," motioned Jimmy.

"Okay, Jimmy, let's go cruisin'," I answered.

Outside the sun was dimming in the western sky. Tangier's narrow main drag, passing in front of our house, was beginning to fill up with descendants of the first cruisers who had come to this island 200 years ago. John Crockett headed that first permanent settlement and a third of the islanders still shared his last name. Little towheads rode rusted BMX bicycles, ten and eleven-year-olds rode balloon-tired one-speeds with crooked baskets and coaster brakes, and teenagers rode double and triple on derailleured machines with tires flattened by the extra weight. Older Crocketts and Crockett cousins rode the same paths with mopeds. A mini Harley-Davidson even sped past us. As we made our way towards "downtown" (where the church, market and ice cream shop were), we realized we had stumbled onto an island without cars, and to us Californians, nothing could have been much more foreign. Not even a Toyota could fit down King Street, but that didn't stop the Tangier kids from their own summer Saturday night procession. As my kids went inside Daley's Gift Shop to buy souvenirs, licorice and ice cream, I sat outside and watched the parade of Tangier cruisers.

Like a fool, I tried to write in my journal. As usual, my pen couldn't keep up with all that was happening in front of me, so after about a paragraph, I threw my journal back in my handlebar bag. My memory would have to get together with my journal later on.

"Hey John, come on in here and see all the neat stuff they've got." Carl didn't give me much time to watch. He grabbed my arm and pulled me inside. The first thing he had to show me was a giant, red, plastic fly the size of a small watermelon. The rest of the kids were each holding one and trying to decide if they would be a wise purchase.

"Yeah, we could attach them to our helmets somehow and they would scare away the other bugs that have been chasing us and eating us up," exclaimed an excited Ethan. Lynn and I had told parents that we would encourage the kids to spend their souvenir money on things that were "meaningful," but I didn't know if Ethan's folks would understand the significance of giant plastic flies.

"Right, Ethan. Except that these flies look pretty macho to me," said Jimmy. "They might attract all the interested female bugs in the area right to you."

"What makes you think these are male flies?" countered Joy, as Ethan contemplated Jimmy's observation. "I think they are female flies."

Jimmy thought for a few seconds, then answered: "Yeah, you might be right, Stick," thoroughly confusing Ethan. "Mother Nature *has* always created the male of the species to be the better looking. And these flies sure are ugly. You're right, they must be females." Jimmy chuckled with a big born-in-Tennessee grin as he finished.

Lynn and I were very used to the loving bantering that had already developed among the kids, and we both laughed as Joy predictably stuck her tongue out at Jimmy. The flies were soon placed back on their shelves, and the kids decided to buy flags, postcards, crab pins and crab pens instead. After the last purchase, I stepped outside and there were Joy and Jimmy sharing tastes of each others' ice creams.

We decided to combine some exploring with our Saturday night cruising, so we wandered off King Street towards the harbor. Boats rattled as they rocked in the waters of the bay.

SWIMSUITS PROHIBITED IN PUBLIC

read the black letters painted on a whitewashed sign nailed to the side of one of the crab shanties.

"Man, this sure isn't California," Ethan mumbled as he read the sign out loud.

We continued walking on the abandoned waterfront, Lynn's hand in mine, our kids walking beside us. Jimmy skipped a rock while Joy and Heather looked at the purple inside of a discarded crab shell. My dad used to take my brothers and sisters and me down to the beach in our red wagon at sunset, and I remember how he always kept us close together. I held Lynn's hand instead of a wagon handle, and our group of five kept close together just like my family used to. That night on Tangier, I think I got to feel a little like my dad must have felt. He must have enjoyed listening to the things we had to talk about on those walks as much as I enjoyed watching and listening to the five kids loaned to Lynn and me, pointing out shells and boats, kidding each other and sharing ice creams. If they kept it up for the next couple months, I knew Lynn's and my next Educational Safari would probably be to the maternity ward.

"Hey John, what's that shack over there with the lights on?" Carl was up ahead and pointed to a wooden shack leaning out over the water. Naked light bulbs hung from black cords strung across the top of an open deck. They bobbed and danced in the breeze like dozens of electric fireflies hovering in formation. We all picked up our pace and joined Carl.

There was a fence around the shanty and we soon saw why. Another of Tangier's many gray-haired women was hunched over large troughs filled with crabs. Water bubbled and gurgled as it was pumped through the tanks. The little lady ignored us as she picked through the crabs, and we just stood there watching.

"I know what she's doing!" Heather's loud whisper didn't seem to disturb her. "She's culling the soft-shell crabs from the others."

" . . . Culling? . . . what's culling mean?" asked Ethan.

"Oh Ethan, remember our friend that first day, back in Maryland?" answered Heather trying to revive Ethan's memory. "Remember how he told us culling was when they separate the crabs?"

"Yeah, kinda . . . She sure is fast."

"I wonder how she doesn't get pinched," said Carl.

"No sweat," answered the ever confident Jimmy. "You just have to grab them from behind. I bet I could do it."

"Not me, thank you," said Heather, shaking her head.

The kids continued their commentary as they watched her. Even with the constant gurgle of the recirculating pump, I knew the woman had heard the kids. When she finished, I expected her to flash the kids a wink or a smile, but no, she just quietly returned to the shed, the wooden door springing to a crooked slam behind her.

We walked a little farther along the water, and as if they had just sprung up, we noticed lots of other lines of light bulbs strung off other gray shanties. It looked like soft-shell crab farming was big business on Tangier Island.

"Hey John, how come there are so many little graveyards here?" asked Joy as we walked along.

"Yeah, I know," agreed Carl. "Almost every other house has one. They're weird too. They're made of concrete and a lot of them look like giant solid bath-tubs. I thought people were s'posed to get buried 5 feet under the ground, not five feet on top of it. All of these graves are above the ground."

"Well, Carl, haven't you ever been to the beach and dug a hole?" asked Joy.

"Yeah, so what?"

"Well, what happens when you're close to the water and you dig down about a foot or so?" continued Professor Joy.

"That's easy! Your hole fills with water," said Ethan, joining in.

"And what would happen if they tried to bury people here under the ground?" asked Joy realizing her class was just about to figure out the mystery of the concrete bathtubs.

"Ooh, that would be gross!" exclaimed Ethan, unable to contain his revela-tion. Joy smiled as she finished her lesson on the burial necessities of Tangier.

"Ya know something else I've been noticing about the tombstones. They all seem to have the same names." Heather was thinking out loud.

"Well, Head, maybe these are family graveyards. There's not much land on the island, so maybe each family decided to have their own plots." Jimmy walked alongside Heather and casually offered his reasoning.

"Yes, I thought that too, but so far I've seen at least four separate Crockett graveyards and a couple Pruitt graveyards and a couple for the Dises and the Parks. It seems like everyone on this island is either named Crockett, Pruitt, Parks or Dise."

I had noticed what Heather had observed too, but just as I was about to get involved in the discussion, the roar of a speeding moped caused us to scatter. We were just crossing one of the narrow footbridges and there wasn't enough room for all of us.

"Hey, that's the girl in the neon outfit!" exclaimed Jimmy. "I've seen her go past us at least ten times so far. Everyone must just go around the island in circles on Saturday night. I don't know if I could get into that." Jimmy didn't seem too thrilled with cruising Tangier-style.

"Yeah . . . I wonder how many people leave the island . . . and never come back." It was Ethan's turn to do a little thinking out loud. "I mean . . . once they've been to the city and been in cars and to movies and stuff, it would be pretty hard spending Saturday nights eating ice cream and going around in circles on a moped . . . These roads are even too full of gravel to skateboard on." I wondered how many Tangier kids felt the way Ethan did.

We continued our circumnavigation of Tangier by foot. The sun set slowly in the direction we would be headed tomorrow. The younger Tangier kids were called in to park their wheels and get in their pajamas, as their older brothers and sisters and cousins turned on their lights. Bicycles and mopeds rolled along the darkened lanes leaving streamers of light behind them. We watched the sky turn from orange to gray to black as we stood in the marsh grass on the western side of the island. We watched the remnants of our afternoon storm glow somewhere over a Virginia we couldn't yet see. Every couple of minutes we could see the flashes of lightning making the horizon light up. Heather got a little frustrated, as she was the only one who couldn't see the flashes. It wasn't because of her height either; her timing was just off. She tried and she tried. She even stood staring west, holding her eyes open with her fingers, trying to prevent herself from blinking, but still she missed the light show.

Before heading home to bed, Carl and Jimmy broke out some sparklers they had found at Daley's Gift Shop, and we tried our darndest to light them in the ocean breeze. We huddled, arms around each other, to try and create a windbreak, but the matches just wouldn't stay lit long enough. On our last match we all locked arms, legs, heads and necks into the tightest human wall I had ever seen, but still the match died before the sparkler could put on its show.

A disappointed bunch of bicyclists bumped and talked their way home to Hilda Crockett's that Saturday night and fell asleep underneath fresh sheets. Tomorrow I'd have to find them some longer matches. They deserved some fireworks.

Our Sunday on Tangier was our first Sunday since hopping on our bicycles. It would begin a set of rituals I hoped we could follow every Sunday between here and home. Our first ritual was our map and journal meeting, and as I called the kids up to our room after breakfast, I had more concerns about the map part of our gathering than the journal part.

I had a large fold-up map of America tucked in the pannier where I carried all the business paraphernalia of the trip: medical release forms, insurance information, state maps, county maps, addresses, stationary—two manila envelopes full of important paperwork. Before the kids came up to our room, I layed out the map of the USA next to our maps of Maryland and Virginia. The kids had already seen our progress on Maryland state and county maps, and our 168.8 miles of progress in five days of riding looked pretty impressive even on the larger state map. Every Sunday, I had planned to get out my fluorescent orange marker and trace our progress on our map of the United States, but, as I looked down on the map of America and saw that the entire state of Maryland was not even as big as my thumb, I had second thoughts about my plan. Even my choice of markers worried me. If I wasn't careful, I would make too big a mark. 168.8 miles on that map with that marker equaled more of a dot than a line. All of a sudden, America looked even larger than it had from up in our jet.

The kids were into the room before I could put the map away, and they couldn't wait for me to take the cap off the marker.

"Hey John, let's see how far we've gone!"

"Yeah John, what are you waiting for? Let's mark this baby!"

I started to show them on the Maryland map, but I didn't get very far.

"No, John, not that one. We've already seen that one, let's see the USA map." Carl didn't have much patience with my diversion.

I don't remember what I said trying to rationalize why our first week looked so short, but whatever I said didn't seem to soften the silence that immediately followed the 'dotting of the map.' The kids looked at each other and then looked at Lynn and me. After a few seconds of silence, their whole mood and posture seemed to change.

"No problem, dudes. We're just gettin' warmed up. Heck, today we'll really be in Virginia, and we're travelling more and more miles every day now." Jimmy broke the ice with his helpful confidence.

"Yeah, remember when Barbara and Larry Savage first started out in Big Sur? They hardly went very far at all," said a smiling Heather. "Remember how they thought they were going to die that first week, and they ended up making it all the way around the world. I haven't felt *that* tired yet, and I know I can start to do more miles each day now that I'm *kinda* getting used to the heat and the humidity."

"Yeah, and remember Peter Jenkins and Cooper. They didn't start off so fast either," said Joy who was now the cheerleader. "We're getting faster and faster with our camping routines: washing our clothes every day, getting our tents and stuff set up, making meals and cleaning up dishes and pans. I think we're doing great."

"Yeah, and I've got lots more room to carry food," added Carl. He was already carrying most of our food, but wanted more. "With me carrying more food, we won't have to stop as much. That means we can go farther each day."

Ethan was the only one who remained silent, but the enthusiasm of his friends soon had him nodding and smiling along with them.

"Well, let's get on with our journals," perked Joy with perfect timing. We folded up the map and put it away until next Sunday, when I hoped our dot would become a full-fledged line.

Phone calls home followed journal writing on our Sunday schedule. On previous trips, Lynn and I had found that too much calling home could be as bad as not enough, so we set up once-a-week Sunday calls as our system of communication with home. Emergencies might arise to change that routine, but I felt strongly that being away from home and out of touch for a week at a time was both necessary and important. I didn't have an easy time convincing kids and parents of that, but my Sunday-Phone-Home-Day plan was eventually adopted.

Everyone except Ethan reached their folks that morning, and no one seemed to be bitten by any homesickness as a result. Ethan tried and tried but couldn't get through. We planned to go to church services at the Methodist Church, so we dressed in our cleanest clothes — the girls each in their one skirt and the guys in their one pair of long pants — and I told Ethan we would try his folks again just before the service started. While the rest of the group tried to find a shop that was open on Sunday, I sat on a wall near the phone where Ethan anxiously dialed through long distance operators. He wasn't on the phone long when I saw him hang it up with one hand and wipe his eyes and nose with the back of his other. I'd seen lots of stains on Ethan in the two weeks we had been together, but those were the first tear stains I'd seen since the airport in Los Angeles. His wet face and trembling little body showed how much he had wanted to hear his mom's and dad's and little sister's voices, but I couldn't do much to ease his pain. Jimmy, who also saw how his buddy was feeling, did a much better job.

"Hey Eeth, did you bring your water camera?" he yelled. "We still got to get the girls back for drenching our tent the other night. C'mon man, let's go find them for a surprise attack." Ethan sucked in some air and wiped his face one last time before reaching into his handlebar bag for his camera squirt gun. Water weapon in hand, he was off and running down King Street with Jimmy.

We filed into church alongside many of the same faces we had seen yesterday on two wheels or behind the counters of shops. We filled up a pew toward the middle of the church, and the kids immediately began thumbing through the hymnal and Sunday announcements. Soon we were standing and singing *Kum Bay Yah* and *Joyful Joyful* with everybody else. Jimmy and Carl already seemed to know the words as they sang without looking at the songbooks, but once the rest of us found the right pages, we were right with them.

At communion time, I noticed Heather, who was sitting at the other end of the pew, working her way over to me. Every 15 seconds or so she would look around her and then change places with one of our group as if she were playing Red Light/Green Light. I wondered what was up — if she had to go to the bathroom or something — and I soon found out.

"John, what are they doing now?" whispered Heather. As usual she didn't want to miss anything.

"They're having communion," I whispered back. I should have known better than to give Heather such a simple answer. After all, she was the one who pointed out that John Glenn looked just like the guy in the movie.

"What's communion, John? Can I do it too?" I remembered that it took me four long years of Catholic catechism to earn my first communion, but as I looked at Heather, I knew she wasn't about to wait that long. I decided if she could sing then she could eat, and gave her a quick lesson in dipping bread into wine. Before I knew it, there she was dipping her morsel in the cup and celebrating her first Last Supper. When she got back to where we were seated, she whispered some more of her young wisdom into my ear.

"Hey John, you were right. All you have to do is dip the bread into the grape juice. It's easier than trying to find the songs in the book." Since God was listening, I figured he was smiling too.

After church, it was time to load up our bikes at the Chesapeake House and get ready to board the ferry to Reedville, Virginia. While I loaded the bikes atop the main cabin of the *Captain Thomas*, Lynn and the kids went to buy lunch. To my surprise, they all returned with soft-shell crab sandwiches.

"What got into you guys?" I asked. I expected Heather to take a bite out of the sandwich I had asked Lynn to find me, but the unanimous support my lunch vote received was a complete surprise.

"Well, Heather said that this would probably be the last time we would have a chance to taste soft-shell crab, so we decided to go for it." I thought that maybe Lynn had used some form of bribery, but instead, Joy let the truth be known.

Just before leaving, we all sat down and rolled back the wax paper around our sandwiches. No one dared peel back the top slice of bread and, reminiscent of the technique I used to employ when taking my mandatory one bite of spinach at the family dinner table, Joy, Jimmy, Ethan, Carl, Heather and Lynn each grasped their sandwich in one hand, a tall Coke in the other, closed their eyes, and took a bite of their "pailer" (Tangier talk for "peeler") sandwich. Gulps of Coke immediately followed those first bites, and pale grimaces of near nausea followed shortly thereafter. Then, one by one, I was handed partially eaten sandwiches accompanied with, "Here, John, you can finish mine."

Carl, his stubbornness admirable at times like that, was the last to admit defeat. "It's not that bad," he said, handing his sandwich over to me. And as the gray crab shanties and white-steepled Methodist Church disappeared to the east, I offered Tangier a fond and filling farewell by eating seven soft-shell crab sandwiches to the amazement of the other passengers on the *Captain Thomas* and to the delight and relief of my own crew.

Merle

"Once you cross the bridge, you're almost there," said the man standing with his family on the landing. Tim Veze was the manager of the Sangraal-by-the-Sea Youth Hostel, our destination for the night. He, his pretty wife and two daughters were at the ferry dock to welcome us to Virginia and give us directions to their hostel.

"I can't believe how friendly people are in the South." Carl was talking to Lynn. "I've heard of Southern Hospitality before, but that man and his family driving all this way to welcome us and tell us how to get to the hostel is pretty incredible."

It was about 3:00 and we were all feeling pretty confident of our first ride along the coast of Virginia. Twenty miles, beds and showers waiting for us at the hostel, and two kids close to their age to talk to — "No sweat," boasted Carl.

"Carl, I think you mean 'no problem,' to be more accurate," said Jimmy. "This is the South and you can't say, 'No sweat.' Just bein' outside makes you sweat."

Jimmy had a point.

Five o'clock found us in Kilmarnock and the kids were hungry from having passed up the wonderful crab sandwiches earlier. Carl's computer said we had gone almost twenty miles, but my map showed our hostel much farther down the road. Even though it was beginning to get late, I decided we had better refuel. I also figured that, although it wouldn't shorten the road, pepperoni pizza and pitchers of soda might help silence any early mutinies. Pizza would make my inevitable "Just a little farther, you guys . . . " a bit easier to take, and as the kids ate, I kept studying and studying my map to see how Tim and I could have miscalculated the distance between the ferry and the hostel so badly. Didn't his car have an odometer? Still, my tenth look at the map showed that we weren't even halfway there.

"Anybody want any more pizza?" I asked just before we left. Five blissful moans from the kids were just what I was hoping for.

Five miles after all the pepperoni we could eat, my plan seemed to be working. No one had asked how much farther, I was a couple hundred yards ahead setting a good pace, and everyone seemed to be riding strong. Then I heard Jimmy riding up behind me breathing unusually hard.

"Hey John!" Jimmy tried to catch his breath. "Joy and Heather crashed. They went off the road into two inches of gravel and both of them went down."

"Are they okay?"

"Well . . . I think so. Lynn's working on them right now. Heather fell on her knee and Joy scraped up her knee and shoulder again. Lynn doesn't look too happy. She said for me to tell you to slow down."

Having ridden with Lynn for a month in Japan, Jimmy knew most of her warning signals. He was right about her not being too happy with me. She rode up to me silently and gave me the "John-what-do-you-think-you're-doing?!-You-better-slow-down!" look. I had seen it a few times before and bowed obediently. I saw fresh tears on the girls' faces and fresh blood on their soft knees. I quietly apologized to everyone for going so fast and slowed the pace way down. Meanwhile, the sun was fading fast and I thought I heard some thunder in the direction we were heading. Carl's computer informed me that our twenty miles were up, but my map showed at least fifteen more miles to go.

"Excuse me, but are you in need of some local intelligence?" came the voice from inside the station wagon. We had pulled into a gas station at the foot of the Rappahanock River Bridge to put on our flashing amber taillights. Twilight was changing rapidly into darkness and the man in the station wagon pulled over to us as we clipped our lights on for the first time in our journey. The owner of the voice stuck his head out the window and repeated his offer.

"Well, no thank you," I answered. "I've got a map, and I think I've got it. We're heading for the youth hostel just across the bridge. Thanks anyway."

"You're sure now?" The look on his face seemed to express some doubt in there being any such place "just across the bridge."

"Yes, thank you anyway," I shot back. I was in a hurry, I could feel Lynn's cold stare already questioning my navigation, and I was in no mood to debate my map. He wished us good luck and watched us as we headed up to the bridge.

Cars were beginning to turn on their lights, and the thunder I thought I heard was now showing itself; even Heather could see the light show as the charcoal sky flashed white over the trees, just up the river. The bridge was over a mile long — our longest so far — but the kids weren't in the mood for any celebrations.

It was after 8:00 when we reached the other side of the bridge. Five solemn and drooping faces — Heather wasn't even smiling — and one less-than-happy wife followed me up and down Virginia's rolling, and very dark, Hwy. 3. They were so tired and angry, no one even asked me "how much farther?".

"HEY CARL!!! GET THE #@*%# OUT OF THE ROAD!!! Jimmy's scream cracked louder than the distant thunder. I stopped and tried to find Carl in the darkness behind me. Hwy. 3 had only two-lanes and very little shoulder. Not more than fifty yards ahead, I saw three sets of headlights, surely blind to our presence, speeding their way towards us in the opposite lane. I jerked my head around in the direction of Jimmy's yell, and behind me, I saw a large silhouette fly across the road. Was that Carl?!!! What would he be doing riding out in the other lane?!!! Damnit, he knew this was a two-way road!!! The silhouette — it looked like two wheels were in there somewhere — literally flew from just in front of the path of the onrushing headlights, back across our lane and landed with a thud on the grass shoulder just behind me. Just after the thud of its landing, I looked in the other lane to see one of our lights still flashing out on the blacktop. Before I had a chance to try and make out any bicycle—or bicycle rider—attached to the light, it exploded underneath the front tires of the first car. I wore my flasher on the back of my shorts, and I prayed quickly to God that Carl wasn't out there somewhere. It was so dark all I could see were headlights and the silhouettes of some of the kids behind me when their lights flashed.

"CARL, WHAT HAPPENED? YOU ALMOST GOT KILLED!" screamed Joy. I looked back to see Carl standing over his bicycle that was thrown on its side in the grass. Before he got a chance to answer, and before I realized all that had really happened, everything was lit up by a blinding light behind us. I squinted my eyes and saw a familiar station wagon inching slowly toward us on the shoulder of the road. It was the man from the gas station.

"John, there's this man in a station wagon and he's been following me ever since we crossed the bridge," said Lynn, sounding very worried. "What's the matter? You guys look like you've just seen a ghost. And why is Carl crying?"

It had been so dark that Lynn hadn't seen Carl go sliding out into the other lane of traffic. "All of a sudden I was lying in the other lane and I looked up and saw two headlights coming toward me. Somehow, I just jerked up my bike and threw it and me over here. It was all like a dream, it happened so fast. Next thing I knew, I heard my tail light being crushed by the car."

"Carl, are you alright?" asked Heather. "That car just missed you. I can't believe how you flew back across the road. I thought you were going to get hit for sure." Heather talked so fast she was short of breath. Carl started shaking and broke down into uncontrollable sobs. He couldn't talk.

Meanwhile, the station wagon door opened and out stepped the "stranger" that had been following Lynn.

"I really think y'all need some local help. Where did you say you were headed?"

I didn't have the guts to tell him we were headed to California. He probably would have flown the kids and Lynn home and had me locked up. Instead, while Lynn ran over to hold Carl, I repeated that we were headed to the youth hostel: ". . . We're supposed to take Route 3 just over the bridge and then turn left onto Route 624 to Route 626. That should put us near a post office. He said the hostel is just down the road from there, on the river. Really, the manager said it was just over the bridge."

"Well, I think I know where y'all are headed. I don't know about the youth hostel, but I do know the post office you're talkin' about. Just don't confuse me with route numbers. Y'all are in Virginia, and we know how to git from one place to another, just don't ask us the road numbers. By the way, my name is Merle and I'm gonna be your escort tonight. Can y'all ride in a pretty close line?"

"Yeah."

"Good, 'cuz I'm gonna put on my high beams behind y'all and lead your way. It's gonna get even darker when we get off this road. I want your tail rider to put on this reflective safety vest I have in my trunk. I use it to jog with at night, and it will make y'all more visible to traffic."

There weren't any street lights on the highway, and I couldn't imagine it getting any darker than it already was, but I wasn't going to argue with Merle. He slipped the vest on Lynn, everyone asked Carl if he was okay and praised him for his bravery. Soon, a shaken-but-steady band of blinking bicycles headed to beds that were proving to be a little farther than "just over the bridge."

Merle's lights were better than pizza, because something magical happened when he turned them on behind us. We turned off the main highway onto a bumpy, pitch-black, one-lane road. It didn't have any stripe to guide us, and howling dogs lurked in unseen farmhouses. Riding at the front with my candle of a headlight, all I could see was a pie-sized area of asphalt just ahead of my front wheel, and all the kids could see was the rider in front of them. Just when I figured the kids were going to vote to have my head and to ride no further, I heard the first effects of Merle's lights. Jimmy and Heather were just behind me and believe-it-or-not, they were singing.

> *"This ole man he played one,*
> *he played knick knack on my thumb.*
> *With a knick knack paddy wack*
> *give the dog a bone,*
> *This ole man came rolling home."*

Jimmy would sing a verse and then Heather would join him for the chorus. Then Heather would sing the next verse and Jimmy would join for the chorus. Their singing echoed in the Virginia night and soon all of us found ourselves humming along with Jimmy and Heather. It sounded like a bunch of kindergartners on their way to the zoo. Hearing my kids singing their way through that darkness behind me had me crying some private tears at the front. I wanted to stop right there and apologize for making us ride into the dark; I wanted to push the bicycles aside and give everyone a big tearful hug.

"C'mon dude!" said Jimmy. It was Heather's verse, so he could talk. "Don't slow down. We're almost to the youth hostel." My hugs and apologies would have to wait.

At 9:30, Merle pulled us into an old gas station/store and told us to wait outside. He said he had to make a phone call. Minutes later, he came walking out with an armful of fruit juices.

"Y'all have been workin' pretty hard, so I figured you could use these. Besides, I'm in no hurry now; my clam dinner has probably all but burned up in the oven at home." He smiled and passed out the juices.

Carl was awarded first choice, and soon we were on the last leg of our long day. Accompanied by his young chorus, Merle lit the way, and at 10:30, Sunday night, June 29, we pulled into the Sangraal-by-the-Sea Youth Hostel in "Just-over-the-Bridge," Virginia.

"Where's Merle?" asked Lynn, as she rode up to where the kids and I were standing at the end of the driveway.

"I don't know," I answered. "I saw the sign to the hostel and, next thing I knew, he had disappeared."

"Shoot, I'm still wearing his fluorescent vest," Lynn continued, as she tugged on its orange piping.

"Man, you know how the Bible talks about there bein' angels on earth that sometimes just appear for a moment to help people out?" Jimmy stood over his bike, looking back down the road as he spoke. "Well, you know Merle? I think he was one of those angels. He helped us, then just disappeared, like the Twilight Zone or something. He sure was a nice guy."

"Well if he was an angel, then I'm glad," added Heather. "I was worried we ruined the clam dinner he said he'd left in the oven. Any angel should be able to fix that, easy."

The Big White Truck

"Hey John, how come you're going so slow?" I looked over my shoulder to see all five of the kids riding in tight formation, followed closely by Lynn. Jimmy was the first to speak.

"Yeah John, is something the matter? We've got over fifty miles to go today. Let's go a little faster." Joy was looking — and sounding — awfully confident.

"Yeah, let's ride," smiled Lynn, as the whole group laid to rest any of my fears about being discouraged by last night. One mid-morning fig bar break and one noontime peanut butter and jelly stop later and suddenly, we were fifty miles down the road at the foot of the gigantic York River Bridge.

The four lanes of rapidly moving cars and semis that had accompanied us most of that afternoon climbed high above the river, and at the foot of the bridge, I discovered that our comfortable shoulder of blacktop came to an abrupt end. The only way for us to get across the wide river was in the "slow lane"— the one where everyone was going 55 instead of 60. I would have given anything for a Southern California style traffic jam, but the cars and trucks just raced by, as I contemplated our next move. I knew the Battle of Yorktown took place on the other side of the river, but as I concluded that the only way for us to cross was to squeeze into that slow lane, I realized we were about to have a battle of our own — the California bicyclists vs. the local motoring militia.

To make matters worse, I saw that the road turned from blacktop to steel grating, as it climbed the bridge. Some steel grating is okay to bike on, but the stuff in front of us was crisscrossed and grooved in such a way that it would grab our narrow bicycling tires. We would either be thrown into the lanes of moving traffic on our left or against the rusted girders of the bridge on our right.

I stopped just as we got to the foot of the bridge, just before our shoulder of road disappeared. "Okay you guys, we're going to take the outside lane, and we're going to walk. It's too dangerous trying to ride on the grating, and there's no shoulder." I had to yell so Lynn and the kids could hear me over the roar speeding traffic.

The kids didn't say a word. They silently got off their bicycles, lined up one behind the other and waited for my next direction. "Okay Lynn, I'm going to take the rear to flag off the approaching traffic. You lead. Just keep it tight so people can pass us and then get back in the lane. The shorter our line the sooner they can get around us. If for some reason we split up, just wait for me where the blacktop starts up again."

You would think that everyone on Rte. 17 that afternoon saw our situation and stopped their cars — or at least slowed down. Wishful thinking! With each truck and trailer flying by us five feet away going 55 miles an hour, our bikes would shake and threaten to be pulled out of our hands by the turbulence created behind them.

"Okay you guys, when I say go, just follow Lynn. You're doin' great. We're almost to Williamsburg." I waited for a lull in the traffic and then rolled my bicycle out into the lane.

"GO!" I yelled. The kids immediately headed onto the bridge in single file behind Lynn, as I stood next to my bike and waved my arms at the approaching line of cars. I figured at 6'6" tall I would definitely be visible. I wrinkled my forehead and watched the entire lane of Virginia traffic slow down and back up like the LA freeway at rush hour. Ahh, there's no place like home. Lights blinked and horns honked, but I had stopped our lane. the kids looked over their shoulders at the honking mass and I yelled, "LET 'EM HONK!" as I fell in line behind Ethan, pushing his bike up the steep incline of the bridge.

Once the cars were taken care of we had to worry about the bridge itself. I watched the kids battling their bikes as the steel roadway took their front wheel one way and their rear wheel the other.

"HEY, WHAT ARE YOU, CRAZY? GET THE *@#%! OFF THIS BRIDGE!!!"

I smiled back at one of our more vociferous admirers who passed by with his head out his window and his fist waving.

"WHAT DO YOU THINK YOU'RE DOING, YOU #%*@?! YOU GOT NO RIGHT HOLDING UP TRAFFIC!"

"Ah . . . yes. Thank you, thank you." I replied, smiling as I bowed.

"GET THEM BICYCLES UP ON THE CATWALK! YOU'RE HOLDING UP TRAFFIC."

"Yes sir, you are very perceptive sir," I said to myself while I smiled his way. "We are holding up traffic, but the catwalk you're suggesting? Well, it's just about wide enough for a cat and not much else. You see — or no, you don't see — anyway, I tried that already and Bud — he's my bike — tried his best, but he just slipped right off, and, weighing about seventy-five pounds, it was kinda dangerous having him fall on top of me. And well, sir, if I fell in front of you and you hit me and the ambulances came and everything . . . well, then you'd really see what LA traffic is like. Our bikes have all our possessions strapped and hanging on them and they are too wide to fit on your catwalk. Thank you for your suggestion, though." My red-faced friend was past me before I got a chance to wave good-bye.

Once at the top of the bridge, boats could be seen as little dots 150 feet below us. I don't think the kids even looked down though, so intent were they on making the other side. Leading up to the top of the bridge, the steel grating had butted right up against the concrete curb and catwalk, so every time our bikes were forced that way, our front tires or panniers just banged off the curb and we struggled on up the bridge. At the top though, a gap just big enough to swallow a bicycle tire opened up just between the grating and the curb. I tried to yell a warning to the line of kids in front of me, but the loud whine of car wheels vibrating across the bridge drowned out my already hoarse voice.

Ethan was the first and only one to get swallowed by the bicycle-eating span. We had been battling the bridge for about 15 minutes when his bike encountered the gap. I watched Ethan try to correct his bicycle's sudden self-steering, but it was no use. It headed right for the slot and was soon sucked toward the water below. I was right behind him and as I heard the scraping of spokes and panniers, Ethan looked over his shoulder at me with a look of panic in his giant brown eyes. He immediately clutched onto his seat and handlebars, thinking it was the only way to save his two-wheeled friend from falling into the water over a hundred feet below. The rest of the kids, unaware of what was going on behind them, continued on, their concentration unbroken.

"Here Ethan, let me help. Are you okay?" I leaned Bud against the catwalk and smiled at another passing member of our fan club. I told Ethan to hop up on the catwalk while I tried to coax his blue bicycle out of the jaws of the York Bridge.

I had to be as gentle as I could. The bridge was no place to have to do repair work.

"Yeah, I'm okay. Is my bike okay?"

I quickly checked Ethan's bike for broken spokes or panniers that might have been knocked off their racks. "Looks okay, Eeth. Are you sure you're alright?"

". . . Yeah, I think so. Thanks for saving Smooth Ruth." Ethan took Ruth from me, looked over his shoulder at the line of traffic behind him, and then, more determined and focused than I'd ever seen him, he pushed his bike up and over the middle of the York River.

The kids claimed victory when we remounted our bikes at the far end of the bridge. Looking back at the giant steel span that had taken them over a half hour to cross, they raised their fists and stuck out their tongues, ignoring the honking cars that still sped by. Some kind of a ferry would have made it easier, but the bridge, now conquered, made us all feel stronger.

The Colonial Parkway began in Yorktown, Virginia, but before following it into Williamsburg, the kids decided to have a celebration commemorating their victory at "The Battle of Yorktown Bridge." Raabi/Father/Reverend Ethan Turpin presided, performing "the blessing of the wheels" on a beach just off the parkway, below the bridge. We filled our water jug with Atlantic water and Ethan baptized our wheels with sprinkles and incantations while Heather did the laying on of hands. As Ethan blessed and Heather touched, Joy, Carl and Jimmy chanted and danced around each bicycle. Lynn and I just laughed and smiled.

"Barook atah, be blessed, have a safe and RAD trip, and we'll bless these wheels with water from the Pacific in October." Ethan removed his bicycle cap for the final blessings.

"Yahoo, Brother Turpin!"

"Amen, Reverend Eeth!"

We completed the ceremony with drinks of warm Tang mixed in our water bottles. Then we hopped on our bikes and headed west toward Williamsburg.

What little traffic there was on the Colonial Parkway seemed to enjoy travelling slowly with us along the cocoa brown roadway. Thick green grass angled up to splitrail fences off to both sides of us. Tall wispy trees shaded the road like a giant green awning. We only had a few miles to go to reach Williamsburg, and we all stopped every half mile or so to read the historical markers. Everyone got a turn to read a sign out loud, and we learned about earlier Indian inhabitants of the river, of settlers from the east who forced the Indians to leave, and of famous battles that took place there, long before the bridge. We even paused for another "YAHOO!" as Carl's computer announced, with its familiar "BEEP," that we had just done our first 50-mile day.

Just after I announced with honest sincerity, "We're almost there, you guys!" a large orange and black sign rudely interrupted the surrounding green and brown. It simply said:

DETOUR AHEAD

"After the bridge, no problem," I said to myself.

Around the next corner, I noticed more of the orange signs, and the traffic that had passed us was beginning to back up. It was 5 o'clock, and I figured a detour at rush hour might be to our benefit. Sometimes we went faster and safer in bumper to bumper traffic. Two gates were locked across the road, and nailed to the crossbars was a large sign reading:

THIS ROAD CLOSED TO ALL TRAFFIC FOR REPAIRS, DO NOT ENTER

We followed the traffic up the hill on the detour. When I got to the top, I realized we were in for a counterattack from the local forces.

Giant green signs towered above a cloverleaf of merging expressways. It seemed that some combination of Interstate 64, State 199 and State 60 was going to lead us into town. I looked around for some way out of the tangle of speeding truck and commuter traffic ahead, but the orange detour signs led us right up and onto our first interstate.

I pulled my second "I-don't-care-let-them-honk" traffic blockade of the day at the first onramp of merging traffic. I wanted to compliment the local drivers for their ability to gather so much speed on the onramps — "Good technique!" I wanted to yell — but instead I had to wave them to slow down and STOP. Heck, I didn't ask for this detour.

After I successfully clogged the onramp with bumper to bumper traffic, I waved good-bye to the less-than-joyous-leader of the motorized pack and rode up to the front of our group. Lynn had them waiting on the litter-strewn shoulder of our first interstate.

"Everyone okay?" I really had to yell to be heard above the roar of the three lanes of traffic. The kids all nodded. "You guys are doing great! Just stay together, ride in a straight, single file line, and hopefully we'll be off this mess soon."

We started up again and did our best to dodge the assortment of road relics scattered all over the shoulder. Every freeway shoulder I'd ever ridden my bike on had been a flea market of rusted nuts and bolts, giant black carcasses of truck retreads, license plates, beer cans and glass. Our section of Rte. 64 in Virginia was no different. We proceeded slowly and surely along our added obstacle course. My only worry for our first few minutes was that the kids might find some interesting souvenir amidst the rubble and want to stop. We were doing great until I noticed the road climbing onto an overpass.

Our shoulder that had been the width of a car shrank to nothing but a white line as the road funneled ahead. The curb and guard railing of the overpass squeezed us close enough to write our names on the sides of the passing traffic. I looked over my shoulder, past the kids and Lynn, to see three solid lanes of metal, all moving at or above the speed limit. With that much traffic, I saw little hope of slowing down our lane without causing an accident, so I decided we would have to go for it. My only hope was that the "slow lane" — remember, the one that goes only 55 — would at least stay on its side of the white line. I said a prayer and forged ahead.

Halfway over the overpass and all was well. Our bikes were buffeted by the turbulence of especially large cars, but so far no semis had used our lane, and I could see the orange detour signs up ahead, leading us off the nightmare.

Then came the unmistakable rumble of an eighteen-wheeler. The roadway started to shake behind me and I dialed God again. Did I say eighteen-wheeler? It may have been my imagination, but that long white monster must have had twice that many, and I swear it was long enough to carry the Washington Monument. The first blast I felt was from the cab; the second came from the sets of wheels toward the front of the trailer; and the third was the incredible vacuum created by the last sets of wheels, as the monster finally passed me. I couldn't look behind me because I was afraid I might be sucked right into the lane of traffic following relentlessly behind him so, I rode on. I just hoped and prayed not to hear any sounds of disaster behind me. I pulled off the freeway on the first offramp going our way and looked back. Not more than fifteen yards behind me, there they were, all six of them. Jimmy first, then Heather, Joy, Carl, Ethan and Lynn, and they were all riding in perfect formation, resolutely following my lead.

Heather's eyes got Ethan-size big as she and everyone else stopped to catch their breath. I could see five little hearts beating through their bicycling shirts.

"Did you guys see that BIG . . . WHITE . . . TRUCK?! As soon as the truck part passed me, the trailer part started pulling me towards it. It was so big, the wheels were taller than me on my little bike." Heather came up for another breath before continuing, and no one said a word as she continued her story.

"I kept saying to myself 'C'mon, Mr. Truck, c'mon. Please don't suck me underneath you.' And all the time its big white side just kept flashing by me. One time my bicycle headed towards the white line, but I fought it back. Even though I knew there would be a terrible suction after it passed, I just wanted to see that last set of wheels. I was really scared."

I had never even thought about Heather and her especially small bike. Its special small wheels and small everything gave her a much lower profile than the rest of us. I didn't realize it had its own special aerodynamic properties and problems.

"And then, when the last wheels finally did come . . . and the suction behind the truck . . . I don't know how I kept from going into the road. It was like riding a bike in a giant earthquake, with the road leaning me and Skittles into all the lanes of traffic."

"Yeah Heather," said a concerned Carl, who had been riding right behind her. "I wondered why you were leaning to the right and your bike was swerving to the left." Heather sighed a smile at Carl and then put her hand on her chest to try and slow her heart down.

"Hey John, that was quite the gnarly back road, dude," said Jimmy, trying to lighten things up. "What was that you said in the *From Sea to Shining Sea* booklet about us riding the 'scenic, little-traveled backroads of America'?" Jimmy was only joking, but I was wondering how many more times we would be faced with the same kind of detour.

" . . . You guys . . . I know we were going to try and find a church to stay at in Williamsburg . . . and if you still want to we will . . . but I was wondering . . . how 'bout if we find a church for tomorrow night? Do you guys have any objections to my finding us a motel with beds and a swimming pool?" We had arrived at the Colonial Williamsburg Visitors Center at about 6. My nerve endings were still suffering the lingering effects of Carl's crash the night before, and my whole body was shaking from our battle at the York River and the Williamsburg Detour. I was emotionally fried and just couldn't find the energy to go knocking on doors or to phone different churches in town, asking for a floor to sleep on.

"Well, John, I don't know if that would be keeping with the spirit of our trip . . . ." Ethan's philosophical response was a surprise to everyone.

"Ethan! Are you crazy?" yelled Carl, unable to restrain himself.

"Eeth, how long do you want to live?" shot an equally upset Jimmy.

"Bathtubs and showers and beds, oh my." Joy and Heather hadn't even heard Ethan and were already dancing their feelings on the matter.

"Well . . . ." Everyone stared in amazement as Ethan tried to continue. He wasn't usually the jokester, but everyone figured he must be pulling their legs with his surprising response. Either that, or the day's battles had really changed him.

"TV, dude." Senator West (Jimmy) said grabbing Ethan by both shoulders and looking him straight in the eye. "T—TELEVISION—V!!!"

"Well . . . if you guys really want to . . . ." Something had changed Ethan that day. Even if he wasn't serious, holding on to his joke for so long and not cracking under the magic word Jimmy had just chanted was abnormal. The rest of the group didn't wait around to examine Ethan's motives. Before you could say "Home Box Office," they were atop their bikes and ready to follow me to the Econo Lodge of Williamsburg. They would do their best to revive Ethan in the pool.

I figured I owed the group a special dessert, so later that night, while the kids finished doing their laundry in the sinks, I walked down to the corner to buy a half gallon of ice cream, some chocolate syrup and some cookies.

How the kids made their sundaes that night was a revelation to me. Their eyes never left the TV screen as they scooped ice cream and poured syrup. They didn't even come up for air during commercials! Once their sundaes were ready, they walked backwards to their beds, constantly staring at the screen, as if in a trance. My video zombies would make it back under the covers complete with bowls and ice cream to zone out some more.

Something woke Ethan out of his zone, because I looked over and saw him spill a spoonful of vanilla and chocolate soup — he liked to stir his up — down his already dirty "clean" t-shirt. It looked like the old Ethan we all knew and loved was returning to normal. My hopes were confirmed when, just before falling asleep, he leaned over to Jimmy, lying next to him, and whispered, " . . . Hey Jimmy, I was just kidding this afternoon about that motel business . . . ."

Jimmy punched him in the arm and soon everyone was asleep — including me. I woke with Carl snoring beside me in our bed and Jimmy and Ethan curled up in theirs. The TV was still on, and so were almost all the lights in the room. I got up and turned ours off, then checked on the girls' room. Except for their neatly hung laundry, their room looked much the same: gooey ice cream bowls resting on the bedside tables, TV and lights still going strong, and Lynn, Joy and Heather curled up tight and catching some much needed rest. I leaned over and gave Lynn a kiss and then turned everything off. I decided then I'd let everyone sleep in an extra hour in the morning. We were all tired.

Not Interested

"Hey you guys, dig this." Jimmy peeked over his section of the *Richmond News Leader* and made sure he had everyone's attention. Then he began reading:

> "According to the latest study, the physical condition of today's teenagers is the worst it's been in this century. Recent fitness tests show America's teenage population in terrible physical condition. In addition, surveys of teenagers show that the vast majority of our youth would rather sit at home watching TV or hang out at the local mall than be involved in some physical activity."

Our dripping rain coats were hanging over the backs of our coffee shop chairs. After sleeping in, we had pedaled our bicycles in the pouring rain that greeted us the next morning in Williamsburg. We ordered all the peach waffles, blueberry pancakes, sausage, bacon, hot chocolate and juice that would fit on the table. We bought two local papers and flipped coins for who got which sections. Jimmy lost out to Joy on the Comics, but had lucked out on Sports & Leisure.

"I wonder when the person who wrote that article rode a bike last?" said Carl, sounding less than endeared to the reporter who filed Jimmy's story.

"He probably grabbed his umbrella and drove to work in a car," grumbled Ethan. Jimmy's reading even woke Ethan up , who was back to his normal self. He had been studying his hot chocolate up close, experimenting with his marshmallow and spoon, seeing how long a marshmallow could stay submerged.

"Hey John, you should call this paper and have them do a story on us," exclaimed Joy. "We're teenagers — well, some of us almost — and look what we're doing. We rode 60 miles yesterday battling guys like him on the road; today we're biking in the pouring rain and we're riding all the way to California!" Joy's mixture of half hot chocolate/half coffee was beginning to wake her up.

"Yeah, call them, John. I hate it when adults put us kids down like that. I do know kids who would rather sit home like he says, but I know adults who would like to do the same thing. He has his right to his opinion, but I just think newspapers should try to tell more of the whole story. He makes our generation sound like a bunch of lazy kids." Heather was very serious.

"Yeah, I bet that dude has never gotten up at dawn to ride a bicycle," said an equally serious Jimmy. "John, I think you should call the paper."

"I bet that guy hasn't even ridden a bicycle lately at any time of the day!" Carl grumbled. "Call them up!"

"I think you guys are right," I agreed. "It sounds like its time for our first encounter with local media. I'll be right back; I'm going to find a phone book and see if I can find out where the nearest office of that Richmond paper is. Just save me some coffee, and don't eat my pancakes."

"What's the matter, man, don't you trust us?"

"Well, James, I won't put down your entire generation, but I don't trust you with my blueberry pancakes." I winked at Jimmy as I left for the phone.

My pancakes were intact when I returned with the good news. There was an office of the Richmond paper on our way to the Williamsburg Visitors Center. It was still raining when we finished breakfast, but the kids seemed to look forward to riding up to the newspaper office dripping wet. Still, I decided it would be best for them to wait outside while I went in to talk.

"Excuse me, but I'm a teacher from California and five of my middle school students, my wife and I are riding our bicycles across America. This morning we were reading your paper at the pancake house and the kids thought you might like to do a story on our trip as a follow-up to your teenage fitness article that appeared today."

I think the secretary turned me off after my "excuse me," because her finger pushed one of the buttons on her phone before I even finished. "Excuse me sir, what did you say your name was and what did you say you were doing?"

I repeated my introduction and then continued, " . . . and here's the story that appeared in our hometown newspaper the day we left. It gives a good overview of what we're doing."

The secretary walked into an adjacent office, armed with our xeroxed article, and returned in three minutes. "I'm sorry sir, but our editor isn't interested." She handed me back our story and with not so much as a thank you or a good luck, she went back to work at her desk.

I was tempted to empty one of my rain-filled shoes on the counter or, better yet, to let the kids come in with their editorial and emotional reply, but a voice inside me advised against it. The divine voice also paused long enough to let me hear the lightning cracking outside. I wanted the lightning to be on our side, so I said that "thank you" and sloshed out to break the news to the kids.

Outside the kids were straddling their bikes underneath an overhang and sprucing themselves up for their interview. I had convinced them to feel that what they were doing was pretty unique, and they were confident that no one would find their story insignificant.

"Sorry, guys, but they're not interested," I announced.

"WHAT?!" Carl was first to react.

"C'mon man, you're kiddin' us." Jimmy winked at me and shook his head.

"Nope, I'm serious. I told them about our trip, and showed them our *Santa Barbara News-Press* story and the secretary told me that the editor wasn't interested. Sorry, you guys." I looked out and saw at least two faces who would have loved to empty their shoes — and helmets — on the counter inside, but before they got their chance, Joy softly changed the subject.

"Hey John, can I go to the bathroom? I've really got to go."

"Sure, let's ride over to the McDonald's, and anyone who needs to go can. Welcome to some of coffee's after-effects, Joy."

The Virginia sky unloaded on us after our bathroom stop, and we splashed through curbside rivers as we plowed our way to Colonial Williamsburg. We pushed our bikes past the long line of station wagons and buses near the entrance, up the loading ramp and parked them right in front of the Visitors Center. Even though we weren't one of the listed *Things to do in Colonial Williamsburg for July 1*, we sure seemed like the first attraction. The secretary and the editor may not have been interested in our story, but the folks visiting Williamsburg sure were. As we locked our bikes to the railing outside the entrance, the kids had a group of interviewers gathered round them. Just as one group of visitors would leave to go inside more would walk up the corridor, see the kids and begin asking the same questions. After about 20 minutes of popularity, I could see the kids getting a little antsy. Heather, who always answered her interviewers with her hands and arms as well as her mouth, hadn't even had a chance to take off her helmet and rain jacket.

"Okay, you guys, lock 'em up. Grab your handlebar bags and zip everything up. I think everything will be safe out here. Let's go see Williamsburg!" My voice broke up each circle of admirers.

"Thanks, John," sighed Jimmy. "Man, I thought we were never going to get out of there. Everyone just kept coming over to us asking questions."

"Yeah, we had people from Missouri and South Dakota and Arizona," said Carl.

"And we had people from Kansas and Wisconsin and even a family from California," said Heather, her helmet finally off.

"Yeah, and I bet we talked to more people about our trip out here than read that stupid ole newspaper," said Jimmy still upset at the *Leader*. Not saying anything, I put my arm around his shoulder and led him through the double glass doors. Satisfied that our story was told, we were off to see the colonial capital of Virginia.

Virginia

Scrabble

"Okay, guys, time for inspection." Our second night in Williamsburg, we stayed in the Wellspring Methodist Church, and on our way into the parking lot, I noticed strange lumps sticking out of the kids' panniers. Some of the bags couldn't even be zippered shut they were so full.

"Inspection? What do you mean inspection?" asked Jimmy.

"Well, you guys, it looks like two weeks of biking has resulted in two weeks of shopping," I answered. "I think Tangier Island and Colonial Williamsburg have taken their toll on our checklist. Lynn, would you take the girls and I"ll take the guys? Here's a packing list. Would you check for numbers of underwear and shirts and everything?"

Heather looked over at me with as much of a scowl as she could muster, and I just stuck my tongue out at her. "I know you love me anyway, Heather." She tried to hold it back, but her scowl quickly surrendered to her smile.

"But John, what about the shirts and souvenirs we bought that are not on the checklist?"

"Good question, Joy. If you bought clothing, then either keep your new shirt or shorts and send the old ones home, or send the new ones home. On souvenirs, check with me. Tomorrow we're going to the post office and we'll send a lot of stuff home. Once we head west at Jamestown tomorrow, Virginia is really going to get hilly, so you'll want your bikes as light as possible."

That night on the auditorium floor I boldly ventured where no man had ever been before . . . inside the panniers and handlebar bags of three 12 and 13-year-old boys. In the recesses of those bags was a story I'm sure even the editor of the *Richmond News Leader* couldn't have resisted.

Jimmy's bags were the most tame. Other than the pair of undies and socks that had missed their daily washing, the mildewed long-sleeve shirt I warned him would never dry in the eastern humidity, and the broken switchcomb and soggy sparklers, Jimmy's bags were still pretty much in order. He organized his things into new plastic bags, separated the things that would be sent home tomorrow and then went downstairs to finish his laundry.

"Five socks, huh, Carl? Do you have two and a half feet, or do I detect something missing here?"

"Well, John, I know I had six socks last week some time." Carl removed one wad of clothing at a time and held it up as if he had never seen it before. Then he would unroll it, first turning it inside out and then outside out. At the end of this process he would sigh, as if he had just been reunited with some long lost buddy: "Oh, I've been wondering where you've been . . . I forgot I even had these shorts; I could have used you guys this morning."

Carl's inspection took almost an hour. I told him that sometimes it works best if you keep shirts with shirts instead of keeping one shirt with one sock, and suggested that old granola bars and half-eaten fig newtons stay fresh longer in plastic bags than they do wrapped up in old tube socks. My experience with Carl convinced me that if we were to make it to California clothed and free of disease, daily laundry and pannier inspections would have to become part of my daily repertoire. If Carl's system was allowed to continue, local rodents and insects would not only have a soft place to sleep, but they would also receive room service. And if we ever came to a state line with an agricultural inspection . . . well, I knew two guys who would probably be jailed right after the fumigation.

All the time I was working with Jimmy and Carl, Ethan was silently meditating on each item he removed from his bags. If Carl's discoveries could be compared to reunions, then Ethan's findings had to be called revelations. His "unbreakable," day-glo Slinky was now in two pieces; he found two brand-new, still-clipped-together pairs of socks, previously unknown to him; and his handlebar bag looked as if he had just burglarized two gift shops and a 7-Eleven mini-market. Gum (chewed and unchewed), buttons, decals and stickers, an assortment of colored pens and markers, post cards (bent and wet), more granola bars, trinkets and plastic rings . . . Ethan had enough stuff to open a little shop of his own.

After that was spread out on the floor, we went into his panniers — yes, that was just his handlebar bag. His trip's worth of vitamins were there, all safely sealed and untouched. He kept them right next to his bike oil, tire tubes and tools.

"Hey John . . . I've got this bicycle computer from my granpa." Ethan pulled a plastic bag out of his vitamin pannier and held it up. "Do you think we can put it on my bike some time."

"Sure, do you have the instructions?"

"Well . . . no, I can't seem to find them, but when I do, will you attach it? Besides, I think I'm still missing a part."

Ethan and I spent the better part of two hours discovering and organizing his amazing panniers. By eleven o'clock, I was able to head down to our room to get our journal meeting going. Little did I know that it wouldn't be until Arkansas that Ethan's computer, its directions, parts and battery would be united.

"You can't use that! It's not even a word." The guys and I were trying to write in our journals, but Lynn, Joy and Heather seemed to be having a loud disagreement next door in their room.

"Z-I-K-A-P-E-E, 'zikapee.' You know the song, *Zikapee Doo Dah*, from the Walt Disney movie." We could hear Heather explaining her latest word in the girls' Scrabble game. Lynn was laughing, crying and trying to object, all at the same time, and Joy was silently trying to figure out why Lynn disapproved of Heather's in the first place. Joy soon joined Lynn in her vocal disapproval.

"I agree with Lynn, Head. I don't think Z-I-K-A-P-E-E is a word."

Heather countered with, "Well, at least its better than your word, Stick."

"Which word?" Joy sounded puzzled.

"U-N-W-A-G, 'unwag'. That word, Stick."

"What's the matter with 'unwag'. You know, like when a dog dies it 'un-wags' its tail."

The girls' wild and crazy Scrabble match prematurely ended the guys' and my journal meeting, so at midnight I turned out our lights. I walked over and asked the girls to tone it down a little, kissed a still hysterical Lynn good night, and went back to fall asleep on the floor of the kindergarten room at Wellspring Methodist Church.

Godspeed

Late on July 1, the kids rode out of Williamsburg with a confidence I hadn't seen before. Maybe it was the York Bridge or the detour, or maybe it was all the people in Williamsburg who were so interested in their journey. Earlier that day, *The Virginia Gazette* got wind of us and sent one of its reporters, Claire, to inter-cept a group of "special kids" seen in front of the post office. She spent over an hour with them, sitting down on the green and asking questions. Lynn and I stood off to the side as observers. Claire wanted the kids' story. We made the front page of America's oldest daily newspaper on the Fourth of July, and I think that interview was the start of the kids' newfound confidence.

One of Claire's questions was: "Why are you bicycling across America?" and Heather had answered it simply, "To meet Americans." The next day we turned our backs to the east for good and headed west to meet some of the wonderful American folks living in the hills of Virginia.

Leaving Jamestown the next morning, we waved to Captain Smith's ship, The Godspeed. It was dawn and the sun cast its rosy rising light on the fog blan-keting the James River. The hint of coolness helped our pace and by 12:30 we had ridden 45 miles. We hadn't even stopped for a snack break and our stom-achs were yelling at us as we pedaled quickly towards the tall sign marking the Hardees fast food restaurant of Hopewell, Va.

Three guys in a Chevy Camaro were just leaving the parking lot when we drove in. Their eyes got big at the sight of our caravan and I watched their heads rotate on their necks like owls, as they stared back in disbelief. Their tires squealed out the exit and they circled back in the entrance. They leaned their heads out of the window and the driver said, "What you all doin'?"

"We're riding our bicycles across America." Jimmy, up near me, was the first to answer. The locals' eyes got even bigger as they poked their heads out the window even further. For a minute they didn't say anything; they just checked out little Heather and skinny and sunburned Carl.

"Why most a yous be just kids! . . . and you all be ridin' them bikes all the way across America?"

"Yup." Jimmy by now was quite nonchalant when describing his journey.

"You crazy!" The guy in the back seat was holding his drink and shaking his head.

"They be ridin' those bicycles all de way across America! . . . Dude, in dis heat too. . . ." The three of them were now talking to themselves trying to convince each other that they weren't dreaming this.

"Y'all really ridin' all the way across America, no foolin'?" By now we were all gathered together and everyone silently smiled and nodded their heads. "Man, you folks be brave!"

"Thanks," I said speaking for my shy band.

"Damn! You really crazy. Good luck." They looked at the kids and their bikes one more time, looked at each other and then slowly pulled out the exit for the second time. The driver kept looking in the mirror, and the other two guys kept shaking their heads as they looked back out the windows and waved. The kids waved back.

What I had hoped would be a one hour— or less—lunch stop turned into a three hour guest appearance at Hardees. First, Dot, the clean-up lady, began talking to us as we downed our burgers. Then she called the *Hopewell News* and filled our paper cups with ice water while we waited for our interview. Hank, the rotund reporter, finally arrived, complete with Texas accent and more than a few stories of his own to share. In the course of the hour he spent with us, he often interrupted his stories (and our interview) with introductions of almost everybody who stopped by Hardees for lunch that afternoon. Dot helped things out a little, because while we were spending time with Hank, she was on the phone calling all the friends she could to come over and meet us. At least a dozen ladies came by to wish us a safe trip and to let us know they'd be prayin' for us all.

A three hour break even gets long for the kids, and I saw them doing their best to accept their umteenth glass of ice water from Dot. I knew we still had a couple hours of riding and some grocery shopping to do, so, with an "Excuse me and thank you, but we still have some riding to do today . . . ." I tried to politely pull us away from all of Hopewell's hospitality.

I only got us as far as the wall outside where our bikes were parked. A little old black lady and her younger lady friend were just getting out of their car when they caught sight of the kids and their loaded bicycles.

"What they all doin'?" The older woman squeaked out her interest and a man, who had already met us inside, answered, "They be goin' 'cross America."

"You kiddin'?" she asked, walking up to Heather to get a closer look.

"Why no, ma'am. Hones' ta God."

"Well, we gotta get a picture then."

While we posed for the photo, Dot came running out of the restaurant and yelled, "Y'all got ice water in them water bottles of yours?"

"Act invisible, you guys," I whispered to the kids. "We've still got over 20 miles to go. Try not to get any more people excited. Stand over your bikes while Dot gets you the water." Lynn and I gathered up the bottles and took them to Dot. In twenty minutes the crowd, led by Dot, waved good-bye to us as we finally left Hardees of Hopewell.

More people greeted us as we waited for Lynn and her two shoppers in front of the Ukrops Mkt. down the road in Chester. One woman stopped her shopping cart by our bikes and visited for about fifteen minutes. As we talked, she kept repeating, "Oh, if I had only known y'all was coming, I would have planned a picnic and party for y'all at our church. Oh, if I'd only known . . . ."

We rode 68 miles that day we left Jamestown. The next day, the Fourth of July, we would top that by doing 71. Even though I had told the kids that our trip was to be measured more in people met than in miles traveled, they were still proud of the distance they were able to pedal each day. 71 miles was indeed something to be proud of, because as we headed west across the hilly Piedmont of Virginia, the heat and the humidity got hotter and thicker. Maryland, now just a memory in our journals, seemed cool and dry by comparison.

Just west of Hopewell, we ran into signs marking the path of General Lee's final retreat of the Civil War.

"Hey John, I think we're following Robert E. Lee to Appomattox," announced Jimmy, who was up front with me. Every time we came to one of the signs, we'd wait for the group, and, just like back at Yorktown, each of the kids took their turn reading one of the historical markers. While someone read, everyone else would douse their frying, sweaty bodies with water from their water bottles. If Carl's computer had a thermometer, I'm sure it would have read somewhere in the nineties. We probably couldn't have read it though because it would have been clouded up with all the moisture in the air.

Although we didn't have an itinerary, I did try and set a destination for us each day. My Fourth of July plan had us riding to a state forest near Appomattox, but each reading on Carl's computer was proving my Virginia map less-than-trustworthy. It was beginning to look like my map's mileages had been measured by some crow.

We ate lunch about 2 PM at Saylers Creek Battlefield State Park. We spread our peanut butter and jelly next to the cannons and the house that overlooked the hills and hollows surrounding the creek and tried to imagine the green expanse being littered with Union and Confederate soldiers trying to end their war. It was an ironic place to be holding class on Independence Day, and I didn't have an easy time explaining how one man's independence was another man's insurrection. Heather wanted to know which war the Civil War was, Jimmy wanted to know how the armies transported everything in these hills and heat, and everyone else wanted to eat. The water was turned off at the visitors center, so we rationed what few drops we had left. Peanut butter on sun-dried bread combined with those few drops of water being warmed to hot from our day's ride made my troops less and less attentive to my Civil War lecture. The only battle they'll probably remember at Saylers Creek was their battle against thirst.

"Sure y'all can have some water. C'mon in. Hey, Mother, come out here and see what just rolled in. It's a bunch of little kids and their teachers ridin' their bicycles across America."

About five hills and ten miles down the road from Saylers Creek, we had interrupted the Carmichael family July 4th BBQ to ask for some water for our now empty bottles. Trucks were pulled up to their hilltop farm and the men were sitting out underneath the shade tree getting the fire ready and drinking some awfully good looking ice-cold beers. More bottles were floating nearby in a galvanized tub filled with ice. Grandpa Carmichael must have noticed me checking it out. "Well, son, can I offer y'all a beer?"

He didn't have to be so kind. Jimmy gave me the evil eye and I gritted my teeth. I managed a polite but painful, "No, thank you, sir, I'd better just stick to water," and as I led the kids into the kitchen I could hear the elder Carmichael and some of the boys laughing at my abstinence.

"Well I'll be . . . " Mrs. Carmichael came into the kitchen and gazed upon my sweaty bunch. "What y'all be doin' bicyclin' in this heat, and on the Fourth of July? My lord."

"We're bicycling across America and we still have 4,000 miles to go, so we have to ride today." Ethan surprised me by being our spokesman.

"Yes, and since the Fourth is today, we're going to take Saturday and Sunday as layover days." Heather was holding her hair up off her neck and enjoying the coolness of Mrs. Carmichael's kitchen.

"Well, would y'all like some ice for those water bottles of yours?" asked Mrs. Carmichael. "You must be famished. I'm feelin' mighty hot today and I'm used to it. Did someone say y'all be from California? Y'all don't have heat and humidity like this in California now do ya?"

"No ma'am, we sure don't," said Jimmy, holding his bottle open for the ice.

"Mother, where's the camera?" interrupted Mr. Carmichael, as he poked his head into the kitchen. "I want to make sure we git a picture of these folks 'fore they leave." Mrs. Carmichael pointed into the living room, and immediately Mr. Carmichael was off. "Father" soon found the camera and, with our bottles filled with ice and sweet well water, we walked outside to pose underneath the big shade tree. "Father" then motioned me over to his truck, where he and three generations of Carmichaels gave me some county maps out of the glove box and suggested some westward routes.

"Sure ya wouldn't like a beer?" The youngest Carmichael tempted me as his uncle traced a route to Appomatox.

"No thanks. I'd love to, but I'd better not." Before I was offered a third and fateful time, I thanked the Carmichaels, gathered up the kids and we headed down the long dirt driveway to our bikes.

"Thanks a lot!"

"Yeah, thanks for the water."

" . . . and the ice." The kids waved and turned around all the way down the driveway. The Carmichaels stood and waved until we were on our bikes and out of sight over the next hill.

"Man, you just walk up to someone's house you don't even know and they invite you in for water and ice, and then they want to take your picture with the whole family." I could hear Carl and Ethan talking with ice cubes in their mouths.

" . . . Yeah, and did you see them give John that whole set of maps for free. They were really cool."

Central Virginia's kindness continued that evening as we pulled into Twin Lakes Campground. Seeing the sign saying snack bar, the kids suddenly blew by me and sped towards the cluster of buildings down on the beach. Our panniers were empty of any food and the kids skidded into the gravel parking lot just as one of the girls who worked the grill was getting ready to turn the open sign over to closed.

"Y'all say you just rode 71 miles . . . in this heat?!" she asked, sticking her head out the screen door.

"Yup. I can prove it to you on my computer," boasted Carl, taking the job as spokesman. "And we're riding all the way to California."

The girl's eyes got as big as the kids' appetites, and as she flipped the sign to closed, she winked and motioned for the kids to follow her. Ten minutes later they came back out to where Lynn and I were sitting with their arms full of burgers, fries, corn dogs, drinks and pizza. The folks at the Twin Lakes Snack Bar had provided us with a 4th of July feast of everything that was left in their kitchen.

The kids, refreshed and inspired by more kindness, were the ones that suggested we have a journal meeting that night before we went to bed. For over a half hour they wrote by the light of our lantern, and Carl surprised us all by asking if he could share his entry.

"Sure dude, go for it," answered Jimmy.

"Okay, here goes:

> "Today we planned to see Appomattox and go to Holiday Lake, but it was too far, so we're staying at Twin Lakes instead. Tomorrow, the Fultons will meet us. They were going to meet us tonight, but we had a communication problem and they didn't find out where we are till dark.
>
> "Today, I saw the other half of America, the kind half, people giving us directions and scouting the area, people giving us delicious well water and people giving us food when we needed it most. I'll never forget the kind side of America."

"Thanks for sharing, Carl," I said softly. "That's a real special entry."

"Yeah, that part about the friendliness is what I tried to write about, but you did it better, Carl," said Ethan.

"Even with all the heat and that stupid spigot being turned off at Saylers Creek, we still had a good Fourth of July," added Heather. "I don't think the people around here will let you have a bad one."

"And you know," said Jimmy, "without that spigot being turned off, we probably never would have met the Carmichaels. They had the best well water we've tasted so far."

"Yeah, and those ice cubes," smiled Ethan. "They were really cool."

"Really *cool*, Eeth?" said Jimmy, shaking his head. "That's a pretty bad pun, man."

" . . . Oh yeah, really cool . . . you mean like ice, really cool . . ." Ethan laughed. "I didn't mean it that way."

"I liked the way Mr. and Mrs. Carmichael called each other 'Mother' and 'Father'," said Joy. "I thought they were cute, him running around looking for the camera, and her filing up our bottles. This was a neat way to spend the Fourth of July, meeting so many people."

"Yeah, even though it was so hot, all the people made this a pretty fun Fourth," agreed Jimmy. "And we still got those sparklers from that kid we met back at the softball tournament. Let's go shoot them off at the lake tomorrow night."

"This time I'll get some better matches for you guys."

"Thanks, John," said Carl getting up. "I'm tired, I'm gonna hit the sack. Good night, everybody."

"Good night, Carl," echoed everyone else as they got up to join him.

"Good night, Lynn. Good night, John."

"Good night, you guys."

"Happy Fourth of July," said Joy.

As the kids walked to their tents, Lynn leaned over to me at the table and whispered, "Yeah John, happy Fourth of July."

Bob and Sulie

Saturday morning, the kids were down at the lake swimming and paddle boating, Lynn was resting in the shade of our tent, and I was visiting with our next-door neighbor, Sam.

Sam reminded me of my grandfather. It didn't take him long to tell me how he had grown up riding his bicycle on the roads around Saylers Creek when they were "still just bumpy dirt carriage paths." He told me how his brother "once bought a Chevy coupe for $730!", and he said he believed Virginia would be one of the friendliest and most beautiful states we would ride through. After each story, Sam would take off his navy blue cap, and, in the course of an hour, I learned he had been a mechanic, a repairman, an auto salesman. He still was an avid salt-water fisherman, and a wild turkey and squirrel hunter.

"And, John, I don't know 'bout your upbringin', but after all I been through, I believe even more than ever in one God, the Lord above . . . ."

Sam told me to watch out for snakes, especially the black ones. "Many years ago, oh I cain't 'member what year, but it was a few years back. Why, my wife, she came upon this big ole black snake, and danged if it didn't start chasin' her." Off came his cap again, and Sam chuckled as he scratched another memory from the back of his head.

"Well, when that big black thang took off after her, she really had to turn on the fan to beat it up onto the porch and into the house. Why, I'll never forget her yellin' and screamin' when she came flyin' through the front door." Sam was just getting warmed up when up drove a silver car with two faces I'd been expecting all morning.

"Excuse me, Sam, but some friends are here to see us," I interrupted.

It was Bob and Sulie Fulton, Joy's folks. Before leaving California, each family had made arrangements with Lynn and me to rendezvous with us for a couple days along our route. Carl's folks had met us on the east coast and Joy's folks were planning on meeting us somewhere in the middle of Virginia for the 4th of July; but yesterday's heat, mileage and my inability to get hold of them until after dark changed our rendezvous to the 5th.

"Y'all remember now, if ya need me to drive y'all into town to the store to get some food, just let me know." Sam had offered earlier to drive Lynn and me to the market to replenish our supplies. "Won't be no trouble neither. Just let me know, ya hear?"

"Thanks, Sam."

Bob and Sulie soon were out of the car shaking hands with me and meeting Sam, his wife and grandkids. During the introductions, Sulie was distracted by someone missing from camp.

"I'm sorry, Sulie," I said noticing Sulie's quietness. "The kids are down at the lake swimming. They walked down earlier this morning."

"Oh . . ." Sulie tried not to sound disappointed. "Then we can set up the decorations and surprise them when they come back." Sulie began to unload the car, but I could tell she was almost ready to hop back in and speed down to the lake.

With some silent help from Bob, Sulie began decorating. First to emerge from the trunk was a giant, red, white and blue sign saying: *From Sea to Shining Sea — Fourth of July Headquarters* . Soon our campsite was draped with streamers, Virginia and American flags, balloons and flowers. There was even a giant cake decorated with an American eagle for a centerpiece. The streamers and decorations would last, but as soon as the kids returned, I gave that cake about thirty minutes.

"John, why don't ya come help me with another table?" said Bob, who had already filled a second and third table with the fixings for our day after the 4th of July feast. Coolers were filled with sodas and beer, steaks were marinating for an afternoon BBQ, vegetables and chips were in bowls next to the sour cream and ranch dips (Joy's favorites), and salad fixins were sliced and ready to go. There was even a hand-crank ice cream maker.

"Bob, don't forget the packages for each of the kids," Sulie said as she and

131

Lynn busily decorated. "What do you think? Should we put them in their tents or should we just set them on the table next to the cake?"

"I don't know if you want to go into those tents," I advised.

"Are you saying it might be less than a pleasant awakening, John?" laughed Bob.

"You got it, Bob," I answered.

"Let's put them on the table then, Sulie."

Sam and his wife watched from their lawn chairs as Bob, Lynn and Sulie transformed our campsite into what looked like the perfect setting for a Fourth of July Coca-Cola commercial. Sulie stood back for final inspection, making sure everything was perfect, and I saw Sam smile. Bob stood quietly by as Mom Fulton tried to stay busy awaiting her long anticipated reunion with Joy. Everything looked perfect and Sulie tried to pass the time talking with Lynn and me.

"They must really be enjoying their swim . . . They knew we were coming today, didn't they?" Sulie was about to burst.

"Why don't you go on down to the lake and surprise Joy there? Lynn and you can walk down, and Bob and I will wait here," I suggested.

"Well, I don't know if I should . . . . "

"C'mon, Sulie. I'll go with you," insisted Lynn. "Joy can't wait to see you, and all the other kids have been looking forward to seeing you too. C'mon, let's go down to the lake. It's a pretty walk." Sulie took one last look at the decorations and was off to the lake with Lynn.

"Has it been tough, Bob?" I asked, once they were gone.

"Shoot yeah. Too tough." Bob sighed and spit some Skoal juice into his styrofoam cup. He told me how hard it was for mom to be away from daughter. It sounded as if things had been kinda silent around the old Fulton homestead for the last three weeks.

"She's been waiting for this moment since you guys walked down the tunnel at LA airport. These last three weeks have been harder for her than I figured they'd ever be — and I figured they'd be plenty hard . . . ."

I sipped my long-awaited Independence Day beer and Bob savored a pinch of tobacco while we waited for Lynn, Sulie and the kids to return. Our conversation that afternoon was the first of many enjoyable ones Joy's dad and I would share over the next few months, and in talking with Bob, I discovered many of the reasons why I enjoyed his daughter so much.

"Sure hope Sulie doesn't hug Joy too tight," said Bob softly.

"What do you mean?"

"Well, I think you and I both know that although these past three weeks may have seemed like an eternity to mom, they more than likely have seemed more like the blink of an eye to daughter . . . Shoot, Joy probably feels like she just got off the plane."

I listened without much to say as he paused between thoughts about mothers and daughters. I was just about finished with my beer and Bob was just about ready to dip into his can for another pinch, when up walked the boys.

"Man, Mr. Fulton, this looks great!" Carl was the first one up the trail.

"How ya doin', Carl?" Bob shook his hand.

"Hi, Bob." Jimmy was next to arrive. "Man, this place looks like Main Street USA, Disneyland gettin' ready for a parade. And those streamers and banners hanging from the trees sure look better than our dirty shorts hanging from the clothesline. Good to see you, Bob." Jimmy walked up to Joy's dad and shook his hand.

"Why, James, how the heck you doin'?" asked Bob as he gripped Jimmy's hand. Jimmy and Bob would develop a good friendship over the next few months, and already I could see they liked each other. Jimmy especially liked the way Bob called him "James."

"Fine, just fine. I mean it, this place really looks good. Excuse me, but did I hear you brought some stuff to eat?" Jimmy looked around and headed to the line of tables as Ethan loped up the path.

The three guys were soon mixing up the onion dip and drinking Cokes. Sulie, Joy, Heather and Lynn came walking slowly up the path, and Joy walked up to her dad and gave him a big hug.

"How ya doin', Pumpkin?" The look on Bob's face as his daughter walked into his arms showed he had missed her too.

Onion dip was followed by the rest of the menu, which was coincidentally filled with all Joy's favorite picnic things. We spent that afternoon eating, visiting, and reading cards, letters and newspaper articles from home. Stuffed and satisfied, I talked with Bob about the possibility of staying over another day and driving to Appomattox to visit the battlefield and courthouse.

"Don't see why not," he said. "I agree that riding your bikes on the Sunday of the Fourth of July weekend would be just as crazy as riding today. I don't think I need to ask Sulie if she would like to stay an extra day."

So, early Sunday morning, the nine of us piled into the Fultons' four-passenger rental Ford and headed off to see where Lee and Grant signed the treaty. All of us sitting on each others' laps — guys on girls, girls on guys, daughters on moms, friends on friends' moms — we were quite a sight. No one fussed or complained as we rolled toward the battlefield. We just giggled on the bumps. As we drew closer and rolled over the silent green farmland that surrounded the little hilltop called Appomattox Courthouse, we asked and wondered what it would have been like over a hundred years ago to have to fight cousins and friends there. A few hours later, even after having seen the moving presentation at the Visitors Center, it was still hard for us to imagine a war took place on those hills.

At the end of Sunday's field trip, on the way back to camp, Bob and I looked into the rearview mirror to see the backseat filled with snoozing bodies. Sulie was surrounded by Joy, Heather, Jimmy and Ethan all asleep with their heads propped up on each others' shoulders. Bob reached for the white styrofoam spittoon he kept on the dash, spit some brown juice into it, and gave me a wink.

When I had set up the opportunity for parents to visit us on the trail, I worried about how it would affect the kids. Later that evening, when we said good bye to Joy's folks, I realized I had it all wrong. I should have worried how it would affect the parents. I almost wished that Joy would cry on her mom's shoulder when they said good-bye, but Sulie was the only one with tears that afternoon. Instead of leaving us with the hollow and homesick feelings in our stomachs I expected, the Fultons left our stomachs excited in anticipation of the Fourth of July leftovers that were packed away in our panniers. Steak sandwiches had replaced peanut butter and jelly, along with three kinds of potato chips, and real milk and cereal awaited us in the morning, instead of powdered white stuff and oatmeal. Handshakes and hugs were exchanged as Bob motioned for Sulie it was time to go. I got the same uneasy smile from Sulie I received at the LA airport, and she hesitantly headed for the car.

"Thanks, Bob, thanks, Sulie. Thanks, Mom, thanks, Dad." The kids all smiled and waved. Carl even ran alongside them as they drove out of camp. We were all glad the Fultons had visited, but as I watched Sulie wave with one hand and dry tears with the other, I wasn't sure if she was glad she had visited us.

Amasta

Somewhere on the horizon loomed the Appalachian Mountains and the Blue Ridge Parkway. When I had read the kids Barbara and Larry Savage's around-the-world bicycling odyssey, *Miles From Nowhere*, Barbara and Larry talked about the Blue Ridge as being one of the toughest stretches of mountains they ever pedaled, and that included the Alps of Europe and the spires of Tibet. We had watched professional bicyclists, who crossed the continent in less than ten days in the Race Across America, speak of the Blue Ridge Parkway as the place that broke everyone's spirits. All of us knew the Parkway was three days ride ahead, but it loomed so ominous in its previews, we half expected to see some colossal green peaks, still over a hundred miles away, etching themselves against the gray Virginia horizon.

Horizons, though, weren't easy to find as we rolled up and down the folded landscape of counties named Prince Edward, Campbell, and Bedford. One minute we would be grunting and sweating our way up the side of what the locals called a hill and we called a mountain, and the next minute we would be sliding down the other side. Trees lined the sides of our narrow two lanes of asphalt, and only when we came upon an occasional parched hayfield did we get any panoramic views. The rest of the time was like riding in a maze of green, with tunnel vision, the trees towering thickly above us, like giant hedges.

"Hey John, are there any flat spots in Virginia?" asked Heather.

"Yeah John, if they call these 'hills', then we're dead meat when we hit the

Blue Ridge MOUNTAINS!" sighed Jimmy.

"Hey John, my back wheel is making that funny noise again." Ever since we left, Joy's wheel had been creaking. "It really does it bad when I'm climbing, which is a lot of the time around here. Do you think you could fix it?"

"I hope so. Do you think you can wait until our cookie and Gatorade break?" I hoped her wheel would too.

"Yeah, I think so. It's just that it's so quiet out here and the birds sound so nice. I wish I could listen to them, but my wheel won't let me."

"We'll be stopping in another twenty minutes or so," I answered.

Joy, in all her quiet, smiling stoicism, nodded to almost every demand I ever made of her. She took a swig of water from one of her three water bottles, smiled, "Okay John," and continued on. I only wish her bicycle had been half as agreeable.

Halfway up some unnamed "hill" near Madisonville, Joy's rear wheel decided to add a new verse to its uphill song. In the middle of one of Joy's pedal strokes the unmistakable ping of breaking spokes rang through the woods. It was soon followed by Joy's voice.

"Hey John, my rear wheel is rubbing against my brakes."

I was at the crest of the hill with Jimmy when I heard Joy. The prospect of replacing spokes had me close to yelling a word I had promised myself — and the powers above — that I would try not to say anymore, and Jimmy smiled, knowing what I was about to scream. Little did he know that broken spokes on rear wheels in 90-degree heat and humidity caused me to question the existence of that same heavenly power I had made that promise to. If Jimmy wasn't careful with his grin, he'd be getting more of an earful than even he hoped for.

"I'm sorry, John, but I don't think my rear wheel is going to make it," said Joy. "I tried to be careful, but I think something broke." Joy was pushing her heavily laden friend up the hill — an effort comparable to pushing a car when someone has left the emergency brake part-way on — and *she* was apologizing. Her attitude in the face of adversity would be very helpful to my relationship with the man upstairs, and Jimmy shook his head in disappointment when he saw me swallow the obscenity Joy's apology had prevented.

Just ahead, a red clay road intersected ours, and just beyond the intersection was Harry's Handy-Mart. So, instead of attempting to fix Joy's wheel in the middle of the road, we rolled our bicycles into the gravel parking lot. It wasn't a bad place for an earlier-than-planned snack break, so as I got out my tools, the kids happily leaned their bikes up against the side of the old market and got out the cookies. Lynn walked inside to buy three bottles of Gatorade, and Joy removed her panniers so I could get at her back wheel.

In front of Harry's, an old, rusty Ford pick-up of unknown color sat parked and broiling in the sun, like some nostalgic piece of sculpture. Alongside it stood a wiry little black man in greasy blue overalls that hung off his shoulders and billowed over his sneakers. On top of his gray-haired head sat a well-worn ball cap, advertising some brand of fertilizer. As I prepared to deal with Joy's wheel, saying prayers that the broken spoke would not be on the freewheel side (requiring me to remove the gear cluster), I noticed him, hands deep in pockets, watching us silently. It didn't look like he'd seen people like us pass through Harry's before.

"Oh #@%*#!" I growled. The spoke *was* on the freewheel side. Joy was drinking Gatorade as I broke my promise, and I saw Jimmy smile and simultaneously move his observation post a little farther away from where I was working.

I got out my freewheel remover and 8" wrench and proceeded to try and remove Joy's freewheel so I could get at that broken spoke. The little man moved closer, while I prayed that I would have enough leverage to remove the cluster of cogs. Joy's legs had screwed it tighter and tighter with each pedal stroke over the past thousand miles, and I hoped my wrench and I were stronger than her legs. I tightened the silver jaws around the freewheel tool and then leaned with all my weight in the opposite direction from that which Joy had pedaled. Sweat streamed off my forehead and down my arms. I grunted like a Soviet weight-lifter, but Joy's freewheel gave no hint of loosening. I shot up another quick silent prayer, leaned on the wrench again, but still not a budge.

"#$@$%#*!!!!" I hoped God was more patient with me than I tended to be with him, because, as that wrench cut its way into the palm of my hand in front of Harry's Handy Mart, the kids and one local observer, I let loose with some more vocabulary I'd used quite often in my own adolescent days. I came awfully close to flinging that wrench — and Joy's wheel — into a nearby Virginia treetop, but somehow I restrained myself. I sponged the sweat from my face and chest with my already soaked bandana, steamed passed the man in the overalls, and walked into the air-conditioned market.

"Excuse me, but you wouldn't happen to have a vise I could use, would you?" The girl at the counter wasn't Harry and wasn't very handy, because I had to explain to her what I meant by a vice.

"I'm sorry, sir, but we don't have anathang like that 'roun hya," she said, shaking her head.

I sighed and walked outside into what now seemed like an oven. I knew it was hot outside, but in the short time I was inside the store, it sure seemed like someone had turned up the heat. I took another deep breath and surveyed the situation one more time. On two of the corners there were old houses, and I noticed an old man working on a 1950 Ford Custom Coup in the shade of his front yard. Surely he would have a vice if he worked on his own car, so I walked over to his yard with new-found hope.

I knew he saw me walking over, but as soon as I neared his car, it was as if I became invisible. He turned a little more of his back to me and suddenly got a lot more interested in the rear wheel he seemed to be working on.

"Excuse me, sir, but I'm a teacher from California and five of my students, my wife and I are riding our bikes across America. One of the kids just broke a spoke, and I was wondering if you might have a vise I could use?"

Instead of turning around right away, the old man continued working on his wheel. Just as I was about to repeat my story and request, he scratched the back of his neck and slowly turned around. The face that awaited me was the spitting image of the man in that old painting of the farmer and his wife. He was a live replica of that bald man standing with pitchfork in hand. I only wished he didn't have that same mistrusting glare in his eye.

"If I was to have a vise, you would be more than welcome ta use it, but I've been sick lately. Well now, George across the street, he's sure to have one. He'll be back home 'round 12:30. He has a black boy workin' for him might be able to help y'all out. Like I said, if I was to have one, you'd be more than welcome to use it."

With that, the bald-headed man looked me up and down one more time and returned to his Ford. As much as I wanted to believe him, I was almost sure he did have a vise, but I would never use it. Maybe I shouldn't have said I was from California; maybe I should have put on a shirt before going over to talk to him, but I just got the feeling he didn't care for me too much.

Back at the bicycles, the kids were finishing off the last of the Gatorade, and I noticed the black man, who had been watching me so intently before, was standing now over Joy's wheel getting a closer look at what I was trying to fix.

I walked back and, like the man next door, he didn't seem to have much to say either. He looked at the wheel, then looked at me. He was even smaller and thinner than he had seemed from a distance. His ebony face was furrowed with wrinkles sparkling from his sweat. Wiry, gray stubble dotted his chin, and when he suddenly smiled, his yellow teeth — minus the one that was missing — filled the bottom of his face. He silently winked at me with his dark, brown eyes, and although I didn't know if he had a vise, I had the feeling that somehow we would have Joy's bike rolling in no time.

"Whatyaneed?" he smiled, adjusting his hat and stroking his chin. I noticed that above the pocket on his overalls the name "Amasta" was embroidered in dirty red thread. I didn't try to pronounce it. I showed him Joy's broken spoke and explained that I needed to get the freewheel off to fix her wheel. He studied my predicament and scratched his chin a couple more times before another smile spread across his face. He raised a long black finger into the air and signaled that he'd be back in a minute.

Amasta, Mr. Amasta or whoever our friend was who wore those overalls, turned out to be the owner of the rusty pick-up. He walked over to rummage through all the stuff — some might dare call it junk — in the bed. He returned with the rustiest and biggest pipe wrench I had ever seen. The jaws were by no means even close to parallel, but all I hoped was that they still opened and closed.

My overalled savior returned wearing an even bigger smile. He held the mammoth wrench high in the air above his shoulder, as if he was carrying the Olympic Torch up the steps of the LA Coliseum. He handed it to me and in a flash, Joy's freewheel was loose. The kids clapped and cheered, I gave our friend the thumbs up sign, and he smiled back with a thumbs up sign of his own. He smiled all the way through my how-to-replace-a-spoke-and-true-your-wheel demonstration, never saying a word, just smiling and occasionally scratching his gray chin. Joy remounted her panniers while I put my tools away, and before we pedaled out of Harry's Handy Mart, the man who will forever be known to me as "Amasta" posed proudly with me so Lynn could take our picture. I put my arm around his strong shoulder, he held his pipe wrench high in the air, and we both smiled. I shook his calloused hand one more time, and the kids waved good-bye as we headed up and over more of Virginia's endless waves of green trees, golden fields and red clay. I hoped my repair would let Joy do a little bird watching.

"Hey John, what did you find out at the jail?" asked Carl. "Do we get to stay in a cell?"

"Hey John, guess what?" said Heather. "We met this really pretty woman and she wants us to be on TV. She's a reporter for ABC in Lynchburg and she wants to do a story on our trip."

"Yeah, she's that pretty black lady over there," added Joy.

Lynn and the kids had stopped for burgers at the Big T Burger in downtown Rustburg, Virginia, while I rode a couple blocks ahead to the sheriff's office and jail to see if we could find a place to stay. Walking into the small jail was like walking into Sheriff Andy's office in Mayberry. I expected to see Barney Fife sitting at the desk with his boots up on the table.

"My name is John Seigel Boettner and I'm a school teacher from California . . . Do you think there are any schools or churches in town where we could stay tonight?" My story of the five kids and their teachers bicycling across America was passed from the deputy to the dispatcher, to another deputy, then to the superintendent of schools and finally on to Bennie Arthur, the principal of Rustburg Middle School. Mr. Arthur told me to go back and have my burger with the kids; he'd meet us in front of the school in 30 minutes.

"You mean we don't get to stay in jail?" moaned Carl, sounding very disappointed. "I was hoping we could stay in a jail the way Peter Jenkins did."

"Yeah, didn't Barbara and Larry stay in a jail somewhere in Asia?" asked Jimmy. "I was kinda hopin' to see what a jail was like, too."

We ate our burgers, and, in between bites, the kids told me about the guy who walked in with a loaded pistol in his back pocket. Carl began the story:

"Yeah John! When we showed Lynn the guy with the gun, she immediately changed our order from an EAT HERE order to a TO GO order, and the guy at the counter got kinda upset."

"We whispered to the manager about the gun," continued Heather, "and the man at the counter said that its legal in this county to carry a pistol — as long as it's not concealed."

"The guy with the gun's order was a TO GO order too," said Joy, taking her turn. "So, as soon as he left for sure, we changed our order to an EAT HERE order again. I don't think the manager appreciated it too much though." The kids caught me up on all that had happened since I left for the sheriff's office. We finished our dinner, made an appointment for an interview the next day with the TV reporter, and waited outside for Mr. Arthur.

"I'm sorry Virginia has been so hot for you all. Heat's even got me sweatin' this summer. I think the gym here will be the coolest place for you all. I'll go and get some big fans from the store room. They might help cool things off a little."

Bennie Arthur, a man about my age, having worked with kids like mine, spoke easily with them as he made things as comfortable as possible on the floor of his gymnasium. He pointed the kids toward the showers ("Sorry, they're cold, you all, but we turn off the water heater in the summertime."), delivered two giant floor fans, and rolled a basketball through the door before saying good bye and good-luck. He said he'd call the sheriff again to have him check up on us through the night, and then was gone. The kids immediately ran into the showers to do themselves and their clothes. From the sounds of the water and their singing, it didn't seem that the cold water or the day's 60 miles bothered them at all.

We spread out our sleeping pads underneath one of the basketball hoops and had our journal meeting. After our meeting, everyone quickly fell asleep, except me. While Lynn sighed, Joy dreamed, Jimmy snored, Heather smiled and Ethan and Carl wiggled, I laid back and thought of all that had happened that day . . . The video camera in my brain wouldn't shut off and it played back all the events of our long day: I watched Joy's smile and her broken spoke. I saw the heat pulling sweat out of my pores and shook my head as I watched a rerun of my search for something to remove her freewheel. There I was, almost throwing the wrench, but instead finding a black friend in blue coveralls. As I watched myself hugging Amasta good-bye, I remembered that somewhere it says something about 'all things working together for the good . . .' I looked up at the dark gym ceiling and whispered a quiet confession for my impatience and extended vocabulary. I fell asleep thanking God for giving angels pipe wrenches.

"Hey John, I think Ethan's sick. Lynn told me to tell you to wait for her and Eeth." Carl rode up to where Jimmy, the girls and I were waiting and wondering what was taking so long.

At Appomattox, we had learned that General Grant would let his troops rest five minutes for every hour they marched. Since then, we had tried to imitate that routine, and so far it had worked. That morning, though, the climbing, heat and humidity, combined with a giant breakfast, slowed Ethan down more than usual.

"I saw him toss his chow alongside the road just after we climbed that first hill. I think all of his biscuits and gravy are now somewhere in the bushes," Carl explained. "When I passed him, he was just sitting next to his bike with his head between his legs. He didn't look too good to me."

Our five minute break had grown to thirty, when a pale Ethan and a smiling Doctor Lynn came riding up.

"Ethan's okay," assured Lynn. "We just need to start off a little slower after a big breakfast, that's all."

"Yeah. I bet General Grant didn't have to march in this heat, and I bet his troops didn't get to have so much food in the morning," said Jimmy. "I know we're supposed to fuel up and everything at breakfast, but sometimes my gas tank is overflowing a little when we hop on our bikes and start riding again right away." Everyone nodded their agreement with Jimmy's sentiments. Ethan drank a little water and we continued on, this time a little more slowly.

"And while I was waiting for the comics, I read the front page of the newspaper and it said that the South is experiencing a record heat wave and drought," said Heather, as we caught our breath at the top of an especially steep hill.

"Yeah, ever since Maryland the crops have looked pretty sick," added Joy. "Even the corn I plant back home looks better than the stuff we've seen. The soil looks so red and dry and dusty; the plants aren't even two feet tall; and did you guys see that field of those really strange looking plants with the giant leaves? You know, the gray-green ones with the yellow spots all over them? They looked like they were burnt or something . . . Maybe they're supposed to look that way, but they sure didn't look very healthy to me."

"Joy, I think that was tobacco you saw," said Jimmy. "They grow a lot of tobacco in Virginia." Jimmy poured water down the back of his neck while he shared some of his local knowledge.

"You know, Senator West, I think you're right," I said, as Ethan and Lynn joined us. "It looked like tobacco to me. I agree, Joy, it sure didn't look like it was enjoying the weather. I think it looked like big bunches of wilted lettuce." We continued talking about local agriculture until I decided it was time to attack some more hills.

"Ethan, if you and everyone else are ready, I think we need to be going. We're supposed to meet the TV cameras in front of the Bedford Courthouse at 1:30, and we still have 30 miles to go."

"30 miles? Piece of cake, dude," boasted Jimmy, as he put his water bottle back on his bike. "It's not even ten o'clock yet."

Jimmy was right, thirty miles wasn't that far for us anymore; but the hills got longer and steeper with each mile we rode west. The red clay was like a vaporizer, and as the day went on the steamy haze got thicker and thicker. We had never ridden through air so heavy, and riding through the "hot fog," as we called it, was harder than riding into any headwind. Our only weapons against the humidity were our water bottles, and when they weren't being sucked on we were using them as squirt guns for water fights. Everyone carried three and I told the kids never to let them run dry.

"Hey John, I'm almost out of water."

"Okay Joy, we'll stop at the first place I see." Just as I answered her, a white car rolled up and over the hill ahead, and I waved down the woman who was driving.

"Excuse me, ma'am, but do you know where we could get some water to fill up our bottles?"

"Well, son, I shore do. Just follow me, you all are comin' ta my house. I got some ice cold well water in the ice box."

I motioned everyone to follow me as she led us the half mile or so to her house. Her name was Mary and she lived in the hills of Bedford County. She had twelve children, twenty grandchildren, and two great grandchildren. She didn't look a day over fifty, and before we had a chance to get up on the shady porch of her house, she'd introduced herself to each of us, had found out our story and had given us all a welcoming hug.

"C'mon inside. You folks look mighty hot. We'll add some ice and fresh well water to those bottles of yours."

We all felt as if we had just inherited a new grandmother. It was nice and cool inside Mary's house, and the kids drank her sweet water and walked around the house looking at the many photos of her clan. The photos were all over the walls and sitting on each of the tables, and at each one, Mary would tell us who they were.

"Would you all like some baloney sandwiches and some cookies?" Mary's open arms and open refrigerator weren't making my task of getting us to Bedford any easier. I had never really had a grandmother and had never been to "grandma's house," but I had heard it was always hard for parents to get the kids to leave. Mary was rapidly making up for any experience I'd missed.

Just as the kids were about to accept her invitation, I had to interrupt their open mouths. "Thanks a lot for your offer, Mary, but we really need to be going. We're supposed to be in Bedford by 1:30 for our TV interview. I think we'll have to pass on the sandwiches."

"Aw c'mon, John," Carl moaned.

I didn't feel much support for my decision. Heather wasn't frowning but her smile drooped a little.

"Whatever you all decide . . . You're more than welcome to cool off here for a while and have lunch, but if you all need to be gettin' on, then I understand. It ain't gettin' any cooler out there."

I started towards the front porch and the kids grudgingly followed me. Lynn took the rear and coaxed the last one, Carl, out the front door. Going inside always made going back outside that much more difficult in the southern heat, and we were practically suffocated by the blast of steamy heat that awaited us out on Mary's porch.

"Mary, is it okay if we take our picture with you?" Joy asked, while Heather ran to get her camera.

"Why sure you can. I'd like to get a picture of you all before ya leave too. John, do you all have the time to pose for a picture for me?"

"Yes, ma'am, I think we can manage it," I answered.

Everyone posed in the shade of the porch with arms around each other, water bottles held high, as I shot pictures with a half-dozen cameras. At times like that, everyone would pile their cameras around my feet or hang them around my neck. Then I pushed all the shutters, while the group smiled their way through my series of "Say cheeses."

Mary hugged each of us good bye. "Remember now, just keep the Good Lord in the right place, and you all will make it to California just fine. My prayers are with ya." Mary waved good bye to her California kids, and we rolled into Bedford refreshed, with a new grandmother, a new friend, a new story and with plenty of time to spare for our TV interview.

We were all so excited about being on TV, we almost didn't notice what looked like a dark shadow on the western horizon. Somewhere between Mary's and Bedford the Blue Ridge Mountains began to show themselves. We knew that in Bedford, besides being on the tube, we would be getting our bikes and our kitchen ready for our 300-plus miles up on the Parkway. After our interview we did our first 500-mile tune-up on our bicycles. Lynn and the kids cleaned their chains and derailleurs with solvent and toothbrushes while I hitched a ride with the TV crew into Lynchburg to get Joy a new wheel. That wheel had the special quality of making friends, because after buying a new one in town, I was given a ride back by a taxi driver who knew as much of Campbell County's local history as I could ask about. With Joy's new wheel in the back, I sat in the front seat with the black cabby as he told me about his family's tobacco farm. He told me what it was like in the forties, when he was just a young boy farming with his family. Back then, they did everything by hand with the help of their horse and their wagon. He smiled dreamily as he told me about his love for the red dirt of Campbell County, and he shook his head as he reminisced about tobacco poles, sheds and "gatherin,' cuttin' and smokin'" the giant leaves. As I listened to him, it occurred to me that someday, when there's a shortage of teachers, we should just hire taxi drivers. I learned more from that Lynchburg cab driver than I learned in lots of classrooms. Class ended when he pulled to a stop in Bedford and I gladly paid the tuition on the meter. Heck, I even tipped him.

I figured celebrities deserved some extra special comforts, so we treated ourselves to two air conditioned motel rooms in Bedford. The motel didn't serve well water and baloney sandwiches, but it did have a swimming pool and restaurant, and my yellow cab dropped me off to find the kids washing the grease off themselves in the pool. That night, we set a record at the nearby all-you-can-eat restaurant, and Lynn and I had another one of our hand squeezing and proud smile sessions as we watched Heather and everyone else smile their way into living rooms all over western Virginia. The kids fell asleep under the covers watching themselves on the 11 O'clock News and dreaming of tomorrow's encounter with the Blue Ridge.

7

I was halfway up a hill when I decided to put on my rain jacket, because it was pouring. I had both my arms in when I found out I had it inside-out. It was too late to fix it. You ought to realize how difficult it is to zip up a rain jacket when it is inside-out. Everything on me was wet, especially my shorts and underwear. All the water had gone through the breathing net and ran down the covering into my shorts. The covering was supposed to cover the netting, but since it was inside-out, it didn't . . . .

Heather's Journal
July 10, 1986

Turtles and Wildflowers

"Ten bags of groceries!!! You-all gonna fit all that on your bicycles and then pedal them up to the Parkway?!"

I didn't know whether it was our bikes or our appearance on the news the night before that made us such celebrities out in front of the Bedford supermarket. A small crowd had made it impossible for me to get any journal writing done, as I sat waiting for Lynn and her two designated shoppers to return with the food that was supposed to get us from there to Asheville, North Carolina. Two shopping carts soon pulled out the doors and over to our bikes, and a new crowd gathered. They couldn't believe we were going to fit all the food on our bicycles.

Jimmy carried oatmeal and bagels; Lynn — dried fruit, rice and soups; Joy took on pasta, cookies and powdered drink mix; Heather — canned chicken, tuna and cream cheese; Ethan took more bread and bagels, peanut butter and jelly; and Carl and I split up stove fuel, spices, cheese, squeeze margarine, bagels, cookies, tortillas, powdered milk — "I'll never drink that stuff," Carl declared — and more of everything else. It took us about ten minutes to perform our magic act, making the groceries disappear into our panniers, and instead of an ovation from the crowd of local onlookers, a silence of disbelief settled over our audience. We rolled out of the parking lot, smiling and waving to the shaking heads who were driving their week's groceries home in the car to pack them on papered shelves and into cold refrigerators. The kids' confidence was always boosted whenever they received such stares of disbelief. Riding up and onto the infamous Blue Ridge Parkway, I figured we'd be needing all the boosts we could get.

The foothills of the Appalachians got steeper and steeper as we rode west toward Roanoke Mountain. Like a modern day Sisyphus, we pedaled up grades — that I'm sure had ruined many an engine and radiator in their time — only to fly down the other side, propelled extra fast by the added weight of a week's groceries packed on our bikes. The folds of land stacked up like the waves on a heart monitor, ending in one great crescendo of green, the now omnipresent peaks of the Appalachians, and the beats of our hearts matched those contours of land.

Hopefully, our hearts would be up for the even bigger beats that the Blue Ridge would require.

At about 6 in the evening on Wednesday, July 9 the Virginia sky let loose with a little thunder and lightning to celebrate our arrival at the sign reading:

YOU ARE NOW ENTERING
THE BLUE RIDGE PARKWAY

We all stopped our bikes, shook hands, hugged and patted each other on our rain-jacketed shoulders. As anxious and excited as we all were, I think our celebration was even louder than the rolls of thunder.

"Ya know, John, while I was ridin' up that last hill, I remembered my first bicycle." Jimmy and I were stopped alongside the Parkway at one of the many beautiful Appalachian meadows that had become a farm. We stood atop our bikes in the wet, dewy grass of early morning, resting after a long climb, and waited for the rest of the gang.

"I haven't thought of that bike for . . . shoot, I can't remember the last time I thought about that bike. It's weird what comes to your mind when you're on a bike all day . . .

"Anyway, it was a red Murray BMX bike, and every day, when I got home from school, I'd run into the garage and grab my water bottle. I'd come back into the kitchen and fill it up with ice cold Coke and run back out and put it on my bike. Then I'd ride all afternoon, all over the farm in Memphis. You should have seen me . . . I thought I was so cool cruisin' all over on that little bike . . . ." Jimmy shook his head as he straddled his new bike. Before he could finish his story, Heather and Joy rode up with big smiles on their faces.

"How ya doin', ladies?" I yelled.

"Did you see all those wildflowers on that last hill?" gasped Heather. "Man, they're even more beautiful than the ones we saw in Canada!" Heather was breathing a little faster than normal, but I couldn't figure out if it was because of the hill or because of the flowers.

"I know the yellow ones are called black-eyed Susans," she continued. "And there are some that look like tiger lilies. When Lynn gets here, I'm goin' to ask her what the pretty little purple and pink ones are called. They kinda look like Johnny jump-ups. I bet she already has some in the flower vase on her handle-bars." Heather talked fast and moved her hands like a conductor, as she got all excited about the new varieties she could add to her wildflower collection. While she was talking, Joy was mysteriously and gently removing something from her handlebar bag.

"Did you guys see those cute little turtles that were crossing the road, back there before the hill?" asked Joy, as she began to unwrap something covered up in her bandana.

147

"I'd like you to meet a friend of mine," she continued. "His name is Sam and I'm giving him a ride so he doesn't get hit by any cars. Don't you think he's cute?" Joy showed us a little turtle that fit perfectly in the palms of her two hands. She tickled Sam on the underside of his marbled shell and began speaking to him as if he was a little kitten.

"And I have one too!" squeaked Heather. "We're not sure, but Stick and I think mine's a girl, so we named her Carmen." Heather pulled Carmen out of her handlebar bag. In each of their handlebar bags, the girls had made beds of bandanas, grass and wildflowers for their turtles to ride in. Heather proudly showed us Carmen's quarters.

"Uh . . . girls . . . Are those turtles house — or should I say — handlebar bag trained?" Jimmy asked as Carl, Ethan and Lynn rode up. "They're cute and everything, but I sure wouldn't want turtle poop on my granola bars."

"Would you rather they get hit by some tourist in a mobile home?" Joy promptly reprimanded Jimmy for his insensitivity. "They were right in the middle of the road, and we saw some that had already got squooshed. Are you saying that your granola bars are more important than Sam and Carmen?"

"But tur—" Jimmy didn't get a chance to finish.

"Besides they wouldn't poop in our bags. We'll let them go for rest stops when we go for rest stops. They'll be fine." Joy was convinced she and Heather had done the most noble thing. Lynn showed us the wildflowers she had placed in her vase and passed out granola bars to everyone. Heather and Joy shared theirs with their shy, shelled friends before we continued south on the Parkway.

"Yeah John, that little BMX bike of mine . . . When I used to ride it after school, I never dreamed I would someday be riding a real bicycle across America." Jimmy continued his story, once we were alone on the next hill.

The Blue Ridge Parkway was two lanes of wonderfully smooth, lightly traveled blacktop that snaked its way along one of the main vertebrae of the Appalachians, and riding it was like bicycling on a 300-mile roller coaster. We'd climb up 1500 feet, then coast down 800 feet, then up another 500 and then down again. There were few, if any, flat spots, but the beauty of the forests, wildflowers, quiet farms and emerald meadows, combined with some breathtaking overlooks, made our riding there much easier than our ride up to it over the steep Virginia foothills.

On one incredibly long hour and a half climb, in a morning drizzle, I stopped alongside the road in the wet grass and opened John's Hot Chocolate and Cookie Cafe. By the time Lynn brought the last two riders in — usually Carl and Ethan — the water was ready and the tablecloth was set with cookies and a wildflower centerpiece, arranged by the girls. I didn't know how Lynn kept her smile, because besides pedaling herself and her bicycle up the long grades, I knew she was doing a fair amount of cheerleading and psychological prodding for our two snail-paced cabooses.

" . . . and now for the beach weather and surf report for Riceville, Virginia Beach and Jonesville. Scattered clouds, chance of afternoon thundershowers, high of 97 degrees, low of 78, water temperature 82, surf about 1 to 3 feet . . . ."

"Water temperature 82 degrees!!! What do they do??? Wiz in the water?!" The guys laughed at my comments and Lynn gave me a half-hearted scowl, as we listened to the radio at one of our Blue Ridge lunch stops. I couldn't believe we were hearing a beach and surf report from the top of the Appalachian Mountains, and I really couldn't imagine a water temperature of 82 degrees. Back home in Santa Barbara, 70 degrees was hot for the ocean, and I stood up on our picnic table hoping to see the ocean the guy with the strange accent described on the radio. I wasn't used to being away from the ocean for very long and I missed it. From my vantage point up on that table I was high enough, but the only waves I could see were the ones we'd bicycle-surfed — the mountains and foothills of eastern Virginia and North Carolina. Even with the rain-washed, crystal blue sky and outrageous view, it was wishful thinking that I might see some ocean from anywhere on the Parkway.

"Wiz in the water . . . That's funny." Even if Lynn didn't particularly like my wit, Ethan seemed to enjoy it. I noticed the girls had tried to hold the line, but they ended up giggling too.

Hang Down Your Head, Tom Dooley, by the Kingston Trio, came playing over the radio as we fought the flies for our peanut butter and jelly sandwiches. No sooner had I mumbled, "Great song!" than the kids sighed, "What's that weird music on the radio?"

"Do you guys know what we're listening to?" I exclaimed in disbelief. "This is an American classic. I can't believe you guys don't know *Tom Dooley*! What do they teach you these days in school anyway? Who's your social studies teacher?"

"You are!" All five of them yelled their answer in perfect unison. I continued to sing along with the Kingston boys on the radio. My distinguished group of younger senators voted unanimously — and kindly — to let me finish my song and then change the station. Their choice was a less antiquated station, and, as soon as they spun the dial, they found the Bee Gees singing the theme song from *Saturday Night Fever*. The boys immediately surrendered their sandwiches to the Blue Ridge flies and began doing their own imitations of John Travolta. I knew the surrounding mountains had inspired many folks to cut a rug, but I had a feeling that Ethan, Jimmy and Carl might have added a few new steps to the Appalachian dancing tradition that afternoon.

"Hey John, I think I have a broken spoke." Remembering my mood at such repairs, Jimmy spoke with a meekness and softness I wasn't used to. We were giving our bikes our daily "Quick Check" (a five minute ritual to inspect them for anything that might have rattled loose, gone flat or come out of adjustment). It was dawn in the Meadows of Dan, and Jimmy had diagnosed a problem with his rear wheel.

"No problem, James, m'man. I bought a larger wrench with more leverage in Bedford. Just get me your freewheel remover and we'll have it fixed before the sun's all the way up." I figured the look of surprise on Jimmy's face was because of my newfound cheerful attitude regarding broken spokes, but his next words proved me wrong.

"Uh . . . what freewheel remover? . . . I don't think I have one, John." Jimmy looked through his tools and I looked through mine. Soon, everyone was looking through their tools for a Suntour freewheel remover. I was sure I had one somewhere in the 10 lbs. of tools that I had packed. When fifteen minutes of searching and searching again proved unfruitful, I could see the two of them that I owned sitting on the workbench at home in my garage.

While the kids wrote in their journals, I spent half an hour trying to dislodge Jimmy's freewheel so I could get at his spoke. In between my "OH #$%*&@!s" and my prayers, I half expected to see another black angel in oversized coveralls coming to my aid, but as the time went by and the sun rose higher, lighting up the haze over the mountains, there was still no Amasta. It looked like the big bicyclist in the sky was going to show himself differently that day.

I unscrewed half of the broken spoke from the nipple that held it to the rim. I then wedged the hooked end of one of Jimmy's spare spokes in the V where two adjoining spokes crossed each other. Then, screwing its threaded end into the empty nipple, I tensioned the new spoke. Each turn of my spoke wrench pulled the hooked end tight into the V, and I trued the wheel the best I could. I didn't know if my invention would work, but I knew the inevitable climbing awaiting us that day would surely give Jimmy and his wheel the ultimate test.

"Just be careful, and try to avoid any bumps or ruts. Try to spin more than usual and, hopefully, it will hold up. There aren't many towns up here, but I'll get on the phone at breakfast and try to find some place with the right tool."

We found a restaurant in Meadows of Dan, and while the kids downed pancakes and shopped at The Country Crafts Store, I called all over eastern North Carolina trying to find a way to get a tool to fix Jimmy's bike. Finally, I called ahead to the Lakeview Motel in Fancy Gap, Virginia located at Milepost 200 on the Blue Ridge Parkway. Fancy Gap was a black dot of "civilization" marked thirty miles south on my Parkway map.

"Hello. Laike-view Mo-tel and Rest-our-rant. May ah help you?" The woman's voice was high and slow. If she had spoken her brand of hilltop English any faster, I wouldn't have been able to understand her.

Although I couldn't see the woman on the other end of the phone, she didn't exactly sound like she had a ten-speed bicycle in her shed. I explained our predicament in my own slow California English, and she said she'd help any way she could.

"We have a Wes-tern Auto Store in Mt. Airy, and I think they sell bi-cycles — at least if they ain't closed down. I thaink one of the boys maight be fixin' to go down into town this after-noon. What kon a tool was it you say ya-all needed?

Say it slow now, and I'll write it down."

I ended up spelling S-U-N-T-O-U-R F-R-E-E-W-H-E-E-L R-E-M-O-V-E-R over the phone twice, and she spelled it back to me twice — "Just ta make sure."

"I ain't never heard of such a thang bafore, but I'll do the best I can. I'll see ya-all this afternoon." Before hanging up, I booked us two rooms at the Lakeview Motel and Restaurant. I figured if we were lucky we'd get some free coffee, but I didn't have much hope of a freewheel tool.

I had to send Ethan to get Lynn and the girls out of the craft shop, and soon we were up and down the road to Fancy Gap. I winced as I followed Jimmy, watching and listening to his rear wheel. By lunchtime, Jimmy's wheel was doing so well I had almost forgotten about it. We stopped at an ancient log cabin alongside the road and Joy read the sign out front:

"Mrs. Orlean Puckett. A busy midwife, she is credited with bringing more than a thousand babies into the world. None of her own 24 children lived past infancy." Joy finished reading, I took a picture and we were halfway to Fancy Gap.

"HEY JOHN, JOY CRASHED!!!" I looked over my shoulder and saw Joy bent up and lying on the grass shoulder up the hill behind me. I told Carl to wait where we were and rode as fast as I could back to where she was.

Jimmy was sitting next to Joy and Heather was stroking her hair. Lynn was talking to her and holding her head. Joy's whole body was heaving with sobs. I looked over at her crumpled bike and then back at her. Most of the skin on the outer side of her left leg had been scraped off by the blacktop and her left shoulder and elbow showed bloody signs of their encounter with the road.

"I was riding along enjoying all the flowers and thinking of that woman with all the children ... I got going about 15 miles an hour and was feeling great, when all of a sudden I saw my wheel had gone off the road—

"OUCH!!!" Dr. Lynn interrupted Joy's story, as she dabbed her wounds with an alcohol swab. Joy yelled at the pain and let Lynn work on, while she continued describing her fall. "I tried getting back on the pavement and my wheel slid right out from under me. I skidded down the road for a long ways and got all tangled in my bicycle." Tears rolled freely down Joy's tanned face, but we didn't hear another OUCH that afternoon.

"When I stopped skidding ... I opened my eyes and got right up. I counted to ten, just to calm myself down. I picked up my bike and got it off the road, and then Jimmy came along ...

"Am I okay? How's my bike, John?"

As Lynn worked on Joy and I worked on her bike, the kids watched anxiously. The looks on their faces showed their concern. They all knew there was a chance that one of us would crash badly in 4500 miles of riding, and they held their breaths, wondering whether their friend would be able to get back on her bike. From the looks of her wounds, I didn't think she would.

But I didn't know Joy ... She slowly rose to her feet, limped over to me and somehow swung her leg over the top tube of her bike. Before getting into her pedals, she hunched over her handlebar bag. We thought she was resting her head and trying to hide the pain, but we were all wrong. She had a giant gold pin of the continental United States attached to the front of her handlebar bag and she just wanted to see how it had survived the crash.

"Oh shoot, I think Florida might fall off," Joy sighed, as she dusted off her bag. She slowly placed one foot in her pedal and then, with a quiet squint of pain, she lifted her injured leg to place her left foot into her other pedal.

"C'mon, you guys. Let's get going," she sniffled. Joy wiped some tears off her face and coasted south to the silent astonishment of all of us.

Joy's unexpected crash was another part of the Parkway that made us all stronger. Watching her ride down the road with skin and part of Florida missing provided an indescribable inspiration for the rest of us. Joy would ride ten more miles that day, sixty more the next, and as many as I asked her to each day after that. The only moans ever heard from her were when Lynn would change the oozing bandages that proved extra stubborn and sticky in North Carolina's own humidity or when she cried in her dreams two nights later. I was up chasing a bunch of raccoons in my birthday suit at two in the morning. As I chased them from our precious food, I heard her sobbing inside her tent.

"Hey, do you guys have a Suntour freewheel remover?" I yelled at the two bicycle tourists who crossed our path five miles after Joy's fall.

"Sure do," they yelled back.

Curt and Peggy, from Montana, were riding their bikes from Maine to Miami. They were the first bike tourists we had seen in our weeks of riding, and while I worked on Jimmy's wheel, the kids proudly told them of their own trip. As it always does among cyclists, the conversation soon turned to food, and Curt and Peggy gave the kids the name of a real, live Mexican restaurant, three days' ride south.

"Do they have chips and salsa . . . and burritos?" asked Ethan, who was already drooling.

"Yup."

"RADICAL! Man, I didn't think we'd be seeing Mexican food for a long, long time," sighed Ethan, as he etched the name Tijuana Fats, Blowing Rock, North Carolina firmly in his mind.

"But there are a few mean climbs between here and there though, you guys," warned Peggy.

"Shoot, a couple big mountains won't keep me from Mexican food," answered Ethan. "I just hope that place has enough chips and salsa. I don't know if people from North Carolina know how to eat them like us Californians do."

I fixed Jimmy's rear wheel and said thanks to our angels from Montana. The kids waved good-bye and confidently wished them a safe trip. The five of them were so excited to have met some other bicyclists, they almost coasted uphill to

Fancy Gap and the Lakeview Motel.

Everyone leaned their bikes against the wall in the parking lot while I walked into the manager's office. No one was inside, but I noticed the side door was open and heard the sounds of *Wheel of Fortune* coming from the TV in the manager's apartment. On the counter was a bell, a card taped to the formica announcing tomorrow's check out time, and a white piece of notepad paper with a familiar-shaped, black object sitting on top of it. I looked down at the tool I had been praying for that morning. Underneath it, in crooked blue letters, was written SUNTOUR FREEWHEEL REMOVER. I shook my head, smiled up at the sky, then rang the bell.

Out limped the lady with the high and slow voice. She lowered her rhinestone glasses to the tip of her nose and handed me the tool. She spoke to me as if she had known me for years:

"Boys had no problem findin' one down at the Western Auto . . . and no, son, I ain't 'ceptin' no tip for 'my time'."

After handing me the receipt — "Y'all maight need it fo yo records. " — she booked us in two rooms, one with a shower and one with a tub for Joy to soak in. She gave me our keys and said, "Now don't ya-all be shy now; if there's any way we can help, ya'all just let me know . . . ."

"Thanks, ma'am, you already have been more help than you'll ever know," I said, as I put the keys in my bag. She walked back to her television set and I walked out to my group. With a giant grin on my face, I tossed one set of keys to Lynn, one set to Carl and then sent the freewheel remover high in the air to my friend, Jimmy. It seemed angels not only rode bikes and drove old Fords, they ran motels and watched *Wheel of Fortune* too.

We spent seven days rising and falling over places like Jumpinoff Rock, Big Laurel Gap, Daniel Boone's Trace and The Lump. The girls collected flowers; Carl sang *Roxanne* and *America the Beautiful* over and over — "Hey John, I only know two songs the whole way through"; Jimmy shared more stories; and Ethan waved proudly to the Race Across America riders who passed us just before Blowing Rock and Tijuana Fats.

"Hey John, you know what?" said Jimmy one afternoon, "I think we're going to make it." We were sitting at an overlook eating cookies and drinking water. Lynn was checking Joy's bandages as we passed fig bars around our snack circle.

I knew from the look I had seen emerge on the kids' faces in their week on the Parkway what Jimmy was talking about, but I wanted him to explain himself anyway. "What do you mean, you think we're going to make it?" I asked.

"Well, you know, when we first started this trip, I don't think we knew what we were really getting into. Yeah, we worked out and listened to stories and studied other pioneers and explorers and stuff, and, I don't know about anybody else, but it never really hit me what we were *really* going to do. But, you know, now that I've ridden over all these mountains and hills and through this heat and humidity, I know I'm going to make it all the way back to California, and I think everyone else is going to make it too. I think we've all got a lot stronger, and although it's not going to be easy, I think we're all going to make it."

"Yeah, I agree," said Carl. "Like, look at Joy's leg and my crash that night back in Virginia. I mean Stick can hardly walk, but she rides 60 miles, day after day, over these gnarly mountains! It's gonna take us some time, but I don't think anything can stop us now." Carl chewed the end of his water bottle and looked out over Tennessee as he spoke.

"Yeah . . . and that couple who rode around the world, what were their names?" asked Ethan, getting ready for his turn.

"You mean Barbara and Larry Savage?" chimed Heather.

"Yeah, Barbara and Larry. Larry said these were some of the most difficult mountains they climbed in the whole world, and really, when you think of it, they're really not that bad."

"Yeah, they're not that bad," agreed Carl. "Larry must have been a wimp."

"Well, I don't know if Larry was a wimp," said Ethan, shaking his head. "He did ride around the whole world. But I do think I know what Jimmy's talkin' about, and I feel the way he does. I didn't really know what I was getting into either, but it feels good now to know how hard riding can be, and to know at the same time, that I can do it. It's cool meeting other people like that couple going to Miami or the Race Across America dudes. And I like the looks on their faces when they find out I'm riding even farther than they are. It makes me feel pretty neat inside."

"Yeah, and that Race Across America rider, the one who passed us, he asked ME how he was doing!" exclaimed Heather, who was so excited she couldn't sit down any longer. "These mountains may be like a roller coaster like you say, John, but they are the most beautiful roller coaster I've ever been on. Going uphill just slows us down enough so we can see all the incredible wildflowers.

"And I sleep with Stick and I know how much she really hurts." Heather continued, letting us know she knew some things only a tentmate could. ". . . If she can keep going with all those sticky bandages tearing off her scabs and stuff, I think we can all make it."

"Yeah, and I even heard Jimmy laughing at Carl's stupid jokes," giggled Joy. "I never thought I would ever hear that!"

"I know," said Ethan, starting to laugh. "A couple weeks ago, I thought Jimmy would kill Carl before the trip was over and, last night, I heard him laugh at one of Carl's stupid jokes too . . . Now, that's pretty radical."

The Blue Ridge Parkway said good bye to us with a 23-mile downhill into Asheville, North Carolina. I didn't know whether it was the long descent or the new spirit everyone talked about, but a group of kids, much different from the one that had ridden up onto the Blue Ridge a week before, was now leaving their roller coaster behind them with fond memories.

"Hey John, my face hurts," said Joy at the bottom of the descent.

"What do you mean, Joy, 'your face hurts'?" I asked.

"Well . . . coming down that hill was so much fun, I smiled the whole time, and I don't think I ever smiled for so long before. So, my face hurts."

Standing at the Asheville City Limits sign, we all laughed and held our hurting faces. I think Lynn was the only one that noticed the tears welling up in my eyes. I knew we were going to make it too.

8

*When we turned the corner, we saw a horse and a black buggy with a man
wearing a white shirt, black jacket and hat and black pants.
He also had a beard . . . .*

Joy's Journal
July 25, 1986

The Ambulance

"What's the matter, John?" Jimmy asked, surprised at the look of fear on my face as the ambulance sped up the mountain. With its red lights flashing and its siren screaming, it scared birds out of the trees and sent unseen animals fleeing in the undergrowth. I had braked to a sudden stop, as the ambulance caused me to swerve off my side of the road.

We were in what the Cherokee nation called "the place of blue smoke" — the Great Smoky Mountains of eastern Tennessee. We had just climbed over New-found Gap, its sixteen miles of switchbacks, our longest and most difficult grade. We'd left our camp in Cherokee before 6 that morning, trying to beat the steady steam of the sky and steady stream of Winnebagoes, tour buses and family-filled station wagons that were sure to climb the hazy ridges later that morning. The Great Smoky Mountains were advertised as "America's Most Visited National Park," and as soon as all the pancakes were eaten in campers and cafes at the bottom of both sides of the grade, I imagined our road would be bumper to bumper and guard rail to guard rail, not leaving much room for us. Inhaling deep breaths of diesel and gas exhaust along with the ever-present humidity, as we huffed and puffed our way up the 16-mile climb, wasn't exactly my idea of a good time.

We made it up to the top of the gap before the traffic thickened, but we didn't make it down. As soon as we shifted into high gear and started down, the Smok-ies started to live up to their reputation. The downhill curves and dark tunnels would be exciting enough without traffic, but with no shoulder for either lane and giant station wagons — the kind with smoking brakes and giant mirrors protruding off the hood so that ma and pa can see their giant radar-dish-equipped trailer swerving behind them — threatening to decapitate us, as they were squeezed into us by busloads of Japanese tourists grinding up the mountain in the other lane, I knew my nerves would be put to another test. To make matters worse, I think some inebriated Army engineer designed the roadway down that moun-tain. In my many years of driving and pedaling, I had seen lots of yellow road signs with curly-cued warnings of curves ahead, but there were a couple signs on the Newfound Gap road that looked like they were diagrams for boy scout knots. At first, I thought the signs were joking, but when the road did a perfect imitation of the sign, my laughter stopped. All the way to the bottom my stomach was tied in knots of its own, worrying if we would all survive.

For awhile, I tried the there's-safety-in-numbers technique of riding in a pace line. I rode in front, setting the pace, and Dr. Lynn rode in the back, telling the kids to stay tight against the edge of the blacktop. After a few too many near misses with the protruding mirrors, I decided to change strategies. According to my map, there was one last steep grade left, and with the tunnels and knots alluded to by the mapmaker, it looked like that drunken engineer was still responsible. To give traffic room to pass us, I dismantled our pace line and had us spread out. I would leave first and then Lynn would call the kids off to leave one minute apart. I hoped a staggered descent, with large gaps between each of us, would give the cars and buses all the room they needed, but I wouldn't know if our new technique was successful until Lynn and the last riders made it to the bottom.

"Don't say anything to me, Jimmy. I hope that ambulance isn't for any of us." As the siren echoed farther and farther up the mountain, I realized for the first time how much my bicycling family meant to me. Sure I had hugged each of them and told them how special they were, but that ambulance — and all the visions of what and whom it might be headed for — started my heart pumping some chemical into my system that made my knees buckle. I started breathing hard, my head got dizzy and I had to hold onto my handlebars to keep myself from falling down. My whole body began to rock and shiver, as all I could imagine was Lynn or one of our kids lying in a pool of blood, unconscious and deathly quiet. My mind raced through images of each their faces, and thinking that they might be really hurt or gone devastated me. They weren't my students or friends any more, they were my family, like my mom or my dad . . . or Lynn.

After Jimmy, Carl rolled in. "Rad downhill! Last time I looked I was going 40!!!"

"Shhh Carl, John's worried one of us might be in that ambulance," warned Jimmy. Carl got quiet and caught his breath. He still couldn't calm the excitement on his face. He liked to go fast.

Next came Joy and Heather, cautiously braking to a slow, controlled stop behind Carl. "Stopping, stopping," announced Joy. Being the lead rider, she was warning Heather that she was pulling over.

"Thanks, Stick. Stopping, stopping." Even though no one was directly behind Heather, she automatically repeated our verbal version of brake lights.

It seemed like an eternity before Ethan and Lynn's dots could be seen back up the shady road. Jimmy and Carl had whispered my concern to the girls and, along with Carl, they were doing their best to keep their excitement quiet.

"Man, that was far out!!!" yelled Ethan, who was smiling underneath his helmet. "That was even better than the downhill into Asheville . . . Especially those curves. Man, they were neat. I don't think I've ever gone that fast before!!!"

"What's the matter, John?" asked Lynn who was also grinning. "You look like you saw a ghost." Lynn rode up to the front and put her arm around me.

"I was so worried about you guys . . . ." My voice quivered and my body was still shaking. "I thought that ambulance that ran me off the road was for one of you, and I was scared I was going to lose one of you guys. As it tore up the hill, I realized how much you guys really mean to me. I couldn't stand losing one of you."

"Ah John . . . ." sighed Jimmy, tilting his head and flashing a theatrical baby-faced smile, while Lynn hugged me extra hard. Back on our bikes, my mind played flashbacks of my nightmarish vision as we rode on into Gatlinburg, Tennessee.

"Man, I was going so fast, my helmet floated off the top of my head," giggled Carl in the pack of excited kids behind me.

"Yeah, I was going so fast, I started laughing and tears started rolling down my cheeks," agreed Heather.

"That ambulance almost ran me off the road too, but I just swerved out of the way. I didn't even use my brakes." Jimmy continued their celebration, and as the kids laughed and reminisced their way into Gatlinburg, I realized that they would always remember that downhill much differently than I.

"Hey you guys, check out the article I found in the newspaper this morning while you were sleeping in," announced Jimmy. "It's about the ten things you should NOT do in lightning storms." Jimmy was reading at the breakfast table again. We had treated ourselves to a family suite in Gatlinburg, complete with two bedrooms, hide-a-bed, kitchen and TV. The kids clicked off their Saturday morning cartoons and came over to the table to check out the article.

Jimmy read it out loud: "Number 1: Don't stand under trees . . . Number 2: Stay away from metallic objects . . . Number 3: Don't crowd into groups . . . Number 4: Don't stand near fences . . . Number 5: Don't stand on hills . . . Number 6: Don't stay outside . . . ."

The kids began laughing before Jimmy could finish.

"Hey John, remember that lightning storm up on the Blue Ridge Parkway?" asked Carl.

"Yeah, the one where you told us to stop and gather in a group, on top of that hill, under those trees?" laughed Heather.

"Yeah, and weren't we right next to a fence?" asked Lynn who had now joined the kids. Tears of laughter were now rolling down her cheeks as well. It was fun for them to see the holes in their leader's armor and they weren't going to let this opportunity pass them by.

"And . . . and before the storm got really bad, remember when you had us roll our bikes over to the side of the road under the trees and stand together? Well, dear, it sounds like you may have flunked the lightning test. So far you're six for six in Jimmy's article."

"Wasn't that storm the same one where Ethan tried to put on his rain jacket upside down?" asked Joy, thankfully changing the subject. "He looked so silly with his hood down by his crotch."

"Well, at least he didn't have his on inside-out like I did," said Heather. "Have you guys ever tried to zip up a rain jacket when it's inside-out?"

"No, Heather, tell us the technique." Jimmy sarcastically sounded like he just had to know. Heather took him seriously:

"Well, first you have to understand that that thing on the end of the zipper is impossible to get to when your jacket is inside-out. That was my first clue that something was wrong, but it was raining so hard I just pushed the zipper up with my fingernail. Then I noticed that the netting in the back, you know, the stuff that is usually on the inside? Well, it was on the outside. I realized then that I had my jacket on inside-out. And as the lightning and thunder got louder and closer, and the rain came down harder, I decided to see if my jacket would work that way."

"Well, did it?" asked Jimmy, who then wanted the whole story.

"Well, not really. You see the flap, which usually is on the outside, makes the rain run over the vent in the back and down the outside of the jacket. But, inside-out, it did just the opposite. It formed a big pocket-like thing, and all the rain ran down my shoulders and into my jacket. It ran down into my shirt and biking shorts and finally got my underwear soaking wet. It wasn't very comfortable, but then, after a little while, I remembered all the crops we saw dying down in Virginia and Maryland and the drought and everything, and I just said to myself, 'The farmers sure could use this rain.' That made things more bearable."

"Heather, you mean to tell me, with lightning cracking over your head and soaking wet socks and underwear under your head, you were thinking about the drought and dying crops?!" asked a disbelieving Jimmy.

"Yes, Jimmy, I was."

Jimmy, chastised by Heather's answer, was silent for a moment and then continued, "Man, if someone was listening to us, they would never believe we've made it almost 1000 miles. John, your expert advice on what to do in lightning storms — are you sure you have naturally curly hair or have you been struck by lightning yourself? — and Heather, your rain jacket technique . . . Our trip would make a great comedy." Jimmy put down the newspaper and shook his head.

We all had so much fun reminiscing over our past comedy, Jimmy never got a chance to finish his article. I secretly read it as we ate breakfast — I was ten for ten.

"Hey you guys, before we turn you loose in Gatlinburg, let's have a journal meeting," I announced after breakfast. "But, before you go get your journals, let's play a quick game of Bright Side." Everyone nestled more comfortably in their chairs, and I began a new round of the game I had made up at one of our meetings in Virginia.

"Everybody ready?" I asked.

"Go for it, John."

"Okay. How 'bout a bright side for Blue Ridge uphills?"

"Simple — Blue Ridge downhills." Carl answered first.

"Alright . . . Heat and humidity," I continued, and Ethan raised his hand.

"Well . . . when its hot and sticky, water tastes much better than it usually does."

"Good, Ethan." Joy was waving her hand, and by the pained look on her face, I could tell she didn't want me to go on to the next event, before she got to say her bright side.

"Joy?"

"And when we need cool water, we have to ask people if we can use their hose or sink, and they usually end up inviting us in. Like Mary, that woman with all the children and grandchildren back in Virginia. I like meeting different people almost as much as getting water." Joy had a wonderful way of reminding me why I loved being a teacher.

"Great answer, Joy. Let's try another one . . . Jimmy's broken spoke . . . Heather?"

"Well, because you had to find a tool, we got to have more time to shop at Meadows of Dan. We probably wouldn't even have had a chance to go in the craft shop if Jimmy hadn't broken a spoke. Can I name a time now?"

"Go 'head, Heather."

"Rain."

Carl waved both his hands, and Heather mercifully called on him.

"Oh, that's easy. The air gets real fresh after it rains, and I like watching the water steam off the pavement. It looks real neat. My turn . . . Suntour freewheel remover."

"Okay, go for it, Eeth."

"Well . . . We got to meet those people biking from Maine. I liked talking biking with them . . . And, oh yeah, I almost forgot. If we hadn't stopped them, we might never have turned off into Blowing Rock to find chips and salsa. Man, I can't believe I almost left that out!" Ethan took his answer very seriously, and he sighed with relief. He couldn't think of a time so I gave Lynn her turn:

"Okay, you guys, one more. Lynn, you name it."

"Mmmm . . . Got it. Joy's fall."

"Jimmy?"

"Motels and showers and beds and TV." Jimmy, connoisseur that he was of the finer things in life, was glad we had occasionally needed to find more comfortable places for Joy to heal than her sweaty tent.

We continued with our journal meeting, and then Lynn and I turned the kids loose in Gatlinburg. Lynn shopped for quilts and American handicrafts while I tried to catch a trout in the Little Pigeon River that ran right through town. Everyone came back to our suite with something to show for their afternoon activities — everyone that is, except me.

"Hey John, where's that trout dinner you promised us?" said Jimmy, sounding less than confident.

"Well, I figured you guys would rather have pizza."

"Yeah, right . . . Is that your way of saying you didn't catch anything," chuckled Jimmy. Jimmy and the gang enjoyed another laugh on my account. As I got on the phone and ordered a large pepperoni and a large cheese, I thought I heard the school of trout down in the river laughing too.

One Thousand Miles

"Hey John, we're going to pass the one thousand mile mark today! My computer says 995." Carl was pushing the buttons of his electronic companion, and it was beeping back. "Let's have a contest. The person who predicts the thousand mile mark the closest wins something."

"Wins what?" Jimmy, who had bet me donuts over many Super Bowls, wanted to know the stakes.

"How about the winner wins their choice of cookies at our cookie stop?" Lynn suggested.

"Yeah, I'm getting pretty tired of fig bars. Maybe we could get something gross like Oreos," said Ethan. Ethan ate fig bars, but he sure didn't enjoy them. "I think I'll even go for the double-stuff kind." Ethan chuckled as he envisioned his choice.

"Okay, Carl," I said, "you let us know when we're on Mile 999, and then each of us will stop along the road when we think we've reached Mile 1000. The winner is the closest person to 1000 without going over it, okay?"

Our discussion of Carl's suggested contest was taking place in the dark at 4:30 AM. We were eating cereal and bagels at our campsite on the muddy banks of the Tennessee River.

An early breakfast was part of our daily routine, and by mile nine hundred ninety-five, we had our system down. I'd wake up at 4, light the lantern in the darkness and get the oatmeal and hot chocolate water going on the stove. I'd reach back into our tent, shake Lynn's foot, and then walk over to the guys' and the girls' tents to wake them up.

"Time to get up, you guys. Breakfast in twenty minutes," I would cheerfully announce. "C'mon, you sleeping beauties, it's time to get up and greet this gorgeous day." Somehow my morning enthusiasm wasn't greeted with the kind of excitement I hoped for in return. The guys moaned and told me to go away, the girls squeaked and questioned how I could tell it was a beautiful day if it was still so dark outside, and Lynn usually rolled over and went back to sleep. The only ones to welcome my wake up call were all the flying bugs that didn't seem to mind having an early breakfast at all. I slapped one on the back of my neck and returned to each of the tents to shake poles and give my "No kidding, you guys, it's really time to get up!" second wake up call.

Once up, none of us tasted much of our pre-dawn breakfast, but as the sky turned from black to gray to orange, the seven of us put enough gas in our tanks to get us on the road by first light.

After agreeing to the contest, Jimmy, bagel in teeth, coordinated the emptying and taking down of the guys' tent, and I had to laugh as I watched him try and speed up Ethan, who operated at one speed below zombie. God wasn't handing out quickness the day Ethan was born, and in the morning, he looked like a super slow-motion replay.

"Hey Eeth!" Jimmy yelled. "This isn't *Wide World of Sports*, dude. Everything's out of the tent, except your stuff. C'mon man . . . What?! You mean you haven't even stirred your oatmeal yet?" Jimmy shook his head and walked away from the tent in disgust. He joined Carl and the girls pulling their laundry off our clothesline.

"These things never dry at night. It's hot enough but all the humidity just keeps them damp." Heather was talking to no one in particular as she pulled yesterday's biking shorts and underwear off the line.

"I just hope we have some downhills today so the wind can dry things out," added Joy, as she held her clothes to her cheek. Despite our clothesline, the real drying was done when we hung socks, undies, shorts, shirts, bandanas and towels off the sides of our panniers in the morning and they were blown dry as we pedaled down the road. With jockey choners and strange-crotched biking shorts flapping next to the state flags also strapped to our racks and panniers, we were quite a sight.

After laundry was collected, the kids did the dishes and brushed their teeth, all without much prodding from Lynn or me. They knew from experience that the least hot time of the day to ride was in the early morning, so once they were up, they moved quickly through their morning chores. Ethan was the only one who still had to be reminded and encouraged and covered for, but there was something about him that made it okay with the rest of the group for him to be the slow one. They pulled his laundry down, helped him with his sleeping bag and tent responsibilities, and would have brushed his teeth for him if they could have, all without any complaints or angry barbs. Had it been anyone else other than Ethan, that person would have probably been strung up with the laundry, but as the sun rose orange and round every morning, we would all stand over our bikes, in some Tennessee driveway, waiting for Ethan to be the last one to roll up. Like a group of little tailors measuring a suit, we would all circle around his bike, check each of his panniers to see that they were all zipped up, jiggle his bed roll to see that it was on tight and tap him on the helmet with an "Are you ready, Eeth?" Once all Senator Ethan's systems were go, we'd finally be on our way.

By about ten o'clock and 20 to 30 miles into our day, we would stop for another meal. By then, all of us, including Ethan, would be wide awake and fully conscious, ready to taste some of the day's fuel. Since their first biscuits and gravy in Virginia, the senators decided unanimously that breakfast should be the meal we'd use to sample Southern Cuisine. We called it "Second Breakfast."

"I'd like two eggs over medium, bacon, cottage fries, a side of pancakes, a large orange juice, hot chocolate . . . and could I also please have a side order of biscuits and gravy?" Ethan ordered and then returned to writing in his journal. His order was typical of the group, and the little waitress shyly walked over to Lynn and me, with a shocked look of disbelief in her eyes.

"Excuse me fo askin', but are these y'all's kids? An' cain they really eat all that food they just ordered?"

"Well, they are *kinda* our kids, and yes, they will eat all the food they ordered." Accustomed to the way most waitresses reacted to their orders, the kids quietly sipped their water and wrote in their journals, as Lynn explained our journey and our group to the waitress. They had heard the same reaction to their appetites many times before. Usually by the end of Second Breakfast, our Tennessee waitresses had befriended the kids as if they were family. At least for us, almost everyone of those smiling ladies made their cafes all-you-can-eat places. Our biscuit baskets and gravy bowls were rarely empty.

Our routine continued with more riding until about one or two in the afternoon, when we would stop for lunch alongside the road or in front of some market. Then it was riding for another two hours, until our mid-afternoon Gatorade and cookie stop. After that break, we'd ride for another couple of hours, hopefully finding our place to eat, do laundry and rest again by five or six o'clock.

I watched in amazement as the kids went through our daily routine. I remembered how hard it was for my mom and dad to get our family in the car on family vacations— and we didn't have to do our own laundry and dishes everyday, let alone pedal sixty or seventy miles. Yet, other than their early morning moans and groans, our family of 12 and 13-year-olds followed the schedule without complaint.

"Did y'all find evrathing ya needed?" said the manager of the supermarket as he came walking out of the glass doors. We were sitting in the shade of the front of his market in Rockwood eating peanut butter and jelly sandwiches, and our mouths were so full all we could do was nod yes. "Where y'all headed in this heat with all that gear?"

Ethan was the first to swallow so he took his turn at telling our story. And, as usual, a small crowd quickly circled around us. After Ethan finished and all the questions from the people were answered, the manager told us about the climb ahead:

"Ya said y'all was headed up ta Crab Orchard? It'd be a bothersome climb on a bicycle. Don't know that anaone's ever done it. Anaway, guess if y'all have made it this far . . .

"Just before the climb, you'll come to a dam. Right after the dam it'll be time for y'all to change yo watches, 'cuz you'll be enterin' Central Time. Then, just before the little town of Ozone you'll start climbin,' and by the time y'all reach

Crab Orchard you'll be up on the Cumberland Plateau. Be a tough climb, but awful pretty."

The manager was right about both. It was tough and it was awful pretty. I was the first to reach the top and as I stood over my bike and watched Jimmy grunting his way to the top I yelled down to him.

"Hey Jimmy!"

"Yo." Jimmy answered, as he pulled next to me.

"What's the matter with everybody in your home state?"

"What do ya mean?" he said as he poured water onto the bandana tied around his neck.

"Well, they're too damn friendly," I answered with a smile. "I mean, if the heat won't slow us down trying to get to your grandparents' house in Memphis, then all the friendly people are sure doin' their best to. I never planned on lunches taking an hour and a half! And I thought Virginia was friendly . . . ."

"Well, boss, it's just good ole Southern Hospitality, that's all." Jimmy gave me a big grin and sucked down some more water. "'Guess we can't help ourselves." Jimmy's California accent was thickening, and with each mile we pedaled west, he was sounding more and more like a local.

That good ole hospitality continued after we grunted our way up the bothersome climb and rode into camp. Waiting for us at Cumberland Mountain State Park was a retired Tennessee couple who came over to our campsite with a paper plate full of chocolates, while the kids were showering and doing laundry.

"We saw you and your kids ridin' in here and we sure enjoyed watchin' y'all get set up and evrathang. Looks to us like you and your wife got an extra special group of young folks there, and we thought y'all might like some chocolates for dessert. Of course you make them eat their supper first." The woman was slightly overweight and wore white shorts and a bright flowered sun-blouse. Her husband shyly stood by, as she did most of the talking. "You do let them eat chocolates now, don't ya? After all the bikin' y'all are doin,' a little chocolate couldn't hurt, now could it? 'Course ifn' y'all didn't want them eatin' any sweets, I'll take these back to the trailer and not cause y'all any trouble . . . Y'all are from Californya, ain't ya?"

I wondered what gave us away. As she said California, she got the strange look we had seen so many times when people realized where we were from. She held the chocolates back apologetically, apparently concerned that we were some of those people who ate yogurt and other strange bacteria for dessert. Our home state didn't always have the best of reputations.

"Of course we'll make the kids eat their dinner first, and thank you, we love chocolate," smiled Lynn. The woman and her quiet husband looked relieved, as Lynn put their fears to rest. "It's hard to carry chocolate on our bikes because it melts so fast in this heat. The kids will be excited about this treat. Thanks." Lynn went on to tell our admirers about our trip, and they stood speechless as they watched the kids coming back from their showers, hanging up their laundry and doing their camp chores. When Lynn finished, they just shook their heads.

"Ridin' all the way across America . . . my, oh my . . . Well y'all look like ya got lots ta do, so we'll let ya be. We just wanted to tell ya how much we think of your group and what y'all are doin'. We know it ain't much, but we hope ya enjoy the chocolates. Have a safe trip now, ya hear." The lady hugged Lynn and the man shook my hand before walking back down the camp road to their trailer.

Lynn looked over to me and smiled. "I still can't believe how friendly the people have been so far in the South. I didn't expect all this friendliness. I knew people said that things had changed down here . . . like Peter Jenkins saying how wonderful the folks in the South were and everything, but still I was a little scared of this part of our trip."

Lynn's fears echoed my own. Growing up in front of a TV set in California in the Sixties, watching the Civil Rights Movement, George Wallace and Lester Maddox, I came armed with my own northern prejudices. I looked for gun racks on pick-ups just like in *Easy Rider* and figured on seeing "Whites Only" signs on backwoods drinking fountains. Even after all my liberal arts education, I still thought a southern accent somehow sounded less intelligent than my own, even on a senator or president. But, as always, my bicycle was changing old preconceptions, and as chocolates, cheerful waitresses and store clerks became as much a part of our daily routine in Tennessee as the laundry and the heat, my view of the South was being rearranged.

Later that night, after burritos and chocolate, our friends from down the way brought us a whole tray of cherries to add to our dessert. Lynn delivered them to the kids who were writing and getting ready to sleep in their tents, and I stayed up for another hour visiting with our neighbors. I still had my own laundry and journal writing to do, but my chores would have to wait until I was done visiting. I got to bed about midnight, and before I knew it, it was 4 again, time to rattle tents and boil water.

Woof, Woof

I worried that as our friendly people per mile increased, our mileage would decrease, but I needn't have. Some other Tennessee residents took care of that. We discovered that each friendly person in Tennessee owned at least a half-dozen coon dogs who were trained to chase anything that moved, and since the July heat wave had fried most every other living thing in the hills of the Volunteer State to a standstill, boy, did those dogs have fun with seven sweet California bicyclists.

"Hey you guys, I have a theory," I announced one morning at second breakfast.

"No, John, not another lecture; not this morning," groaned Carl. "I'm wiped out from out-racing that last pack of dogs."

"No, really. I think you guys might be able to use this. I mean, when you get to college, a lot of thesis topics will already be covered, but I've got one for you that no one has ever done, and one that you will have already done research on."

"Oh boy, sounds like fun," frowned Jimmy. "Okay, John, get it over with quickly. Put us out of our misery."

"Alright, here it is . . . This is for those of you who will be majoring in Canineology—the study of dogs . . . Hypothesis: the number of dogs per capita increases as the number of stripes on the road decreases. Furthermore, on roads with no stripes and less than two lanes most dogs tend to be left unchained."

No one seemed interested in my theory as they hid themselves behind their comics and shook their heads. They were too tired from their research to joke about it.

The dogs of the Tennessee back roads made sure that, regardless of heat, humidity or hospitality, our pace across their state would not be slowed. In July of 1986, when we weren't pausing for stories, gifts and directions from friendly Tennessee homo sapiens, we were being chased at a high rate of speed across the entire state, from Gatlinburg to Memphis. Canines of all shapes and sizes strengthened our vocal chords, our legs and our aerobic capacity as they ran up to us to show us their ivory. Our dawn miles were the dogs' favorite, because the temperature before ten in the morning was still only in the 80's, and their tongues weren't dragging as they would be in the three-digit heat of the afternoon. Even Tennessee's best woof-woofs had trouble catching us in the broiling afternoons, but in those hazy mornings, we approached every stretch of small farmhouses as quietly as possible, trying not to wake up the local chapter of the "Man's Best Friend Club." My group of senators decided that whoever made up that expression for dogs definitely did not ride a bike, and I was in total agreement. After five hundred miles of dog races I, an avowed hater of domesticated felines, would have given my last bottle of Gatorade to be able to ride some roads with signs reading: BEWARE OF CAT.

Coming off the Cumberland Plateau, on a downhill that was as wonderful as the climb up the other side had been bothersome, I heard the all too familiar sound of barking. Down at the bottom of the hill I saw a pack of hounds that looked like they had chased their fair share of varmints up neighboring trees. There were at least a dozen locals, it was still early in the morning, and it didn't look like any of them had yet surrendered to the heat. All their holes dug into the cool earth and their spots in the shade of the rocking chairs up on the porch were vacant. As I looked down at them in the distance, I contemplated my possibilities. I almost decided to go for the go-slow and smile "nice-doggie" technique, but I was going so fast, and the speed felt so good, I decided the heck (well, close enough) with the sons of dog mothers; I'd see if I could outrun some of Tennessee's finest. I put my head down, took one last look at my unscarred calves, and went for it.

Before the leader of the pack could bark, "Get 'em," I was by the two houses in a blur. I didn't look back, but I could hear that old hound sing the call to alarm. Soon I had the entire pack chasing after me. Their pursuit lasted a couple hundred yards before they gave up.

Well, maybe giving up wasn't quite the right word, because screaming down that same hill behind me, some ways back, were Jimmy and the rest of the meat — I mean — crew. The pack of hounds slowed down, sniffed the air, spun around and headed back in the other direction at full speed. I slowed my bicycle, said a quick prayer for my wife and friends, and listened for the sounds of the inevitable skirmish.

"Hey John, thanks a lot." When Jimmy finally caught up with me, the words coming out of his gasping mouth sounded less than sincere. "What did you do, wake up every dog in Grundy County? It was like they were having a bike-chasing convention back there or something." Jimmy was having trouble breathing as he explained how he had made it through the pack. "It was like a roadblock, man. They all lined themselves across the road like they were in formation. Some places they were even two and three deep. Up at the top of the hill I heard all this barking, so I got ready to try and out-sprint whatever was chasing you, but when I saw them stacked up across the road, I changed my plan. They were smilin' and sayin', 'Here comes breakfast, dudes,' in dog language. I slowed down and tried to weave may way through them, and luckily they just barked at my heels. Man, you're the lucky one. You just wake everyone up, and then they get ready for me and everyone else behind." Jimmy shook his head and managed to laugh.

Jimmy caught his breath while we listened for the rest of the group to have their encounters. Heather and Joy rolled up smiling. Jimmy and I were surprised that we hadn't heard anymore barking.

"Did you see those cute dogs back there?" asked Heather, who wasn't even breathing hard. "Stick and I stopped and petted them for awhile. They were so cute."

"Yeah, they just licked our legs," smiled Joy. "Remember that book you read us about that boy growing up in the Ozarks with Rowdy, his coon dog?"

Jimmy and I were still speechless, so Joy continued. "Well, there was one dog back there that looked just like I imagined Rowdy to look. He was all jumping around and licking my knees and stuff. Didn't that one dog remind you guys of him?"

"Well, Stick," said Jimmy. "We didn't really try to get up close and personal with them, cuz' . . . uh, they were chasing us down the road, if you know what I mean?"

"Well, you guys just don't know how to handle animals, that's all," smirked Joy. Just as she finished, we heard another chorus of barks, the kind Jimmy and I expected to be hearing.

"That must be Carl," Heather laughed. Carl was even more notorious in his relationship with local dogs than Jimmy or me. Some dog in the Tennessee hills already had a California souvenir from Carl. The day before, Carl had left a piece of his biking shoe in the mouth of an especially gregarious hound on one of our early morning dog races. Carl's dog techniques included: The Classic Italian Pump Swinging Method; the Yell and Scream: "BAD DOG, GO HOME" (which usually brought on uncontrollable fits of laughter from the chasing canine); and, among many others, the "Okay, If You're Going To Be That Way, Then How Would You Like A Kick In The Face" technique, which Carl had executed perfectly the day before, except for the fact that this particular dog grabbed hold of Carl's shoe and tried to pull him to a halt. Carl parted with his new found friend only by pulling his shoe out of its mouth and leaving behind a little piece of his sole. Like Joy, Carl proved very popular with the local pups, but for very different reasons, and, to this day, Carl's right shoe still has a little hole in the bottom.

"I hope Carl isn't trying his shoe technique again," Jimmy moaned.

"He's so stupid to do that. Those cute dogs aren't going to hurt him," Heather said, as the barking continued. Finally Carl rode up with an angry scowl on his red face.

"Stupid mutts. The people in Tennessee sure may be nice, but their dogs sure aren't. Why don't they tie them up?!" growled Carl, as Jimmy and I nodded our agreement. Heather and Joy just laughed.

We didn't hear any more barks while we waited for Ethan and Lynn. They both rode up together, enjoying the traffic-less country road. Lynn couldn't believe why we had stopped at the bottom of such a good downhill. "Wasn't that downhill great?" she smiled. "It's so beautiful dropping down into this valley. Ethan stopped with me to get some fresh wildflowers for my vase." Ethan smiled and Lynn showed us her new purple and yellow decorations. She had a special bike built for our trip and she asked our framebuilder friend, Mike, to design a flower vase for the handlebars. She was always stopping alongside the road and freshening up her flower arrangement.

"You mean, you guys didn't see that pack of dogs at the bottom of the hill?" Carl couldn't believe their nonchalance.

"What dogs? All Lynn and I saw were some flowers and that guy walking down the road in the overalls and straw hat. Man, he looked just like Mr. Greenjeans." Ethan poured some water down the front of his shirt as he talked. "We didn't see any dogs, did we Lynn?" Lynn shook her head as Joy helped her with the flowers.

"John?"

"Yes, Heather."

"I'm getting pretty low on water. Can we stop pretty soon to fill up our bottles?"

"Sure, Heather, next farmhouse. Let's make it a quick stop though; we've got a long way to go before Lynchburg."

"Lynchburg? Are we going to Lynchburg?" asked Carl. "Hey John, isn't that where Peter Jenkins almost got lynched?"

"Yeah, didn't they think him and Cooper were drug dealers or something?"

Ethan added.

Jimmy was next, "Yeah, and that's where they make Jack Daniels, the original Tennessee whiskey."

"Yahoo, then let's get going," exclaimed Carl, as a big eyebrow raising grin spread across his face. Inspired by Jimmy's information, he hopped back on his bike and yelled, "C'mon you guys, what are you waiting for?!"

78 And Still Plowin'

"I thought y'all was hippies when I saw the first one comin' down the road," chuckled the man with a big grin. His name was Uliss Meeks, and I was standing outside his small Tennessee farmhouse while the girls were getting water. "Why sure, y'all can have all the water ya can fit on them there bicycles." Mr. Meeks ("you jus' call me Uliss") — well, Uliss and his friend, Vernon Bonner, lived just down the road from where we had stopped to discuss dogs and wildflowers. It was the first place we came to that looked like it had water, but from the look of these two friendly and talkative men, this wasn't going to be the quick water stop I had hoped for. Vernon was a wiry man with bald head and black rimmed glasses. Unlike Uliss, who was wearing the southern uniform of overalls and cap advertising fertilizer or chewing tobacco, Vernon wore jeans and an old t-shirt.

"Yes sir, we done had our share of hippies 'roun here. Why, Uliss, 'member that ole boy use ta live up on the hill? Never knew how he could live up in them woods. Why it's so damn thick up there, dogs even get tangled."

"Yeah, Vern, I do remember 'm. Most folks thought he was growin' some of that mary-gee-wanna up there, but he never bothered me. 'n fact, never saw him much." Uliss removed his cap and wiped away the sweat with his bandana. Vernon crossed his arms and kicked pebbles around on the ground while Uliss continued.

"Ya say y'all is ridin' them bicycles all the way to California? Why shoot, that's a mighty piece to be pedallin' . . . Why, as soon as my grandson was old enough, he traded his bicycle in for one of them Ja-pan-ese motorcycles. I can hear him comin' from a mile away that thang makes such a racket."

"Mr. Bonner—"

"Damn it, boy, I said ya can call me Vernon."

"Vernon, you mean to tell me you're a grandfather? You look in awfully good shape to be a grandfather. You must be doin' something right." I figured we weren't going to be leaving soon, so I decided to enjoy the conversation.

"Maybe so. All I know, son, is I'm 78-years-old and still plowin'!" Uliss laughed as Vernon boasted his age. "I think it may have sumthin' to do with the country 'round here . . . It may be hot, but ya sure cain't beat these Tennessee hills for peace and quiet."

"I agree with you there. It sure is hot, but it has to be some of the most beautiful country I've ever seen."

"Just like a picture, ain't it? Corn fields risin' into the hills, thick with all them trees . . . Lots of birds and deer and coons . . . Some of the best huntin' and farmin' land there is. Ain't never left for long and don't never plan to." The girls were back now and listening to Vernon and Uliss as they talked about their home.

"Yes sir, y'all ought ta come back sometime 'n October. Why . . . at that time o' year, these hills look like they're on fire with all the colors. And the October nights? . . . why, they're cool enough for y'all to get a good night's sleep . . . Bugs slow down a might then, too . . . ."

"Ya know, son, I got me a nephew, and he was in dat dere Vietnam War," said Vernon changing the subject. "He was a helicopter pilot and for a while they had him stationed out in California. Damned if they didn't give him a black boy for a co-pilot. 'magine that! A black boy sittin' raat there next to him . . . Oooh mama!" Vernon lifted his hat again and both he and Uliss spit a little tobacco juice off to the side. "Ya know what? Ma nephew got to be real good friends with that boy . . . Yep, real good friends. I guess travelin' will do that for a fella . . . ." Vernon got silent for a while and then asked, "Where y'all stayin' at nighttime?"

"Oh, sometimes we camp, but a lot of times, especially in Tennessee, we just ride into a town at the end of the day and ask someone at the market if there's a church or school we can stay at."

"Bet y'all had no trouble neither."

"You know, you're right. People have been incredibly friendly."

"Well, I don't know 'bout y'all, but I ain't never found a church that was unfriendly, you, Vernon?"

"No sir, Uliss, I cain't say I ever found me an unfriendly church."

"Do you guys mind if I ask you some directions? I've got these Tennessee bicycling maps that have been real helpful, but I always like to ask some local people if they think I'm taking the best route. Today we're headed for Lynchburg." I got my map out and spread it out across my handlebar bag. "What do you think?"

"First of all, if ya don't ask questions, ya ain't never gonna meet folks. So, if ya care to take a bit of advice from me, don't y'all ever be too shy or too proud to ask someone a question." Uliss looked me in the eye as he talked to me. I knew my map would have to wait.

"Ya know . . . I had me a friend and he asked more questions than two men ought to . . . ." Vernon thought for a second before he continued. "And, boy, was he intelligent."

I was enjoying our long water stop and hated to get down the road. Vernon and Uliss debated for a little while over which was the best way to Lynchburg, and as I folded up the map, they offered to give us a short tour of their honey operation. They took us into the shed and told us how to gather honey, "Tennessee style." We returned to our bikes after visiting for almost an hour.

"I know y'all have got ta be gettin' on down the road, but would y'all send

172

us a post card when ya get to California? Sure would like ta here how y'all fared goin' 'cross." Vernon surprised me with his request.

"Sure, Vernon, but only if you'll let me take your picture," I answered.

Uliss and Vernon spruced themselves up with their bandanas and a little spit on the back of their hands applied to the hair and foreheads. They then posed for one of my most priceless pictures. They stood arm in arm and leaned up against each other, smiling proudly in front of their honey house. When the picture taking was finished, I went over to my bike to get my address book. As I searched through my handlebar bag, I noticed that Vernon had disappeared into the shed.

" . . . No, I mean what's your mailing address?" I asked Uliss, as I wrote down their names.

Uliss laughed at my question. "Address? Why, son, we don't have any street address or box number out here. Just you write down our names and 'Pelham, Tennessee.' We'll get it."

"But don't you have a zip code?" I insisted.

"Hey Vernon, John here wants to know our zip code . . . Ya know that thang with the five numbers."

Vernon yelled from inside the shed. "Yeah, I knows we's s'pposed to have one, but danged if I ever used it. It starts with a three, but that's all I remember."

"Well, just put our name and town like I says, and we'll get it. They know us down at the post office." I closed my address book and out came Vernon with a big five pound glass jar of honey under his arm.

"I know it ain't much, but we'd like to give y'all a jar of our honey for y'all's trip. Y'all like honey now, don't ya?" Vernon asked with a shy look on his face. He handed the honey to me and I insisted on taking another picture of our friends and their honey jar. Uliss readjusted his hat and Vernon again pushed whatever hair he had left back against the sides of his head with his wet palms. Automatically they put their arms around each other and held the honey in between them. I didn't even have to say "cheese;" they just held their heads back proudly and flashed two million-dollar, Tennessee country smiles.

As we waved and rode away, I thought of all they had shared with me. I, the California liberal with all my veiled prejudices, had just stopped and visited with two white, good ole boys from the South. I even shook their hands and patted them on the shoulder . . . It's amazing what travelin' can do for a fella. Oooh mama!

The Way It Is

"Hey John, I'm confused," sighed Heather. It was five in the morning and Heather sat in Lynn's and my room at the Lynchburg Bed and Breakfast, eating her muffin.

"What are you confused about, Heather?"

"Well, you know last night, when Lynn asked the owner if there were any churches around? I was listening, and he told her there were four white churches and two black churches . . . Lynn got all quiet, and when he saw the look on her face, he said that's how it's always been and always will be . . .Wasn't that what the Civil War was all about?" I could tell by the look on Heather's face that she was really puzzled, and she continued. "All the people around here seem so nice, but then he talks about those churches. And then, yesterday, when we were at breakfast, we read that article in the paper that told about how the day before the Ku Klux Klan had marched right by where our bikes were parked. I didn't think they could do that anymore. It's almost like the North never really won the war."

Jimmy, who had spent the first ten years of his life growing up in Memphis, looked like he wanted to say something, but like me, he couldn't find any words to help Heather.

Carl then took up the conversation: "And like yesterday, when we took the tour of the Jack Daniels Distillery . . . I mean, how can it be legal to make all that whiskey here and then have it not be legal to buy it. The lemonade did taste good at the end of the tour, but it seemed pretty silly for adults not even to be able to taste it. A dry county with a giant distillery right in the middle of it . . . seems pretty hypocritical to me."

"Yeah . . . it sounds like one of our paradoxes back in science class," said Ethan.

Lynn looked over at me and I looked back. We had grown to love the South we'd seen, but still little headlines and old ghosts would pop up, daring us to renew our old prejudices. As teachers, we wanted to give Heather and everyone an answer, but as people who had met the same friendly folks the kids had the past weeks, we were finding it harder and harder to pronounce any verdicts. Instead of answering, we just listened and passed the muffins. Getting the kids back out on the road to meet some more people was the only answer we could give them.

Simple Gifts

"Hey John, where are we going to stay tonight? Doesn't look like there are any towns around here, only cornf—" Jimmy's question was interrupted by a strange sound coming from over the little rise in the road about a hundred yards ahead. For some strange reason, all of us immediately slid our bicycles off the road and stopped to listen. Even the crows playing in the cornstalks stopped, and the fields became silent except for the distant sound.

"Clip-clop, clip-clop, clip-clop . . ." the approaching sound repeated itself, accompanied by a steady grinding sound growing closer and closer. None of us knew why we suddenly stopped, but in the still haze of that Tennessee sunset, a magical calm came over us as we waited for the invisible noise to show itself.

First a black line rose on the horizon, followed by the shape of a black roof, growing into the shape of a buggy and the nodding head of a horse pulling it. The driver of the wagon was at first just a silhouette, but as he drew closer we could make out a straw hat, wiry beard, blue shirt and black pants. Chills ran up and down my body as scenes of Gary Cooper racing his buggy in the movie *Friendly Persuasion* flashed through my mind.

"Wait here, you guys," I whispered. "Let's see if this man might know a place for us to spend the night." The kids' jaws dropped as I rolled Bud over to the approaching buggy.

"Excuse me, sir." I waved and motioned to the man whom I now saw was about my age despite his beard and wire glasses. "Excuse me, sir."

At first he just gently tapped his horse on the backside with his whip and proceeded to turn right down a rocky dirt road. I turned down the road to follow him. "Excuse me . . . Sir? But-I'm-a-teacher-from-California-and-my-wife-and-I-and-five-of-our-students-are-riding-our-bicycles-across-America-and-we-were-wondering-if you-might-know-a-place-where-we-could-set-up-our-tents-for-the-night.-We-just-need-a-field-or-something-and-we'll-be-gone-first-thing-in-the-morning." That was the fastest I had ever done our introduction, and I was just about ready to turn around and give up when I heard a gentle "Whoa" and saw the wagon come to a stop.

His name was Danny, and when I offered him my handshake at our introduction he hesitated, not in an unfriendly way, but as if he wasn't quite sure what I was doing. Finally he set down his whip, reached down from the wagon and grasped my still-gloved right hand. My exposed fingers could feel the hard callouses on his hand as he looked over at the line of Lynn and the kids watching silently. He turned back to me, looked me in the eye and smiled. He looked at my wheels, spoked with shiny steel and I studied his, spoked with weathered wood. He looked back at me, grabbed the rim of his straw hat and nodded; I grabbed the visor of my plastic helmet and nodded back.

"So you be riding bicycles, eh? Where did you say now?" His English was halting with a rhythm far different from the thick as sorghum, one-word- sliding-into-the-other rhythm we'd (almost) grown used to in the Tennessee hills.

"Well, I'm a teacher and my wife and my students and I are riding our bicycles across America." I repeated myself, more slowly this time. "We started in Washington, D.C. about six weeks ago, and we're riding home to California." Danny leaned out of his wagon, studied my bike, and gazed back at Lynn and the kids one more time.

"Hello, my name is Danny Beiler, what's yours? I think you say it already, but you say it too fast." He grinned as he stroked his beard.

"Oh, I'm sorry. My name is John Seigel Boettner, and I'm a teacher from California, and that's my wife Lynn over their on the red bicycle and our students Jimmy, Heather, Joy, Carl and Ethan. We've been staying in churches and schools and people's yards. Do you think there might be anyone in your community who would let us set up our tents in their fields?"

"Those younguns over there . . . you say they are riding those bicycles all the way to California? They look like they be carrying a mighty big load. Dey must be very strong children, eh." Danny gave his horse orders in a language I didn't understand. He slid over on his seat, nearer to where I was standing, and started asking all kinds of questions about us. He got more and more interested with each of my answers.

"My people, we are called Amish. We have a community in this part of Tennessee." He paused on most every word, as if he was trying to make sure each one was correct. As I listened I was enchanted by many things about him, his buggy, his Abe Lincoln beard, his wire glasses, his clothes, and his strange mixture of twangy English and some foreign language I still couldn't quite figure. "Most of de fields around here be part of our community. You vould be more than welcome to stay with my wife and my family on our farm, but two more miles down this bumpy road it be. Such a road not be too good for your wheels, I think."

"Do you know of anyone else nearby who might let us camp in their fields?"

"Well, yes . . . I think mebbe I know someone. I can't be saying for sure now, but I be pretty sure that it might be fine for you to stay there. My wife's mother and father and their family live on down the road you were on about six more miles. You will have to ask him, but I tink you would be more than welcome to stay there. You will know his farm by a big red barn and a very tall vindmill next to it on the right side of the road." Danny pointed down the road and then decided it was his turn to offer his hand, and he reached down and grasped mine. Before picking up his whip and continuing home, he leaned out of his buggy, looked over at Lynn and the kids, tipped his hat and gave a smiling wave to my family.

I said, "Thanks again," and coasted back over to the group, who were all still speechless. Before I told them where we were headed, we all silently watched and listened as Danny and his buggy clip-clopped, clip-clopped and disappeared down the red dirt road.

"Okay everybody, I want you all to pinch yourselves," I ordered with a smile.

"Pinch our—"

"No questions, Carl; just do it."

"Everybody still here?" I asked when we were done.

"Yeah," they answered.

"Oh, I get it," smiled Heather. "You wanted to see if we were just dreaming what just happened." I smiled and nodded Heather's way.

"And we're not!!!" exclaimed Joy. "That was a real Amish guy! Just like the ones Harrison Ford met in the movie *Witness!*"

"Yeah John, I thought they just lived in Pennsylvania," said Heather. "What did that man tell you?"

"Yeah, John, what did he say?"

. . . Danny's father-in-law's farm was just like he described it. Six miles down the road, the tall windmill appeared, followed by the roof and sides of a big red barn. We pulled over to the side of the road, and I told everyone to wait there while I rode down the dirt driveway to introduce us. The dirt drive was bordered by a large garden full of sweet corn, squash, tomatoes, melons and plants that this city boy didn't recognize. Next to the barn were two smaller tin-roofed barns, and off to the right was the house — a white two-story wood house with a crooked porch hanging off the front. On the porch sat two rocking chairs that looked like they were well used. Everything was quiet though, just like the road had been before we saw Danny. There wasn't a breeze, so even the windmill was still. I looked over by the barn and saw a black buggy much like Danny's parked next to it, but I still couldn't find any signs of life as I slowly rolled Bud into the yard between the big barn and the house.

The stillness was finally broken by the sound of pumping coming from near the windmill. I looked over and saw a tall man working the pump that sat underneath the windmill tower. His dark britches, straw hat and light blue work shirt with rolled-up sleeves looked identical to what Danny had been wearing. His back was to me, so I rolled my bike quietly over to where he was working.

"Excuse me . . . excuse me . . . Could I bother you for a second? . . . ." He turned around, let go of the pump handle, and stared as I hit him with my 30-second, nonstop and nervous version of my introduction. He took off his hat when I finished and took a deep breath as he looked me and my bike over. I caught my breath too, and checked him out. In addition to his clothing, I noticed he was barefoot. He didn't have a beard and he looked a little younger than Danny. He pumped the pump one more time and then walked over to me. I continued my story by telling him that I had met an Amish man in a buggy down the road who said his father-in-law lived on the farm by the big windmill, and that he thought we might be able to camp in his corn field.

This young Amish man had his hand out and ready to shake mine before he even got to where I was standing. "Good to meet you, John. My name is Aaron, and surely we can find a place for your family to sleep. Where they be?" Aaron spoke more quickly than his brother-in-law and didn't seem as concerned with the correctness of his speech.

I backed up my bike and motioned down the driveway for Lynn and the kids to come on in. I introduced Lynn and each of my blushing kids to Aaron, and he excitedly shook each of their hands. He pointed us to the corn field where he said he thought would be the best place for us to stay. As we walked around the barn, we noticed a woman in a dark blue dress, white apron and white bonnet. She was hunched over an old milk pail washing clothes by hand. The sound of our bicycles caused her to look up, and as soon as she saw us, she dropped her wash and walked over to check us out.

"Mother, this is John and Lynn and Jimmy and Heather and Joy and Ethan and Carl." Aaron pointed to each of us as he made his proud introduction. "They are riding their bicycles across America. John said they need place to sleep, so I said they could use the corn field."

Aaron's mom was a round, rosy-cheeked woman, much shorter than her son. She wore a quiet smile that almost looked as if she had been expecting us. She dried her hands on her apron and wiped the perspiration from her forehead with the long sleeve of her dress before she spoke. "Hello . . . my name is Anna and I be Aaron's mother. Yes, you are welcome to stay here with us." As Anna spoke she looked us all over. I'm sure we looked as odd to her as she did to us. Dressed in our tight lycra shorts and bright t-shirts, we must have been quite a sight, and I thought I noticed Anna trying to hold back a giggle as she spoke. "You younguns look very hot and thirsty. Would you like some water?" Anna looked over at the kids who nodded shyly.

"Aaron, why don't you draw our friends here some water from de well. I surely hope you will be comfortable in the corn field. We have just cleared it and there still be some stubble there." Like Heather, Anna accompanied her words with motions from her hands. Her words waltzed out in her blend of German and hill talk, and there was no mistaking the fact that she was the mother around here. Something about her drew our affection and respect immediately. I'm sure if she would have asked us to clean a chicken coop or rake some hay, we would have done it without hesitation. Even Aaron paused before speaking, making sure his mother didn't have something to say first.

Aaron and I started over to the pump, when, just like the scene in the *Wizard of Oz* when all the little munchkins appear out of nowhere, a bunch of Amish little ones appeared from behind the barn, behind the tree and under the buggy. All of a sudden we were surrounded by almost a dozen munchkins of various shapes and sizes. Anna must have given some kind of signal, because they all came out at the same instant. The girls looked like little Annas, wearing their maroon or blue dresses, black aprons and bonnets, and the guys looked like their big brother with their black barn-door britches, suspenders, blue shirts, straw hats and bare feet. Heather gasped in surprise, covering her mouth and trying to swallow the "Oh my gosh" I saw on her face. Joy did a 360-degree turn and smiled. And Ethan's eyes did their expanding act, setting a new trip record for size. From the look on the barefooted munchkins' faces, their eyes set some records that evening too.

"Oh yes, these are some of my children," laughed Anna, seeing our surprise. "We Amish have large families. See out there in the field? That be my husband, Jacob, and more of the children gathering the last load of hay for today."

I barely had time to count all the kids in the yard when Anna pointed our attention out to the fields, now amber in the sunset. Not quite darkened to silhouettes, a large wagon, stacked high with hay, was being pulled by a team of two large horses. On top of the hay we could see two girls and one boy receiving and arranging the hay being tossed up to them by two boys with pitchforks out in front of the wagon.

Coming up the road and motioning for the wagon to follow him was a man with a beard. "The man coming up the road . . . That be my husband, Jacob. Dey be finished soon, and then you meet dem also. You be the first folks ever asked if they could stay here . . . Most folks, why they be afraid of us. They think it strange the way we dress and talk and go about our lives." Anna stood with her hands tucked beneath her apron. All her little ones were gathered around her and studying us. Aaron pumped water into our water bag and explained to me that when the wind was calm he had to use the pump to get water from the holding tank.

"I don't reckon you use a windmill where you all come from, eh?"

"No, Aaron, you're right; we don't."

"We dig this well ourselves by hand, and most time the wind, it draw water up from the well and stores it in the holding tank over by the barn there. It has a spigot and we just turn de handle to get water. But, oh the weather, it be so hot and still late, and I must pump water by hand." I held our nylon water bag under the pump and Aaron filled it with cold water. "You sure you and those youn-guns of yours won't be needin' more? You make a big sweat from pedaling those bicycles of yours. I can fill you a bucket of water, eh?"

"Thanks, Aaron, but I think this will be enough." Before we left the pump, Aaron, still worried about our water supply, gave me a lesson on how to prime and work the pump and showed me where the buckets were. I grabbed our cool and plump bag and we rolled our bikes through the gates and out into the corn field. Before we had a chance to park and unload our bikes, Jacob and the rest of the family came up the road on the hay wagon. Aaron motioned us back to the barnyard, so we leaned our bikes up against the wood fence and walked over to meet Father.

Standing next to the hay wagon was a man much smaller than myself. His shirt was dark blue with sweat, and when he lifted his straw hat off his head I could see he was bald. He wore a beard with no moustache, like Danny's, only his was a blonde color. He, like all the children, was barefoot, and his feet looked tougher than those of any barefootin' beachbum I had ever seen.

"Hello, my name is Jacob. Welcome to my farm." He stood next to the wagon and I walked up to him.

"Hello, sir, my name is John." I held out my hand to shake his and I saw the same look on his face that I had seen on Danny's back down the road when I had tried to shake his. He didn't reach his hand out to me, he just asked me another question.

"John? . . . John how much?"

The silence was awkward. His kids were lined up silently next to him and Anna awaiting our first words, and Lynn and mine were grouped behind me almost holding their breath. His question 'John how much?' flashed in my head as I quickly tried to figure out if Jacob was some Amish comedian or if he was trying to ask me something I just didn't understand. Lynn leaned over to me and whispered in my ear. "John, he means 'John who?' He wants to know your last name."

"Oh, I'm sorry. My name is John Seigel Boettner and this is my wife, Lynn." I sighed and again held my hand out to him. He followed my lead this time and we shook hands in front of both of our families.

"John See . . . gull . . . bait . . . ner . . ." Jacob looked deep into my eyes as he slowly tried to pronounce my name. With my long last name, maybe he was right thinking how much. "Please excuse my poor English. We learn to speak what we call low-German, eh . . . When we try to speak English . . . we don't do so good . . . Sometime we get all backwards things and sometime we mix our German wit de English. So I am sorry." I could see his forehead wrinkle in effort with each word. Like Daniel down the road, he wanted to be so correct, and as the minutes went by, and he looked me deeper and deeper in the eye, it seemed he was growing excited about our visit. He took his hat off again, rubbed more sweat off his forehead and smiled with a twinkle of his own in his eyes.

"We don't have no visitors here, and if it not be imposing on you, I would like to ask you many questions about your family . . . And please ask me all the questions you would like to. But, first, before we do any of those things, we must be getting hay into de barn. It be getting late." Jacob motioned to the boys and said something in German. Quickly, the boys were unhitching some harnesses and off around the side of the barn hooking something up. Then Jacob continued talking to me.

"We don't gather the hay into bales . . . We gather it by horse and hand and then we load it into the barn. Would you like to watch?" Jacob asked us shyly. "Maybe you be tired and have more important things to do, eh?"

"Oh no, Jacob, we'd love to watch, as long as we aren't in your way." I spoke and the kids and Lynn all nodded. Our kids and Jacob and Anna's kids, except for Aaron, had remained silent in the half hour we had been together so far. Both groups were checking each other out, mine awed by all the kids and the farm and the hats and bonnets, Jacob's big-eyed over our colorful biking outfits, sparkling bicycles and strange helmets.

One of the sons led the two horses over to the side of the barn while Jacob went inside and lowered something from the loft. Soon, one of the other boys appeared from the small door above where the hay wagon was parked. He lowered a set of hooks to another boy standing on top of the stack of hay. Watching their teamwork, we were beginning to see one of the reasons why Jacob had a large family. The hooks were placed into the stack of hay and, as the boy and the horses on the side of the barn pulled a large rope hooked to a pulley hanging from the roof, the hay was lifted into the loft. It only took four hookloads to empty the wagon that had been stacked at least twelve feet high with loose hay. We couldn't believe they did it in only four loads, and as we gasped and shook our heads, Jacob and his family giggled at our amazement.

As soon as the hay was loaded, Anna came out of the house with a basket on her arm. Jacob and the kids promptly jumped up on the wagon while we leaned on the nearby fence. From the looks on the Amish kids' faces, they knew what was in the basket.

"Do you like peanuts?" asked Anna. "I have some fresh roasted ones here I thought we could share." Anna walked up to each of the kids and peeled back the cloth covering her basket.

"They're still warm!" exclaimed Joy, and all the kids on the wagon giggled again.

"Yes, I just now took them out of the oven. I hope they be warm. Help yourself." Anna's eyes sparkled above her rosy cheeks. It didn't look like having five more kids was going to bother her a bit.

"I want to know everyone's name here." I talked to Jacob and his kids as Anna passed out the peanuts. "First of all, Jacob, you said you wanted me to ask questions. Well, here's my first one: How many children do you and Anna have?"

"Well, John See-gull-bait-ner, we have fourteen. Two of them, Isaac and Verna, is married now, and these ones live at home."

I didn't know if it was the way they always sat together, but as Jacob introduced each of his children, it was if they were in order of age. If he stood them all up there in front of the wagon they would have looked like a human staircase, each one a year or so older and a couple inches taller than the next.

"You know my son, Aaron. Then dere be Elizabeth and Abraham and Elijah and Rebecca . . . and little Anna and little Jacob and Ruth and Mary and . . . the littlest one there be Noah." Each of the kids, except Aaron, blushed as their dad called their names.

"Okay, let's see if I can remember everyone's names. How about if I try and guess your ages as I say your names?" All the kids looked at each other and, having already handed out the peanuts, Anna joined them up on the wagon. Everyone shelled the warm nuts as I proceeded down the line.

"Let's see now . . . Aaron, you already told me you were eighteen, so that's easy. Elizabeth . . . I'd say you're . . . about sixteen." She nodded shyly that I was correct. "Okay . . . Abraham . . . let's go with fifteen." He nodded. "Elijah . . . I'd say fourteen." He shook his head.

"No, I am only thirteen, but I will be fourteen soon, eh." Elijah was the first of the kids other than Aaron to speak with me. He smiled and seemed glad I had guessed him older than he actually was. I'd learned long ago it was better to guess adults too young and kids too old. It worked with Amish kids too.

"Okay . . . Rebecca. I was going to guess your age as thirteen, but now I have to say twelve. You and Elijah are the same age as our kids." She smiled into her hands, glanced over at Heather and Joy and then tried to hide her blush on her sister's shoulder. "Well . . . am I right?" I could see her nodding yes from behind her sister.

"Alright, Anna . . . You have got to be ten or eleven. You look eleven, but I'm going to guess ten." I was right again. Anna put her hand over her mouth and nodded.

"Jacob . . . I used to teach third grade and you look just like one of my old cub scouts—well, almost. I would say you must be eight."

"You be right!" In just a short time, the gleam in blond Jacob's eyes had let me know that, unlike his sisters, he wasn't the least bit shy, and his answer was quick, loud and clear. I bet he knew every good tree to climb on the whole farm, and as I'd seen him eyeing the kids and their bicycles with particular interest, I worried about the effect of our visit on his dreams.

"Okay, three more . . . Ruth, you look just like my niece who is six-years-old, Mary, you look like you're about five, and Noah . . . I'm sorry, but I can't guess your age."

Little Jacob answered for the last three. "Yes, John Seegullbaitner, Ruth is six, but Mary is only four. Noah, he's one and a half." Little Jacob smiled proudly, and as I looked over at his dad, I saw he was smiling at his wife. I think they were proud of their family.

"How does you folk eat and sleep with your bicycles and all?" Father Jacob asked.

"Well, we carry everything on our bikes. Would you like to see us set up camp?" I figured a demonstration would be better than words and besides, we needed to be setting up our stuff soon anyway. The kids were getting tired and it was getting dark. Jacob's kids all had that "Please, Dad, can we?" look on their faces, but Jacob didn't want to impose on us.

"Yes, I would like to see that very much. But . . . please, do not let us be a hindrance to you. I know you must be very busy with all that you have to do, and I do not want us to get in your way." From the look on Father Jacob's face, he was as interested in seeing our set-up as his kids.

"Oh no, it would be no bother at all," I answered. "I just don't want to be an imposition to you and your family. It looks like you are busier than we are, and I bet you've put in just as long a day as we have."

"Well, yes, we do start early in the morning with the milking and everyting, but as long as we don't be a bother to you all, my family would like to see how you live on dem bicycles."

"Okay, let's go." I led Jacob and everyone over to the corn field.

"Anna," Joy was walking next to her as we headed over to our bicycles, "I don't usually like peanuts, but those peanuts we just had were some of the best things I have ever tasted. Thank you very much."

"You're welcome, Joy."

"How do you roast them?" Joy wanted to know.

"Oh, it not be that hard. I just put them in a pan in the oven at a low fire so they not burn," Anna answered, as we got to the bikes.

"I want to try that when I get home," Joy told Anna and they both smiled.

Jacob, Anna and their family stood back and watched us take our tents and sleeping sacks off our bicycles and lay our stuff out on their corn stubble. Watching us set up was as amazing to them as watching four loads of hay being hoisted into the hayloft had been to us. This time it was the Amish kids' turn to gasp and our kids' turn to giggle at something so routine to one and so alien to another. Watching our nylon tents suddenly stand up was more than even older Jacob could take, and he immediately walked over from where everyone was standing by the fence to touch our blue tent. The rest of the family stood back as Father had to do some pinching of his own.

" . . . This be your . . . portable home?" Jacob touched the mosquito netting, stroked the nylon and crouched to look inside.

I tried not to laugh at his description of our tent, but I couldn't stop myself. I patted him on the shoulder and said, "Yes, this is our portable house . . . We call it a tent, but I like your name better."

He didn't have time to be embarrassed, he was too interested. Anna, Aaron and the rest of the family came over to be next to Father. Little Jacob voiced what everyone including Father was wishing: "Can we go inside?"

I nodded, "Yes," and little Jacob was the first one in. Right behind him were his brothers and sisters. Even Papa Jacob got in the act as his kids waved and asked him—in German—to come see. They all edged their way to the back of our tent, and Jacob crawled in on his hands and knees. He couldn't stand up so he just kneeled on top of all the little Amish footprints on the floor. He looked around and looked up at the sky through our netted roof, and smiled something in German to his kids. More than satisfied with their tour, they all followed their crawling dad out the door and chattered excitedly in German, as we got out our sleeping pads and nighttime gear.

Every so often, before he said something to me or answered one of my questions, Jacob would speak quietly to Anna or Aaron in whispered German, as if asking for a translation. Then he would turn to me with his question or answer.

"What time do you folks rise in the morning?" he asked.

"Oh, usually sometime before dawn. We try to get on the road by first light."

"That is when we rise also. We must get an early start on our work. It looks like your children are ready to go to sleep. I think it best we let you finish your evenin' chores and get them to bed, but I would like to talk with you more in the morning, if it be okay with you."

"And I would like to visit with you some more tomorrow as well. I just don't want us to get in your way."

"John, please do not be worried about us. We will go on about our work. We will get up at our normal time, and you, you please get up at your normal time. Are you sure you do not need a lantern or some light? Aaron can fetch you one of our kerosene lanterns."

"Oh no, that's alright, we have a lantern we carry. We'll use it to light our dinner by."

"Oh, have your children not eaten their supper yet?" Anna asked with a worried look on her face. "They must be very hungry, and all I offered was peanuts. I'm sorry. If I knowed you had not had supper, I would have fixed somethin'."

"That's okay, don't worry," insisted Lynn. "We're going to have some sandwiches. We have lots of food in our bags, and if we don't eat it tonight, it will go bad."

"If you say . . . I still wish I knowed you had not eaten. You must be starved. Jacob, let's let them be now and have their dinner." Anna was already gathering her brood back over to the gate. "We will see you in the morning. Abraham? . . . Elijah?" Anna's English words speeded up and soon transformed into her German dialect I couldn't understand. She seemed to be asking them something.

"The boys have tied up the horses that usual run in the corn fields at night. Please do not be worried about them tonight. We will see you in the morning." Jacob herded his kids through the gate and said good night for his whole family. Our kids had been pretty shy and silent since we first met Aaron over two hours ago, but as soon as Jacob's family disappeared around the barn, they all started talking at once.

"I can't believe we are here! This place is like going back in a time machine," Jimmy exclaimed.

"Yeah, I know, it's like we are in 1886, not 1986," said Heather.

"You mean, 1786 is more like it," giggled Ethan.

"The girls are so cute in their aprons and bonnets." Joy was next to get a chance to speak. "And the guys with those straw hats and dropseat britches . . . and their bare feet . . . I just can't believe they all walk around barefoot. I know my hay at home scratches me. I can't imagine walking all over the farm with no shoes on."

"Yeah, even Papa Jacob was barefoot. The only one wearing shoes was Mother Anna," added Heather.

Lynn interrupted with a little mothering of her own. "Why doesn't everyone get out the food from their panniers. I think we have enough stuff for a late peanut butter and jelly dinner. You guys haven't eaten since lunch and we should really eat something before going to bed. John and I will spread out our tarp and we can talk about the Amish while we eat."

Carl, who looked exhausted from his two flat tires and derailleur difficulties earlier in the day, raised his hand. "You guys, I'm really tired. Is it okay if I skip dinner and hit the sack? I'm not really hungry, and I'll get you the food out of my panniers before I crash."

"Are you sure you wouldn't like something to eat?" Lynn asked.

"Naw, I had some peanuts. I'm okay."

"Okay, good night, Carl," said Lynn, as she walked over and gave him a hug.

"Good night, Carl," echoed the rest of the kids.

We spread out our orange plastic tarp, lit our lantern and greased up with insect repellant before we ate our PB&J in the Amish corn field. We talked for over an hour about bonnets and britches, strange languages and shyness.

"Well, you guys were pretty shy too," I suggested.

"Yeah, I guess we kinda were," said Ethan. "I hope we get a chance to talk with the kids tomorrow."

"John, it looked like you and Jacob got to be pretty good friends," smiled Joy. "I also noticed how Aaron was always standing next to you guys. He looked like he kept wanting to say something. He did get to talk a couple of times. But really, it looked like you and Jacob liked each other real fast."

"Did you really notice that, Joy, because I sure felt it. After he looked me in the eye and we *finally* shook hands, I felt a special closeness with him. I don't know if it's fair to say in such a short time, but I think he's a very special man."

"What do you guys think of Anna, the mom?" Lynn asked.

"Oh, I think she's so pretty." Joy jumped right in with her answer. "She doesn't wear any make-up or anything and her cheeks are so rosy red. She has a beautiful smile."

"Yeah." Heather's answer was next. "And she's had fourteen children! She's so patient and kind with everyone. It looks like the older girls help her out a lot, but still, fourteen children . . . . "

"Well, do you guys think you could live here?" I asked the big question.

"Whoa . . . I don't know . . ." Jimmy wondered. "They look really happy and everything, but man, they don't have electricity or cars or anything. There wasn't even any chrome on their buggy."

"The only thing I ever knew about the Amish was from Harrison Ford in *Witness*," said Joy. "Those were Amish people in that movie, but they seemed to be fancier Amish. I don't know if I could live here, but I sure would like to spend some more time here tomorrow. I'd really like to see more of what their lives are like."

"Me too, John," said Heather. "Do you think we can stay here for awhile tomorrow?"

Lynn seconded the motion with a hopeful glance.

"Well, I hope so." I answered. "It seems like they have lots of work to do, but as long as we don't get in their way and Jacob says it's okay to stick around, we'll stay as long as we can. I think, though, we'd better get to bed now. Their day starts as early as ours, so it will be an early rising again tomorrow."

Jimmy and Ethan helped me fold up the ground cloth, while the girls arranged the food back into the food bags. I moved our lantern from the tarp up onto the fencepost holding our water bag, and everyone gathered in a circle around it to brush their teeth.

It was almost eleven o'clock, and all of us were tired, but we kept talking about our hosts as we fought tooth decay.

"You know what?" Ethan mumbled through his mouth filled with foam and toothbrush. "I wonder if the Amish brush their teeth?"

Jimmy immediately shoved his friend with his shoulder. A white stream of foam dribbled down his chin as he mumbled himself, "Yeah, Eeth, I bet they use Crest."

Still Ethan continued, "No, man, I *really* wonder if they brush or not. Brushing teeth is a hassle and if they don't, then maybe I could get into being Amish."

"Here, Eeth, since you're not Amish . . . yet, I think its time to rinse." Jimmy handed him the water bottle we were sharing, and with that the toothbrushing topic ended.

"Hey John?"

"Yes, Joy."

"Thanks a lot."

"You're welcome, but what for?"

"For finding us this place to stay with the Amish and all. I never thought we would ever be able to do anything like this, so thanks."

"Yeah, John, thanks." Jimmy was serious this time, and Heather and Ethan thanked me too.

"Well, you guys, thanks for comin' . . . Sleep tight and we'll see you in the morning," I answered as Lynn grabbed my hand in one hand and my toothbrush in the other.

"Yeah, thanks, Papa John," she whispered in my ear as we climbed into our "portable house." We laid down on our backs and watched the Tennessee stars twinkling through the roof of our tent. We fell asleep holding hands, stargazing and listening to Joy and Heather as they talked about all they had seen at Jacob's and Anna's that evening and all they hoped to see in the morning. Those two never quit.

The high-pitched electronic alarm of my watch awakened me at 5 o'clock the next morning, and I half-expected to wake up back in the nineteenth century. I stretched my arms as far as I could within the confines of our tent, rubbed my eyes and slid into my shorts that were hiding somewhere near my feet. Lynn, as usual, was still sleeping as I unzipped the tent and poked my head out the door. I had grown used to surrendering to my alarm before dawn every morning, and my private quiet time stretching outside the tent and greeting the sky was one of my favorite daily rituals. That morning, though, when I stuck my ugly head out our door, I found that, for the first time in our trip, someone had risen before me. I also discovered that my visions of buggies and straw hats hadn't been just a dream.

Standing in front of the gate, just ten yards from our portable home, were three angels in bonnets and aprons. The corn field and barnyard were enveloped in the haze of dawn, and I rubbed my eyes once more just to make sure I wasn't hallucinating. Rebecca was on the left, smiling quietly and holding her apron up at the corners, cradling something I couldn't see. On the right stood her next youngest sister, Anna, smiling also and holding a liquid-filled canning jar tight to her chest. In the middle, squeezed in between her two sisters, stood giggling little Ruth, and she was hugging what looked like a loaf of bread tightly to her chest. She cradled her gift as if she was holding a little baby. I shook my head again and blinked my eyes — had I gone to heaven? — and all three of the girls giggled at my tall form dressed in no shirt and skin tight shorts as I slid out of the tent and stood up.

"Well, if you aren't the three most beautiful young ladies I ever laid eyes on . . . I'm sorry I'm probably the ugliest man you ever laid eyes on . . . Good morning, girls." I smiled and stretched as I greeted the three maidens.

"Good mornin'," said Rebecca shyly. It looked like she was the designated spokeswoman. "Mother thought . . . Mother thought . . . you might like some breakfast . . . . " She seemed to have already practiced her speech, but she still had trouble getting the sentences out as fast as she would have liked. These were the first words I had heard from any of the girls, and I was glad it was taking her so long. Her sisters were nudging her to keep talking. "I have some tomatoes from our garden . . . and um . . . Anna has some milk . . . and . . . and Ruth, she-has-a-loaf-of-bread-Mama-just-baked-yesterday." I don't think little Rebecca took a breath the whole time she talked, and she said her last sentence as if it were one word. After catching her breath, she smiled proudly at her two sisters, and I smiled back at her. Talking to my ugly form early in the morning was a difficult task even for Lynn, and Rebecca had done a courageous job.

"Why, thank you, Rebecca . . . And thank you, Anna and Ruth. Did you get up this early just to bring us breakfast?"

Rebecca hesitated. I think she thought she was finished talking. " . . . Uh . . . oh no, we always gets up early. Papa be getting ready to do the milkin' soon. Says you be welcome to come watch if it be no trouble." She breathed much easier this time.

The girls slowly walked closer to me and handed me their breakfast offerings. Just as Ruth handed me the bread, we were interrupted by Abraham and Elijah walking one of the horses through the barnyard, "Hey girls, Mama says it's time to feed the chickens now, eh. Better you be a hurryin'."

The three of them wheeled around and ran barefooted back towards the house. "Thanks again, girls," I yelled after them, but they didn't even turn around.

Abraham and Elijah paused and waved at me. "Hey guys, you got a minute?" I said, motioning over to them. They looked like they wanted to talk, and they hitched the horse to the fence and came through the gate. "Good morning, guys. Let's see . . . I'm sorry, but I don't remember your names."

"I'm Abraham."

"And I'm Elijah."

Elijah was definitely the younger one. His face was still round and soft, while his brother's was a bit ruddy and had signs of hair. Abraham's muscles had started to show some definition, and although Elijah was strong too from all the farm work, his face and arms still showed a child's softness. The two boys must have been up for some time already because they were already sweating. I noticed them checking out our lantern on the fence post, so I asked them if they wanted to see how our Coleman stove worked.

"Sure, we would very much like that," Abraham said.

As I put on my shirt and got the stove from my pannier, I started in on some of the hundreds of questions swirling around in my head: "Do you guys like working on the farm?" I began.

"Oh yes, I like working on the farm very much," answered Abraham. "I could not wait until I finished school so that I can work on the farm all the time."

"And I have only one more year at school and then I work on the farm all the time like my brothers and Father," Elijah said proudly.

I got out the stove and explained how I pumped and lit it. The boys watched quietly and then continued telling me about school and the farm. "When we turn 14, we work on the farm den," smiled Elijah. From the giant smile on his face, it looked like Elijah couldn't wait to leave school.

"And sometimes, when the farm work it need to be done, we boys we stay home from school and help with the planting or harvesting," Abraham continued.

The stove lit and I began boiling the water. Aaron soon appeared around the windmill.

"Abraham . . . Eli . . . you best be getting that horse pastured now. We be milkin' soon." The boys thanked me and were off following Aaron's orders.

Aaron was definitely the older brother, and from the way I figured it, he was soon to be the next to leave the family farm and begin his own. That morning he wasn't barefoot; he was wearing black high-top shoes, the same kind I used to be so ashamed of when I was five. Mine were brown and I had to wear them for my flat feet.

"I be off to work early this mornin' and I just wanted to visit with you before I had to be going." Aaron leaned on the fence as he talked. "Did you sleep well last night?"

"Oh yeah, Aaron, we slept great. In fact the kids and my wife are still asleep. I told them I would wake them up in time to see you milking this morning. Is that okay?"

"Well, sure. My father be glad to show you our milking barn."

"This sure is a beautiful place you have here. It's one of the most beautiful places we've seen." I looked out across the rolling fields to where they had been haying last night. "I'm used to staring out across the ocean, but I sure can see how someone could get attached to this."

"I never see the ocean and I do not think I ever will," Aaron said as he too gazed out over his home. "I have been to the city when our family takes the bus to visit our relatives in Ohio, but I never cared for it too much. I just likes to look out over the land that we plow and plant. In wintertime, those fields be covered white with snow and, in the fall, they be a beautiful sight all covered with orange and yellow. I like seeing the way the land changes each season. It gives me good feeling watching the fields grow from the work of our hands."

"So you wouldn't ever want to leave here?" I asked.

"I be very happy here. I hope to have my own farm someday soon. Sometimes, our people be leavin' to start new communities and we helps them move. We packs up everything in our wagons and moves their things . . . Maybe someday that might be me moving somewhere else, but I sure like this place."

"Hey John, is it time to get up yet?" We were interrupted by one of my troops. "Have they started milking yet?" Heather's voice was groggy, but concerned.

"Excuse me a second, Aaron; I better get the kids up. Hey Heather, is that you?" I laughed as I stood over the girls' tent. "Unbelievable!!! One of my sleeping beauties is up, even before I had to shake the tent."

"Well, we just didn't want to miss the Amish, John. Joy's up too. We've just been lying around waiting for you to tell us to get up," Heather continued.

"Yeah John, we've been up too," Carl's voice rose from the boys' dome. "Even Ethan's halfway awake. I've been up for a long time. I've been listening to you talk."

Soon Lynn's drowsy head was peeking out of our tent and everyone was up. They all staggered over to the water bag and splashed their crusty faces. Aaron watched the procession and said good morning to everyone.

"Hey John, should we start taking our tents and everything down?" Carl asked.

"No, let's just wait. Just get yourself dressed and then I think we're going to go watch the milking. I'll meet you guys out in front of the barn, okay." I turned off the water bubbling on the stove and told Lynn we had some gifts for our breakfast.

"Why don't we wait to have breakfast until after we see the milking?" Lynn suggested.

"Okay, I'll meet you over in front of the barn."

While we waited for everyone, Aaron kept talking. A lot of dreams and feelings had fermented inside him for a long time, and he seemed to enjoy his opportunity to share them with me. I was all ears, but he often stopped in the middle of one of his descriptions to ask about where I lived. He enjoyed driving a buggy and although he admitted his enjoyment of an occasional faster-than-necessary buggy run to the neighbors, he assured me he had no interest in cars. In fact, he told me his grandfather had been killed by a hit and run automobile driver while driving his buggy home one evening in Ohio. Aaron loved his land and his family and the lifestyle of his community, and, as I listened to him, I couldn't help worrying if we had invaded his home wrongly. When he asked me questions, I intentionally tried to keep my stories brief, because the last thing I wanted to do was bring my disease of progress to his simple and seemingly satisfying way of life.

"How come you're wearing shoes today?" I asked.

"Oh, I'm helping some neighbors raise a barn, so I must wear them. In fact, I must be making soon, so I must say good-bye early." The boys had hitched up the buggy and one of the girls came out of the house and ran up to Aaron with his lunch.

"Good bye, Aaron," she waved.

"Good bye, Aaron," waved his mother as she leaned out the front door. "Good morning, John, ' sleep well?"

"Yes, ma'am, we slept great." I waved to Anna as she held the door open. "Thanks for the milk and bread and tomatoes."

"You be surely welcome. I be heating water on the stove while you be watching the milking. After morning chores are done, you be welcome to join us for breakfast on the porch." Anna was wiping her hands on her apron as she talked. "I would invite yous to eat with us at table, but it would be quite a crowd. I think you and Lynn and your younguns be more comfortable on the porch."

"Thank you. We can eat out in the corn field, if that makes it easier," I said.

"Oh no. Don't you be eating out there now. The porch is fine. You might find yourselves a patch of shade up there. You go watch the milkin' now and then we see you on the porch." Anna had breakfast all worked out and I didn't argue.

Aaron was ready to go, but he waited until his mom was through with me. He reached down from the wagon and shook my hand.

"John . . . I sure be glad you stopped by here last night. I enjoyed talking to you very much . . . 'specially this morning. I wish we have more time to visit, but I must go to work now. . . ." Aaron never let go of my hand as he spoke. "Maybe, someday . . . you come back by this way again. By that time, I have my own farm."

"I would like that, Aaron. I do hope we make it back here someday. Thank you for being so much help to us. We'll never forget you." I squeezed his hand and then we both let go. He straightened his hat, grabbed the reigns and gave the horse a click-click from his mouth. The horse immediately was in motion. Aaron leaned out the side, smiling and waving back at us as he headed off to work.

"Good mornin', John." Jacob came up behind me as I waved to Aaron. "I hear you slept well. Would you care to come watch us do the mornin' milking?"

"Good morning, Jacob. We sure would. The kids are on their way."

The milking barn was just to the side of the main barn, and Jacob led the kids and me over to where their six cows were doing their daily duty. Flies were everywhere, and the non-dairy products that flowed from the cows' rear ends were much in evidence. Jacob and his kids barefooted their way comfortably through puddles of urine and manure, and if you were a fly in this part of Tennessee, that milking shed seemed like the place to be. The cows whipped their tails, swatting the insects; we flapped our hands and shook our heads; Jacob, Elizabeth, Abraham, Elijah, Rebecca and Anna rolled up their sleeves, hiked up their britches and dresses and used their hands to grab the cows' udders. They acted as if there were no flies. They just sat down on their wooden stools and started milking.

Jacob leaned over his shoulder as we watched. "We do this once every morning and once every evening. Please ask questions if you would like."

"Does everyone milk?" Lynn asked.

"It take very strong hand to milk a cow. We teach the children how to milk when they are very young, but we don't let them really milk until they can be helpful." As Jacob answered, his kids smiled to each other. "There is much to be done on the farm and we do not have much time for play. Once we finish one ting, we must move on to the next ting." Jacob milked and talked over his shoulder at the same time. What he was doing looked about as easy to me as riding a bicycle backwards, but his cow never missed a shot into his pale. "It be the same way with the other chores. Anna teach all the girls to sew, but they not be allowed to do real sewing work until they can be helpful."

Jacob was the first to finish milking. He spanked his cow on the behind and stood up. Behind me, on top of a barrel, I noticed a pink blob. Elizabeth was the next to get up, and, as she carried her full pale over to the milk can, she reached behind me and grabbed the pink lump. She quickly plucked it into her mouth, and, as she walked away, I realized that what I thought had to be some salve or liniment was actually just what it looked like — it was bubble gum. Our jaws all dropped at our realization that the Amish chewed gum. Elizabeth walked away and smiled over her shoulder when she saw the look of surprise on our faces. She looked like she was tempted to blow a bubble and have us all faint, but instead, she headed into the house.

"They never said anything about that in *Witness*," whispered Joy. "I didn't think the Amish did things like chew gum!"

Once finished with the milking, it was time for breakfast. Lynn and the kids went back to the food sacks to bring our food, and Jacob's kids ran into the house to get ready for theirs. Jacob and I had some time to visit while breakfast was getting ready.

"Jacob, I don't know how you do it . . . You have a wonderful family, but I can't imagine all the work you must have to do."

"John, we Amish are very used to having large families and a farm to take care of. My father and his father and his father before him, they be Amish people. My family have been Amish as far back as I knows. We are what be called Old Order Schwartzentruber Amish.

"My children, they be very helpful, but sometimes I get headaches from my large family. I be worryin' about them many times." Jacob lifted his hat and rubbed his wrinkled forehead. "Sometime . . . it be great burden to tink about how my children will carry on. Right now my oldest daughter, Verna, she be the one married to Danny, the man you met last night. I be helpin' her and her husband to raise their barn and start their family and farm, and I tinks they do well, but sometimes, when I tinks of all my children and their lives ahead of them I get worried. I love farming, but it be very hard business. Now I must do more than just farm. I must do some carpentry to help our family to survive . . . .

"Much has changed since I be a younger man. More and more outside people be moving around these parts all the time, and it make it hard on our way of life. I hope my children can keep these ways of ours . . . I trust in our beliefs, but sometimes . . . oh sometimes . . . my head just get to be pounding at the end of the day when everyone else they be asleep. I just lay awakes and not be able to go to sleep. Soon, it be morning again and I goes back to the fields and my carpentry . . . There not be much time for worryin'."

Jacob's life seemed simple, but he showed me that didn't mean easy. The more he spoke to me, the more admiration I felt for him. I looked at him and his wife and family, and his beliefs manifested themselves in more than just his dress and appearance. His faith showed in everything he did, including his bald and wrinkled forehead. As I visited with him that morning before breakfast, I wondered what faith I had and if it showed anywhere in my life.

"Papa, it's time for breakfast." Little Anna came running over and tugged on her father's pants.

"Thank you, Anna. We be right along." Jacob then walked me up onto the porch.

Lynn and the kids had set up our breakfast things on the porch, and the Amish girls had set a plastic tea cup for each of us on the ledge. Jimmy informed me that Anna was making us a pot of coffee to go with our breakfast. Jacob and I walked up onto the porch just as Lynn, Joy and Heather came walking out of the house.

"We gave them that jar of honey those men gave us the other day." Lynn said.

"Guess what, you guys," Heather whispered. "They are eating cornflakes."

"Man, I wish we had some cornflakes," said Carl. "I'm getting tired of oatmeal."

"Do you have everything you need?" Anna poked her head out the door.

"Yes, thank you very much," answered Lynn. Anna smiled as she looked at the group sitting on her porch steps. She motioned Ruth and Elizabeth out with a tray, adding fresh butter, more tomatoes, more bread and more milk to our morning feast. She checked on us one more time before returning to her family who sat packed around the large, wooden table in the kitchen.

"I can't believe it." Heather tried to talk as softly as she could. "Anna cooks for everyone three times a day. And you know what? . . . They don't even use electricity or gas. They have a wood burning stove."

"I can't believe they eat cornflakes," said Carl.

"Or chew bubble gum," laughed Ethan.

"I know, man," agreed Jimmy. "Could you believe it when she picked up that piece of gum?"

"Hey everyone," said Lynn. "When we gave Anna the honey, she told me about one of their favorite things for breakfast. They take a thick slice of tomato, put in on a piece of buttered bread, and then cover it with honey. Let's try it."

"Well, if it's half as good as this coffee, it will be delicious," exclaimed Carl.

"I think it's the milk that makes the coffee taste so good," said Joy. "Could someone please pass me the tomatoes and some honey?"

"Hey, when I read the *Little House on The Prairie* books, they did that too," said Heather. "They put tomato and honey on big slices of bread just like Jacob's and Anna's family."

We ate our own tomato and honey sandwiches along with oatmeal and coffee. In the middle of one of her bites, Joy, who was leaning against the side of the house underneath the window, looked over her shoulder and saw a whole window full of little Amish faces watching her and all of us eat. Joy waved and they all disappeared giggling. When breakfast was done, my bicycling senators called for a special vote and agreed unanimously that the food was the best they had ever tasted — even better than pizza.

Our morning with Jacob and Anna and their family went by much too quickly. We traded as much culture in those few hours as we could. Jacob's and Anna's kids showed us the chickens and the sheep, and then our kids showed them how to take down a tent. Papa Jacob was amazed at our velcro and collapsible tent poles.

"Excuse me, but could you please show me how dem tings work again?" he asked, as he got down on his knees on our tarp. I handed him one of the telescoping aluminum poles, and everyone gathered around him in a silent circle as he snapped it into its full eight foot length and then collapsed it into its smaller pieces. He did it a couple times, the only sound in the corn field being his mumbling to himself in whispered German. He did the same with our velcro fasteners. I wondered how he envisioned he could use our space age portable house technology on his farm. He finally handed the poles back to me and laid our tent down on the ground. He got up, rubbing his beard and shaking his head. He nodded a smile at me and I nodded back. We finished stowing our gear and then we split up into smaller groups.

Lynn helped Anna with the dishes, while the kids visited on the fence. I followed Jacob and his older boys as they did some chores around the barn. The girls showed Joy and Heather their kittens and the boys showed Jimmy, Carl and Ethan their rope swing. Walking around with Jacob and the boys, I saw they had lots to do, and in the back of my mind I realized we had some miles of our own to work on that day. I looked back across the field at my kids swinging and visiting, and Jacob did the same.

Jacob had to be going to help his daughter and Danny with their barn, and I didn't want to slow him in his chores. I excused myself from Jacob and the boys to walk over and make my announcement that it was time to leave, and it proved as unpopular with Jacob's kids as it did with mine.

"Sorry you guys, but we really need to be going." I hurt as I said it, because I would have loved to stay longer and perhaps help with some of the work around the farm. Looking back at Jacob as I said it, I thought I noticed a bit of sadness in his eyes too. I think he would have enjoyed helping me set up the portable house for one more night.

"You are welcome to stay another day," insisted Anna. Her voice hinted at mixed emotions, as she looked over at little Jacob, who had momentarily traded his straw hat for Heather's helmet and gloves.

I remembered Jacob's headaches and how he had talked to me about the difference between work and play, so I had to turn down her offer. "I really wish we could stay, but I think we should be going. Thanks anyway."

"Well, you'll just have to wait a few more minutes," barked a very disappointed and disapproving Lynn. "Anna said she would show me some of their quiltwork." Knowing Lynn's love for quilts, I didn't argue. "It won't take long." I had heard those words before, and, as Lynn disappeared into the house with Anna and Elizabeth, I didn't rush to put my gloves and helmet on.

Jacob needed to be going, but he waited to say good bye to us. He put his shoes on and gathered his tool belt into his buggy. Lynn and the girls returned with Anna, and Lynn wore the telltale smile that meant our checkbook was about to receive a dent, but I didn't mind at all, because quilting was one of Anna's ways to reduce Jacob's headaches. I probably would have bought two.

Boy, did I feel like Captain Bligh as I told the kids to mount their bicycles and get ready to leave. Before we left, Jacob shyly asked me a favor.

"John, would you please take our address and write us a letter sometime? I would like very much for my family to hear from our friends again. If it would not be a bother to you, would you write us a letter from your home sometime?"

I got out my address book and wrote down his address. We shook hands firmly — and quickly this time. My stomach and heart ached at having to leave, and the waving smiles of Jacob, Anna, Elizabeth, Abraham, Elijah, Rebecca, little Anna, little Jacob, Ruth, Mary, and Noah didn't help much either. We rolled ever so slowly down the driveway we'd just entered the night before. It was probably the most difficult stretch of road we ever pedaled.

The kids were silent for the next ten miles. Their heads hung low, and if their hearts felt as heavy as mine, I understood their silence. We pulled into a mini-market for a bathroom and water stop, and I decided that maybe some donuts might lighten up the mood.

"Hey John, I sure wish we could have stayed longer." Joy spoke for everyone gathered around the wood table out back of the store. "We know why you thought it was best for us to leave, but we sure wish there was some way we could have spent another day."

"Yeah, the kids were just starting to open up," said Carl. I passed out the donuts and juice, and the discussion began.

"Especially little Jacob," smiled Heather. "You should have seen him trying on my helmet and gloves. He took out all the velcro pads and then rearranged them in different patterns. He's not shy at all."

"And while you were talking with Papa Jacob, the girls took me out to see the sheep and the chickens," said an excited Joy. "They even showed us where the baby kitties hide under the house."

"I still can't believe they chew bubble gum," said Ethan shaking his head.

He then took a swig of orange juice, and half of it dribbled down his chin onto his shirt. "Shoot, this was a clean shirt."

"Are you kidding, Ethan?" laughed Jimmy. "You don't have any clean shirts!

"Did you guys hear Lynn when she saw Mary chewing gum out by the chicken pen?"

"No, Jimmy, I didn't," I said. "What did you say, dear?"

"Well, I just saw her chewing her gum and I said, 'Gum before breakfast???' She smiled up at me and just kept on chomping."

"You guys missed it by not coming into the house to see the quilts," continued Heather. "Anna told us that when an Amish girl moves out of the house to get married, she gets three quilts. And she showed us how they make the quilting patterns from ordinary stuff in their house; it was really neat! They trace around cups and saucers and kitchen tools and come up with these beautiful patterns."

"Well . . . we couldn't see everything," sighed Carl. "There were so many of them. The reason we couldn't see the quilts was because we were out playing on the swing and talking with little Jacob."

"When Anna took us inside . . . We saw this sock on the stairs, stuffed with straw and tied with yarn. Anna told us that Old Order Amish don't have toys, but that she still couldn't stop the girls from making simple dolls."

"Well, Joy, we found out that only men who have been baptized wear beards," said Jimmy, not wanting his discoveries to be left out. "John asked Father Jacob when Amish get baptized, and he said sometime when they're around eighteen."

"Then why doesn't Aaron have a beard?" asked Joy.

"I was getting to that," Jimmy continued. "That's the funny part. Jacob said Aaron has been baptized, and the reason Aaron doesn't have a beard is because he has trouble 'raisin' hair.'"

"Kinda like you, huh James?" I couldn't resist my chance to poke a little fun at my friend. Ever since Maryland, Jimmy had been taking a daily count of the peach fuzz beginning to sprout on his chin and under his arms.

"C'mon John, I'm only thirteen and three quarters," Jimmy moaned. "Give me a break."

" . . . You know . . . " Ethan thought for a moment, " . . . I wonder if their whole family will stay Amish . . . I mean, little Jacob looked like he was ready to hop on one of our bikes and join us."

"Yeah," said Joy, "I'd be worried to take my kids into town like they do for shopping . . . And I would be especially afraid to take them on the bus all the way to Ohio like they do when they go visit their relatives. When you laid out our map of the United States in the corn field this morning and showed Jacob and the kids our route and our home and the ocean and everything, he got this strange look on his face. I wonder if it gets harder to stay Amish after they see the outside world . . . ."

"Didn't you ask Jacob about running away, John?" asked Carl.

"Yeah, I did, and he said that there are runaways, sometimes. Abraham told me that his best friend ran away and now lives in Atlanta. He said that ever since he knew him, his friend was always restless, and that he couldn't handle school and everything. He said that his friend never really settled into the rules of the community."

"It's got to be tough," said Jimmy.

"I also asked Jacob if anyone ever converts to their way of life."

"What do you mean by convert?" asked Joy.

"I mean, does anyone like us ever try to join and become Amish," I answered.

"Oh, I get it. What did Jacob say?"

"Well, he said that some people have tried to convert, but that they usually don't stay with it. He said that unless you are born Amish, you're too old." My answer quieted everyone. I remembered how I had responded the same way when Jacob had given me that answer. Jacob's wisdom was as simple and hard as his work.

After everyone contemplated Jacob's words for a while, Jimmy changed the subject. "Well, if we have to get on down the road, let's do it. I think I can smell Memphis out there somewhere."

"Hey John," chirped Heather. "Will you make sure you give us extra journal time the next couple days? Stick and I have got a lot to write about yesterday and this morning. We're still writing about when we first rolled into Jacob and Anna's driveway last night. It's going to take a lot of pages to write down everything."

"Okay, I'll try to give us an extra fifteen minutes or so at meal time for journals . . . Is that okay with you two?"

"Thanks, John," they both answered, and soon we were back on our bikes and on the road towards Memphis.

When Ya Gotta Go, Ya Gotta Go

"Excuse me, but is Pastor Morris at home?"

"Why I'm Pastor Morris, may I help you?" Pastor Morris was a tall and slender man. His brick house stood right next to the First Baptist Church in Olivehill, Tennessee. The people up at the little market had said his was the closest church, and being that it was already past 6 PM, I decided to walk down and see if the Baptists had any place for us to sleep. By then, we had stayed in Methodist, Episcopal and Amish churches, and since we were in the "Bible Belt", I figured it was time to give the Baptists equal time.

"Well, son, the Baptist church is organized as a democracy with a pastor and a board of deacons." I had introduced myself and our trip and asked Pastor Morris if we could stay in his church and use the bathrooms. Heather was dancing up the hill, and although everyone was more than used to using the bushes, now that we were in town I asked everyone to wait until I found a more private place to relieve themselves.

Pastor Morris continued: "I realize y'all have spent some time in other churches, but I must give ya a lesson in our ways. First of all, the deacons of our Baptist congregation have made it policy not to let strangers use the church facilities for overnight shelter, and second of all, I can't even let y'all use the bathrooms, unless I got me a majority of the deacons' approval. All our decisions must be taken to a vote; I may be the pastor, but I'm just another vote when it comes to decisions like the use of our facilities. What subject did ya say ya taught?"

"Social studies, sir."

"Well then ya ought to know that democracy isn't always the fastest way to make a decision, but it sure is the best."

I had to bite my tongue as I envisioned Heather dancing and humming a little faith of her own — that John would find her a bathroom. I understood the democracy thing and all, but making my kids wet their pants or someone else's bushes seemed pushing things a bit far. But, from the look on the pastor's face, he didn't seem to be joking.

"Well, pastor, we have stayed in lots of churches and schools and my kids have very good manners. If you would have a patch of grass where we could pitch our tents, we'd really appreciate it. And if you could possibly call some of your deacons to see if we could use your bathrooms, I promise you that we'll keep them clean. I know it's a bother, but it's getting late and I don't really want to make the kids ride to the next town in the dark."

"Well, let me give some folks a call. If you can give me twenty minutes or so, I'll have an answer for y'all." I knew that I could, but I wasn't so sure about my kids. Still, I bit my tongue, thanked Pastor Morris politely, and he disappeared into his house. I headed back up the hill to my anxious family who were confidently waiting on top of their bicycles, ready to follow me to our new church home away from home. Little did they know they were about to get a lesson in church civics.

As I tried to explain to them why they had to hold their bladders for twenty more minutes, I realized in the back of my mind that this might have been the reason that old Roger Williams had encouraged our founding fathers to keep matters of church and state separate. I could also see the kids demonstrating that when you gotta go, ya gotta go, so I decided to share some of our own popular democracy with the Olive Hill Baptists.

"Tell you what, you guys. Let's quietly roll our bikes down the hill to Pastor Morris' place and wait on the lawn. I think once he sees you guys demonstrating your need, he'll exercise some executive privilege." The kids danced and bit their lips as they rolled their bikes down to the church. I don't know if Pastor Morris had time to get hold of all his deacons or not, but as soon as he put his head out the screen door and laid eyes on the kids, his whole tone and posture changed. He walked outside, grabbed the keys from his pocket and opened the door to the church school. Shaking his head in disgust with himself, he escorted the kids to the bathrooms. He checked on the toilet paper supply and then surveyed his front yard to find the nicest places for us to set up our tents.

"Hello, Lynn, you must be John's wife. I'm John Morris, and I apologize for making y'all wait so long. I'm sorry I can't let y'all use the church, but that's out of my hands. I do think over here on this side of the house might be the most comfortable place for y'all to set up your tents. It's shady and the least hot place in the yard. Also, I think y'all might find the ground a little flatter and softer over here. It should make it easier for y'all to stake down your tents."

Like many other doubting Thomases along our road who had first balked at the mention of twelve and thirteen-year-old kids from California visiting them, I think Pastor Morris' heart was changed by his first sight of the kids. After he first laid eyes on my crew, giant waves of warmth burst from the tall pastor. The kids used the bathroom, set up camp and walked down with me to Indian Creek to bathe and do laundry. When we returned, we found Pastor Morris stirring our dinner over our cookstove while Lynn mixed up the punch. After taking a few spoonfuls himself and adjusting the spices, he introduced us to his shy wife and then returned inside his house to give us "a bit of privacy." It wasn't much later that he came back out the screen door to check that everything was alright, and he didn't go back inside for another couple hours. After he said good night to each of the kids, he stayed up to talk with Lynn and me.

He told us how he'd lived in this area almost his whole life, and how our kids and their tents reminded him of his old boy scout and church camp days back in the thirties. All he knew of California was what he saw on television, and it didn't look like the kind of place he would like to visit. He and his wife "didn't travel often anyways", because they had an invalid daughter who had been handicapped since birth. She was over twenty-years-old and most of their last two decades were spent caring for her. She was in bed inside the house.

Pastor Morris talked and talked that night, telling us of his life and asking us questions about ours. His world was as far apart from ours as was Jacob's and Anna's, and the love and dedication I could feel pouring out of his words and recollections had tears welling up in both Lynn's and my eyes. Around eleven o'clock, he looked down at his watch and apologized:

"Is it eleven o'clock already?! Why I'm awful sorry. Y'all must be plum tuckered out from your riding today and all my ramblin' on. Ya should have been in bed a long time ago. Y'all got miles to ride tomorrow and all I have to do is preach my sermon. I sure apologize for keepin' y'all up. I didn't realize it was gettin' so late. I must have got carried away . . . Don't get much chance to visit with folks like y'all too often . . .

"I'll leave that night light on and the door ajar for y'all in the morning. Y'all go head and make all the noise ya need to to get your breakfast fixed and your tents taken down. Noise won't bother us a bit. I was so glad to meet y'all, and my prayers will be with ya." Pastor Morris shook Lynn's hand and then shook mine. He waved good-bye under his porch light before going inside, and Lynn and I crawled into our tent.

"John?"

"Yes, dear . . . ."

"I don't know how to explain it, but I'm getting awfully full."

"Well, don't eat so much."

"No, not food full, *people* full."

"What do you mean?"

"Well, we've met so many wonderful people and we've heard so many of their life stories and everything . . . I don't know how much more my heart can take. Everyone's so different from us and everyone's so different from each other, yet they're all so friendly and caring and . . . I don't know. Just when I get to have some time to start thinking about someone we met, we go and meet someone else. I don't want to get numb to all this kindness, but I'm about to burst with all these people who help us. And tomorrow—"

"Lynn—" I tried to interrupt, but she just kept on.

"Or the next day, I just know we're going to meet someone just as giving as Anna or Pastor Morris. Someone I haven't even dreamed of yet—"

"Good night, Lynn."

"John, don't you understand? Don't you have anything to say?"

"Yes, dear. Good night."

Lynn crossed her arms across her chest in disgust, but I couldn't say anything. She didn't know it but I fell asleep in Tennessee counting friendly faces instead of sheep, and I knew I had a lot of counting to do before I'd be getting any sleep.

"Honey, I got this teacher here from California, and his wife and five of their students are riding their bicycles across America. He wants to know if they can stay down at church." We were in the little convenience store and gas station that marked the turnoff to the small town of Pocahontas, just three miles from the border of Mississippi and one day's ride east of Memphis. The lady at the counter was yelling to her husband in the back room.

Her husband yelled back and slowly came up to the register. "Well, even if I was able to get hold of all the deacons, I couldn't let them in without Pastor's approval." I said to myself, "Uh, oh here comes that ole Baptist democracy again."

"That's right, honey, I forgot," said the lady, looking honestly disappointed. "We just got ourselves a new pastor and he been splittin' his time between here and his home in Mississippi. We got him a house here but he don't use it much. Why don't y'all ride on down there and see if he's home. Just go on down this road a couple blocks and you'll see the church on yer right. The house just this side of the church is the pastor's house. I'll watch y'all's groceries here and keep them cold while my husband tries to get hold of the other deacons."

We rode down the little lane that was the main street of Pocahontas, and it looked as if the whole town had seen better days. Broken windows and broken cars lined the streets. I walked up onto the porch of the pastor's house and even his front door glass was broken. A pile of mail lay in the broken pieces of glass. Pocahontas was the first town that looked the way I'd imagined all back roads southern towns to look, and the ghosts I thought I'd said good bye to after weeks of southern kindness started stirring in my mind again. I was almost relieved that the pastor wasn't home, because then we'd have to leave town, and as we headed back up the street to the market, I almost didn't even stop.

"Well darn it, honey, if ya can't get a hold of Pastor and if all the deacons ya got a hold of say it's okay for them to use the bathrooms, then I say let 'em use the bathrooms. They's just kids. Heck, I say let 'em use the refrigerator and the kitchen too. If Jesus was pastor, he'd surely let them use whatever they needed. Look at those kids, two of 'em is even girls! Who's got the keys, you or Henry?" It sounded like the lady of the house was starting to adjust the family pants.

"Henry does," her husband said meekly.

"Well then, get Henry on the phone and tell him to meet us at church. We're gonna let these people use our bathrooms. Sir — I'm sorry I forgets yer name — ya put those kids and yer wife back on them bicycles o' yers and meet us at the church. Pastor or no pastor, I ain't gonna have y'all ridin' any farther tanight. Least we can do is let you use the toilet and the grass out back. If we can get hold of the pastor before dark, we'll even try and find a way for you to sleep inside. Heaven knows, might be a storm blowin' in tanight."

I reached over to grab our bags of groceries off the counter. "Now don't y'all lay a finger on those. We be bringin' them over in the car. Just give me a chance to close the store, and we'll meet y'all over at the church."

Thank God for mothers. It was probably some mother who inspired the concept of a veto. We rode back down the road and found we had a welcoming committee waiting for us at church. Standing out front was Mr. Henry Hudson, a retired truck driver and a staunch and proud son of Tennessee. He wore a stained golf shirt that barely covered his round stomach, a pair of well-worn, gray plaid double-knit slacks, and hush puppy shoes — just like the kind my dad gets for his birthday. After introducing himself to us before we even dismounted our bikes, it didn't take him long to inform us that he didn't like any of the Kennedys and that he felt that separation of the races was the way God meant things to be. Almost in the same breath though, he told us he couldn't believe that anyone would ever not let us use their facilities, and I shook my head trying to figure him out. My head kept spinning as he unlocked the doors while telling a few very pointed jokes that told us just how he felt about "colored people." My ghosts were up and dancing.

The woman from the market and her husband pulled up while we were inside, and they stayed around long enough to see that we knew where the bathrooms and kitchen were and had found suitable places for our tents. Henry stuck around to join us for dinner, and after over an hour talking with him, I still couldn't figure him out. The kids were tired and dreaming of Memphis, so they gobbled down their food and hit the sack early, leaving Lynn and me to talk with our host. Henry's politics were miles apart from ours, but somehow we managed to steer clear of any debate, as we finished dinner. He offered to help Lynn and me do the dishes, and we spoke of our travels while he talked about his hobby of restoring Civil War houses.

Henry left after dishes and said he would be back to see us in the morning. Lynn and I crawled into our muggy tent, and I took off all my clothes and slid onto my sleeping pad.

"What's the matter, John?" Lynn asked.

"I still don't like this town," I growled. "It's not because of Mr. Henry Hudson either. I think I can handle him even if I don't agree with all his politics and prejudices. At least he wants us to be able to use the church. This stinking heat and humidity is really getting to me tonight, and . . . hear that thunder in the distance? If some thunderstorm blows in here tonight and all our stuff outside gets blown around and sopping wet, I'm gonna be pissed."

"Yeah, but Pastor Morris only let us use his yard and you didn't get ticked off at him."

"Yeah, I know, it's just this town gives me bad vibes. A couple people down the street and back at the market, they look like they thought we were the enemy from Mars or something. I don't know, maybe it's not them . . . I'm just tired and I can't stand this stinking heat and humidity. I'll never get to sleep."

My complaining was soon interrupted by flashlights, footsteps and voices heading our way around the church.

"Hello . . . excuse me . . . are you the bicyclists from Californya?" It was a woman's voice coming from over by our bikes.

"Yes, ma'am, we're the bicyclists from Californya," I mumbled to Lynn, sarcastically imitating the woman's southern accent. "I wonder if she would like to shake the hand of a naked California schoolteacher? I bet she expects something weird to be going on inside here anyway, 'bein' that we'all come from Californya and all' . . . . " I got up, started unzipping the tent and prepared to fulfill our visitors' wildest dreams.

"JOHN, what are you doing?! Put some clothes on!!!" whispered Lynn as loud as she could.

"Just a minute," I said, getting hold of my senses and my shorts.

When I emerged from the tent, I found we had a committee of six church members who had come to check us out. Lynn threw a shirt out of the tent to me while she made herself presentable, and the six of them stared at me while I stared back.

"Excuse me, but I have a big apology to make to y'all." The tall woman with the most suspicious look of the group stepped forward and spoke. "I din't want to come over here tonight. In fact, when I heard a group from California wanted to stay at church, I objected as loud as I could. Ya know, livin' here in Pocahontas and not really travelin' much, all I ever heard about California was what I seen on TV or read in magazines . . . ya know, all yer weird religions and evil habits and things like that. I never had no desire to go to California, and I really din't want any strange Californians in our town, least of all my church . . . didn't want any of our kids dealin' with anybody from out where y'all come from. They almost had to drag me over here tonight, I was so scared of comin', and now I see those little bicycles with all that stuff hanging off them, and hear y'all's kids sleeping in them tents o' yers . . . Lord, forgive me for my callous heart. I hope y'all will forgive me too." She held her chest tight and then reached out both hands to me. As she held on to my hands and squeezed them, Lynn emerged from our tent.

"And this this must be your wife; nice to meet you." She grabbed Lynn's hand and then everyone else started shaking our hands.

"We're all sorry we ain't been more hospitable to y'all. We hear lots of strange things about Californya, and we were afraid to have y'all in town. We got children of our own and . . . well, that don't matter none now. Welcome to Pocahontas and tell your kids we're sorry we weren't more hospitable. We just couldn't go ta bed knowin' we hadn't greeted y'all.

"So please forgive us, and we'll be goin' now and lettin' y'all get yer rest."

Lynn elbowed me, and before they left, I made a confession of my own.

"Well, ma'am, I've got an apology to make to all of you as well. You know, I was raised my whole life along a beach in Southern California, and I never really wanted to have anything to do with folks from the South either. I thought you were the ones who were weird, and when I rode into Pocahontas this evening, I must admit I was scared to stay here. After all the kind people we've met in this part of the country, I should have known better, but I don't know who was more afraid of having us stay in this town, you or me."

While the eight of us stood there baring our souls and shaking hands, up drove the pastor. He apologized for his absence and said he'd unlock the door if the storm blew in as hard as he'd heard the weatherman on his radio predict it would. We all said good-night, and soon Lynn and I were back in our tent shaking our heads up at the sky. A half hour later, the sky did a little shaking of its own as the storm arrived in Pocahontas as advertised. The next morning, when Henry Hudson came to join us for oatmeal, he found our camp deserted and us and all our wind-blown and rain-soaked gear asleep on the linoleum of one of the church classrooms.

"Glad y'all got out o' that storm last night. It blowed pretty good even for 'round here. After we finish our oatmeal, why don't y'all come over and see my house. Used to be a field hospital in the Civil War and thought y'all might like to take a peek."

Henry cleaned his dish, told a few more "colored" jokes, and shook each of the kids' hands good-bye after showing them his house. I rode out of Pocahontas shaking my head.

A Tennessee Homecoming

"Hey Jimmy, slow down!" I yelled, as Jimmy passed me and increased his lead on the climb ahead. The closer we got to Memphis, the faster he rode. He was the first one up that morning in Pocahontas, and if he had his way, there wouldn't have been any breakfast or lunch stops.

"C'mon John, you guys are slow!" he yelled back. I rode up to him and asked him to stop and wait for everyone else.

"Hey James, you hardly even touched your biscuits and gravy back there in Moscow, and it didn't look like you read the sports page . . . Shoot, you even let Carl have the comics first, when you could have had them. Are you sick or something?" I asked.

"I don't know, John, but my stomach is just going crazy. Back in California, I dreamt about riding my bicycle into my hometown and seeing my dad and Gram and Gramps, but I never thought I would be this excited." Jimmy looked like the little kid I had met a couple years ago instead of the young man he was becoming on the road.

"Well, just try to keep in my sight, okay . . . I ain't never been to Memphis before and neither has anyone else in this family, so don't lose us. I need you to show me how to get to that Memphis BBQ place you've been braggin' about since we first met."

"Got it, dude."

I let Jimmy lead once we reached the outskirts of Germantown, an affluent suburb east of Memphis. As we approached the Germantown City Limits sign, small groups of people gathered on their front lawns and began waving. After about three lawns full, we realized they were waving at us.

"Hey, I know those people!" Jimmy yelled, and again he picked up the pace. The rest of the group shifted and did their best to keep up. We hadn't been in any city traffic since back in Asheville, North Carolina, and I was as worried about the kids riding in traffic as I was about them keeping up with Jimmy. I hoped they remembered how careful they needed to ride with all the trucks and stop lights and turning lanes they now encountered. As I followed Jimmy, I looked behind me to see them all sweating in the 100-degree heat, heads down and in perfect single file formation. Back beyond Ethan I saw Lynn wink and give me the thumbs up sign; my worries were in vain, my senators knew how to ride.

Parked under the Welcome to Germantown sign was a wood-paneled station wagon where Jimmy skidded us to a stop. The doors opened and out stepped a silver-haired lady with tears streaming down her suntanned cheeks. She ran over to Jimmy and threw her arms around him.

"That must be Jimmy's grandma," Ethan observed from the back of the pack.

"Well, I hope so," joked Carl.

Out of the other door hopped a young woman with a camera around her neck. She was smiling, shaking her head, and taking pictures. "Well, Two Bits, I

can't believe you did it. Only bike I thought I"d ever see you ridin' in Germantown was your tricycle." She walked over to Jimmy and gave him a hug.

Jimmy introduced us to his grandma and his sister, Tasha. Jimmy's grandma,
"Mrs. Taylor" to us, "Grams" to Jimmy, checked us out again to make sure we
were for real. "I just cain't believe y'all are ridin' in this heat . . . And my word,
ya look so tan and strong. We got a little lemonade and some refreshments waitin'
for y'all up at the house. I'll go up and make sure evrathing's ready."

"Two Bits, ya know the way to the farm from here, now don't ya?"

"Yeah Tash, I know the way." Jimmy's tone of voice convinced me that Tasha
was indeed his sister. Brothers and sisters communicate in their own special tone,
and it sounded as if it was no different in Tennessee than it was in California.

Nailed to the trees leading up to the Taylor's farm, Tasha and Mrs. Taylor
had attached big signs. In giant letters we read:

WELCOME TO MEMPHIS! FROM SEA TO SHINING SEA BIKERS.
1500 MILES DOWN, 3000 TO GO . . .

Wildwood Farms, the Taylor's polo pony farm, was straight out of *Gone With
The Wind*. Bowing trees dotted the pastures as groups of horses played on the
undulating green carpet. Our single lane of blacktop was lined with freshly painted
white fence, weaving its shady way past the barns and stables. Up on the hill
ahead stood the replica of every vision I had ever had of a southern mansion —
two stories, with tall white columns reaching from porch to roof, the faces of the
house a dignified mixture of brick, white wash and shutters.

"Hey Jimmy, is that your grandparents' house?" Ethan yelled up to Jimmy.

"Yeah Eeth, but that's the back of the house," Jimmy replied casually, leading us up the drive.

"The back of the house! Jimmy, are you kidding?" I gasped.

"No man, honest truth. That's the back."

The Taylor's driveway, just in front of the house, was strung with rainbows
of triangular flags. We rode underneath them and stopped as Jimmy's grandma,
sister and other, yet-to-be-introduced friends and relatives applauded our arrival. When the clapping stopped, all of us remained silent, waiting for Jimmy to
give us a demonstration of the southern manners he had told us were observed
at his Memphis house. Over the past few days he had managed to tutor us in the
proper uses of "yes, sir," "yes, ma'am" and "excuse me, sir" and "excuse me,
ma'am." Jimmy had learned California casual with its assortment of "yeahs",
"heys" and "mans" very quickly since moving to our state, and he was hoping
we would learn proper Memphis formality just as quickly.

First out of the garage was Mrs. Taylor's housekeeper, Nootie, a big black
woman whom Jimmy had told me many stories about. Nootie had played a big
part in helping raise little "Two Bits," in his old training wheel and BMX days.

"Oh, Jimmy!" she screamed as she ran out to him with her arms open wide.

Her black skin and black hair were a sharp contrast against her white house dress. "How's my little Jimmy," she said, throwing her arms around him. Jimmy crumbled in the big woman's arms, wrapped his arms as far around her as he could and stayed there for a few extra seconds before turning around and introducing us.

After a few more introductions and a few photographs, we went inside where we met Jimmy's "Gramps"— Mr. Taylor. He was waiting in the dining room and standing over a giant sheet cake which read: *Welcome Home, Bikers*. He stood over the cake trying to look unaffected, but as soon as he saw Jimmy, he broke into a big smile, set down the knife and gave his grandson a big hug. We all shook his hand, and then he proceeded to cut the cake, while Nootie and Mrs. Taylor dished out ice cream and lemonade. While Jimmy caught up with his grandparents, we just stared and ate cake in the tall-ceilinged dining room. A giant chandelier hung over the dining room table, and the room was wallpapered with a mural of an ancient Chinese polo match. When the kids got Jimmy alone, I was sure they would have some secret questions about the place where Jimmy grew up; I knew Lynn and I did.

There were rumors of a pool nearby, and after wolfing down their first piece of cake and first glass of lemonade, the kids politely pressed Jimmy for the truth:

"Hey Jimmy—" Ethan caught himself before continuing. "No . . . I mean . . . excuse me, Jimmy, what about that pool? . . . Please?"

"Yeah sure, Eeth, it's right out back," answered Jimmy. "You want to go for a swim, man?"

Ethan nodded and the guys didn't even bother to go get their trunks off their bikes. They set down their plates — "Don't put those in the sink; we'll be back for more later," announced Jimmy — then ran out the back door and dove into the pool with their biking clothes on. I noticed Mr. Taylor smile as they ran for the water, and I could tell he was glad to have the kids around. Joy and Heather excused themselves to their bikes to get their swimsuits and soon joined the guys in the pool. Within an hour of their arrival, the kids had splashed a few inches of water out of the pool, emptied two pitchers of lemonade and polished off the entire sheet cake.

"They sure do know how to eat," exclaimed Mrs. Taylor. "Nootie, looks like we are gonna need all that food we bought at the market and then some." From Mrs. Taylor's laughing smile, it looked like she was glad to have the joyful noise of kids echoing through her house and yard again too.

That night at Sunday dinner, we were served elegantly in the dining room — china, silver, crystal — and as we finished, I figured that Nootie or Charles, one of the other black helpers, would be doing the cleaning up. Just when I was expecting the kitchen help to come and clear off the table, Mr. and Mrs. Taylor, stood up and took over kitchen patrol.

"Little Muscles . . ." announced Mr. Taylor, smiling at his wife, "it's time to get to work." Jimmy's grandad rolled up his sleeves, grabbed Mrs. Taylor by the arm and walked into the kitchen with her, as if he was leading her in a waltz.

Moments later he appeared from behind the swinging door wearing the funniest looking pastel yellow flowered apron and snapping a giant dish towel. Jimmy's grandad in an apron was the last thing I expected to see.

"Little Muscles," he continued, "let's get those dishes cleared. I'll wash and you dry. I hope the swimmin' keeps them busy long enough for us to get these clean and get dessert ready."

The kids stayed around the table to smile at the action for a few seconds, but when they saw they were relieved of any duties they were immediately back in the pool. Lynn and I stayed a little while longer in our chairs, trying to figure our place. I must have left my jaw wide open, because when Mrs. Taylor, who had been studying me too well all afternoon, passed by me with an armful of dishes, she winked and said, "He does the dishes evra Sunday night . . . likes to mow the lawns too." Little Muscles laughed her way to the kitchen, and Lynn gently pushed my jaw closed.

We planned to spend four nights and three days with the Taylors in Memphis. For the kids it would mostly be a time of relaxing and visiting. For Lynn and me, it would be a time of chores, business and visiting on the run.

Joy and Carl needed to see an orthodontist. Somewhere back in the Appalachians while I was fixing broken spokes, Dr. Lynn was using the pliers from her tool kit on their braces. Some of the metal wires that were attempting to true Joy's and Carl's teeth had snapped and Lynn had needed to break off the protruding ends. Her labor didn't help their teeth any, but it saved their cheeks and gums from getting all cut up. I often wondered if the pioneers would have ever made it west if they were burdened by our twentieth century "necessities."

Dentist appointments were just the first things on a long list. Joy needed socks and underwear; Heather needed film. In addition to all the bikes needing their 500-mile cleaning and tune-up, Heather's needed new shifters, Carl's needed a new freewheel and chain, and Jimmy's and Ethan's needed new handlebar tape. We all needed new toiletry supplies. And last, but not least, Lynn and I had to get our next six weeks worth of funds exchanged into cash and travelers checks. My brother Jay, back at *Headquarters*, had sent us a check, thirty rolls of film, and maps for Arkansas, Missouri, Kansas and Nebraska, and I needed to send him thirty rolls of exposed film and my already used maps of the Southeast.

Monday was dentist, bike stuff and sit down dinner with Jimmy's grandparents, dad, sister, uncles and cousins. The kids and Lynn got to sleep in, but I knew I had to get an early start on things to get everything done. I also didn't want to leave Memphis without getting a chance to get to know Mr. and Mrs. Taylor better, and before going to bed Sunday night I had found out that another one of their rituals was an early morning breakfast together. I hoped I wasn't intruding as I hesitantly asked Mrs. Taylor if I could join them.

"Why sure, John," Mrs. Taylor smiled, "what time would ya like me to wake ya?"

"Whatever time is best for you and Mr. Taylor, ma'am." I was getting pretty good at that ma'am stuff even that first night — in fact I kinda liked it. Wearing my dress outfit of grease-stained nylon windpants and musty and wrinkled Hawaiian shirt, if I couldn't look dignified, I could at least sound the part.

Mrs. Taylor softly woke me up bright and early Monday morning and I walked out to their enclosed veranda looking out over the lower pastures. Mr. Taylor, dressed in neatly pressed polo shirt, tan summer slacks and the classiest pair of brown and white wing-tip shoes I had ever seen, sat quietly at the table, sipping fresh squeezed orange juice and reading the sports page.

"Good morning, Mr. Taylor."

"Good morning, John. Did ya sleep well?"

"Yes sir, I slept great. It sure is nice to sleep in a cool house."

"Yes sir, I bet it is. This is near the hottest summer I can remember in these parts." Mr. Taylor and I dispensed with the usual introductory conversation about weather, while Mrs. Taylor brought out fresh home-brewed coffee, more orange juice and peaches and cream.

"John, how would y'all like your eggs?" she asked.

"Over medium, thank you ma'am." I placed my order and Mrs. Taylor disappeared back down the hall to the kitchen.

"Mr. Taylor . . . Jimmy tells me you started a company called the Federal Compress Company?" I asked, beginning the first of many questions I wanted to ask Mr. Taylor. I may have had time to be proper, but I didn't have time to be shy.

"Yes sir, originally it was called the Federal Compress Company. Most of the cotton grown 'round here passed though our compresses on its way to market. Our machines compacted the cotton into large dense bales ready to ship. That business changed, though, with the changing of the market. Synthetics and imported cotton forced us to change our business. Now the Federal Company is a large corporation that controls a lot of smaller agricultural companies."

"I think Jimmy told me that Holly Farms Poultry is one of those companies."

"You're right, sir, it is." Jimmy's grandpa put down the newspaper and began telling me all about his chicken operation. In ten minutes I learned everything that happened "from the rooster to the roaster," and I found out that he ran his business the same way he ran his household. In addition to his dishwashing and landscaping, Mr. Taylor made sure he dirtied his shoes in chicken coops, processing plants, truck yards and supermarkets. I had a bunch of other questions to ask, but the kids were up and ready for breakfast before I got a chance. He excused himself to an appointment he had with his lawn mower, and I think we both looked forward to tomorrow's breakfast.

The kids and Lynn circled around the table, sleepy-eyed and hungry. After witnessing the disappearance of the cake Sunday afternoon, Mrs. Taylor was braced for the vast amounts of food it was going to take to feed the crew. She wisely distracted the kids with giant bowls of fruit while she took egg orders. When she left I noticed there was some whispering and giggling filtering around the table that seemed to be embarrassing Carl.

"Okay you guys, what's up?" I asked.

Joy and Heather looked at each other and then looked at Carl. Finally Heather spoke, "Well . . . you see . . . Carl walked into our room this morning and asked if he could borrow our razor." She and Joy began giggling again as Ethan and Jimmy looked at their companion in disbelief. Jimmy looked worried that his fellow male had beaten him to the mirror for his first shave.

"What did you do, Carl . . . have a sudden spurt of hormones? You didn't seem to have a beard yesterday." I laughed.

"No, John, I didn't," Carl sourly answered.

"Well, then, why did you need the girls' razor?" Jimmy quickly asked, dying to know.

"He said he was going to shave his legs!" Joy burst out laughing.

Carl slid his legs under the table as far as possible, as it seemed the girls had broken some sort of secret pact. Carl's covert plan to remove the blonde fuzz on his calves and thighs was now revealed, and everyone immediately ducked their heads under the tablecloth to check out his work.

"Hey Carl, good job," I congratulated him. Other than a few nicks and scabs of clotted blood, Carl had done pretty well. "You're braver than me. I know hard core cyclists shave their legs and everything, but shoot, I never had the guts to shave mine."

The kids pulled their heads out from under the table and stared at Carl who was slowly recovering from his embarrassment. I'm glad they didn't stay under the table much longer, because Mrs. Taylor was just down the hall returning with the next round of food. I could just see her returning to a table full of five kids and two supposed adults, hunched over with their heads under her tablecloth She knew we were a close-knit group and everything, but I didn't want her to get the wrong idea.

Tuesday it was up early for our longest day. Jimmy's grandma had landed us a spot on the *AM Memphis* morning television show, and we all had to be up early for breakfast that morning. I missed my visit with Mr. Taylor because we had to be downtown at the studio by 7. The girls took an extra twenty minutes getting ready, as we all donned our nicest bicycling outfits to greet the cameras. Lynn tried to help the boys with their hairdos, but finally surrendered to the generation gap. Knowing better, I just stayed out of it. All ready for stardom, we piled into the Taylors' station wagon and headed to the studio. On the way into town, we paired off in groups of hosts and guests, and everyone practiced for their debut on ABC's Memphis affiliate.

"Hey John, how are we all going to fit around that little table?" asked Carl looking at the set.

"Yeah John, it doesn't even look like they have enough chairs for all of us set up," worried Ethan.

The kids seemed to be right. I hadn't bothered to consider that perhaps not all of us would get to be on camera. The production assistant walked over and said, "Which three of you are going to be on camera? We want the leader and two kids."

Oh, the realities of the media. I turned around and saw one anxious wife and five anxious friends. It was time for another one of my no-win decisions.

"Well, I have to go with Jimmy, because he is from Memphis . . . and don't you think we should have a girl up there too?" Carl and Ethan drooped their heads in disappointment, but they understood my reasoning. "And, Heather, since you were on TV in Virginia, don't you think it should be Joy's turn?" Heather smiled and agreed.

Lynn looked over to me with a little disappointment in her eyes, and said, "Go 'head John, you are the leader. I understand. C'mon Ethan and Carl, there's nothing we can do, so let's go sit and watch."

The lights clicked on and before we knew it, our spot was over. The kids, always quick to bounce back, critiqued the performance and then said, "Hey John, we're hungry, can we get something to eat?" Even though they weren't on their bikes they were addicted to our second breakfast routine.

Jimmy's dad, Jim, met us and became the pied piper of Memphis. I discovered where Jimmy had received his enthusiastic spirit, as Jim took us all over town. He must have seen the riverboats, Beale Street and Mud Island a thousand times, but he cheered for more stale popcorn aboard the Delta Queen and insisted on "one more rack" of ribs at The Rendevous. Lists of chores would have to wait, as he put his arm around his son and led us all over town that day, finishing with more popcorn and a late night movie. We returned to the Taylors' after midnight, and the kids, exhausted from their day, collapsed onto their beds before they even got their clothes off.

Early the next morning, Jim took the guys off for haircuts while Lynn and I finished all our errands. Once haircuts were done, Jimmy spent much of the afternoon alone with his dad. Ethan, Carl, Heather and Joy spent the afternoon finishing their bike maintenance, riding Jimmy's go-cart, and submersing themselves beneath the cool water of the pool. That evening the Taylor family threw a good-bye party for us. Friends and relatives all stopped by for Memphis BBQ, homemade slaw and fresh-baked chess pie out by the pool. Everyone wished Two Bits good luck, and I had a hard time breaking up the party to get the kids to bed early. Our three days of rest and relaxation were almost over, and early in the morning we would be getting on our bikes again and heading into Arkansas.

"You guys have everything packed in your panniers and ready to go on your bikes tomorrow morning?" I asked a less than enthusiastic group in their rooms upstairs.

"Yeah, John," answered Joy. "Can we pack our toiletries in the morning?

Heather and I want to take a shower before breakfast."

"Sure Joy, you guys have everything else organized already anyway, don't you?"

"Yeah, Lynn gave us all our liquid soap and shampoo and deodorant and toothpaste and stuff this afternoon," Joy continued.

"Are you two ready to get to Arkansas tomorrow?" I asked. I shouldn't have pressed my luck.

"Not really," Joy frowned. "It's gonna be hard to leave this place. The rooms and TV and everything have been great, but it's going to be even harder to leave the Taylors. They really made us feel at home. I know we have to keep heading west and everything, but that still doesn't make leaving any easier."

"Yeah, I know," agreed Heather. "Just think of Jimmy. I could tell by looking at him tonight that it's going to be a hard day for him tomorrow. He always tries to act so cool about everything, and I've never seen him like this. He's really going to miss his dad and his grandparents."

"Well, if you two can think of any way to make tomorrow easier for him, please let me know. Tomorrow's ride isn't going to be easy for any of us, and I agree with what you said about Jimmy's day being especially difficult. Thanks for thinking of him."

"Good night, John," they said together. "Where's Lynn?"

"Oh, she's downstairs visiting with Mrs. Taylor."

"Well, tell her good night too, okay?" The two girls disappeared as they shut the door slowly.

"Good night, girls. See you in the morning."

9

It was very hot — about a hundred and seven degrees. It was so hot that when you poured the water on yourself to cool yourself off, it just burned you, and it hurt to drink it also.

Ethan's Journal
July 31, 1986

JC

Thursday morning dawned hotter than any day we'd experienced. Mr. Taylor shook all of our hands at breakfast and took a quiet walk with Jimmy before he disappeared to some chore around the farm. Mrs. Taylor kept us around as long as she could and sad tears flowed down her face when she finally had to say good-bye.

"Good-bye, Grams," waved a tearful Jimmy as we pulled out of the driveway. Just a couple of (too short) days before, Jimmy had led us up the same driveway, but this time he reversed his position. "Hey John, can I ride at the back behind Lynn?" he sniffled, not too proud to show his tears. Of course I said yes, and Jimmy slowed our pace out of Wildwood Farms and into downtown Memphis.

Jimmy's dad had routed us the quietest way possible through Memphis, and we met him at his house downtown. He then led us to the base of the "Old Bridge" that crossed the giant river, where two Memphis motorcycle patrolmen were waiting to escort us across. It turned out to be our easiest and proudest river crossing of the trip, as they closed off both lanes of traffic going our way and gave us two carefree lanes of bridge. We smiled our way across the Mississippi into Arkansas with one motorcycle policeman leading and one tailing our procession. I even had time to stop my bike in the middle of the bridge to take a picture.

"Hey John, how 'bout if these guys lead us the whole rest of the way to California?" beamed Carl, excited to see semis and buses yielding to him.

"Well son, don't ya say that too loudly, cuz we're half tempted to join y'all," said one officer.

The two officers shook each of the kids' hands, posed for a picture and gave us their address so that we could send them a postcard from "out west." It seemed we had picked the right two patrolmen, as they unbuckled their helmets for a few minutes and told us how they liked to go touring on their motorcycles on their vacations.

"Sure would like to ride our (motor)bikes out in your part of the country some day," continued the other officer. "You folks have yourselves a wonderful time and ride safely, ya hear."

"We sure will, officer," saluted Carl. "Thanks for the escort."

A few miles down the road, at the Roadrunner Truck Stop in Marion, Arkansas, we ate lunch with Jimmy's dad and then said another good-bye. All the kids had stomach aches from all the giant soft drinks they downed in our half-hour sitting, but, pulling out from the station, Jimmy had a stomach ache for his own reasons. Tears poured down his face and he didn't want to let go of his dad. After a long embrace that was hard for us all to watch, Jimmy hugged his dad one last time, wiped the tears off his cheek with his biking glove and bravely got onto his bike. The rest of the group was silent as Jimmy rode up to me at the front of our paceline.

"I'm not feeling too good, John." Jimmy was still crying. "I've said good-bye to my dad before, but for some reason this time it hurts really bad. I feel like my chest is going to break open . . . Have you ever felt like that before?"

"Yeah Jimmy, I have . . . anything I can do to help?"

"Oh, I don't know . . . I think I would just like to ride alone for awhile."

I gave Jimmy directions to stay within sight, and off he went. With the mercury reading a record 112 degrees and the humidity matching it, no one went very fast that day. The dancing gray haze steaming out of the rice fields had us all hallucinating. We tried to cool ourselves off by tying bandanas around our necks and soaking them with water. It had worked earlier in the trip when the temperature was only in the nineties, but that Arkansas afternoon was different; every time we poured water on ourselves it literally burned our necks. The water in our water bottles went from cold to warm to very, very hot, and drinking or pouring it on ourselves was like trying to refresh ourselves with tea — the hot kind. As we broiled and boiled our way along the western bank of the Mississippi that afternoon, Jimmy's misery got all the company it wanted.

"What'd those niggers want? They givin' y'all any trouble?" scowled Mr. Carroll as we parked our bikes outside the Sharecropper Restaurant in Earle, Arkansas. "Them niggers give y'all any trouble and y'all jus' let me know; I'll take care of it."

We had met Mr. Carroll later that afternoon as we rode through the rice fields that fan out from the banks of the Mississippi in the flatlands of eastern Arkansas. Dilapidated, tar-shingled shanties dotted the sides of the road. Doors hung crooked on rusty hinges, windows with and without glass were propped permanently open, and underneath the sagging front porches slept listless dogs, their skin stretched tightly over bony skeletons. Eastern Arkansas was the hottest and the poorest part of the country we had yet seen. We had seen poverty on other back roads, but the blank, black faces of old men and skinny young children that stared at us from behind those shacks showed no signs of any hopes or dreams. It was the South I had always imagined, and riding through the rural ghetto didn't help the heat any. Just past the row of shacks, our road turned. I was trying to cool my brain with some daydream of the ocean when I looked up to see two trucks and a giant tractor blocking our path. I blinked my eyes and slapped my cheeks hoping it was just another hallucination wrestling for my attention. It wasn't.

I saw a very large man get into his truck and start to drive away, but when he saw us in his rear view mirror, he drove back into place and blocked our path. When he stepped out I saw how large he really was. I stopped my bike and motioned for the rest of the group to stop theirs. The man in the truck opened his door and stared coldly at us as he leaned against it. He seemed to have no intention of moving.

"Well, I'll be damned! Boys, y'all have got to git yerselves over here and see this." He must have weighed three hundred pounds! His blue shirt bulged at the buttons, opening to his sweaty white t-shirt underneath, not much of which made it over his large belly and into his matching blue pants. He wore the proverbial ball cap advertising fertilizer, and I could see myself in the highway-patrol-style, mirrored sunglasses which seemed to be permanently attached to his face. He looked just like the southern redneck I had sitting on the shelf of my California mind, and I imagined he never wore anything different. Shoot, he probably even slept with his shades on.

"What the hell y'all doin' out here?" he asked, but I wasn't sure I had permission to answer. "Boys, have y'all ever done seen nothin' like this here bafore?"

"No, JC, cain't say as we ever has?" One of the other white men snickered, as JC and the other boys out in the middle of the road enjoyed checking us out from head to toe. Two black men in their twenties stood nearby and a young black boy, who looked as if he was Jimmy's age, looked on from inside the tractor. Even though we hadn't passed through any gate or fence, I had the feeling we had entered this large man's territory. Everyone else in his group — black and white — seemed to follow his lead, and Lynn and the kids looked at me, puzzled why I hadn't said anything yet.

"What in tarnation are y'all doin' out here?" The big man still hadn't smiled, and as I went through my normal introduction of myself, Lynn, the group and our trip, I felt like a kid who had been discovered searching for the baseball he had hit in the mean old man's backyard down the street. After I stammered my way through our introduction, he turned to his buddies, told them some private joke that had them snickering, and then turned back to me.

"M' name is Johnny Carroll, but you call me JC . . . Now let me get this straight: you say y'all are from California and you're ridin' them bicycles all the way across America?"

"Yes, sir." I was in good practice from our stay with the Taylors.

"Now why would ya want to do a thang like that?" His voice was deep and hoarse, and no one else made a sound when he spoke.

"Well, I'm a social studies teacher and I wanted the kids to get a feeling for all the different kinds of people that make up America . . . and I thought that traveling across it by bicycle would be the best way to get to meet people . . . So far we've ridden across Virginia, along the Appalachians, across Tennessee and now we're heading up towards Independence, Missouri where we'll begin to follow the Old Oregon and California Wagon Trail. We're going to be reading an old pioneer journal from the Gold Rush and follow the paths of the wagons west to see what going west was like over a hundred years ago." I tried to gauge his feelings toward us as I talked, but those sunglasses made it awful difficult. He didn't crack a smile, but he did seem to be listening. After a long silence he spoke:

"Where y'all stayin' tonight?"

"We're staying with a friend of Jimmy's grandmother. Her name is Betty Bernard and she lives somewhere on the outskirts of Earle." As soon as I mentioned Mrs. Bernard's name, Mr. Carroll and his friends started to laugh again. "Did I say something wrong?"

"No, no, don't mind us, just a little joke, that's all." Mr. Carroll laughed again to his friends. "I just does me a bit a fishin' in Mrs. Betty Bernard's pond when I ain't s'posed to, that's all . . . What are y'all doin' for breakfast tomorrow?"

"I don't know. Do you know a place that serves good biscuits and gravy? We haven't tasted any Arkansas-style yet."

"Yeah I do, and they're on me. Y'all meet me at The Sharecropper Restaurant in Earle tomorrow morning and I'll buy y'all the breakfast ya can eat. What time y'all eat, anyway?"

He still hadn't smiled at me or changed his gruff tone of voice, so I proceeded hesitantly with our breakfast plans. I wasn't quite so sure I wanted to see him again. "Oh I don't know . . . I'm not sure if Mrs. Bernard has already made breakfast plans for us."

"Well, you just tell Mrs. Bernard that Johnny Carroll is takin' care of breakfast tomorrow. Now tell me, do you all eat breakfast early or late?"

"Well, I like to get us on the road early so we can try and beat this heat." It didn't seem like our plans were up for a discussion.

"How's 7 AM then?"

"Okay, 7 AM. Will I need directions to get there?"

"Naw . . . if ya have any questions just ask somebody in town. Should take y'all about twenty minutes by bicycle from Mrs. Bernard's house. Y'all be about ten miles from her place right now."

"Well, thanks for the breakfast offer, Mr. Carroll—I mean JC. If you don't mind, I'd like to get us down the road to some shade and some water. We're all pretty hot and tired, and things don't seem to be getting any cooler."

"'know what ya mean. Just keep goin' straight on this road for another six miles or so and then take yer first right. I'll move my truck and let y'all be on yer way."

"Thanks again, JC."

"Ain't nothin'. See y'all in the morning."

We didn't shake hands; JC just tipped his cap. I let out a big sigh of relief once we'd cleared inspection and were past our roadblock. I picked up our pace as fast as I could in the heat, and I didn't look back over my shoulder as I tried to think of some way to get out of our breakfast engagement at The Sharecropper.

"John, are we really going to have breakfast with that man tomorrow?" Lynn asked after a few minutes of riding. "He scares me."

Mr. Carroll and the boys were three miles behind us by then, but as I looked over my shoulder to answer Lynn, I noticed a large tractor speeding its way towards us.

"John, don't you think Mrs. Bernard is going to have some breakfast for us tomorrow? Aren't you going to answer me? Are we really going to have breakfast with that man tomorrow?"

I still didn't answer because I was studying the rapidly approaching tractor. Finally, I recognized the green and yellow John Deere monstrosity as the same one that had been part of our roadblock. I could tell because it had the same four giant wheels in the back that spread out like those on some tinkertoy tractor. I had never seen one that tall and wide before, and as it barreled down the road at full speed toward us, I saw that it took up the entire road from ditch to ditch. Maybe I wouldn't have to worry about that breakfast at all; maybe we wouldn't be around for it. Riding along that, all-but-deserted, Arkansas back road, I had a terrifying vision of JC or one of his boys taking a break from their rice work to harvest seven Californians. Out there in the middle of nowhere we would make some very humorous fertilizer.

When the tractor slowed down behind us and the black boy in the cab smiled and waved, I realized that I had seen too many movies. He motioned me over to the cab and we all stopped our bikes.

"Mr. Carroll, he tell me to show you all da way to Mrs. Bernard's house. He say he don't want y'all to be gettin' los'." The young boy sat tall above me in his air-conditioned cab. He was wearing a holy white t-shirt, dirty jeans and a navy baseball cap that said "New York" proudly across the crown in gold letters. "M' name's Leon and I work for Mr. Carroll. I does what he done tells me to. So y'all follow me."

I shook my head and introduced each of the kids to our escort, Leon. Even though my kids worked for me, they often dictated the pace, and before we started riding again, they decided that they wanted to ask Leon some questions of their own.

"Hi, Leon, my name's Carl. How old are you? I'm twelve."

"I be fourteen."

"How long you been driving that tractor?" asked Ethan who was sitting on his bike and hanging onto one of the giant wheels. Even sitting up on his bike, the wheels were a foot taller than he was.

"Been drivin' for Mr. Carroll for five years now."

"Whoa, dude! . . . You mean you've been driving tractors since you were nine-years-old?! Is it fun to drive those big things?" Carl continued.

Leon lifted up his ball cap and scratched his head. "I guess at first it be fun. . . now, it just be work."

Mr. Senator Jimmy ("you can call me James") West

Mr. Senator Carl Fagerlin

Mr. Senator Jimmy ("you can call me James") West

Ms. Senator Heather Deutsch

Ms. Senator Joy Fulton

Mr. Senator Carl Fagerlin

Mr. Senator Ethan Turpin

Doctor Lynn Seigel Boettner & Carl

Mr. Pipewrench "Amasta" & John Seigel Boettner

a Nebraska classroom . . . .

"Okay, John, let's go," announced Carl.

"You guys ready?"

"Sure thing, boss," laughed Jimmy.

"Okay, Leon. After you."

Everyone fell in line behind Leon and drafted him all the way to Betty Bernard's. Before Leon stopped, we saw what we figured to be her place up on the left side of the road. In marked contrast to all we had seen since arriving in Arkansas, a large white mansion stared out across the rice land. Leon slowed his tractor and pulled over across from the long driveway that led up to our home for the night.

"Dis be da place," Leon announced staring up at the house.

As he idled the large machine, Heather and Joy tugged at my shorts from behind.

"Hey John, do we have any t-shirts left? You know, the ones we give to special people we meet along the road." They cupped their hands to my ears as they whispered. "If we do, let's give Leon one."

So, with the sweltering green rice fields saying good-bye to us on our right, and the cool, columned porch of Mrs. Bernard's mansion awaiting us on our left, we presented Leon with a brand new *From Sea to Shining Sea* t-shirt. He turned off the John Deere, came down from the cab and held his shirt in one hand as the kids all shook his other hand. As hot and thirsty and tired as the kids were after riding twenty-five miles in the heat, they decided that Mrs. Bernard's pool would have to wait until they said good bye to their new friend.

"C'mon John, get out the camera," ordered Carl. "We've got to get a picture for our slide show."

After waving good-bye to Leon, as he disappeared down the road clad in his new shirt, we all managed to switch channels and enjoy the incredible dose of southern hospitality of Betty Bernard and her son Harbert. We were still waving and only halfway down the driveway, when Mrs. Bernard came running out of the door welcoming us with hugs, kisses and a bottomless pitcher of ice cold lemonade.

Early the next morning, even though I had explained to her about our breakfast engagement, Betty insisted we join her for sweet rolls, coffee, hot chocolate and orange juice before getting on to Earle. After stuffing us, she kissed each of us good-bye, Harbert shook everyone's hands, and we were off through the early morning clouds of mosquitoes and on our way to our appointment with Johnny Carroll at The Sharecropper Restaurant.

We got an escort through Earle, but it wasn't our friend Leon. As we rode through the small town that didn't even seem to have any stores or businesses, all the resident dogs announced our arrival on the outskirts of town. A group of little black kids sitting on one front porch looked at us, wiped the sleep from their eyes, and immediately hopped on their own bicycles and followed us through their town like we were grand marshals of some parade. Little kids, barefoot and looking like littler Leons, rode three to a rusty bike or ran as fast as they could, laughing and yelling and screaming alongside us. In a block or so, the news of our arrival had awakened more excited natives, and some older brothers or sisters or cousins hopped into their old, beat-up silver Ford Pinto and joined the parade.

"What you all be doin'?" one of them shouted, as he stretched his slender body out the window towards Jimmy. From their clapping and the big smiles on their faces, everyone — the little kids on their bikes and the kids in the car — seemed to be having the time of their lives. Jimmy was the first to answer.

"We're riding our bicycles across America," he said with a smile and a wave.

"Say what?" yelled the kid as he stretched himself even further out of the window. One of his buddies was holding onto him so he wouldn't fall out of the car.

"We're riding our bicycles across America," repeated Ethan. "We started in Washington, D.C. and we're heading for California."

"Ridin' 'cross America? . . . to California? . . . Say what?! Why, you be crazy!" This time he almost did fall out of the window and his friends yanked him back into his seat. Once back inside the car, I saw him start talking to his friends, all the time slapping their shoulders and wildly waving his hands. We couldn't hear the words he was saying or the questions his friends were shouting to him, but it sure sounded like that old Pinto had some excited passengers. They followed us all the way to The Sharecropper, their bicycling relatives not far behind. We pulled into the parking lot and the guys in the Pinto pulled in alongside us. They didn't say anything and their animated excitement changed to quiet disbelief as they studied us dismounting our bikes. Soon their stares turned into pointing and whispering, and, not being able to resist their questions any longer, they inched up closer to us.

"Now y'all don't be jivin' us now. Y'all really ridin' them things all the way to California?"

Heather was giggling, but she still managed to answer, "Yup, we're riding four thousand, five hundred miles from sea to shining sea. Here, see Ethan's t-shirt." She showed the guys in the car our logo. "That's us riding our bikes across America. That big guy's John and we're the smaller ones."

The guys in the car broke up into laughter, punching and bumping each other. "Why y'all be crazy," laughed the astonished driver.

"Yes sir, y'all be jus' plain crazy," pointed the guy who had leaned out the window. The little kids on their bicycles were hiding shyly behind the Sharecropper sign, and our kids were enjoying the attention, when up drove Johnny Carroll. At the sight of his truck the expression on the faces in the Pinto immediately changed. They quickly rolled up their window, didn't say a word, and peeled out of the parking lot without a good-bye or a wave. I looked over to where the little kids had been watching us on their bikes, and they too had vanished. It seemed like they knew something about JC we didn't.

Our kids were still smiling when a sleepy Mr. Carroll stepped out of his truck and assured me he would take care of any niggers that bothered us.

"Oh no, sir, they weren't bothering us. They were just wondering what we were doing riding through their town. I think they were just having fun."

"Well, like I said, if any niggers 'roun here give you or any of your kids any trouble you just let me know, ya hear?"

I didn't answer and my stomach, which never before had hesitated at the thought of some biscuits and gravy, suddenly felt ill. We followed JC inside. Three of the tables had been shoved together and a group of farmers sat around as if they were having a morning meeting. Smoking cigarettes and drinking coffee, the half dozen men, some my dad's age and some not much older than me, sat talking about the weather and what they'd seen in their dawn rounds through their fields. They all wore the same kind of clothes that Johnny Carroll wore — ball caps, sports shirts and jeans or slacks. The only other people inside besides the waitress and them were two truck drivers in greasy coveralls sitting together at the corner table. Everyone obviously knew our escort, because as soon as we entered the room, they all stopped their conversations and said, "Mornin', JC," as if in salute.

Mr. Carroll pointed to the two tables in the middle of the cafe, and we understood from his gesture that we were supposed to sit down. JC silently walked over to his place at the head of the tables where the other local boys sat and motioned to the waitress. She immediately came over with a bunch of menus and ice water for our group. Mr. Carroll still hadn't said anything to me since he had first questioned me outside, and as we studied the menu, he spoke in muffled words to his friends at the next table. I couldn't even read the menus I was so uncomfortable. JC seemed to be whispering about us to his buddies, because every so often he would pause and they would all turn and check us out.

Finally Johnny turned to our table and said, "'member what I said now, y'all git whatever y'all want. Johnny Carroll is buyin'!"

The kids could tell I was nervous, and they looked up at me with anxious eyes. "Go 'head, you guys, get whatever you can eat."

The kids all looked at me again with eyes that said, "Really?" I nodded my head and they studied the menu in earnest. Soon they were ordering their usual assorted mounds of pancakes, baskets and baskets of biscuits, bowls of gravy, sausage, eggs, hot chocolate and juice. The kids silently wrote in their journals and wrote postcards while they waited for their orders to arrive. They didn't even ask if they could get a newspaper, they just plugged themselves into their writing. My stomach was still nervous and I tried to look busy with my own journal as the men at JC's table and the two truckers in the corner continued their whispers and stares.

As soon as our food came, we set a *From Sea to Shining Sea* record for the fastest breakfast. We wolfed down our food and still we didn't hear a word directed at us from anyone at the other groups of tables. I knew we weren't invisible, because we sat right in the center of the small and otherwise empty cafe. I kept telling myself that I was being unfair in my fear of these men, but they kept looking at us for almost a half-hour, and never said a word or asked us a question. Our first Arkansas biscuits and gravy may have been the best in the country, but I don't think Lynn or the kids even tasted them — I know I didn't. By the time we finished, Johnny Carroll had pulled a chair up to the two truckers' table and was talking with them. Lynn and the kids asked me if they could be excused — a first! — and headed for the restrooms. After they finished with their duties, each one of the kids meekly walked up to Mr. Carroll, thanked him for buying their breakfast, and then tried not to run out the door to their bikes outside. Just as I was about to get up myself, Johnny, who still hadn't removed his mirrored shades, motioned me over to where he was sitting with his index finger. I walked over and readied myself for the worst.

"Son," Mr. Carroll began, "I wanna tell ya how much I admire what ya are doin' there with them kids a yers. Now I know ya haven't felt all that comfortable bein' round me, shoot, it's written all over yer face, but I got to tell ya I think what y'all are doin' is the greatest damn bit of education I ever seen." Johnny leaned back, crossed his arms across his giant girth, and the whole restaurant listened. He looked me dead in the eye with his mirrors and continued, "Ain't no book learnin' or lecturin' that cain teach these kids what ya be teachin' them by bein' out on the road . . . meetin' folks white and black, takin' the time to stop and talk ta 'rednecks' like me, seein' where folks live and how they live . . . Damn it, that's worth more than any piece of paper. That's what evra kid should be learnin'.

"John, I also know that what you and your wife are doin' caint be easy. It takes work to be learnin' these kids how to take care of theirselves and how to talk to folks and then ya get them on their bicycles day after day. I ain't never done anathang like it maself, but I know it got to be damn hard work."

"Thank you, sir," I interrupted.

"Now don't y'all be thankin' me. I just wanna be sure that you and yer kids got enough ta eat and have some good membrances of Johnny Carroll and this neck of the woods. I know we be different than y'all out in California, but I'm glad I got the chance to meet y'all and for my friends here to meet y'all, too. Before ya leave I want ya to promise old JC two things."

"Damn," I whispered to my ghosts.

"What's that?" asked JC.

"Oh nothin'. Sure, JC, be glad to. What would you like me to do?"

"First of all, I want ya to send me a postcard when y'all reach California."

"Shoot, I'll send you one before that to let you know how we're doin'."

"Nope, ya jus' listen to me now. I said I wanted ya to send me one from California and not before. Y'all got too much to be doin' 'sides writin' me a postcard. No, you just send me one when y'all get home and have some time. You spend the rest of yer time on the road bein' on the road, not writin' me some silly post card. I don't want to hear from y'all til y'all reach yer final destination, ya hear?"

"Yes, sir."

"And second of all, I was damned impressed with yer bunch of kids. Y'all have done right well with them. Just promise me one thing: y'all keep bein' good to each other, ya hear. I cain tell ya've been good to each other so far, cuz I knows what I sees and you got yerself one damn fine bunch o kids there. Shoot, even looks like ya taught them a few things 'bout eatin'! Ya jus' be sure ya keep bein' good to each other the rest of the way.

"Now, you bes' be gittin' outside now, and don't bother with no more thank yous or nothin' else. Ya got a bunch of kids and a good wife out there waitin' for ya, so git goin'. I already took too much of yer time up already. Have a good trip and remember, be good to each other."

Mr. Johnny "JC" Carroll, still seated between the two truckers, never got up from his seat, and to this day, I don't know what color his eyes are. He just reached out his ham hock of a hand and shook mine. He gave me the kind of grip my dad had always told me to give — strong, firm and not like "some wet dish rag". In five short minutes, JC had told me what I hoped that everyone we met would understand about our trip. His politics were far different than my own and he had different names for different colors of people, but tears rolled out of my eyes as I walked out of The Sharecropper Restaurant that morning. I just hoped I had given him the same respectful grip that he had given me.

The kids and Lynn saw my face and wondered why I came out smiling and sniffling.

"Hey John, what's the matter?" Carl yelled.

"Yeah John, what's the matter?" asked Lynn.

"Oh, I'll tell you later. We've got to be getting down the road." JC had told me to get goin' and I planned to follow his orders. We hitched up our toe straps, rolled slowly through the gravel of the dusty parking lot and headed west toward our next lesson.

Damndest Wind I Ever Saw

Our next lesson wasn't too far away. That night the sky gave us a live demonstration of what TV weather people call a "Tornado Watch & Severe Thunderstorm Warning." JC was right. The textbooks, the TV and the weather pages in the newspapers just didn't do the heavens justice. That was the night the tidal wave of a storm broke with full force on our campsite at Jacksonport State Park — the night we spent dodging lightning, trying to hold on to the ground, abandoning camp, and sleeping in the women's room.

The following morning, after asking the cows in the nearby pasture if we could have our socks back and after removing other pieces of laundry from the barbed wire fence at the far end of the campground, we gathered in a circle and held hands. Soggy but safe, we thanked each other for being strong the night before, and Heather decided she wanted to play a quick round of Bright Side.

"Okay Heather," I said, "let's play . . . but just two rounds."

Heather stood there with a silly smile all over her freckled face. Her eyes wore dark circles like everyone else's, but still they twinkled. "Well . . . you guys . . . someone has to say the bad thing, so I can say my bright side . . . Gee wiz!"

"Okay. . . tornado," moaned Jimmy.

Heather jumped on her chance. "Well, with the rain and everything last night it should make our ride today much cooler. Remember how hot it's been so far in Arkansas?"

"Yeah, and I have a bright side too," beamed Ethan. "You know the magnet for my computer that we've been searching for since back in Virginia? Well . . . in all the tumbling around of our bags and our tent, guess what I found?" Ethan held up a small black disk about the size of an M&M.

"Alright, Ethan!" Everyone broke hands and cheered as they gave a smiling Ethan a standing ovation. We ended our game and headed up the White River towards Batesville and the Ozark Mountains.

Ethan's mom, Sue, and his sister, Amber, had their three-day rendezvous with us in Arkansas, and even though Sue had planned to follow us from campsite to campsite, she wasn't the least bit disappointed when I decided we deserved a Ramada Inn the night after the storm. Ethan asked to sleep with his mom and his sister in their room rather than with Jimmy, Carl and me, and Sue was delighted. Before seeing his mom, though, he wanted to shower and do his laundry in our bathroom, so while I surveyed the storm's damage to our equipment, Ethan went inside to clean up. I was outside in the parking lot laying out shredded tents when I heard Jimmy yelling.

"Hey John, you should come inside and see something."

"I can't right now. I'm busy," I yelled back.

"No, John, really. I think you really should come and check this out."

I wasn't in the mood for fun and games, but Jimmy sounded concerned. I threw some wet panniers on top of the tent I was inspecting so it wouldn't blow away in the afternoon breeze, and then I walked back inside our room. Jimmy rolled his eyes, held one hand over his mouth and then pointed in the direction of the bathroom, where I could hear Ethan taking his shower.

"Yeah, you'll just have to wait until Ethan is done to take your shower," I barked. Jimmy didn't say anything; he just silently pointed in the direction of the bathroom. I walked around the corner and noticed a wet strip of carpet at the threshold of the bathroom door. A steady flow of water was pouring out of the bathroom.

I knocked loudly on the door so that Ethan could hear me over the shower. "Hey Ethan, open up! Are you playing Noah's Ark or something?" I yelled.

The shower turned off and after a few moments a naked and puzzled Ethan poked his head around the door. He was standing in two inches of water, and as he opened the door all the way, I could see that what I suspected was true; he had created a new lake in north-central Arkansas. I looked over at the shower and discovered the meteorological cause for the new body of water. The shower curtain was completely outside the tub, causing all of Ethan's excess to pour out onto the floor. I frowned while Ethan stared at me with his giant brown eyes. The puzzled look on his face told me he still had no idea why I had so rudely interrupted him.

"Did you say something about Noah or something?" he asked.

"Ethan . . . look down at your feet."

Ethan looked down at his submerged toes.

". . . Yeah, what's the matter?"

"Well, don't you see the lake of water you're standing in?"

Ethan looked down again.

". . . Oh . . . that . . . ."

"Hasn't anyone ever taught you how to use a shower curtain?" I asked trying to contain the anger that was being fueled by my exhaustion.

". . . Well . . . uh . . . no, is there a special way to use a shower curtain?" By this time Ethan's shuffling feet had caused little waves of water that were causing the damp strip of the carpet to spread. Now a four foot square section of the carpet was completely soaked.

"You're supposed to PUT THE CURTAIN ON THE INSIDE OF THE TUB SO THE WATER DOESN'T GO ALL OVER THE FLOOR AND RUIN THE FLOOR AND THE CARPET!!!" My voice was a growing crescendo, and poor little Ethan was bearing the brunt of my sleepless impatience. "SO GET OUT YOUR TOWEL AND START MOPPING UP THIS FLOOR BEFORE YOU CONTINUE WITH YOUR SHOWER. AND DON'T YOU DARE USE THE OTHER TOWELS. THOSE ARE FOR JIMMY, CARL AND ME TO SHOWER WITH . . . .

"Carefully mop up the floor so that no more water gets to the carpet. Wring the towel out in the tub and then soak up some more water until the floor is as dry as you can get it. That means no puddles!!! Then when you get back in the shower be sure to put the curtain INSIDE the tub. I can't believe you could be so stupid." I shouldn't have said stupid there at the end, but I was about out of energy and gentleness. I had enough storm damage to worry about outside without Ethan causing some of his own.

I walked back outside trying to figure out how we were going to continue with what I had discovered had happened to our gear. The girls' tent was thrashed beyond repair (four-foot gashes were ripped through the ceiling, poles were broken and their rain fly was in pieces), the boys' could be repaired with a roll of duct tape (their gashes were only two feet long and their fly was still holding together), and Lynn's and mine had a broken pole and rips that would take a few hours of mending. Our tarps looked like swiss cheese, and many of the nylon stuff sacks that held our tents, pads and food were probably floating down the Mississippi.

Before leaving Batesville the next day, I called my brother Jay back home at

Headquarters and asked him if he could get a hold of all the new equipment we needed. He could send it along with Joy's folks who would be meeting us in a week or so in Missouri. We would have to make do until then with some new sleeping arrangements. I would sleep with the guys in their tent and the girls would join Lynn in ours. I had repaired it enough for it to last a few hundred more miles — weather permitting.

Our first night camping in the Ozarks proved my new arrangements possible and very educational — for me. It was an understatement to say that the guys' standards of organization and cleanliness didn't quite match what I was used to sleeping with Lynn. The aroma of adolescent sweat socks perfumed the already stale air inside their nylon abode; all three of them snored to the beat of their own drummers; and although they *were* cute, I didn't get the same thrill cuddling up behind Carl, Jimmy or Ethan as I did from wrapping my arms around Lynn. I just hoped my natural nocturnal instincts wouldn't get the best of me in my sleep . . . so did the guys.

The girls had just the opposite problem. They were a little too organized for Lynn, and she had to clean up her act. Heather and Joy got out their little orange broom and dust pan and gave our tent its first sweeping out in over four years of faithful service. Lynn did suffer from the same nighttime desires as I, and one night in our campground in Blanchard Springs, Joy woke up to find Lynn's arm wrapped around her waist and Lynn's knees tucked up tightly underneath hers in what we called, our "spoon" position. Joy just rolled Lynn over. If I had spooned one of the guys, I have a feeling they wouldn't have been quite so gentle.

My Arkansas bicycle guide described our route as 'extremely difficult, for very experienced cyclists only, full of steep climbs . . . ", but the kids had no problems. Riding the Ozarks was just another bicycling roller coaster, and they just laughed at road signs like the one outside Mountain View that said:

HILL USE GEARS

"No kidding," yelled Carl at the yellow and black sign, as if it could hear what he was saying.

The kids' strength helped them enjoy the beauty of the hills, and our faster pace allowed us to stop and explore many of the fascinating little hill towns that appeared out of nowhere. Dots on the map named Fifty-Six, Pleasant Grove, Hasty and Evening Shade beckoned us to stop for a spell. A place called Loafers Glory seemed to hold a special lure for some members, as did Booger Hollow — home of the Booger Burger.

"C'mon John," laughed Jimmy, "there ain't really a place called Booger Hollow."

"Check out my guidebook, James!" I smiled.

"And a Booger Burger?"

"Yup, says so right here on page 53."

Ethan and Carl wanted to go for a Cheese Booger Burger, but Booger Hollow was just a bit out of our way. Our map meetings in the Ozarks provided lots of laughter, and I often found the kids studying my map to see if they could find more places with unique names. After one morning's break, the guys discovered a town called Ralph.

"Hey John, do you think they named a town Ralph because everyone there throws up?" laughed Carl.

"You guys are gross!" Joy moaned.

Quite pleased with Joy's reaction, my three new tentmates did their best impressions of what they thought a Ralphian might be doing, and off to Ralph we rode.

In the small patch of blacktop outside the Locust Grove General Store, we stopped for some Gatorade, watermelon and a journal break. A hunched over old man in his sixties studied us from under a shady tree beside the store and then ambled over to us as we dripped watermelon juice on our pages. He walked up to where I was sitting on the ground and leaned up against the storefront. With his wrinkled hands resting on the back of his hips, he rocked back and forth. About every dozen rocks he would lean off to the side and spit some brown tobacco juice away from where we sat. He looked at me, rocked, looked down at Lynn and the other writing-and-watermelon-sucking kids, spit, looked back at me and then rocked some more. Finally, after a couple minutes, he lifted the straw hat off his white-haired head, wiped some sweat off his brow with his bandana and spoke.

"I don' mean to be interruptin' you folks or nothin', but what in tarnation you be doin' bicyclin' in these hills. Might steep and hot, ain't they?" He spit when he finished.

"Yes sir, they are that, but they sure are beautiful," I said. It didn't look like I was going to get much journal writing done, so I closed up my book and stood up. Sometimes I was so busy writing about what had happened the day before, I missed meeting the people and places that I had a chance to meet right in front of me.

"Where you people headed?"

"Oh, we started in Washington, D.C. and we're headed to California," I answered.

"Naw . . . if that ain't the damndest—oh 'xcuse my lainguage, there bein' kids 'round here and all—but if that hain't the darndest dang thang I never heared of. I hain't never been out there to Calfornya . . . ." He paused as some old memory seemed to occupy his mind. "But I had me a sweetheart back when I was a younger man and she went off to Calfornya. I done went 'way ta war and came home to find her gone off with some other boy. Last I heared she was out some place called Baker's Field or somethin'."

"Yeah, there's a place called Bakersfield out in the Central Valley of California."

"Well, hit was many years ago an' caint say as I ever heared a word from her since . . . probly better off just as well. Sure loved that girl though. Never loved no one bafore her and hain't never loved no one since."

"You mean, you never married?"

"Nope. Plenty for a man to do 'sides be married. Yes, sir, plenty to do."

He faded off again and I saw a sadness in his old eyes. The clothes he wore, the suntan brown work pants and matching sweat stained tan work shirt looked like they once were shiny and new, but now looked as if he had worn them to work and to bed for a long, long time. The end of his belt ran way past the buckle and wrapped half-way again around his waist. Those ole pants bunched up belt loop upon belt loop, just like I remember my grandpa's pants used to do. He had missed one button hole in his shirt so the collar was all cock-eyed, and the fly on his pants was at half mast. He was as weathered and stained as the old Locust Grove Store, and his hill country accent and nostalgic stories soon had the kids listening from over their closed journals.

"Would you like some watermelon, sir?" offered Joy, as she held up a giant chunk of the bright red and juicy fruit.

"Thank you, I's wunderin' if you-uns would ever ask. Et a lot of watermelon in ma days and caint says as I never grown tired of it." The old guy grinned with a smile that revealed he now had a few less teeth than he was born with. He accepted the piece from Joy's hands and immediately took a large bite, red juice drooling down his chin and adding another spot to his shirt. He made a slurping sound as he downed his first bite, and before continuing, he wiped his lips with his forearm.

Jimmy leaned over to Ethan and whispered, "Hey Eeth, he eats just like you do, man." Ethan laughed and elbowed Jimmy as the old man continued.

"You-uns had yerselves any bad weather yet?"

"Yeah!" Carl jumped up as he answered. "Our second night in Arkansas . . . we had a tornado and spent the night in a girls bathroom." The way Carl emphasized the last part of his answer I couldn't tell what he was more proud of: weathering the storm or spending some time in the Ladies Room.

"Yup we git them things roun' hyer . . . 'member one time . . . just down the road hyer . . . back when it used t' be jus' a dirt wagon path. Not many cars come up hyer back then. Well, anyways, my frens, Tommy and Lennis and me, were havin' us a good ole time playin' checkers out underneath this big ole gum tree one evenin' when all of de sudden things git real quiet like." By this time, Lynn and all the kids were circled around him listening. ". . . Yup, things got real quiet like, and we knowed that didn't mean no good. 'Fore we had chance to do sumthin', damndest wind I ever saw blows the table — checkers and all — right over into Tommy's lap. 'Shoot!' yells Tommy and bafore we knows what hits us, dang saahclone comes dancin' over the hill and rat up the hollow. Tommy, Lennis and me we jis dives for a ditch nearby and holds tight to the brambles. Twister made itself a gosh-a-mighty racket and dang near tore up evrathing for miles around. Boys and me were lucky, though; that old gum tree wasn't gunna let no saahclone take hit for no ride. Never saw that checkerboard agin though and, ifn' I remember correctly, I was winnin' that blasted game."

He stopped long enough to take another chunk out of his piece of melon, and we had just enough time to laugh before he continued.

"Yes, sir, we get saahclones often enuf roun' hyer. One other time I was workin' out in the barn and twister came blowin' right through the farm. Done blowed a bit of fence post right through my hand. See the scar right hyer." He held out his hands and the kids crowded even closer to check it out.

We stood around trading watermelon for stories for almost an hour that afternoon. He told us about the days before cars, of coon hunting and possum stew, and ended it all with a warning about Ozark mosquitoes. "You-uns be careful now, got mosquitoes so big 'roun hyer been known to carry young-uns away for supper." We all laughed again, but after that none of us ever went to bed in Arkansas without annointing ourselves with a thick layer of insect repellant.

One afternoon, while Heather and I napped on the lawn in front of the Berryville drugstore, we were approached by a man wearing a tape recorder around his neck. Lynn and Joy were looking at quilts across the street and the boys were in the drugstore trying to find some alternative to the roadside bushes that had served as outhouses earlier that day.

"Hello, my name is Tim Pointer. Are you part of the group that I saw riding their bicycles just outside of town?"

Heather and I both moaned and slowly got up from our naps. Sometimes, we just wanted to be invisible. The incredible heat, humidity and friendliness of the Ozarks had taken their toll. Heather managed a half smiling "yes" and we both got up.

The young man with the tape recorder didn't look or sound like a local. He had on nice slacks and a sport shirt that looked as if it had even seen an iron that morning. He spoke with only an occasional twang and was one of the first people we had talked to in many miles that didn't use some form of "you all."

"Where you guys headed?" he asked Heather.

The "you guys" part woke Heather and me up immediately. Was this guy from some familiar territory?

"Well, we're from California and we're riding our bicycles from Washington, D.C. to Santa Barbara, California," Heather answered.

Tim may have talked different from most of the people we had been meeting lately, but as soon as Heather finished her answer that old familiar look of disbelief lit up his face.

"You're riding your bicycles with all that stuff on them all the way to California . . . and you've ridden here all the way from Washington, D.C.?"

"Yup," Heather smiled. She had heard all these questions before and was ready for the next question.

"Why?"

She didn't have a chance to answer because at that very moment, Carl and Ethan came running out of the Berryville Drugstore yelling, "Hey you guys, the man at the drug store says he'll buy us all the ice cream we can eat!!! They've got this really neat soda fountain inside just like in the movies, and the man in the white suit fills prescriptions and makes ice cream sodas. You've got to come and see it to believe it."

"Yeah . . . and he's really nice," continued Ethan. "He says 'it ain't no 31 Flavors,' but he's got all the chocolate, vanilla and strawberry we can lick."

Tim must have eaten a few ice creams at the same drugstore because he said, "Go 'head you guys, but can I get an interview with you when you're all done? I'm with the local radio station and I do an interesting people spot on my daily news broadcast. I wish you were going to be around in a couple of days, because I also do a weekly half-hour talk radio show. I sure would like to have all you guys on and hear what your impressions of America are . . . Go get your ice creams now. Believe it or not, I used to work there stocking shelves when I was your age, and I know how good that ice cream tastes. I've got a phone call to make anyway. Take your time, and I'll meet you out here when you're all done."

Inside, the drugstore smelled like a drugstore, but it didn't look like the giant discount drugstores the kids had been brought up with back home. The lighting was soft and dim, and above the giant jars of colored liquids on the top shelf hung black and white pictures of Berryville's past pharmacists. Each of the few short aisles was neatly arranged, and at the end of each one stood a different woman. They were all dressed in bright white smocks that hung past their waists and had big pockets in the front.

Off to the left of the aisles was a chrome and formica-topped bar with six stools lined up like a row of giant metallic mushrooms. Each stool had a vinyl seat that spun on top of a chrome pedestal bolted to the floor. Behind the counter were all the milkshake machines and ice cream cones. The chrome spigots and dippers were so perfectly clean you could see your face in them. The place may have only had three flavors, but it looked prepared to make some mean sundaes and banana splits.

Behind the counter, standing proudly with his arms crossed, was the pharmacist and soda chef. He was either very short or he was standing in some kind of a gutter, because he seemed to be about the same height as Lynn. His white smock had only one pocket and it was stuffed with two pens and the case for his spectacles. Two wonderfully kind eyes twinkled over the top of his bifocals as he welcomed our group. His bald head glistened almost as much as his fountain.

"Looks like you all are in need of somethin' cold," he smiled. I pinched myself to make sure I wasn't dreaming, because I felt thrown back in time again. I half-expected Andy Griffith, Barney Fife and Opie to jingle the bell on the front door as they walked in and joined us for a chocolate sundae. The gentle, little man looked like he was born behind that counter, and I couldn't imagine him not ever being there, smiling and giving kids scoops of ice cream. He probably gave their dogs scoops too.

"Well, what'll it be. Cat got yo tongues?"

We licked cone after cone that afternoon as we visited with the folks at the Berryville Pharmacy. We were the only customers, and the ladies even joined us for a few cones of their own. By the time we finished and had spun around on the squeaky stools for the last time, Heather and I were feeling much friendlier. That little old pharmacist had just what the doctor ordered.

10

We saw a huge, and very dark, black cloud coming towards us with lightning and rain off in the distance. We got our raincoats ready and then we saw a bunch of bright white birds fly across the sky which was very dark. It was very beautiful. Then we rode on in the rain . . . .

Ethan's Journal
August 7, 1986

Mizzou

WELCOME TO MISSOURI said the sign at the top of the hill. We stopped for our usual triumphant picture, as we always did upon entering a new state. The sky just ahead of us looked like it had a welcome ceremony of its own in mind, and not a mile into the Show Me State, it turned from flannel gray to nighttime black.

"Looks like we're gonna get wet, guys," said Jimmy as he unzipped his pannier and got out his rain jacket. Usually we just rode out Ozark thunderstorms in shirt sleeves, because a shower from the sky almost always felt better than the shower of sweat caused by the combination of our rain gear and the humidity. This time, though, it looked like we were in for quite a deluge. We could smell the rain in the sky ahead, and the sudden gust of wind that almost blew Jimmy's jacket out of his hands and back to Arkansas gave us all the weather report we needed.

"Well, I would say the thunder and lightning should be here in just . . . about . . . ." CRACK went a bolt of lightning, interrupting Carl and etching a sharp white squiggle across the black mass across the road. "Now," finished Carl. The kids were getting pretty good at understanding the weather patterns in this part of the country. In addition to geography, linguistics and all the other courses the road had taught them, the kids were becoming pretty well versed in meteorology as well.

At that first crack of lightning, a giant flock of white birds took off from a marsh hidden in the trees. The flock rose over the oaks and spread across the sky like doves at the opening ceremony of the Olympics. Everyone let out a long sigh, in awe of the show in the sky above us. The birds flew towards us, their white forms flickering across the black sky. Another bolt of lightning and crack of thunder caused them to change course, and they fluttered their wings over our heads and turned north, as if to show us the way through their state. We watched them disappear into the darkness, and then the rain started. We finished zipping up our jackets and got back into our pedals.

The rain fell in sheets that day. The Ozarks in southern Missouri seemed less wooded than those in Arkansas, at least on the road we were traveling. In Arkansas we had trees for umbrellas, but in Missouri, we had more open sky. Our road became a swiftly flowing creek and giant plumes of water spewed out from

234

behind us and waterfalls of rainwater streamed off our noses as we cut our way north through the constant downpour. In a way, it was an enjoyable day's ride. Once everything on our bodies got completely soaked and our shoes were squishing like sponges on top of our pedals, we just blinked our eyes to see and stuck out our tongues to lap up the fresh water pouring down our faces. Our water bottles didn't get much attention that first day.

"Man, I can remember when I used to get in trouble for riding my bicycle in the rain," Jimmy said as he rode alongside me. "My friends and me, we used to love throwing roostertails of water on each other as we splashed through every puddle we could find. Then our moms would spoil everything and yell for us to come inside. Moms . . . they're always afraid you're gonna catch a cold. This is kinda fun."

"Yeah, except for the lightning," I answered. Lightning and thunder rattled the dark rain every couple of minutes.

"Man, John, you're always worrying about being struck by lightning. You know what the chances are?" Jimmy didn't sound too concerned about the electricity.

Just past Table Rock Reservoir and Mark Twain National Forest, our schizophrenic hills smoothed some and spread themselves out onto rolling dairy farms. Through the gray veil of rain, we saw large, neatly kept barns and fields of staring cows. No one else was out on the road that day to wave or ask us questions, so the cows mooed hello in their place and interrupted their hunched over lunches of grass to follow us down the road with their big brown eyes.

"Hey, Mr. Cow," I yelled at one cow who seemed to be particularly interested in us, "don't they teach you that it's not polite to stare?"

"Hey John, I hate to tell you, but . . ." Joy was smiling as she rode up next to me, " . . . but that's not a Mr. Cow, but a Mrs. Cow. You don't get milk from the guys!" Joy giggled and then dropped back in the pack. My city roots were showing. I looked back and could see Lynn at the back talking with Joy and laughing herself.

A rather damp and grungy looking group of bicyclists dripped into the town of Mount Vernon, Missouri that evening.

"Let's find us a church, you guys," I said as we stopped at the lights on the outskirts of town. The first steeple we came to was that of the First Baptist Church of Mt. Vernon. I asked everyone to stay outside while I went in trying to find the pastor. I found out the pastor was away at youth camp, and I don't know if it was my squishing shoes or unshaven face, but the secretary, who was holding down the fort in his absence, was a bit skeptical of my proposition that she let us use a classroom or social hall to spend the night. Remembering the Southern Baptist democratic approach to ALL decisions, I wasn't too optimistic myself, and just as I was about to ask if there were any other churches in town, in walked Jimmy, the janitor.

"What's goin' on? 'jus' talked to a group of younguns outside that look like they've had themselves a mighty wet first day in Missoura." Missoura . . . I had heard my great aunt say Missouri that way. It was where my ancestors first settled in America, and Jimmy the janitor sounded just like Aunt Katherine when he said that. From the smile on his face and the tone of his voice, it sounded like he wasn't going to let me go to another church to find shelter. "The woman out there — that must be your wife — she tells me y'all need a place to spend the night tonight. Why, we got plenty of classrooms here ain't bein' used during the week. I'm sure we could find one ta suit ya."

As Jimmy spoke, the secretary didn't look too happy, but I could see that soon we'd have a place to stay. I never met a janitor that I didn't like, and Jimmy was no exception.

"Now, Mabel, I knows Pastor, he ain't here and all, and I cain see ya hesitatin' lettin' these folks stay here without his permission, but they done rode all the way from Eureka Springs in the rain today and we cain't very well turn them away. You gotta see these younguns outside all soaked and wet. Why, their fingers are so puckered up they look like they've been soakin' in a bathtub all day long. Who cain we get hold of to get permission?"

"Well, I think Deacon Miller, he's at home. Think he came down from camp last evenin' . . . 'magine ya could talk to him 'bout it." Mabel wasn't smiling, but she did help us.

"Raight . . . raight . . . 'should have thought of him maself. I'll drive this man over there and we'll talk to Paul. I'll have him call ya when he says it's okay." Jimmy grabbed my arm and whisked me out the door before Mabel had too much time to think things over. "Sorry 'bout that, but Mabel, she jus' don' want to make too many decisions, the pastor not bein' here and all."

"Oh, I understand. Thanks for helping us out. By the way, my name is John." I reached out my hand and Jimmy wiped his on his Levi's before shaking it.

"Sorry, but I'm a might dirty. Some hoodlum threw a dead possum in the church van last night and I've been spendin' the whole day tryin' to clean it up. Done got the possum and all out of there, but, shoot, that van shore smells a might foul. Don't know as I never gonna get that smell out of things. Smells awful. Shore would like to catch them that did it and lock 'em up inside so theys have to smell it for a day . . . Be fittin' punishment."

We went out to where Lynn and the kids were sitting. The rain had stopped and the Missouri sun was already back at work. A steamy fog rose off the wet sidewalks and streets as the water headed home to the sky. Just as I was about to ask the group to wait while I went with Jimmy over to the deacon's house, Jimmy gave the group directions of his own.

"Why don't y'all roll your bicycles inside and I'll open some bathrooms and a room for ya to rest in, out of this sticky weather. Y'all have seen enough moisture for one day. John and I'll be back bafore ya know it, and I'll have a place for ya to roll out yer stuff and make yerselves mo comfortable. Sorry 'bout the delay." Jimmy led us and our dirty bicycles right across the floor he kept so clean.

Like one of the cows we'd met earlier, Mabel stared blankly from the office, and Jimmy led us on to some wonderful ice water and an air-conditioned classroom at the end of the hall. "Jus' make yerselves at home; be back shortly."

"Don't see no reason why eight folks cain't use one classroom," smiled Deacon Miller from his doorway. "Matter of fact, practically the whole town spent the night at church when the tornado siren went off other night." He wanted to visit longer, but Jimmy, knowing Lynn and the kids were waiting back at church, said something about having to get more possum out of the van and whisked me back into his car. Back at church, he showed us the bathrooms and our preschool suite. Before he left later that night, he checked in on us just to make sure we were comfortable. After he tucked us in, we took his picture and promised we'd send him a card when we got to California.

It had been a month since Joy had said good-bye to her mom and dad back near Appomatox, and although I knew the rest of the group — including me — was looking forward to their upcoming second rendezvous, I was a little worried about how Joy would receive them. Visions of that hurt look on Sulie's face as she drove away kept flashing through my mind.

We met the Fultons at Stockton Lake, just a hundred miles south of Kansas City. When Bob and Sulie drove up, the kids were down at the lake fishing and a hesitant Sulie hopped out of their rental car.

"Hi, John, where are the kids?" I could see Sulie had a hug ready for Joy.

"Oh, they're down at the dock fishing. Jimmy's out renting a jet-ski."

"Do you think it's okay if I interrupt them?"

"Go 'head Sulie. They'll be glad to see you." Sulie headed down the hill and Bob got out of the car. As usual, he was his relaxed self. Like a local, he wore a tractor cap and had his styrofoam spittoon in hand, ready for his Skoal juice. Looking quite at home, Bob walked over and sat on the table next to me.

"Well, Captain John, how goes it?" he asked, winking as shook my hand. "Heard you folks ran into some weather back in Arkansas." Bob chuckled and spit into his cup. "You made it here just like you planned, so everything must be okay."

"Yeah, Bob, we made it here, but I never knew how scary weather could be. That night back in Arkansas when that storm blew in . . . I don't think I have ever been so scared in my entire life. Funny thing was, I didn't have time to show it. Everything happened so fast and everyone was looking to me for the decisions. I sure hope I made the right ones . . . . "

"Well, like I said, you're all here safe and sound, so you must have done somethin' right. Other than the weather, how do you feel like you're doin?" Bob didn't usually waste any time, and it was good to have him back again to talk to. In our conversations I usually discovered myself saying something that had been on the tip of my mind for a lot of miles.

"Got a beer?" I asked.

"Sure do. Just wait here, I'll be right back." Bob returned with a tall cold one. "So tell me, how's the journey goin'?"

"Well, Bob . . . this country has shown me — I mean us — more than I ever imagined. You know how sometimes you have this dream of how great things are gonna be . . . and then when you get there, you're kinda disappointed? College was that way for me and turnin' 21, but this trip it's been just the opposite . . . I can't tell you all we've learned — and I don't even know if 'learned' is the right word.

"Remember how I told you once, that when I'm back at school in my classroom, I'm always more excited when kids leave class with more questions than answers?"

"Yeah."

"Well, this trip is kinda like that, only on a much bigger scale. I've got so many more questions in my mind about this country and its people and everything, I can't keep up with them. Every time I sit down to write in my journal, some new person steps up and wants to talk to us. I gave up trying to ignore them for the sake of my journal. I know when I try to write my book I'm going to leave a lot of wonderful things out because I didn't have time to write them down. I just hope my memory does a good job, because there have been so many incredible things that have happened to us.

"Like, we met this guy coming into Arkansas . . . I guess I'd call him a redneck — well, maybe I'd used to call him a redneck — he looked just like one of those bigoted old southern boys I used to poke fun at when I was eighteen. He called black people 'niggers' and I didn't want to have anything to do with him. He bought us breakfast one morning, and, after we were all done, he called me over to his table. I thought he was going to order me out of the county by sundown, but, instead, he just went on and on about how special he thought our trip was.

"Shoot, Bob, he knew my dream as well as I did! He sat there and told me that what we were doing was what every school kid should have the opportunity to do. He even told me how hard it must be sometimes to be doin' what we do everyday. Bob, he was the coolest red-neck I ever met.

"I knew his politics were far from mine, but I found myself liking that man very much. I still shake my head whenever I think of him.

"God, we've met so many wonderful people . . . And they're all so different from each other. The way they talk, the places they live, the things they believe in. I must sound like a commercial or something, because I had heard all those things before, but they're true. America is full of so many different folks and most all of them are just waitin' for a chance to be friendly."

Bob nodded his head as I paused for air. "How are the kids doin'?" he asked.

"Wait til you see them, Dad . . . They're the most incredible little Americans of them all. You know, a lot of our friends thought Lynn and I were crazy spending four months, twenty four hours a day, with a group of five teenagers. 'You'll go crazy,' they said, 'that's the worst possible age . . . As a matter of fact, you won't go crazy, you *are* crazy for even attempting such a thing!'

"Well, Bob, this is the most wonderful asylum I've ever been part of. I watch those kids wiping the sleep out of their eyes at 4:30 in the morning; swatting bugs and eating soggy oatmeal in the dawn rain; riding their bicycles so confidently over these hills and mountains; stopping to talk to locals; asking questions; and writing their remembrances down in their journals. Then they get on their bikes and do the same thing the next day.

"Now, every Sunday, when we get out the big map and mark another couple hundred miles and remember another couple hundred wonderful folks, I get tears in my eyes. I used to be scared to take out that map because it made everything look so big, but now, even though we all know this country's even bigger, I get the map out with no fears at all. Those kids have pedaled almost two-thousand miles! They've learned America's not only bigger than advertised; it's better.

"This group can handle anything. Lynn and I couldn't have made it this far without them. We love them more than we ever imagined we would, and your daughter, Joy — Where can Lynn and I get another one just like her?"

"She's been doin' well, huh?"

"I know I've told you how special she is before, but I'm not kidding. That day she fell on the Blue Ridge . . . she was in a lot of pain, but she just bit the bullet. Her riding sixty miles the next day meant more to all of us than I can ever say.

"She always tries to make things easier. If there's a disagreement, she always sees how she can help. Her only problem is getting up in the morning. Heather isn't always so excited about having to roll her out of bed, but I understand, I have the same problem every morning with Lynn.

"And Heather and Joy . . . what a pair. Watch them and the way they handle their camp chores and their riding these next couple days and you'll see what I mean."

I would have probably gone on with my monologue well into the six-pack if Sulie and the troops hadn't returned from the lake. Even Lynn had been fishing and she showed me her catch. She held up a bluegill that looked more like a piece of bait than something someone would catch.

"Hey, sweetheart, how did that little thing open its mouth wide enough to swallow one of those night crawlers?" I asked.

Lynn stuck her tongue out at me and said, "Well, dear, you've been fishing in every state since Virginia and you haven't caught anything yet. One little fish is better than no fish at all. Besides, the girls and I think this one is especially cute."

Surprisingly, my once-vegetarian wife (who later admitted to me that Carl had baited her hooks for her) wanted to know immediately where the frying pan was, and if I would get out my knife and clean her fish.

"Me? . . . clean *your* fish? I think the Official Missouri State Fishing Guide says that each fisherperson needs to clean their own fish, aren't I right, Bob?"

"Sorry, Captain, I'm much smarter than to answer that question. Being a married man myself, I'll have to plead the fifth."

"Thanks a lot, Bob," I laughed.

Carl gladly volunteered to clean all the fish. Joy and Heather showed us their fish and explained theirs were for looking not cooking. They were going to return their catch to the lake: Joy tried talking hers back to life and Heather tried tickling hers. They only surrendered their fish to the frying pan after their attempts to revive the "cute little bluegills" failed.

We hadn't seen any turtles since the Blue Ridge, but they returned to the road somewhere around a place called Jericho Springs. Joy and Heather found one precariously plodding across the road, adopted it and named it Mizzou. Sulie promised to smuggle it on the airplane home, and the last time I checked it was still being fed California lettuce and bugs in Joy's backyard.

The Fultons spent three days fishing and following us through the Ozarks of southwestern Missouri. Bob marveled at the changes in our group, and Sulie was happy to see how glad Joy was to see her. One afternoon, as we stopped for a picnic lunch of just-fried fried chicken (the secret recipe used Kellog's Corn Flakes), I happily watched Joy lean up next to her mom as they both ate. Two months of pedalling had done another one of the things I'd hoped it would . . . Joy missed her mom and she wasn't afraid to show it. The next morning, after our last biscuits and gravy in Missoura, it was time for the second Fulton Rendezvous to end, and Joy showed much different emotions saying good-bye this time. Tears fell freely from her eyes, and she sobbed as she held her mom in one of her I-won't-let-go hugs. Bob winked at me as we shook hands, Sulie whispered something in Joy's ear and then kissed her on the forehead. Joy finally let go and wiped her face. Before getting in the car, Sulie came over to Lynn and me and gave us both strong hugs. We all waved good-bye as Bob, Sulie and Mizzou drove away. Everyone, especially Joy, looked forward to Fulton Rendezvous Number Three, one month and fifteen hundred miles down the road, somewhere near Oregon.

Jim

Joy's eyes were still wet when, just a mile west of our breakfast with Bob and Sulie, we were waved off the road by a young man in an old green Dodge. I saw him first, waving his arms wildly from a gravel driveway. He appeared to be about my age and wore jeans, tennis shoes, white t-shirt and a beaming smile. He looked like a little kid watching a parade and I suddenly found myself smiling back at him and pulling to a stop. Jimmy wrinkled his eyebrows, wondering why I had stopped so soon after we had just left, and four confused kids and one confused wife soon stopped behind him.

"M' name is Jim and I saw y'all back in town when I was doin' ma chores earlier this mornin'. I was hopin' ya'd be comin' out this way, so I bought some cold drinks to refresh ya." He hopped around nervously as he talked to us. "Don't get a chance to see folks ridin' through here on their bikes, and from the looks of all that stuff ya got there on yers, I figured ya must be goin' a long ways, and I was hopin' I would get a chance to talk to ya. Only a couple ways to go comin' out of town, and I just hoped I was lucky enough to be on the way y'all were headed."

I explained our trip to Jim, and with each state I mentioned, he got more and more excited. I wouldn't have been surprised if he had asked us for our autographs.

"Ya know, back in '76 a large group of cyclists crossing the contry came right through here and stayed in a church in town. I was able to get off work and visit with some of them. Ever since then, I've wanted to see this contry from a bicycle." There was something about Jim that made me want to laugh and cry at the same time. Possessing the spirit of a child in his adult body, I bet he waved to everyone who drove by and said hello to everyone he passed back on the sidewalks in town.

As Jim began talking about the Schwinn back home in his garage awaiting its day to see America, I noticed the kids looking with less-than-enthusiastic eyes on the twelve ice-cold sodas sitting on the hood of his car. I was overly full myself from all the biscuits, gravy, sausage and pancakes Joy's folks had treated us to just fifteen minutes before, and although my group was almost always up for drinking vast quantities of carbonated beverages, from the rolling eyes I saw that morning, I could tell Jim's two six-packs would be a struggle. Fighting back a burp myself, I spoke to the kids for the first time since we had stopped.

"You guys, this is Jim and he saw us back in Butler before we had breakfast. He bought us some cold drinks to cool us off." As I spoke, I gave the kids my don't-ask-questions look, and they seemed to get the message that, full or not, it wouldn't be wise to turn down this hospitality.

"Could I please have a Coke?" asked Carl.

"Yeah, I'm so thirsty I bet I could drink a whole sixer myself," groaned Jimmy. Recognizing Jimmy's sarcastic tone, the girls rolled their eyes and Ethan giggled, as he nudged Jimmy. Jim, not recognizing any of these hidden messages, immediately started taking orders.

"Oh, I'm awful sorry, I got carried away with myself and forgot to give y'all your drinks. What would you like, girls?"

Joy and Heather went for Sprite, and I had no trouble extending my conversation with Jim. Although I didn't want to take this much time out of our riding time today, I knew that unless I took this stop slow, the kids would soon be spraying the Missouri roadside with their breakfast.

"So you're riding all the way to California . . . I never been there, but I'm gonna be there this fall," Jim continued proudly. "Yup, I've saved myself enough money to go there by train . . . Ain't never been on no train before neither, and I'm kinda excited. I hear California's a mighty big place. I'm gonna get myself a window seat and see all I can." Jim's eyes got bigger and bigger as he talked, and I saw the kids smiling as he described his first train trip with as much excitement as a five-year-old.

"Well, why don't you come and visit us in Santa Barbara?" asked Lynn. "The train station is right near our house."

"Well, I don't know if they'll let me get off the train," answered Jim.

"What d'ya mean, 'if they'll let you get off the train'?" asked Jimmy. "Are they keeping you locked up or something?"

"Oh noo, they just said that there will only be so many places that we'll get to go sight seeing, and I can't remember if Santa Barbara is one of those places . . . You see, with my job and everything, I could only afford a short trip, and I guess it's kinda rushed. I know I won't get to see everything like you all are getting to, but at least I'll get to see the Pacific Ocean and I'll get to meet some new people on the train."

"I think trains are neat," said Joy. "And I bet you'll have a wonderful time. Maybe someday, when you've saved enough money for that bike trip of yours, you'll get to California again, and then you'll get to see it slow like we are."

"And if you can get off the train, I'll buy you dinner," said Lynn. "John and the kids won't be home yet, but I have to be back in California September first to start my first grade classroom, so I'll be home." She reached into her handlebar bag and pulled out one of our business cards. "Here, here's our address and phone number. You just call me when you get to Santa Barbara. If you can get off the train, I'll take you out for some Mexican food, and if you can't, I'll come down and wave when you stop to pick up passengers. The train station is an easy bike ride from our house."

"Well," Jim hesitated. "I don't quite know what to say. I wouldn't want to inconvenience you or anything. You wouldn't really want to come down and just wave to me on the train now, would you?"

"Sure, why not?" answered Lynn. "After all, look at us here with you sipping nice cold drinks. You didn't have to go out and buy us these."

"Yeah, but that's different . . . You all are riding your bikes across America, and I'm just riding a train . . . Do you really think it would be okay if I could call you?"

"I'd be hurt if you didn't," insisted Lynn. "I'll be waiting for your call." With Lynn's answer, Jim tucked our card safely away in his pocket and blushed.

"Hey Jim," said Carl. "Thanks for the drinks. What should I do with my bottle?"

"Oh here, give it to me, I'll throw it away. Anybody want anymore? I've still got some left."

The kids, who were politely holding back the burps they usually let fly on the open road, looked around at each other.

"Thanks anyway, Jim," I answered. "But I think we had better be getting down the road. We're going to enter Kansas today, and we've still got a ways to go."

"I understand." Jim got a sad look on his face, as he collected all the bottles from us. "I sure enjoyed meeting you all, and I sure hope you have a safe trip. You're sure it's alright for me to call you when I get to Santa Barbara and everything?"

Lynn smiled. "Like I said, I'll be expecting your call."

"Gosh, I sure wish I could join you all in what you're doing," Jim continued. "But, ya know, someday I will . . . Well, you folks best be gettin' a move on. I've done held ya up too long already. Thanks for stoppin' and takin' the time to talk with me."

"Hey, thanks for the drinks," said Jimmy, as he looked up from tightening his toe strap.

"Yeah, thanks for the drinks," chorused everyone else. Jim stood waving at our westward parade as we disappeared over the rolling hills of Missouri. We smiled and burped our way all the way to Kansas.

11

There was a storm brewing. We biked for a while and somehow we started singing songs from The Wizard of Oz.
. . . Something to do with Kansas, Toto?

Jimmy's Journal
August 13, 1986

Black Cats

Just after our photo session at the Kansas state line, we celebrated the 2000-mile mark of our journey. Sometime later that afternoon, Lynn and the kids decided to add a new member to our traveling band. Maybe everyone figured our two milestones that day would put me in an "easy" mood to approve their addition, and that evening at dinner in Spring Hill, Kansas, I noticed everyone huddled around Lynn, whispering and covering something in Joy's handlebar bag. As soon as I came around the corner, everyone got quiet and stood up straight as if nothing was going on.

"Should we tell him now?" Joy's whispered question to Lynn wasn't intended for my ears, but I heard it anyway.

"Tell John what?" I queried.

"Oh nothing," smiled Lynn, as all the kids lined up behind her.

"Now I may look stupid, but I know that look on your face, dear. What's going on?" At that point I was in a good mood for the very reasons the kids assumed. I just wanted to know what the big secret was.

"Let's tell him," said Joy. This time she didn't whisper, but she looked worried.

"Okay, I'll tell him you guys." Lynn walked up to me gingerly and gently grabbed my arm. "Now, John, I want you to be calm, okay?"

"Calm about what? Is something the matter?"

"Oh no, nothing's the matter, I just want you to promise to be calm." The kids were deathly silent as Lynn spoke to me. "You see, this afternoon, Joy and Heather found a little black kitten on the side of the road all alone —" Lynn paused and the kids all took a deep breath. They knew I liked cats as much as Snoopy did and had heard that I had repeatedly refused to allow a kitten in our house at home.

"So . . . ." I interrupted.

"Well, they didn't want the kitten to die out there all alone, so I told them they could keep it and try to find it a home." Lynn's last words went by real fast, and the kids let out a sigh of relief as they awaited my reaction.

"You what?!!!"

"So, I told them they could keep the kitten until they found it a new home." As Lynn repeated her explanation, I saw Joy open her bag and take out a scrawny and mucous-eyed little black kitten.

"You let Joy put that cute little kitten in her handlebar bag?! The same place she puts some of *our* food?" My voice was neither calm nor soft at that point. "Do you know where that cat has probably been? We are not going to have a kitten traveling with this group!"

"But don't you want to see it? The kids said that they would feed it every-day and make sure it was clean?" Lynn continued her argument.

"No, I want that cat out of here. The kids have enough to do feeding them-selves and keeping themselves and their own laundry clean. We don't have time to be caring for a pet." In a few short seconds I had become really angry, and neither Lynn nor the kids could understand why their cute little ball of fur had brought out my worst side.

"Listen, Lynn, we are trying to get to Jackson Hole in time for you to see the Tetons before you have to fly home and leave the trip, and we can't afford any more diversions than the ones that will naturally occur over the next three weeks. We have a lot of pedaling to do, and seeing that I'm the one who gets us up every morning and gets our first meal going before everyone is up, and hangs the clothesline and finds the food stops, I don't want to add something else for the kids to do along the way. I don't want any cute cat getting in the way of the things we need to do, and I won't allow it." I was shaking with anger.

As far as everyone had come in taking care of themselves and each other, there still were the many times each day when I definitely had to lead, when I had to remind everyone of chores to be done and then had to remind them again. I didn't want the milk going to the cat instead of to Joy's oatmeal, and I didn't want our attention being distracted from our journals to our kitten. Many times I allowed decisions to be made by discussion, but this time was not going to be one of them.

"But I told the kids that they could keep the kitten until they found it a new home," countered Lynn.

"Listen, Lynn, you're not hearing what I'm saying. We are trying to make it to California, and trying to get you over the Continental Divide before you have to go home. I'm the one whose responsibility it ultimately is to get us there. I will not, I repeat, will not have a cat in anyone's handlebar bag. WE DON'T HAVE TIME!"

"Well, I told the kids what I told the kids, and I'm not going to break my promise." Lynn matter of factly defied my decision and waited for my reply. I was beside myself with anger, but no one seemed to understand. I was as alone as I was every morning before I woke everyone up, but that evening I wish I had had some company. Knowing that soon I would get even louder and more angry, I threw down my helmet and took off down the street.

"But what about your dinner?" Lynn yelled after me.

I didn't even turn around; I just kept walking. Tears rolled down my face as the exhaustion of leading finally caught up to me. I cussed out Lynn and I cussed out the stupid cat that had made me show a side of myself to the kids I had prayed would never surface. I cussed and then I sobbed, trembling from having come to the end of my rope. If there was a low point to my trip, that evening had to be it. Could we travel with a cat??? Yeah, Joy could probably handle it, but I knew it would slow us down, and with the second part or our journey coming up following the Oregon Trail, and with less than three weeks to go twelve hundred miles, and Lynn leaving the trip and all . . . damn that cat. Why couldn't Lynn have seen that before she let the girls keep it? Who was this trip for, John? I asked myself. Was it for the kids? . . . Was it for Lynn? . . . Or was it just for you? You just don't like cats, that's all.

No, no, but it wasn't that.

I walked and walked while Lynn and the kids did something about dinner. It was getting dark and I still had to find us a place to stay — why couldn't I just get a little silent cooperation from the troops and my wife? When I got back to where the group was having their hamburgers, I wasn't raving, but I was still mad.

I had never before seen the look the kids wore on their faces when I returned. Even Jimmy, who had seen more of my moods than anyone except Lynn, looked scared of me, and I got even more mad at that cat for bringing that fear to their faces. Lynn told the kids to sit still and walked over to me.

"What you just did was really unfair, John. I made a promise to Joy and Heather, and you had no right to break that promise. The kids are really upset. Joy even started crying when you walked away. You know what she said?" I stared blankly and Lynn continued, "She said this was all her fault, that if she would have known that you would get so upset that she would never have dreamed of helping that cat. She loves you a lot, John — all the kids do — and she didn't want to do anything to upset you most of all. While you were gone, the kids didn't even get dinner; they spent the entire time trying to find the cat a home and you know what . . . they found some people to take it. I think you owe everyone an apology." When Lynn was finished she crossed her arms like an Indian chief. She was a little angry herself.

Even with the cat gone, I was still wiped out. From the look on Lynn's face, I could tell she still didn't understand my concerns about adding another chore to the journey, so I surrendered myself to the fact that I would just have to swallow any more attempts at an explanation. It was sometimes lonely at the front, and this would be one of those times. I knew that Lynn and I wouldn't be doin' much cuddling, wherever we slept that night, but that in time, we'd be back snuggled together. The kids, those five scared faces I'd grown to love so much, were another matter. I had hurt them and their eyes showed the bruises. I hoped they'd let me hug them again soon.

I apologized to the kids, and then we went inside the Tastee Freeze for dinner. I ordered one of my favorites: two corn dogs. You'd think, of all places to get a corn dog, that Kansas would rank up there with the best, and although they may have been very good, those two dogs I ate on the corner that evening in Spring Hill were the worst two I ever tasted. I think I ruined everyone's dinner that night.

Wagon Ruts

The logo for *From Sea to Shining Sea* was an outline of the continent of the United States. It was dotted with caricatures of American people — farmers, loggers, fisherman, kids, politicians, mothers and fathers. Those caricatures were supposed to symbolize all the folks we hoped to meet on our journey across the America of 1986. Also on that continental USA, bold and black across the middle, was a covered wagon heading west, followed by a rather tall bicyclist and a line of much smaller bicyclists. That image traveling west was supposed to symbolize the second part of our trip — the part when we would be trying to meet some of the America and Americans who traveled and inhabited the band of land known as the Oregon and California Trail. In the spring of 1848 and 1849, thousands of Americans journeyed towards the Pacific, and we wanted to see if we could experience a little of that history ourselves.

Earlier that year, in my social studies class, we had read about all the men, women and children who had packed up their belongings and made their way to Independence, Missouri to set off across the Plains, and after two months of pedalling we finally arrived at what those pioneers called "The Jumping Off Place." Armed with the journal of an old gold rusher named William Swain and maps marking his route, we prepared to relive America's great migration west; only, instead of walking alongside a wagon pulled by oxen, we would be riding on top of two-wheeled wagons, pedaled by us.

In the two years of planning that led up to our crossing, I had read dozens of pioneer journals describing coming west in the nineteenth century. I settled on the journal of William Swain to be our guide because the book in which it was published, J.S. Holliday's *The World Rushed In*, was unique. Not only did it contain Mr. Swain's journal, but it also contained the letters of his family, who had to stay at home back in the spring and summer of 1849, while William went to California in search of "shiny rocks." I could be reading what it was like out on the trail to the kids, while their parents and brothers and sisters could be reading what it was like to stay home. I threw my dog-eared copy of Swain's journal into my panniers and gave each of the kids' families copies of the Swain family letters, excited that they could become part of the second half of our journey in their own special way. When I had seen Carl's mom in Williamsburg; during Sulie's first rendezvous at Appomatox; and when Ethan's mom visited us in the Ozarks, I kept remembering what William's wife, Sabrina, had said about miss-

249

ing her husband. On April 15, 1849, she wrote:

> ". . . William, if I had known that I could not be more reconciled
> to your absence than I am, I never could have consented to your
> going . . ."

I wondered if my five *From Sea to Shining Sea* moms found any solace in realizing that, over a hundred years ago, Mrs. Swain shared their feelings.

On the eve of our crossing William's wagon path near Topeka, I was nervous and excited at the prospect of our experiences matching his. Having read and re-read his journal and having almost memorized all his trials and tribulations, if I had known, that night, how close our experiences would come to his over the next two months, I might not have continued the journey.

"Hey John, Kansas ain't flat!" remarked Carl as we sat in Audra's Cafe in Baldwin City.

"Yeah John, I've always heard that Kansas was flatter than a pancake," said Jimmy. The kids seemed no worse for last night's encounter with my darker side, and at second breakfast, they were already asking questions and providing commentary on the morning's ride.

"Hey John, do you think every state's going to welcome us with rain our first day?" asked Joy. "Because the last two have."

This second breakfast was actually our third breakfast that morning. It was only eleven o'clock, but I decided we needed to stop again before lunch. I ordered a third breakfast stop not only because we were soaking wet from the thunderstorm we'd been riding in since dawn, but also because I was still feeling a little guilt over my rough treatment of the kids last night. That day, I was going to be a softy. I just hoped we didn't come across anymore stray kittens.

"Well, I can't argue with the weather, and, Joy, that is pretty interesting that we have had rain our first full days in Arkansas, Missouri and Kansas. As for the flatness, William Swain describes the plains in Kansas as 'undulating.'"

"What does 'undulating' mean?" asked Heather. Her face was spattered with mud that passing traffic had thrown all over her. The rest of the group, too, looked as if they had been out playing in the mud, and, even though we'd only just sat down, puddles of muddy water were forming underneath our tables.

"What are you kids doin' out in this rain?" barked the large lady who had been standing behind the counter. She came over and with both hands on her wide hips, she stood over us like a mother hen. When Jimmy told her that we were riding our bikes across America, she immediately ran over to the door, poked her head outside and saw for herself our bikes leaning up against the fence and getting drenched in the downpour.

"Well, them bicycles shore look like they're headed a long ways. How 'bout some hot chocolate for you kids and some coffee for your parents?"

The kids giggled when the woman unknowingly called Lynn and me their parents. "These aren't our parents," insisted Jimmy. "John's our teacher and Lynn's his wife."

"You mean ta tell me that yer out here riding in the rain, across the country, and these ain't even yer parents!!! Why . . . yer parents and these two adults here, they must be very special folks to let you be doing this." Our mother hen, still hands on hips, was now shaking her head. "Now, before I go and get you that cocoa, why don't you all take off those wet shoes and jackets of yers. Don't you mind if the floor gets wet neither. You being kids and all, ain't nobody in *my* restaurant gonna complain. You just make yerselves comfortable and warm. Here are some menus, and I'll be raight back with those hot drinks."

Audra's was just a small one room cafe with a half dozen tables and a counter with the grill right behind; it seemed to be the only place in town. Even though we sat off in the corner, our waitress and the cook, who looked like our waitress' twin sister, soon had the whole place informed of the group of kids from California biking across America. I was in the middle of my explanation of the word 'undulating' when our waitress returned with our steaming mugs.

"Ma daughter, she moved out to California just outside a Sacramento, and when she had her first child I went out to visit . . . Been out there for holidays evra Christmas since . . . I don't care too much for the bigness of everything out there. I always look forward to gettin' back home. Find folks a lot friendlier back here. Sure wish I could convince my daughter and her family to move back. They just say: 'Grandma, why don't ya come out here and live near us?', but I just can't bring myself to leave here. Folks in Baldwin are the friendliest folks I ever been around. Even my own daughter and grandkids can't get me to move away.

"Oh yeah, I almost forgot, ma name's Jackie," she added, as she turned to get our orders from the cook. Audra's had the best restaurant pancakes we had ever tasted.

Lynn and Jackie got into a lengthy discussion about the friendliness of the people we had met so far in the Midwest. Jackie took notes and even got out her camera, and her notes and photograph appeared as a story in that week's edition of the Baldwin paper.

I was hoping that our third breakfast that morning might give us and the sky a chance to dry out, but we had no such luck. The rain continued to pour down outside and I gave everyone the command to squeeze their wet socks back into their wet shoes. Our shoelaces dripped as we tied them into squeaky bows. Even the hardened, weather-proof farmers having breakfast at Audra's couldn't believe we were heading out into the storm. They shook their heads and wished us good luck as we velcroed our leather gloves still heavy from all the rain. Ethan turned his helmet over to place it on his head and water came pouring out all over the floor.

"Good move," chided Jimmy.

"Oh don't worry about it," smiled Jackie, "got lots of moppin' to do anyway. You kids be careful now, storm's not s'posed to let up 'til late this afternoon."

The kids walked out to their bikes with their hands turned up to the gray sky to catch the pouring rain. Everyone, except for Joy and me, had yellow nylon rain jackets with long tails that covered their fannies and large-billed hoods that fit over their helmets. When their hoods were cinched down over their helmets, they looked like pumpkin-headed aliens, their eyes peeking out of the little opening in front. Occasionally, the kids would lay their heads back, look up at the sky, and I could see a little tongue poking skyward. I couldn't decide whether they were exhibiting some gesture of disapproval towards the heavens or if they were merely taking a drink from the clouds.

Lynn was the last to exit Audra's as she wound up her conversation with Jackie and the cook. We waved good-bye as we stood next to our bicycles ankle-deep in the puddles of the parking lot. Thunder and lightning rumbled and flashed in the distance, and as we turned west at the corner, it looked like we were heading right for it.

"Hey John," yelled Heather as we rode in formation through town, "you know what the worst part of riding in the rain is?"

"No, Heather, what?"

"Well, I think the worst part is when you first start riding. You know, when you're still kinda dry. Those first drips of water down your neck and into your underwear are the worst, but once you're completely drenched and your fingers are all shriveled up and your shoes are all squooshy, then it's kinda fun."

"Kinda fun?" moaned Carl. "Heather, are you crazy?"

"Yeah, I agree with Heather . . . " grinned Ethan. "I kinda like getting wet too . . . except when trucks come by and splatter us with all the dirt and junk from the road." A not-so-distant bolt of lightning cracked as Ethan finished.

"Alright!" cheered a smiling Heather. "I like the lightning. It's neat to watch the patterns it makes across the sky. Sometimes I just miss seeing it off to the sides of us. But sometimes I'm lucky to be watching just the right part of the sky to see it. When the rain gets boring, it's nice to watch the lightning."

The miles rolled by as the kids continued their discussion of the water and light show that surrounded us. Jimmy and I were soon off the front of the group riding a quarter of a mile ahead of everyone else. We used what we called our "Peel Off Technique." I would wait for Jimmy, tell him which way to turn and then head off; then Jimmy would wait for the next person (usually Heather or Joy) and they would wait for the next person. It was kinda like a game of bicycling telegraph. Our system allowed us to ride alone or with a partner, never having to worry about getting lost. Some days we'd ride as a tight group and other days we'd spread out to get some time and space to ourselves. That day leaving Baldwin, everyone seemed to want some privacy so we spread out.

Heather and the rest of the bunch may have enjoyed rolling underneath the arches of electricity, but I was suffering from visions of electrified bicycles. Other than the occasional van or truck that splashed us with road muck, we seemed to be the tallest things on the hilly farm country of eastern Kansas. And with each thundering crack, I imagined little piles of smoldering yellow nylon beside the road, melting like the Wicked Witch of the East. I looked up at the sky, careful not to extend my tongue, and said a quick prayer, "Hey God, please not us, okay?"

I thought I heard him laugh and say, "Would I do that? I'm helping you guys get to California . . . You wanted a little adventure, didn't you?"

I smiled and said, "Thank you", but I have to admit I still jumped a little when the next bolt exploded like a cannon off to the north. The angels on lightning duty that day must have laughed at me all afternoon.

Steve

"Guess what, you guys." The storm had broken and we were sitting on a patch of green prairie about ten miles south of Topeka. "We just passed William Swain."

"What, are you kidding?" asked an excited Joy. "I didn't see him. I mean, I didn't see any markers or ruts or anything."

I pulled Swain's journal from my panniers and the kids hurried over to sit in a circle for sandwiches and one of our first readings from our pioneer friend's diary. "Believe it or not, you guys, when Swain came rolling through here with his wagon train, he had a thunderstorm just like the one we just had.

"Listen to this:

> "May 24, 1849. This morn our camp was well enough to travel, and we started early from campground. We had before us one half-mile away the Wakarusa River—

"The Wakarusa River!!!" exclaimed Joy. "Wasn't that the river we crossed just before the storm ended and we took off our rain jackets? I thought it had a strange name."

"You're right, Joy," I answered, "that was the Wakarusa." Then I continued with William's account:

> ". . . a thunderstorm commenced as we were ascending a hill or bluff about two hundred feet high. Our captain rode forward to reconnoiter and viewing him through the mist from the vale, he looked like a sentinel—

"Hey John, that means you're kinda like our captain, huh?!" observed Ethan, who had been listening so intently he had both jars of peanut butter and jelly stalled in his lap.

253

"Yeah, Captain John," laughed Jimmy. "Hey Eeth, hurry up with the PB&J!" I continued again:

> ". . . As we raised the hill, thunder, lightning, rain, hail and tremendous wind made the elements 'war.' . . . I turned with reluctance from the sight and walked after our teams, wading through flowers and through peltings of the storm, which, with our oilcloth suits on, were harmless to us."

"Hey John, that *does* sound just like us," said Heather.

"Except we need to get some of those oilcloth suits!" sighed Carl. "I don't know about you guys, but even with all my zippers closed, I got soaked." Everyone nodded in agreement with Carl.

"Hey Lynn, what's oilcloth?" asked Heather.

"Well, I don't know if anyone uses it anymore, but I can remember oilcloth when I was in elementary school. Whenever we painted, we painted on tables covered with green oilcloth. It almost seemed like rubber or plastic."

"Oh yeah, I know that stuff," said Jimmy. "It kinda smells weird and they staple it or tack it underneath the tables. At my school they covered the easels with it."

"Is it kinda thick and woven underneath, like canvas?" asked Heather.

"That's the stuff," Lynn answered.

"Man, I can see how a suit like that would keep you dry, but can you imagine how hot wearing that stuff would be?" said Jimmy. "It'd be like wearing a wetsuit!"

"Keep reading, John," insisted Ethan.

> "May 25, 1849. This morn we are all soaked out by last night's heavy rain. About midnight the wind commenced a rookery such as you find nowhere but on these 'land seas,' and the rain fell in streams, literally. Tents blew down; the boys yelled, sang, laughed, swore, and turned out of their beds in their shirts, pants and socks, drenched in rain. Our tent was strongly staked and stood the storm, but the rain found the bottoms, and we were lying in the water before we could get up. Beds wet, shirts and stockings, too. We scratched up, put on clothes, and stood it till morn, when we changed clothes, made fires and had a fine day."

"Sounds like our night back in Arkansas," giggled Heather.

"Yeah, but it sounds like his tent stakes were a lot better than ours," said Carl. "Hey Jimmy, are you finished with that peanut butter yet?"

I closed up William's journal and the kids spent the rest of their lunchtime comparing their adventures to the pioneers'. Lynn and I, two silent teachers, sat back and listened, as proud as we could be.

"What you folks doin'?" The man's red face poked out of the window of his Chevy and interrupted the kids' discussion. For some reason, I didn't like the look in his eyes, and I waved, hoping he'd drive by. His was the only car that had passed us since we had sat down over a half hour ago. He sped past us, made a screeching u-turn and then headed back to where we were eating. His car came to a skidding halt in the gravel over by our bicycles.

"Hey John, that man looks like he's as tall as you are," gasped Ethan.

"What do you think he wants?" asked a concerned Lynn. She, too, didn't like the looks of our visitor, and when he came weaving over to our little group with a half empty bottle of whiskey in one of his large hands, I got a little nervous.

"I asked: 'What are you folks doin'?', and all I got were some waves . . . ." His eyes were blood-shot and the odor of alcohol surrounded him. Lynn started to pack up lunch and tried to give the kids silent messages to do the same. "My name's Steve and I grew up around here. Ain't too often we see many travelers come through here."

"My name is John, this is my wife Lynn and these are my students, Jimmy, Heather, Joy, Carl and Ethan. We're riding our bikes across America. We started in DC and now we're following the Oregon and California Trail back home to California."

"Oh, you mean this is some sort of school or somethin'?"

"Yeah, you could call it that."

"When I was these kids' age I hiked and swam and fished all 'round this place. Born and raised right here. Didn't leave until I got drafted into the god-damned war." Steve had carrot orange hair and matching fu-manchu moustache. He looked to be about my age, and as he told his story, I began to feel sorry for him. "Yup, went to Vietnam, just like my friends, and came home all screwed up. Didn't get nothin' for servin' my country.

"You know . . . when I was little, I used to *play* army in these hills and creeks. Playin' weren't nothin' like the real thing. We were all so stupid. We didn't know crap about fightin' a war over there . . . ." Steve stopped to take a swig from his bottle, then continued:

"Where do you stay on this cross country trip of yours?"

"Oh, we stay in campgrounds and churches and schools; sometimes we stay in motels." Lynn and the kids were glad to let me do the talking that afternoon. They saw the bottle and smelled the alcohol as well as I did.

"Well shoot, why don't you stay at my house tonight? I'll even buy the hot dogs for a cookout. My friends and me, we used to go canoin' down in the river and then have a cookout and overnight on summer nights when I was younger. I'm sure your kids would enjoy a cookout in my back yard."

The kids stared silently and looked to me for some signal whether they were supposed to smile or not.

Steve continued, "And tomorrow I can show you Topeka. It's the most beautiful city I ever been to. Not many folks talk about it, but I was sure glad as hell to get back to it after bein' in the service. Got us a nice park downtown with a lake and a beautiful rose garden. The girls, they would probably like the rose garden . . . And there's the capitol building . . . Yeah, there's lots to see in Topeka and I can show you tomorrow."

"Well, thanks for your invitation, but after riding in the rain today, I promised the kids a motel and showers."

"Hell, my house has got a shower," he insisted.

"Well, most of our stuff is really wet and we need to do some laundry and get some supplies for the next week. We don't get a chance to be in a large town very often, so we really need to head all the way into Topeka today." Luckily, Steve lived out here, still miles from Topeka. I was afraid he was still going to push his invitation, but he just took another gulp from his bottle and remained silent for a few very long seconds.

Screwing the cap back on the bottle, he looked into it and continued, "Drank an awful lot of this stuff since comin' home . . . yeah, just can't seem to get off it . . . I understand about your needing to get to town and all, but let me be your escort anyway. I know these roads like the freckles on the back of my hand, and I'll get ya to Topeka the easiest way possible." There was a sad look in Steve's red eyes and I wanted to go along with him, but as tame as he seemed out in that open field, I was afraid that his bottle would get the best of him. He seemed to have some anger lurking beneath his sadness, and I was afraid it might explode. I also worried about his driving. I certainly didn't want a drunk escort taking us into the largest city we'd visited since Memphis.

"Oh, that's okay, but I think I can find our way into town. I've got a good map here that marks the route really well. You don't need to escort us in."

"No, damnit! I insist, and don't you worry none 'bout my drivin'. I can drive a straight line a lot more sauced than I am right now." He stood up suddenly, grabbed his bottle and took another large swig, spilling some, Ethan-style, down his shirt. "Damn!" Lynn and the kids looked at me with fear I rarely saw in their eyes, as the tall, red-haired man stumbled over to his car. "Let's go!" he yelled.

"Okay, everyone, just stay cool and stay together," I whispered. "We'll take it real slow and easy. If you need to stop, just say so and we'll all stop together."

Lynn couldn't hold back her fear. "John, I don't like the way he looks at me or the girls. What if he tries something? He's really drunk."

"Just stay together and follow me. I'll take care of things."

"Hey John," said Heather with a pained look on her face, "I've got to go to the bathroom." She wiggled and from the look on her normally smiling face, I could tell she really had to go. "I don't mind going in the field — I mean, Stick and I have done it a million times so far this trip — but should I, with that guy around? It's so barren around here, there isn't anyplace for privacy."

"Can you hold it?" I asked.

"I'll try, but I've got to go pretty bad."

"Okay, you try your best, and I'll try to get you some space or some bushes or something so you can go. If it gets unbearable just say something and then I'll handle it, okay?"

"Okay," she said. Heather bit her lip, buckled her helmet and gently mounted her bicycle.

Steve's choice of roads didn't help Heather any. It was full of potholes and gravel patches, and the bumpy ride was showing on Heather's worried face. Steve would speed ahead, spin a screeching u-turn and then circle back behind us. It was hard to stay together as we rode up and down the rolling hills leading to Topeka. On one of Steve's long drives ahead, I told Heather to quickly head over to a ditch that ran alongside our road. She handed me her bike to hold, grabbed some tissue from her handlebar bag and ran over to the ditch. If Steve did come speeding back, all he would have been able to see would be her white helmet as she squatted as low as she could in the soggy ditch. Luckily, Heather was back on her bike and riding in line before our bewildered escort returned.

"Boy, you sure do ride them bikes slow. I won't go so fast on this next stretch," he mumbled out his window.

We still hadn't seen any other cars. I was hoping as we got closer to town we'd see some cars or homes that would save us in case of an emergency. If Steve exploded out in the fields, there would be no one to go to for help. At least with some cars or some farms around, we could scream. He hadn't done anything dangerous yet — other than driving all over the road. I wanted to trust him, but with his breath and his bottle, I just couldn't afford to.

In a couple of miles, some houses did appear and suddenly Steve, just ahead of us, started to slow down and honk his horn. People seemed to know Steve's horn, and they came out onto their front porches and waved to him. I thought of stopping and asking for help, and Lynn looked at me wondering if I would, but I felt it best to keep going. We had made it this far, Heather had been to the bathroom, and it looked like up ahead we were coming to a major road with lots of cars and perhaps even some that were black and white.

At one point, Steve drove way ahead, almost out of sight. When we caught up with him, he was standing in a driveway with a young woman holding a baby. I don't know if it was his family or not, but they all waved as we paraded by. Steve motioned for us to stop, but I gambled and motioned that we were going to keep going. We passed the house and I hoped that we might have seen the last of him, and for a while only the open road lay ahead and behind us. We sighed our relief at not having Steve and his Chevy hovering around us, but just as we thought we were rid of him, he came speeding by — this time even faster than before.

We made a left turn onto a two-lane highway and proceeded along the shoulder. In traffic, Steve couldn't rip a u-turn anytime he wanted. He tried one, almost crashed into another car and ended up in a ditch up ahead of us. We kept on riding, picking up our pace as he tried to get back on the road. A big green sign up ahead said:

TOPEKA

in big white letters, and a large arrow pointed to a road that led toward a large green clump of trees on the northern horizon. Steve was nowhere to be seen, so we speeded up even more and turned onto the four-lane highway that had no shoulder.

Heads down, the kids pedalled furiously alongside the five o'clock traffic pouring into the south side of Topeka. We hadn't seen traffic like it for weeks, but the prospect of losing our escort energized everyone into high cadence. Up ahead, we saw traffic lights, and behind, still no Steve. We pedalled even faster, and beyond the lights, we saw a Ramada Inn. We sprinted through the light and then walked our bikes safely and quickly across the four lanes of traffic and under the entranceway to the motel. I found an open hallway behind the lobby and had everyone follow me, walking themselves and their bikes to where they couldn't be seen from the street or the parking lot.

"Do you think we lost him?" asked Carl, who along with the others was pale-faced and breathing hard. Joy had her hand on her chest feeling how fast her heart was beating as I answered.

"I don't know, but I hope so.

"You guys . . . I'm not sure if this place has HBO; you sure you want to stay here tonight?" I said trying to sound as serious as possible. "You know, if you don't like this place, we can always get back on the road and look for another . . . After all, Topeka is the capital of Kansas; I'm sure it must have more than one motel to choose from."

"Are you kidding?!" exclaimed Carl, not detecting that I was kidding. "That Steve guy might find us again. We're hiding out right here!"

"Yeah, that guy gives me the creeps. Do you really think we lost him?" asked Heather.

"Well, I hope so. You guys stay here out of sight while I try and get us some rooms. I'll make sure the manager doesn't let anyone know we're here. You catch your breaths and I'll be back as soon as I can.

"Lynn, if you've got some change in the budget, why don't you all get your-selves something to drink from the coke machine right here while I'm gone. You guys did really great!"

Cling Free

"Hey Lynn, can I borrow the sewing kit when we get to the laundromat?" asked Carl.

Lynn looked surprised that it was Carl asking to borrow her needles and thread. It's only use so far had been when Heather had borrowed it to sew up the brand-new bathing suit she had ripped in just the wrong place on a water slide in Williamsburg. Heather's sewing skills proved faultless because 2,000 miles of lakes, creeks and rivers later, her posterior was still covered. In fact, her stitches couldn't even be seen.

"Did you ask me if you could borrow the sewing kit, Carl?" asked Lynn, just to make sure.

"Yeah, what's the matter? . . . ' you sexist or something? I got a rip in my gloves and I want to sew it up. Boys can sew too, you know."

I laughed at Carl's go-for-it spirit. I'd stuck my fingers and wrestled with threading a needle a few times in my days and I agreed. "Yeah, boys can sew too, dear."

With curtains closed, bikes inside and doors locked, we had all taken showers and sorted laundry while anxiously waiting for enough time to pass to feel sure that our intoxicated escort had given up on us. We were now looking forward to our evening and overnight in Topeka without worry. I'd found out there was a laundromat a couple of blocks away, a shopping center across the street with a Mexican restaurant, and a nearby movie theater that was playing the popular movie, *Running Scared*.

"Man, the name of that movie sure fits our day," sighed Carl.

"Hey John," smiled Jimmy upon hearing my scouting report of town, "maybe that Steve dude was right about Topeka. Sounds like a pretty cool place to me."

"Laundromat, Mexican food and movies, oh my!" Heather and Joy were chanting again.

"Man, I hope they have more chips and salsa than that place in North Carolina," said a concerned Ethan. "I could eat three baskets all by myself."

"Just think about William Swain, you guys," said Lynn. "He didn't even know what Mexican food was."

"And I bet there wasn't a big town out here when he came through," said Carl.

"John told me that this used to be an important river crossing for the pioneers," said Jimmy. "I bet that's why it grew into a town. All those wagons lined up and waiting to go across . . . Some wise old business dude probably started sellin' stuff to all the people who had nothin' to do but wait, and then more dudes started sellin' stuff. I bet that's how a lot of towns started out here."

"Not bad, James . . . you'd make a pretty good historian," I commented.

"Not me, man. I'm gonna be one of those smart business dudes," Jimmy answered without hesitation. "Who knows, maybe I'll even start a city."

"Yeah, Jimmy, where? . . . on the moon?" Heather and Joy interrupted their laundromat-Mexican-food-and-movie-oh-mying to get in their dig at Jimmy.

"Okay, you guys. I think it's safe to hit the laundromat. Are all your dirty or wet clothes in these two stuff sacks? After Topeka, it'll be back to sinks and spigots. We won't be hitting washers and dryers for a long time."

"*All* my clothes are wet and dirty," grinned Ethan. "So I think all my junk is in there."

"Okay, grab your journals then and let's get going. We'll have a journal meeting while the clothes are washing." I grabbed one of the bags and Jimmy grabbed the other. We were off to paradise.

"Hey Eeth," shouted Jimmy as Ethan, as usual, was the last one out the door. "What did you throw in this bag, dude, your bike? This thing weighs a ton!"

The kids took turns dragging the heavy bag across the park between our hotel and the laundromat. While our clothes spun in washers for the first time in weeks, we sat outside in the Kansas wind and wrote in our journals. On the second part of our trip, I usually preceded our writing with readings from Swain's journal and then presented the kids with a topic they had to write on to begin that day's journal entry. Having already read them Swain's account of his travels in the Kansas downpour, our topic that afternoon was: RAIN. The time it took for our clothes to wash and dry gave us just the right amount of journal time.

"Hey Lynn, what's this thing?" asked a puzzled Ethan, as he held up a pink piece of foam and studied it carefully.

Before Lynn had a chance to answer, Heather was there. "Oh my gosh, Ethan, you don't know what that is?!" First she laughed and then she placed her hands on her hips, readying herself to give ole Ethan a lecture on the finer points of doing laundry.

"You mean you honestly don't know what that is?" Heather's lecture was about to begin, and two other male bicyclist friends of mine shyly hid behind their dryers and watched over their shoulders. From the looks on their faces, they didn't appear to know what that "pink thing" was either.

"Uh . . . no, I honestly don't know what this thing is. Did someone's panties get shredded or something?" Ethan answered with a style Carl and Jimmy seemed to enjoy.

"That's Cling-Free, Ethan," Heather continued.

"Cling what?" asked Ethan.

"Cling-Free," answered Heather, this time slowly and deliberately. "That pink thing comes in a box full of other little pink things, and you put one of them in the dryer when you are doing a load and your clothes come out without static cling and they smell real fresh."

"Smell's pretty weird to me," said Ethan as he held it up to his nose. "You mean my shirts are gonna smell like this thing when they're done?"

"Yeah, you'll smell real nice for once."

"Right . . . 'for once'," mused Ethan. "What was that other stuff you were talking about? . . . Something about static?"

"You mean static cling. That's what sometimes happens in the dryer. All your clothes get full of static electricity and stick together. Those pink things not only keep everything smelling fresh, but they keep your clothes from sticking to each other."

"Oh, you mean like sometimes when I put on a clean t-shirt and I find that sock I thought I was missing stuck in one of my armpits." Ethan was the perfect subject for Heather, and she smiled proudly as her student continued. "When I get home, I'll have to tell my mom about this Cling-Free stuff. Man, doin' our laundry everyday and washing dishes three times a day and sewing things up and everything . . . I never realized all the things that moms do everyday. I hope I remember that when I'm home from this trip and things are back to normal. I don't think I ever appreciated my mom as much as I have since being out on the road."

"Do you miss home, Ethan?" asked Lynn.

"Well . . . yeah . . . kinda . . . I don't want to go home or anything, cuz' I want to finish this trip . . . There's lots more things to see and do and all . . . But I still miss some things at home like my mom and dad and my skateboard and Amber."

"You miss your sister?!" asked Carl.

"Yeah, I do," answered Ethan without hesitation. "You see, it's like . . . like Amber and I are brother and sister and everything, but we're also good friends. When I talk to her on the phone Sundays and stuff, it sounds like she misses me a lot . . . It's kinda sad when I talk to her." Ethan set down the pink strip and started handing out the socks and underwear that sat finished in his dryer. After he talked about missing home, everyone got strangely quiet. We quickly folded our fresh clothes and headed across the street for some Mexican food, a taste of home.

No Brains, No Headaches

"The National Weather Service has posted a Severe Thunderstorm Warning for northern Kansas and southern Nebraska." I was drinking my morning cup of instant coffee and listening to the man on The Today Show, as I sat at the end of the bed in our Topeka motel room. The man on the TV stood in front of a map that showed two pressure systems colliding. The kids weren't the only ones who had learned a lot about weather this trip; I could have turned the sound off the TV set and given a pretty accurate forecast myself.

Everyone was still sleeping soundly, and I walked over to the window and pulled back the curtain to see what the sky had to say about its plans. In our months on the road, I had also learned that the sky has little respect for weathermen. I still couldn't decide whether the sky's often blatant disregard for weather maps and forecasts was the result of the angels' dislike of meteorologists or whether they just liked to laugh. Anyway, when I peeled back the curtains, it looked like, for once, the angels and the weatherman were in agreement. The blue sky that had followed yesterday's storm had changed to battleship gray and the accompanying gusts of wind were testing the trees' ability to bend. It was only six in the morning and little dust devils were already playing in the parking lot. Despite all the signs otherwise, I hoped that the forecast would be wrong.

The pioneers had to wait in lines to get across the Kansas River, and believe it or not we did too. There was some construction going on and we had to wait our turn in a detour line to go across one of the bridges that cross over to the north bank of the river. I didn't think the Kansas Highway Department had any interest in the historical accuracy of our journey, but I thanked the man with the flag and orange helmet anyway.

Swain and thousands of other "emigrants" followed the Kansas River west, made a right turn at the Little Blue and Big Blue Rivers and headed north along Big Sandy Creek to Ft. Kearney on the Platte River, in what is now Nebraska. We tried to envision wagons strapped to barges, ferrying across the river as we looked down. Just as the water stopped and the north bank appeared below us, our visions were disturbed by the glimmering silver rails of many train tracks. They sparkled in patterns of pairs running beneath the giant concrete grain elevators and silos that dwarfed the black railroad man who drove his little cart along the tracks.

"Hey John, do they really fill those things with grain?" shouted Carl from behind me.

"Yup."

"Man, those are almost the biggest buildings I've ever seen, and they're for corn," Carl continued.

As we turned north, rows of those colossal concrete towers blocked our view of the river but shielded us from the wind. When they disappeared on the outskirts of Topeka, we were in for another lesson.

When the wind got bad for the pioneers, they would take down the canvas coverings on their prairie schooners and, much like a sailboat, shorten their sails to survive the heavy winds. Our bikes, with panniers over both front and rear wheels, had sails of their own, except, unlike sailors and settlers, we couldn't take them off. We had to lean into the gusts and hope that we guessed right. If the wind let up or the gusts changed direction, we would either weave into the middle of the road or topple over onto the gravel shoulder that graced the right side of our asphalt-topped Kansas trail.

Our leaning method wasn't a lot of fun, but it worked pretty well on roads that didn't have much traffic. We were soon to discover, though, that the tracks of those earlier pioneers had not only created large cities in their wakes, but that many of the major roads that now cross the midwestern United States are just old wagon trails paved over. My map showed a wide red line called Highway 24 as our only road if we wanted to follow the Kansas River. I only hoped that, with the winds and our corresponding riding technique, those highway workers in the orange helmets had spent some time giving it a nice, paved shoulder.

We soon found out that they hadn't.

"William Swain may not have had Cling-Free and *quesadillas*, but he didn't have to mess with highway traffic either," I growled to myself when we looped down the ramp onto Hwy. 24.

"What did you say, John?" asked Jimmy who was right behind me. "Man, with this wind and all this traffic, it looks like we're entering the gust zone."

Two lanes of pavement stretched across the endless fields in front of us — one lane going our way and one lane going the other — separated only by a yellow line. The blacktop ended, dropping off into deep gravel, a car's width from that centerline. The white line that signaled the end of the blacktop and the beginning of the gravel would occupy our attention more that afternoon than any imagined wagon trains. Jimmy and I carefully pulled into the gravel and waited for the rest of the group, while cars, pick-ups and giant twin-trailered semis flew by us doing their own versions of the 55 mph speed limit.

"I'm sorry, you guys, but this road doesn't look like much fun," I said as Lynn pulled to a stop behind everyone. Dangerous was a better description for the forty miles of trail ahead, but I didn't use that adjective. The kids concerned faces already told me they understood the situation, and I didn't bother them with my so-far-secret knowledge of the day's weather forecast. "Just stay low and slow, and ride with your ears. Let the person in front of you know if you hear a car or truck coming so they can brace themselves. Remember what those semis do after they pass you, and be careful. Tomorrow, when we head north, this wind will be behind us."

It didn't take long for us all to realize that tomorrows and just being careful wouldn't be enough. Less than a mile from where we had stopped, we were riding along in a line trying to lean as little as possible, when an eighteen-wheeler came flying by us going at least sixty.

"TRUCK!" yelled Lynn from behind. "TRUCK!" yelled Ethan, "TRUCK!" yelled Carl, and the word truck traveled forward to me like in a game of Telegraph at a birthday party. The only problem was it wasn't a party, and the faces of the kids relaying the message weren't smiling. In turn, everyone quickly lifted their heads, yelled warning to the person in front of them and then immediately braced themselves head down in the best aerodynamic position they could muster. Our sails were trimmed the best we could trim them, and our hearts pounded in anticipation, wondering if our formation would be intact after the speeding, bicycle-sucking beast stormed past us.

The explosion of speed was followed by an aftershock of wind that shook even my bicycle. I held on for myself and said a prayer for my family behind me. The truck couldn't give us a wide berth because with only two lanes of blacktop and traffic coming from the other direction, he had no choice but to stay on his side of the line. That combination forced us into a bicycling tight rope act on the white line on the outside of the road. Swerve to the left and we become hood ornaments and retreads; swerve to the right and we dive off the shoulder into bicycle-swallowing gravel just waiting to embed pebble souvenirs in the knees and elbows of passing cyclists. Riders who rode in lines like ours got the extra added bonus of proving that the domino effect was truly something to be feared, because if one of the lead riders fell, then everyone behind who wasn't some acrobat would tangle themselves into the heap . . . Oh, the joys of bicycling . . . .

Bud, my bike, was struck first by the shock waves. We wiggled, wobbled and fell off the edge of the road, coming to a less than graceful stop in the gravel. Somehow, I managed to jerk my right foot out of its toe clip and brace myself before I fell over. Suddenly, I remembered the dominoes and looked behind me to see six bicycles and their riders pull off the road in varying degrees of control. Luckily, no one went down, but as I looked back at those frightened faces, I realized, with only a half-mile down and thirty-nine and a half to go, I needed to do something or someone was going to get hurt.

I took a deep breath and looked back again at my silent brigade giving me that *"Hey John, what should we do?"* look I had seen many times before in the last few months. Even Lynn looked scared. "Take a drink, you guys, and give me a second while I try and think of something."

The human mind is an incredible thing. In the minute or so that we all stood there drinking and letting our adrenaline return to wherever it goes after an alarm, my mind took me back to a river raft trip we had taken on Joy's and Heather's bike tour in Canada. When my mind decided to run that memory while I was searching for a solution to our road problem, I immediately tried to override its selection. My mind, sometimes having a mind of its own, disregarded my request and continued with the raft trip. I remembered all of us in our raft coming around one bend in the river where the current got going pretty fast. Out in the middle was a large mother elk escorting her wobbly-legged baby across the raging water. The guide on the raft explained how the mom would place herself just upstream of her child and shelter it from the onrushing current. A relatively calm flow of water would surround the baby and the two would be able to cross the river safely. They made the journey many times daily, surviving the rapids every time, and if it weren't for the mother's position, the baby would have surely been dragged down the river to drown.

I took a drink, thought for a moment and sighed to myself, "So that's what you wanted . . . ."

The kids looked at me and wondered whom I was talking to. I woke from my little trance and said, "Okay, you guys, I got it. I'm gonna be mama elk, and you all are going to be fawns or elklets or whatever they call baby elk."

"What?" asked a confused Jimmy. "Hey John, did you hit your head on that truck or something?"

"Well, I don't have time to explain but we're going to try a new formation . . . one I learned from a mama elk in Canada." Heather and Joy wanted to talk about the raft ride, but I didn't let them get started. "We've got a long way to go today, so I don't have time to explain, but we're going to ride with Lynn at the point and me at the back. We're going to ride in a tight pace line, and I'm going to ride out in the middle of the lane, zigging and zagging so that any approaching traffic can see us and slow down."

"But what if you get hit," asked Joy.

"Well, if they hit me, they'll dent their car," I joked. "No . . . really . . . even with two lanes this is also a road that tractors have to take, so people who drive it have to slow down for them. I'm just going to try and act like a big, wide slow-moving tractor, and hopefully people will slow down for us too. Then they'll pass us when they can go way around us."

"Well, what if they don't slow down?" asked Carl, not sounding very optimistic.

"Okay, if they don't slow down, we'll have to be like Barbara and Larry when they were riding their bikes in Florida. Remember the chapter in their book called "Dive or Die?" The kids nodded. "If I can see that a car or a truck is not going to slow down or doesn't have a choice, then I'm going to yell, 'OVER!' giving you plenty of warning. As soon as you hear me yell, then you yell 'OVER!' too. Then I want you all to slow down carefully and roll off the road, onto the shoulder and brace yourselves for the aftershock. You're gonna have to be very careful when you slow down and get off, because I want us to ride in a paceline, and, if someone stops too quickly or doesn't stop at all, we'll all end up in a pile. I'll give you plenty of time to get off, so just follow the lead of the person in front of you, okay?"

"Can we practice it once when there aren't any cars behind us?" asked Joy.

"Sure, Joy, that's a good idea," I answered.

I think that mama elk would make a good bicycle rider. Our practice run and her technique worked for most of the drivers who drove Hwy. 24 that day. I say it worked for most of the drivers, because it didn't work for all of them. We waved kind thank yous to those that slowed down but still got very familiar with the gravel when I had to yell, "OVER!"

I must have had to yell it twenty times, and the kids perfected a system of bracing themselves over their bikes based on the size and speed of the passing vehicle. We learned that just being off the road often wasn't enough to protect us, because the gusts of wind teamed up with the blasts of air following the traffic and threw dirt and gravel into our faces. When we were forced over by an American car, the amount of turbulence warranted a moderate grip on the handlebars, and a slightly bowed head. Japanese cars were easy — we just held our bikes with two hands and sneaked drinks of water while we waited for them to pass. Semis with one or two trailers drew the respect of full battle stations — legs spread, bracing bike and lower body, hands holding tight to handlebars, and heads laid on top of handlebar bags with eyes closed to protect eyeballs. When the big monsters rumbled by, gravel shrapnel ricocheted off our bikes, our helmets and our bodies, and our stretch of gravel echoed with sounds that accompanied the rock fights I used to have when I was in third grade. The record for flying debris that day is held by a rather large truck that pulled half of a giant, prefabricated home. The kitchen, dining room, living room and half a bedroom hung over the trailer on both sides and its large yellow warning banner announcing "OVERSIZE LOAD" didn't do much good.

When its dust cleared and while the rest of us coughed, Carl managed to gasp, "Man, even those guys pulling houses go the speed limit around here. That trucker must be crazy."

Despite the gusts and the gravel, the kids were riding tough and strong, and their confidence in our new system seemed to be growing with each mile. It wasn't much fun having to mount and dismount every mile or so, but, like most situations, they learned to cope with things as they were. I wished I was just half as patient as they were, because just outside of St. Mary's, I lost my temper.

We were cruising along and I saw a semi approaching us from the rear on one of my zig-zags. I waved my arms and saw the trucker slowing his rig down and looking ahead to find a place to pass us safely. I waved my thank you just as he started to pass us, when suddenly he veered over to our side of the road forcing us immediately off onto the shoulder without warning. I looked ahead and noticed that a woman driving a blue sedan had suddenly passed him from behind, forcing him into our lane just as he tried to pass us slowly. Halfway by him, she discovered that another car was coming from the other direction so she fell back and abandoned her attempt to pass.

We watched this whole maneuver from our surprised position in the gravel. The kids came to a stumbling stop, looked back at me wondering why I hadn't given them the usual warning, and were more scared than hurt. When the truck was past us and the lady in the sedan had resumed her position behind him, I let fly a hand motion that was my best attempt to communicate that I thought someone in the vicinity was absent the day brains were handed out. The woman driving the car was one heck of a charades player because she immediately slammed on her brakes and ripped a u-turn in the gravel ahead. She had apparently deciphered my message in record time and was returning to receive her prize. The kids saw fire in my eyes, and after our encounter with the Spring Hill Kitten, they didn't look as if they envied this woman's position at all.

Carl did manage a "That truck almost killed us," and I thanked him. The woman was behind us on the shoulder with her head out her window before Carl had a chance to tell me I was welcome.

"THAT HAS GOT TO BE THE MOST STUPID DRIVING MANEUVER I HAVE EVER SEEN. WE HAVE BEEN RIDING OUR BICYCLES ALL THE WAY FROM WASHINGTON, D.C., OVER TWO THOUSAND MILES, AND LADY, YOU RECEIVE THE AWARD FOR THE WORST DRIVING WE HAVE SEEN!" I was fuming and I wasn't about to let her get in a word edgewise. "Do you like taking target practice at kids on their bicycles? My mom used to say, 'No brains, no headaches.' and I bet you never need aspirin. I can't believe anyone would pull such a bonehead stunt. The truck slowed down and everything, and then you forced him right into us. Lady, I can't believe you."

I came up for air, and the woman, who appeared to be in her late thirties and had a young child in the seat next to her, got her chance to reply.

"You bicyclists! You just think you own the road. I live around here and I pay my taxes. Why there ought to be a law that prohibits bicyclists on this road. If ya can't handle the traffic then get the heck off the road."

"WELL, LADY, IT SURE SEEMS LIKE YOU TOOK THE LAW INTO YOUR OWN HANDS, BECAUSE YOU DID A GREAT JOB GETTING US OFF THE ROAD. HECK, YOU ALMOST GAVE US THE DEATH PENALTY AS WELL. WHAT'S THE BIG HURRY? WERE YOU LATE FOR A HAIR APPOINTMENT OR SOMETHING?" I was still yelling at the top of my lungs and the kids looked a bit embarrassed.

"I don't have to take that kind of talk from you." The woman pulled her head back in the window and turned the ignition key.

"I hope your daughter in the seat there never rides a bike around here. Not with people like you on the road. Don't be late for that appointment now." I yelled my last good byes, but I don't think she heard me. She gunned the accelerator and the gravel flew as her wheels searched for traction. She sped away and I shook my head. The kids were staring at me as I trembled in anger, and Lynn looked away. Even she had never seen me that mad.

"Are you guys okay?" I asked in my voice that was hoarse from yelling, "OVER!" and my recent encounter.

"Yeah, we're okay," said Jimmy. "The question is: Are you okay? Man, John, you were pissed off."

I caught my breath, and we got back up onto the road. When no cars were coming, Carl, who was riding towards the back, asked, "Hey John, did your mom really used to say, 'No brains, no headaches'?"

I laughed and said, "Yeah, Carl, I remember her saying that when somebody did something stupid, and what that woman did was not only stupid, but it was also incredibly dangerous. I'm sorry I got so loud back there, but I was angry that someone might hurt you guys."

"That's okay, John. I get angry and loud sometimes too."

Off to See The Wizard

At lunch that afternoon, I pointed out that the gathering of gray on the western horizon was predicted to contain some nasty thunderstorms and maybe even a twister.

"You mean like Arkansas?" asked a worried Joy.

"These crosswinds are going to get worse?!" asked Jimmy.

"Well, that's what the weather man said this morning."

"Where were you planning to stop us tonight, John?" asked Carl.

"Well, I was hoping we could make it to Manhattan, but I didn't expect to be diving off the road all day today. I'm really sorry this is the only road, you guys."

"That's okay, John," said Joy. "I bet we can still make it to Manhattan. How far is it anyway?"

"According to my map, about twenty-five or thirty miles, " I answered.

"Shoot, it's only a little after one," said Jimmy. "I bet we can make it there by five, easy. We can beat those thunderstorms, if we push it."

"Yeah, we're getting pretty good at bailing off the road together and then getting back on when it's clear," said Heather. "Let's go for Manhattan." The kids wolfed down their lunch in record time, and before Lynn and I knew it, they were back on their bikes and raring to go. In a few miles the road entered corn fields so tall and thick it was like riding through a corridor in a giant maze. About the time the corn started, the road widened to give us our first paved shoulder all day, and three feet of wonderful blacktop became our yellow-brick road to Manhattan.

I was riding along at the front sighing with relief and enjoying the quiet of being out of the wind, when, from behind me, I heard Jimmy whistling a melody I had grown up with. Soon the girls joined in, supplying the words, and Carl and Ethan were right behind, adding harmonies at the top of their lungs. Not all the words were exactly as I remembered them, but that afternoon, on the road to Manhattan, we did the most inspired renditions of *Wizard of Oz* music Kansas has ever heard. We sang some songs in rounds, some in solos, some in duets and some even in full chorus. Occasionally, we would do a little dialog to break things up — the kids taking the starring roles and Lynn and I filling in with Aunty Em or the munchkins. With a shoulder of asphalt leading our way to Manhattan and no impending shouts of "OVER!" to worry about, we sang and carried on, oblivious to the outside world.

Our performance that afternoon had only two interruptions. One was a corn field bathroom break, and the second was the final curtain call announced by the sky. The wind slowed to an eery stillness like someone taking a deep breath before blowing out their birthday candles.

"Hey John, I think it's getting ready to blow, man," warned Jimmy from behind me. "The sky always seems to get real still just before it lets loose. Remember that night . . . ."

"Yeah, Jimmy, I sure do."

Like time lapse photography speeded up, the sky over what we hoped was Manhattan shifted and rolled into position for its own finale. Within minutes, masses of clouds joined forces and turned the sky a dark gray. One by one, the cars around us started clicking on their headlights, as if to signal each other of the approaching storm. In the distance, the canons of the sky went off and a breeze gusted across our path, scattering leaves and garbage across the road.

"Here it comes, you guys!" shouted Jimmy. "We better jam."

Automatically, and without a word, the kids started to pick up the pace, and faces that moments before had been wearing animated smiles and singing songs of Oz changed. Heads down and toe straps tightened, they wore the determined gaze that I had seen earlier that day when we were dodging cars and trucks. With the sky now threatening to float us off the road, we tried to race the storm to Manhattan. But when all of a sudden the stop lights about a half-mile ahead disappeared in a curtain of falling water, we conceded the race and just attempted to finish. Cars around us had their visibility so impaired that they were pulling over to the side of the road. I thought I had seen the familiar black and yellow sign of a Best Western Motel up past the set of stoplights before everything became a blur, and when the kids shouted and asked if they should stop to put on rain gear, I just shook my head and waved my arm, giving them the signal to keep going.

We made it through the light and into the parking lot of the motel with no interference from traffic. The road was like a river and white fountains of water flew off the corners of the driveway. It wasn't easy pedaling a loaded bicycle through five inches of rushing water, but with the protection of the overhang ahead in sight, the kids took a little extra time to splash each other with the giant rooster tails spewing out from their rear wheels.

"Man, we got here just in time," smiled Jimmy.

"Yeah," said Heather matter of factly, "I would have to say that's the hardest rain we have ridden in yet. I think that weatherman was right."

As if to confirm Heather's opinion, a giant bolt of lightning snaked across the sky and a prolonged crack of thunder shook the windows of the motel office. Even more rain emptied from the black sky and the wind cranked up its velocity a couple more notches.

"Hey, you guys," said Ethan, pointing to the roof, "check that out!" Water was cascading off the eaves in walls of transparent gray. Whenever the wind would gust the right direction, it would part the water like it was blowing open the curtains on a big window.

After watching the show for a few minutes, we checked into the motel and walked our bicycles to our rooms. The lightning was still playing overhead, and I didn't especially enjoy pushing our two-wheeled lightning rods through the parking lot's ankle-deep water. But, with bathtubs, sheets and my promise of pizza awaiting us, the troops didn't seem too worried.

"I just hope this storm doesn't black out the electricity," said Carl. "I heard Arnold Schwarzenegger is on TV tonight in *Commando* . . . ."

Later that evening, as we dined on pizza delivered by a brave girl from the local Domino's, I read from Swain's journal:

> "May 21, 1849. The roads were slippery from the recent rain; but the wind, which often blows on these vast plains, blew from the east, and as we traveled to the west our wagons rolled along very easily, the wind blowing so hard that we had to brace ourselves against it as we rolled along . . . ."

"Yeah, just like us," nodded Ethan between bites.
I continued:

> "May 20. The wind is quite high on the plains, like that on our own lakes, and the clouds look like rain . . . This afternoon we had a heavy thundershower, which makes camping disagreeable both for men and beasts. We are obliged to turn the cattle out of the corral onto the plains and keep guard around them all night."

"And we are obliged to find a motel," joked Jimmy. "Ole William, he sure stays cool about things. He always seems so calm and uses such big words."

"Yeah, I know," agreed Joy. "I wish he would show more emotion. I mean, his storms sound just like ours, but he . . . he writes about things like they were no big deal and he sounds like an English teacher or something. It was bad enough for us when we rode through conditions like his, but he was in a wagon and he didn't have any towns or places to escape to."

"Yeah, and I bet he never even heard of pizza," laughed Carl.

"Well, what do you think, everybody?" I asked. "Who had it harder: the pioneers or you guys? Or should I say, was it as hard for the pioneers as you thought it was when we studied the Oregon Trail? . . . or easier?"

"Oh, I can't tell yet," answered Joy. "I need more time out here to answer that."

"Yeah, I think we all need more time for that question," said Heather. "Keep reading."

"Okay, I've just got one more thing before we start our own entries. This is from a letter that William wrote home to his wife that same May 20. Since it was the Sabbath, he had more time to write than on a regular day.

> "Dear Sabrina,
>   We have had a high wind today, which we generally have on this ocean of plain, accompanied by a heavy rain which beats through our tent and has dampened my paper so that I can hardly write. I shall send this by the first chance to Independence and will write every opportunity . . ."

My readings ended. We all sat down in the comfort of our motel room and wrote in our journals. Our topic that night was: WIND, and we had no trouble filling up our pages. Some of the kids even took some extra time to write postcards home to sunny California. Once the TV was on, though, the only other duty their pens would see would be as weapons. That day, the kids had switched from swerving onto the gravel to singing on the shoulder, and that night they had no trouble switching from visions of wagons and windy thunderstorms to Channel 12 and its video views of muscles and machine guns.

Lynn wasn't too excited about the movie, so we ate cold pizza and privately drank our own root beer floats in the next room. We sat in bed listening to our kids shooting and dying as they swapped their roles of Tinman, Lion and Dorothy for guerillas and commandos. I was tempted to go die and moan a few times myself, but Lynn, realizing my temptation, held me a little tighter and told me to stay put. I would have to be content with my afternoon performance as the Mayor of Munchkin Land.

High Plains Rendezvous

Sometime that night the storm passed, and we woke before dawn the next morning to a damp parking lot scattered with leaves and branches. While I warmed hot chocolate water, the kids stepped outside to breathe some of the fresh and cool morning air.

We rolled through Manhattan long before most folks were up, passing the medieval-looking campus of Kansas State University. The streets smelled wonderful after the storm, and as the sun slowly cast its pink glow on the hills around us, Heather gave her weather forecast for the day:

"Well, I think that we are going to have a beautiful day's ride today. If you'll look off to the south of us you'll see the clouds from yesterday's storm. The wind is very calm and up ahead I see only gentle puffs of cotton ball clouds. I think we will stay dry all day today . . . ."

Heather gave her forecast on the road that headed northwest out of Manhattan through a beautiful little valley called Keats. Immaculately kept stone barns and lush green pastures reminded the kids of the valley in California where they first learned to bicycle, and, with little or no traffic and lots of confidence, they abandoned their single file formation. I looked behind me and watched the five kids and Lynn zigging and zagging all over the deserted road, talking and riding with no hands. Sometimes three of them would ride abreast, and other times one of them would peel off and drop back to enjoy some quiet time alone. It was the first day we could really enjoy the Plains.

At three o'clock that afternoon, after an easy seventy miles, we reached Washington, Kansas, a very special stop for us. Not only did it mark Mile 2,250 (half of our predicted 4,500), but it was also the sight of our High Plains Rendezvous, where we would outfit ourselves for the second half of our journey.

Before leaving California, all the kids and their parents had delivered their cold weather gear to my house, boxed and ready to be shipped to some then-unnamed destination in Kansas or Nebraska. In reading William Swain's journal I had noted his description of the chilly nights on the High Plains, and I decided that when we reached them, I would have my brother ship us all our gear. So far, we had travelled without the unneeded weight, bulk and heat of sleeping bags, wool socks, leg warmers or ski caps. One layer of skin had been more than enough in the steam baths of the Southeast and the Mississippi Valley, but now it was time to prepare for the cooler temperatures that awaited us as we climbed toward the Continental Divide.

The exact point for our rendezvous turned out to be the Park Hill Motel in Washington, Kansas, and as soon as our crew of bicyclists pulled up to the motel office, the smiling manager brought out a bouquet of metallic balloons that Ethan's mom had sent to celebrate our halfway point. All our cardboard boxes were soon to follow, and we splurged for three rooms instead of two. The boys would have theirs, the girls theirs and Lynn and I would sleep alone in a bed for the first time in a long while.

I figured once I gave the kids their keys and their boxes they would retire to their rooms to open them in privacy, but I was wrong.

"Hey John, let's all open our boxes in your room," suggested Jimmy.

"Yeah, opening them alone will be no fun," said Carl. "That would be like having Christmas all by yourself."

"You guys want to be together?" I asked.

"YEAH!" It sounded unanimous.

"Alright then," I continued, "Carl, why don't you mix up some drinks, and girls, why don't you go find the ice machine. We might as well make a party of it."

Refreshments made and Swiss Army knives cocked and ready to rip open the boxes, we sprawled out on the two beds to open our packages. Old sleeping bags were greeted with smiles that I thought were reserved for pets and old friends, and every new change of clothes caused a fashion show. Heather strolled across the room modeling her wool jersey and long underwear and Ethan strutted around the room in his new electric-blue tights. As Heather spun around at the end of the room, stopping at each quarter turn, she received thunderous applause. When Ethan attempted the same, he received a barrage of cat calls and flying socks.

My sister and brother-in-law had sent us giant, homemade chocolate chip cookies, and we devoured all two dozen of them — or I thought we did. Later that night, Lynn and I found a few uneaten chocolate chips and crumbs under our "fresh" sheets.

Every item pulled from box or envelope was cause for celebration, and although I had specified item and number on my High Plains Rendezvous Checklist, I could see that I was again going to have to step in and ask the kids to send some extra things home. It seemed that many of the moms and kids had again read a typical checklist item like: "long pants, sweats or wool legwarmers" and translated it to mean: two pairs long pants, assorted pairs of sweatpants *and* legwarmers. I didn't want to spoil the party that afternoon though, so I decided the clothes editing would wait until morning.

Friends had also heard of our High Plains Rendezvous, because each of us also received a stack of mail that brought more smiles and more than a few show-stopping, out-loud recitations. Our celebration was as exciting and joyous as any Christmas, and for two hours that afternoon, we danced and laughed and held up our packages of home. Chunks of uneaten cookies lay around like half-eaten candy canes, and as the sun set, the kids got ready to retreat to their rooms for their showers.

"Dinner and journal meeting at about seven, okay, you guys?"

"Sure thing, John," answered Jimmy.

"Why don't all of you go and enjoy your showers and your presents," said Lynn. "John and I will clean up all the wrappings and stuff."

"But, Lynn, we left a pretty big mess," said Joy.

"That's okay, you guys go enjoy yourselves. We'll clean up."

"Are you sure?" Joy asked again.

"See you at seven, Joy. Now get out of here and go enjoy your bathtub."

"Oh yeah, our bathtub." Joy smiled and looked over at a likewise smiling Heather. Soon, Lynn and I heard the tub running next door.

"What's the topic for tonight, John?" asked Carl.

"Well, I thought we would read about Swain's daily routine and see if you guys think it comes very close to our own.

> "June 7, 1849. We are traveling through one of the most beautiful countries the eye ever rested upon . . . our hour of rising in the morning is four o'clock, hitch up and start at half past six, drive until eleven, rest until two, and drive until six in the evening. The roads are now first-rate, and we are making from seventeen to twenty miles per day . . . .' "

"Seventeen to twenty miles per day?!" exclaimed Carl. "No wonder it took them so long to get west."

"Yeah, but they got to stop for three hours for lunch and a rest, and we only get thirty minutes for peanut butter and jelly," said Jimmy.

"Didn't they call that rest a noon-something?" asked Heather.

"Yeah . . . I think they called it a 'nooning,'" answered Ethan. "We did that in one of our wagon train situations back at school."

"Well, I think that other than their mileage and having to take care of their animals, Swain's wagon train had a schedule a lot like ours," said Joy. "We get up at the same time and leave at just about the same time. And I know our lunch isn't very long, but our second breakfasts sure are. I just can't imagine how much the lightning and thunderstorms must have slowed them down. At least our bicycles don't spook and we don't have to go out and chase them across the prairie."

We wrote in our journals about our daily schedule, and when we finished, I read another entry from Swain about a change in routine:

"June 10. Sabbath. Today we are enjoying ourselves by laying abed late to rest. The sun was high when we got up and got breakfast, which we all enjoyed well, as we got some extras: pudding, apple pie, etc."

"You mean we get to sleep in tomorrow?" yelled Ethan.

"Thank God for ole William's Sabbaths," smiled Jimmy.

"Was that a pun, James?" I asked.

"Yeah John, a little humor . . . a little humor," chuckled Jimmy. "Man, I can't wait to catch some extra zees."

"You guys can sleep in as long as you have all the stuff that needs to be sent back home labeled, boxed and in this room by noon. Remember to check the checklist, because I will before Lynn and I head to the post office tomorrow. No duplicates or extra shoes, socks or undies, okay, Heather?" I cast a knowing glance Heather's way, as she tried her best to scowl. Heather was the only person I knew who could scowl and smile at the same time.

"John?" she asked. "Can we go back to our rooms now? I haven't finished reading all my letters yet."

"Yeah, I want to read mine again," agreed Ethan. "I don't think I've ever got this much mail before."

The mood of the kids changed as they slowly got up. I had never seen them so subdued before.

When the pioneers were discouraged by weather, disaster or homesickness — many to the point of turning back — they called it "seeing the Elephant." The story goes that, once upon a time, when the circus was coming to town, a certain farmer, never having seen elephants himself, hitched up his wagon and rode into town to see the circus parade. Upon seeing the big black animal leading the parade, his horses spooked, turned the wagon around and high-tailed it home. So, when something upon the trail spooked the emigrants, they said they had "seen the Elephant."

Later that night, Lynn and I visited the kids and found them propped up in bed, reading and re-reading their letters from home. As we tucked them in and clicked off the lights, I wondered if the Elephant would be visiting any of them that night. Closing the door to the boys' room, I thought I saw a large, dark shadow moving slowly down the hall.

"Hey Carl, what are you doing up so early?" It was only 8:30 the next morning and I didn't expect to see any of the kids up when I stepped outside to get the newspaper.

"Oh, you know how it is, John. Whenever you're told you get to sleep in, no matter how hard you try, you just can't keep your eyes closed?"

"Yeah Carl, I know the feeling. It usually happens to me on Saturdays during the school year."

"I even already went through all my stuff and went over the checklist. Me and Ethan and Jimmy did all that stuff last night when we couldn't get to sleep."

"You mean Ethan's all ready too?"

"Yeah, hard to believe, isn't it?" laughed Carl. "We thought we'd beat the girls at something for once. You know . . . it's kinda good that I'm already up, because I wanted to get an early start today cleaning up my bike. Those rain storms have got it looking and sounding pretty gross."

"Ole Bud is looking pretty funky too," I said. "I need to spend some time on him this afternoon. Why don't you come with me across the street and help me pick out breakfast? Then I can take a look at the stuff you're sending home."

When Carl and I returned with breakfast, all the rest of the troops were waiting for us. It seemed that no one could stay under the covers much past nine o'clock that morning, and by 10:30, all the guys' stuff was checked off, boxed and ready to return to California.

"Hey, girls!" chided the boys as they stuck their heads into the girls' open doorway. "We even got less underwear than the checklist says." Ethan was hit by the flying pillow Joy and Heather threw as their answer. Next, the door slammed shut and the guys retired proudly to some morning cartoons in their room.

At eleven, I knocked on the girls' door and was let into a room with clothes all neatly laid out on their beds. "You ladies have one hour til noon. I need to have all your stuff ready by then."

"But, John . . ." moaned Heather. "I can't decide which shirts to take. Can't I just take one extra?"

"Nope. All that warm clothing is going to take up more pannier space and we're still going to need lots of room for food and water," I answered. I loved Heather, but I hated those moments when we discussed clothes.

"And I can't decide which sweater I like best, John," sighed Joy. "Which one do you think I should take?"

"I think you should definitely take the wool one."

"But it's not as pretty as this other one," Joy insisted. As rough and ready as Joy and Heather now were, they still had some problems with wardrobe planning. I decided to leave the final choices up to my female half. I shook my head and returned to Lynn, in our room.

"Lynn, I need you to take care of the girls. They got stuff all spread out and Heather can't decide which shirts to wear and Joy can't decide which sweater to take. Here, here's the checklist. I want you to go over there and get them done in forty-five minutes. And no exceptions to the checklist — I don't care how cute they smile. We are going to need all the room we can get when we have to pack food and water across Wyoming. Plus, with just their sleeping bags and wool stuff, they've added at least ten pounds to their loads."

"Okay dear, calm down, I'll take care of it." Lynn walked out of the room laughing at my frustration.

Ten minutes later, she returned with a somewhat anxious look of her own. "John, Heather wants to know since the list says four pairs of underwear and four shirts, can she bring three pairs of underwear and five shirts?" Lynn saw her answer immediately on my face and started backing out the door. "Umm . . . yeah . . . four underwear and four shirts . . . that's what I thought . . . Just checking, though. Sorry to have bothered you, dear. You go back to your map, okay? We're almost ready."

"Hey Ethan, you missed a spot," commented Joy, as she sat Indian-style facing her bike. On the way back from our journey to the post office and market, Lynn had gotten sidetracked at the corner antique store, and I returned alone to find the kids lined up along the motel wall, scrubbing, cleaning and lubricating their bikes.

"Hey John, we're having a clean contest," continued Joy. "We cut off some Coke cans with our Swiss Army knives, just like we saw you do back in Asheville, and filled them up with solvent. One of the maids said she had all the old rags we needed so we wouldn't mess up any bathroom towels."

"How long have you guys been out here?"

"Oh, since right after you and Lynn left," answered Jimmy as he scrubbed his chain with the old toothbrush from his tool kit. "We decided not to go swimming until after we finished cleaning up our bikes."

"Hey Joy . . . ." said Ethan, who looked like he had transferred all of the grease and the grime from his bike to his face. "I can't find that spot you said I missed. I've been looking all over for it."

"Hey Eeth," laughed Jimmy. "She doesn't mean you missed a spot on your bike, man. She means you missed a spot on your face. You've got this one little tan place left on your chin. Other than that, you're whole face is black!"

"Yeah, Eeth, you look just like a coal miner, man!" laughed Carl.

I walked over to inspect Heather's cleaning job on "Skittles," her little Nishiki. "Hey Heather, you don't really need to clean the freewheel. It looks pretty good to me."

"Nope, I think I should clean it," Heather disagreed. "Skittles always shifts better with a clean freewheel. Besides, she rides quieter and I can hear more country sounds. After all, that's one of the reasons I'm here."

I rubbed Heather's shoulders, smiled and moved over to Joy and her bike, "Mad Mountain Mike Bike."

"John, Carl told me that my bike doesn't have a clearcoat. I think that's why my Schwinn decals are all chipped up. When I outgrow Mike, I'm gonna make sure my next bike has a clearcoat. It will keep it looking nicer." As Joy talked, she didn't even look up, she just kept scrubbing and shining. She and all the kids talked to their bikes and treated them like good friends. They knew how to adjust their brakes and derailleurs, and thrown chains were old hat. Joy and Heather even had a technique they called the "two-finger technique" which enabled them to remount a chain in seconds and keep their hands clean, at the same time. "We can even do it without getting off our bikes," they boasted.

Carl and "Pack Rat" were next down the line and Carl, for all his efforts and expertise, seemed to have a problem that needed my help.

"Hey John, guess what?" he said. "My rear rack is being held on with three bolts instead of four, and . . . I think I've got a broken spoke."

"You *think* you've got a broken spoke?"

"I mean, I know I've got a broken spoke. Can you help me fix it?"

"Sure, do you have your spares?"

"Yup, I got them out right here waiting for you. How do you like my new handlebar tape job?" Carl paused to point out the new red and black stripes gracing his handle bars. He looked proud.

"Pretty RAD, dude," I answered in my best impression of his generation's largest compliment.

"Thanks, I did it all myself. I'm sure glad I got started early this morning. Taping handlebars is harder than it looks, especially when you use two colors."

Also staying at the Park Hill Motel were racers and crews for a National Midget Car Race being held that weekend. The parking lot was full of large trailers painted with flames and names of sponsors. While I was working on Carl's wheel, a middle-aged man came out of one of the rooms and walked over to where we were working. He wore a t-shirt that had a picture of a red, yellow and orange race car speeding across his chest in a cloud of dirt.

"Ma name's Vallie Schneider and I've been watchin' these kids work on their bicycles for the last two hours. I've gotta tell ya, it gives me a good feelin' to see young people respecting their machines like that. What are you folks, a church group or something?"

"No, we're kind of a school group from California," answered Carl.

"From California?! What are you doing way out here in Kansas? We're from Illinois, and I thought *we* had a long drive."

"Well," continued Carl. "We started in Washington, D.C., and we're headed back home to California."

"By bicycle?" asked Mr. Schneider.

"Yup. Right now we're following the Oregon/California Trail. We're reading the journal of an old goldrusher and following his route."

"You got a van following you, carrying everything?"

"Nope, we carry everything ourselves . . . about thirty pounds of stuff, depending on how much food we're carrying. Our weight just went up though, because we just got our cold weather gear shipped to us here."

"Why, I haven't ever heard of such a thing. Who's leading the trip, one of your parents?"

"No, this is John Seigel Boettner and he's our social studies teacher at school. He and his wife Lynn are our leaders." I stopped my repair and stood up to shake Mr. Schneider's hand.

"Well, John — is it okay if I call you John? Your last name sounded like quite a mouthful — I've got to compliment you on this undertaking. Takes special people to even dream of doing such a thing. At first, I thought you were just on some week-long outing with a church group or scouts or something, but now that I hear you're crossing the whole country — why, I wish more young people today had the same opportunity."

"Thanks, they're a great bunch of kids. My wife and I couldn't have made this trip without them."

"Their parents must have a lot of trust in you. They don't look to be much past eleven or twelve."

"Yes sir, the oldest is thirteen and the youngest, Carl, here, is just twelve." Carl gave me a what-d-ya-mean-just-twelve look, as I realized I should have chosen different words.

"Like I said, their parents had to put a lot of trust in you and your wife to let them go. How long will your trip take?"

"Four months and 4,500 miles," answered Carl. "This is our halfway point in miles . . . See, my computer says 2,250." Carl beeped his computer for Mr. Schneider and continued telling him about our trip while I trued his wheel. After I replaced the bolt on his rear rack and inspected the other bikes, the kids went swimming and Mr. Schneider, still watching nearby, reached into his back pocket and walked over to me.

"I still can't get over what you're doing with these kids. I sure would like you to be our guests at the races, but Carl tells me you're getting on the road tomorrow. He sounds pretty excited about crossing into Nebraska in the morning. I wanted to be part of your halfway celebration, so here, here's ten dollars. I want you to go across the street and buy some ice cream and root beer. Kids still like root beer floats, don't they?"

"Thank you, they sure do," I smiled.

"Also, since you can't come to the races with us, I want to give each of you one of these t-shirts with our car on it. That's my son, Robbie, driving. He should do pretty well this weekend. Anyway, you let those kids swim now and when you have your dinner, you ask them their shirt sizes. You just leave a note on our door with the sizes, including yours and your wife's, and we'll leave the shirts on your doorstep late tonight when we get back. I just wanted to say that I think what you're doing is great, and I feel lucky to have met you and your kids. You all have a safe trip, and enjoy them shirts and those floats."

Mr. Schneider shook my hand like my dad and Johnny Carroll had done, and I got some more goosebumps as he looked me in the eye and squeezed my shoulder. Our handshake was interrupted by the kids yelling for me to come join them in the pool. I said good bye to our friend from Illinois and ran over to the pool, doing a cannonball and splashing Joy and Heather who were sunbathing on the deck. I could only join them for a short dip, because after about five minutes, I realized I still hadn't cleaned my bike.

"Hey John, is it time for our meeting yet?" Five helium-induced, high-pitched voices, sounding like the Lollipop League in Munchkin Land, came from our open doorway. The kids had inhaled some of the gas from their balloons to achieve their new accents and had them hidden behind their backs. They all turned around and tried to reload for their next words, but uncontrolled laughter reduced them to giggles.

"As soon as you guys get in here, we're going to do a little artwork for our meeting tonight." The kids took their balloons back to their rooms and soon returned with their journals.

"Did you say something about artwork, John?" asked Jimmy. "Was Swain some kind of artist, too?"

"Well, I don't know if he was an artist, but each of the wagons had slogans painted on the sides of their canvas covers, so I thought we would do the same thing. Here's what Swain writes about the ones on his train:

"May 16, 1849. . . . With our wagons all regularly numbered, we made a grand appearance. Using axle grease, the members had printed 'Wolverine Rangers (the name of Swain's company of emigrants), Mess No. __' on each wagon cover. In other companies the wagon covers are nearly all painted with the names of owners, and their residences. Many of them have various mottoes and devices. . . . such as Wild Yankee, Rough and Ready, Live Hoosier, Never Say Die, Patience and Perseverance, and Have You Seen The Elephant? Others have drawings — a sprawling eagle or huge elephant, a tall giraffe, a rampant lion, or a stately ox, done in charcoal or black paint with an artistic skill that is bold if not accurate."

"We're going to use magic markers to draw our slogans on pieces of Lynn's ripped up sheetsack and then we'll pin them on our bikes. But, first, let's do some brainstorming in our journals."

"Hey John, what was William Swain's motto?" asked Carl.

"You guys aren't going to believe it . . . His canvas said: 'No Great Evil Without Some Good.'"

"You mean Old William knew how to play Bright Side too?" smiled Jimmy. "John, I think you picked the right dude for us to follow . . . ."

Everyone eagerly opened their journals and worked late into the night. It was past midnight when finished scraps of sheet were neatly folded and taken back to rooms. Everyone voted to wait 'til morning to unveil each design, when they'd be properly displayed on our two-wheeled wagons.

The next morning, at about six, I opened our door to find seven race car t-shirts neatly folded in a plastic grocery bag on our door mat. Looking next door,

I noticed the kids had already lined up their bikes outside their rooms. All five of them had awakened early and made sure their slogans were where Lynn and I could see them. I put the t-shirts back in the room and called Lynn out to take a look at the wagons.

The boys' bikes were first. Safety-pinned to Ethan's sleeping bag, atop the rear rack, was his artwork: a skinny bicyclist was drawn, leaning over his bicycle with beads of sweat dripping off his head; large bolts of lightning were striking all around him and a cloud of smiling mosquitoes was in hot pursuit. In the corner of the banner was a road sign reading:

CALIFORNIA... 4,500 MILES

Ethan had left about as much white space on his piece of sheet as he had on his face when he was cleaning his bike. Carl's sheet displayed a large cartoon caricature of a bicyclist, yelling:

"WHERE'S THE DOWNHILL?!!!"

Jimmy's banner had a long road disappearing over a hilly horizon. His motto at the bottom was:

"OVER THE HILL."

The girls' bikes were next. Heather's clean and shiny Skittles not only had her slogan attached to her sleeping bag, but also had her helium balloon tied to the top of her bungee cords. Snoopy danced on the foil sphere, floating above her bike, ready to root her on to Nebraska. Heather also had added a pinwheel to the end of her handlebars. One of her friends had sent it to her and she said the green palm trees swirling around on its clear plastic wings reminded her of her final destination. I knew better than to argue about the aerodynamics of her new decorations. Heather's banner had a picture of the Capitol in one corner and a picture of a palm tree in the other. In the middle, in giant block letters, she had written:

WANTED IN CALIFORNIA
ALIVE OR DEAD

Joy's bike had her balloon attached along with her banner, but she didn't have a pinwheel. Her banner had a simple stick figure of a person riding a bike. In crooked letters, lovingly placed above it, was the phrase:

THE MORE I SEE THE COUNTRY,
THE LESS I CALL THIS WORK.

Upon seeing it, I put my arm around Lynn and let out a deep sigh.

Lynn smiled up at me and said, "You know, John, I think Joy's parents named her just right, don't you think?"

"Hey John and Lynn, what do you think of our balloons?" I didn't get my chance to answer as Heather poked her smiling face out from behind the girls' door.

"I think they're great, Heather." said Lynn.

"I think I got the pinwheel on there real good. I must have used a whole roll of tape, but I think it'll stay on now."

Joy joined Heather outside with us and asked to see Lynn's and my banners. Lynn, almost always being the tail rider of the group, had written

CABOOSE

in large western style letters on her sheet and had pinned it to the rear end of her bike. For my motto, I had drawn two large lightning bolts slashed diagonally on the sides of my sheet and, in the middle, black and bold, I wrote:

WHAT ELEPHANT . . .

"I like yours, John," said Joy as she walked around to the front of my handlebar bag.

"Oh, I don't know, Joy," I said, putting my arm around her shoulder. "I really like yours."

"You do?"

"Yeah, I really do. I like what it says a lot." I quietly gave her a long hug as we looked at our line of bikes. I squeezed both her shoulders and went to get the t-shirts.

The light of dawn came reluctantly that morning as a thick fog hung wet and low in the Kansas sky. We sat on the edge of our beds watching early morning TV, waiting for enough light to ride.

"Let's get going, John," said Carl as he watched the morning news for the third time. The troops were restless and ready to ride, so we decided to cut a path through the fog. We mounted our blinking amber tail lights that I hoped would make us look like moving road hazards. If the cars could just see those lights through the fog, they would steer around us, faked into thinking we were some automobile-eating ditch. My only worry was whether or not the cars could see us in time. The visibility outside wasn't much more then ten yards, and it didn't look like it was getting much better.

"Hey John, this is fun," beamed Heather from her position right behind Jimmy. We were riding in a tight group and I was at the back again playing mama elk with two of our lights mounted to my large behind. I was trying to listen in the foggy distance for oncoming traffic, but was soon distracted by another one of the kids' what's-there-to-worry-about conversations. I had long since stopped playing our game of Bright Side with the kids, because I had learned that, to them, it wasn't a game; it was just the way they saw most everything.

"What's this about you liking this fog, Heather?" I asked.

"Yeah, it's neat. I can see all the hairs on my arms, because they're covered with little droplets of water."

"And did you see all those pretty spider webs?" exclaimed Joy. "With the fog and the dew on them you can see all their different patterns. They're all different . . . like snowflakes."

"I like this fog because it feels so cool," said Carl. "It reminds me of the early morning fog back home on our ranch. It feels good when you stick out your tongue and breathe in the cool wet air. I remember dreaming about fog like this when we were going through all that hot weather in the East and the South. Now here it is and it feels great."

"Hey you guys, look at Jimmy!" laughed Ethan. "He's growing a moustache."

Jimmy looked back at us, astonished and disappointed at the same time. "Hey, no fair, you guys. I don't even have a mirror!" The water did as good a job on Jimmy's face as it did to the hair on our arms, and Jimmy didn't want to miss the show.

"Does it really show?" he asked as he tried, in vain, to look over and under his nose as he rode along.

"Not bad, dude," complimented Ethan.

"Yeah James, not bad," I laughed. "I wonder if they sell razors in Nebraska . . . but then again, old William Swain said that "moustachios" were quite popular among the men going west — you may want to keep it. I know what a conscientious student you are and I think trying to be historically accurate with your upper lip deserves some extra credit."

"Oh, most definitely," nodded Joy, trying not to laugh.

As frustrated as we had ever seen him, Jimmy didn't say anything. He just reached up with his fingers and tongue trying to feel his fuzz, all the while contorting his face, trying to get a peek over his nose.

"Hey Lynn," said Joy. "I can even see the hair on my legs now from the mist. All these little drops are dancing on my thighs."

"Hey Carl, can you see any drops on your legs, or did you shave back in Washington?" I joked from behind.

"Oh, cut it out, John. I haven't done that in a long time," he scowled. "Besides, the girls won't let me borrow their razor anymore."

"I'll let you borrow ours, anytime," offered Lynn. Carl just shook his head.

"Hey, you guys," said Heather. "Try closing your eyes every so often. The dew on your eyelashes will roll down your cheeks, and it tickles!"

For fifteen miles that morning — all the way to the Nebraska state line — we played with the fog, as oblivious to the occasional cars as those cars probably were to us. As I pedaled behind and listened, I imagined another generation of kids, perched atop or walking alongside creaking wood wagons, playing similar games. I wondered if they noticed themselves growing older as they crossed the same stretch of openness, in some earlier morning's fog.

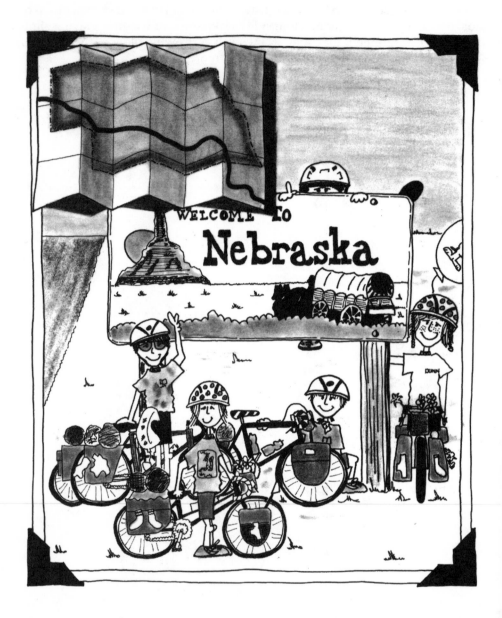

12

You could see the eroded away wagon wheel marks as you crossed the prairie that hundreds had done before. I stared up at Chimney Rock, a definite landmark for the pioneers . . . .

Heather's Journal
August 21, 1986

100 Miles

"Hey John, how far do we need to go today?" asked Carl. The kids had promised Lynn that they would try and get her over the Continental Divide by September first. She had to be back to her first-grade classroom for the start of her school. They knew I had a pretty good idea how far we needed to go every day to make it over the prairie and mountains to Jackson Hole. We had left Memphis on the thirty-first of July and had exactly one month to go 1700 miles. The folks in Tennessee didn't give us much chance of making it, but they didn't know these kids as well as I did. My five young friends didn't take promises lightly, and I knew they would do everything they could to get Lynn across the plains to see the mountains before flying home to the ocean. Still, I hesitated when I gave Carl his answer that morning.

"Well . . . what do you guys think about trying to do our first century today?" I asked.

"Yeah, let's go for it, we can do it." Carl sounded pretty confident.

"I think we can, too," agreed Joy. "We've already done over thirty miles and it's only ten o'clock, and . . . and we haven't even been going that fast."

Ethan watched the discussion silently. Jimmy and Heather, hearing the mention of a one hundred mile day, put down their breakfast funny papers and joined the discussion.

"Why not?" said a cocky Jimmy. "It seems pretty flat in Nebraska so far."

"And if the wind stays calm, we should be okay," said Heather. "I bet we can do it. It will help us get Lynn closer to the Tetons, so I think we should all go for it."

We were having our conversation at our first breakfast in Nebraska. We had ridden down the red brick streets of Fairbury to The Kettle Restaurant, which was right next to The Chicken House Antique Shop. Lynn and the girls smiled when they saw the treasures next door, and I wasn't surprised when the three of them finished their breakfast before the guys and I even got a chance to dent our stacks of pancakes.

"See you later, dear," smiled Lynn. "Would you handle the check for me?"

"Where are you going?" I asked, pretending not to know.

286

"Oh, Joy and Heather and I are going to check out the antique shop next door. I'm running out of time on my quilt collection."

"Well, just remember, we only have one bed and you've already bought three quilts so far."

"Yes, dear, I know, I know." Lynn flashed me a look I'd seen many times before. She didn't see why having only one bed should limit the number of quilts in the family.

"And remember, we only have one closet . . . ."

"Oh, John, don't worry, they probably don't have anything good anyway."

"Famous last words," I mumbled, and the guys laughed. "Really, guys, marriage is wonderful — sometimes — Hey Jimmy, you done with that sports page?"

"Sure, John, you may not be able to afford another one after Lynn is through next door."

"Thanks, James. If she buys too much stuff, I won't be able to buy you and me donuts anymore when we get back home."

While the guys and I finished our breakfast, we also had a chance to study all the Nebraska Cornhusker football paraphernalia on the walls of the coffee shop. Banners, pennants and schedules saying GO BIG RED! and BEAT THEM SOONERS! covered the walls like wallpaper and announced we were, most definitely, now in Cornhusker Country.

"Oh, John, they had the neatest stuff in that store." Outside, Heather was beside herself with excitement. Realizing Lynn was still inside the shop, I was beside myself with concern.

"I got these neat antique clothes." Heather's arms danced in the air, as she continued describing her purchases. "I got this really neat dress and this cute jacket and . . . and these really cute shoes that are leather and go up your ankle and have all kinds of buttons going up the sides. I've always wanted to get a pair like them and this lady — oh, she was so sweet — she brought out this box from the back and said she had something she thought I would really like. And she opened it up and there were these brown shoes, just like I had always dreamed of. They were just like something from *Little House on the Prairie*. I just couldn't resist them and they were really reasonable, so I bought them. The lady — you know, the one who was so nice — is going to ship them home for me . . . Oh, I could spend a lot of time and a lot of money in there. I wish we could stay longer; I really like this town."

"How's Lynn doing?" I asked, as Heather paused long enough to catch her breath.

"Oh, John, you should see her! She's got quilts spread out all over everywhere in there. That nice lady, she has lots of neat old quilts."

"Uh . . . Heather? . . . Could you go in there and tell Lynn that we need to hit the road? I don't want to go inside and see the damage."

"Damage? . . . What damage, John? We were careful not to knock any of that neat stuff over."

"Oh, Heather, never mind. Please just go inside and ask Lynn to hurry up."

"Okay, but you're missing a really neat shop."

Lynn did buy three more quilts that day at the Chicken House, but we also rode our first hundred mile day. Just outside of York, Carl's and Ethan's computers flashed the magical three digits and we stopped for a celebration.

"Hey Heather, I think it's time," said Joy, looking through her handlebar bag.

"Yeah Stick, let's get them out," answered Heather.

Heather and Joy got out the party poppers they had been saving for an extra-special occasion. They held the little plastic champagne bottles in the sky and pulled the strings dangling out the bottom. With a loud "POP!" the streamers burst from the exploding bottle, and we continued our hugging and dancing as the streamers rained down upon us. Before leaving, we all yelled our ceremonial "YAHOO!" for the only audience nearby — the corn and the clouds — and I told the kids they could choose the celebratory meal when we got to York. Upon spotting a pair of Golden Arches on the outskirts of town, their choice was unanimous.

"Let's go see Ronald!!!" they all yelled, and we rolled into the McDonald's in York, Nebraska. I was hoping for some cuisine more unique to the area, and the kids, knowing me pretty well, did their best to convince me of the appropriateness of their choice.

"Hey John, this place is perfect," said Carl, pointing to the playland in the center of the parking lot. "It's made just like a wagon train — only it's plastic."

I wasn't much of a McDonald's fan, but the kids seemed as excited about finding the Golden Arches as they were to have ridden a hundred miles, and Carl was right; it did almost look like a wagon train.

"I wonder what William Swain would have had," laughed Ethan, as he stepped up to the counter.

"My order? . . . Yes, ma'am, I'll take a Big Mac, large Coke and fries."

Passing Trains

"Hey, you guys," said Carl at breakfast the next morning. "Remember all the bicyclists back home who told us we were crazy riding from east to west?" They said all the prevailing winds on this side of the Mississippi would be blowing against us . . . Well, so far they've been wrong, and, anyway, if the pioneers could do it, then so can we. Shoot, if the settlers only went where the wind took them, I wonder if there ever would have been a California?"

We didn't do any more hundred milers in Nebraska, but the kids' promise to Lynn, combined with the Nebraska tailwind, helped us average over ninety miles a day as we followed Swain and the Platte River across the endless prairie.

"Hey John, you know how we used to look for water towers to find the next town off in the distance?" asked Joy one day as we were riding.

"Yeah."

"Well, in Nebraska it's different. Instead of looking for water towers, now we look for corn silos."

"Yeah, it seems like all they grow around here is corn, milo and soybeans," said Heather. "Back in Virginia, I was sad when we saw all the corn dying, but now, all I can see is corn and milo."

"And that man back there at that store, under the silo that said CO-OP," added Carl. "He said that the silos are already overflowing with grain."

"No kidding," exclaimed Ethan. "Every time our road comes close to one of those silo things, there's corn all over the road. It looks like big popcorn."

"And it's not even popcorn!" said Jimmy. "All this grain is for animals, not people. I always thought all the corn in Kansas and Nebraska was the kind we bought in the store."

"And I never even heard of milo before," said Heather.

"Hey John, is this where all the farmers are going out of business and stuff?"

"Yeah, I think so, Carl. Remember that big open stretch we saw a while back? You know, where all those tractors and harvesters were lined up and parked for as far as your eyes could see?"

"Yeah."

"Well, I think that's equipment that the farmers have to sell when they go bankrupt."

"If farming is so bad, and if there is such a humongous supply of corn and stuff," wondered Ethan, "then how come there are all those fields we keep seeing where the farmers are trying new varieties of plants? At the same time people are saying there is too much grain, they're trying to grow more and more of it . . . I don't understand."

"That's okay, Ethan. I don't understand either."

"John, isn't Nebraska one of the states where there were a lot of homesteaders?" asked Joy, changing the subject.

"Yup, Joy, you're right. In fact, Homestead National Monument was back there, just east of Fairbury. That's where they say the first official homestead was claimed under the Homestead Act."

"So, do you think all these farms were originally homesteads?"

"I don't know for sure, but what are some of the things we've seen so far that might give us some clues?"

"Well, first of all, there sure are a lot of farms around here," she answered.

"I've got a big clue," boasted Jimmy. "Remember in class when we acted like we were homesteaders and we settled that imaginary land?"

"Yeah." Everyone answered Jimmy in chorus.

"Well," Jimmy continued, "remember how most of our quarter sections had perpendicular property lines, and how the roads would only run along those lines?"

"Yeah," everyone answered again. "Yeah, so . . . ."

"Well, what have you guys noticed about almost all the roads we've been on so far?"

"They're all at right angles to each other!" yelled Carl.

"How neat!" beamed Joy. "Just like our homestead game. This really must be homestead country."

"And the other day," Jimmy continued, "when John and me were stopped and waiting for you guys, I checked out his map of Nebraska, and you guys should see it! It looks like a checkerboard. The county lines and the road lines almost all intersect at ninety-degree angles. I bet if we had time to measure these roads and fences, we'd find them divided up in acres, quarter sections, half sections and everything, just like we learned."

Carl waited to make sure Jimmy was finished before he began: "You know, all that time we studied the pioneers and the homesteaders and stuff, I got into the simulations and everything, but I never really tried to imagine what the land looked like. Grazing land and prairie land and valley land didn't really have much meaning to me, but, now, the more I ride and feel the changes, the more I think about what settling out here must have been like. Nebraska's a pretty big place."

And none of us knew it, but the bigness had just begun. The further west we rode, the bigger and broader Nebraska got. Grain fields and green swells of feed, rolling in the wind, gave way to brown hills and expanses interrupted only by our ribbon of blacktop, barbed wire fence — and the railroad.

Yes, the railroad. The road along the North Platte was a train chaser's paradise. Almost every half hour, the giant steel centipedes would rattle by us and we'd all be mesmerized. At first, we would all come to a stop, lift our arms and wave the international kids' signal asking the engineer to blow his horn, and then we'd count the cars in the train. Our first train caused the senators to develop a set of rules for counting cars:

"Hey you guys, I think we should make it a rule that we have to count the cars silently, 'cuz I get all messed up when I hear someone else counting out loud," suggested Ms. Senator Fulton.

"Yeah, me too," agreed Mr. Senator Fagerlin. "I get all screwed up when I'm on one number and I can hear someone else on another number."

"But . . ." hesitated Ethan, ". . . I don't count silently too good."

"Oh, Ethan," laughed Heather, "then just try and whisper your numbers."

"But . . . I don't whisper them too good either," sighed a disappointed Ethan.

Pretty soon the kids learned to count the trains while they rode alongside them on their bicycles. Joy and Heather would each lift one hand off their handlebars and point their index finger at each car, counting each one silently. Jimmy and Carl simply nodded their heads with each car and Ethan, well, as usual, he had a technique all his own. Whenever I looked back at ole Eeth, I saw his lips moving and his head bobbing with each passing car. His nose took the place of his index finger because he kept his two hands firmly attached to his handlebars, just in case any dusty, bicycle-swallowing ditches tried to lure him into their jaws. I was still amazed every time I watched Ethan ride his bike. And every time I looked back at our group, waving at engineers and counting trains, and saw him at the back so intent on mouthing each number, I'd end up grinning such a giant grin, I'd lose track of what number I was on.

Oh California

"Okay, you guys, tonight we are going to write a song." Like most of the trains, our stop that night was North Platte. We found a cheap motel with showers, sheets and a television, and I figured the indoor acoustics would be perfect for a special journal meeting I'd been planning.

"What?" asked a surprised Carl.

"Remember when I told you guys that the pioneers took the tune to *Oh, Susannah* and wrote their own song called *Oh California*? Well, I thought it was about time for us to write our own version. I'll read you some of the pioneers' verses and the chorus I wrote for us, and then we can each take some time to write our own."

"Then are we going to get to sing them?" Ethan asked excitedly. Ethan liked to sing.

"Yup," I answered. "We're even going to record them into this tape recorder I've been carrying."

Everyone got out their journals and I dictated some lines from the emigrants' version of *Oh California*. For almost an hour the room was silent, except for some whispered humming, as the kids tried to match syllable and rhyme. Our chorus was:

> *Oh California!*
> *Now don't you cry for me,*
> *For I'm coming home by bicycle,*
> *From sea to shining sea.*

When verses were finished — or as finished as they were going to get that night — we practiced the chorus in an inspired and never-heard-before seven part harmony. We featured Joy covering the entire range from bass to soprano (sometimes in the same line); Jimmy showing why young men who are trying to sprout their first whiskers don't make much money as singers; and Lynn on uncontrolled giggles and laughter. As much as Lynn tried, she couldn't contain her response to our rather unconventional sound. Nonetheless, after over an hour of trying to record our musical and historical genius, we did come out with a cassette copy of our *Oh California*.

"Who knows, John?" joked Jimmy. "Our version may be studied and imitated a hundred and fifty years from now by future young scholars. I bet Swain and the boys didn't sound much better than us."

Here are some of the words, and you may sing along if you'd like. The group and I guarantee that unless you have a collection of seven completely different and crazy voices (one of them on soprano laughter), your version will only be a distant approximation.

OH CALIFORNIA
(Recorded August 18, 1986 North Platte, Nebraska
. . . all rights surrendered)

CHORUS:
Oh California!
Oh don't you cry for me,
For I'm coming home by bicycle,
From sea to shining sea.

ETHAN:
Oh as I ride along the road,
I think of William Swain,
Cuz he's the one who came this way,
With his old wagon train.
John reads us William's journal,
It talks of homesick pain,
It also talks of lightning storms,
I guess we're much the same.

CARL:
We get up around 4 AM,
But I sleep in til 5,
So I must really hustle then,
To catch up with the guys.
We bike all day in the hot sun,
The weather it is dry,
We hate to see the clouds roll in,
That darken up the sky.
CHORUS

JIMMY:
I come from California,
My mind upon a quest,
To cross this country, bright and blue,
From the East to the West.

I've gone half way and I can say,
It's been a lot of fun,
But I can't wait til that glorious day,
When I'll be all done.

JOY:
We started out in Maryland,
This country we would see,
Four long months of pedaling,
From sea to shining sea.
We met a lot of people,
We saw a lot of land,
We can't wait to get home
To California's sand.

HEATHER:
We've traveled over 2,000 miles,
And seen a face or two,
I've never seen so many smiles,
Saying wish I could come too.
We stayed a day with Amish friends,
A special family,
They showed us how to milk the cows,
Which was a sight to see.

CHORUS

The next morning, as the kids showered, I could hear them humming and singing each other's verses from the night before. And for twenty miles, aided by another tailwind, we cruised along the Platte River, composing new verses to our song. Like the night before, each verse's rhythm and/or rhyme might have been in question, but the emotion was irrefutable. Every so often, at some cross-roads or in front of some Pioneer Trail marker, we'd stop for an impromptu concert, and more than a few people who passed us that morning gave us strange gazes from their windows as we sang and clapped — and Lynn laughed hysterically — on the side of the road.

We were still singing when, just outside of a little town called Paxton, we climbed an especially large brown wave of prairie marked suspiciously by a lonely tree at its summit. The sun bounced off the blacktop as we climbed and the asphalt seemed to vibrate in the midday heat. Any humidity had been blown ahead of us by the incessant winds that blew us across the plains. I laid my bike down in the dirt — there was nothing to lean it against — as I told the kids to go ahead of me so that I could take a picture of them. I crouched down on the road and tried to get in good position for the picture, but, as soon as I looked through my lens, I knew I couldn't do the scene justice. Framing the view that afternoon was absurd; it was like putting blinders on. What made that place so immense wasn't just what we saw ahead, but what surrounded us. If ever the earth and sky seemed like it could swallow us up, that was the spot. I snapped my pitiful pictures quickly, took off my blinders and returned to my 360-degree view.

I watched as Jimmy was the first to crest the lonely hilltop, then Heather, Joy, Carl, Ethan and, finally, Lynn. As each of them disappeared over the top, I wondered if perhaps Columbus was wrong; maybe the earth did have an edge. I honestly expected to crest the hill myself to find that the rest of the group was falling into a deep chasm of sky on the other side.

My fantasy didn't last long, but what awaited me on the other side of the hill was just as spectacular. The kids had all laid down their bikes and stood, jaws dropped open and silent, staring due west. Old Chris was right, it seemed the earth *was* round.

"Hey John, look out there," gasped Joy as she pointed. "Out there on the horizon, if you look carefully, you can see how the earth curves."

"I don't know about no curving," said Carl, " but this place is so big, I'm gettin' dizzy standing here and looking at it. It's like I can feel the earth spinning underneath me."

The prairie of Nebraska stretched itself out for as far as we could see — and we could see a long way. Just below us, we could see the North Platte River winding its way to the northwest, with scrub brush and an occasional tree marking its banks with isolated splashes of green in a sea of brown. If we were quiet and could ignore the pounding beats of our hearts, we could hear the wind whistling across the open spaces.

"Hey John, we're going to ride out there past where our eyes can see, aren't we?" said Joy after a long silence.

"Yeah, Joy, past where we can see, and then some," I answered.

We pitched our tents that night across from Ash Hollow, a famous camping spot for Swain and thousands of other emigrants.

"Hey John, we read about Ash Hollow when we studied the Donner Party," said Jimmy. "Didn't they bury some of their members there?"

I couldn't recall if they had or not, but the next morning, as we got on our bicycles, I wondered if we would be burying any of our party along the bulge in the North Platte called Lake McConaughy.

The wind that had blown us west howled all night long, and, sometime in the darkness, it had changed direction. Our normally encouraging morning breeze was cranked up to a dawn crosswind much stronger than any we'd yet experienced. We pushed our bikes into the blowing sand and up onto the road.

Our road sat atop the bluffs that rise high above the north shore of the lake. With not as much as a tumbleweed to block that wind or a guardrail to keep us on the pavement, we were a good bet to be blown off the cliffs.

"Be careful, you guys," I warned the kids as we began our pedaling, and a few hundred yards later, I looked over my shoulder and saw them struggling to keep their bikes from capsizing. They leaned into the wind and, like sailboats, tacked diagonally across the roadway.

For the first hour that morning we were all pretty fair land sailors. We were eight miles down the road, no one had fallen and we were almost ready to start enjoying the adventure when things got drastic.

As the sun rose higher, the wind blew harder and harder, and every time we rolled down into a ravine, it would be funneled even more. The onslaught of dust and air at the mouths of those little canyons felt like someone was shooting us with a giant fire hose of air. To make matters worse, the traffic, which had been almost non- existent in the early hours of morning, started to pick up. When a sudden gust from the north threw all three hundred combined pounds of me and my bike across our lane and almost to the shoulder on the opposite side, I could only imagine what a similar gust of wind might do to the kids and their bikes. They had much the same sail area on their bikes as I did, but their weight was less than half of mine. If some unsuspecting car happened to be in their vicinity when that happened, we would soon be burying one of our party. Even if there wasn't any car nearby, I could see Heather suddenly becoming airborne and flying like some metallic and nylon tumbleweed over the bluff and down the steep cliff into the water below.

"Hey Jimmy, I think we had better stop and see if we can do something about this wind," I said to my partner at the front, after I came back into my lane.

"Yeah, this is pretty dangerous. That last gust just missed me, but I saw it blow you across the road. I wondered if you were doing it on purpose to get in position to take a picture or something." Jimmy caught his breath and laid his bike down on the ground off the road.

"Hold onto your bike, Jimmy! It might blow away." I wished I was joking as I yelled at Jimmy. We both held on tight and waited for everyone else.

The rest of the group slowly but surely fought their way up the hill. Normally, from her vantage point at the back, Lynn saw all the wiggles and wobbles and near misses, but from my vantage point at the top that day, I saw how the kids were struggling to keep their bikes upright. Heads down in their most aerodynamic position, they tried to keep from steering into the ditch on their side of the road or being blown across two lanes and off the cliff on the other.

I saw a large pick-up truck approaching from behind Lynn and the girls and said a quick prayer. The driver seemed very aware of the bicycles as he drove very slowly out in the other lane. He passed the girls and pulled up to where Jimmy, Carl, Ethan and I were waiting.

"You folks shouldn't be bicyclin' up here in this wind." He looked a lot like our Arkansas friend, Johnny Carroll. The ball cap atop his head must have been held down with glue, because the only thing keeping my helmet from being blown south was my chinstrap.

"It's still early, too, and its only bound to get worse," he continued. "There's a couple stretches ahead just been plowed, and in addition to this wind, the dirt and dust will blind ya and make it awful tough to breathe. "May I make a suggestion?"

"Sure can," I said.

"I just talked to your wife and the two girls back down the road, and they explained to me about you riding all the way across America and everything, and even though they looked a little worried, when I offered to give them a lift in my truck, they said that you wouldn't let them accept it. Said you were riding the whole way and couldn't accept no rides.

"I understand that reasoning and everything, but I'm from these parts and I know how wicked this ole wind can git. Not much stoppin' it between here and the Dakotas. Better to take a lift from me down off these bluffs, than to have one of these kids git themselves hurt."

By the time he had finished his proposal, Lynn and the girls had pulled up and laid down their bikes. When I told him I would accept his offer, the entire group looked at me as if I had gone nuts. They whispered to each other and asked me if I was all right, and I assured them I was. After all, the land seas were as rough that morning as any river, and I was sure I could find some journal entry of Mr. Swain's that described a ferry crossing.

Our friend took our bikes and us to the cafe in Lewellen. As the waitress (nominated by five wind-blown senators as the nicest waitress of the trip) kept pancakes coming and hot chocolate cups filled up, I prayed for some calmer waves on our ocean of land. The wind was calmer down off the bluffs — thank God — because we had over sixty miles more to go and no tailwind to help us.

"Hey John, it took us over two hours to go less than sixteen miles," observed Jimmy. "We'll never make it to Bridgeport today at this pace."

Jimmy was right; despite being out of the wind, our pace was really dragging, and I could see, from the droopy posture of the group, that it was time for me to break out a little handlebar bag psychology. I motioned Lynn to the front of the group and asked her to stop for lunch in the next town. In the meantime, I needed to lighten the spirits and speed the pace of the rear guard.

"Hey kids!" I yelled, as I rolled back alongside Joy and gave my best Groucho Marx eyebrow imitation.

"Oh no, John," moaned Carl. "Please tell us you're not going to do one of your corny comedy routines." Heather and Joy rolled their eyes, and Ethan didn't even raise his head. Jimmy and Lynn were spared my humor, only because they were about a quarter-mile ahead of us.

"Did you say corny, Carl?" I asked. "That's pretty funny. Is that a Nebraska joke or something?"

My captive audience moaned, and Carl sped up to join Jimmy and Lynn rather than listen to me. My plan was working already; either the kids would have their minds taken off the road by hysterical laughter, or they would hate my jokes so much they would pedal even faster, bridging the gap up to Lynn and Jimmy.

"Hey Joy, how come they call a certain variety of corn Dumbo corn?" I didn't know where the joke came from because I made it up right there on the spot. Lynn always said that I tended to get hysterical when I was exhausted, and that morning's blustery encounter had driven me to the edge in more ways than one.

"I don't know, John. Why *do* they call a certain variety of corn, Dumbo corn?" Parroting back my opening, Joy was the perfect straight person.

"Well, because it has . . . big . . . ears!!!" I answered loud and slow. I got a big kick myself out of the joke I'd just heard for the first time. I laughed and laughed and pretty soon Joy, Heather and Ethan couldn't help but laugh along , as tears rolled down my cheeks.

"Hey John, that *was* pretty funny," chuckled Joy as she looked over at my red face.

"Pretty funny?!!! That was even a better joke than I thought I was going to have for you guys. I bet you guys didn't know I was so funny."

"Oh no, John," said Heather. "We knew you weren't so funny already. You and Jim (another teacher at school) tell the worst jokes, but I have to admit that one was pretty funny."

Eight of the next ten miles to lunch was spent discussing what was funny and what was not. I created a few more jokes, shed a few more hysterical tears, and the three kids shared a few silly jokes of their own. When the grain silo marking our lunch stop appeared on the horizon, I decided to speed our final few miles by breaking out the cookies in my handlebar bag. I rode up alongside each of the kids, held a cookie just out of reach in front of them, and then I speeded up. My bicycling carrot technique worked, and out of cookies and out of breath, we soon rolled beneath the silos at Lisco, having ridden the last ten miles in under an hour. Bridgeport was still thirty miles away, but we would make it if we kept up our new pace.

Even though we were following the river, our road seemed to always be on the opposite side from where Swain's train had driven. Fourteen miles past lunch, at a crossroads called Broadwater, we had a chance to take an alternate road into Bridgeport, one that followed the same side of the river that our friend William had. We turned left and excitedly crossed the North Platte River.

As if by instinct, all the kids stopped just as we reached the south bank of the river. Looking down river to the east and up river to the west, everyone got deathly quiet, listening for the squeaks and rattles of approaching wagons. There were no cars, just us and the ghosts of pioneers past.

Joy finally broke the silence. "Hey John, do you think Swain came close to here?"

"Yeah, I think he crossed where we're standing right now." Everyone's eyes got real big and I was sure I wasn't the only one with goosebumps that afternoon. "Wouldn't be surprised if he didn't stop and camp somewhere real close by. He might have even stopped here for a swim or to do his laundry . . . ."

"You really think so?" asked an excited Ethan.

"Do you think you could read one of his journal entries from around here, so we can hear how he describes it?" asked Joy.

"Sure, I'll read one tonight when we get to Bridgeport—"

"No, no, not tonight, read one now, while we're right here," insisted Heather.

"Okay, okay. Let's pull off the road and see what I can find . . .

"June 17, 1849. . . . First I washed the dishes and gathered chips for the next three days; then went in swimming, which I found pretty much fun. On plunging into the river, which I supposed three feet deep, I found I could but just stand on the bottom, which being of sand, would slip away from my feet as soon as the force was applied to it necessary to sustain myself against the current, which was very strong; and in place of standing where I expected, I found myself sweeping along down the river. I was obliged to swim with the current, which took me along like fun. After having a fine swim, I washed some clothes, and then I made a bag to keep my clothes and gun in. Attended preaching at seven o'clock."

"Sounds like us swimming in the lake last night," said Carl.

"And that preaching stuff . . . that's like you reading to us at our meetings," said Ethan.

"Keep reading," said Joy.

"June 20, 1849. After traveling about three miles . . . the wind, which had blown all day from the southwest, suddenly changed to the northeast, and the clouds changed their course with it and came directly upon us."

"Go on, go on."

"June 26, 1849. We started early this morn and had a good day's work over sandy roads. I bathed in the North Platte at noon. Elk are along the road today. Graves are also frequent.

During the forenoon the road passed through many steep ravines and sandy bottoms just under the line of the bluffs, which are high and rugged and properly named Castle Bluffs for they appear like ruined castles. The road is almost all sand, the day hot, the mosquitoes abundant and unmerciful."

"It sure looks like this is the place," observed Joy. "Look how sandy it is this close to the river. I'm sure glad we get to ride on this side for a while."

"Yeah, me too," agreed Heather. "But I bet the mosquitoes really do get awful down here by the river. The sun is getting ready to go down. If Swain is right, we should start getting down the road to Bridgeport before they attack."

"Are these bluffs around here those Castle Bluffs he was talking about?" asked Carl.

"Yeah, I think so. Do you guys think they look like castles?" I asked.

"Well, yeah, kinda," answered Joy, getting back on her bike and looking across at the bluffs. "They were probably taller then, because the wind and the rain has probably eroded them a lot since the pioneers were here."

"Well, everybody, be looking for Courthouse Rock and Jailhouse Rock up ahead, when we get close to Bridgeport."

Before leaving, we looked up and down the river one more time — just in case there were any late arriving wagons.

After our pause along that stretch of the Platte late that afternoon, I didn't need any more cookies or comedy. Anxious to see the two stone landmarks reported to be ahead, they set a record pace to Bridgeport. Like many before them, they were excited to see something to break up the monotony of the naked Plains.

Wagons Ho

"I think this is it, you guys," I said as I pulled off the road at the intersection. Off to the side of the road, a sign read:

OREGON TRAIL WAGON TRAIN

and it had a silhouette of a covered wagon being pulled by a team of horses. My directions said to turn right at Chimney Rock, but we almost missed the turn because we were so taken by the stone sentinel towering above the prairie.

"Boy John, that sure is big," said Jimmy. "Even bigger than all those pioneer descriptions made it sound. It kinda looks like Mother Nature's Statue of Liberty . . . Ya know, when I see something like this and realize how many pioneers actually came by here and got the same view of it as I am . . .Well, it just makes me think a lot . . . This is a very special place."

Jimmy faded off into thought as he pushed his bike down the sandy dirt road and looked off at Chimney Rock.

Our next stop was two days off our bicycles and two days on a real wagon train with Gordon Howard. We were all excited to see what riding a wagon was really like, but Chimney Rock was so amazing that even the anticipation of a sail in real prairie schooners couldn't stop us from twisting our necks toward the rock as we approached Gordon's corrals.

"Wow John," exclaimed Carl. "Look at those wagons! Do you think those are the ones we're going to ride in?"

"Yep." Before I had a chance to respond, Carl's answer came from a stocky, bearded man who poked his head around one of the circled wagons.

"Gonna ride in one just like these," he continued. "My name is Gordon Howard. You must be the group bicyclin' across America. Been lookin' forward to meetin' ya." Gordon looked a lot like Jacob, our Amish friend. He wore a floppy leather hat instead of one made of straw, wire rimmed glasses with small round lenses, had a nineteenth century beard without an adjoining moustache and wore brown boots instead of barefeet. He wore long, brown britches, and his long-sleeved, checkered shirt was topped with a well-worn leather vest. He motioned us over to the front of his cabin and told us to lean our bicycles against the rail fence.

"You can all call me Gordon because you're all gonna get to know me real well in the next two days. I'm your wagonmaster and John, your schoolteacher here, is going to be my assistant." He shook hands with everyone and herded us over to lunch.

"Takes lots of energy to cross the prairie in a wagon. Do you kids eat a lot when you're ridin' them bicycles of yours?"

"Yes, sir, we do," answered Jimmy in his most respectful tone, and we all nodded in agreement. In just ten minutes Gordon had us in the palm of his hand.

"Well, I ain't never ridden a bike too far, but I'm willing to bet that drivin' wagons takes about the same amount of energy, so I think before we set out, we had better put some food in our stomachs."

Rows of wooden picnic tables sat under a tall wooden awning built in the middle of the yard. Gordon's camp consisted of several log cabins, some stables, the pasture with the circle of wagons and the large picnic area. Sitting on the edge of the North Platte, the grass and the trees of his spread were like an oasis.

Spread before us were two plates stacked high with bread, one bowl with potato chips, one bowl with Cheetos, two plates heaped full of thick slices of barbecued beef, one plate of cheese and two large pitchers of lemonade. Dessert was mountains of cold melon slices.

"Now I don't want anyone bein' shy about eatin'," Gordon said as he sat us down. "If ya finish this, then my wife, Patty here, will get some more."

Patty smiled as she watched the kids listen to her husband's orders. She started pouring the kids lemonade, and as she filled each of their cups, she asked them their names. I saw the kids shyly hesitating to dig in, but I knew that once I led the way, Gordon would be amazed at how many trips Patty would soon be making to keep those plates full. He didn't realize who he was dealing with, and I knew of a few waitresses who would put money on the kids if they ever got in an eating contest with any pioneers — past or present.

While we ate, Gordon spoke to us about the rules of the trail: "Now I ain't a very schooled individual, but I do know something about traveling by wagon. Been studyin' the ways of the trail now for many many years, reading old journals and studying sketches done by the people who crossed this prairie.

"If ya ain't discovered it by now, you'll find me to be short with my words, because I believe a person learns a lot more 'bout things by doin' them than by talkin' bout them.

"By some accounts, there was a grave for every mile of the trail, by some others one for every half-mile. Some of those deaths were caused by sickness and accident, but then some others, they were caused by carelessness. I'm gonna be askin' you to do a lot of the work when we get on the wagons, and I want ya to listen to me real good, because I don't want to be adding any more graves to this section of the trail.

"When I show ya how to get up on the wagon, then I want ya to remember how to get up on the wagon. Don't got no time to be showin' ya twice. When ya get out and walk alongside the wagons and I tell ya to watch for rattlesnakes, then don't get careless — ya got to watch for rattlesnakes. And, when ya get your turn to ride the horses, then ya got to be extra careful of those snakes, because, believe me, there are lots of them around here.

"I want ya to have fun, but I also want ya to have a safe trip. Usually I take folks out for three and four days, and on those trips I have more people and more than the two wagons we are gonna take. I always take my two sons and some other help to cook and drive, but this time it's gonna be just John, you guys, you ladies and me. This is going to be a test run to see if this kind of trip is possible, and from the looks of you guys I think it will be, just as long as you're careful and listen along the way.

"John, how are you with horses?" As soon as Gordon asked, the kids started to laugh, and Lynn laughed even louder.

"Oh, alright I guess," I answered quietly.

"Sounds like your group here might disagree," chuckled Gordon. "Well, anyway, you're gonna be drivin' one of the wagons, and my son, Murph, is gonna show you how to hitch it up. As soon as you're finished with your lunch, I want you to go with him over to the wagon and get hitched up. While you're doin' that, I want everyone to get the clothes they need and put them in these duffel bags to be put in the big wagon over there."

News of my driving may have been humorous to Lynn and the kids, but to me it wasn't so funny. My upbringing made me much more comfortable on a wave than a horse, and although I had had a few successful pony rides as a young child, Lynn and the kids knew that horses had a tendency to laugh whenever I came near them. Walking with Murph over to the wagon, I hoped my animal would be wearing blinders.

"Go get 'em, John," laughed Jimmy as I left.

"Yeah, go get 'em, dear," laughed Lynn, who I could tell was on the brink of suggesting a change of drivers to Gordon. She knew she was a better horseperson than me and was a little jealous that I had been chosen solely because I was the male leader of the group. She had trouble with the woman's place in pioneer society but figured watching me struggle with a horse might be even more fun than being my equal for the next couple days. She was satisfied to bite her tongue and join the laughter.

Murph was waiting for me over by the wagon, and I walked gingerly over to the horse he was preparing to hitch up to it. I stroked the animal's neck with all the confidence I could fake.

"John, you don't got nothin' to worry about. Pixie here is one of the sweetest tempered team horses we got." Murph sounded like he was telling the truth, and so far I hadn't seen Pixie laughing at me.

"Looks pretty easy," Jimmy's voice surprised me from behind. "Gordon asked for a volunteer to ride with you and I'm it."

"Thanks for the faith, Jimmy," I said.

"Oh, I don't know if I'd use the word 'faith,' John . . . I just figured I could use a few laughs," Jimmy grinned. "How come this wagon's only got two wheels? It looks like somebody cut it in half."

"Well, sometimes that's just what happened," said Murph as he moved Pixie into position. "This here is called a Dearborn wagon. Only has two wheels. Lots of pioneers traveled west in Dearborns; some by design and some by predicament. Some people who had small families or were on their own and traveling light left Missouri with wagons just like these; others . . . well, they may have had an accident or their animals got real weak or maybe even they had to speed up to make it over the mountains before the snows. Whatever the reason, they just cut their original wagon in half and ended up with something like this. Not everyone traveled across in wagons like are in all the pictures. More people traveled in Dearborns than you might think."

"Shoot, I never even heard of a Dearborn before," said Jimmy.

Murph had me do the hitching while Jimmy threw his duffel and mine inside the back of the wagon. Our only other cargo was a five gallon water container and a canvas awning. Once we were all hitched and packed, Murph held Pix while Jimmy and I went across the yard to watch the others get into the big wagon. It looked like all the ones we had read about and was pulled by two giant black horses. They looked like the ones in the beer commercials. Their names were Fern and Casey and I thought I saw them wink at each other when they saw me coming. I sure was glad I wasn't driving that wagon.

"Everyone's duffels loaded on?" asked Gordon, as the kids and Lynn stood around him waiting for his next order.

"Yeah, I think so," quickly answered Carl.

"Well then, who wants to be the first one to climb in the wagon?" Before Gordon even finished his question, five hands shot up into the air, and I saw him fight a losing battle with a grin before he continued.

"Now I don't think we need to be raisin' our hands. As I sees it, there be only eight of us altogether, and although I aim to have ya learn a lot more than ya could in school, this ain't the classroom, so I think if ya just speak up instead of raisin' those hands of yours, we'll all do jus' fine. 'Sides, might be needin' those hands for somethin' more important . . . ." Gordon chuckled to himself, and the kids held their hands behind them.

"Could I go first?" Joy asked politely.

"Why sure," said Gordon. "First thing is ya got to be careful with the animals. Don't want to spook them when yer gettin' on or off." Gordon reached for Joy's hand as if he was going to lead her out onto the dance floor.

"Place one hand gently on Casey's rear end." Joy reached out and did just as Gordon asked. "Now place one foot gently on the tongue of the wagon and then the other. Lightly now. . . that's it . . . Good job, Joy. Then grab onto the front of the wagon with your other hand . . . perfect. Now, pull yourself up and onto that seat in front." In one smooth lunge, Joy was sitting atop the seat with a big smile on her face.

"Great job, Joy. You look like you've done a little pioneerin' before," said Gordon, winking up at her. "Okay, who's next?"

I saw a few hands begin to go up, but the kids caught themselves and quickly formed a line behind Carl. Not all of them were as smooth as Joy, but they all made it. Lynn sat next to Gordon at the reins, and poking their heads out of the space between the canvas cover and the sides of the wagon were four of the cutest pioneers I had ever seen.

"Let's load up that Dearborn, gentlemen," ordered Gordon. "Got to make Chimney Rock 'fore sundown."

Jimmy and I ran over to our wagon and did our best to duplicate Joy's technique. Then, with a shake of the reins and the shouts of Gordon and the kids yelling, "WAGONS HO!," we were off down the trail.

When our wagon started to move, I think I knew how Ethan felt that first day on his bicycle. Gordon's wagon, in the lead, drove a straight course down the dusty road leading to the stretch of prairie we were going to cross. Pixie, Jimmy and I seemed to be taking a rather scenic and slow route down that same driveway. After just fifty yards, Gordon stopped and waited for us to come alongside him. He and all his passengers were already laughing at my style — or lack of it. Gordon gave me the equivalent of my telling Ethan not to try anything fancy. He showed me where the brakes and handlebars were and asked me to stay out of ditches. Like Ethan, I held on tight with both hands and I didn't figure I'd be scratching my nose for a long time.

We headed off down the road, a little straighter this time, and I didn't credit our straight course so much to my skill as I did to the little lecture Gordon had given Pixie when he finished with me. Jimmy patted me on the shoulder and assured me that everything would be okay.

Just as we left the long dirt drive, two buckskinned men on horseback approached us at full speed. One had two horses in tow and the other had two large saddle bags hanging behind his saddle, and they looked like they were in a hurry to see us. With a big, "WHOOOOA!" Gordon brought his wagon to a stop. Just as I was about to pull back on the reins and do a WHOA of my own, Pixie and the Dearborn came to a stop right behind Gordon's wagon.

Our visitors were Murph and Gordon's other son, Kevin. They were disguised as two riders from the Chimney Rock Pony Express Station and they had a few deliveries for our party.

"Got some packages for a Miss Heather Deutsch," announced Murph, as he reached into his bags and pulled out two small boxes and two crumpled envelopes. "I hears she's on this train."

Heather leaned out under the wagon cover to receive her packages, and at that moment I wished her parents could have seen her face. She looked like a little kid who had just found out that Santa had brought her exactly what she wanted. She looked around for somebody to hug, and then just hugged the packages to her chest, so excited to have these things delivered by the bearded man on horseback. I had seen her excited every day for almost three months, but I don't think I ever saw her as excited as she was that afternoon. I'll never forget that look on her face.

"Also got two horses here for your wagon company," said Kevin. Gordon handed Lynn the reins and hopped down off the wagon.

"I know you boys are busy, so I'll let ya be on yer way," said Gordon, grabbing the leads from Kevin. "Thanks for the deliveries." Their business done, our two Pony Express riders spun their horses around and were off.

Joy and Heather volunteered to ride our two horses, Queenie and Meano, and we were off again. As we rolled along the road, Gordon pointed out the spot where the old, sod Chimney Rock Pony Express Station stood. About a mile after our deliveries, our dirt road ended at a gate opening onto the yellow grass of the open prairie. Gordon opened the gate and our wagon wheels left the road for the first time.

"Let's switch riders, okay girls?" he said to Joy and Heather. "Also, let's have two of you walk alongside the wagons. Most of the emigrants walked to Oregon and California. The wagons were mostly for carrying possessions."

Jimmy and Carl hopped on the horses, Heather and Joy stretched their legs and Ethan bravely came and joined me in the Dearborn.

"Hey Gordon?" asked Carl. "How come there's that line of green grass over there, when all the other grass around here is dry?"

"Anyone got a guess for Carl's question?" asked Gordon. Gordon may not have been "very schooled", but he was a natural teacher.

"Could it be wagon wheel ruts?" asked Joy, anxious for Gordon's answer. Since Missouri we had seen lots of roadside markers and signs talking of wagons and ruts, but we hadn't yet seen any.

"Yep, and they ain't mine," he replied. Everyone's eyes got the same look they'd had when they'd felt the ghosts of William and his wagons back at Broadwater.

"So many wagons came through here on their way to Chimney Rock that this is one of the places where there was almost a road leading west. The wheels of thousands of wagons plowed up this stretch of prairie, and places where you see furrows or bands of green grass are actually the ruts left behind by all those wheels heading to Chimney Rock. Later this afternoon, we'll do a little explorin' for artifacts left behind and scattered all around here. Ya can't hardly walk ten feet without stumblin' over somethin'."

Gordon gave everyone time to take some pictures and then continued, "Just one more thing before we head on. I want everyone to look up at Chimney Rock. If you look real careful, you can see that it's shaped like an Indian brave."

We all cocked our heads from side to side trying to see the figure of the Indian.

"Look real close and you can see him sitting, holding his knees and looking west . . . Some folks say you can even see him shedding a tear.

"Well, you keep lookin' as we get along. We'll be seein' lots of Chimney Rock, but we had better be goin' now.

"Boys, you got them horses?"

"Yes, sir," answered Carl and Jimmy.

"Girls, you be careful of snakes now. They're all over in these weeds." Gordon hoisted himself back up into his driver's seat. Once back at the reins, he asked, "Okay, now what do we say everyone?"

"WAGONS HO!" Seven voices echoed across the plains, and two wagons, two horses and two walkers headed west again.

The wagons rocked and lurched as the prairie proved not to be as smooth and flat as it looked from a distance. Each hole and hidden furrow in the grass was magnified by our wooden wheels. I tried to follow Gordon's path the best I could, figuring that he knew the smoothest route, but I didn't do so well. After one of my detours took us into a ditch and rocked us pretty good, I leaned over to Ethan and said, "I wonder if this thing has a roll bar . . . ."

Ethan laughed nervously and we continued on. At first, we kept pretty close to Gordon. Joy and Heather would walk back and forth between the wagons, relaying some of the stories that Gordon was telling up front. We learned about the most popular wagon colors, about how Chimney Rock had been much taller in the 1800's, and about the new kitchen that was strapped to the back of the big wagon. Each time the girls returned with a story, their hike got longer. Slowly but surely, Pixie, Ethan and I were falling behind.

One time, while the girls were walking alongside the lead wagon, Pixie stopped dead in her tracks. Gordon and the girls kept on going as Pixie laid herself over with a thud to take a nap. I didn't think a siesta was part of the day's program, and from the surprised look on Ethan's face, it didn't appear that he did either. Gordon's wagon was getting farther and farther away, so I jerked at the reins and asked Pixie to proceed. I learned later that you don't *ask* horses to do things, you *tell* them, but I was still in the asking stage. After a few "pleases" and "pretty pleases" and a timid "Come on, you stupid animal, get going" did nothing, Gordon thankfully stopped his wagon and looked back to check our progress.

Pixie must have seen Gordon turn toward us, because as soon as he looked back, she immediately got up and proceeded on. We caught up to Gordon and the others, and while Gordon gave Pixie a threatening lecture, the kids and Lynn told me how Gordon had let them have a chance to drive.

"Yeah, John, you just have to hold on real tight to the leather reins and be firm with the horses," Heather said, making it sound so easy.

Before tackling our last stretch to camp, Joy took Ethan's place alongside me, and Ethan took Jimmy's place up on Meano. As we rolled our last half-mile to camp, Joy told me about the figure of a pregnant Indian woman Gordon had showed her, silhouetted in the bluff to the south. Gordon stopped to lead the wagons down a steep embankment, and while we waited at the bottom, Joy pointed her out to me.

Just ahead, in a narrow draw that sat a quarter-mile away from Chimney Rock to the west, Gordon "WHOAED!" us to a stop and told us this was to be our camp.

"Picked a spot where we wouldn't be able to see any man-made changes in the landscape," he said as he helped the kids down off the wagon. "I also picked a spot that wasn't up high, so we'd be protected from lightning. At the same time I had to be careful not to pick a ravine that might be prone to flash floods. What d'ya folks think?"

"I think it's great," said Heather.

"It feels like you can reach up and touch Chimney Rock!" exclaimed Jimmy. "And I thought it looked big from down on the road . . . ."

"Well, let's unhitch these animals; we got lots of work to do. When the pioneers corralled their wagons for the night, their work wasn't over. For some of them it was just beginning."

"Carl? Ethan? Here's a shovel, you guys got the first chore." Gordon handed them the shovel he grabbed from the wooden toolbox on the side of the big wagon. "I want you to find a good place for the john. You're going to have to use it, so the spot is up to you. Dig it deep enough for all of us, and here's a roll of pioneer toilet paper to set beside it."

The boys disappeared laughing around the little bank behind the Dearborn.

"Gordon," asked Heather, "how far did we just go?"

"Oh 'bout three and half, maybe four miles."

"In four hours?" exclaimed Joy. "Man, we were slow."

"Yep, we sure were," said Heather in her best Gordon imitation.

"Okay everyone, while the boys are diggin' the latrine, we need to gather fuel for the fire tonight. With no trees around for wood, what do you guys think the pioneers used for fuel?"

"Didn't they use buffalo chips?" answered Jimmy.

"Yep, and that's just what we're gonna use," Gordon answered quickly.

"But aren't the buffaloes extinct?" asked Joy.

"Well, there aren't too many around anymore, but there's lots of cattle that run this range. Besides, I've been told the only way to tell between a buffalo chip

and a cow chip is to taste it." The kids wrinkled their noses as Gordon continued. "You'd be more than welcome to try. Might just be some old buffalo chips
around here somewhere. You just let me know if you taste a difference.

"One of the first things pioneers did when settin' up camp was to gather fuel
for the fire. Now, there's all kinds of fuel around here so we won't have any problem.
Just fan out and gather all you can. And make sure you get the dry ones . . . the
wet ones are kinda messy."

"Oooh gross," moaned Heather.

"Just bring them back here and pile them up," Gordon continued as we set
off in search of cow pies. "Remember, just the dry ones now. Pretty soon we're
gonna need your hands to knead the bread . . . ." Gordon laughed as he watched
us kicking the mounds of cow dung before we picked them up. Lynn, with reck-
less abandon, seemed to enjoy this chore the most, as she came back with more
armfuls of chips than anyone else. Soon there was a large pyramid of poop ready
to cook our food and keep us warm long into the night.

Before Gordon had a chance to give us our next chores, Ethan and Carl returned proudly with the shovel, their chore completed. I really had to go and
was glad to see them come back so soon. My journey with Pixie and the Dearborn had a laxative effect on my lower tract, and I was off to christen our pioneer
john. I excused myself and headed around the corner to where the boys pointed
me.

The location was a good one: out of sight of camp and down wind. Ethan
and Carl had even constructed a make-shift paper dispenser by mounting the
roll of tissue on a stick stuck into the ground. I lowered my shorts and positioned
myself over the hole, only to realize that they had overestimated the necessary
width of their trench. Luckily, I was the first to use it. Otherwise, I would have
fallen into a very messy predicament. I stretched as wide as I could, carefully
did my business and returned to camp.

"Nice job, guys; I almost fell in," I said sarcastically upon my return. "Is that
a john or a booby trap?"

"I guess it is a little wide," grinned Carl, as Ethan giggled.

"A little wide?" I exclaimed. "It's more like a grave than a toilet! Did you
guys test it out?"

"Nah, we didn't have to go," laughed Carl, shovel still in hand.

"Well, just be careful, everyone, when you do go." Having returned successfully myself, I was now laughing with the diggers. "If we hear screams in the
night, we'll know what happened."

"Okay, since you guys seem to be pretty good with a shovel, I want you to
dig the fire pit," said Gordon, changing the subject. "Right over there, by the buffalo
chips, I want you to dig a pit three feet long by one foot wide by one foot deep.
Then, Jimmy, would you go over to the tool box and get us five flat pieces of
iron? They should be stacked together in the bottom of the box. They're about
yeah long and about an inch wide."

Jimmy sorted through the tool box and came back with the five strips. The boys, having finished digging in the soft ground, watched as Gordon took the five pieces and placed them across the pit, forming a grill.

"Just right, guys," he said, as he picked the pieces back up. "Now we need to get the fire started and start some cooking."

Gordon took some chips and some wood he had in the wagon and stacked them in the pit. He then took one of the lanterns hanging in the wagon and used some of its kerosene for lighter fluid. Soon our fire was crackling and we were off to the kitchen.

On the back of Gordon's wagon was a tall chuckwagon chest he'd built just for our trip. We walked over behind the wagon, and Gordon unhooked the door that folded down to become our work table.

"Wow Gordon, that's great," marveled Heather. "It's just like a counter."

Next Gordon asked me to get the canvas awning and poles out of the back of the Dearborn. We stretched the awning and lashed it down to give our kitchen some shade.

Inside the chest were shelves and drawers filled with more things than our kitchen cupboards at home. Brown earthenware crocks and jars of ingredients sat alongside all Gordon's pots, pans and kettles. All fit tightly and perfectly so as not to spill or break, and Lynn, who loved looking at country kitchens in her magazines at home, edged her way in front of the kids to get the closest look.

"Anyone here ever made sourdough bread?" asked Gordon.

"Sure," boasted Carl, "I've made garlic bread before."

"I'm not talkin' about toast," said Gordon. "I'm talking about making bread from scratch." No one said a word as he pulled out a small brown crock and continued. "This is sourdough starter. It contains the yeast and stuff that will make the dough rise and give the bread its flavor. We're going to combine it with flour and water to get some of the best loaves of bread you'll ever taste. Lynn, I'm gonna have you and Jimmy and the girls work on the bread. First, though, I want Ethan and Carl to get the stew started.

"Okay guys, John here just shot us a buffalo, and we're going to have us some buffalo stew. I want you two to cut up the stew meat and then put it in this bowl." Gordon grabbed a large bowl and handed it to Ethan. "Then I want you to dust the meat in a mixture of flour, salt and pepper that I'll show you how to mix when you're ready. Cut the meat up in small chunks, and be careful with those knives while I'm getting Jimmy and the girls ready."

Carl and Ethan began right away, alternating chopping meat with swatting the flies that were joining us for dinner.

"John, you're in charge of beans," Gordon continued. "The pioneers, they used to catch some pretty bad cases of dysentery. Killed many of 'em. Well, they thought it was beans that turned their bowels, so they emptied their bags of pinto beans right here on the plains. Too bad they didn't realize it was the water causin' their problems. Beans woulda been a good source of protein. Anyway, here's an iron kettle, a sack of beans and some ham hocks. You need anything else?"

"Yeah . . . ," I hesitated, "do you have an onion?"

"Was hopin' ya'd ask. Why, you bet I got onions." Gordon reached into one of the drawers in the chest, pulled out a sack of onions and threw me one.

"After I get you guys started on the bread, I get to work on the main course," Gordon said with a sly look on his face.

"What's the main course?" asked Ethan.

"Pioneers' delicacy . . . buffalo tongue," Gordon answered with a faraway look in his eyes that immediately told us how much he liked it. Everyone looked at Gordon to make sure he was serious, especially Lynn who didn't even eat hamburger. Gordon pulled out something wrapped in paper that was stowed in one of the drawers at the bottom and unwrapped it. Sure enough there it was: the biggest, pinkest, bumpiest lump of flesh I had ever seen, and, from the looks on the kids' faces, that any of them had ever seen.

"Uh . . . is that really a buffalo tongue?" asked Ethan as he touched it with his finger and leaned over to study it up close.

Yep," answered Gordon. "Buy my buffalo from a good friend of mine in Colorado. Best buffalo meat there is . . . a real delicacy."

As everyone stared silently, Gordon filled another cast iron pot with water and plopped in the tongue. "Takes a long time to get it cooked just right, so I'd better get it over the fire.

"Ethan and Carl, you two keep at that stew meat, and I'll be right back to get started on that bread."

Jimmy, Joy and Heather passed around the crock and took a whiff while Gordon was at the fire. I worked on the beans, and Lynn went over to help Ethan and Carl with the stew. When Gordon returned, he had the bakers measure flour, starter and the other ingredients with a dinged-up, tin measuring cup. Soon, six sticky hands were busily kneading the dough.

"If it gets too sticky, just add a little more flour to it," suggested Gordon. All three of the kids' hands were so full of dough by then, they couldn't decide who or how to grab more flour.

"Hey Gordon, could you throw a little more flour on this bread?" asked Jimmy. "All our hands are too full of gooey stuff to grab the measuring cup."

"Sure can," nodded Gordon. In less than twenty minutes, the stew and the beans were ready for the fire, and the bread dough was ready to rise.

"Next business is to set up your tents." Gordon never wasted any time. "Most of the tents used on the trail were fashioned after military tents. I've studied every charcoal sketch, drawing and old army manual that I could get my hands on to design the replicas you'll be using. Had a tentmaker in Colorado make these up for me, and I think you'll like 'em. Course now they'd be a might heavy to carry on your bicycles, but for their day they were the best a pioneer could git.

"One of you boys climb up in the back of the big wagon and throw me down those white canvas bundles. Should be four of them altogether. Another one of you go into the toolbox and grab the bag of tent stakes that should be in there."

Before Gordon even finished, Carl was up into the wagon and Jimmy was opening the toolbox. Gordon demonstrated the art of setting up pioneer tents by using his own as an example. We all circled around him as he transformed his roll of canvas into a spacious A-frame home.

"Wow. . . those things are giant," said a wide-eyed Ethan.

"Shoot, we could all sleep in one of those," agreed Carl.

"Look Heather, they've got those flaps that come off the sides and the doors that tie together and everything," Joy whispered. "Aren't they neat?"

"Yep," nodded Heather, continuing to sound like Gordon. "Stick, let's find our tent a spot with a good view."

"After you get your tents set up," continued Gordon, "I'll give ya each a sleeping bag and a sheet to set inside it. Think you guys can set up your own now?"

We all nodded anxiously and went to work. Unlike the guys who immediately chose their spot, the girls took some time surveying the landscape. Gordon watched for a few minutes, and convinced they had things under control, went to check on dinner.

"Hey Gordon, John read to us from the journal we're following that the pioneers used to climb Chimney Rock." The boys' tent was up, and their sleeping bags were tossed in, in their usual casual style. Jimmy led the boys over to where Gordon was heating the dutch oven.

"Yeah, Jimmy, you're right," he answered. "They used to like to see who could climb the highest and leave their autograph."

"Like pioneer graffiti?" laughed Ethan.

"Yep, like pioneer graffiti," smiled Gordon. "Sounds like you boys would like to carry on the tradition."

"Yeah, now that we're set up, do we have time before dinner to go do some climbin'?" asked Jimmy. "And as long as you don't have any more chores for us to do," he politely added.

"Nope, got no more chores for ya to do, and I think it's gonna take some time for the bread to bake. Tongue's still got a ways to go yet too." Gordon stroked his beard when he talked, just like Jacob did. "Matter of fact, why don't you boys saddle up Queenie and Meano and give Chimney Rock a try? It's farther away than it looks, and, if I remember correctly, the east side of the rock is the best for climbin'."

The boys were off in a cloud of dust. They worked out the details of who would walk and who would ride as they ran over to the horses. In a few seconds they were mounted, and I watched them disappear up and over the bluff toward the giant stone Indian.

"Our tent is so neat and cozy," announced an excited and smiling Joy. She had just emerged from her tent with Heather and they came running over to Gordon. "Gordon, would you come and see how we have it set up? It feels just like home." I watched as the girls led Gordon over to their tent.

"Oh, just a second," insisted Heather, "just one more thing. We need some flowers." Joy held Gordon at the doorway while Heather ran over to some flowering weeds. She carefully picked just the right bouquet and hurried back to the tent, arranging them as she went.

"Okay, now we're ready," she announced, after she set them inside. "Can't have an open house without flowers."

Gordon got the grand tour and came out shaking his head and smiling. Lynn and I then walked over for a tour of our own. Their sleeping bags were neatly laid in the center of their tent, their sheets tucked squarely around the corners. Instead of using the bags separately, they had decided to use one as the mattress, covering it with their make-shift, fitted sheet, and to use the other as the quilt, using their other sheet as the top sheet. They even left little folds at the top of their bed to expose the ducks, geese and bears on the flannel liner of their bags.

"Aren't these sleeping bags cute?" said Heather. "They're so big and comfy. They're so much nicer than our nylon ones."

At the head of the bed were duffel bag pillows stuffed with clothes. Off to each side, neatly arranged, were their journals, pens, cameras and Heather's two little bunches of flowers.

Lynn looked inside, then looked back at our tent and said, "John, I think I'll sleep with the girls. This place looks like a country inn."

"I'm sorry, ma'am, but we're not open for business," joked Joy.

"And besides, we have to close now," added Heather. "Our wagonmaster said we have some loaves of bread to make. I think our dough is through rising."

The girls closed their tent and Lynn and I went over to watch them finish the bread. They divided the dough into three pieces and rolled it out on the pine chuck wagon top like three pizzas. They added butter and cinnamon and were just about ready to roll it up and put it into the dutch oven when they had a suggestion:

"Remember that dried fruit we saw in the cupboard?"

"Yes," replied Gordon.

"How 'bout if we make one of these cinnamon loaves a cinnamon fruit loaf? It would make a nice dessert, don't you think?"

"Yep, I think it would at that," answered Gordon. "Surprised no one — including me — has ever thought to do that before." Gordon was beginning to have a hard time holding back his smile. Our five kids were casting their enthusiastic spell on him, and Lynn and I held our arms around each other and smiled as Gordon reached up and grabbed the jars of dried fruit.

I don't know if the boys smelled it or not, but they were back just in time for dinner. Gordon showed the girls, Lynn and me how to make pioneer coffee, and the aroma of brewing grounds, steaming buffalo stew and baking cinnamon fruit bread floated through the air. The buffalo tongue was taking an extra long time and Gordon announced, to a less than disappointed crew, that we would have to wait 'til breakfast for our taste of his delicacy. Everyone grabbed their blue and white speckled metal dishes from the back of the chuck wagon and lined up as Gordon dispensed the vittles.

Sitting around the campfire in the shadow of Chimney Rock, the kids attacked dinner just as they had attacked lunch. Gordon didn't have to do any encouragement. The kids piled spoonful after spoonful of beans and bread and stew onto their plates. They plopped themselves down on the dusty ground and ate silently, staring up at Chimney Rock, their tents and their own tiny corral of two wagons.

". . . You know. . . ," Ethan sighed, breaking the silence, "I know it's really 1986 and everything . . . but . . . ." He cocked his head and looked around again. "But . . . it sure seems like 1849 to me."

No one said a word. I looked over at Gordon quietly stroking his beard and wondered if crusty old Nebraskans got goosebumps.

"Quiet everybody!" Gordon ordered as we were doing our dishes with water and weeds at the back of the wagon. "Look there, up on the hill."

On the hill above our tents stood the figure of an Indian walking a horse. He wore leggings, a blanket and a headband that had three feathers hanging crooked at the back of his head. Gordon motioned for us to walk over to where our visitor was descending the hill towards camp. When Gordon quickly told us that Indians didn't pose a very real threat to the early wagon trains, the kids told him that they had already learned that. He seemed pleased that their less-than-shy approach to the brave was an educated, as well as enthusiastic, one.

He spoke to the Indian in a language that we couldn't understand, and the Indian, who looked very old, spoke back. Gordon translated that our visitor was searching the plains for buffalo, but that he couldn't find any. Gordon asked us if the Indian could join us for dinner.

The kids ran back to the fire to serve the Indian some of our food. While he sat at the fire and ate, he pointed out that he had boxes strapped to his horse that were filled with Indian artifacts. Gordon then explained that our visitor was actually a friend of his who was part-Indian. He had asked him to visit us and share his knowledge of local Indian lore.

We finished all the dishes while he spread a large buffalo skin on the ground. Once everything was neatly stowed back in the chuckwagon, we joined him on the rug of buffalo hide. We gathered cross-legged in a circle, and he passed around a beautifully carved, black, stone peace-pipe. It was filled with tobacco and lit. Each of us silently took a long chestful of smoke and then passed it to our neighbor. No one choked and no one laughed — it was still 1849.

For over an hour Myron, our part-Indian friend, passed more things around the circle: headdresses of eagle feathers and porcupine quills; chestpieces of bone and sinew; beautifully beaded dresses and moccasins; and bracelets, anklets and pouches that rivaled any museum collection. Unlike any museum though, we got to touch everything, and the kids treated the artifacts with the gentle respect

312

usually reserved for infants.

All the while he passed things around, Myron told stories of the peoples that used to inhabit the Plains, and the kids asked questions. In the background stood our tents and two wagons, lit only by the campfire flickering in the distance. In slow motion, the wisps of clouds that were scattered in the sky behind Chimney Rock changed from white to orange to pink and finally to purple, before giving way to the first twinklings of stars overhead. The rock was soon just a dark form in the distance, and as they finished the pow-wow, Myron's and the kids' hands and faces darkened into silhouettes against the sky. The boys thanked Myron and Gordon, and headed off to bed, tired from their climbing. The girls joined Myron, Gordon, Lynn and me around the fire for a few cups of coffee.

The thousands of stars that must have been looking down on us from that Nebraska sky never got a chance to put on their show. The girls had hoped to do some shooting star gazing, but off to the east rose the giant, buttery ball of a full moon. It lifted itself slowly over the plains, coming toward us shyly, as our Indian friend had done earlier that night. Chimney Rock to our backs, we stared silently as the moon filled the sky with blue light.

"Gordon, did you plan that full moon for us too?" I asked.

"Yep, ordered it just for you," he answered smiling. "Kinda pretty, ain't it?"

"I think it's the prettiest moon I've ever seen," answered Joy. "Do you think it will be bright enough to light up our tent for journal writing?"

"Well, I don't know about that. Why don't you take one of the kerosene lanterns and use it if you're gonna do some writing." Gordon took one of the lanterns off the side of the wagon and lit it. "You girls really gonna do some writing now? Aren't you tired?"

"Yeah, I'm tired," said Heather, "but so much has happened today, I don't want to forget it. The wagon train and the tents and the food and the Indian. I've got to write it all down. Oh yeah, and I've got to write about this coffee too. Even though it has chunks floating in it, it's sooo good. It doesn't even need sugar."

"Gordon," said Joy. "Thanks for everything. I can't believe I'm out here doing all this. I want to go write everything down too."

"Good night, Joy," Gordon said tipping his hat. Heather and Joy said good night, and I watched them contemplate giving him one of their good night hugs. Still not quite sure of his reaction, they hesitated, repeated their "good nights" and went off to bed.

Lynn, Gordon and I sat around talking and drinking coffee for a little while longer. I looked around again — at the wagons; up at Chimney Rock; and finally over at the tents. The guys' was dark and whistling with snores, while the girls' was illuminated by lantern light, revealing two shadows bent intensely over their journals. I then looked back at Gordon, who was studying the sky. I was sure our wagonmaster would be getting at least two big hugs in the morning.

"Hey Gordon, what's for breakfast?" I heard Carl's voice outside our tent. I looked out and saw that Gordon had already started the morning fire and had some coffee brewing. His early morning activities reminded me of my own.

"Well, as soon as everybody's up we'll start cooking," answered Gordon. "How good are you at frying salt pork and bacon?"

"I've never cooked salt pork before, but I think I can handle bacon," answered Carl. "I've had bacon lots of times."

Soon everyone was up and reporting for duty. It was a beautiful blue-sky day, and the kids were anxious for another day's lessons.

"Well, I thought that before we started breakfast, we should have a little appetizer." Gordon smiled as he lifted the pot with the buffalo tongue onto the tailgate. The kids were anxious to learn, but their enthusiasm waned slightly when he pierced the tongue with a fork and plopped it down on the boards.

"Snuck myself a little taste this mornin'," Gordon grinned as he began to slice into the gray lump, "and ya know it tastes even better than I remembered. Okay, who wants the first slice?"

He held up the slice on a fork, revealing that inside the gray outer layer of flesh the tongue was a pale pink color. I expected the kids to start running toward Ethan's and Carl's outdoor restroom, but Carl bravely stepped forward and said, "I'll go for it."

A hush fell over the crowd as Carl doused his slice with salt and pepper. He held it up to his mouth, took a deep breath, paused long enough for just the right dramatic effect and bit into it. He chewed quickly and swallowed it down in seconds. Still conscious, he smacked his lips, took another bite, this time more slowly, and announced, "Hey, that's not too bad, Gordon. I'll take another piece."

At Carl's announcement, the line quickly formed behind him. All of our company—except Lynn—decided they didn't want to miss out on anything that Gordon had to offer. Before breakfast got a chance to get started, the buffalo tongue disappeared.

Carl proceeded to cook the salt pork and bacon with great skill, followed by Heather and Joy frying eggs in his grease and Jimmy flipping flapjacks. Gordon fried up some hoecakes and Ethan kept the coffee coming. We sat around the morning campfire trying to keep all the food from overflowing our plates. Jimmy reheated last night's beans and, grabbing one of his pancakes, showed Gordon how to make a burrito. The girls' leftover bread was buttered and used to soak up the wonderful combination of egg yolk, honey and bacon grease coating the bottom of our blue plates, and although we weren't sure whether or not burping was historically accurate, a few award winning belches were heard after breakfast as we did the morning's dishes.

"I sure am going to be sad to say good bye to these tents," said Joy as she and Heather took theirs down. "I slept so good."

"Yeah, me too," said Heather. "The wind made such a pretty sound whistling through and flapping our door. It's the best I ever slept in a tent."

After all the tents got rolled up, the boys helped Gordon pack up camp and the girls did their ride and hike up Chimney Rock. When they returned, Gordon gave us a lesson in shooting a muzzle-loading, black powder rifle. He placed a block of wood about thirty yards away against one of the hills and had us sit down behind him. He loaded the rifle for each of us and then had us aim and fire. White puffs of smoke exploded from the barrel as the ball flew forward and the kids flew backward. After five shots, the piece of wood still stood tall, unscathed by the marksmen. It was my turn.

I had earned my NRA Marksman patch at summer camp when I was eight, but hadn't shot a gun since. Lynn and the kids looked about as confident in my marksmanship as they did in my horsemanship. I remembered that when I used to shoot those old BB guns at camp, I'd aim at the lower right corner of my target. So I stepped up, took the rifle from Gordon, aimed at the lower right hand side of the block of wood, pulled the trigger and . . . BAM, the ball flew and the block of wood did a complete flip.

"I don't believe it," yelled Carl.

"Give me a break," moaned Jimmy. "That was either the luckiest shot in history or Gordon has somebody hidden on one of the bluffs who shot it down for you."

I had to admit I was a bit surprised that I had done it, but I confidently agreed to a search of the block of wood. The investigation proved that I had indeed hit the mark, and I proudly walked back to camp with the kids shaking their heads. Little did I know that my pioneer skills were soon to be put to an even greater test.

We soon had all the wagons packed up. All that needed to be done before heading back was for Gordon to hitch up the horses. While he hitched up Fern, he had Joy hold Casey. Fern started dancing around and spooked Casey. Casey jerked at his bridle, pulled himself out of Joy's hands, ran across camp, and disappeared over a nearby hill.

"Dang!" said Gordon as he slapped Fern on the rump. "Now look and see what you did."

"I'm sorry, Gordon," said Joy with a worried look on her face.

"Oh, don't worry, Joy, it wasn't your fault." Gordon put his arm around her shoulder. "These animals should know better. I'm gonna have to go and fetch ole Casey. We can't make it back home without two horses to pull the big wagon.

"John, leave Pixie hitched to the Dearborn; Heather you hold George (Pixie's son who had come to visit us in the night); and, John, I'm gonna have you hold onto Fern here while I go and get Casey."

Lynn and the kids cast less than confident glances my way as Gordon handed me Fern's lead. "Now don't ya take nothin' from her now. Be firm, and if she gives you any trouble, just whack her real hard."

I didn't say anything, but my heart went right to work. Fern wasn't your regular old riding horse. She was big. In fact, she made my friend Pixie look like a pony. I held her lead rope and reached up and stroked her neck. As Gordon headed off after Casey, I looked up at Fern and hoped Pixie hadn't already talked to her about me. I had the worst visions of Gordon retrieving one horse only to return to have to retrieve another.

"Hey John, you're doing great except for those shaking knees of yours," laughed Lynn from her seat in the shade of the wagon. She was writing in her journal, probably something about Gordon turning the animals over to me instead of her.

"Yeah John, just keep sweet talkin' ole Fern," joked Jimmy. "Although if you keep strokin' her neck like that, she won't have any hair left when Gordon gets back."

Every minute I waited for the sight of Gordon returning over the hill seemed like an hour. Sweat beaded up on the back of my neck, and, in minutes, my entire shirt was wet. Every so often, Lynn would throw a half-hearted compliment on horsemanship my way, and the kids would laugh along.

I was just getting confident again when George started jerking Heather around. Pixie seemed to be egging him on, so Joy went over to help. George danced and jerked, but the girls held on tight and even whacked him a few times. He maneuvered himself so that his halter got stuck on the tongue of the Dearborn hooked to his mother's harness. Maybe he thought he could free her, but, instead, he just got himself stuck to the wagon. The girls tried to lead George off the tongue, when all of a sudden he bucked wildly and broke it clean off. Seemingly satisfied with the damage done, he immediately calmed down and stood like an angel next to Heather, waiting for Gordon's return.

During the commotion I helplessly held onto Fern who, thankfully, didn't pay George much attention. After a very nervous forty-five minutes, Gordon appeared over the hill with Casey in tow. I broke the news gently about the broken wagon, and Gordon assured us we really hadn't hurt anything. He whacked George, lashed the tongue back into service with some leather thong, and then hitched up Fern and Casey.

Everything and everybody ready and loaded, Gordon complimented us on our morning chores as he climbed into his seat. Then he lifted the reins, hesitated a moment and with another resounding "WAGONS HO!" booming from all seven of our voices, we were off and on our way back across the Plains.

I don't know if it was because we had really improved our trail technique or what, because even though we followed our old ruts back to Gordon's cabins, we sure got back fast. Too fast, in fact, for seven California-bound pioneers.

"I wish we could keep going on the wagons," said Carl when he stubbornly dismounted back at Gordon's headquarters.

We helped Gordon unload the wagons and he watched us reload our own two-wheeled ones. To lengthen our stay, the kids asked if they could invite Gordon for an early lunch in his front yard.

"Hey Gordon, want a sandwich?" asked Jimmy. "The bread isn't as good as what we make out on the trail, and peanut butter and jelly isn't quite as tasty as buffalo tongue, but it's brought us almost three thousand miles so far."

Gordon sat down on the grass and tried the sandwich the kids had made especially for him. "You're right, it ain't quite as good as tongue, but it ain't half bad either. Thanks for the lunch.

"I want to tell all you kids that it was my pleasure sharin' this section of the trail with you. Try to remember some of the things I showed ya, and remember me when ya roll into Oregon. You're a special group of kids, doin' somethin' I wish every kid in America could be doin'. Don't you ever forget that."

The kids finished their sandwiches in record (slow) time, and I had to do a little "Wagons Ho" of my own to get them up off the ground. Gordon, the master wagonmaster himself, saw my predicament and rose to his feet.

"Looks like it's time to hit the trail," he said as he dusted himself off. "Better get movin' if ya want to make camp by sundown."

I walked over, looked him in the eye and gave him a long handshake. "Thanks for all the teaching; you taught me a lot about real schoolin'. . . I hope our trails meet up again sometime."

Lynn was next with her hugging good bye, and behind her the kids all lined up to say good bye to a man whom, in only a few miles of trail, they had grown to love. The boys went first, getting strong handshakes as Gordon thanked them all by name. Heather was next, and last came Joy, who threw her arms around him and held on tight, burying her head in his shoulder and beard. Tears ran down her cheeks, and it didn't seem like she was going to let go. Gordon hugged her tightly, patted her on the back and then let out a booming"WAGONS HO!" Joy let go, looked up into his bespectacled face and walked slowly to her bicycle.

Gordon and his wife stood at the edge of their dirt driveway as we pushed our bikes down the sandy road, past Fern, Casey and Pixie. We waved back at our wagonmaster and his wife, and Joy leaned over to me and said, "Hey John, you know what you said about 'seeing the Elephant'?"

"Yeah."

"Well, when I had to say good bye to Gordon, I don't know if I saw it, but I sure saw its shadow." Joy's eyes still wet as she looked up at me from beneath her helmet. I put my free arm around her, squeezed her shoulder and hoped the wind coming out of the west would dry her tears. The road and time *did* have a way of doing that. Soon we were heading west again on our wagons of nylon and steel, leaving Chimney Rock and a bearded friend to mark the trail behind us.

13

Today we climbed Togwotee Pass, 9700 feet high. I caught a little elevation sickness which later got worse on the downhill, but was cured by a pudding pop at the end of the 26-mile downhill . . . .

Carl's Journal
August 28, 1986

Ice Water

"Hey John, how does William Swain describe Wyoming?" asked Heather. It was our second night in "Cowboy Country" and we had treated ourselves to a motel in Glenrock.

"Heather, there wasn't a Wyoming back then," said Jimmy.

"Well, you know what I mean. How did William Swain describe the place that we now call Wyoming? . . . Because it sure seems different than Nebraska or Kansas."

"Yeah, I know," said Joy. "Nebraska was big and everything, but Wyoming is huge. I can't decide what is bigger, the land or the sky."

"I think it's kinda ugly," said Carl.

"Well, first of all, you guys, before I read William's journal, in Indian, Wyoming means 'end of the plains.' Why do you think they named it that?"

Everyone thought for a few seconds and then Heather started talking. "I think they named it that because we're really starting to climb now. I mean, when we first crossed into Wyoming, everything looked flat, but the more we rode the more I could feel us going up."

"Yeah, even when it's flat it really isn't," added Carl. "It's like everything is tilted down toward Nebraska, so even when we don't see any mountains or hills, we still have to shift down and climb."

"I know," sighed Joy. "If it wasn't for you, John, talking to Heather and me about the pioneers as we rode, I don't think we would have made it to Douglas this afternoon. Some of those hills were really long, but you took our minds off them. I can't even remember shifting."

"So what did William Swain have to say about the place we now call Wyoming?" asked Heather, emphasizing the end of her question for Jimmy's sake.

"Okay, you guys, here goes:

> "July 9. We soon passed a flat of good grass, and then, leaving the Platte, commenced our way across the hills.
>
> The appearance of the soil, vegetation, and road changed with our ascent. The soil, sandy and gravelly, was dried to powder

320

and the vegetation crisped. Nothing but the bloodless wild sage showed its head, and the road was macadamized with sharp gravel which wore the cattle's feet badly.

We halted on a barren hill to noon, at the foot of which the cattle got some water and some little picking. Our road through the afternoon was a succession of ups and downs. At dark we reached La Bonte Creek, where we encamped without feed for our teams."

"I was wondering where they got feed for their teams around here," said Jimmy. "I'm sure glad we found that pizza parlour here in Glenrock."

"I can't imagine going to bed hungry and then having to ride early the next morning," said Joy. "It must have started getting really tough for their animals around here."

"And if they had weather like we've been having, it must have been even worse," added Heather, our resident weather person. "Did the clouds smoosh together in the afternoons for them too?"

"Well, Swain doesn't call it 'smooshing,' and it happened a little before here, but I have a reading from his journal that I think you guys might enjoy. Tell me what this reminds you of:

"June 20, 1849. After traveling about three miles, a line of clouds in the west which had been advancing some time gave greater evidence of an approaching storm of no ordinary character. The men all clad themselves in India-rubber or oilcloth, preparatory to a rainstorm . . . as the clouds advanced, a noise like the rushing of heavy wind grew louder and louder, until the whole air resounded with a noise resembling a shower of stones falling on a floor of boards. In an instant the air ahead appeared full of falling white spots, and in an instant more the pelting of heads and the bounding ice balls convinced us that a tremendous hailstorm was upon us. The fury of the storm can only be imagined by a minute description of itself and its effects. In a moment after the first hail fell, the air was literally filled with balls of ice from the size of a walnut to that of a goose egg, falling like drops of rain and rebounding from whatever they struck; while bursts of thunder broke out in tremendous peals and forked lightning shot through the sky, streaking it with vivid lines of light.

. . . All who could, sought safety in the wagons, and those who could not shielded themselves from the fury of the descending ice by any means in their power. Some clung to the reaches of the wagons and allowed themselves to be drawn along under them; others crowned themselves with camp kettles while the horsemen who were lucky enough to retain their animals placed the saddles over their heads and awaited as best they could the termination of the storm. It lasted about fifteen minutes.

... All the wagon covers, which were either painted or oiled, looked as if they had been used during the Mexican War. ... The cattle were many of them cut through on the hips and back by the hail .... this storm was decidedly severe, a touch of the terrific, something of the Elephant.

We soon repaired our breaks and were on our course again in good spirits, remembering the past with many a hearty laugh over the various freaks of fortune in her dealings with us. 'No great evil without some good' was our motto, so we filled our pails and kettles with hail and had ice water the rest of the day, a luxury we little expected on this route."

"I still can't believe ole William played Bright Side," said Jimmy, shaking his head. "I can just see all his buddies runnin' around with those buckets on their heads ... And makin' ice water after a storm like that ... I think it would be a kick travelin' with his train."

"Hey John, his hail storm sounds like the one we had last night," said Carl.

"Yeah ... when your Chinese chicken and vegetable stir fry turned into Chinese chicken, vegetable and ice stir fry," laughed Ethan. "And your friend Billy told us there wouldn't be a storm."

"He may be a news reporter, but I bet they don't let him do the weather," smiled Joy.

Bill Huddy, a friend I had known since elementary school, was the evening news anchor for a Colorado Springs TV station and he'd driven up from Colorado to spend a night with us in Wyoming. Just before dinner, Heather looked up at the sky and predicted the arrival of some smooshing, but Bill disagreed. He shook his head and said we had nothing to worry about; he didn't think the storm would be coming our way. Trusting Bill's word over Heather's, Lynn and I continued cooking and the boys continued their haphazard tent raising. Heather and Joy, on the other hand, quickly put up their tent and staked it into the ground, pulled their panniers off their bikes, brought them inside their tent, covered their bikes with their tarp, and put on their rain jackets. Seconds later, when the wind gusted and the first bolt of lightning flashed overhead, the girls could be heard laughing from inside their tent, while the guys chased most of their worldly possessions and their half-pitched tent being blown toward the river. Hailstones almost immediately started dancing on our picnic table, and while Billy disappeared into the safety of his jeep, I tried to keep the falling ice from ruining dinner — Lynn loved cold Chinese food, but it wasn't really what I had in mind. Much like Swain's, our smooshing that evening only lasted for about fifteen minutes.

Billy left the next day, offering Heather the job as weatherperson on his show; but she declined, saying she had promised her mom that she'd be biking right home. Billy offered Heather a rain check and we all booed as we waved him good-bye.

"Hey John, what was the longest ride you and Billy did when you were our age?" asked Carl.

"Oh . . . we probably rode fifteen miles at the most."

"Man, you guys were wimps," Carl continued. "We can do that in an hour."

I nodded my head with a smile for Carl, and then changed the subject: "We've got a long way to go tomorrow, so I think we'd better hit the sack, you guys."

"How long is long?" asked Heather.

"Oh, I'm not sure exactly where we're going to stop, but we'll be going at least seventy-five miles; maybe more . . . ."

"Sounds like you're right," nodded Heather as she got up.

"Good night, Lynn. Good night, John." Each of the kids headed to their rooms when they heard we would be in for another long day. Just as we turned out the lights and the boys prepared to begin snoring, we were jerked out of our beds by a loud emergency siren that suddenly blared from the center of town. The only siren like that we had heard was in Missouri, warning of an approaching tornado. Everyone came running into the living room where Lynn and I were sleeping.

"Hey John, do they have tornadoes in Wyoming?" asked a frightened Carl.

We all gathered around the phone as Lynn tried to call the sheriff. She couldn't get a line out, so she ran to ask the manager. Lynn returned smiling, informing us that the siren went off every night announcing curfew for everyone in Glenrock under 18. The kids then shook their heads disgustedly and hurried back to bed. They didn't want to lose a second's sleep, because they knew that sometime around 4 AM the siren of my voice would announce a curfew of a different kind.

"Ain't much between here and Shoshoni 'cept maybe a few gas stations," said the man who had befriended us at our second breakfast in Casper. "Got me some good friends, out in Powder River though, think it's some of the most beautiful country in the world. Say they wouldn't trade their place for livin' anywhere else.

"Once you hit the high desert just out of town here, be careful for a couple things: rattlesnakes warmin' themselves on the road, trucks barrelin' along the highway and . . . the wind." The man smiled and shook everyone's hand as he headed for his car. Before getting in, he looked back at us on our bicycles and added, "But don't you worry, you kids look plenty prepared. You just enjoy all that wide open space out there, and have yourselves a good time."

William Swain's party headed south from Casper (then known as Upper Mormon Ferry) along the North Platte, through the Rattlesnake Hills towards

Independence Rock and their crossing of the Continental Divide at South Pass. We would continue reading his journal, but rather than pedaling along his string of "shortcuts" across the deserts of northern Utah and Nevada, we'd be taking a northern diversion to experience the Tetons of Wyoming and the Sawtooths of Idaho.

"See you in California, William," the group yelled as they waved to their friend at the Casper City Limits sign. "Bye, bye North Platte River. . . ."

"Man John, I can't imagine Swain's route being anymore desolate than ours," observed Jimmy as we waited for the rest of the group ten miles later. "Even the weeds look lonely out here."

"Hey John, what did you say our first stop was?" asked Heather as she rolled to a stop with Joy.

"Natrona; it's in about fifteen more miles."

"Do you think it will have a bathroom?"

"I don't know, Heather, can't you use the side of the road?"

"Well . . . yeah, but . . . there aren't many bushes around here, if you know what I mean. Stick and I are pretty good at using the great outdoors, but there's not much privacy out here. I really don't want to put on a show for the truckers . . . And besides, we don't want the rattlesnakes paying us any unexpected visits . . . you know?"

"Yeah, did you see that one back there on the road that got run over by a truck?" exclaimed Joy. "It was still moving!"

"Well, can you girls hold it for another hour or so?"

The girls looked at each other, bit their lips and quietly nodded.

"Did you guys see that snake that was half-dead?" Carl asked as he skidded to a stop. "Wasn't it gross with its guts comin' out and everything?"

"Let's go, Carl," said the girls giving him the evil eye.

"But didn't you see that snake?"

"C'mon, Carl, let's go," snarled Heather, as she got back on her bike.

"But—"

"We're out of here." Jimmy cut Carl off before he could ask again. Lynn and the last two boys didn't even get a chance to grab a drink of water. Carl shook his head and mumbled something about girls as Joy and Heather led us to Natrona.

For about ten miles, all we saw was dusty brown dirt interrupted occasionally by a lump of gray sagebrush. Then, off in the distance, we spotted something reflecting the sun growing larger and larger as we approached it. Finally we discovered it was a town — or what folks in Wyoming call a town.

NATRONA

POP. 8   ELEV. 5420

The black and white city limits sign had been our friendly beacon, and we pulled up and thanked the little piece of sheet metal for giving us a distraction.

Beyond the sign stood the booming metropolis of Natrona — a weather-beaten little market, a gas pump and a solitary white outhouse.

The wind had cranked up so that the crooked shack rocked back and forth and the door slammed open and shut. Heather learned the hard way if you weren't careful the wind would blow the door open, even when the outhouse was occupied.

Returning with a blush and our roll of toilet paper, Heather said, "I think I'll use Mother Nature's outhouse, regardless of truckers or rattlesnakes. Going to the bathroom in that thing rocking back and forth in the wind was pretty exciting. It was kinda like a ride at Disneyland."

The boys whispered some grossities and then, one by one, went to ride the outhouse. Once everyone had taken their turn, the senators unanimously agreed to fertilize the Wyoming landscape outdoors from then on.

With a confident, "READY OR NOT, ALL YOU RATTLERS, HERE WE COME!" a temporarily relieved bunch of bicyclists headed toward Powder River, Wyoming.

According to its sign, Powder River also had eight residents, and we stopped for lunch at the gas station oasis.

"Hey you guys, I think I've created something new to add to our lunch menu," announced Jimmy. "Remember those chips we were saving for lunch?"

"Yeah, man . . . I've been dreamin' of those chips since Casper," said Ethan.

"Well, I just invented a new flavor," Jimmy continued. "You've all heard of nacho cheese and BBQ flavored . . . Well, it gives me great pleasure to announce the newest taste sensation . . . James West's Kerosene Flavored Corn Chips. It seems the old fuel bottle in my pannier has developed a leak, and the chips are soaked."

"Oh no!" moaned Ethan. "Not my chips!!!"

"Sorry dude, but you should see my pannier. It's a major fire hazard right now."

"That's okay, Jimmy," said Joy. "We've got plenty of bread and cookies and stuff. If you'll take everything out of that pannier, I'll help you clean it."

"Thanks, Stick. Let's do that after lunch. Sorry about the chips, everybody. I was looking forward to a few hors d'oeuvres myself."

We set out our picnic in the gravel alongside the gas station. It was about three in the afternoon and the wind had picked up even more since our adventures in the Natrona outhouse. Powder River's name became self-explanatory as we tried to shield our sandwiches from the sand and grit that joined us for lunch. Everyone ate their sandwiches with extra care, biting down gently and hoping to get early warning of any grains of sand that had stuck to their gooey lunch. As they slowly chewed bite by bite, and occasionally stopped to pull a grain off one of their molars, I couldn't resist going to my bike and getting Swain's journal.

"Hey you guys, believe it or not, ole William had a few meals like this," I announced as I sat back down.

"You mean the pioneers ate peanut butter and jelly?" asked Carl.

"No, I don't think so, but they did have their share of SANDwiches. Listen to this:

> "July 18. . . . We traveled late and encamped in a driving storm of wind, which took up the sand and gravel and carried it along like shot. In these storms it is impossible to look up for a moment, as the eyes become immediately filled with sand, so that the teamsters are obliged to fasten their handkerchiefs over their faces to enable them to see where they are going . . . . the wind, in addition to its furious violence, is so very hot and dry as to render perspiration . . . quite difficult. The throat and fauces become dry, and lips clammy and parched, and the eyes much inflamed from the drifting dust.
>
> We almost made our supper from sand tonight, as the wind had spiced our victuals."

"It sounds like his wind was a little worse than ours," said Heather. "Where was he when he wrote that?"

"Believe it or not, he wrote that one day after leaving Upper Mormon Ferry," I answered.

"That's really weird," Ethan continued as he looked around. "That means he wrote that right around here somewhere.

"Hey John, where would the North Platte be from here?"

"Well, if we looked due south . . ." I said, pointing across the road, "and over those mountains called the Rattlesnake Hills, about fifty miles from here we would see Independence Rock.

"Independence Rock was another landmark like Chimney Rock, and it sits real close to where the North Platte River hits the Sweetwater River. Right around there, Swain's party began following the Sweetwater, because the Platte turns south and the Sweetwater heads west."

"Can you get out the map and show us?" asked Joy. The rest of our lunch was spent eating and following William on our new tablecloth — my map of Wyoming. It didn't solve our sand problem, but it took our minds off it for awhile.

At the end of lunch, we decided to spend the night out in the middle of the prairie and camp as we had with Gordon. The kids were all excited at the prospect, at least until about five miles out of Powder River, when the wind started to do a pretty impressive imitation of Swain's journal. The sky on the western horizon looked like a big bruise, as it turned an angry mixture of black and blue. And even though it was only four in the afternoon, the cars approaching us from the west all had their lights on. To make matters worse, our road tilted steadily upwards into the unfriendly sky and, as hard as we tried to stay in a tight formation, our paceline was soon in pieces.

Jimmy was up front with me giving it all he had, his shoulders rocking back and forth above his handlebars. Joy and Heather were a couple hundred yards behind us, trading the lead and breaking the wind for each other. Somehow they seemed less labored than Jimmy, and somehow they were still smiling.

Way back in the distance were three dots. Ethan, Carl and Lynn had fallen back fast and seemed to be losing their battle with the wind.

The sky ahead groaned as echoes of distant thunder were blown our way. I looked out across the desert for some place that might shelter us from the storm, but there wasn't a canyon or a ravine to be seen. As Heather had pointed out earlier, there weren't even any bushes.

My only hope was a tiny tooth-shaped area on my map labeled: *Hell's Half Acre*. I had seen it before, but with its letters marked even smaller on my map than Natrona, and with its name, I'd hoped to blink and be past it. But as the wind gusted stronger and stronger and the lightning flashed for real on the horizon, I figured we'd soon be knocking on the Devil's door and asking if he had any accommodations.

"Hey John, look up there!" yelled Jimmy. "It looks like a sign or something."

Sure enough, it was a whole group of signs and small billboards. Painted in a hideous combination of pumpkin orange and pea soup green, the signs said:

HELL'S HALF ACRE MOTEL AND CAMPING, JUST THREE MORE MILES . . .
COME VISIT OUR ROCK SHOP AND CAFE

Jimmy and I pulled over and waited for the rest of the group. The wind, the climb, and the headlights warning us of the approaching storm had dampened the kids' excitement about pitching their tents atop the barren sand along the highway.

"John, do you think we could stay at that place on the signs?" Joy asked shyly. After seventy miles of wind and desert, even she was beat.

"We'll really have to hustle to make it there before the storm does," I answered. "Do you guys think you can push hard for three more miles?"

Everyone except for Carl nodded their heads and tightened the straps on their pedals, signaling they were ready to go. Carl, who already had tear stains running down his dirty face, wiped his nose with the back of his bicycling glove and said, "I don't know if I can make it. My whole body hurts."

Sometimes we all forgot that Carl was the youngest, and oftentimes, with the whole group, I forgot my riding partners were only twelve and thirteen- years-old. Almost always, they had been up to the challenge of our days, but that afternoon, in the middle of Wyoming, Carl was about to break. I remembered breaking a few times myself when I was twelve, in circumstances much less frightening than Carl's. There he stood, over sixty pounds of bicycle and gear, in the middle of nowhere, with a howling wind blowing sand into his face, and the biggest, blackest electrical sky rumbling its way right for him. And all the pinching in the world couldn't have changed things.

"Carl, you're just going to have to gut this one out." Brave and easy words coming from me, but wrapping my arms around a little boy right then and taking any of our precious time wouldn't be fair to him or the rest of the group.

"But— "

"Sorry, Carl, no 'buts' now, except the one I want you to put on your seat and pedal as fast as you can to Hell's Half Acre." My callous orders brought more tears from Carl.

"C'mon, Carl, you can do it," said Jimmy.

"Yeah, it's only three more miles," added Joy, patting him on the shoulder as he strapped himself in his pedals.

I didn't get a chance to yell,"WAGONS HO," because the sky shattered our privacy with an arching crack of lightning that rattled the water bottle cages on our bikes. It spurred us on better than any cheer of mine, and suddenly I found myself being pushed into the storm by six, quickly-pedaling cyclists. I couldn't tell if they were scared or inspired, and I didn't stop to ask.

The road climbed and climbed and we kept looking for signs of civilization. Could those billboards be advertising some oasis long since been blown off the landscape? Was it our chance to relive what the pioneers experienced when they reached a non-existent outpost? I was sure I could find some journal readings describing it, but I told God I'd rather pass on the opportunity. Besides, where would I hold the meeting? Our tents could never stand that storm.

Our group stayed together for about the first mile and a half, and then we splintered again. Jimmy and I blazed the trail in search of a sign; Ethan joined Heather and Joy; and Lynn cheered Carl on the best she could, but their two shapes just shrank smaller and smaller behind us.

Jimmy and I crested the hill and there it was, Hell's Half Acre.

"Yahoo! We beat the storm!" Jimmy yelled as we pulled under the sign. Before he could finish his celebration a strong gust of wind blew both of us and our bicycles across the parking lot. "Hey John, this wind is worse than Lake McConaughy . . . . "

"Jimmy, you lean your bike up against that bungalow, out of the wind — or at least out of the worst of it. I don't want any bikes becoming airborne up here. I'm going to see how everyone else is doing."

Jimmy nodded proudly, and I ran up to the edge of the road. Cars coming from the west were all pulling into the parking lot to get out of the raging storm. Lightning exploded constantly overhead, and a hunched over, but smiling Joy, Heather and Ethan crested the summit and waved. I warned them about the gale up top, and they nodded silently, carefully pedaling downhill to where Jimmy was waving his arms.

I had to walk over the top of the hill to get my first view of Lynn and Carl. They still had a quarter-mile to go and I could see Lynn yelling. I jumped up and down like a high school cheerleader waving my arms and yelling at the lightning and thunder. Just as they crested the top, the gray above us surrendered to black and the rain began. I ran down the driveway beside them yelling and screaming and clapping. A little water didn't matter; Lynn and Carl had beat the storm too.

"Hey John, do you know you still have your helmet on?" Joy laughed as I reached up and tapped it.

"He's just playing William Swain," said Jimmy. "Remember the guys with the pots and pans on their heads?"

"Oh yeah," smiled Joy.

"Yeah . . . One guy in a car just told us that just up ahead it's hailing really bad . . . ." As Ethan spoke, I noticed he still had his helmet on too. "Another guy told us that the winds get over a hundred miles an hour up here . . . Said we were pretty smart to stop here and wait out this storm."

"Hey John, are we going to camp?" asked a trembling Carl.

I looked over at the plywood sign that pointed to the campground. A solitary silver trailer, rocking in the gale, seemed to be the only thing brave enough to inhabit the space for campers.

"That trailer must be bolted to the ground!" exclaimed Ethan.

"Yeah, either that or it's some wind tunnel testing ground," added Jimmy. "Anyone who would camp up there has got to be crazy. There's no way you could pitch a tent up there."

"Well, senators," I answered. "It seems like we're going to have to see what kind of motel rooms the Devil is offering tonight." The kids' reaction was unanimous. I accepted my standing ovation with a quick bow and went to find us some rooms.

I returned to find the kids (all of them wearing their helmets) out in the rain and hail, seeing how far they could lean into the howling wind. Lynn was out with them too, looking like she was hinged to the ground, and I threw the keys in my handlebar bag and ran out to join everyone. Anyone who drove into the parking lot at Hell's Half Acre, Wyoming that afternoon probably thought they saw seven crazy kids stupidly playing in a raging thunderstorm. Little did they know, they were actually witnessing seven kids spending a little extra time after school, studying the pioneers.

Candy Bars

"What's the matter, John?" Lynn asked as we sat on the bed alone. We had finished our journal meeting and the kids were over at the gift shop buying candy bars.

"Oh, I'm still pissed off about yesterday's phone calls home." I looked at Lynn sitting next to me and realized that this was our last week together. I wondered if knowing that had fueled my anger, but I was hurting and had to tell her when the kids weren't around.

"Why, what happened?" she continued.

"Well, first of all, the kids call home and as soon as the 'hi, how are yous' and 'I miss yous' are over, some moms are asking the kids why they haven't been keeping up in their journals or why they haven't written aunt so-and-so the post card they promised. And then, they wonder why we're staying in a motel instead of camping out or why we didn't ride ten miles out of our way to go to the post office to pick up some mail. The kids get off the phone feeling bad because they haven't written down every candy bar they bought in their personal budget book — I'd like to see their mom's personal budget book! — Or the kids are upset because they got in trouble for not taking their stinking vitamins!

"Dammit, I wish some of these parents could just watch their kids for a day. Seven hours of sleep, breakfast dishes, lunch dishes, dinner dishes done everyday . . . Can't leave the dishes in the sink here, because they'll get left behind! And they wonder why they didn't get their postcard! . . . The kids do *their* laundry *every* day, ride their bicycles seventy-five — maybe even a hundred — miles a day, and somebody back home wonders why they're watching TV in Nebraska rather than being blown across the prairie in their tent like some nylon tumbleweed.

"I just can't believe that parents would lay trips on their kids like that. They sit at home watching the TV weather or looking at it in the newspaper, and what do they know about bicycling through 'scattered severe thunderstorms?!' They just turn the page and read Ann Landers or the sports page while their kids get blown off the road.

"Lynn, I'm so proud of these kids, and I love them so much . . . I just hate to see their sad faces when they get off the phone, thinking they let somebody down. They haven't let anybody down . . . They're the hardest working kids I have ever seen; I just wish some of their parents would acknowledge that to them instead of complaining about stupid vitamins and postcards . . . ."

"John . . . why don't you tell them that?" Lynn asked smiling.

"Tell who? the parents?! You want me to tell the parents how ticked off I am?"

"No, not the parents, John. Tell the kids. Tell the kids how you feel about them, and what they're doing."

"But, don't I tell them that already?"

"Well, yeah, you do, but usually you do it when everybody is so busy. Take some time tonight while you're feeling so strong and let the kids know how you're feeling — your anger and your love. They need to see that from you, too."

"You think so?"

"Yes, I think so. And I think you should try and understand the parents a little bit more too. They don't get to see their kids everyday and that probably hurts them a lot. Not knowing what it's really like on the road . . . all they can ask are questions about things they know about, and their questions may sound stupid to you, but that's all they have. It's also probably very hard to talk to their kids and hear that they are so busy, so busy that they don't have time to miss home. So understand how the parents are feeling too. Get angry if you want to; but also understand. We are really lucky that these five families let us have their kids for four months, and no matter how we're feeling, we can't ever forget that.

"Also, it's not going to be easy for me to ask all the 'right' questions when I get back home and you call me on Sundays from somewhere out on the road. I'm going to need a little understanding too, and *I* know what it's like to be riding everyday . . . ." Lynn got real quiet as she finished. We both got tears in our eyes as we reached across to hug one another. We held each other tight, trying to put out of our minds that we only had three more days together before she would have to fly home.

"Hey John, do you want a taste of my Snickers?" asked Joy as the kids burst through the doorway in the middle of our embrace. Carl flew in next, oblivious to an embarrassed Joy trying to back out the door.

"Oh, it's okay you guys," laughed Lynn, brushing away her tears. "Come on in."

The kids saw our tears and whispered to each other. "Okay, you guys, what's the whispering about?"

"Oh, I was just telling everybody that with this being Lynn's last week and all, that you were probably starting to feel down, that's all," said Jimmy. "I know how I felt when I had to say good bye to my dad, and I'm used to it. It's gonna be really hard for you guys. Here, John, have a drink of my Coke, it'll make you feel better."

"Thanks, Jimmy. Would you all sit down for a second so I can talk to you about something?"

Everybody sat down on the bed and I started my speech:

"I don't know if I show it all the time, but I hope you guys know how much you mean to Lynn and me. I wake you up every morning and tell you to turn here and stop over there and to hurry up before you get struck by lightning. I hope I also do enough hugging and shoulder rubbing and smiling to let you all know how much I love you . . . .

"Last night, after some of you called home, I got really angry because I saw you feeling sad after talking to home. You looked like you had let somebody down. Now you guys know I try to give you time to write in your journals and write post cards and do all those things that everyone expects you to do. And some of you take better advantage of those times than others." I looked over at Joy and Heather and smiled and then over at the boys and winked.

". . . And other times we get so busy with all we have to do that we just don't have time, and nobody should make you feel bad about that. Remember . . . remember when we first got together for this trip and I told you that we would be riding an average of fifty miles a day, and for every three days of riding we would take one day off? Well, when is the last time you can remember us doing that?"

"Never," answered Carl.

"I wish the people back home could understand how hard you guys are working everyday, but they won't ever be able to understand. I mean, how can anyone describe how hard it was today to ride in that wind or how fun it was to have that hail bounce off our helmets. That's what makes us all so special to each other. No one will ever get to know what it was really like, and trying to tell family and friends what we're *really* doing will always be difficult — probably impossible . . . .

"Anyway, you guys, please don't get discouraged, because what you're doing is unbelievable — even to me. Sometimes I look ahead and go, 'what am I doing out here? I'll never make it.' And then I look back and see you, Jimmy, rocking back and forth; and you two, Heather and Joy, talking about the number of speckles on some ugly lizard; and you, Ethan, hunched over and spacing out under those glasses of yours, and finally you, Carl, back there with Lynn, singing that same stupid verse from *Roxanne* over and over again.

"Without you guys, Lynn and I would never have been able to make it across this country, and don't you ever forget that.

"We love you all a whole bunch, and I just had to say that tonight, because I wasn't feeling too good while you guys were gone . . . .

"So enough of John's sermon for today; what's the candy bar selection like in the gift shop?"

The kids laid out the Milky Ways and Reese's Peanut Butter Cups and ancient postcards they had found in the gift shop. People say that candy gets kids wired and silly, but long before nine o'clock and any distant siren went off, our kids were fast asleep in the lumpy beds of the Hell's Half Acre Motel. Joy and Heather were snuggled together in their double bed; Lynn and I in ours; and the boys were, all three of them, packed into the same double bed — Jimmy and Carl on the outside snoring away and Ethan the sardine smiling on the inside, lost in some distant dream. Lynn and I crawled into bed and snuggled close.

"John?" she asked, rolling over and facing me.

"Yes, dear."

"I'll take these kids as our family any day."

"Yeah, me too," I agreed. "It's too bad we only get them for four months."

It's the Water

"Looks like leg warmer and mitten weather," announced Jimmy, as we ate breakfast and waited for the sun to chase the stars from the sky the next morning. "It's so nippy out there, you can see your breath."

We finished breakfast, and donned our wool in time to get on the road for sunrise. Sage, unnoticed or unappreciated the day before, was now painted a golden yellow by the rising sun, and with each cool breath, we inhaled its wonderful scent.

"Hey John, my fingers are frozen," exclaimed Heather, as we rode down the deserted highway.

"Blow on them, Heather, and don't forget how they feel right now. As soon as it gets warm this afternoon, you're gonna need some memory to keep you cool."

Our bodies soon began to warm up. Steam puffed from our mouths and nostrils and rose off our shoulders as we climbed the hills. In the early morning, we had the road all to ourselves, and the cool air, combined with the still dozing wind, quickened our pace.

After about ten miles, Jimmy and I stopped to strip off some layers of clothing, and in the middle of our wardrobe change up rode the girls.

"Well, I count sixty-three so far, how 'bout you guys?" asked Heather as she rolled to a stop.

"Sixty-three? . . . sixty-three what?" asked Jimmy.

"Sixty-three antelope, that's what," answered Heather in disbelief. "Don't tell me you guys haven't seen the antelope. You go so fast that you miss all the good stuff. There are antelope all over the place around here, but you gotta watch really careful; they have perfect camouflage."

"Yeah, there may not be many people in Wyoming, but there sure are lots of antelope," said Joy. "Heather already thinks she can tell the difference between the males and the females."

"Yup, they seem to travel in families or packs." Heather began her antelope lecture as Lynn, Ethan and Carl rode up. "Like back there about a mile or so, just off the side of the road, there were four of them — one big one with weird-shaped antlers, one medium-sized one and two baby-sized ones. I bet the one with the weird antlers was the daddy."

"When they saw Heather and me, they walked over to check us out and then they just shot off across the desert," exclaimed Joy.

"And man, are they fast runners! First the papa one bounced and took off, then the mama and then the two little ones. I've never seen any animals go so fast . . . . "

"Are you talking about the antelope?" asked Carl.

"Yup, did you guys see any?" asked Heather.

"Heck yes," said Carl. "They're all over the place." Jimmy looked at me, and I looked at Jimmy. We decided to go a little slower on the next stretch and let the girls give us the tour.

Finding a town in the Wyoming desert was like looking for a spouting whale on the ocean, and just like sailors up in the crow's nest, the kids would interrupt their antelope census by craning their necks up and looking for a metallic reflection on the horizon. As usual, a couple miles from Moneta, we saw the speck of a white box off in the distance, and the cry of "Town Ho!" echoed across the desert.

Moneta's sign boasted a population of 6, and it consisted of two dilapidated wood buildings. On one side of Main Street was a combination cafe, gas station and motel, and on the other was what appeared to be a house. We leaned our bikes against the motel, joining the tumbleweeds parked against it.

"Sign says 6, but don't you believe it." A short, wiry man opened the rusted screen door and poked his head outside to check on the commotion. "Haven't been that many people here in years — even with someone stayin' at the motel. Ain't had many of them neither, far as I can remember. Population should read: '3'."

"Are you serving breakfast this morning?" From the looks of the Moneta Motel and Cafe, I wondered if it was still in business. Doors and windows were boarded up and the only letter in the neon sign that had light in it was the M in Motel.

"Sure am, I'm the cook. Come on in." The little man's face folded up into a warm smile. His rough, ruddy complexion was as weathered as his motel, but most of his wrinkles looked like they were caused by many years of enjoying himself. Despite his smile, he looked a wee bit suspicious of us, and we soon found out why.

"Hope ya got better manners than the last group of bicyclists that came through here. Must've been over a dozen of 'em college kids."

Our host continued talking as he led us through the lobby and into the dining room. "Yup, they came stormin' in here like they owned the place, grabbing candy bars and demandin' food . . . why, I fixed them real good . . . gave them some of the well water I save only for waterin'. Ya see, we have to have all our drinkin' water trucked in here because the ground water is so alkali, and I just poured them all big glasses of it. Now, normally, anyone would be able to tell the water weren't any good after the first drink, but these college kids they just gulped it down fast as they could . . . They were headin' east, and so far as I can figger . . . probably took them thirty miles or so before it got real uncomfortable to sit on them bike seats o' theirs. They probably had themselves some mean cases of diarrhea all the way from here to the Mississippi." He chuckled as he finished, and the kids all straightened up and started polishing up their 'pleases' and 'thank yous.'

"Now you kids seem pretty nice to me, so don't you worry none about me servin' any bad water. Besides, we just got our tank filled yesterday and you look awful thirsty. I'll get ya some water and some menus, and you just make yerselves at home right here at this table."

As he walked into the kitchen, the kids sat themselves down without a sound. They lifted up their chairs and slid themselves gently under the table. They tucked their handlebar bags neatly under the table, out of the man's way, and when he returned with our seven glasses of ice water, they all waited for me to take the first drink.

"Now, what's the matter? You kids don't trust me? I told ya I wouldn't be servin' ya any of that bad water and I meant it. Now drink up."

Fearing reprisals for hesitation, everyone drank quickly and heartily. The skinny man with the suntanned face laughed again as he watched us down our first glasses. He returned to the kitchen to crank up the grill, while we studied our menus.

"Are you our waiter, too?" asked Ethan.

"Yep, I'm the waiter, the plumber, the manager, the postman, the mayor and about everythin' else around here. Why, with a population of three, a fella learns to do just about everything. If I'm cookin' your order and someone drives up in their car, you'll have to excuse me while I go and fill up their tank. We run a full-service gas station here and ain't nobody fills up any tanks but me. If I'm in the middle of anybody's eggs when someone pulls in, I may have to ask one of ya to come into the kitchen and take over for a second."

The kids were warming up to the mayor of Moneta and he was rapidly warming up to them. Ethan was the first to order and his order was typical of the rest:

"Uh . . . I'll have . . . two eggs over medium with . . . home fries . . . bacon . . . toast . . . a large stack of pancakes . . . and a large orange juice and coffee."

The mayor looked at his pad and then down at Ethan and then scratched his head. Just as he was about to move over to Heather, Ethan continued his order:

"And . . . do you have any hot chocolate?"

"Yep, I think we have some back in the kitchen somewhere."

"Well, then I'll have a hot chocolate too." Ethan quickly closed up his menu and smiled up at our friend.

"You mean, you want hot chocolate instead of the coffee?"

As always, Ethan thought for a second, then answered, "Nah, I'll have the coffee and the hot chocolate."

"Do the rest of you order as much food as this guy?" he asked looking down at Ethan's order.

"Yes, I'm afraid we all do," answered Lynn.

"Well, ain't no problem for me as long as you don't mind waiting for me to cook it all. My wife usually does most of the cookin', and I tend to be a little slower than her in the kitchen."

"Oh, that's fine," answered Lynn. "We're a little ahead of schedule today anyway. So, if its okay, we'll wait."

"Why sure, like I said, make yerselves comfortable. I'll be right back. I think I'm going to need another order pad."

As soon as everyone was finished with their orders, they all got out their journals, postcards and address books. I hadn't said anything, but it seemed like my sermon last night was having some effect. Joy and Heather, who had kept up with their postcards, were thankful for some time to add to their already lengthy journals. Jimmy joined them in his journal, and Carl and Ethan wrote some post cards. While Ethan was trying to unstick some stamps that had been floating around in his handlebar bag through Kansas and Nebraska, I noticed that he and Carl were sending postcards that they had bought back in Washington, D.C. and Virginia. In front of them they spread out mildewed collections of shots of the Washington Monument, White House and Williamsburg.

"Are those the first postcards you've sent?" whispered Heather, as she tried to cover her giggles with her journal.

"Yeah, and what's so funny?" barked Carl, as Ethan nodded.

"Well . . . let's see . . ." continued Heather philosophically. "It's only been two months since we were in Virginia and DC . . . But I guess it doesn't matter when people get the postcard. It's the thought that counts."

"Yeah, it's the thought that counts!" Ethan and Carl both whispered their answer together and then proceeded to work on their cards. Ethan's address book seemed to have been in the same leaky bag as his stamps, and he spent about twenty minutes just separating his stamps and addresses. When breakfast finally came and the postcards were finished, I hoped the people on the receiving end of the messages from my two young male friends appreciated all the time and effort that went into them. Those few postcards, however bent and stained, were definitely collector's items.

"Hey John, didn't the pioneers have trouble with the water on the desert, too?" asked Jimmy. "And I don't mean getting water. I mean, didn't they also run into alkali water that messed up them and their animals?"

"Good memory, Jimmy," I answered. "They really did. Do you guys mind if I read something from Swain's journal while we eat?"

"No, go for it," said Carl with his mouth full of pancakes and syrup.

> "July 17. We passed over the bluffs, and our road, having been heavy and sandy, became hard and gravelly. We passed many saline lakes which were dry, their beds covered with alkali. Those with water are dangerous for the teams, as they often die from the effects of drinking it.

> "July 18. This morn we started late and soon found our cattle sick from the effects of drinking from the saline springs. We doctored them by giving them large pieces of fat pork and had the good luck not to lose any of them. The poisoned oxen were immediately unyoked and chained to the wagon wheels. We then tied pieces of fat bacon to the ends of sticks or whipstocks and shoved it down the throats of the suffering creatures. It formed a sort of soap in their stomachs which neutralized the effect of the alkali."

"Hey dudes, I won't be gettin' the runs," announced Jimmy. "I ate all my bacon and right now it's forming the soap in my stomach."

"Yeah, right," snickered Carl.

"Hey everybody, listen to this. Here's how another emigrant describes the effect of the water:

> ". . . I saw more than one hundred dead oxen and two or three horses. As soon as an ox dies, he bloats as full as the skin will hold, and sometimes it bursts, and his legs stick straight out and he smells horrible . . . . When they are nearly decayed there is frequently three or four bushels of maggots about the carcass."

"Three or four bushels. . . Yuck!" said Joy, trying to keep her food down.

"Yeah, can you imagine seeing a group of bicyclists lying dead on the desert, their legs sticking straight up in the air, with millions of maggots crawling through their rotten lycra shorts?" Carl got a devilish gleam in his eyes as he tried to describe the scene in grossest detail.

"Who needs diarrhea when Carl is trying to make us throw up?" said a pale Heather.

"Well, I think it's time to change the subject," I interrupted. "How much farther to our 3,000-mile mark, guys?"

"About nineteen more miles according to my computer," said Carl. "Can we have a celebration when we hit it?"

"Well, what do you guys think?" I knew what the answer would be, but it was always good to use a little democracy wherever possible.

"Let's party, dudes!" smiled Ethan, and from everybody else's smiles, I could see my prediction was correct.

"Okay, we'll celebrate at the first town we come to after crossing the mark. If we have nineteen more miles, then it looks like the town of Shoshoni is just two miles past our mark."

"Hey John, before we go, do you think we can get our picture taken with the guy that runs this place? I think he's cute," whispered Joy.

"Well, why don't you ask him?" I suggested.

". . .Would you do it for us? I feel kinda weird asking him."

As soon as breakfast was done, Joy and Heather had him over by the cash register. With Joy on his left and Heather on his right, and two tan California arms held tightly around his waist, the mayor, postman, cook and jack of everything in Moneta, Wyoming smiled his biggest desert smile as the cameras flashed and he joined two of his admirers in a laughing "Cheese." Instead of him infecting the kids with his water, they had infected him with their smiles. After the photo, he walked with us out to the wooden-planked sidewalk by our bikes, and he stood and waved goodbye as we rolled west, out of the Moneta City Limits.

Right on schedule, two miles from Shoshoni, we hooted and hollered as Carl's and Ethan's computers flashed magically from 2,999.9 to 3,000.0. Not willing to wait until town, water bottles were unleashed and we spent five minutes drenching ourselves and each other with all the water we had.

"Hey John, I hope that map of yours is right, because if Shoshoni isn't in two miles, we could be in deep trouble," warned Carl as he emptied the last of his water down my back.

My map was accurate and the town of Shoshoni seemed like New York City compared to where we had been. It had a main street, complete with sidewalks and cross walks, and the gas stations were separate from the cafes — amazing! We found a pharmacy and soda fountain advertising: *The Best Malts in Wyoming!*

"Probably the *only* malts in Wyoming. . . ," commented a skeptical Carl on his way inside. He promptly grossed everyone out by ordering a combination cherry and root beer malt. The waitress asked him to repeat his order to be sure, and when he did, she mumbled something about him probably coming from California. She didn't think Carl had heard, but he did, raising his eyebrows and smiling as wide as he could.

At first, I thought Carl had ordered such a strange flavor because he was enjoying being on a roll at grossing everyone out, but when he began to down his malt in record time, without any added dramatics, everyone was soon asking for a taste.

At approximately mile 3,010, Heather's rear tire decided it had had enough of our transcontinental blacktop. With a loud, KABOOM, followed by the rhythmic flapping of loose rubber being sandwiched between rim and road, Heather and Skittles thudded to an unexpected stop.

"Whoopsy," smiled Heather as she looked back at her wheel. "I think I have a flat tire."

Her words were an understatement. Not only did she have a flat tube, but she also had a tire that had an inch-long slash where the nylon and rubber casing had split open. Normally, such mechanical difficulties were just occasion for me to get out my tools and for Lynn and the kids to get out their journals. The same scene of me hunched over a bike and the kids hunched over their diaries had happened countless times in the past three thousand miles; but this was the first time that one of Heather's tires had failed. I carried folding spare tires for everyone except — you guessed it — Heather. Heather, still a couple inches shy of the five foot mark, was riding a bike with small wheels, and since none of our kids had ever destroyed a tire on any previous trips, I thought that Heather's would do fine. Besides, I figured that when I saw they were wearing thin, I could find what we needed. Well, I was wrong. I scanned the desert for a 24-inch tire and, seeing none, I knew it was time for a little creative mechanics. Shoot, we only had a few miles to the giant town of Riverton, and we would surely be able to scare up a spare for Heather there. Until then, I could rig something up.

It turned out that I was right on one count and way wrong on the other. I put in a new tube and constructed a new casing for her tire with a little duct tape and an old piece of tire I carried in my tool kit. The kids caught up on their journals and we all rolled — Heather with a little added bump — into Riverton. The row of hotels and shopping centers that blinded us as we entered town gave me hope of finding Heather's tire.

In honor of our 3,000-mile mark and of Lynn's upcoming departure, we decided to go out to dinner. Our friend back in Moneta had recommended a combination steak house and Chinese restaurant that sounded like the perfect place to throw Lynn a goodbye party on almost her last night on the trip.

The restaurant was great except that Lynn had to go home early, suffering from cramps; but before the kids would let her leave, they all made toasts and gave little speeches thanking both Lynn and me for getting them so far. When Lynn left the restaurant, we were both near tears.

The shopping center had just about everything, except for a tire that fit Heather's rim. I bought another roll of duct tape and worked til midnight trying to reinforce her reluctant tire.

"Heather, how's your tire doing?" I asked at our second breakfast the next morning.

"I think it's doing okay," she answered. "I'm even getting used to the little kerplunk that happens every time my wheel goes around." Heather smiled and continued working in her journal as she waited for her food. The cafe was a haven for cyclists, but not our kind. With its Harley Davidson mirrors, pool table, and some of the most interesting bathroom graffiti we'd read, it was used to riders with leathers and beards not lycra and peach fuzz. It was ten in the morning and the menu consisted of burgers and beer — no pancakes, no juice, not even Cokes, just burgers and beer; so the kids ordered burgers and Lynn, who doesn't eat beef, ordered a cheeseburger without the burger. The kids got their water bottles off their bikes and mixed up some of our drink mix. I had my earliest beer of the trip and the kids begged for a sip while letting me know that it was a form of carbohydrate and that carbos were good for bicyclists. I held my ground, left them to their fruit punch and soon we were off again.

Heather's tire held its ground a little too well about five miles after brunch. I heard a familiar sound reverberating from behind me and looked back to see Heather slowing to a stop in the gravel alongside the road. I told Lynn and the kids to go on up ahead and find a shady place. The same sun that had heated my patch job beyond its melting point threatened to do the same to the kids, and we still had sixty miles and 2,000 feet of climbing to do.

I unbolted Heather's rear wheel and discovered that the slit in her tire was growing. What yesterday had been an inch-long separation was now over an inch and a half. I rewove some of my makeshift reinforcement from more duct tape and my old piece of casing, and the whole time I worked Heather hummed and smiled at the surrounding view. My countenance wasn't quite so bright, but soon she had me remounting her rear wheel with a little less scowl on my face. I didn't know it at the time, but our roadside repair meetings were just beginning.

My patch job lasted another thirty miles before exploding again. Heather smiled

"Whoopsy," and I spent another half hour repairing the damage before we could continue toward the mountains.

The land changed drastically as we left the Wind River Reservation and entered the Shoshone National Forest. The Wind River gurgled at us as it streamed out of the mountains down a deep, red rock canyon.

We sweated up the long grades, enjoying looking down on something for the first time in a long time. Stopping at the top of each climb, before each downhill, I would ride over to Heather to check on her tire.

"I want that smile to make it to the Pacific by bicycle, okay Heather?"

"Okie, dokie," she would smile back, and thumpity-thumpity she would carefully coast down the road. Heather's tendency to make me smile caused more than a few winged insects to lose their lives on my teeth, as I followed her down those Wyoming grades.

At Dubois, Wyoming, one day's ride shy of the Continental Divide and the Tetons, the kids decided to have a special celebration. It was August 28, less than one month since Memphis. The kids had pedaled across the Plains and — Heather's tire willing — they would get Lynn to the Tetons and Jackson Lake with one day to spare. They had chosen a menu of camp burritos, chips, salsa, salad, Cokes for kids, beers for adults and brownies and real milk for dessert for their own special farewell banquet.

Camp was set up in record time, and Lynn had all the kitchen volunteers she could handle. Vegetables were cut up, salad was tossed and the table looked as good as one at any Mexican restaurant. Before we sat down to eat, Jimmy ordered everyone to crack open a drink for a toast. He looked at Lynn, walked over and put his arm around the side of her that I wasn't already holding, lifted his Coke and toasted.

"To Lynn, our *From Sea to Shining Sea* mom . . . Us kids — and I'm pretty sure your husband here — couldn't have made it here without you. Thanks a lot."

We clanked our cans and swigged down our drinks. In the emotion of continued toasts to Lynn, we failed to notice that our table, however beautiful, wasn't balanced too well. When Jimmy finished being toastmaster and sat down at the far end, the whole table flipped up, sending beans, tortillas, salsa, and everything else flying his way.

Three months on the road had instilled us with an intense appreciation for food, and the speed with which everyone dove for that flying feast probably set a world's record. A few *frijoles* (beans) may have found the grass and a little salsa may have splashed on Jimmy's shorts, but everything else was rescued and rebalanced. As we sat around eating burritos and brownies, we all reminisced about some of our other memorable meals with "Mom." It was Lynn's last night with the kids, and one of the few since I've known her that she had trouble going to sleep.

Rendezvous

"Hey John, is it true that you can smell a donut shop from thirty miles away?" asked Ethan as he bit into his jelly donut at the shop in downtown Dubois.

"Well, with favorable winds, maybe from twenty-five," I answered with my mouth half-full of apple fritter.

"Yeah, he even found us a donut shop in Japan!" laughed Jimmy. "But let's not get John talking about donuts now, Eeth. Let's finish up and go climb the Continental Divide."

"Yeah, it's about time we had some mountains," smiled Heather. Let's see how these compare to the Appalachians."

Our ride that day was going to be over sixty miles — twenty-five miles and almost three thousand feet of climbing up to Togwotee Pass and then another thirty-five winding down to Jackson Lake. The kids were raring to climb, not only because they were so excited to see mountains after weeks of the Plains, but because they had something special awaiting them in Jackson Hole.

Back in the early 1800's, long before any caravans of wagons headed west, men with names like Jim Bridger and Jeremiah Johnson spent their lives hunting and trapping for beaver in the mountains of western Wyoming. Once a year these bearded mountain men would gather to have a party and swap meet in a valley in the mountains called a "hole." Jackson Hole, at the base of the Tetons, was the perfect spot for one of these gatherings known as "Rendezvous." Having studied the mountain men in my class along with the pioneers, we had planned a little Rendezvous of our own at Jackson Lake. We weren't going to chew buffalo intestine or have any orgies, but Carl would be seeing his family for the first time since Williamsburg; Ethan would be seeing his mom and sister he hadn't hugged since Arkansas — and seeing his dad for the first time all summer. Joy's grandparents were driving up from Colorado, Jimmy had some family friends meeting him, and Heather had Mom, Dad, two sisters and Grandma and Grandpa all lined up for their hugs somewhere on the shores of Jackson Lake. She hadn't seen any of her family since Los Angeles Airport and she was even more excited than usual that morning.

My "WAGONS HO" followed by six loud "YAHOOS" echoed through downtown Dubois that morning as we pulled out of the donut shop. We were just across the road when an open, tan jeep driven by a man wearing a stocking cap and waving a bicycle tire, came honking by from the west. He slammed on the brakes in the middle of the street and made a screeching u-turn.

"Hey, you guys," shouted a surprised Heather, her eyes as big as Ethan's. "That looks just like my granpa's jeep . . . and . . . that's my dad and Gretchen and Heidi!" We all pulled to our own sudden stop as Heather's dad and two sisters jumped out of the jeep. Heather dropped her bike on its side and ran into her dad's arms. Wrapped in his daughter's hug, Ray was smiling as big as his frozen face would let him. Heidi and Gretchen were right beside him, and Heather warmed them next with her bear hugs.

Ray ran back to the car and came back with the tire in his hand. "I heard you guys might be needing this." Ray immediately got a big hug from me — I had done an extra thick patching job on Heather's rear wheel earlier that morning, but I happily forfeited any further road testing. I changed her tire as everyone enjoyed visiting with some faces from home. I had never seen Heather so excited to see her family, and in no time, she had a new tire. With a "see you on the other side" and another set of "hos" and "yahoos," we headed off — smoothly this time — for Togwotee Pass, almost 10,000 feet up in the sky.

Our climb began almost immediately as our donut shop disappeared behind us. The cool of the mountain morning was perfect weather for climbing, and before long we'd all stripped off our wool gloves, legwarmers and long-sleeved jerseys. The lower slopes of the mountains were cleared for cow pasture, while up at higher elevations we could see forests of blue-green fir and spruce trees. To our left, a mountain stream jumped down the mountain, and, up above us, the sky was a deep blue that grew deeper and deeper as we climbed into it.

Our enthusiastic pace slowed once we entered the tree line. The grade got steeper and steeper, and soon we found ourselves in our lowest gears. The stream was invisible now, hundreds of feet down the canyon, obscured by the trees and our elevation. White popcorn clouds sped across the incredible sky and the wind whistled off the peaks towering all around us.

"Hey John, check out these trees," said Jimmy who was riding up front with me. "We haven't seen trees since . . . shoot, I can't remember the last time we saw trees. This shade and this air sure feel good."

I could see Heather and Joy riding behind us, and from the looks of things, they were again marveling at mother nature. They were pointing out trees and wildflowers and clouds, and every so often, when we slowed down and the wind was just right, I could hear them behind, talking excitedly about some new discovery.

After about six hours of climbing, Jimmy and I came around a corner to a sign that read:

THE CONTINENTAL DIVIDE
TOGWOTEE PASS   ELEVATION 9,658 FEET

"YOW!!! This is it!" shouted Jimmy, immediately picking up his speed and cresting the top. We both pulled into the turnout and hugged each other in triumph. Jimmy then leaned himself proudly against the sign and sat down to drink from his water bottle, while I ran up to the road to greet the girls.

A sweating but smiling Joy and Heather soon appeared down around the corner. I ran down to where they were and ran up the last few yards with them. At the top I threw my arms around them and kissed them on the cheek.

"Man, John, how come you didn't give me a kiss?" asked Jimmy sarcastically. I immediately ran over to my seated friend and throwing my sweaty arms around his sweaty body, planted a loud and wet one on his cheek.

It took Carl and Ethan a little longer than Jimmy and the girls to reach the top. I was surprised when I saw Lynn appear around that corner with no signs of the two boys. "I just couldn't go any slower," she gasped, as she pulled over to the sign. "And there was no way I was going to stop in the middle of that last steep section. They should be coming soon. Ethan first and then, behind him a ways, Carl."

I gave Lynn a hug before she even had a chance to get off her bike. Ethan appeared about five minutes after her, going so slow I wondered how he balanced his bike. A red-faced and quiet Carl came soon after , and as soon as he caught his breath, he announced that he didn't think it was that bad. Lynn looked at me and smiled.

Once Carl laid down his bike, Jimmy led everyone in a dance around the sign.

"9,700 feet . . . not too bad," he boasted.

"Yeah, I bet some cars have trouble going over that mountain," chuckled Ethan.

"I don't know if I've ever been this high, other than in an airplane," grinned Carl.

"Okay, you guys, ceremony time," I announced. "Everybody go and get a water bottle and meet me back here at the sign." Soon everyone was back with full bottles. "Jimmy, I want you to get down on your hands and knees, and everybody else, I want you to gather in a circle around him." Jimmy dropped to the ground, like a wrestler in ready-position.

"Okay, who can tell me what 'The Continental Divide' means?"

Heather's hand immediately shot up. "It's the dividing line where all the streams and rivers on one side flow into the Atlantic and all the ones on the other side flow into the Pacific."

"Good, Heather. Remind me to put an A on your transcript next to Geography." Heather blushed and bowed to the applause of the group.

"Our Continental Divide ceremony is going to be a simulation of what Heather just explained. When I say pour, I want everyone to empty their water bottles over Jimmy's helmet — he's going to be the Continental Divide. Now, some of the water from our water bottles will flow off Jimmy's eastern side to the Atlantic and some of it will flow off his western side to the Pacific. I don't want any of you dudes or dudettes to pour until I say so, because I want to get a picture of this momentous occasion."

Jimmy scowled up at me from his position, but being the good sport that he was, he didn't move. Besides, he liked having his picture taken. I yelled "pour" and the kids enjoyed emptying every last drop of their water bottles over a once dry Jimmy. They always were enthusiastic to further their understanding of geography, and somehow, thanks to Jimmy and their bikes, I don't think they'll ever forget the significance of the Continental Divide.

Our long awaited downhill into Jackson Hole wasn't to be forgotten either, but not because it was a lot of fun. Almost as difficult as the uphill, it was twenty-five miles of downhill alright, but it was also twenty-five miles of road construction. Gravel stretches appeared out of nowhere around steep descending curves; smoke-spitting dump trucks rumbled by, leaving us coughing in their trailing clouds of dust and gravel; and road crews waving orange flags stopped our progress every couple of miles. By the time we reached the bottom, our eyes were bloodshot and our arms ached.

I rode way off the back and Lynn was waiting with the kids at the bottom of the descent, smiling and holding a box of fudgesicles in her hand.

"We didn't want to start until you got here, dear," she said as I rode in. "What took you so long? We were beginning to worry about you."

"Oh, nothing. I was just trying to slow things down, that's all."

No one seemed to understand my answer as Lynn passed out the ice creams.

"What are you laughing at, John?" asked Jimmy a couple minutes later.

"Well, I was just looking at your faces and thinking of what William Swain did when he crossed the Divide at South Pass."

"What did he do?"

"He took some samples of the rocks at the top and put them in his wagon for souvenirs," I answered. "If you guys could see yourselves in a mirror, you would see all kinds of dirt and junk stuck to the places where your eyes watered and your mouth drooled on the way down the mountain. You guys are just like ole William. Your faces are full of Togwotee Pass souvenirs."

Everyone then did their best Ethan imitations, wiping their faces with the backside of their hands to check out my accuracy. A cleansing water bottle fight soon erupted and when bottles were empty, we headed towards Jackson Lake.

We had no trouble finding our campsite. It was the one decorated with streamers and giant signs welcoming us to our Rendezvous. Everyone in the surrounding campsites seemed to know us too, as they interrupted their dinners to applaud our triumphal entrance.

But what was a reunion for most of the kids was separation for Lynn and me. We tried the best we could to be part of the celebration that night, but after joining Heather's family for the wonderful lasagna dinner they had prepared, Lynn and I borrowed Ray's truck and headed off to Jackson Hole to spend our last night together for a long time — alone.

While I loaded Lynn's bike into the back of the truck, she said a tearful goodbye to each of the kids. They had kept their promise of getting her over the mountains before the first of September, but that didn't make their goodbyes any easier. Joy quietly stayed off to the side, hoping that her turn wouldn't have to come, and when Lynn had only Joy left, they ran up to each other and held on. Joy didn't want to let go of her favorite doctor and riding friend, and Lynn's well burst when her favorite patient wouldn't let go. Watching her say goodbye from my seat in the car didn't help matters any for me, and by the time Lynn joined me in the cab, I was a mess too.

Lynn and I didn't get much sleep that night in Jackson Hole. Over and over again, my mind played back all the times I had taken her for granted. For over 3,000 miles, if I had left out a "please" or a "thank you," it was Lynn's. And if a hug was forgotten in the group, it was the one I should have given her. I knew we'd sat together, back on the pier in Santa Barbara, and said we wouldn't have much time for "us" once we were on the road; but how long would those hugs and thank yous have taken? Did all those times really get us that much further down the road? I stared at Lynn's back a lot that night, and by the time the sun came up, I was a wreck. When we arrived at the airport and were called to the departure gate, I completely fell apart.

Lynn walked with me to her gate and then stopped and held onto my fore-arms. The same knees that had so strongly pedaled me this far, suddenly felt like they were going to buckle beneath me. A few tears found their way down Lynn's tan cheeks, but she didn't tremble like I did. She was going to lead through this storm.

"John . . . you've done an incredible job with all of us. Thanks for getting me to the mountains. Everything we hoped would happen on this trip so far has happened, and you're the one who has got us this far." How Lynn talked with-out having her voice crack I didn't know, but it sure helped me that afternoon in the wet airport. "Now don't you get all sad and homesick or any of that stuff, you hear? You've still got a few more miles to pedal and we've got a little dinner engagement on the Pacific Coast, remember? . . . Who knows, we might even get to rendezvous some time before then, so dry those tears and get back to our kids."

Lynn threw her arms around me and dug her fingers into my back. Both of us trembled like never before. We held on as long as we could, finally broken up by the referee on the loudspeaker announcing the last call for Lynn's flight. Lynn whispered "Wagons Ho" into my ear and kissed me one last time. I watched her head down the hallway and run across the runway to her plane. She waved once before ducking inside, and then she was gone.

In my handlebar bag, I had a list of chores that needed to be done, and as I waved to Lynn's plane speeding down the runway, I grabbed it, half because the chores had to be done and half because I hoped that my being busy would take my mind off Lynn. Lynn had made me the list and I was doing great, until I got to the market.

I was cruising through the aisles filling up the basket and crossing things off the list, when I came to "liquid soap." I didn't have any trouble finding the soap, but where I found it set me off to crying again. You see, Lynn loves health food stores almost as much as she loves quilts, and the Safeway in Jackson had one whole aisle (both sides!) devoted to health foods. Four kinds of bran, a dozen different kinds of granola, bottle after bottle of the grooviest sounding lotions and potions I had ever seen. Lynn would have loved that place, and if we had been shopping together, I probably would have been left standing over our shopping basket watching our perishables perish as she checked out that one aisle. That afternoon I would have loved to, and after finally getting our liquid soap, I completely messed up the rest of the list. I got this suffocating feeling in my chest, and I could hardly even read it anymore. I had my own Jackson Hole where my heart was supposed to be.

I backtracked all over the market trying to find easy things like milk and cheese, and when I rolled our groceries out to the truck, I discovered that I had forgotten a bunch of things. I went back into the market and shopped a second time for the items I had left out. I even ended up stopping one more time, at a little market on the way back to camp, when I realized I had forgotten the wine for that night's dinner — and I never forget wine. I may forget the noodles, but I never forget the wine.

"Hey John, did you say goodbye to Lynn?" asked Carl as I pulled into camp. "I already cleaned and lubed my bike; come and see it. It didn't even have any broken spokes or missing screws!" I walked over to Pack Rat and it was the cleanest I'd ever seen it — even its spokes sparkled in the afternoon sunshine.

"Check out my chain too, John." Carl got down on one knee and turned his cranks. "I got it so clean it hardly even makes noise anymore. I wanted to get it good and clean before my folks get here, so I can spend as much time as I can with them.

"Was there a good bike shop in Jackson? I want to take my mom and dad there if there is."

While Carl was showing me his bike, Ray Deutsch came through the trees with a glass of wine, a little less oblivious to the condition of my heart. "Here, John, I think you probably need this. Did everything work out okay at the airport?"

"Yeah, Ray, everything went fine. Thanks for all your help with everything."

"Oh, my pleasure." Ray came up and gave me a squeeze on the shoulder. A small, warm man with a great recipe for daughters, his company would help me keep the Elephant at bay.

The kids hadn't had a layover day since Kansas, over a thousand miles ago, and they loved our three days in Jackson. We had polar bear meetings in Jackson Lake early each morning, leaving a ring of prairie dirt around our giant bathtub. The kids lounged around camp, and Jimmy even employed Heather's sister and Ethan's sister as masseuses. Early Saturday morning, Carl's parents arrived, and Carl spent his next two days staying with them at the Jackson Lake Lodge, taking two warm showers a day, eating in the dining room, horseback riding, canoeing and fishing. Later Ethan's family found us, and after Ethan gave his amazed dad a bike maintenance demonstration, they were off to their lodge for some time alone. Joy's grandparents and cousin drove in Saturday afternoon and added some of the best apple pie I have ever tasted to all the wonderful menus Heather's folks had planned for us in camp. At nighttime, the kids would wolf down some of Ray's famous linguica burritos or some of Heather's mom's great

346

lasagna, burn some marshmallows and then be off to play flashlight tag or hide-and-go-seek. I visited with Heather's folks and grandparents in the quiet of their camper, listening to them share the changes they saw in their daughter, while the kids enjoyed their late nights without worry of some pre-dawn wake up call. It was a restful time for us all, and as the three days drew to a close and I began to make sure things were ready for the last third of our journey, the gnawing hole in my chest slowly began to go away. It only got bad when I crawled into my nylon home with nothing to cuddle but my four blue panniers.

The night before we left Jackson Lake, I gathered up my journal and every-one's laundry and took off for the camp laundromat. As soon as the four-wash-ers-worth was loaded, I sat down and my pen took off. Thoughts of Lynn, of the road ahead and the road behind rushed through my head. It started to sprinkle outside, where I was writing, but I just hunched over my book and tried to keep the drizzle from smearing my racing thoughts. As I filled and turned each page, I grew more and more excited about all we had accomplished so far, and I heard the words Lynn spoke to me at the airport. I cried again that evening as I lis-tened to Lynn's words echo through my head, but my tears that night were much different than the ones back at the airport. I was so proud of Lynn and the kids and myself, and excited about preparing to continue to the Pacific. I closed up my journal and walked back into the laundromat with a big grin on my face. I hummed and talked to each sock and pair of underwear as I put them back in the laundry bag. The call of the road had me excited again, and I had trouble sleeping that night. I couldn't wait for my alarm to go off again at 4 AM.

The kids' equivalent of Lynn and my airport goodbye happened on a stretch of blacktop at the foot of the Grand Tetons. Joy waved goodbye to her grandpar-ents and cousin; Carl hugged a tearful goodbye to his mom, dad, brother and dog; Heather made the rounds, throwing her arms around everyone in her family; and Ethan, poor Ethan, his goodbye was the hardest of all.

Before the trip, Ethan's dad had planned to join up with us in Jackson and ride with us through Idaho and Oregon to the California border. Bill had outfit-ted himself with a new bike, racks and camping gear, and had trained with Ethan all spring to be able to join us. Ethan spoke often of how he looked forward to meeting up with his dad so he could show him how much stronger he was and how much he had learned. He even joked about whether his dad had trained hard enough to be able to keep up with the group. Ethan's dreams were ended when his dad arrived in Wyoming without his bike. Bill had become seriously ill over the summer and almost didn't even make the flight to the Rendezvous. That morning in Jackson, when it really hit him that his dad wouldn't be coming along, Ethan crumbled. He ran into his dad's arms and held on like a kinder-gartner on his first day at school. Ethan's thin little body shook and quivered as he burst into tears against his dad's chest. He held on and he held on, not want-ing to let go, not so much worried about not riding with his dad, but afraid that he might never see him again. I stood back and saw the kids watching their friend trying to say goodbye, and I wouldn't have been surprised had they all ignored my next order.

I motioned for them to wheel their bicycles back onto the road, and they silently buckled their helmets and formed a line heading west. I felt so awful as we waited there for Ethan that I couldn't look the four of them in the eye. A few long minutes later he joined us, trying to control his sobs, but not doing a very good job.

"Are you okay, Eeth?" As soon as I said it, I was reminded that teachers ask some of the dumbest questions. Ethan just sobbed, as his trembling hand reached for his toe straps.

With Lynn gone, I was now going to be riding in the back of the group, so I motioned for Jimmy, our new point rider, to head towards the Snake River. I followed behind Ethan, as he stretched out over his bike and painfully pedaled to school with his classmates. I knew he was on his way to learning so many wonderful things, but still, as his little body shook and quivered, I couldn't help but cry along with him . . . . Although the stretch of asphalt leaving Jackson Hole, following the Snake River into Idaho, was all downhill, Ethan would tell you it was the toughest mountain he climbed anywhere in America.

14

We camped next to a beautiful little stream, that you could watch and hear while eating your spaghetti and chocolate pudding. As the light faded, we wrote in our journals and played a little Spoons and Hearts under the glow of the lanterns . . . .

Heather's Journal
September 13, 1986

ABC's

"Hey John, it doesn't work!" Carl pulled to a slow stop off to the side of the road and looked back at me, shaking his head.

"What doesn't work?" I asked, as I stopped alongside him. "Is something the matter with Pack Rat?"

"No, nothing's the matter with my bike. It's just that I figured since we crossed the Continental Divide and that all rivers now flow to the Pacific and everything . . . Well, I thought I'd see if if I could be just like one of those rivers — maybe I could coast all the way to the ocean. But I guess the Continental Divide is different for bicycles . . . It didn't work." Carl shrugged his shoulders, flashed me a smile and then was back on the road, pedaling this time.

Following the Snake River, as it plunged its way towards Idaho, could easily have given anyone the impression that it was all downhill to the Pacific. We sped down the canyon out of Jackson and soon found ourselves at a sign that read:

WELCOME TO IDAHO — THE GEM STATE

As we stopped for our mandatory state line picture, I motioned the kids over to my bike and, placing my hand on top of my handlebar bag, I recited an oath: "I, John Seigel Boettner, being of sound mind and carrying a long fishing pole, hereby and solemnly swear that this group will not leave the state of Idaho without my first catching an Idaho trout. A trout on the end of my line will be our passport to Oregon."

The kids moaned and I think I heard all the fish in Idaho laughing at my pronouncement.

"Hey John, we may never get to California," laughed Jimmy.

"Yeah, we may be here for the rest of our lives . . . can our budget afford a long stay in Idaho?" added Carl.

"I think we better buy a frozen trout at the next market and hook it to your line the next time you go fishing," said Heather. "So far, in all the states we've been through and all the times you've gone fishing, what have you caught? . . .

352

Four or five little bluegill in Missouri? If you added up all the money you've spent on fishing licenses and tackle, those are some pretty expensive little fish." Everyone laughed in agreement with Heather.

"Well, I thank you guys for your unwavering confidence in my angling skills, but you mark my words, no Oregon until I've caught myself that trout."

"Hey John, I hate to say it, but you fish about as well as you take care of horses," giggled Joy. "I second the motion for the frozen trout."

We followed the Snake River to Idaho Falls, and all the little streams that crossed under our road feeding into the giant river looked like the perfect place to catch our passport. At the market in the little town of Swan Valley, trophies of beautiful fish adorned the wood walls above dusty rolls of toilet paper and tin foil. I grew excited to catch mine.

"Hey John, hurry up and come on outside," whispered Joy, as Heather, Carl and I shopped for lunch. "There are three cyclists who just pulled in, and they are riding from Portland, Maine to Portland, Oregon."

We finished shopping and walked outside to meet some fellow bicyclists. They were gathered with the kids around their bicycles, swapping stories of the journey across the continent. The kids introduced me to the three bicyclists, who were in their mid twenties, and then continued sharing stories. I excused myself from the conversation and went around to the other side of the market to set up lunch.

"Man, did you see their faces when they saw us?" said a beaming Ethan. "I saw them checking out our loaded bikes and wondering who was riding out here. When the three of us kids showed up to get the lunch stuff off our bikes, they couldn't believe they belonged to us."

"Yeah, and when the one woman asked me where we had started," smiled Joy, "and I told her we started in Maryland, she got this real strange look on her face. I think she thought we were from around here somewhere."

"Yeah, her friends got the same look," said Jimmy. "I think they were kinda disappointed. I think they were ready to tell their story of all the miles and everything they have done, and then they see a bunch of kids who have done more miles than they have. And we're not even in a hurry to get the trip over like they are."

"Yeah, they sounded pretty thrashed," added Ethan. "The one guy who planned to ride all the way to San Francisco says he may hang up his bicycle when they get to Portland. He sounded like he was tired of seeing his bicycle seat, and they even bailed with their bikes and hitchhiked in cars for some of their miles . . . Still, it was fun to talk with other bicyclists . . . even if they are kinda discouraged . . . What's for lunch, John?"

"How does tuna sandwiches, chips and lemonade sound?"

"Does tuna count as your fish?" joked Carl.

"You guys are gonna be sorry when I pull a beautiful trout out of one of these Idaho streams," I answered.

"I'll take my tuna with pickle relish." Joy changed the subject.

"I'll take mine without," said Jimmy.

"I'm gonna put chips in my sandwich," smiled Ethan. "Corn chips work best, but the ones you guys got will work fine."

Joy made up the bowl of tuna salad with pickles while Heather made up the other, and the kids crunched their tuna and chip sandwiches while they continued talking about the three bikers. Meeting the other cyclists bolstered the kids' confidence, and even Ethan seemed to have put his painful parting back in Jackson behind him.

"What did they do, nuke this place?" asked Jimmy, as we pulled to a stop just outside of Idaho Falls. "This makes the eastern part of Wyoming look scenic."

"Yeah man, I think this must be Hell's other half-acre," agreed Carl.

We knew from our look at the map that we were leaving the Snake River behind us at Idaho Falls and heading across another one of those parts of the map that looked stark even on paper. All that was noted on Highway 20 in the sixty-five miles between Idaho Falls and Arco were a few extinct cinder cones and some place called *The Idaho National Engineering Laboratory*. It was supposedly the site of America's first nuclear power plant, but as the sun rose behind us and heated up the vast stretch of lifeless dirt, it looked more like the sight of America's first nuclear disaster. For as far as we could see in any direction — except behind us — there was dusty, gray-brown dirt. Our road went straight ahead and disappeared in a vanishing point somewhere in the distance. Our only companions that morning were the occasional buses ferrying workers to the Laboratory and an occasional tumbleweed blowing across our path. From our wildlife study in Wyoming, we had concluded that antelope love only the most barren landscapes, and the barrenness of that stretch of Idaho was even too desolate for them.

Still, with all the monotony of our road that day, the kids started off pretty well. Jimmy was doing a good job as our new point rider, and our strawberry, peach and chocolate chip waffle breakfast seemed to be having a beneficial effect on our pace. Soon, though, two volcanoes poked over the horizon like pyramids of Pharaoh, and as we neared them, our pace slowed to a crawl. Everyone had already exhausted all the songs they knew, and if the two landmarks on the horizon didn't hypnotize the kids to sleep soon, the steady band of the painted white line that wiggled as we rode along it surely would. I was even beginning to feel the effects of the monotony, and I decided it was time for a diversion.

When my brothers and sisters and I would get restless on family vacations, my dad would always come up with some road game to make the miles go faster. Although my troops weren't getting restless, I didn't want anyone falling asleep at their handlebars, so I combed my memory for some of my dad's old games.

"Hey Jimmy!" I yelled from the back of the pack. "Pull over."

Jimmy pulled to a stop and everyone pulled over behind him. I told Ethan to pass out cookies while I explained our game.

"Okay everybody, the name of the game is ABC, and here's the way you play: You start with the letter 'A', and then go all the way through the alphabet to 'Z' by trying to find the letters on something alongside the road, like a sign or license plate. You've got to get each letter in order."

"Oh, I know that game," smiled Heather. "My family plays it all the time."

"Yeah, I know that game too, but where are we going to find letters?" asked a less than enthusiastic Jimmy. "There ain't no signs out here, and the only cars are those big busses that go by every half hour or so. It will take us forever to get to 'Z' — if we *ever* get there."

Not having a good answer for Jimmy, I silently buckled my helmet and motioned for him to lead on. We agreed we couldn't pull off to the side of the road and dismantle our gear, looking on labels and maps for our letters. I knew that it was going to take us a long time to complete the game, but as I looked at the endless stretch of nothing ahead of us, I was glad it was. We were going to need a long diversion.

It took us about a mile for someone to find the first "A". No busses were in sight and no signs were anywhere to be seen when Carl called out, "A — Coca Cola — right over there in the ditch on that old Coke can."

Everyone jerked their necks around looking for the red and white piece of aluminum, and for the rest of that day everyone was thankful for man's poor manners in regards to litter. The busses helped only if the letters on the sides, which the kids had memorized, happened by at the right time, and discarded soft drink cans, juice bottles and milk cartons were welcomed with enthusiastic shouts from a revitalized group. It took longer than any game of ABC that I have ever played before, and the smooth but slow flow of letters came to a standstill when we got to the letter "J". Heather took the early lead when she was the only one to spot the sunbleached consonant on a tiny orange plastic bottle cap alongside the road. The rest of the group grumbled as it disappeared behind us, and their desire to get through the wasteland ahead stopped any of them from circling back to catch up with Heather's lead.

Over the next ten miles, Heather sped ahead, "L, M, N, O, P. . . ," stopping at that toughest of all letters,"Q," while we combed the sands for another orange juice cap or some grape juice can that hadn't had all its letters erased by the constant glow of the sun. Heather got stuck on that "Q" and we all got caught up with her before she could find one. Once the game was tied again, our pace picked up as we scrambled for letters. Carl found the golden "Q" on a can of Squirt and sped ahead.

"Hey John, I didn't know rattlesnakes ate omelettes," Carl yelled, as he pulled us over and proudly held up an abandoned styrofoam egg carton he spotted. "But I'll take this "Z" right here in 'dozen'. I win!"

Carl's prize for winning was an extra drink from our supply of boxed juices, and everyone's consolation prize was that by lunchtime we had ridden forty-four miles closer to Arco and had only thirty more to go.

Carl received first prize at one of our more spartan picnic spots — a triangular island of blacktop that marked the junction of our road and the road leading to a place called Atomic City. We decided to pass on any side trip and have lunch instead. We had to eat our lunch standing up, because the asphalt was too hot to sit on. The heat, rising through the soles of our shoes, made it almost too hot to stand on.

The name of the game after lunch was "Names," and instead of trying to find the entire alphabet, we had to try and find the letters to our names. Carl was again the lucky winner in the contest that lasted about ten miles, and instead of a box of drink for his prize, he awarded himself with a crash on the roadside. He was so excited about winning the second round that he lifted his arms in triumph. His victory signal immediately caused him to run off the road into the gravel, and he tumbled over and tangled himself in his bike. I got out Dr. Lynn's first aid kit and cleaned him up. Carl's crash ended our road games for the day.

The scenery improved shortly after Carl's victory, and we even found a river. The Big Lost River suddenly stops out in one of the lava flows that make up the Idaho laboratory, but, lucky for us, where we crossed it it was still flowing. The kids changed quickly, threw off their shoes and jumped in the cool water, splashing and trying to wash away any memories of the fifty miles we had passed through that long morning.

After our swim, the wind began to pick up, blowing dust into our faces and blowing our biking clothes dry in less than a mile. The headwinds for the last fifteen miles were so strong that Jimmy asked me to take the lead, so that everyone could draft my wide berth the rest of the way. Everyone fell in behind me, and at about 5:30, almost twelve hours since we had first hopped on our bikes in Idaho Falls that morning, we rolled into downtown Arco, Idaho.

"Wow, this place looks nice." I recognized Joy's voice behind me, and when I looked back, I saw a big smile on her dusty face. Arco was a weathered collection of motels, gas stations and pastel stucco houses, a place that on almost any other day of our trip wouldn't have prompted much enthusiasm. But that day, after riding through the nuclear laboratory, it was heaven.

"Yeah, this place is pretty neat," agreed Carl. "You could play the ABC game and win in less than five minutes. I've already seen a couple of J's and Q's, just standing here!"

Milestones

There were many milestones in the four months of our journey. People milestones — like meeting Amish friends and "HO"ing with Gordon; geographic ones — like the Blue Ridge Parkway and the Continental Divide; there were adventure milestones — like Joy's fall and the Arkansas tornado; and there were the actual miles themselves, accumulating on Ethan's and Carl's computers. Some were occasions to celebrate, some were stories to be noted in journals, and some were just left to memory to be recalled in the flicker of some future campfire or in the all night reminiscing of some future slumber party. Others I don't think the kids even realized, like the one that set my goosebumps dancing and my tear ducts flooding the next morning when we left Arco.

It started off as just another normal morning. We ate oatmeal and drank hot chocolate as we waited for the sun to stretch itself over the horizon and for Ethan to find his last sock.

The sun and Eeth's sock showed up at just about the same time, and I fell in behind the kids as Jimmy led us through the outskirts of town. It didn't take the crisp desert air long to finish waking up the kids, and, in less than a mile, they fell into a tight pace line.

It was a Saturday morning and all over America kids their age were rising and stumbling down hallways to turn on the morning cartoons that would hold their attention like zombies as their parents got some morning peace and quiet; and that morning I too got some peace and quiet, but it wasn't because my kids were spaced out.

"Gravel," Jimmy's voice was loud and clear as he announced the upcoming road hazard.

"Gravel," echoed Joy who was riding just behind him.

"Gravel, be careful." Heather was next and she pointed, fulfilling her duty to pass the word.

"Gravel," followed Ethan.

"Gravel, John." Carl completed our warning system and we all veered safely around the gravel. We had used our system hundreds of times and Heather held the record for the most creative warning. Once, while she was leading, she'd come upon a road kill. Pointing down at the shoulder of the road and steering her bike around it, she casually yelled, "Carcass!" and led us around the dead animal. Jimmy's warning was a more routine one, but, nonetheless, it did the job.

After I thanked Carl, some subconscious messenger of mine told me to slow down, and soon the kids were a couple hundred yards ahead of me. All five of them rode together in perfect formation, using Jimmy's proud lead and each other to ease their forward progress. They pedaled confidently, like some bicycling caterpillar, and no Tour de France professional cycling team could have been more in tune with each other. With every rut and gravel fan that Jimmy called out, they echoed his words and line, and with every lizard or cactus that Joy and Heather pointed out, I saw the boys crane their necks to check it out. I felt like a mama bird watching her kids confidently take off on their first solo flights. Watching my group of fledgling bicyclists flying down the road, on their own without me, made me proud and sad at the same time. Sure, I had the map and the stove and the frying pan, but the zigging and zagging, wiggling and wobbling group that had pulled out of Tuckahoe State Park had grown up. They were now more experienced and efficient than even I had been just a few months before. Like parents, Lynn and I had tried to teach them all we knew, and they had learned their lessons well. After three months and almost four thousand miles, they could do most everything on their own.

"HEY JOHN!" Jimmy stopped the group ahead and yelled back at me. I gathered myself together, blew my nose in my bandana and pulled up behind Carl. "Man, John, you're slow today. You're riding like an old man."

"Yeah, I guess I'm just feelin' a little old today . . . Sorry if I slowed you guys down."

"Oh, that's okay," said Heather. "We were going a little faster than usual this morning."

"Do you want me to slow the pace down?" asked Jimmy.

"Oh no, that's all right; just stop when we get to Craters of the Moon National Monument. Don't mind me if I trail off the back. It's nice watching you guys from behind . . . You've become real strong riders, and I like watching you work so well together."

"You know what, John?"

"What, Joy?"

"Well, I kinda like the landscape around here. You can see so far. It used to be when we would see the road stretching out so far ahead of us, or see a bunch of mountains all stacked up ahead, I would get a little discouraged knowing I would have to pedal even farther than my eyes could see, but not anymore. Now I get kinda excited, because I know me and my bike are gonna go right over the edge of that horizon and a lot more after it . . . It's a neat feeling."

"C'mon, you guys, let's go! I was just getting warmed up," ordered Jimmy. "Besides, I think the ole man here needs some time to himself." Jimmy winked at me and soon had everyone back on the road.

"Are you kidding, John? It's only ten o'clock and we've only ridden thirty miles!" Carl couldn't believe I'd asked everyone if they wanted to end our day's ride at Craters of the Moon.

"Well, it looks like a great place to do some exploring. We got Lynn to Jackson on time, and we don't have to meet Joy's folks in Boise for another week. I just thought you guys might want to slow down and take it easy for a little while."

The senators looked at me in disbelief and went behind a huge black fold of lava to hold a meeting.

"Well, John, the decision is unanimous." Joy, as usual was the spokesperson for the senators. "We've all decided to explore the moon, but we still can't believe you're letting us stop after only thirty miles."

"Yeah, John," said Jimmy. "Are you sure you're feeling okay?"

"Yeah, I'm sure I'm okay. Just get back on your bikes and go pick out a campsite, okay?"

"Sure thing, dude." Before I knew it, the kids were off through the entrance of the campground looking for a place to land their tents.

Whoever named Craters of the Moon National Monument probably has received many letters complimenting them on their perfect choice. For miles, dark black rock was piled and folded all over the golden desert. It looked like thick fudge dumped out on a fudgemaker's table, the lava being the fudge and the dry sage brush off in the distance the table. Except for a few determined pine trees, all we could see as we descended into the campground was rock so black that it made our strip of asphalt seem pale. We set up our tents in the crunchy cinders of our chosen spot, our blue and gray nylon domes looking like space-ships in a lunar parking lot.

"Hey John, we're going to go and do some exploring," announced an excited Joy. I looked up and saw her and the rest of the kids putting their helmets on.

"You mean you guys are going to explore this place on bikes?"

"Sure," said Heather. "I looked at the map we got from the Visitors Center and it shows a bike path right through the park. Sounds to me like the best way to see this place."

Heather, never real easy to argue with, left me shaking my head. She and her fellow explorers didn't return to camp to retire their two-wheeled friends for another two hours.

The rest of the day and night was spent napping, journal writing, and eating. Dinner was followed by a dessert of pump wars, where the kids, using their bicycle pumps as ray guns and light sabers, fought and died, miraculously came back to life, and fought and died over and over again. Late that night, as the stars of the Idaho sky did some shooting of their own, five, dusty kids crawled into their nylon space stations, tired and satisfied with a well-earned day of rest.

But What About School?

"Don't lose him, John!" Carl yelled at me from the bank of the Wood River in Ketchum, Idaho.

"Yeah, don't lose that fish; he's our ticket to Oregon," laughed Jimmy from across the river.

We had ridden up into the mountains to stay with the Simmons family in Ketchum, and I immediately rigged up my fishing pole to try my luck in the river running through their backyard. Ed Simmons had been headmaster back at my school in California, and one of his sons, Mike, had gone with Lynn and me on our first bike trip through New England when he was thirteen. Mike was now a senior in high school, and he and his brother Patrick had guaranteed me a fish from their favorite spot.

"Most people in Idaho don't really call fishin' with worms fishin'," said Mike as he led us down to the river. "Unless you're fly castin', some folks think you're a criminal. But, if you're as bad a fisherman as the kids have told me, I think we'd better use worms."

"Yeah, I think you had better use worms for sure," agreed Carl, as he walked alongside us.

It didn't take long for the rainbow to hit my line, but when he first hit, all my kids were off along the river doing some exploring of their own. They weren't about to hold their breath to watch me fish. When I first yelled that I had one hooked, they just continued skipping rocks and soaking their feet, responding to my call as if I was crying wolf for the tenth time. When they saw my fish come to the surface, they all ran over and to offer support.

"Now don't get him caught in the rocks, John . . . easy now," coached Carl.

"Man, I can't believe you finally caught a trout," said Ethan as he scanned the water for my rainbow fish.

"Looks like a pretty big one," said Patrick as he watched my rod bend.

"Yeah, big and stupid," said Jimmy who loved to poke fun at my angling skills. "Didn't Darwin say something about the survival of the fittest. Well, if you catch that fish, you must have caught the dumbest fish in Idaho. Fish all over America are never gonna believe it."

I pulled my prize catch from the water and, before photographing it for posterity, I had each of my senators inspect it for proof of its authenticity. It wasn't a giant rainbow, but it was about twelve inches long — a veritable whale compared to my previous bluegill catch. Patrick and I fished for another half hour, and I must have caught some mutant, because Patrick kept pulling in more rainbows while I kept reeling in empty hooks.

"Hey John, you ought to work in a zoo," laughed Jimmy. "You'd be a great fish feeder!"

I winked a nodding scowl back at Jimmy as I used my last worm. It too was sucked off my hook by some laughing trout. Every rainbow in that stream but one was sad to see me leave.

Ketchum and Sun Valley received their first slush and snow storm of fall the day we left. A cold north wind blew in our faces as we headed into the Sawtooths to climb Galena summit, elevation 8,701 feet. Ethan and Carl had trouble breathing as we began the long climb up the mountain, and at one of our rest stops Joy sighed, "John, I just can't seem to get started today. My thrust button is stuck." Carl and Ethan were still catching their breath, and they nodded in agreement as they tried to suck some water from their water bottles.

"Hey Jimmy and Heather, you two can go ahead if you want to. I'll ride with Joy, Carl and Ethan. Just wait for us at the summit. From my map it looks like we have another ten miles or so. If it starts raining or snowing again, make sure you put on your wool and rain gear, okay?"

Heather and Jimmy nodded and headed off confidently, disappearing around one of the tree-lined switchbacks as I told Joy, Carl and Ethan to take a few deep breaths of the pine scented air before heading on up the mountain.

"Hey John, the air sure smells neat up here," said Joy, sounding better. "I was worried when we got to the mountains in Ketchum. They seemed so brown and barren, like the rest of Idaho, and I was really looking forward to seeing some forest."

"Yeah, it is kinda pretty up here," said Ethan. "And I think I'm getting used to the altitude again. I just hope it doesn't snow."

Overhead the sky looked like it could soak us or dust us whenever it felt like it. It was a thick gray and we could hear echoes of thunder and lightning bouncing off the hidden peaks above us. The three kids with me picked up their pace but still weren't setting any records. Carl eventually got a burst of energy and disappeared ahead of us, but Joy and Ethan were content to shift into their lowest gear and spin up the mountain.

Ethan, whose back tended to tighten up on big climbs, would pull over to the side of the road every mile or so to stretch his muscles, and Joy and I would hold his bike as he laid himself down on a bed of pine needles. Bringing his skinny legs over and behind the top of his head, he'd hold his position for about thirty seconds, roll back over and stand up. Then, dusting himself off, he would run back over to his bike, sigh, "That's better," and continue up the switchbacks.

"Hey John, I think the same person who named Craters of the Moon must have named The Sawtooth Mountains," said Heather as all of us caught our breaths after descending Galena Summit.

"Yeah, these mountains are incredible," agreed Jimmy. "They look like a giant handsaw leaning against the sky. Only the saw is green and gold . . . . "

"That's what I meant," continued Heather. "Craters of the Moon looked just like the moon, and the Sawtooth Mountains look just like a saw."

We made our first overnight stop after Ketchum at a wonderfully isolated community of cabins and campgrounds at Redfish Lake. Another aptly named spot, it was named for the scarlet salmon that come home to spawn there. We found an old log cabin near the lodge and treated ourselves to a night of burritos and journal writing in front of our own crackling fireplace. Hot chocolate and roasted marshmallows easily made up for our cabin's rustic lack of a television.

"Hey John, what was William Swain doin' about now? We haven't heard from him since the middle of Wyoming?" asked Carl, giving us our topic for the night's meeting.

"Yeah, let's hear about ole William tonight," said Jimmy. "Didn't you say that his train tried to take some short cuts that weren't quite so short?"

"Yup, Swain and his buddies were struggling across a lot of high desert south of here in northern Utah and Nevada." I got out our United States map that showed Swain's route in yellow and ours in orange. "Just about now they were following the Humbolt River."

"Wasn't that the river they said was like a mixture of horse urine and salt, and didn't some pioneers call it the Humbug River?" Carl laughed as he remembered the description he had read back in social studies class.

"Good memory, Carl. The Humbolt doesn't sound like a real scenic spot. That's one of the reasons why we parted company with Swain back in Wyoming. Listen to his description of life on the Humbolt:

> "September 20. 'A man can get used to anything' is an old saying, the truth of which is pretty clearly demonstrated on this journey. . . . We have seen a man eating his lunch, gravely sitting on the carcass of a dead horse. And we frequently take our meals amidst the effluvia of a hundred putrescent carcasses. . . . We see some of the most grotesque figures, living caricatures of the human species, some of them mounted on poor, dusty looking mules, others on miserable looking worn down horses, all dressed in dusty ragged clothes, as most of us are. Well, they say misery loves company, so we can have some enjoyment after all, for there is plenty of that kind of company here."

"Sounds pretty bad," said Joy. "What is eff-whatever you said, and what does putre-something mean?"

"You mean 'effluvia' and 'putrescent'?"

"Yeah."

From the look on Jimmy's face when Joy asked her question, I could tell he had a good idea about the meaning of those two words. Teenage boys usually have excellent vocabularies when it comes to describing the grossities of life, and Jimmy was no exception. In fact, he had one of the best such vocabularies I had ever been associated with.

"Hey James, you look like you know. How would you like to give Joy some definitions?"

"Well, John, as long as you won't get mad."

"Just try and keep it clean," I suggested.

"I don't know . . . that's gonna be tough in this case, considering the two words." Jimmy sounded like he had the right meanings.

"Well, just do your best."

"Okay, let's see now . . . first I'll start with 'putrescent.' It means something that is rotting and smells really bad, I mean REALLY bad like . . . well, you know what like."

"Good job, James, you're doing great. Keep going."

"Well, this next one's gonna be really tough . . . 'effluvia' . . . Well, you know how Swain always uses big words when he could just as easily get away with words much smaller and simpler? Well, 'effluvia' is the stuff that comes out of humans or animals' rear ends . . . you know shi—I mean poop. It's usually used for sick animals or people and sometimes refers to the stuff that comes out of their mouth when they're really sick. So Swain is describing some pretty funky, smelly stuff they had their lunch in."

"And I thought we had it pretty bad sometimes," sighed Joy.

"Listen to this, you guys," I continued. "It wasn't written by William, but this guy in his train named McKinstry was taking some journal time, somewhere along the Humbug, and another guy comes up to him and says:

'My God, McKinstry, why do you write about this trip so you can remember it? All I hope is to get home alive as soon as possible so I can forget it!'

"It sure doesn't sound like they were having much fun," said Heather. "Didn't they ever get a chance to enjoy themselves?"

"Well, I've got a reading that doesn't come from the Humbolt, but it talks about some evening entertainment."

"Read it to us, John," requested Joy.

"Okay, here it is:

> "June 21. When we halt at night, we are usually too tired for games or sport of any kind. We smoke our pipes, talk when we feel like it, and before we examine the Odometer, we do some guessing about the number of miles made during the day. In true American fashion, if we have anything to bet, and there is sometimes a little extra tobacco, we back our opinions regarding the speed of the train with a wager. This is about the extent of our gaiety."

"Well, we're kinda like that too," said Joy. "We don't bet tobacco, but sometimes we do try and guess hundred mile marks and we do play cards for extra cookies or who has to do the dishes."

"Speaking of which, how 'bout a little game of 'Hearts' after we write in our journals?" suggested Jimmy. "For tomorrow's breakfast dishes."

"Yeah, let's finish up, I'm feeling lucky tonight," grinned Carl. Soon our journals were put away, and, in the flickering orange glow of our fireplace, we sat on the floor dealing cards and trying to shoot-the-moon. When the fire burned so low we could hardly see anymore, and when droopy eyes and minds started to fade, we added up our points and awarded the next morning's kitchen duties to a rather bewildered Ethan, who hadn't quite seemed to catch on to the finer points of playing Hearts yet. He was still asking questions when he crawled under the covers between Jimmy and Carl.

"YAHOO, PARTY TIME!" I heard Jimmy singing with delight from the small bathroom of our cabin. "Good bye, James, my boy; hello, James, my man." Jimmy seemed to be very pleased with himself for some reason that morning, and his gleeful chuckles echoed through the thin bathroom door. I sat on the edge of my bed trying to imagine what was so exciting in there. Jimmy continued hooting and sang a few verses from a song I was too old to recognize, and when he euphorically strolled out of the bathroom, he was surprised to see me watching him.

"Sounds like you were having a pretty good time in there, my friend. What happened? Did you get another pimple?"

"No, better than that, John. And we don't call them 'pimples', we call them 'zits.' Get with it, man." Jimmy was never very shy about his quest for manhood, and I could tell I would be getting a full report on his progress that morning.

"I am very proud to report that James West, right here this very morning at Redfish Lake Cabins, discovered a major patch of hair underneath both of his arms. It's as if I became a man overnight, and I think, in all due respect to this major event, that it is time for the members of this bike trip to call me by my proper and more mature name. I would like everyone to now call me 'James', not 'Jimmy'."

I nodded my head silently, trying to contain the laughter threatening to explode from my insides, and Jimmy, oblivious to the humor in his pronouncement, lifted his arm and continued, "Here, John, check this out."

He was right, it wasn't the indistinguishable growth of peach fuzz that he had had me inspect many times before. He did have some legal-size black hairs. I promised I would try and do my best to respect his request for a name change, but I still tend to call him "Jimmy."

"I think the trip you're taking these kids on is great. I loved talking to the two girls — weren't their names Joy and Heather? — they told us about all the people you've met and all the places you've seen. And the way you're following that pioneer's journal and writing your own . . . but what about school?"

I was talking with the couple in the campsite next to ours. Heather, who had taken over Lynn's duties as the manager of our budget book, had informed me that our budget really couldn't afford two nights in a cabin, so, after Ethan finished the dishes, we moved our stuff into the campgrounds nearby. The boys were wading in the lake and the girls were in their tents eating two pounds of M&M's, while I visited with the young couple from Boise. I was looking forward to visiting with them because they looked like people whom I'd have much in common with. They were my age, and appeared to be married for about as long as Lynn and me. They wore the same brand of shirts, sandals and shorts that were Lynn's and my daily uniforms back home in California, and I was enjoying our conversation, when they asked a question that had been popping up lately when we met people — a question I didn't think would come from them: "But what about school?"

"Are the kids getting some sort of credit for this trip?" they continued. "Will they be be making up all the work at school they are missing? Isn't six weeks away from school a lot of time?"

And they had looked so cool . . . like they would immediately understand how much more important than any textbook or classroom our trip across America was. So many folks who didn't look half so hip had seemed to understand how important a little horse sense was, how much more could be learned from seeing the land and meeting its people than reading some textbook's watered down version. A rather round redneck in Arkansas had seen that, and so had a barefoot, bearded Amish man, who had stopped going to the schoolhouse when he was thirteen. Our friend, Gordon, although he admitted "not being very schooled", never once worried about the kids falling behind in their books. But because we were entering the sacred month of September — or maybe because we were getting close to cities — people began asking us about "all the school we were missing." Each time I heard that question, my heart dropped like a stone, and I was ashamed to be a "teacher."

When people first started asking us, I would take over the conversation and justify our journey by explaining about how the kids were keeping daily journals and figuring out our budget; how we had two bike computers that we played math games with; and that we were reading an old pioneer's journal. Then as I listened to myself, and played back the wisdom of Johnny Carroll and Jacob and Gordon and all the other people of the heartland who had winked at us in understanding, I suddenly became angry, because I felt myself explaining away the real lessons and fruits of our labor. I wished my college educated and citified colleagues and fellow citizens could break out of their modern day mindset that the only place we learn things is in some classroom with four walls and a chalkboard and some teacher at the head of the class. If it wasn't in a book, forget it and if it was, learn it for the exam and then forget it. Grades, grade point averages and levels were more important than real people, real places and real interactions. We even met a drunk in front of a suburban supermarket who asked me from his place against the wall: "How come these kids ain't in school?" And as I shook my head and we followed a schoolbus out of the shopping center, I wanted to let all the air out of its tires so the local kids would get to see what it was like to walk to their school; it was such a beautiful day. I contained myself though, because their teacher probably would have been very upset at their tardiness.

I finished talking with the Boise couple and tried not to seem too upset at their question. I didn't try to justify our trip with any academic jargon describing our daily activities. I was still glad that I got to talk to them and glad they got a chance to meet my kids. I just hoped that someday they might stumble across some "uneducated" countryboy or enlightened plowman who might make them pause and think twice about what they'd like their kids to learn and remember some day. I shook their hands good-bye, asked them if they knew of any more good camping spots between Redfish and Boise, and then returned to our camp.

"Melts in your mouth, not on your journal," giggled Joy from inside the girls' tent.

I let out a long sigh and listened to Joy and Heather reading their journals to each other. Then I looked over at the boys studying the lake and the best way to skip a rock. "Hey ladies, you got any more of those M&M's?" I asked, walking closer to their tent.

"Sure, John, they're scattered all over the floor, just a second," answered Heather in her usual perky voice. "We're getting pretty full now anyway."

Heather's hand reached out of the tent handing me my candy, and I looked up at the sky and thanked God for my kids and my teachers. If it was okay with Him, it was okay with me to have M&M's scattered on my classroom floor.

"No brains, no headaches," exclaimed Carl, as I watched our frying pan and its *huevos rancheros* breakfast fly slow-motion through the air above our stove and then land with a splashing splat all over my shoes and the ground around them. One of my mom's favorite expressions had become our description of any clumsy or bonehead maneuver, and, that morning, at Warm Springs Campground, the kids—especially Carl—enjoyed using it on me.

We had passed over Banner Summit after leaving Redfish Lake and come around another aptly named place in central Idaho called Cape Horn. Heading southwest toward Boise, we were planning on spending our last three days in the mountains of Idaho, following the Payette River as it descended into the Snake, near the state capitol. We had bought frozen eggs, tortillas, cheese, salsa and even fresh tomatoes at the market in Stanley, and had planned on celebrating our first hot springs of the trip with our favorite breakfast.

"Yeah John, no brains, no headaches," giggled Joy, as she pretended not to hear the single syllable word beginning with the letters 's-h-' that had burst from my lips when our breakfast spread itself all over my shoelaces. Jimmy tried not to pretend he hadn't heard my choice of words, and he winked his approval before surveying the damage.

"Looks like another *From Sea to Shining Sea* creative breakfast," suggested Heather. "I say we make *quesadillas* (tortillas filled with melted cheese) and cinnamon tortillas."

"Hope the bears like Mexican eggs," said Jimmy. "Cinnamon tortillas sound good to me. Do we have any oatmeal left?"

As usual, the kids made the best of the situation and we had a bright side breakfast before hiking up the canyon to the hot springs. After about a half-mile of hiking and anticipation, the trees cleared and we saw clouds of steam leaking from the gray rock hillside ahead. Underneath the clouds, large patches of green moss and algae could be seen shining under the curtains of water that shimmered down the rock faces and into the river.

Sitting on top of one large boulder was an old wood structure that looked like an outhouse. We walked over to discover that it was actually a bathroom in the truest sense. Someone had brought in wood and nails and constructed a bath house complete with tub and hot and cold running water. Pipes ran down from the hillside, and out of one ran ice cold water and out of the other ran steaming hot water from the springs. The temperature was controlled by a beer can placed on the end of each pipe. When you rotated the cans, hot and cold water gurgled out and into the wooden tub. Carl immediately stripped to his shorts and decided to be the first one of us to take a bath. Ethan, Jimmy, the girls and I decided to explore the hot springs closer to the stream. We hiked down the hill and found three large pools with several steaming hot waterfalls splashing into them.

"Man, these look better than the bathhouse," exclaimed Jimmy.

"Hey John, come and feel this," yelled an excited Heather. "Each of the three pools is a different temperature! The one closest to the cliff is the hottest and the one closest to the river is the coolest." Our two little Goldilockses had their shoes off and were testing the tubs.

"Aren't you supposed to go skinny dipping at a hot springs?" asked Ethan.

"Yeah, that is a tradition in many hot spring lovers circles," I answered.

"Well . . . I think I have a way where we can all go skinny dipping and nobody will get embarrassed," Ethan continued. "The girls can walk in backwards; the boys can walk in frontwards; and we'll go in first."

Ethan seemed very confident of his plan, but not seeing the world through exactly his perspective, the rest of us needed an instant replay.

"Uh, excuse me, Ethan, but could you run that by us again?" I asked, as Heather, Joy, and Jimmy wrinkled their foreheads along with me.

"Well . . . uh . . . it's really simple. The girls walk in backwards . . . The boys will walk in frontwards . . . And we'll go in first." Ethan smiled proudly at his plan, but the kids and I still couldn't quite picture it.

"Eeth, you're spaced," observed a thoroughly confused Jimmy. "Your plan may work fine, but, for the life of me, I can't figure it out." Joy and Heather were repeating Ethan's plan over and over to themselves, but it looked like they were just getting more confused. My brain was drawing all kinds of diagrams but was getting about as far as the girls.

"Well, you guys can go skinny-dipping if you want, but Stick and me, I think we'll just keep our suits on," announced Heather. Ethan looked disappointed that no one seemed able to visualize his plan, but he just shrugged his shoulders and walked over by the girls to test the three pools.

"Promise not to look if we decide to?" asked Jimmy, who seemed to be very worried.

"What's there to look at, Jimmy?" laughed Joy.

Jimmy didn't answer, and Joy and Heather headed off to do some more exploring while the guys and I laid our shorts on the bank and went to bathe in our birthday suits. Carl must have heard our moans and groans of pleasure as we lowered ourselves into the hottest pool, because he came running down the hill to join us. The steaming water rose up to our shoulders as we sat on the smooth hot rocks at the bottom or our tub.

"You know what, guys? I think we should go rinse ourselves in the river after we soak here for awhile."

"You're crazy, John," said Carl. "That water is freezing!"

"Aw c'mon, what's the matter? You guys wimps or something?" I knew the 'wimps' part would get them.

"Alright, but only if you go first," answered Jimmy. "That way you'll not only be the first one to freeze, but also, if the girls are spying on us, they'll see you first."

The water was freezing, but the girls weren't spying, so the guys and I spent the next half hour going back and forth from the hot tub to the freezing river, yelling and screaming and hooting so that the entire canyon echoed with our hollers. I even managed to grab my camera on one of our journeys and snapped a wonderful slide of Jimmy's and Ethan's posteriors for posterity. The girls never peeked, but my camera did.

Joy's parents were planning to meet us for their final rendezvous in Boise, and in one of our Idaho phone conversations, Sulie had asked me if we could "see the barn yet." I wasn't sure if the kids were looking homeward yet, but on the road leading out of our hot springs campground, I heard the kids talking about redecorating their bedrooms, reserving school lockers, and wondering what their friends were doing in algebra class. I followed behind, trying to ignore their conversation and tried to let the deep, turquoise waters of the Payette winding beside us hypnotize me away from thoughts of our journey's end; but still I couldn't seem to block out the kids' conversation. Finally, an hour before I had originally planned to stop for lunch, I pulled us over to a spectacular overlook of the river and told the kids to unpack the peanut butter and jelly.

"Do you guys mind if I give a little sermon before we eat?" I asked, as the kids sat in a circle in the pine needles.

"Sure John, go ahead," said Jimmy. "What's the matter?" All five of them got quiet and turned their eyes toward me as I sat down to join them.

"Thanks, you guys . . . Does anyone remember where our 1500-mile mark was?"

"I think it was somewhere in Tennessee," answered Carl. "Why?"

"Do you guys remember all the things we saw in those first 1500 miles?"

"Yeah," answered Joy. "We met all kinds of people. The Amish and the black guy with the wrench and we saw the Blue Ridge Parkway and Virginia and the Chesapeake Bay and all the dogs and friendly people in Tennessee."

"And we went to Williamsburg and we met Merle," added Heather.

"And the black guys and the waitress at that Hardees and the Smokey Mountains and all the churches we stayed at," said Carl.

"Okay, okay, good you guys," I interrupted. "Guess how many miles we have left to go?"

"Uh . . . About 1500?" answered Ethan.

"Right. Just about 1500, and I'm worried that we might miss out on a lot of America if we don't give these last ones a chance."

"What do you mean, John?" asked Joy.

"Well, the closer we get to home the harder it is I think for us to not start just thinking about getting home and all the things that are waiting there for us. School and clothes and books and lockers and stuff like that. There are still 1500 miles of people and places and adventures ahead of us, and if all we think about is home in those miles, we'll miss out on a lot. I don't think you guys would want to throw out all the things that happened to us in the first 1500 miles, and I think that, once you're back home and you have your lockers and your bedrooms and your algebra books, you'd be really upset if I let you pass up the 1500 we still have ahead of us.

"I know how much you guys love your friends and your families and everything, and don't get me wrong, I think that's great. But don't miss out on the next five weeks by having your minds walking through your bedroom or through some textbook. It won't be long until you are home and this trip will be over, and you may never get out here again. Home and school aren't going anywhere and they'll be waiting for us when we get there; but everyday, out here on the road, miles and people are passing behind us we might never get to see again. Let's not miss out on them, okay?

"I'm sorry if I'm sounding heavy and everything, but when I heard you guys talking about the school lockers, back there when we were riding along such a beautiful stretch of road, I got really scared. I'd never heard you guys talk like that, and I just had to stop us.

"Just think of the kids back at school, and where their minds will be after they've been in school for about a week and the old routines are back in motion. Where do you think they would rather be — in the classroom, or out here taking a shower under a hot waterfall?"

"I'm sorry, John," said Joy with a sad face. "You're right about everything being there when we get back. It's kinda like Barbara and Larry in *Miles From Nowhere*. Their book seemed to end so fast. All of a sudden it was over, and I was kinda sad they weren't still on the road."

"Yeah, like Christmas," said Jimmy. "You can't wait for Christmas and opening presents and everything, and then before you know it it's Christmas Day night and everything is over. It's kinda sad. You've opened all your presents and everything, but you know there won't be another Christmas for another year. Getting home will be exciting and everything, but it will mean that the trip is over. And there won't be another one in three hundred and sixty-five days either. I think I'll stop worrying about my locker and what I'm missing in Latin class, and get into Idaho, Oregon and California. Sorry, dude."

"I'm sorry, you guys, for another one of my lectures, but I just had to say something. You guys know I love you more than I can say, and I'm gonna really miss you when this thing is over. I'd really be mad at myself if I didn't help you get the most out of the trip. It's okay to talk about home and school sometimes. Shoot, I still talk about Lynn, 'cause I love her and miss her a lot, but she'd be mad at me if I spent all of the next three states thinking about her. Let's see how many more neat people and places we can discover in the last part of our journey, and let's not have the last chapters of our book end too quickly, okay?"

"Okay," nodded my five senators.

We ate a rather quiet lunch that morning, and, before leaving, we all paired up and gave each other neck and shoulder massages, as we listened to the Payette crashing over rocks and making a sharp westward turn below us.

It didn't take long for the kids to take our discussion to heart. We were climbing the corkscrew of road that wound up into the mountains above the little town of Lowman and I was following behind Ethan. We had spread ourselves apart and were silently climbing towards the summit, when I noticed a red-tailed hawk perched on a bare branch that overhung one of our steeper switchbacks. Almost close enough to touch, he watched each of the kids, as each of the kids watched him. Slowly making their turn around him, they smiled and talked with the big bird sharing their mountain. My five senators were back in Idaho again, and I thanked Mr. Hawk as I passed by him, happily bringing up the rear.

"Man, I can't believe it," Ethan shook his head as he walked over to the table at our campsite.

"The ranger said urinating under a tree is a hundred dollar fine, but have you ever tried to stop in mid wiz?" giggled Carl. "I thought the voice behind us this morning was kidding anyway, so I just kept wizzing. When I turned around to see this very serious looking ranger, I got kinda embarrassed, and then he repeated his warning. I freaked."

"Can you imagine a fine for wizzing?" Jimmy laughed in disbelief. "I wonder if they fine the bears . . . ."

"Are fines for wizzing in public covered in our budget, John?" laughed Carl. The kids were well trained in the etiquette of outdoor potties — the guys even perfected a technique for emptying their bladders without getting off their bikes — it involved good knowledge of wind direction and good balance — and they just couldn't believe being told they couldn't water a tree.

"Yeah . . . I wonder if the ranger takes Master Charge. . . ," laughed Ethan.

"I . . . I hate to change the subject, gentlemen, but where are the girls?"

"Oh, they took off early this morning to go exploring," said Jimmy. They didn't want to hear about our encounter with the ranger — something about it 'serving us right' and us being gross — so they grabbed their cameras and headed up the creek to take some pictures . . . I think they're just jealous."

"Yeah, Joy fell in the creek again and soaked her second pair of shoes," laughed Ethan. "And Heather's only pair are still wet from their hike last night."

"We may be gross, but those two . . . they're nuts," exclaimed Carl. "They're always off exploring and taking pictures or writing things down in their journals. Man, John, you should have heard those two squishing off through the creek with their soaked shoes. By the time we get to Boise today, their feet are going to be either freezing cold or all puckered up from all that water in their shoes."

"Yeah, but I bet you they'll both be smiling either way," Jimmy said, shaking his head. "I wonder how they do it. I'm no grouch, but those two . . . they're always smiling."

As it turned out, Joy and Heather weren't the only two with frozen feet and puckered toes that day. Instead of growing lighter that morning, the sky thickened to block out the sun, and, just as we got ready to ride out of camp, it began to rain. We paused to pull on our rain gear from head to toe, and by the time we rolled into Idaho City, it looked as if all of us had fallen into the girls' creek.

The evergreen trees disappeared just south of Idaho City, and we entered a new landscape of chocolate brown ravines and ochre canyons. We screamed down towards Arrow Rock Reservoir, just outside of Boise, as a convoy of pickup trucks streamed up into the mountains, each carrying chain saws and tarps to cut firewood for the winter.

"Hey John, they even work on weekends in Idaho," said Carl at one of our water stops. "Everywhere, except in Southern California, people seem to be getting ready for the next season . . . gathering feed and grain, canning fruit and vegetables and now cutting firewood. I wonder when they get time to mess around."

"Yeah, back home I'd be riding my skateboard or going to the beach," said Ethan.

"That's because we hardly have any seasons," said Heather. "Where we live it's usually pretty warm, and we can usually get almost any kind of food year-round from the supermarket."

"Most other places in America, people have to worry about the weather," said Joy. "People say they worry about earthquakes in California, but we don't have earthquakes every year like they have blizzards, and floods and tornadoes and stuff. We hardly ever have lightning, and almost everyday of the year we can wear shorts. Most other places it's freezing cold in the winter and hot and sticky in the summer. I think I would like to live in a place where they had seasons, though."

"Uh . . . I don't know about me," said Ethan, deep in thought. "With seasons, I don't think I would be riding my skateboard as much."

"Yeah Eeth, it's pretty tough to skateboard with a chain saw," laughed Jimmy.

"Or in the snow and ice," added Carl.

Ethan got quiet again and didn't say a word until we reached the Boise City Limits, miles later:

"Uh . . . you know what, you guys?"

"What Eeth?"

"Well . . . I'm appreciating California more and more every day."

"One more state, dude," grinned Jimmy.

15

The top looked like it was just around the bend about three times, but it really wasn't. The downhill was pretty bad because of the wind and rain . . . My red gloves were collecting water and made my hands colder every time a raindrop fell on them. My legwarmers got cold and wet and my feet were cold and soaked . . . .

Carl's Journal
September 17, 1986

Stinking Water

"Hey John, I thought Oregon would have a much cooler sign than this," Ethan said, shaking his head. "My family goes to Oregon all the time, and it always seemed like a beautiful place to me. I figured they would have a sign with mountains and trees and ferns, and all kinds of green plants and things."

A morning's ride west of Boise, the plain green and white sign had said:

WELCOME TO OREGON

No sunflowers like on the Kansas sign, or covered wagon like on the one welcoming us to Nebraska — just green and white letters. Coming from California, and constantly hearing how beautiful their northern neighbor was, the kids were a bit surprised at both the sign and the land beyond it.

"The sign's not the only thing that is dull around here," observed Carl. "I don't see anything green except for it, and those mountains way out there ahead look pretty dry to me. I thought it was supposed to rain all the time in Oregon."

Jimmy winced when he heard Carl say that. In four months of riding, he had learned not to dare the sky.

Both Jimmy's respect for the sky and the purported wetness of our new state were confirmed just after lunch that afternoon as we headed over Carl's "dry" mountains. The sky of Oregon turned from blue to gray to charcoal, and all of us finished that day in full rain gear as the Oregon state birds — the clouds — pelted us with big drops of rain. Little did we know that for the rest of the week, the Oregon sky would live up to its reputation and keep us soaking wet.

Our first Oregon campsite was behind a long-since-closed little store in a deserted cow pasture, scattered with lots of cow leftovers. We pitched our tents carefully and walked gingerly around our camp that had two new members. Joy's folks had returned for their third and final rendezvous and would be riding alongside us across Oregon in their truck.

With the added food and energy the Fultons always supplied, I figured we could do some long days across the high desert of southeastern Oregon. That first day we had done 92 miles, with Bob and Sulie cheering out of their pickup

374

and making us the best picnic lunch any pioneer ever had.

Tuesday morning, Bob and I woke up at dawn in our pasture campsite to roust the kids. As I stretched my neck out of the entrance to my tent, I was immediately greeted with "Oregon Sunshine." Drops of rain danced off my head and down my neck. Waking up to a wet sky wasn't our favorite way to start a day, but, nonetheless, the kids rolled out of their tents and packed up their sleeping bags and soggy tents cheerfully, as Bob and Sulie tried to keep breakfast from floating away.

"You guys want us to take your gear in the back of the truck?" asked Sulie. Bob stood next to her over the pan of scrambled eggs, and I saw him look over at me, curious for an answer.

"Are you kidding?" shouted Carl. "You and Bob can carry extra food and your gear, but we carry our own stuff. Heck, I've even got some tortillas and fig bars I'm still carrying."

"Yeah, and I've got some salsa," smiled Ethan.

"Hey Bob," Jimmy laughed, walking over and nudging him on the shoulder. "Are you sure your truck can handle carrying everything? . . . I mean, if it gets too heavy, we'd be glad to carry some of the stuff on our bikes."

"Well, thank you, James," answered Bob, putting his arm around a wet Jimmy. "But I think the old truck can handle it."

"Like I said," Jimmy continued, "just let us know if we can help."

"I'll do that, Jimmy, and you know what, there is something you can help me with. I've got this pan full of eggs and potatoes that's gettin' awful done and awful heavy. What do ya say you guys sit down and eat?"

"We'll be right over as soon as we get our tent and sleeping bags strapped to our bikes," answered Carl. "Can those eggs wait that long?"

Bob smiled over at the boys and winked over at me. "You bet they can."

As we ate, the rain turned from mist to drizzle to drops, and by the time we rolled out of the pasture, we were all decked out in rain pants, rain jackets, wool gloves and wool socks. It was seven o'clock, and our tentative destination, Burns, Oregon was one hundred and twelve miles away.

By noon, we had sloshed our way over fifty miles to Juntura, where we had our lunch at a roadside cafe. Gloves and socks were heavy with water; yellow rain suits were gritty and black from all the grease, gravel and mud splashed upon us by cars and semis; and runny noses dripped on pink faces, as the kids parked their bikes and slowly walked inside the warm coffee shop.

"I'll take a cup of coffee and a cup of hot chocolate," Jimmy motioned the waitress before sitting down.

"Yes, may I have that too?" asked Joy, as she sat down in the puddle she created on her seat.

"Coffee *and* hot chocolate?" asked the waitress.

"Yup, one cup for each hand," answered Jimmy. "I don't know if I'll ever be able to squeeze again, they're so frozen. I need those two cups to thaw me out."

"And we also like to make chocolate mocha," smiled Joy. "But not until after we thaw out."

It was two cups of something steaming all around, as the kids ordered anything and everything hot on the menu. By the time we finished eating, a small lake had formed beneath our table, and a high-rise city of plates was stacked on top of it.

Outside the rain had continued to come down, but the kids just put their wet, but warm, gloves and shoes back on, remounted their bikes and headed west.

"Got your watches ready, everybody?" asked Heather.

"I've got mine," shouted Jimmy from the front.

"I've got mine too," smiled Joy, holding her wrist in the air.

"We've got ours on our wrists and on our computers," added Ethan and Carl just ahead of me. The kids had a date with the Pacific Time Zone, ten miles up the road, and they weren't going to let any rain keep them from it.

"It was really weird, John. I was just kinda staring at Heather's rear tire in front of me, when I saw this big, black bubble form. Then all of a sudden it just got bigger and bigger and exploded right in front of me. I was so surprised to watch it all happen, that I couldn't even say anything 'til after it went boom . . . ." Joy shook her head as we all stood around Heather's bike to inspect the damage.

"Hey John, it looks like Wyoming revisited," sighed Jimmy, shaking his head. "It's got a slit, just like before. I thought this was her *new* tire."

"Yeah, so did I," I moaned, looking at the all too familiar looking inch- long gash.

"Well, at least it's stopped raining," said you-know-who.

The Oregon sky did manage to stop raining just long enough for me to change Heather's tube and form a new casing with duct tape for her tire. Eastern Oregon was about as desolate as Wyoming, and I had the strangest feeling that, even with the Fulton mobile nearby, I would be spending a lot of time with Heather's rear tire in the next five days.

About five minutes after we got back on the road, the sky grayed over and continued its wet performance:

"Isn't it neat how the sky sounds whenever it rains like this?" Heather, unaffected by the bumpy ride created by my tire surgery, was just in front of me, talking with Joy.

"Yeah, it sounds just like the clouds or the angels or whoever lives up there is clapping . . . Like we're on a stage and hundreds of people are clapping for us."

I didn't say anything, but the sky did sound just like the girls described. And with the riding the kids did that day, they deserved a standing ovation from every cloud and angel stationed above Oregon.

We passed mile 75 at about three o'clock atop Drinkwater Pass (elevation:

4230 feet). Still damp and cold from the rain, we tried to warm ourselves with the hot chocolate the Fultons had waiting for us in the back of their truck. The kids, still decked out in wool and nylon, seemed undaunted by the rain, but, with Stinkingwater Pass another thousand feet up and the horizon looming even blacker, I wondered how much they had left. We still had forty miles to go before we planned on sleeping.

"Hey John, can we ride ahead and meet you at the top of Stinkingwater Pass?" asked a half-thawed and confident Jimmy.

"Yeah, us too," agreed Joy. "I feel really strong after the hot chocolate and bananas. We'll wait for you guys at the summit. Thanks Mom and Dad."

Before I knew it, Jimmy, Joy and Heather disappeared down the mountain. Ethan and Carl, less revitalized from our rest stop, took a much slower pace than their friends.

At the bottom of Stinkingwater Pass, the balcony filled with more clouds and applauding angels as the rain came down louder and harder. Ethan got a sudden burst of energy and shot ahead, disappearing into the large gray cloud. Carl slowed down and began to moan as the rain saturated his gloves. Soon both of us entered the cloud to see our breaths turn into clouds themselves, smoking out of our mouths and nostrils. I kinda liked acting like a fire breathing dragon as we climbed, but from the look on Carl's face, he wasn't the least bit amused.

Sometime in between my puffing and Carl's pouting, the rain turned into hail. The clapping clouds and angels turned into a bunch of drummers pinging our helmets and pitting our skin with frozen pellets. I rode up alongside Carl to see how he was doing. He looked over at me and I could see drops of tears had joined the flow of water down his rosy-red face.

"Hey John, I hurt real bad." Carl winced at me as he spoke, and then he returned his gaze to the road. He continued up the mountain, further into the cloud.

A biting wind joined the hail about a half-mile from the top, and as I cheered Carl on, I wondered how the rest of the gang was doing. At their pace, they were probably an easy fifteen or twenty minutes ahead of us, and if they'd stopped at the summit, they were probably freezing by now. When Carl and I reached the top, my fears were relieved when I saw Jimmy, Joy, Heather and Ethan huddled around their bikes dancing and bear hugging each other.

"All right, Carl, way to go!" they all yelled, running down the road to escort us to the top.

"Wasn't that hail neat?" said Heather.

"Didn't you like the sound of it bouncing off your helmet?" asked Joy. "I was getting kinda tired of the rain."

Our four fearless leaders immediately hopped on their bikes and headed down the other side of Stinkingwater Pass. They didn't want to give Carl a chance to freeze on the lonely mountaintop.

"Hey John, how much farther to Burns?" asked Jimmy.

"Oh, not much further," I lied. My map said twenty-seven miles, my watch said 6:30, and the oncoming cars, with their headlights and windshield wipers on, said we were in for some wet darkness if we were going to try and make Burns that night. "Just keep riding, you guys, you're doing great." I don't know what was going through my mind at that point. I knew how dangerous riding in the dark was and had been for us, and riding twenty-five more miles in a freezing rain storm was definitely crazy.

"How are you guys doing?" came the familiar voice from the blue pick-up that pulled alongside us just outside Buchanan, Oregon. It was Sulie and Bob in the Fulton-mobile. "You guys are looking pretty good. We found a motel in Burns complete with jacuzzi, color TV and pizza. Think you guys can make it?"

I don't know whether it was the jacuzzi, the TV or the pepperoni, but suddenly the kids speeded up. The sun set quietly behind a black wall of clouds ahead of us, and I prayed that visions of sitting in steaming hot water in front of the tube, eating endless slices of pizza, could carry us through the darkness.

"Hey Bob, how much further to heaven?" asked a smiling Jimmy.

"Please lie, Bob," I prayed. I had learned to tell the kids it was much shorter than it really was whenever they asked me "how much further?" It was much better to blame the map and be called a liar at the end of a day than to tell the kids how far they really had to go.

"Only twenty-three more miles to go." I winced as Bob made his all-too-honest announcement. He could have at least said twenty, and I would have probably gone for twelve or fifteen, but he smiled as he rode alongside us. The group looked back at me in disbelief at the number of miles that still lay ahead.

Bob and Sulie had raced off-road in Baja California and knew what it was like to test their physical limits. Many parents would have stopped the ride much earlier that day — throwing bikes in ditches, kids in the truck, and me in jail; but the Fultons recognized a determined look in their daughter and her friends and decided to encourage us to Burns.

The rain began again shortly after dark, and we all donned our flashing tail lights to be able to see each other in the blur. The Fulton-mobile turned on its high beams and flashers behind us and lit our road the best it could. Jimmy rode point, followed by Joy, Heather, Ethan, Carl and me, and soon I could hear everyone but Carl singing, "*One hundred bottles of beer on the wall* . . ." It took about twenty bottles per mile as the rain continued coming down harder and harder. Whenever a car or semi would pass us, a giant plume of water would spray us with rode grit and make it even more difficult to see, but Joy was still able to play Bright Side.

"Did you guys see how that truck's headlights lit up the water? It was really neat . . . like a rainbow that glows in the dark!" Something had gotten into Joy that night and, next to Jimmy, she was the strongest rider on the road. She was our main cheerleader, talking to everyone about pizza flavors and telling us how great we were all doing. "I can't believe we're doing this, you guys! Remember when we used to have trouble doing fifty miles in the sunshine back in California!"

Despite Joy's best attempts at encouragement, poor Carl seemed to be succumbing to the cold and wet darkness. There wasn't an ounce of fat to insulate his wiry body, and, as I rode alongside him at the back, I noticed that he was shivering more and more each half-mile.

"John, I really don't think I can make it. I hurt all over."

"C'mon, Carl, you can do it. We only have fifteen more miles to go."

"Yeah John, I know your fifteen miles; it's probably more like twenty. My hands are so frozen that I can hardly hold onto my handlebars, and my feet can't even feel my pedals." Lynn and I had pushed Carl beyond what he thought he could do many other times in the trip, and for the next five miles I pushed Carl on with equal doses of encouraging words and harsh orders. Finally about 8 o'clock, with ten miles to go, Carl pulled over to the side of the road in the darkness and collapsed in tears, laying his head on his handlebars.

"I'm sorry, you guys, but I just can't go any farther." Carl sobbed as he looked up at the rest of his friends huddled around him.

"Hey, don't worry about it, dude," said Jimmy. "You did the best you could; we'll see you in Burns, man."

Wasting no time, Bob and Sulie lifted a quivering Carl into the cab of the truck, threw "Pack Rat" in the bed and continued following us towards Burns. With five miles to go, we could see the fuzzy blur of lights on the horizon. It was 9 o'clock and Heather and Ethan were about out of gas; only Jimmy and Joy could be heard singing the bottles of beer off the wall. I had no words of encouragement left, as I myself had long since lost the feeling in my fingers and toes, and my body did a little trembling of its own trying to stay warm. Silently, I followed my four kids toward the light.

Three miles from downtown Burns our road joined with Interstate Highway 395, and as we floated to a stop at the intersection, the sky gave us a standing ovation. What had seemed like a downpour the past twenty miles gave way to a cloudburst that sent sheets of water from the sky. We couldn't hear ourselves, and the rain was so thick it was hard to make out the person riding just a few feet ahead of us. Bob and Sulie tried to help us out by clicking on their high beams, but we were only more blinded by their white reflection.

Turning onto 395, we found the road covered with two inches of water, and steering our bikes became a concerted effort. It wasn't long before our first semi blew by and I yelled, "TRUCK!" as loud as I could. The rain drowned out my warning and a blinding wall of water splashed over us as it sped by. Joy may have had some optimistic description of the experience, but if she did I sure didn't hear it. We rode on along Highway-turned-River 395 and finally entered the Burns city limits. Joy's dad clicked his lights off and on and took over the lead, as the street lights did a better job lighting our way. Bob honked when we passed the pizza parlour and then signalled left into the parking lot of our motel.

No sky, no matter how loud, could have drowned out the yells and screams that the five of us let out as we saw Bob pull in that driveway. After his cheer, Jimmy patiently looked both ways before leading us across the four lanes of highway. We pulled outside the doors of heaven and Sulie grabbed up a sleeping Carl and carried him into the guys' room. Soon two steaming showers were filled with frozen kids thawing out after 112 freezing wet miles. Just before she left with Bob to pick up three giant pizzas, Sulie helped Carl off with his shoes and tucked him under the covers of one of the double beds. Carl was too tired, even for pepperoni and Coke, and I tucked him in even tighter as I listened to Joy and Heather describing rooster tail rainbows from their shower in the next room while Ethan and Jimmy continued singing *One Hundred Bottles of Beer on the Wall* from theirs.

"Hey John, you won't believe the dream I had last night," said Heather, as she tried to conquer the mountain of whipped cream on her hot chocolate at breakfast the next morning.

"Oh yeah, Heather, what did you dream about this time?" I asked.

"Well, I hope you don't get mad at me, but I dreamt we were in our motel room, and it was nighttime. In my dream, I woke up to find you moaning and groaning and crawling across the floor in nothing but your underwear."

"Heather, that's really weird," interrupted Joy. "I think you've been on the road too long."

"What was really weird though, John," Heather continued, "was that you would stop every so often and try to touch your toes like you were doing some exercise. It was really strange."

"Heather," said Jimmy, "I think you had too many pieces of pizza last night. That Italian sausage probably got to you."

"Either that, or those mushrooms," laughed Ethan.

Little did Heather know that she actually *had* seen me crawling my way towards the bathroom. Around two in the morning, on what began as a routine trip to the toilet, both of my thighs and both of my calves had tied up in cramps. Heather had seen only half my struggle, and that morning I felt lucky to be alive. I shyly hid behind the sports page as Heather went on to describe her "dream"— and my crawl — in detail to her laughing audience. I decided I'd tell her the truth sometime when she was a little older.

The Oregon sky was abnormally kind to us for most of that day as we rode across more sand and sagebrush, through garden spots named Riley and Wagontire. Late that afternoon, the wind began to howl and the sky thickened to its familiar charcoal gray as we rode our last ten miles in blowing rain and hail. It stopped as we rode into the gravel pit campsite Bob and Sulie had found for us, but the prospects for a dry night didn't look too good. The wind was blowing some nasty looking clouds our way, and with the gravel pit making it impossible to drive our tent stakes into the ground, my final prayer that night was for the assortment of rocks and shoes holding down the corners of our tents to stay put.

I was up long before dawn the next morning, excited that we had been graced with a dry night and at the fact that Lynn would be flying in that afternoon to rendezvous with us for the weekend. I had planned that we'd ride 110 miles to Lakeview, where I would hop in the Fulton's truck and drive to the Reno airport, while the kids and the Fultons took a layover day. Bob and Sulie already had a bottle of champagne chilling in the back of the truck, and with the prospect of a motel for two nights, I figured the kids would have little trouble riding one more long day to Lakeview.

I must have forgotten to pray for the sky's kindness to last into the daylight, because although not a drop of rain had fallen that night, the black clouds had received reinforcements and they filled up the sky in all directions for as far as I could see. The heavens stayed still and dry all the way through breakfast, but as soon as we rolled out onto the highway from behind our mounds of gravel, the wind whistled, the clouds shook and the rain fell in big drops that bounced off our helmets.

"Hey John, do you think we should put on our rain gear?" asked Heather.

"What do you think? Rain jackets and rain pants? Or just jackets?" asked Jimmy.

The kids were already wearing every layer of wool they had. Even before the wind kicked up, camp had been close to freezing. The only skin visible on Ethan was between his eyebrows and the top of his nose. In addition to his wool mittens, legwarmers and socks, he had wrapped his head in a wool scarf that made him look like some bedouin bracing for a sandstorm.

"Well, I think we should go for it all, you guys," I answered. "With the couple of cars that have passed us so far having their headlights still on and the black sky ahead, it looks like we're in for a long day." As I pulled us over to the side of the highway to change, my face must have given away my disappointment.

"Hey John, don't worry, we'll get you to Lakeview this afternoon," said Jimmy, placing his hand on my shoulder. "We won't let a little rain keep you from seeing Lynn."

"Yeah, besides, we want to see her too," said Joy as she zipped up her jacket. "You're not the only one who's missed her."

I wanted to stop and hug each of the kids as they all told me not to worry about the miles ahead, but they wouldn't let me. "Hey John, c'mon, hurry up with your rain pants; we're gonna get you there, but let's not take all day, okay," yelled Carl. "Remember, I don't ride too well after dark."

We weren't on the road but ten minutes when Heather's rear tire exploded with a bang like a gunshot. She flopped over to the side of the road as I waved the rest of the kids to ride on for five more miles. Heather, happily humming another song I didn't know, shifted her bike into tire-changing gear, released her rear brake and got out her spare tube. The cancerous rip in her rear tire had spread beyond my makeshift casing, and I cut out more nylon from my tool kit and tried to keep the duct tape dry enough to rebuild my patch job.

"John, should I fix my tube while you're finishing up?" she asked, interrupting her song.

"Oh, I don't think you'd better in this rain, Heather. According to my map, there's a rest area in ten miles or so. Maybe there we can find some shelter from the rain where you can patch it better."

"Okie dokie," Heather replied before continuing her song and packing her tube in her handlebar bag. The new patch on her tire made her bike thump even more, but still, as I rode behind her, I could see her checking the roadside for new discoveries and hear her singing in the rain.

The rain increased with each mile we traveled that morning, and Heather and I came upon a completely drenched group of friends when we finally caught up with them a half hour later.

"Granola bar, banana and jerky break at the rest area ahead, okay, you guys?" I announced to a less than enthusiastic crew. "Just five more miles."

Silently, except for Joy and Heather's duet, we remounted our bikes and splashed through the steady stream of water covering the highway. There was a rest area five miles down the road, but it consisted only of a few bathroom stalls and some picnic tables covered by awnings of corrugated metal. The wind made those awnings useless, as it whipped the water off the eaves and all over us, but we still stopped for our food break. Between her granola bar and her banana, Heather used me for an umbrella and patched her only spare tube, while the rest of the group alternated eating with blowing into their frozen gloves, hoping to thaw their hands into some workable state. When the food was gone and Heather's tube was patched, we rolled back out into the torrent and proceeded to climb into the clouds that awaited us on Hogback Mountain.

"KAABOOM!" A half-mile into the climb Heather's tire exploded again, and I motioned for all the kids to stop and wait for us this time. Their wet bodies started to shiver as the wind howled down off the mountain. I did my best to repair her tire as fast as I could, but my fingers were hampered by being a bit cold themselves. The skin on my thumb, frozen and hard from all the previous work on Heather's wheel, finally cracked as I hurried to get her tire back on the rim. A deep gash opened alongside my thumbnail, and I sucked the end of my thumb, trying to ignore the pain. Five freezing kids were waiting to get me to Lakeview and all I could do was jam that wheel back up into Heather's bike and hope that the tape I used to patch myself would last along with the tape patching Heather's tire.

I don't know if it was the cold or the rain, but in another half-mile Heather's rear wheel exploded again and so did I.

"Dammit Heather, how can you still be hummin' and smiling?" I yelled as I sucked on my thumb and pulled us over to the side of the road. It was still raining and blowing and the kids hadn't had a chance to build up much heat since our last stop. I was worried about hypothermia as I watched them huddle together, waiting for their steaming leader to patch Heather's tire *and* tube. Between the throbbing pain in my sliced and frozen thumb and my wondering how I was going to fix Heather's tire, I was about at the end of my rope. Before wrapping my crescent wrench around the all-too-familiar bolts on Heather's rear axle, I turned my back on the kids and walked out into the sagebrush, trying to calm myself down. If I worked on Heather's wheel right then, I probably would have heaved it into the desert, and the cautious gazes the kids shot my way showed they knew I was on the verge of cracking more than just my thumb.

I counted to ten with my head to the sky. All the kids were now shivering and cuddled up with each other in the pouring rain, so I took a final suck on my throbbing thumb and went after Heather's wheel. After patching the tube and the tire, I gave it one final benediction and thrust it back into the dropouts of her bike. Without a word, the kids climbed back on their bikes and headed up the mountain behind Jimmy. The kids were so unsure of my emotional state that they didn't even look up at me. They just hunched over their handlebars and rode in perfect formation over 5039-foot Hogback Summit. No pig had ever been so ugly.

Just over the top the rain stopped, and off to the side of the road we saw the Fulton-mobile. Sulie and Bob were working on something in the bed of the truck, and when we pulled into their turnout, we found them pouring us bowls of hot soup. They had ridden ahead and found a cafe that had homemade soup on the menu. They bought the entire pot and we all wrapped our frozen hands around steaming mugs of vegetable beef. The kids were so frozen they didn't even start shaking for about five minutes. I couldn't even feel my fingers, and when I looked at my thumb I saw that the slice had grown even longer and deeper. Sulie cut me some white tape from the first aid kit, while I walked over to inspect the slice in Heather's rear wheel.

"Hey you guys, I'm really sorry about my tantrum back there," I said as I put my arm around Heather. "It's just that my thumb was really hurting and I saw you guys all suffering and I didn't know how I was going to keep Heather's tire from exploding every five miles . . . and Heather, I wasn't mad at you for smiling, I was mad at your tire. I love your smile; I just can't believe how you keep it up all the time." I gave Heather an extra squeeze, and she smiled up at me and hugged me back.

"Hey John, we understand," said Joy, "don't worry about it. But you better take a look at Jimmy. His hands are really hurting and his fingers are turning dark blue."

Jimmy had hopped right in the cab of the truck when we arrived, and he hadn't yet been out. Our most confident and vocal member hadn't said anything since we fixed Heather's tire the last time, and that worried me more than Heather's tire or my thumb. Sitting with his hands over the heating vents of the truck, Jimmy looked like a wet and battered dog that had done its best to find its way home but had finally exhausted itself. There was no fire in Jimmy's eyes, no sarcastic or heroic statements on the tip of his tongue. Sulie was trying to force him to drink some soup, and seeing my young friend silent for the first time buckled my knees and made me realize how much I relied on his bravado.

"Hey John, I'm sorry I didn't listen to your advice about the wool gloves." Jimmy's voice sounded slow and weak. "You're right about my cotton ones being stylish but not much good for keeping fingers warm. I can't even feel my fingers yet, and back there on the road I was really having trouble holding onto my handlebars."

"C'mon man, you can't die on me now; we haven't even reached the California border yet . . . And didn't you promise to get me to Lynn tonight? It'll cost you a few donuts back in Santa Barbara if we don't make it." I hoped some bravado of my own might thaw him out, but Jimmy's body just continued shaking as he sipped the soup from Sulie. I gave him a hug and went back outside to talk with Bob.

"I figure it's about forty-five more miles to Lakeview, and if the weather keeps up like it's been, I'm not sure we can make it," I said. "Is there anything between here and Lakeview, in case we need to shorten the day?"

Bob pulled his cap off and scratched the back of his head. "Well, 'bout half way to Lakeview there's Valley Falls, and Sulie and I passed a big ranch that might be a stopping point. Other than that, we'd just have to pull off and make our own camp like we did last night."

"Making our own camp is out of the question . . . We need some place where the kids can thaw out and dry their clothes. They're wearing everything warm they own, and camping out in this wind and rain might really do them in."

"John, you're the boss; you just let Sulie and me know what we can do to help."

I looked up at the sky and thought for a while, as I blew on my hands that were slowly coming back to life. The throbbing in my thumb started to grow and reminded me that in addition to the weather, we had a tire with a throbbing of its own that threatened to slow any pace I planned for the rest of the afternoon.

"You think the kids are really in that bad o' shape?"

"Yeah Bob, when Jimmy stops braggin', I know we're in trouble, and Heather even stopped sparkling back there on that last climb . . . Tell you what, I'm gonna give Jimmy my wool gloves, and we'll try to make it to Lakeview, but if we can't make it, would you help me out with this alternate plan?"

"Sure, John, you name it." Bob put his daughter and her friends completely in my hands, and his quiet confidence in me helped make up for Jimmy's silence.

"How 'bout if you and Sulie go to that ranch you told me about and ask them if they have a barn or something where we could store our bikes in an emergency? That way, if we can only make twenty-five more miles today, we can park our bikes there and drive to Lakeview in the truck. Then tomorrow afternoon, we can drive back to the ranch and get on our bikes to ride the last twenty-five miles. We'll be giving up one day of being off our bikes, but that may be the best we can do."

"Whatever you say, John. Sulie and I will drive ahead and check out the ranch, and then we'll come back and follow you guys the rest of the way."

"Let's just hope Heather's tire hangs in there," I said as Bob patted me on the shoulder.

Our soup stop lasted about a half hour, and thank God it didn't rain at all that entire time. Before getting on their bikes, all the kids went over to Jimmy and rubbed his arms and shoulders, trying to give him some extra warmth. I blew into my wool gloves one last time and then helped Jimmy guide his fingers into them. I would be riding with bare fingers, and I hoped the chill of late afternoon would numb my thumb but not my fingers — I had handlebars and brakes of my own to hold onto.

The Oregon sky must be allergic to dryness, because not five minutes into our ride down the pass toward Lake Abert, the floodgates of heaven opened and the rain resumed. It was only 1:30, but the few cars that passed us on that lonely stretch of Hwy. 395 all had their headlights on. The storm was so dark, it seemed like night was just around the bend.

As we approached Lake Abert we could see giant flocks of Canada geese overhead, and looking at a struggling Jimmy up at the front of our flock, I had to decide whether to play mama elk or father goose. Jimmy was trying his best to set a good pace into a strong and chilling headwind, but as the miles wore on, I could see him weaving more and more and laboring to turn his pedals. At the same time, it was so dark that I felt I needed to protect my flock from the semis that roared out of the darkness behind us every ten or fifteen minutes. I finally had to do both, in order to protect the kids from the wind and the eighteen-wheelers. I would look over my shoulder searching for any approaching headlights. If I didn't see any, I would sprint up to the front of the group and lead like the head gander, the kids tucked in tight behind me, protecting themselves from the vicious headwind. When I saw a set of lights approaching us from behind, I would peel off to the side and fall back and take my place like the mama elk, protecting the kids from the rear with my waving arms and large body signalling the approaching lights to slow down and not blow us off the cliffs. Like Indian Running in reverse, I changed positions many times that afternoon, and after three hours, we were almost to Valley Falls. It wasn't the most enjoyable three hours of riding I'd ever done, but I could still feel a few tingles of life in the tips of my fingers and, with twenty miles down and five to go, Heather's tire hadn't blown up yet.

"Hey, you guys!" I stopped the group at the southern tip of the lake. I looked into their red, frozen faces and told them of my alternate plan for the first time. It was almost five o'clock, and I didn't think it would be very wise to try and ride the thirty more miles to Lakeview.

"You guys are unbelievable. I think, though, we had better resort to Plan B or Plan C."

"I didn't know there was a Plan B or Plan C," said Carl as he struggled to move his frozen jaw.

"Well, the way I figure it, it would be pretty crazy to try and make Lakeview tonight. I don't think we should try another night ride in this weather." I pointed up to the rim of rock a couple hundred feet above us and the kids noticed, for the first time, the line of snow that had been following us.

"Joy's folks are checking with a ranch about five miles up the road to see if they will let us store our bikes there for the night. Plan B calls for us to leave our bikes there and drive to Lakeview in the truck, and then tomorrow, when I get back from Reno with Lynn, we'll drive back up to the ranch, pick up our bikes and ride them the twenty-five more miles into Lakeview. Plan B would mean giving up Saturday as a complete layover day . . . .

"The only other way I can see us doing things would be to park the bikes there, let you guys have your layover day, and Saturday, when Lynn and I get back, Bob and I would drive back to the ranch, pick up the bikes and drive them into Lakeview."

"You mean we wouldn't ride those twenty-five miles?!" exclaimed a disbelieving Joy. "So far, we've gone over 4,000 miles and you're thinking of letting a little — well, a lot of — cold water stop us from riding all the way across America? No way! Not for me. I vote for riding all the way to Lakeview tonight or for Plan B."

"Shoot, John, we're not going to give up now," agreed Carl. "I vote for Plan B too."

"Yeah, we can have a half a layover day tomorrow and ride in the afternoon," said Ethan. "That way we can still watch Saturday morning cartoons, and riding twenty-five miles in the afternoon will be easy."

"Yeah, big leader . . . ." Jimmy was speaking for the first time since he had moaned in the truck. "We didn't ride all this way to hitchhike. If you put our bikes in that truck, it'll be you owin' *me* those donuts back in Santa Barbara!"

My five senatorial friends voted unanimously for Plan B, and soon the Fulton-mobile pulled alongside us to guide us the final few miles. The friendly owners of the River's End Ranch led us down the muddy road to their aluminum barn where our bikes would be spending the night.

". . . if I had known they were really little kids I would have never hesitated to let you all store your bikes here," said the somewhat embarrassed owner. Bob had told me that he had had to do some convincing when he had approached the man about our use of his barn. "I can't believe these kids have pedaled all the way from Washington, D.C., and today . . . in this storm? Why, I gave my hands the day off, cuz we couldn't get nothin' done rain was blowin' so hard . . . You folks can keep your bikes here as long as you want. 'magine you all have grown mighty close to them bicycles and don't you fret one bit. We'll take good care of them."

Bob and I talked to the rancher and his wife while Sulie tried to make room in the cab of the pick-up for six soggy cyclists plus Bob and herself. Somehow, by sitting three-deep on each other's laps, we were able to squeeze in and still give Bob enough room to steer. Our arms were pinned down so, instead of waving, we had to nod and yell our goodbyes to the folks at River's End Ranch, as we bounced out their muddy driveway.

"Hey John, wake up, wake up." It was Joy. I jerked my head up and discovered I had spent the whole ride from the ranch to Lakeview asleep on her shoulder.

"Did I sleep the whole way?"

"Yeah, you didn't even make it out the driveway. You must be real tired." Joy smiled and wiped my drool from the shoulder of her rain jacket. I blinked my eyes a couple more times and tried to free my hand to open the door so we could get out. I dizzily hopped out and hugged each of the kids as I helped them down.

"Hey pillow," I said to Joy as I held her tight. "Thanks."

"That's okay, John, you needed some sleep," she said, smiling up at me. "Be careful driving to Reno, all right?"

"Yeah, be careful dude," said Jimmy heading to his room and the first shower. "And John?"

"Yes, Jimmy."

"Well . . . I'll understand if you don't bring me back any champagne . . . ." With a sly grin on his face, Jimmy looked like he was well on the road to recovery.

16

We left school and I drove home, not rode. It was only 5 minutes and I missed them already, but I knew what happened with the trip, that I would <u>never</u> forget them — ever. You know, the guy in Stand By Me was right! 'You never have friends like the ones when you were 12 and 13 . . . .'

Joy's Journal
October 17, 1986

Blue Skies

We made it! Glad to be here, California.
                                        Love,
                                        Joy

Joy stood tall and proud as she wrote with a big black marker on the back of the WELCOME TO CALIFORNIA sign. Jimmy stood back from the sign and showered us with the confetti the girls had purchased back in Idaho and had somehow managed to keep dry across Oregon.

Earlier that morning, as we ate Lucky Charms and Safeway Danish in front of Lakeview's Old Perpetual Geyser, the sky had pulled back its curtains to reveal one of the deepest and clearest blue skies we had yet seen. Even though they had fourteen miles to the long-awaited border, the kids craned their necks around each corner, hoping to be the first to sight the California State Line. Ethan's anxious anticipation caused him to fall behind, and we both lost sight of Jimmy and the others as they sped ahead.

Ethan's and my first hints of home were the series of signs bidding us good-bye from Oregon. The one that said: COME BACK SOON! drew a sarcastic, head shaking, "Yeah, right . . . ." from Ethan, who remembered the past week's weather all too well.

A quarter-mile beyond that last Oregon marker, we could see a large, green road sign with our friends gathered around it. Ethan picked up the pace and we rode across the border to cheers, back slaps and an enjoyable downpour of confetti. After the kids finished dancing around with each other, they looked over at me for my reaction to their most recent milestone. I silently smiled and held up my index finger, signalling them to wait just a minute. Reaching into my handlebar bag, I fished out my ceremonial California sunglasses, dusted off the prairie dust and granola bar crumbs, and placed them dramatically on my ears and nose. Then, after a moment's silence, I yelled a "YAHOO!!!" that scared every honker on nearby Goose Lake into the sky, and called every goosebump on my body into action. Hugs were next, and although the kids thought my sunglasses were symbolic of California, I knew that, in actuality, they were just covering the tears flooding my eyes. I held on long and hard to each of them, and Lynn, who stood off to the side wondering when she could break in, was the last and longest in my arms.

"Hey John, do you think it's okay if we write on the back of the sign?" Joy had asked moments earlier. "It's so dull . . . plain green and white . . . I think it needs a little artwork."

"And besides," added Jimmy, "didn't you tell us that the pioneers used to carve their initials and messages in the landmarks along their route . . . like at Chimney Rock and Independence Rock?"

I nodded my head in agreement, and soon the kids were decorating one of their own landmarks. Heather, who couldn't quite reach the sign even with tip-toes and full arm extension, ended up climbing onto my shoulders so she could pen her memorial to our crossing.

Other than the geese honking overhead and the occasional car speeding by, there wasn't much of a crowd to celebrate our special accomplishment, but by the time we left that sign, it was covered with balloons, streamers and the graffiti from some twentieth century pioneers.

We rode on to Goose Lake campground and continued with a celebration of another kind. September twenty-first will go down with each of the members of our group as the day they crossed over into California. Joy will remember that too, but she'll also remember it was her thirteenth birthday. Pedaling her bicycle over 4,000 miles and finally entering her home state was a pretty special way to celebrate becoming a teenager, and it couldn't have happened to a more special girl. If I could have planned her thirteenth candle and our thirteenth state to happen on the same day, I would have, but somehow our clapping angels had taken care of that part of Joy's itinerary. As Jimmy secretly snuck into the girls' tent with confetti of his own, and as Carl, Ethan and Heather hung up dancing bear balloons, wishing their friend happy birthday, I looked up at the sky and smiled. We spent the next couple hours celebrating with a Mexican brunch cooked up by Bob and Sulie, chocolate cheesecake flown in by Lynn, and presents that included more bears from Joy's parents and mine, some interesting pink flamingo salt and pepper shakers from Lynn, and some even more interesting mushroom earrings from Ethan.

"Hey Ethan, where did you find those?" I asked, as he proudly watched Joy try them on.

"Oh . . . I found them back in Jackson. I thought they were really cool, so I bought them." Ethan couldn't hide his big grin, as everyone marveled at his purchase.

"And you kept track of them for two states? How did you do that?"

". . . Well . . . uh . . . I don't know how I did . . . I just dumped out my handle-bar bag a couple of minutes ago and they were on the bottom. I was kinda surprised myself to find them down there . . . ."

Our party continued until it was time for Lynn to get back to Reno to catch her plane home. We all hugged her good bye before she hopped in the truck with Bob and Sulie. She would rendezvous with us two weeks later at the Golden Gate Bridge, and Joy's folks would meet us somewhere down Hwy. 395 the next afternoon with lunch — and hopefully a new tire for Heather.

"Hey John, what's been happening with William Swain?" asked Carl at our journal meeting later that afternoon.

"Yeah, didn't he come over the mountains somewhere around here?"

"You're right, Jimmy. He came over Fandango Pass, just east of here. I can't believe you remembered this was where we would meet up with him again."

"C'mon man, we're your students aren't we? What did you expect?" Jimmy chuckled.

"How long did it take Swain's wagon train to get from where we left him at the Platte River to here?" asked Heather.

"Well, William and his buddies decided to take a few 'short-cuts' along their way and it kinda slowed them down." I spread out our map and continued: "Their route took them from Wyoming down into Utah; back up into southern Idaho; across the desert of northern Nevada; and finally, across those mountains you see over there to right here at Goose Lake. It took them almost three months."

"Some short-cuts those were," said Joy. "Looking at my journal . . . the last time we read about William Swain was . . . just over a month ago. That means it took him three times as long to get here as us! . . . Was his weather as bad as ours?"

"It might have been worse. They had some days in the desert when the temperature got over 105 degrees. When it got that hot, they would drive their wagons at night. And other days, they woke up with an inch of ice on their water barrels. The weather and the dust and the bugs were taking their toll, and many of their animals and some of their people died between Wyoming and here. Remember the Humbolt River we talked about? Well, they followed it in Nevada."

"You mean the Humbug River," said Ethan. "Wasn't that the one that was really gross? We talked about it back at Redfish Lake."

"Good memory, Ethan, you're right. Let's catch up with William with a couple of his journal entries before we write in ours, okay?"

"Go for it," said Jimmy. "I've missed hearing from old William."

"Okay, here's one from the Humbolt:

> "September 17, 1849. Last night was cold — ice an inch thick in the wash basin. The day is clear and the sun shines out warm. The lady in the neighboring camp is no more.

"And here's what Swain wrote after crossing Fandango Pass:

"October 10-11. Up we ascended, slowly but surely, by the toilsome climbing of the teams and by the lifting of the members of the mess at the wheels. Dreadful was the lashing our poor teams received, and many a drop of sweat was lost by our men.

"And another pioneer wrote:

"... In the very center of the very broad, sandy, dusty road men were urging their heavy ox-trains up the steep hill with lashes, imprecations, and shouts ... Across the road about midway up ... lay an ox on his knees, dying and covered with an old gum, oilcloth coat by his compassionate owner. But it was unavailing, the dust was suffocating and the animals and wheels went over him in the haste and trouble of the steep ascent ...."

"You mean, they ran right over it?" asked Heather.

"Well, did things get any better once they got to California?" asked Joy. "Did the weather get nice like it did for us?"

"Yeah, it did for a while; he even did a little hunting and swimming around here. Listen to this:

"October 18, 1849. ... I shot a goose in the river and had to swim to get it — and it was COLD. Mr. Crosby shot two deer. I rambled along the river a long time and only overtook the train at noon when they were cooking the venison. Far to the west of us, solitary, rises to an immense height a gigantic mountain (Mount Shasta), the top and sides clear to the base covered with snow — a magnificent sight ...."

"Hey, I saw that too when we were riding into camp!" exclaimed Ethan. "Everything else was dry and this giant white rose above everything. It was on the mountains on the far side of the lake and kinda to the south ... or at least I think it was south. It was toward the direction you said we would be heading tomorrow. Was that it?"

"Yup, Ethan, you saw Mount Shasta." I answered.

"Just like William Swain ...." Ethan chuckled proudly to himself, as the rest of the kids stood on their toes and tried to get their view over the row of trees surrounding camp. The trees were a little too tall, and their view of Ethan's and William's mountain would have to wait til morning.

After a few more journal pages and few more pieces of birthday cake, we hit the sack early, excited about our first full day of California cycling in the morning.

"Hey John, how far are we gonna ride in California?" asked Carl at breakfast. "If we don't plan to get home for almost a month, we still must have some riding to do."

"Well, yeah we do . . . ," I answered hesitantly, not wanting to spoil the kids' feeling of having reached their home state. "California's a big place . . . and we've got almost a thousand more miles to ride."

"A thousand miles?!" Carl stopped in mid-mouthful of his breakfast burrito.

"No problem, dude," Jimmy promptly cut in. "This is California, land of sunshine and ocean. A thousand miles here will be a piece of cake." Jimmy pulled off his sunglasses and wiped them clean with his bandana before slowly remounting them atop his nose. "Heck, I'm planning to ride the rest of the way without taking off my shades! I got to work on my tan for our final-mile celebration . . . ."

The rest of the group, including Carl, were bolstered by Jimmy's brash confidence. Their initial shock at my mention of a thousand more miles was erased by his encouragement.

"Yeah, a thousand more miles should be pretty easy after all we've been through," added Joy. "I can't wait to ride a full day in California; it's been a long time since I've been here. Let's hurry up with breakfast and ride."

Soon camp was packed and we were heading south on the bluffs high above Goose Lake. Our first California destination was the small town of Likely, forty miles away. Joy's parents had some friends who ran a large cattle ranch there where we would be spending the night.

"Hey John, I can't wait til today is over," Heather said, as she rode alongside me.

"Why's that, Heather?"

"Well, the Fultons are bringing me a new rear tire today, aren't they?"

"Hey, you're right, Heather. I can't wait til today's over then either. I'll be glad to say good bye to that old tire of yours."

"Me too. It's really getting bumpy with that last patch of nylon and duct tape you added."

"Sorry about the bumps, Heather. Let's try and make it to the Fultons without any blow-outs, okay?"

"I'll do the best I can." Heather smiled and then pedaled ahead of me, her body bouncing every two feet.

The sky continued more blue than we could remember, and for the first twenty miles, we coasted, blown south with the wisps of clouds. Everyone got their view of Mount Shasta, as Ethan's snow-covered pyramid was our constant companion that morning.

Our effortless ride was rudely interrupted by a shotgun-like blast exploding from the rear of Heather's bike. I was riding behind her and watched helplessly as she tried to gain control of her bike that suddenly had a mind of its own. We were riding down a long hill and she was riding slower than usual because of her rear tire, but even at twelve miles an hour, the explosion made her heavy machine ride like a rodeo bull. Skittles wiggled, wobbled and headed for the gravelly shoulder of the road, that, after ten feet, dropped off steeply and deeply into a canyon. Heather pumped her brakes and somehow managed to stop just a few feet before the cliff, and when I pulled to a stop alongside her, she had laid Skittles down and was holding onto her chest trying to keep her heart inside.

"John, that was pretty scary," she said in between breaths. "I couldn't get control and I thought I was going to go down. I can't believe I'm standing on my feet . . . I think my heart stopped there for a minute!" Heather's knees were shaking and her eyes were as wide as I'd ever seen them. Still, out of the corners of her mouth, she managed that sparkling smile of hers.

"Let me catch my breath, and then I'll help you change my tire again, okay . . . I'm sorry I got another flat, but I was doing the best I could to be careful."

I laid down my bike, walked over and wrapped my arms around her. "Heather, you're unbelievable. You just tell me where your spare tube is and you sit this one out. Just remember, you owe me."

"Owe you? Owe you what?" she asked.

"The recipe for your smile."

As I devised another patching plan for her rapidly deteriorating tire, I looked over to see her sitting up against a road sign and writing in her journal. When she caught me staring, she explained:

"Well, I've got to write that flat down in my journal . . . After all, it *was* pretty exciting."

"Hey John, what took you two so long?" Jimmy asked. Tire patched, Heather and I caught up with everyone a couple miles later.

"Well, three guesses. And the first two don't count," I answered, as Heather tried not to blush.

"Oh wow . . . ." answered Ethan. "Was that the loud explosion I heard? . . . Heather had another flat?"

"On that downhill?" asked Joy. "Heather, are you all right?"

Heather nodded.

"Hey John," Jimmy continued, "how's your thumb?"

"I don't know, James, I'm afraid to look. If I don't think about it and it's not freezing cold out, it doesn't hurt too bad.

"I think I've got her tire fixed for the rest of the day. This time I sandwiched a piece of aluminum can between the layers of duct tape and her tire. I hope my new design will hold until we see Bob and Sulie with the new one."

"Hey John, that's rad; you just invented the first steel belted bicycle tire!" exclaimed Carl.

"Yeah, I guess you're right. I just hope it works. You guys should have seen Heather wrestling her bike on that downhill. We almost lost her. Everyone say a prayer that she doesn't have another flat."

"Are you guys ready for a little math problem?" I asked, before we started riding again.

"Math?! what d'ya mean math?" asked Carl.

"Well, some people are worried about you guys missing school and everything by being out here on your bikes everyday, and I thought I'd give you guys a bicycling math problem, so they wouldn't have to worry."

"But, John, I thought you told us about how those people upset you?" asked a puzzled Joy.

"I'm just kidding about doing it for 'school' or any of those people who can't see how much you're learning. I just was watching Heather bump along the road when a problem popped into my head. Maybe, because it's September and everything, the classroom teacher in me just couldn't resist — I don't know. Do you guys want to hear my problem, or not?"

"Shoot, dude; I'm ready," answered Jimmy. "But the 'popped into your head' bit is a pretty poor pun."

"Oh, I get it . . . ," Joy laughed as she thought over my unplanned choice of words.

"What pun?" asked a confused Ethan.

"Later, dude. I'll explain it to you on the road? What's the math problem, John?" asked Jimmy.

"Okay, here it is: Every time Heather's rear wheel goes around she gets a bump from her bike, right?"

"Right," everyone answered.

I continued: "So, if Heather gets jolted with each revolution, how can she reduce her bumps between here and lunch . . . by going faster or by going slower?"

I saw Carl ready to answer me right away, but I stopped him. "Don't answer me yet. I'll get each of your answers between here and Alturas. I'll ride up alongside you, and then you can explain your answers."

I could see the kids talking to themselves over the next few miles, and by the time we got to our lunch stop I'd visited everyone. Only Joy had the correct answer, and her explanation to the rest of the group at lunch was one of the better math lectures I have ever attended. The kids combed the Fulton's truck for their favorite kinds of cookies for dessert, and Heather found a dessert of her own, a brand new tire that I mounted with great ceremony on her rear wheel. I said a prayer that it would be the last time that I would touch those axle bolts on Skittles, and Joy's folks put the old tire, complete with aluminum belt and duct tape, in a spot for safe keeping. It would definitely be a piece for our transcontinental museum, and someday Heather will be sitting in her armchair, with grandkids in her lap and that same circle of rubber in her hands, telling them the stories hidden beneath its bandages.

A Special Pleasure

"Well, John, our ranch runs for about as far as you can see and then some." Bill Flournoy drove his old Ford truck along one of the many dirt roads that crisscrossed his pastures. "Why, we got some cattle up grazin' on the far side of that mountain over there." He pointed his leathery hand up against the windshield, and I tried to imagine caring for all the acres and acres that stretched across the broad valley.

It was just after dawn on the Flournoy Ranch and Bill was giving me a talking tour of his place, while the kids sat on hay bales in the bed of the truck, blowing on their freezing hands and keeping lookout for all the wildlife that shared Bill's place. The kids would gasp as deer ran alongside the truck and then leapt effortlessly over the pasture fences, and they'd all point excitedly at the giant birds rising without warning from hidden irrigation ditches.

"Yessir, John, the Flournoy family's been farmin' this land since 1872. Had us a family reunion here back in 1972 to celebrate our centennial and darned if 1500 people didn't show up!" I marveled at the man sitting next to me in his Levi's, boots and black cowboy hat. He carried a bandana that he really used, and he rolled down the window every so often to spit some brown tobacco juice out into the cold morning air.

Bill Flournoy called himself a buckaroo proudly — in fact, I'd rarely heard a profession pronounced with such dignity. "Cattle ranchin'" was his life, and in the few hours that I had spent with him, I'd already learned more about cowboys and buckaroos than I'd learned in 33 years.

"My work takes up 365 days a year, and as hard as it gets to be sometimes, I wouldn't rather be doin' anythin' else. I just hope we can hold on through these tough times we're havin' right now."

"What do you mean?"

"Well, the beef business ain't quite what it used to be. Times keep on bein' the way they've been much longer, and I'm afraid I might be the last Flournoy to make a livin' from this land. The banks are making it awful tough these days . . . Used to be, we'd call up the bank and they'd loan us money over the phone. I can remember the time we had our banker up for a visit, and I took him for a drive like this one we're on, and when he saw all our bucks and does, he forgot all about the fact he wanted to visit about our account. Only thing he ended up askin' me was when he could come up and do some huntin'.

"Yessir, things aren't quite like they used to be. Got big banks speculating on property and plowin' it up, and the Sierra Club and those other citified environmentalists getting after me about hunting or fishing on my own land. Why my wife, Athena, has got a family of deer that return to her porch step every year since she nursed one of them back to life—Look there! See that bird liftin' itself into the sky. That's a Great Blue Heron. Got plenty of them around here; beautiful birds aren't they?"

As we drove over the pastures, Bill talked with equal parts reverence and knowledge about all the animals living on his ranch. I couldn't imagine any college-trained naturalist knowing or caring more about the land and its inhabitants, and I didn't have enough room in my journal to write down all I learned in our hour-long truck ride.

"You kids ready to do some eatin' buckaroo style?" Bill asked, pulling to a stop in front of the ranch house.

"Yes, sir, as soon as we thaw out," answered Jimmy as he moved his fingers away from his mouth just long enough to answer.

"Well, I think we got some good food fixed for you all down in the bunk-house. Should be warm down there too. Let me help you kids down." Bill reached up and swung each of the kids to the ground and then led them to breakfast.

The bunkhouse was warm and the kids' eyes got wide as they saw the long table piled high with food. Six extra chairs were pulled up to the table that must have been fifteen feet long. We had the rare privilege of joining Bill's brother, his dad, and the half-dozen other buckaroos and ranch hands that gathered every morning for their breakfast ritual. Bill introduced the kids to the all-male gathering, but my kids didn't seem to draw much attention, as all the men seemed more interested in the business and work of the day than my frozen little bicyclists.

Their indifference changed as soon the kids started to eat.

"Excuse me, but could you please pass me the sausage and eggs?" Ethan began, and before long each of the kids had called the platters their way. Their plates were soon stacked chin high with buckaroo-sized portions of cereal, eggs, sausage, ham, canteloupe, biscuits, gravy and maple bars. Cereal bowls were filled, coffee was poured all around and "moon juice" (what Likely buckaroos call Tang) and milk filled the kids' glasses. I noticed the men at our end of the table watching with wonder as the kids went about loading their plates with "pleases", "thank yous" and platter-emptying portions. Ethan was the first to finish his plateful, and when he wiped the maple frosting from his face and asked, "Excuse me, but are there any seconds?" all conversation at the far end of the table stopped and the buckaroos stared our way.

One of the ranch hands quickly jumped up and gathered each of the serving trays. He ran into the kitchen and refilled each of them. While he was gone, the questions began from the astonished men as Bill and I leaned back and smiled at each other. Bill's dad began the questioning, asking us what we were doing in Likely, and Joy answered with a wonderful explanation about us following the pioneers and our desire to meet all the different kinds of people who live in America. Heather answered the question about our gear and how we carried everything, and for half an hour the kids alternated eating and explaining to the Likely buckaroos. Every detailed answer caused the cowboys to shake their heads in wonder at our adventure. I didn't answer once as the kids handled every question better than I ever could have.

"Well, I think we all had better be getting about our work for the day," Bill

Flournoy interrupted as he saw that the kitchen had long since been emptied by the kids. His dad, his brother and his ranch hands got up and shook each of the kids' hands before they grabbed their cowboy hats hanging near the door. "I hope you all don't mind if I watch you close up camp," Bill asked as the kids got ready to leave.

The kids were amazed that anyone would want to watch them break camp, but Joy answered, "Sure, if you'd like. I hope you don't get bored."

Bill looked anything but bored as I caught the look on his face watching us roll up sleeping bags, pads and tents. In all of fifteen minutes, the kids had everything loaded on their bikes and were asking where they could fill up their water bottles.

While they were all inside Athena's kitchen, Bill pulled me to the side of the water tower to speak with me in private:

"You know, John, when Bob Fulton first phoned me about a bunch of kids on their bicycles stayin' on our place, I really didn't pay him much mind. I guess he told me about you all crossing the country, that you were carrying all your gear and that the kids were only twelve and thirteen, but, until you rode in the driveway yesterday evening, I really didn't pay you all much attention. Then I see you all setting up camp, and hearing those kids sayin' 'please' and 'thank you' and 'yes sir' . . . and this mornin' when they emptied the kitchen and spoke so articulately about what you all were working so hard at doin' . . . Well sir, I'm impressed. You've got one dandy bunch of kids there, John, and I want to congratulate you on what you've done and let you know that I consider it a privilege gettin' to meet you and your kids. Again, let me say you got one dandy bunch, and I don't use that word too lightly."

I hoped my silent handshake let him know the feeling was mutual.

I rode at the back as we left the Flournoys, waving from their front yard. As I basked in pride and said a prayer for the future of Bill's place, Dave, one of the ranch hands we'd met at breakfast, came running out to stop me near the gate.

"John . . . it is John, isn't it?" he asked, catching his breath.

"Yes, it is."

"Hi, I'm Dave, and I didn't get a chance to tell you this morning after breakfast, but I just wanted to tell you what a special pleasure it was to meet your kids and hear them tell their story this morning . . . Ain't had such a good feeling about kids and this country for as long as I can remember."

"Thanks for stopping me to say that," I answered, shaking his hand.

"Well, again, the pleasure is mine. You all be careful and enjoy the rest of your trip. I wish you the best of luck."

The kids were just up the road at the entrance, yelling and waving at me. I finished shaking Dave's hand and I tried my best not to smile too proud as I rode up to them.

"C'mon, John," yelled Jimmy. "We've still got to stop by the Likely School today. We can't have you talking to everybody and his brother along the way . . . ."

I managed a somewhat serious, "Okay," and Jimmy immediately led us to the small elementary school at the edge of town.

My kids quietly rolled their bikes into the cafeteria as I told the school secretary we had arrived. Ethan and Carl asked for our map of the United States that showed our route alongside William Swain's:

"Hey John, I bet the kids would like to see where we've been and see how we've been following an old pioneer," they said. "I can remember the first time I studied about wagon trains back in elementary school."

The teachers brought their classes into the cafeteria in single file, and my kids smiled proudly as each class "oohed" and "aahed" at their loaded bicycles. Soon there was a half circle of kids sitting silently "Indian style" waiting for the adventurers to speak. I didn't get a chance to say anything before Jimmy stepped to the front to take charge. He introduced his friends and explained that we had ridden over 4,000 miles so far across America. Like twin Vanna Whites, Heather and Joy held up our map between them and, while Jimmy spoke, Ethan and Carl traced our route along it. When Jimmy finished his talk, Heather stepped forward and explained the other route traced on the map, and she even told the spellbound audience how William Swain had probably rolled right through Likely with his train of ox-pulled wagons. Goosebumps of pride danced up my spine as I listened to my kids explaining their journey just as they had at breakfast.

When Heather was finished, Joy asked the kids if they had any questions, and one little guy towards the back, who must have been about eight, immediately shot up his hand:

"Did you guys eat like the pioneers did? Like, did you cook over a campfire and everything?"

Carl stepped forward to answer. "Well, sometimes we cooked over a fire, but usually we cooked over our campstove . . . ." And as Carl continued to list our typical menus, Heather came over and asked me if she could take the stove and frying pan from my panniers. Soon she was back giving a demonstration of our bicycling kitchen.

"Did you carry all of your food?" the little guy continued, and Joy and Jimmy were soon into their panniers, pulling out our plastic bags of hot chocolate and oatmeal and our containers of peanut butter and jelly.

"And . . . sometimes we would go out for pizza." Ethan's contribution to Carl's answer drew enthusiastic approval from the entire audience. Encouraged by his response Ethan continued, ". . . and we've been having a taste test . . . You see, we make sure we go out for pizza in every state. . . and sometimes we even go two or three times. We've been having a contest to see which place has the best, and so far I think it was a Pizza Hut we went to on the Fourth of July, back in Virginia." Obviously relishing his moment in the spotlight, Ethan smiled and laughed to himself when he saw how much the audience was enjoying his pizza explanation.

My kids continued answering the enthusiastic questions of the Likely school-children. Jimmy showed them how he dressed when it was raining; Joy and Heather demonstrated how they packed their panniers to make sure things wouldn't get wet; Carl showed them how his bike had 18 gears; and all the kids shared the stuffed animals that had traveled with them since leaving Washington, D.C. I noticed a woman walk into the assembly late, and from her posture and business-like appearance, I figured she must be the principal. When she raised her hand to ask her question, I knew I was right.

Ignoring every kid in the auditorium, including mine, she asked, "Excuse me, but aren't these children missing school?"

Her question went off like a bomb, destroying every smile in the room. I stood silently and didn't answer, trying to prepare myself for the questions I was sure would follow.

"Are they going to be making up all the work they're missing when they get home?" she continued, speaking even louder. My knees buckled, my goosebumps disappeared and I did my best trying to count to ten, as my sunburned face turned even more red. I looked over at my kids and saw they too had been stunned by her blow. Looking at me with wounded eyes, they immediately started to put away the map, the kitchen and all the other things they had unpacked to share. With just two questions, the woman had pulled the carpet out from underneath them. Even Heather stopped smiling, and the hurt looks on my kids' faces made me even more angry than the principal's questions. Still she continued:

"Six weeks seems to be a long time for these children to be away from school. Are they going to be tested on what they learned when they get back? Are they going to write a report on their trip?"

Ms. What's Her Name or Dr. So and So, whoever she was, continued her barrage, and each succeeding question blurred in my mind. I became sick to my stomach and managed some stupid reply about how the kids were writing journals and keeping a budget. I said a quivering "thank you" to the audience as I tried to get to my kids, who were packing their bikes as quickly as possible, out the door of that cafeteria. I was about to say something that might get the six of us thrown out of town.

"Who cares about journals and budgets?!" I said, seething with anger, as I got to the kids, silently waiting outside beside their bicycles. "Damn that woman and teachers who do that to kids.

"She thinks the only place kids can learn is in some four-walled room with state-approved textbooks and study questions and unit tests and all that other junk.

"You guys were so fantastic in there. The way you answered the kids' questions and demonstrated everything. You didn't even give me a chance to talk, and those little kids loved it. I bet there were more than a couple of them who would have loved to join you guys." Tears were flowing down my cheeks, as I looked at my kids whose heads still hung low.

"Don't you let anyone — principals, teachers or anyone! — take away all you've accomplished and learned by being out on your bicycles. You guys know how much you've learned and how important it has been to jump out of those books to meet all the people you've met. And you know how it really felt for the pioneers who settled our country. That woman doesn't care about that. All she would have you do is read a couple pages and then regurgitate some dates and facts about them on some dittoed test, and then move onto the next chapter.

"I love you guys so much, and I'm prouder of you than I can ever tell you, so please don't let that woman get you down. I want you to ride out of this parking lot knowing that you've got a lot of little admirers sitting back in their classroom, probably not paying attention to their worksheets and dreaming about riding down the road with you . . . You've got some big admirers back at the Flournoy Ranch I know about, too."

The kids were listening hard to my outburst and they slowly raised their heads toward me. Heather's smile eventually returned and, as usual, Jimmy couldn't stay silent for long:

"Hey John . . . Don't worry; it's cool. we know what you're sayin' . . . Ya know, I've been thinking about what you told us back there in Idaho somewhere, and I think I've finally got it wired. Listen to this:

"The road is our classroom. Our bicycles are our textbooks. And the people are our teachers . . . Sounds pretty good, doesn't it?"

"Yeah, Jimmy, I'd have to say I couldn't say it better myself . . . Thanks."

Jimmy puffed up his chest and pointed proudly at himself. "Well, just remember one thing, if you use it in your book, I want a share of the royalties."

"Get out of here, Jimmy," I laughed. "You're leading this group, aren't you?"

"Yeah."

"Well, let's get going. We've got an appointment with the Sierras this afternoon. We'll talk royalties on the other side." I blew my nose and mounted my bike. As the kids did their usual quick recovery, I rode behind them trying to fight off what my colleague had said. Still, she ruined the next forty miles for me — I hadn't yet learned Heather's recipe for smiling.

Jingle Bells

"Hey John, there's enough blue up there to sew a Dutchman's pants," Heather exclaimed at our granola bar stop. The next sign to us said,

NARROW WINDING ROAD NEXT 14 MILES

and as we saw the band of blacktop wind its way up through the pines, we decided we had better fill up our gas tanks before the climb.

"I remember when your brother, Dan, used to always say that in Canada," said Heather. "Whenever the clouds would let a little bit of blue show through, he'd talk about the Dutchman's pants."

"Do you think it might snow today?" Joy asked. "I think it would be neat."

I looked up at the pine trees whipping underneath a blustery blue and gray sky. "I don't know, but it sure seems cold enough, and if it rains like it did yesterday, we could be climbing high enough to get some white stuff."

"Snow in California? . . . in September?" exclaimed Jimmy. "Nooo, I don't think so; I'm working on my tan."

As we headed up the mountain, I prayed that Jimmy would be right, but the Dutchman soon lost all the fabric for his pants. In not more than a hundred yards, the sky darkened and the trees stopped swaying.

"Hey John, it's getting awfully quiet," whispered Joy as she rode alongside me at the back of the pack. "Quiet, just like the way it got quiet when we rode in the snow in the Canadian Rockies."

The road narrowed as it criss-crossed its way up the eastern slope of the Sierras, and the only noise that could be heard on our deserted stretch of it was our huffing and puffing. Soon after the trees stopped their dance, a light gray mist began falling from the sky, and Joy, with cold, rosy cheeks, looked over at me in excited anticipation.

Soon after her smile, the mist turned into large drops that quickly turned into pellets of ice that promptly broke the silence as they banged off our helmets and bounced off the blacktop all around us. Jimmy was a few switchbacks ahead, and I knew I wouldn't hear his reaction until I met him at the summit; but Joy, Heather, Ethan and Carl seemed to be enjoying the whiteness that danced like frozen popcorn all around them. With another corner's gain in elevation, the hail turned into lightly falling snow, and again we were surrounded by the quiet that accompanied the soft flakes of white. The kids examined the snowflakes that sat for an instant on their handlebar bags before melting. Our climb upward brought more and more snow and before we knew it, the road ahead had turned from wet black to translucent white, and soon the trees around us were covered with white frosting.

"This is fun," said Joy, her cheeks growing rosier and rosier.

"I'm taking a break," said Ethan, pulling over to the dirt shoulder just before an especially steep and narrow curve. Carl and Joy joined Ethan to catch their breaths.

"Don't wait here too long, you guys, you'll get cold," I warned, as I passed them. "I'm going to ride with Heather. I'll see you up ahead."

I approached Heather from the rear, and I marveled at her smooth pedalling up one of the steepest grades we'd yet challenged.

"John, do you think that's the top up ahead?" she asked, as I greeted her with a compliment on her style.

"Well, I hope so," I answered. "I don't know how much more climbing I want to do in this weather."

"Me either—" Heather's answer was interrupted by the groaning of a pickup truck approaching the summit from the other side. It was still invisible but its headlights illuminated the falling snow. It was the first vehicle other than our own we'd seen in six miles. The truck crested the top and peeked over at us like some four-wheeled dragon. Steam billowed out its mouthlike grill, and its headlights made us realize how dark it actually was around us.

The driver must have panicked at the sight of us climbing toward him or at the snow-covered road suddenly heading steeply down into the canyon behind us. I think he tapped his brakes, because as soon as his back wheels got over the top, he started to spin and skid. Before Heather and I knew it, the truck was sliding broadside and out-of-control down our lane. Heather, who was still ahead of me, froze in her tracks and straddled her bike as the truck came hurtling straight toward her.

"DIVE, HEATHER! THE DITCH, DIVE!!!" I screamed.

Not more than fifty yards from where she stood, the driver of the dragon somehow gained enough control to slide to the other side of the road. My sigh of relief was only momentary as, right beside us, the truck pitched over onto its side and slid toward the steep cliff that dropped off into the canyon on the other side of the road. The truck rolled over onto its roof and then rolled over again. It finally slid onto its side and headed off the slippery road towards the cliff. There was no guard rail that could save the truck from plunging over the side. I only hoped the four-wheeled monster would slide towards one of the sections of shoulder with trees that might stop it, and luckily it did. It came to a sudden halt, no more than ten yards from where Heather and I were standing, and everything became eerily quiet — no moans, no nothing coming from the overturned cab. The dragon lay motionless and smoke rose from its hood.

"Did that really just happen?" Heather's eyes were open wide and she held one hand to her chest. "And I thought I almost died when my tire blew up the other day . . . ."

"Are you all right, Heather?" I asked, putting my arm around her.

"Alive, yes; but all right? . . . I don't know if you'd call this all right . . . Right now, my heart feels like it's going to jump out of my chest again, and my knees are rattling so hard they're are going to bruise themselves.

"At first, I thought the driver was drunk or just trying to scare me, and then he started getting closer and closer . . . and then I heard you yelling, 'Ditch', and then he slid back over and started flipping over . . . It all happened so fast, yet it all seemed to be happening in slow motion."

"So, you were ready to hit the ditch?"

"Yeah, even before you yelled at me I was ready to dive." Heather looked up at me.

"John . . . ."

"Yes, Heather."

"What about the people in the truck?"

"I just wanted to check you out first . . . and I'm scared to go look. Before I go over there, though, you better get back on your bike and head on up the road. After sweating for the last half hour, I don't want you catching cold standing here in the snow. Just tell Jimmy to wait at the top, and if you have to wait long for me, do some dancing and jumping to keep yourselves warm, okay?" I gave her a big hug, and as she remounted her bicycle, I laid mine down and walked over to the smoking pick-up.

Heather's heart may have slowed a little, but mine speeded up as I approached. I couldn't tell whether it was smoke or steam that seeped through the grill and mangled hood. The skyward wheels spun silently, and my head spun through every first-aid lesson I had ever taken. Being the only car we had seen in several miles of lonely road, I figured any help would have to come from me. And while I worried about what awaited me inside the overturned cab, I also worried about the effects any delay might have on my sweaty and sky-soaked kids. Five cases of hypothermia scared me almost as much as one downed dragon.

Before I had a chance to walk around to the side of the truck where I could look into the windshield, five fingers and a hand slowly clawed their way out the window. To my relief, they were followed by the arms and body of the man who had been driving. He pulled himself up and out of the window and then hopped down onto the road.

"Are you okay?" My voice quivered, as if I'd seen a ghost.

"Yeah, we're all right. My wife and son are still inside, but I think they're just shaken up."

I remembered some of the horror stories I'd heard about people going into shock after accidents, so I slowly approached the man and reached for one of his hands, while putting my other hand on his shoulder.

"Are you sure you're okay?" I repeated.

"Yeah, I think so. I'm awful sorry about what just happened. The last thing I expected to see when I crested the summit was a little girl riding her bicycle, and then when I saw the snow on the road, I guess I must have touched my brakes . . . Is she okay?"

"Yeah, she'll be all right. I had to keep her moving, though. It's not good to be standing around in this cold after heating up. Let me help you with your family."

"Hey John!" It was Carl, along with Ethan and Joy, coming around the corner below. "What happened?"

"I'll tell you later. You guys just keep movin' and I'll meet you with Heather and Jimmy up top. While you're waiting, keep moving. Try to stay warm; I'll be there as soon as I can."

The man's son was the first one out, and then, with help from the three of us, out came his wife. She immediately started dancing around the road yelling, "Praise the Lord! Oh, thank you, Lord!"

I agreed with her completely, but I was worried that she might be as hysterical as she seemed to be thankful. While her son and husband were inspecting the damage to their truck, I approached her slowly to see if she was okay. I grabbed both her hands and looked into her eyes, trying to calm her down, and slowly her eyes lost their glaze and her feet eventually stopped dancing.

"Yes, I'm okay. Thank you, oh thank you for stopping."

"Well, I just wanted to make sure you were okay before I left. The first car I see I'll wave down and ask to phone for help. I'm sorry I can't help anymore, but I have got to get to my kids. It's awfully cold for them to be standing around up here." I shook everyone's hand and headed up the hill, as the men continued surveying the damage and mom danced a few more praises to the Lord.

". . . it was like I was watching some weird video on MTV! There was this truck coming right at me, and there was the wonderful snowy forest, and John was yelling behind me, and I just knew I was going to die, and . . . and my entire life story was playing." I reached the top to find everyone hopping and dancing in a circle around Heather as she shared her story. They didn't even notice my approach.

"The really strange thing was that it was happening in super-fast and slow-motion, both at the same time."

". . . Like the Twilight Zone, huh Heather . . ." said Ethan.

"Were the people all right? Did you see them?" Heather asked Joy, Ethan and Carl.

"Yeah, I think so," answered Joy. "Just as I rode by, this lady jumped down from the side of the truck and started dancing around the road yelling, 'Praise the Lord!'"

"Are you guys okay?" I interrupted.

"We're a little cold, but we're okay," answered Jimmy. "I hear I missed some excitement back down the road."

"Yeah, I guess you could call it that, but there's no time to talk about it now, we better get moving. This weather doesn't seem to be getting much better. Blow on your hands a couple more times and get them warm for the downhill."

Our seven miles of downhill proved more miserable and dangerous than I could've imagined. The sky hurled snow, hail and slush into our faces, and without any climbs to provide us with heat, we began to get dangerously cold.

"Hey John, I'm having trouble grabbing my brake levers," cried Carl, as I rode up alongside him a mile into our downhill.

Jimmy, feeling more of the pain he had felt that awful day in Oregon, stopped the group a mile later.

"John, it's getting really cold, man," he said, shaking his head and blowing into his soaked gloves. "I feel like my face and fingers are about to fall off."

"Yeah, and it's getting hard to see," said Joy, who didn't seem to be enjoying the sky as much as she had earlier. "If that Highway Patrol guy back there hadn't had his lights on, I don't know if I would have seen him."

"Well, you guys, I wish I could do something about the weather, but I'm sorry. Just go real slow and pump your brakes. It will take us longer to get to the highway, but you won't get as cold and you won't have to worry about getting out of control. Just try to think warm thoughts like bathtubs filled with hot chocolate and fireplaces—"

"Yeah . . . and Virginia in June," interrupted Heather with a smile. "Try singing some song to take your mind off things, if you can. I've been singing and it seems to be helping me."

I don't know if any of the kids took Heather's advice, but after a half hour of freezing descent, five red-cheeked and silent faces awaited me at the stop sign, marking Highway 36.

Originally, I had planned on turning west on Hwy. 36 and heading over 5,750-foot Fredonyer Pass to Lake Almanor, where we would spend the night; but it was only two o'clock in the afternoon and the busy highway was crowded with dragons with their headlights on. Logging trucks, semis and greyhound buses rumbled past us, pedal-to-the-metal, throwing slush, diesel exhaust and red volcanic gravel in our faces. There was so much water on the road that each vehicle left a wake that blinded us as they roared past. Lake Almanor was a warming climb and fifteen miles to the west, and Susanville was a freezing and seemingly blind three mile descent to the east. In almost four months of pedaling, we hadn't yet backtracked, but with my senators not interested in any vote, I decided we'd better seek shelter back down the mountain.

"Okay, you guys, we're going to change plans and ride down into Susanville. I think we need a motel." My promise of sheets and bathtubs received no cheers, just blank stares. Tears ran down Carl's face, and it looked like a few of his friends were about to join him.

Somehow, we managed to cross the four lanes of fifty-five mile an hour traffic. "Be careful, you guys," I warned the kids stupidly — as if they would be anything but careful. Once on the other side, we remounted our bikes and began to ride down the mountain.

6% GRADE NEXT THREE MILES warned the sign ahead of us. The black and yellow sign with its truck speeding down a black triangle was usually one of our favorites, but not that afternoon. Just as Jimmy passed it, a giant gray bus blew by us, and I watched the kids ahead of me wobble and struggle to gain control in its blinding aftershock of wind and water. Soon they all disappeared, as I too was blinded. I held on for life as my bike was shaken by the blast.

"STOP SLOWLY, EVERYBODY! PULL OVER AND STOP!" I yelled at the top of my lungs.

Pulling over to what little shoulder there was, the kids looked back at me, their faces frozen with terror.

"John, that was dangerous," Jimmy said. "I couldn't see nothin', and that bus sure came close."

My brain worked as fast as it could, weighing our options. The kids were standing up to their ankles in water, and Ethan was now crying with Carl. What little shoulder of asphalt there was was now covered with the run-off of red cinder being washed from the mountainside. Highway 36 would be dangerous in dry sunlight, and, in the downpour that afternoon, it threatened to end our journey.

"Okay, you guys, we're going to play Peter Jenkins and walk down this mountain." I tried to sound confident as a logging truck tried to drown out my announcement. "Someone give me their flashing tail light and I'll add it to the one I'm already wearing. Any truck that tries to take you guys out will have to hit me first . . . and I'll dent the @#%#* out of it." No one laughed, but Heather managed to get to her light and tossed it to me.

"Just keep your brakes on and walk as close to the guard rail as you can without running into it."

It was harder than I thought walking our bikes down that road. I had forgotten how hard it was for the kids to push bikes that weighed almost as much as they did. Bicycles were designed for riding, not pushing, and we had more than one life-threatening loss of control, as the kids tried their best to wrestle the gusts, their gear and gravity.

We had hiked downhill about a quarter-mile when Joy suddenly pulled to a stop.

"John . . . I'm really cold. I don't know if I can make it." All the sparkle was now gone from Joy's eyes, and her shoulders stooped over as she tried to hold herself and her bicycle upright. The rest of the group pulled to a stop, and I leaned my bike on the guard rail. As I tried to warm Joy with a bear hug, I looked over her shoulder to see Jimmy blowing into his gloves, Heather rubbing her arms and shoulders, and Carl and Ethan shivering. Ever since her skin-stealing crash back on the Blue Ridge, the kids had looked to Joy for strength. Her stoic smile had led them through many painful miles, and if she could do it, then they always could as well. Her knees were beginning to buckle for the first time, and we were all shaken seeing her that way.

"Hey you guys, remember what my mom used to always say?" I said, trying my best to sound cheerful.

"Yeah . . . 'No brains; no headaches' . . . so what?" barked Jimmy.

"Well, I shouldn't be getting any headaches today. Look what I've got us wearing on our heads right now." Everyone reached up and touched their helmets.

"You know, bike helmets may be made out of part styrofoam, but I don't think they're the best insulation, you know what I mean? And since we're not riding our bikes down this stupid road, there's really no reason to be wearing them . . . So . . . why don't each of you take turns holding each other's bikes, and let's swap helmets for our wool hats."

"Hey John, you're brilliant," said Jimmy.

"John, can we put on dry sweaters if we have them?" asked Heather.

"Sure, go for it." I continued rubbing Joy's back as the other kids paired up.

She slowly reached down into her panniers and grabbed her sweater, and soon she'd swapped her dripping helmet for her pink ski hat, embroidered with dancing reindeer.

"Okay, everybody, give your partner a squeeze . . . blow three more times into your gloves . . . and James, take us to Susanville." I squeezed Joy's shoulders one more time, she reached around and squeezed mine. Two more miles to go.

> " . . .Sleigh bells ring are you listenin',
> down the lane all is glistenin',
> a wonderful sight we're happy tonight,
> walking in a winter wonderland . . ."

Maybe it was the dancing reindeer on Joy's hat — I don't know — but after a few more minutes of our descent, I began singing every Christmas carol I could remember. I began with *Winter Wonderland* and followed with my best impersonation of Bing Crosby singing *White Christmas*. Jimmy managed to turn my way and roll his eyes. Still, I continued with *Jingle Bells* and my own composition, *Rudolf the Red-Nosed Biker*, but no one joined in on any of the choruses. We were making progress though, and after an hour of my terrible singing, the rooftops of Susanville appeared around a bend in the road. Town looked just a half-mile away.

"Hey John, your voice isn't too good, but I tried to do a little dancing as I listened, and guess what . . . I think my toes are waking up." Heather was smiling again, and with more and more rooftops coming into view, the kids started cheering.

"Hey John, can we ride our bikes once we get to town?" grinned Carl, as he turned and wiped the last tears from his face.

"Sure, let's go for it!" I answered.

We got off at the first side street that entered Susanville and stopped to decide the best way to ride into town. Water was running from sidewalk to sidewalk, and it was so deep, it was hard to tell where the curbs were. At one intersection where two especially deep streets of water collided, giant brown plumes of rainwater, as tall as the kids, shot up from each corner. As we stood ankle-deep underneath the Susanville City Limits sign, Carl surveyed the road conditions and then amended his suggestion:

"Well, on second thought, maybe we'd better walk."

We walked our bikes through town to the first motel I could find. Folks sheltered in coffee shops and businesses on the main street stared in disbelief as the kids pushed their bikes through the downpour. Almost as if on cue, the minute we floated into the parking lot of the motel, the clouds spread apart to reveal a dazzling blue. Heather grinned a giant grin as she shouted a laughing: "Hey John . . . enough blue to sew a Dutchman's pants, don't you think?" I ran over and gave everyone big hugs before I went into the office.

After securing our two rooms for the night, I returned to find the kids doing a wild splash dance in the water-filled parking lot. Holding hands in a circle of triumph, they were singing at the top of their lungs.

"Hey John, where's your camera?" yelled Carl. "I think we deserve a picture!"

They posed their silliest pose, complete with rabbit ear fingers placed behind each others' heads. Ethan took off one of his shoes and emptied a foot's worth of waterfall onto Jimmy's head. I clicked the picture and then pointed over their shoulders at the sight that had just opened up behind them.

"Whoa, dude, that's beautiful," sighed Jimmy, and the kids, with arms around each other, looked to the west. It seemed the Dutchman needed some bigger pants, because the sky cleared completely to reveal the mountains covered with a thick white blanket of snow.

". . . and we rode right through that stuff," boasted Ethan.

Indeed they had. I called it our toughest day of riding in my journal that evening. I wrote something about how my kids held their own against the dragons of the Sierra, as I sat in the pizza parlour waiting to pick up our dinner, while the kids sat in hot bathtubs and thawed out in front of TV. My fingers were still so stiff, I had trouble holding onto my pen.

While the kids slept the next morning, I continued my journal session across the street at the laundromat. Almost all of their many layers of clothing were heavy with rain and sweat, and I figured we might be needing all of those layers again soon, as the weatherman predicted "continued unseasonal snow in the mountains of Northern California . . . ."

We left Susanville later that morning under blue skies, and it looked as if the weatherman might be wrong. But before we had reclaimed all the altitude we had lost the day before, the sky clouded over and the Dutchman again lost his pants. By eleven, the sky was again falling, and as we climbed towards Fredonyer Pass, rain turned to hail and hail turned to snow. The many-wheeled dragons were again doing their best to blind us in their wakes, and those of us who had room underneath their helmets were wearing their wool hats for extra protection against the cold.

We made it over the pass, and at a little market in Westwood, I broke out the stove and cooked up a steaming pot of chicken noodle soup. As we danced and sipped underneath the overhang, a white pick-up truck pulled up. We were about to meet Fred and Marie Bennett.

Fred stepped out of the truck first, adjusting his collar and logging cap to keep the sleet from going down the back of his neck. He was a wiry man, had gray hair and looked old enough to be a grandad and strong enough to cut his own firewood. Marie, bundled up in the cab, stayed inside and tried not to look too obvious as she stared at the kids.

"Howdy," Fred said, shyly nodding as he walked into the market.

After a couple minutes, Marie couldn't stand her curiosity any longer, and she rolled down the window. "What are you kids doing out here in this awful storm?"

"Oh, we're just riding our bikes across America," Jimmy announced nonchalantly. Marie choked on her chewing gum and immediately brought her hands to her cheekbones in surprise.

"You mean to tell me you little ones are riding your bicycles across the United States? You're going to ride from here back east? Where are your parents?"

Jimmy and Heather walked over to her window to answer.

"Well, ma'am, we're not riding from here to the East Coast," smiled Jimmy. "We've ridden from the East Coast to here. Shoot, we're almost finished."

"Yeah, so far we've ridden over four thousand miles since we left Washington, D.C. back in June," added Heather. "And our parents aren't with us. That tall guy over there is John, our teacher."

"Yeah, he's the big ugly one over by the stove," Jimmy laughed.

"And your parents know you're out riding in weather like this? Why, this storm is so bad, my husband Fred, who works for the highway department, isn't even working today."

"Oh, the weather *is* pretty bad, but I guess we're kinda used to it," answered Heather. "We're following the trail of the wagon trains and trying to be like the pioneers. They had some pretty bad weather too, and they didn't even have any places like this to stop. My parents knew we would have some bad weather, but they still wanted me to go."

"Yeah, my mom knew that too. Shoot, we've already been through a heat wave in the South, a tornado on the Mississippi and some pretty awesome lightning in Kansas," said Jimmy.

I watched Marie marveling at Heather and Jimmy's explanation, and when old Fred returned to the truck, Marie slid over to the middle of the seat and gave him an excited replay of all she had heard.

"Well, you kids be careful," she warned, as Fred started up the truck. "The road gets awful narrow and windy between here and Chico. We'll be prayin' for ya."

Fred backed the truck out onto the street as Marie finished. He looked over at me through his foggy windshield and nodded his good-bye quietly. I had a sneaking suspicion we might be seeing them again.

The rain and snow limited us to forty miles that day, and we rolled into Chester, hoping that one more day's ride would take us out of the mountains and down into California's Central Valley.

It did turn out to be one day's ride, but it was one long day's ride. The next morning, the digital sign outside of the bank on Chester's main drag alternated flashing 9:00 and 40 degrees, but as the day grew older, the sky only grew darker, and I'm sure that thermometer dove into the thirties as we pedaled out of Chester and headed toward Deer Creek Pass.

"Hey John, will you help me with my drawstrings? I've got to go to the bathroom really bad," Joy asked as she slowed her bike to ride beside me.

"Sure, Joy. Just wait till you see a place with enough room to pull over."

Joy finally found a place where the road didn't just drop off into oblivion or butt up against some wall of rock. The rain had made a mess of the knots in the strings that held her rain pants and sweatpants around her narrow waist, and it was my job to get them undone before we had an accident.

"I'm sorry I can't get them undone myself, but my fingers are too frozen to grab them," Joy apologized, doing her best not to dance too wildly as I attempted to untie the impossible knots. The rain had swollen the cotton ties and, to make matters worse, Joy had them tied so tight that the knot was half in and half out of the two tiny slits at the front of her sweatpants.

"I'm sorry this is taking so long, Joy, but my fingers are pretty wasted themselves. Could you suck your breath so I can get a little slack on this string?"

"Okay, I'll try, but I think I'm already sucked in as far as I can go . . . and . . . John . . . I really have to go . . . I don't know if I can hold it much longer."

"Well, Joy, I would say to try to think dry thoughts, but with this rain and these waterfalls pouring down from the rocks—"

"JOHN! I'm not kidding!" Joy smiled in pain, sucked on her finger and knocked her knees together. Just when I thought I'd have some gap to work with in her stubborn little knot, she'd let out her breath or change her dance step, and it would tighten itself back into a ball, just like one of those little bugs that tightens into a ball when you roll it over. My poor, slit thumb was useless, and I had to blow on my fingers every minute or so to keep them working. Finally I made it through both layers of pants and Joy ran over to water a pine tree.

It wasn't long after Joy's "thank you" that I approached Ethan, who was off the road and looking at his bike.

"Hey John, can you change a flat tire in the snow?" he asked. ". . . because I think I have a flat tire on my back wheel."

My fingers were called back into service, and Ethan watched as I showed him the proper method. By the time I had finished and returned my fingers back into my gloves, all the *insulating-while-wet* power of wool seemed to be gone, and blowing as hard as I could into those frozen finger covers only made me dizzy.

"You know what?" announced Heather, when Ethan and I caught up to her, "I think these mountains would be a beautiful place to camp."

Ethan echoed a "yeah" after taking a few seconds to look around. Usually I could join the kids in their games of Bright Side, but that day, switchbacking in the cloud-shrouded mountains above Chico, all I could do was pray for some sight of the big valley below. The gash in my thumb had become a canyon of open flesh, and the freezing temperatures may have kept it from bleeding but did nothing to numb the screaming pain. I had to go to the bathroom myself, but I didn't have time. Each time we stopped, I needed to untie one of the kids' pants or fix one of their bikes, and then get them moving again before they froze. Besides my bursting bladder and throbbing thumb, I was worried about the way our narrow road was disappearing into the pea soup clouds. Cars and trucks were roaring up behind us on the blind corners, and my nerve endings were rapidly unravelling. Just as I was about to break down in tears, I heard a car honking from behind, and I was just about to give the driver and his horn a less than considerate bit of sign language, when I heard a familiar voice over my shoulder.

"Hey, you guys are looking great!" It was Marie Bennett with her head and shoulders hanging out the window. Fred had his emergency flashers on and was slowly pulling up alongside me.

"I said my prayers for you all this morning, and I just knew you would be doing just fine," Marie announced with a smile. "I even called all the TV stations to tell them all about ya."

"Hi, Marie!" yelled Heather and Joy, as they looked over their shoulders and noticed our truck driving cheerleaders. Fred waved from behind the steering wheel, and I noticed even he was smiling.

"You guys keep it up, you've only got twenty miles to go." Fred leaned over Marie's shoulder to give us the mileage. I knew from my map that he was correct, but I was hoping he'd lie and make Chico a little closer. The kids waved and Marie cheered as Fred drove alongside us. I just looked down at my map and tried to blow the pain from my thumb.

Cars began turning their headlights on even though my watch said it was only 3:30 in the afternoon. I didn't want us spending another day in those mountains, but I also didn't want to be coming down the mountain into Chico at night. As we crested each ridge, I prayed for some view of the valley below, but each turn only revealed another ridge. *"Faster, you guys, faster,"* I chanted to myself. *"It's getting darker and darker . . . ."*

Just before Forest Ranch, the last bastion of civilization before Chico — and the last possible place to abandon our plans to make it out of the mountains that day — I saw Jimmy and the group pull over to an unscheduled stop.

"Hey Jimmy! What do you think you're doing?" I yelled. "We haven't got time for anymore food stops or bathroom breaks. I thought I told you no more stops until Forest Ranch. If you're gonna lead this group, then do what I tell you."

"But John—"

Just as Jimmy was about to justify his stop, I saw the white truck coming towards us, honking its horn loudly. Marie was hanging out the window again despite the rain, with a giant smile on her face and her arms waving wildly. Fred and Marie pulled to a stop at the turnout across from us, and Fred ran across the road carrying two fluorescent orange vests.

"Here, John and Joy, you two need these. Why, up there on some of those misty gaps, a driver can't even see you with your dark rain gear and all. These other kids are visible in all their yellow, but you two can't be seen until somebody's almost right on top of ya." Fred helped Joy on with her vest, carefully bringing it around her shoulders and tying it snuggly in the front. Marie helped me on with mine.

"Fred wears these all the time when he's out working. Helps folks see him from quite a distance, even when it's sunny out. We ran down into town to pick these up after we passed you back there." Marie straightened the shoulders on my vest, as if she was getting me ready for church.

"Okay, you all best be goin'," announced Fred. "Sun ain't gettin' any higher, but you're almost there. Marie and me, we'll be gettin' ourselves back home now too, so we'll have to say good-bye. We'll see you all on TV."

"But what about your vests?" asked Joy.

"Oh, you just keep them as souvenirs from Fred and me," smiled Marie. "You kids just get along now. The Lord promised me he'd get you to Chico before dark."

Just as Fred turned toward his car, Joy tapped him on the shoulder. She threw her arms around him, and old Fred blushed as she hugged him like a grandpa.

Forest Ranch was just a few more ridges away. I don't know if it was Marie or God who had spoken to Lyn DuMond, the woman who ran JR's Restaurant there, but she had bowls of hot clam chowder waiting for us. While we warmed our frozen insides with her soup, Lyn got out twelve empty, long-neck beer bottles and placed them in front of the crackling fireplace.

"Why don't you hand me your gloves and I'll get them on these bottles," she said. "Might help to dry them a little bit. I can't believe you kids are out in this weather."

"Hey John, do you think she might let us dry our socks out there?" whispered Ethan.

"Are you kidding?" Jimmy cut in, while I swallowed my mouthful of soup. "You don't want this place smelling like our tent. We hang our socks out here and she'll never have another customer. Chowder's gonna have to warm our toes."

Just as Lyn was telling us that snow-covered bicyclists get free soup in her restaurant and that we'd better get going if we wanted to make Chico by dark, one of the Chico TV stations showed up delighted with our situation. I told the excited reporter we didn't have time for retakes and sit-down interviews, so he just followed alongside us in his car, his cameraman sticking the camera and microphone out the back window and he sticking his head out the front. I smiled as I watched him interview the kids in the pouring rain.

At the crest of a long grade, I saw another car pulled over with two women waving their arms out their windows at us. It was another one of Fred and Marie's TV crews, and Jimmy pulled us to a stop. As the two women approached the group, I noticed a particularly bright patch of land down below the clouds. Our first opening of the sky all day revealed a broad valley at the base of the canyon.

"Hey, you guys!" I yelled, startling the two reporters. "I think that's Chico down there!"

Jimmy started the "YAHOOS," and soon the kids were dancing over their bikes and slapping each other on the back, oblivious to the cameras.

I tried to roll my bike back away from the kids' celebration so the reporters would talk to them and not me. With all the hugs and smiles going on from my frozen little friends, I think the two women noticed there was indeed something very special happening in front of them. They did an about-face and began interviewing the kids without saying a word to me.

"Are you the kids who have ridden across America?"

Jimmy looked ready to answer with one of his sarcastic barbs, but, instead, he smiled over at me and turned on his manners. "Yes, ma'am, that's us," he nodded.

"And you've been riding your bikes in this storm for the last three days?"

"You bet," answered Carl. "It's been raining and snowing since we left Eagle Lake."

"And you rode your bikes in the snow?"

"Sure, the pioneers could push their wagons through it without any roads, so we could at least ride our bikes through it . . . Noooo problem."

The kids laughed at each other as they heard themselves describe their last three days. The reporters were captivated as each of the kids in turn went on about our journey. Heather talked about our Amish friends; Joy about William Swain; Carl spoke of our mileage; Ethan of our tornado and lightning; and Jimmy of how important it was to be seeing the country and meeting Americans. My thumb didn't say a word as I listened smiling from my vantage point a little ways away from the group, and finally the two ladies walked back to get to me.

"The kids tell us that you're their teacher and leader. We were wondering what made you want to do something like this?"

"Well, I don't mean to sound too corny, but you just met the five reasons. I dreamt for a long time about doing this, and now that I'm almost finished living that dream, I realize I had it almost all wrong."

"What do you mean?"

"Well . . . I left California thinking the most important thing our trip would do would let my kids meet their country, and now I think the most important thing was that the country got to meet these kids . . . .

"I mean, those five kids up there just spent the last three days riding their bikes through the snow. Three days of eight to ten freezing hours, trying to hold onto their handlebars to make it up the mountains and then trying to hold onto their brakes so they wouldn't get killed on the way down. And why? Because it was fun . . . or because they were going to get A's on their report cards? Shoot no. My kids wanted to learn something about America, and they've spent the last three and a half months — day and night — working harder than any classroom I know of to do that. And I think every American who has met them or watched them from their porches and windows has learned something too.

"What can I say about those guys up there? I never thought I could love a group of kids so much. If it wasn't for them, I don't think I could have made it over these mountains . . . and you know . . . I hope you put them on TV; not me.

They're the real story you should be talking about, okay?"

"Can we get a shot of your group heading down the mountain?" the reporter asked.

"Yeah, sure, go ahead. Just be careful where you decide to pull over. We can't be stopping anymore. This road is getting darker and more crowded, and I owe those kids bathtubs, TV and pizza. Thanks for coming up in this storm. I think the kids deserve it." With that, I slid my foot into my pedals, motioning for the kids to get ready for the downhill. As we rode past the camera and the kids waved, chills of pride replaced the ones caused by the cold, and salty tears rolled down my face along with the raindrops falling from my helmet. We rolled into Chico, California, on Friday evening, September 26 . . . finally out of the mountains.

"Hey John!" Heather had a huge grin on her face as she stood over her bike at the stop light in downtown Chico and pointed to the sky. "Enough blue to sew a Dutchman's pants."

Good-bye William

The next morning I rose early to find a donut shop where I could be alone. The kids were all tucked deep underneath the fresh sheets of our motel, and I had an hour to myself at Helen's Donuts, reading the newspaper and trying to do some justice in my journal to our mountain passage. I returned to the rooms to find the kids propped up on their pillows and mesmerized by Saturday morning cartoons. They didn't even notice me when I walked in.

"Hey you guys, I've got donuts." Attention immediately turned my way as my five crusty friends dove into the box of breakfast. It didn't take them long to grab their favorites, and I was soon forgotten. Within thirty seconds they were all back on their pillowed perches, entranced with the characters dancing across the screen.

"Uh . . . excuse me, you guys," I said, jolting them back to earth by turning off the TV, "but does eleven o'clock give you enough time to watch cartoons and get showered? I would like to have a journal meeting and bike cleaning session."

"Sure dude, I think we can handle it," said Jimmy. "Now, could you please turn the TV back on? Scooby Doo was about to escape."

"So, eleven o'clock, on those tables outside?"

"Yeah, John, eleven o'clock. Please turn the TV back on!" The way Jimmy sounded and the way everyone else was dancing around, Scooby must have been in deep trouble. The kids sighed with relief when I clicked the set back on. By eleven o'clock, the dozen and a half donuts were gone, Scooby had escaped safely, and everyone was showered and waiting for me around the pool with journals and pens.

"Hey John, isn't Chico where William Swain ended up?" asked Heather.

"Well, as far as I can tell by my maps, this is close to where he ended up. I know he crossed the mountains where we did, and the place he finally ended up he called 'Lawson's Ranch.' Actually, it was called Lassen's Ranch and I think it was pretty near here. Wait til you guys hear his journal entries about coming over those mountains."

"I'm ready. Go for it, John." Jimmy sat back and everyone listened to our friend Mr. Swain with as much attention as they had paid to old Scooby Doo.

"Nov. 6. Never shall I forget the scenes of that day.

The storm increased as the day advanced. The clouds were dark and lowering on the mountaintops. The snow descended as it descends only in a mountainous region, and the thick foliage of the dark, mammoth firs and pines was loaded and bowed down with snowy crescents rising one above another, as limb succeeded limb, to the tops of those magnificent spires, among which the driving clouds frequently mingled. Snow fell deep and melted fast when fallen.

. . . Here might be seen a mother wading through the snow and in her arms an infant child closely and thickly wrapped with whatever would secure it from the storm, while the father was close at hand exerting to the utmost in getting along his team, wagon, and provisions – the last and only hope of securing the life of the family.

During the whole afternoon our party waded through two feet of snow with no path, alternately leading an hour each, guided by the blazes on the trees by the sides of the road, while the fresh track of the grizzly bear plainly told the character of the mountain natives.

. . . The ridge was . . . barely wide enough for a road. It was frightful to look down into the dark gaping gorges . . .

The soaking of the melting snow had by afternoon compelled me to abandon half my pack, together with my rifle. I had left all else with but little regret, but when I leaned my rifle against a tree with my belt and sidearms, I felt I was leaving an old friend behind me."

"No, man, not his rifle," sighed Jimmy.

"That would be like leaving our stuffed animals behind," said Carl with a pained expression all over his face. "Keep reading, John."

"Eight o'clock found us almost out of the line of snow, gathered around a blazing campfire, preparing our pinole and coffee.

We stood around the fire till morning, while the rain fell in streams . . .

"Nov. 7. Daylight found us on bare ground and passing along
the first oaks we had seen since leaving Missouri—"

"I remember those!" said an excited Joy. "Just after Forest Ranch, when we
started coming downhill."

"Yeah . . . remember when we yelled and pointed at the oak trees!" Ethan
exclaimed, completely absorbed in his vision of himself and William coming down
the mountain. "That's where we had that gnarly headwind."

I continued:

"We traveled all day in the most drenching rain that I ever saw
and over the worst road that ever was. I was often in the mud
up to my boot tops.
     . . . Rain and wind beat one almost unprotected, for the
mountains here are bare of trees with the exception of scattering oaks. On we went, with sore feet, giving ourselves no time
even to eat or rest, in the hope of reaching the settlement by night."

"Did they make it?" asked Joy.

"Nope. It took them one more day. They arrived at Lassen's on November 8,
1849, and that made their journey twenty-five weeks long since leaving Independence on May 16."

"Man, I can't believe they made it over those mountains . . . ." Jimmy shook
his head, deep in thought.

"Yeah . . . Swain's weather was just like ours . . . and he didn't have a road
. . . ." sighed Ethan, his eyes especially wide.

"John, I know we crossed the mountains at the same place William did, but
are you sure you didn't order our storm so we could be even more like him?"
smiled Heather.

"I still can't believe he left his gun up against that tree," sighed Carl. "I mean,
he carried that thing for six months and then he left it with just a day or two to
go . . . Man . . . ."

"Hey John, is that the last time we are going to hear from him?" asked Heather.

"Yup, this is where we leave ole William behind."

"Shoot, I'm going to be sad to say good-bye," said Carl. "It was kinda neat
hearing how he was doing. Even when we didn't read his journal everyday back
in Idaho, I wondered where he was and if his weather and scenery were like ours
. . . ."

"Yeah, it's pretty unbelievable how much his days were like ours," said Jimmy.
"It made me feel like a pioneer too. Even if he did sometimes write like an English teacher, I'm gonna miss him. Leaving him here makes me feel like I'm saying goodbye to an old friend, too. When I get to heaven, I think I'll look him up."

"You mean, *if* you get to heaven," laughed Carl.

Joy hadn't said much during this discussion because she was already writing in her journal. Soon everyone else joined her, writing about their trail over the mountains, and that afternoon in Chico — somewhere near "Lawson's Ranch" — we shook ole William Swain's hand and said goodbye.

. . . To Shining Sea . . .

"Hey John, shouldn't we be at the ocean by now?" sighed Jimmy as he pulled the group over to the side of the road. Sweat poured down his face onto his already dripping wet tank top. The Saturday morning we woke up in Chico, the sun had made a solo performance in the sky, and now, three days of riding later, we were back into our sleeveless summer cycling clothes and more than ready to see a beach.

"Yeah, John, I can't believe California is this wide!" said Carl as he poured a water bottle over his head. "I knew it was long, but it's pretty far across too . . . ."

"It's not so bad that it's wide," said Heather, "but it's so scrunched up . . . It's like the earth has wrinkles. I think it has something to do with earthquakes."

"Yeah, I think I'd call those 12 and 16 percent grades out of Calistoga this morning major wrinkles," said Jimmy. "I keep thinking that on the top of the next hill I'll look down and see the ocean, but every hilltop seems to lead me to another one. This has got to be the longest 'short' day of riding we've had."

Even I was tiring of the geography lesson that California was giving us, and I was as ready as the kids for its chapter on waves and beaches. "Well, you guys, according to my map we should—"

I never got a chance to finish my lie, because the kids weren't about to listen to any of it. They just drew their loaded water bottles, aimed and fired at their (sometimes) less-than-accurate leader.

"According to my map . . . we should just keep riding and get there when we get there."

"Thank you, oh wise one," Jimmy grinned, as he shot me with one more burst from his bottle. "Let's ride; I think I can smell the ocean."

At 4:30 PM on October first, James "Jimmy" West crested a hill just west of Bodega Bay, California. Upon reaching the top, his awaiting view was accompanied by a loud ringing "YAHOO!!!" that echoed through the windswept canyon and woke up every sea gull for miles. After four months and 4500 miles of pedaling, he had reached the sea, and he wanted the entire world to know about it.

The rest of us, following behind him and hearing his shout, quickened our pace. Soon we joined him atop the same rise, and after gently laying our two-wheeled friends down beside the road, we joined arms and did a land-sailor jig, laughing and shouting uncontrollably. It was a moment we'd dreamt about for a long, long time.

"Hey, you guys . . . ." I had trouble holding back the tears cracking my voice. "You're pretty incredible . . . ."

I looked over at Jimmy and noticed he was wearing a few tears himself. He stopped his dance, spread his legs wide and, with hands on hips, stared off at the water.

"We did it, man, we did it!" shouted Carl, as everyone traded hugs. Joy and Heather then joined Jimmy staring out at the blueness, and Ethan stood between them, gazing through his giant glasses, his eyes as big and brown as I'd ever seen them.

"Hey John," said Joy, "thanks for getting us here." She started to say something else, but was interrupted by Ethan, who spoke as if he'd just awakened from a dream.

"Hey you guys . . . you know what?" Everyone awaited Ethan's words of wisdom. "I think we should go to the beach." In a perfectly serious tone, he said it as if he thought we might make a left turn and continue south without touching the water.

"Gooood idea, Eeth!" shouted Jimmy, as one more barrage of water from everyone's water bottles was emptied on Ethan, who couldn't quite understand why he deserved the honor.

I managed to hug everyone once more before Jimmy led them downhill to the sea. Trying to savor the long-awaited moment, I used my brakes all the way down the hill as I watched my kids race towards the ocean.

I reached the parking lot at Doran State Beach to find it deserted, except for five bicycles. Next to each bike — well, in three cases, *almost* next to each bike — were the rider's shoes and socks. Joy and Heather had their shoes side by side, socks neatly tucked in each shoe, and the boys had one shoe here and one shoe there, one sock another place and the other who-knows-where.

I laid Bud against the brick bathroom and tossed off my shoes and socks guys'-style nearby. I ran out onto the beach to see my five friends running with the wind and the sea birds.

It was the perfect day to hit the coast. The wind had swept the sand clean, and the sky was so blue and clear you could see the curve of the horizon off to the west. The kids floated across the sand at full speed, as if something had broken loose inside them. Joy and Heather did cartwheels at the water's edge, and Ethan and Jimmy had already run a half-mile down the beach, splashing rooster tails behind them as they cut through the water. Off by himself, Carl stopped to wade in up to his knees. He looked out at the horizon, then back over his shoulder and let out a "yahoo!!!" louder than any I had ever heard. Then he leaned over and scooped up a long strand of seaweed, and fastened it around his arm, just above the elbow.

I was almost afraid to interrupt his private moment, but I did anyway, "Hey Carl, what's that for?"

"C'mon, John, this is my seaweed ceremonial arm band . . . I've been waiting a long time for this!" He then took off down the beach, kicking and spinning through the waves. Down the beach, I saw Jimmy run towards him, and when they met, they both leaped high in the air and slapped each other's hands in slow motion.

Maybe someday man will invent film that can capture special moments like that afternoon at the ocean. I snapped away at my leaping, jumping and shouting kids, trying to catch their elation, but every time I looked through my camera and saw those four sides of the frame, I knew my technology wasn't coming close. The tears pouring down my face didn't help much either. Finally, I abandoned my camera on the sand to do a little flying and splashing of my own. I wanted to jump and roll and dive through my old friend's waves as I had done so many times before, yet I didn't want my moment to end. My toes approached the foam at the edge of the water like my mom always used to approach me after not seeing me for a long time. I walked slowly, one step at a time, just like she used to before putting her arms around me.

"Hey John!" Jimmy and Carl ended my moment. Splashing and kicking water, as they ran towards me, they yelled: "Let's christen this dude!"

"Yeah John, we've christened a lot of land seas," laughed Jimmy, out of breath, "and now I think we ought to christen the real thing!"

"I thought you guys would never ask. Where's Ethan? We've got to do this together."

"YO, ETHAN!" Jimmy yelled to his friend, who was walking towards us as if in a trance. Ethan stared out at the water and then down at his feet, skating his legs through the ankle-deep foam. "YO, DUDE! WE'RE GONNA WIZZ IN THE OCEAN!"

Joy and Heather, who were doing some kind of drawing on the wet sand, heard Jimmy before Ethan did. "I can't believe you guys." Joy tried to sound disgusted, but she couldn't help giggling.

"You guys are gross!" added Heather, doing a less than satisfactory job holding back a giggle of her own.

Ethan finally processed Jimmy's proposal and started running towards us for the ceremony. Jimmy invited the girls to join us, but they didn't seem interested. We didn't even have to ask them to turn their backs, because they turned away on their own and tried to imagine we weren't there.

We solemnly held hands, and in (almost) complete seriousness, looked to the person on our left, nodded; looked to the person on our right, nodded again; and then, with a piercing "YEE-HAW!!!," we four guys christened the Pacific. Uncontrolled laughter soon got the better of us, but thanks to the strong offshore breeze and our experienced good aim, no damage was done. We placed our shorts back in proper position with an extra snap of the elastic and then proudly walked back to the girls.

"I still think you guys are gross," smirked Joy.

"Thank you," said Carl, enjoying the compliment.

During our ritual, Joy and Heather had been drawing a giant map of the United States in the sand, and the boys ran to get pieces of driftwood to help them with the finishing touches. The five of them danced around in the middle of the sculpture and then recalled some of their adventures as they slowly drew their route across the continent:

"Oh, there's where we met that crab guy . . . and there's the Blue Ridge Parkway . . . and the Smokies . . . and Jacob . . . and Anna . . . and Memphis . . . ." They reminisced all the way west to where they were actually standing, and then got suddenly quiet, as if realizing their accomplishment for the first time.

". . . Hey, you guys. . . ." Ethan broke the silence, before the tears could begin. ". . . I think it's time."

"You're right, Brother Ethan," agreed Jimmy in an unusually soft voice, "but what are we gonna put the water in?"

"I've got that taken care of, you guys, but you'll have to help me empty it first, before we can fill it back up."

"What do you mean, John?" asked Carl.

"Well, back at that market in Sebastopol, I bought us a bottle of champagne. I figured you guys deserved a special toast today."

"Right on, dude!" said Jimmy. "Break it out!"

I grabbed the bottle I'd hid in a pile of seaweed, and we all walked hand-in-hand down to the water. We went in up to our knees and I popped the cork. Just like the winners of the World Series, the kids shook the bottle and squirted each other, and soon it was empty. Ethan then filled it with ocean, and all five of them joined hands high in the hair. They faced to the East, then to the West, and screamed one last time before heading back to the Blessing of the Wheels. After dropping each others hands, they each hesitated before leaving the water, and they got quiet again, realizing their party was about to end.

Back at the bikes, the celebration was much more subdued. Ethan took the bottle of salt water and once more everyone joined hands as he anointed each bicycle wheel. When it was all over, I asked everyone to gather in a circle, just like we had done that morning after the storm in Arkansas.

"You guys, I know I joke lots of times about things, but before we go, I think we owe the sky and the powers up there a quiet thank you for letting us get here. I don't know about all of you, but I believe we could never have made it without the help of God and all the angels He placed along our way. And I know that this trip isn't over yet, but I would like us to take a quiet moment together in thanks for all the people and all the weather and all the roads that have made this such an incredible journey. And . . . I'd like to thank God for each of you, because I could never have found a more special group of friends than you guys. I couldn't have made it to the ocean without you. So, let's squeeze each others hands and give some quiet thanks . . . ."

"Hey Heather, what are you doing up so early?" It was the next morning and she was up before I was.

"Oh, I couldn't sleep. My mind was going really fast all night, and I had to get up and write some things down in my journal."

"It was a pretty heavy day yesterday, wasn't it . . . ."

"Yeah, it was. I mean, I knew it was going to be exciting and everything getting to the ocean, but I don't know how to describe all the stuff that was happening inside me. I've never had such a hard time writing things down before."

"Could you read me some of what you did write? You don't have to, but I'd sure like to hear it."

"Okay, but don't mind if it doesn't sound just right. My pen's been going pretty fast, and I haven't read back over it myself yet . . .

"October 1, 1986 . . . The wind was blowing strong as we pedaled down the worn-out road leading to the water. We leaned our bikes and took off helmets, gloves and shoes and ran through the sand to the ocean at last. Jimmy and Carl ran and jumped and hit hands. We ran along the beach with strength we never knew we had. We made a map of where we had been, but I knew it wasn't necessary because I knew we had already made one — a life-sized one. We left our mark with everyone we stayed with and every driver that waved and we waved back . . .

We had a ceremony with champagne and pouring the salt water on our tires. The wind blew the sand that stuck to our wet, salty bodies. We stayed in a room that overlooked the great blue ocean. I sit here now, the next morning writing this, watching our flag blow from the winds off the water, thinking what a hard trip this has been, but I'm glad that I did it . . .

"And that's as far as I've gotten. There's lots more I want to say, but I can't get the words from my insides to my head and then out into my journal. I know what I wrote sounds okay and everything, but it just doesn't describe all the feelings going on inside me yesterday and today . . . ." Heather looked back out at the flag and then back at me.

I had a little trouble myself getting words out of my mouth to say to Heather. I looked at this little girl, sitting there contemplating what she'd just done, and I wondered if she really knew the marks she had made. I wanted her to know how she had fueled my spirit and how important her sparkling smile and enduring spunk were to me and Lynn and the four kids sleeping in the room. I wanted to give her a hug and cry on her shoulder, but I couldn't do it that morning. Instead, I held back my tears and said something stupid about having three more weeks to ride and sift through her feelings. She thanked me and went back to staring at the ocean and the flag outside. I excused myself to the bathroom where

I could cry alone.

Golden Gate

"Hey dudes, check it out!" Jimmy yelled, from the top of the hill. "I think that's San Francisco."

"Where's the Golden Gate?" asked Carl. "Shouldn't it be down there somewhere?"

"It's over there alright, but I don't think we'll be able to see it from here. We've still got a few little hills to climb over before we'll get a shot at it." I lied about the steep headlands we still had to cross to get to Sausalito and the bay.

"Hey John, what are you shaking your head about?" asked Jimmy at one of our rest stops later that afternoon.

"I can't believe you guys! Five months ago, these hills would have killed you without any stuff on your bikes, and now you're just cruising . . . ."

"Well . . . I guess we're just gnarly . . . ," chuckled Ethan.

"Yeah, we're just gnarly," agreed Carl.

Nighttime found us in Mill Valley riding a bike path along the San Francisco Bay. San Francisco glittered in the distance, an orange sunset painting itself all over the glass of its skyline, but we still hadn't caught sight of the Golden Gate. We ended up spending the night at a Howard Johnson's there, and decided to get our first sight of the bridge in the morning.

I remember the first time I crossed the Golden Gate Bridge — my family was taking its first real vacation, and my mom and dad had piled my five brothers and sisters and me into the old white station wagon and headed north. All fights, card games and songs stopped immediately as soon as the Golden Gate came into view — a reverence previously held only for a first sighting of the Matterhorn on trips to Disneyland. Our little hearts pounded and our jaws dropped as dad drove us over that orange span of cable and concrete. "Do it again, Dad! Do it again!" I can remember us cheering in unison, as we reached the other side and looked back at one of the wonders of our world.

That same silence descended on my group the next morning as we rounded a bend in Sausalito and caught our first glimpse of orange cables. Electricity flowed through our veins and the hair on our arms stood high above the goosebumps. We climbed the final grade to the northern entrance and stood silently looking up at the two towers at the mouth of the bay. We rolled into the parking lot hooting and hollering, but none of the hundreds of sightseers even noticed us — except one.

Jimmy hadn't seen his mom in over three months, and when he saw her drive up and get out of the car, his eyes welled up with tears. He tried to run towards her, but his feet seemed stuck in the pavement. Audrey, his mom, had to do the running herself, and after everyone in the group yelled, "GO FOR IT, JIMMY!"

he finally got his legs moving. He hugged his mom long and hard, just as he had hugged his dad that hot afternoon at the foot of another bridge just this side of the Mississippi. None of the kids poked any fun at their boastful point man; they all knew how he was feeling.

When Jimmy and Audrey were finished, she came over to check us all out. I offered her my sweaty bandana, but she just let the tears run down her face. We shot some more pictures, and then it was time to cross "The Bridge."

There probably were hundreds of tourists and visitors driving across the Golden Gate that day, but as far as we were concerned there was no traffic during our crossing. Any young lovers, tourists or suicidal thrillseekers were invisible to us, because for a few fleeting minutes that morning we owned that bridge. I watched them, their sparkling faces and strong bodies gleaming in the sun, and we all felt pretty famous as we rolled off the other side. The kids looked at me and then back at the bridge, as if they wanted to ask permission to make the crossing again, but they held their tongues. No cheers echoed from the San Francisco side of the bridge, as we were all quieted by a strange sadness. The Golden Gate part of our dream had passed from something to look forward to something that could only be looked back upon, and our faces fell as we realized that memories often weren't as exciting as hopes.

"C'mon John, let's go for it, we might never be here again together!" yelled Joy.

If it wasn't for my five young friends, I might have been content to sit in San Francisco and mourn over the fact that our journey was rapidly coming to a close. The kids, however, used that realization to inspire them to grab every opportunity and hour to explore San Francisco.

"Yeah, man, I want to hit that punk rock shop!" yelled Ethan.

"I want to go to a movie," said Carl.

"And I want to go shopping," said Heather.

We spent the next four days enjoying San Francisco as if we could never come back. We stayed with Joyce and Angelo Piccinini. Joyce had been my master teacher during my student teaching days of college. She said she always knew I would do things differently as a teacher, and when she saw me ride up her driveway with my classroom on wheels, she smiled, gave me one of her big Irish-Italian hugs and said, "Well, John, at least you got your hair cut." She didn't mention my scraggly on-the-road beard; she just stood me at arms length to get "a good look at me." Joyce showed us our rooms and the refrigerator, then told us not to get home too late.

"Man, John, this place is great," sighed Jimmy as we waited for a cable car. "Now, every time I look up at the skyline or we pass through Chinatown or something, I feel all special inside. I mean, it makes you see things all different when you realize we crossed the whole country to get here. I don't know, but I've never felt this way before . . . ."

"Hey John, c'mon, here comes the cable car!" shouted Heather. "Hurry up and get on."

Heather jumped up onto the running board and found herself a spot with a handrail. She leaned back and looked up at the towering buildings. Lost in her own dream, she looked like she was feeling just like Jimmy.

Lynn joined us for the first two days of our stay, and Saturday morning, after the two of us had a chance to have a private breakfast and the kids had a chance to watch cartoons with Joyce, she took Joy and Heather on a shopping safari through the urban jungle of boutiques and department stores. The girls knew their designer labels as well as I knew my landmarks, and I spent much of the day photographing the kids running in and out of stores and jumping on and off cable cars.

Sunday morning had us off to the Hyatt Regency Hotel for an all-you-could-eat brunch celebration with family and friends who had driven to San Francisco for the day. Heather's family would be there, along with Carl's, Jimmy's, my mom, dad, sister and brother-in-law. There were even two surprise guests, my teaching partner and fellow Educational Safaris' leader, Jim Brady and his wife, Robin. Lynn had spent weeks organizing the party, and I almost messed the whole thing up.

I was planning on putting on my best on-the-road clothes, ones that had been good enough for everyone and every place we had visited in the past three and a half months. I had my nylon rain pants, clean *From Sea to Shining Sea* t-shirt and fresh socks all ready for our Sunday celebration, but when I emerged from my shower that morning, Lynn had pressed slacks, a shirt with buttons, saddle shoes and brand-new brown "designer" socks with polka dots lying on the bed. I looked at the outfit that I saw she was telling me was "appropriate," and anger welled up from deep inside me. She didn't realize it, but putting those clothes out was like telling me the trip was over; that it was time to get back to the *real* world; that I could no longer explain my scruffy appearance with my bicycle or live only on the clothing it could carry. I hadn't worn a shirt with buttons in months or a belt or brown socks, and I wasn't ready to that morning. I wanted my friends and family to see me in my best across-America clothes. She and the kids could wear their fancy pressed outfits, but I wanted to be dressed up, bicycle-style. I didn't realize it, but my refusing to wear those clothes was like telling Lynn I didn't want to come home.

We argued a lot that morning, and as much as Lynn couldn't understand my wanting to stay on the road, I couldn't understand the fact that she, who had been "home" now for over a month, wanted me to come home and live out of our closet. She wanted me to hang my panniers for a while and sleep next to her in our bed, not our tent.

Ethan, Joy and Heather were getting ready in the next room as we yelled at each other in our loudest whispers for a half hour. In protest, I put on *my* outfit, but Lynn's icy stare and threats to leave the seat next to me empty at our gathering soon had me wearing those awful slacks and shirt. By the time we left Joyce's house that morning, we were both red-eyed from crying, and my insides were tied in knots.

Joy, Heather and Ethan looked worried when they saw us come out of our room, and they kept a frightened distance all the way to the hotel. Brave Joy tried to compliment me on how "nice" I looked, and seeing the Kansas-black-kitten-look in my eyes, even she cowered and didn't try talking to me the rest of the morning. Lynn did sit next to me at breakfast, but she didn't sit very close.

Although Lynn and I didn't taste much that morning, the kids and our guests did. Carl set the pace at the brunch, showing everyone in our party all he had learned about nutrition. He downed five full plates of food and everyone else did just about the same. After four hours of eating and visiting, it was time for another celebration to end. The kids said goodbye to their families and I said goodbye to mine. Lynn and I went for a walk before she had to head home, and we talked painfully about the work we had to do for my re-entry, after the confetti and fanfare of homecoming were over. There were lots more socks and slacks at home in my closet . . . .

That night, the kids, Jim, Robin and I decided to go see some theater — "I mean, if we're in the city we should get some culture," Heather had suggested. I picked out *Greater Tuna*, a comedy about life in a small Texas town, but the kids didn't laugh much — and it wasn't because they didn't understand it.

"Hey John, that was supposed to be funny?" frowned Jimmy, as we left the theater.

"Yeah," said Joy, "I thought it was kinda mean."

"I think whoever wrote that must live in California or New York or something," Jimmy continued. "Those characters in that play were different than city people, but I don't think the play should have made fun of them."

". . . They were kinda like . . . ," said Ethan, stopping to think for a moment, ". . . kinda like a lot of the people we met crossing America. I mean they lived in their little houses with their dogs and different ways of talking, but they were nice people."

"Yeah," said Heather, "I don't think the person who wrote that play or the people who laughed so hard at those characters ever took the time to meet those people. All the time the audience was laughing I kept thinking of all the people who filled up our water bottles, or gave us that honey back in Tennessee, or let us stay in their churches. If I laughed in the play, I would have been laughing at them."

The kids continued their review all the way to the bus. Jimmy sat next to me, and, after a few blocks of quiet thought, he turned to me and said, "Now I know why you took us to that play . . . you dog." Little did he know that after my difficult morning, I hadn't planned more lessons. Still, I just winked at him as he punched me in the arm.

Dear Friends,

    Come join us as we celebrate the last mile of our journey across America. We will be riding into Dunn Middle School in Los Olivos, California on Friday morning, October 17 at 11 o'clock.

    Your friendship and help has made our trip possible and we would love to share our last mile with you. If there is any way you can join us — please do. If not, please know we will be thinking of you.

Our love,

Jimmy, Heather, Joy, Carl, Ethan, John and Lynn

    Our last two days of sightseeing and shopping flew by, and soon it was time to head south on the last leg of our journey. Before leaving, we spent our last morning addressing and mailing invitations to our homecoming celebration two weeks away. State by state, we went through our journals and our recollections of all the friends we had met between the oceans, and our list of people deserving invitations was so long that the kids had to go outside the post office for their water bottles when their tongues ran out of saliva to lick all the stamps.

    We took one long last look at the Golden Gate as we pedaled our bicycles homeward along the southern shore at the mouth of the bay. A day's ride south had us halfway to Santa Cruz, where Carl had some friends living in a spectacular house overlooking the rocky shoreline at Pescadero. The Foresters had a redwood hot tub that was made to order for six sweaty bicyclists, and after welcoming each of us with a hug, Linda Forrester led us all to the bubbling tub, where she had stacked six giant, fluffy towels, five Cokes and one beer.

    "Hey you guys, let's give each other massages like we did back in Idaho," suggested Heather. "If we each trade feet with the person across from us, we can give each other foot massages."

    "Oh yeah, those are the best kind," sighed Jimmy, and soon all was quiet, except for the gurgling of the tub and the occasional sighs of one of us. Linda came to the window to check on us, and when she saw us rubbing each others heels and toes, she just winked at me and went back inside. She could tell this was a private ceremony.

    "I think we should rotate partners so that everybody does everybody else's feet," suggested Joy. "After all, our feet have done a lot of work, and I think they deserve it."

    "Sure, I'm up for that," smiled an ecstatic Jimmy. "Let's see . . . five massages and 4600 miles so far—"

    "Four thousand, six hundred and twelve," Carl corrected him.

    "Okay, four thousand six hundred and twelve, divided by five massages . . . that's a little over 900 miles per massage . . . Yeah, I think we deserve five massages."

There was no giggling or tickling that evening as we rubbed away the miles. The fog, drifting in patches over the ocean, muffled the sound of the pounding surf below the bluffs. We changed partners about every ten minutes, and at every change I could hear the kids quietly ask, "Where does it feel the best?" before they proceeded with new feet. When everyone was finished, Heather and the boys got up to watch TV, while Joy and I soaked a little longer.

"Hey John, I'll rub your toes for five more minutes if you'll rub mine."

"Sure, Joy, my feet won't mind a bit."

"John . . . ." Joy waited til everyone else was back inside, and then continued. "Thanks for getting us here." Her voice was quiet and she looked down at the water as she talked. "I don't think I ever realized how hard it would be to get this far . . . I can't believe we've done everything we have, and I don't think we could have made it without you and Lynn . . . .

"Things are going by so fast now, since we got to the ocean, and although I want to get home, I don't want the trip to end either. I miss my bed and my room and Bubbles, my dog, but now, after almost four months, I don't want this all of a sudden to be over."

"Is that why you have been staying up so late at night this past week writing in your journal?"

"Yeah . . . that's one of the reasons . . . ."

"Does your stomach hurt sometimes?" I asked.

"Yeah, like there's a big hole under my ribs." She nodded and tried to hold back her tears. I squeezed her foot hard and let a few tears fall myself.

"Well, we can't stop getting home, but maybe we can ride our brakes the rest of the way and slow things down a little bit . . . okay?"

"Okay."

I squeezed her foot again and she gently squeezed mine. She got up to join the others and I took some time alone before turning off the tub.

The next day we rode south to Santa Cruz. Terraces of green fields dotted with bright orange pumpkins spread themselves out above the ocean, while surfers carved the faces of the head-high waves below. From behind, I watched the kids as they rode slowly, trying to pick out the biggest pumpkin, and I laughed along with them as they stopped to watch the surfers who got the biggest wipe-outs.

Our next stop after Santa Cruz was Carmel, and in a few hours' time, my band of bicyclists became celebrities in the town of golf courses and art galleries. We parked our bicycles along a stone wall just off the main street, and when I reported back for my bike-watch, I found Jimmy, Heather and Ethan gathered on the curb talking to a rather affluent looking, older woman. They were giving her their usual description of our journey: the route, William Swain, tornadoes, rain and Amish corn fields; and the woman, with her gold jewelry and silver hair, was spellbound by the kids' story.

". . . and who is your leader? I would like to meet the person responsible for this wonderful journey," she asked.

"Well, he's standing over there next to the lamp post. That's John, our teacher," smiled Heather.

I had tried to be as inconspicuous as possible. The kids were cute, but I was a different matter. I was afraid that my scraggly beard and weathered face might scare away their admirer.

"So, you're the man who has been taking these kids to see their country." The woman didn't seem to mind my appearance at all. "I'd just like to shake your hand. I know you've got a pretty special group of children here, and from all they've told me about your travels, you must be a pretty special man yourself." She walked over and grabbed my hand with both of hers. After shaking it, she suddenly reached down and squeezed my hairy leg.

"Just had to feel those muscles," she laughed. "Well, you all are getting pretty close to home now, so don't you get careless. The road gets pretty windy between here and where you're headed, so be careful . . . Heather, Jimmy and Ethan . . . and John, it's been a pleasure visiting with you. I expect there to be a book about all this when you get home; you just make sure we get some up here in Carmel, because I want to read it." She waved her well-manicured hand at the four of us and then disappeared around the corner.

"Hey John, what was that lady doin' grabbing your leg?" shouted Joy, as she came running across the street to where we were.

"Oh, she just wanted to touch somebody famous," I laughed.

"Well, she should have touched me," smiled Jimmy.

"Yeah, right," smirked Joy, as I went over and pinched Jimmy's thigh. "Really, who was she?"

"Oh, just a lady who was excited about our trip," answered Heather.

"Gosh, this whole town is excited about our trip," said Joy as she put down her shopping bag. "Everywhere I go, somebody asks me if I'm one of the kids who bicycled across America. I thought one lady was going to ask me for my autograph."

"You should have seen this one woman who came by here when Ethan and I were on watch," said Heather. "She asked us to pose next to our bikes so she could take our picture. And from the look on her face, I think that one picture of us made her day."

"Well, you guys are doing a little better than me," said Jimmy. "I know what you mean about being stopped all over town, except I was stopped by this one lady who said she was a teacher, and she got this real angry look on her face. She asked me what school I went to, and why I wasn't there instead of riding my bike."

"And what did you say?" asked Joy.

"I didn't say anything. She had that look on her face that told me nothing I could say would make any difference. Then, before she walked away, she told me she would like to find our teacher and give him a piece of her mind about keeping kids out of school to ride their bicycles. She growled something about wanting to drive us back to our homes, and I just split."

"WHOA, I think I've had a teacher like her before," said Ethan, shaking his head.

"Me too," said Heather. "She sounds like she's related to that woman back at the Likely Elementary School."

Jimmy looked over at me and continued, "Hey man, don't worry, I didn't let her get me down. I know how much we're learning out here in our pedaling classroom. It actually felt kinda good walking away from her . . . ."

I walked over to Jimmy, put my arm around him and gave him a kiss on the cheek. "Thanks, Jimmy, I needed that."

Jimmy pushed me away and wiped my slobber from his face. "Yeah, but you didn't have to go and kiss me. You can't go around ruining my image this close to home." Everybody laughed and then took off for some more shopping, while I took my bike watch.

We left Carmel Sunday morning, October 12, with less than a week left of pedaling. Five years earlier I had coasted down the same hill in Carmel, heading south with my first group of bicycling kids. Thoughts of that rag-tag and ill-prepared bunch tried to find their way into my head with all the other emotions that were dancing around there, as shadows of "the barn" began appearing around each corner.

"Hey Stick and Head, you two actually made it, huh. Has the Dutchman been followin' you guys?" My brother Dan joined us at Big Sur Campground, and his voice was very familiar to Joy and Heather. The three of them exchanged hugs, and the two girls smiled as they told Dan of some of their adventures. He listened quietly, while Joy and Heather set up camp for one of their last times.

"Hey Dan, I even learned how to put film in my camera!" joked Heather.

"And every time it rained or snowed, we'd be looking for the Dutchman's pants," smiled Joy.

The girls had put in a lot of miles since their Canadian summer with Dan, and he was all ears that afternoon beneath the redwoods. Like an uncle who hadn't seen his nieces for a long time, I think he noticed how much his two friends had grown.

It didn't seem possible, but the sky seemed to grow brighter and bluer each day as we glided up and down the Big Sur roller coaster. With the ocean on our shoulder and familiar scenery coming more and more often, it seemed that our bikes had motors, and as much as some of us tried to slow that last week down, we gobbled up miles in record time. Joy was seeing the barn more and more along with me, and her emotions got the best of her one night on a bluff near Hearst Castle.

"I don't want to hear any more talk about home or school! I'm tired of riding along and hearing some of you guys talking about your rooms at home or your school lockers." It was the first time in four months that I'd heard Joy get mad in front of the group, and that evening she was so angry she had to fight back the tears.

"We're going to be home in three days, and our trip will all be over . . . Then we'll have our bedrooms and our lockers and our school books. I think we should all enjoy these last couple miles as much as we can, because I don't think we'll get another chance like this again, and we'll have lots of bedrooms and lockers. I miss home and everything too, and in a way I can't wait til we ride into the Middle School, but at the same time I don't want this trip to end . . . I don't know; I feel all mixed up inside right now . . . But please, you guys, let's not talk about home anymore; we'll be there soon enough . . . ."

Joy's outburst changed our topics of conversation but didn't slow us down any. The next afternoon, at about three, Morro Rock came into view, and everyone pulled over behind Jimmy to get a view of California's miniature Rock of Gibraltar.

"Hey John, I've seen that rock at least a hundred times before," shouted Heather.

"Hey, you guys, guess where we are?" I grinned as I reached down into my panniers for the can of warm beer I'd hidden there. Carl started to say Morro Bay when he saw me lift the red,white and blue container.

"Hey, that means we're a hundred miles from home!" he shouted. "This is the Henry's Crossroads of the west!"

Heather gave a rather confused Dan an explanation of the celebration we had had months ago, marking the 100-mile mark of our trip on that dirt road back in Maryland. I popped open the can and each of us took a lick of the white foam that came spewing out. Everyone insisted that Dan join in the ceremonial toast, and then I poured the rest of the can on a very special patch of California asphalt.

The next day found us backtracking an especially familiar road — the road we had ridden on our shakedown cruise the spring before our journey.

"Hey John, that's the market where Joy and I got the first banana stickers for our helmets." Heather smiled underneath her bicycle helmet that was now covered with weathered stickers from produce departments all over America.

"Yeah, and I remember the box boy there who didn't believe us when we told him we were going to ride across the United States," laughed Carl. "I wonder if he's workin' today . . . ."

". . . And over the hill there at Montana de Oro," said Ethan lifting his hand off his handlebars and pointing west, "over there is where you tried to teach me how to wash my lycra shorts for the first time." Ethan chuckled and then grew silent as he rode on.

That night, at Pismo Beach, we said goodbye to my brother and hello to Lynn. My dad had driven her and her bicycle up from Santa Barbara for our last night of camping and our last two days of riding. That night at our last campfire, no one seemed to want to say much, but no one seemed to want to go to bed either. A somber bunch of bicyclists crawled into their "portable houses" that night, and

I put my head down on Lynn's chest and broke down in uncontrollable sobs. She didn't say anything about socks or shirts; she just quietly stroked my head as it trembled on her chest. Though there wasn't a cloud in the sky, it rained a lot inside our tent that night.

"Hey you guys, you see that, that's our land!" A giant, Heather-sized smile broke out on Joy's face as she topped the last hill before her house. After a ceremony at Santa Maria City Hall, we'd pedaled ten miles to Carl's house for cake, and then fifteen more to Joy's. We had decided to spend our last night before riding into school with Bob and Sulie.

After a tearful hug for their daughter at the front gate, Joy's folks showed us to the hot tub. A dinner of barbecued steak and lobster soon followed, and then the Fultons asked us to come into the living room for a special ceremony. Bob did the talking, and his voice cracked for the first time in the two years I had known him:

"Well, seeing as you guys are almost finished with your trip, and having been across a few finish lines ourselves . . . Well, Sulie and I just felt that you needed something special to wear tomorrow when you ride that last mile into school. It's traditional for finishers to get finisher's jackets, so we had these made up for you."

Bob wiped his nose, and Sulie pulled seven blue satin jackets, printed with our red, white and blue logo across the back. On the front, over the heart, each one had our name embroidered in white thread.

"We got one made up for each of your moms," Sulie said as she put one on herself. "We figured they were pretty brave for four months too . . . I know I was."

After each of us got our jackets on and modeled them proudly around Joy's living room, Bob and Sulie got hugs from each of us. Dessert was served and eaten slowly, and when everyone had licked their bowls as clean as dog dishes, it was time to say words I'd said almost every night for the past four months.

"Good night, you guys. I think it's time we get some sleep. We've got some riding to do tomorrow." Somehow, I don't think any of us thought we would be hearing those words for the last time, and Lynn and I walked around the room getting the quietest good night hugs we had shared in many miles.

Early the next morning, Sulie cooked up some biscuits and gravy that I'm sure were delicious, but none of us ate much. With the difficult ride ahead of us, our stomachs had butterflies where the food usually went.

We came to our last hill just a mile and a half shy of school and the end of our road. At the top, I stopped everyone for one last meeting. I spread out our weather-beaten, scotch tape-reinforced map and everyone joined hands around it, while I uncapped our orange highlighter.

"Man, remember the first time we got that thing out?" said Jimmy.

"Yeah, it was in that hot and sticky upstairs room on Tangier Island," added

Carl. "It was storming outside, and I remember how little the mark you made looked and how big the country looked . . . I was kinda scared."

"You know what, you guys? . . . I was pretty scared myself."

"Well dude, don't be scared to mark it now; cause we did it," boasted Jimmy. "From sea to shining sea and then some . . . what's that computer of yours say, Carl?"

"Four thousand, nine hundred and seventy," Carl answered, as his computer made its last electronic beeps. "And you told us we were only going to ride four thousand five hundred."

"Yeah, but now we know better," said Jimmy. "John bein' four hundred and seventy miles off in a total of forty-five hundred ain't too bad. Go 'head and mark that thing. And I say, with rounding off to the nearest hundred, we just say we rode five thousand miles even. What do ya say, senators?"

Jimmy's motion was passed unanimously, and, with our usual ceremonial hugs and yahoos, we marked and folded our map for the last time. The kids smelled school and their friends in the valley below and were quickly back on their bikes and asking if they could go for their last downhill.

"Sure, you guys, go 'head. Just wait for me at the highway. I'll be down in a minute; I want us to ride into school together."

After the kids sped down the mountain, Lynn came over and held me. She noticed the tears in my eyes, and told me to take as much time as I needed. She would wait with the kids down below.

I looked down at school and then looked back over my shoulder, realizing that it was time for the dream to end . . . time for me to give the kids back. The downhill did its best to blow the tears off my face, but the kids didn't mind my red eyes when I finally reached them. We rode past Mattei's Tavern in Los Olivos, and soon the big old oak tree — the one Ethan had crashed under, in a cloud of dust — came into view. We rode down the driveway where we'd first learned to ride together, only this time it was covered with a red carpet and lined with hundreds of cheering friends and relatives. There were even TV crews and newspaper people.

Once our wheels touched the carpet — I rode point and Lynn rode caboose — streamers and confetti flew, and I only saw glimpses of the kids as they disappeared into the throngs of people. Jimmy was off giving a TV interview, leaning back against his bicycle, and from his hand motions and confident grin, I was sure he had everything under control. Carl was over by the willow tree, posing for a family photo in front of a map of our trip, with a "Hey Mom, I told you I could do the whole thing!" smile, as friends and classmates looked on, trying to imagine riding all the way across the giant map. Joy and Heather were alternating giving hugs and interviews, and Ethan was over standing next to his dad, already catching up on lost time.

I felt like I was the groom at a wedding — there were so many people I wanted to see. Somewhere in the throng were six very special ones I wanted to dance with all morning, and five of them would soon have to leave. It was all such a blur, and before I knew it, I found myself standing alone in the driveway. I looked over at Lynn and she nodded her head.

"Yes, John, everyone has gone home and it's time we headed that way, too. Put on your helmet and let's ride. I think it will make you feel better."

We rode, just the two of us, those thirty miles over the mountains, from school to Santa Barbara. We stopped at my old beach for what I thought would be a private reunion for my favorite ocean and me. But as I rode up to the sand, I discovered that my family had planned a surprise celebration at the water's edge.

After riding our bikes home at sunset and putting them in the garage, Lynn held my hand and walked me up the stairs to our house. After showering, we decided it would probably be best if we got out of the house and went to a movie. We thought it would take my mind off being away from the kids, but instead my first reaction when we walked into the theater was to look for five extra seats.

Lynn noticed my hesitation. "John . . . ." She kissed my cheek and gently led me to the seats right in front of us. "We only need two seats now . . . ."

The movie did a pretty good job of taking my mind off my aching insides, but on the walk home, I was pretty horrible company.

"John, you haven't said a word for almost a mile. You really miss them, don't you?" Lynn said, stopping me in the middle of a block.

"Yeah, I do . . . I wonder if they miss us?"

When we got home, I found out that at least one of them did. There was a message waiting for me on our answering machine, and Lynn watched me smile as I recognized Joy's voice.

"Hi, John. I just called to tell you you're missing a great TV show. I guess you're not home, though. Well, anyway, good night . . . and . . . and thanks again for the trip."

Maybe it was my imagination, but I thought I noticed a hint of sadness in Joy's voice. Hearing her made me feel better and worse at the same time, and that night, as I crawled into bed next to Lynn, I didn't sleep very much. I was little John again, having trouble going to sleep. I'd left home four months ago wondering how I would get any sleep being around five kids, and now that I was back, I wondered how I'd ever sleep without them . . . .

Epilogue

" . . . Have you thought of a name for your baby yet?"

Everybody we knew
Feb. — Oct., 1987

It's been over a year and a half since the morning we rode our last mile, and I'm not quite sure if I'm proud or sorry to say that I'm sleeping a lot better in my own bed now than I did that first night home . . . It's been a while since I went into a movie theater and looked for five extra seats, and I've grown used to wearing shirts with buttons, pants with belt loops and shoes with colored socks . . . But even with the domestications living at home has lulled me back into, not a day goes by that I don't check out a weather map to see what the skies are like over Tennessee or Kansas, and when I wake up in the middle of the night, memories of some Midwestern campsite or Southern church floor take the place of any sheep counts to relax me back to sleep. Our trip across America is part of me like some new middle name, and from all I hear from time to time from the kids, it's an undeniable part of them too.

Jimmy wrote me the other day from where he is attending high school. He was watching the video tape of our *From Sea to Shining Sea* slide show as he wrote, and he said he was just approaching Manhattan, Kansas and pedaling his hardest to beat the storm. "Ya know, John, not a day goes by that I don't think about our trip across America . . . ." He went on and on about how hard times or certain people or certain smells or weather bring something about our journey back to mind, and his letter had my old goosebumps dancing again.

Ethan told me he's been giving Smooth Ruth, his bicycle, a rest, choosing instead to push and coast the four wheels of his skateboard. Every couple months he asks me how the book is doing, and he blushes beneath his glasses when I tell him that every new bicycler at school knows about "his tree" and itches their face for the first time while pedaling, inspired by the legendary "Reverend/Rabbi/ Father Ethan."

Carl moved to Indiana where he stopped shaving his legs, and promised to find me some Hoosier-style biscuits and gravy. At Christmastime, he called and asked for a copy of the picture of him riding his bike across the Golden Gate Bridge ". . . to go on the wall next to my map of our trip," he said. "Come on out to Indiana sometime and bring your bikes; they got some neat country roads back here. And even the dogs are nice . . . ." We sent him some new bike gloves along with his picture and someday we'll follow him through his new state.

Heather made me a tie-dyed t-shirt with a flag of the United States on it for my birthday this year and she wrapped it up in plain white butcher paper because: "I wanted it to look like one of the packages one of those small town country stores would make . . . you know, just like back in Tennessee or the Ozarks . . . ." And earlier this spring, she sent our Amish friends some home-baked cookies she had made to look "just like watermelons . . . I had to bake a second batch though, because our dog got to the first ones and ate them all up . . . ." I could hear her smiling over the telephone as she continued, "I hope they'll like them."

438

Epilogue

Joy called me last summer to ask me if I would help her find a new bicycle: "John, I think I've outgrown Mad Mountain Mike Bike, and I want to get a new one. I'm planning on using the money I get from selling my 4-H steer at the County Fair, and I sent out announcements to a lot of our friends telling them that my across-America bike had gotten too small and that their bids would help me get a new one . . . So, could you help me pick out a new bicycle?" This summer she'll be joining me, Heather and some more friends on a three week journey through New England. "We're only going to do thirty miles a day? Man John, that will be easy . . . ."

And what about Dr. Lynn, our caboose and my wife? . . . Well, right now she's changing a diaper and wiping some banana off the little bicyclist who came into our lives on October 14, 1987. Jacob John was born early that Wednesday morning and rode home from the hospital the next morning, sleeping in the trailer being pulled by his dad's bicycle (according to both head-shaking grandmothers, his "crazy dad's" bicycle). And every night since, he has fallen asleep underneath the story-filled, blue, maroon and black diamonds of the quilt, stitched for him by a very special family in the hills of Tennessee.

Over the last eight months, Lynn has changed a lot of diapers and wiped a lot of banana from little Jacob's face, and she's been more than patient, giving me the time and the room to write our way across America.

From Sea To Shining Sea has continued to be part of our lives in many, many ways, and it's sad to be coming to the last page of our ride. In fact, I wouldn't be surprised if tomorrow morning I wake up looking for a few more paragraphs to write. In time, though, I'm sure I'll get used to riding my bike again instead of writing about it — Jacob and Lynn already have the bananas and the bike trailer ready.

And if what other parents tell us is true, it won't be long before Jacob comes running up the stairs yelling: "Hey Mom! Hey Dad! Can I ride my bike across America?"

Lynn and I have already practiced our answer a couple times . . . She'll look at me and then I'll look at her — just for a little suspense — and then we'll both say: "Hey Jacob, we thought you'd never ask . . . ."

Thanks for riding along with us,

John Seigel Boettner
Santa Barbara, California
June 5, 1988

PS. On July 25, 1989, the day after his birth, Isaac followed the trail of his older brother home from the hospital. And there are now two blue and yellow bike trailers in the Seigel Boettner garage.

We are traveling through one of the most beautiful countries the eye ever rested upon . . . Our hour of rising in the morning is four o'clock, hitch up and start at half past six, drive until eleven, rest until two, and drive until six in the evening. The roads are now first-rate, and we are making from seventeen to twenty miles per day . . . .

William Swain's Journal
Thursday, June 7, 1849
Little Blue River

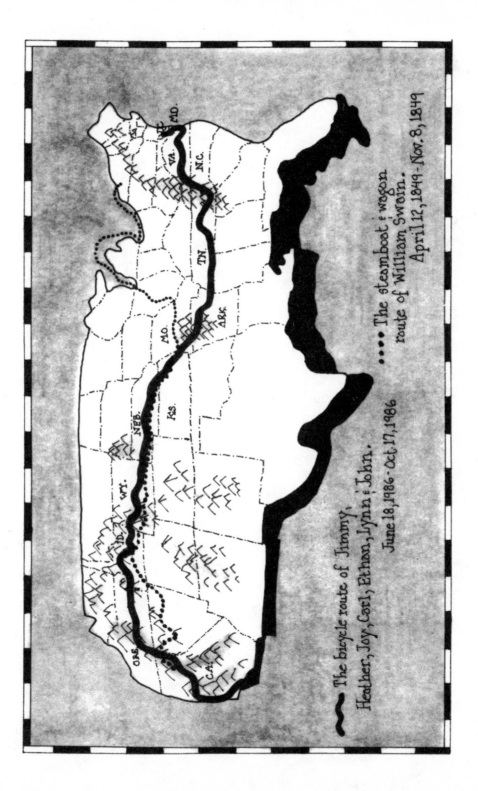

The steamboat & wagon
route of William Swain.
April 12, 1849 - Nov. 8, 1849

The bicycle route of Jimmy,
Heather, Joy, Carl, Ethan, Lynn, John.
June 18, 1986 - Oct. 17, 1986